Baltazar,

Congratulations on your graduation and best wishes for a fruitful future.

José Angel
June, 1971

BEETHOVEN: BIOGRAPHY OF A GENIUS

Books by George R. Marek

PUCCINI—A BIOGRAPHY

RICHARD STRAUSS—THE LIFE OF A NON-HERO

OPERA AS THEATER

Beethoven

BIOGRAPHY OF A GENIUS

by GEORGE R. MAREK

FUNK & WAGNALLS · NEW YORK

Acknowledgments

Quotations from *The Letters of Beethoven* (3 vols.),
copyright © 1961 by Emily Anderson, ed.,
by permission of St. Martin's Press, Macmillan & Co. Ltd.

Quotations from *Beethoven As I Knew Him,* by Anton Felix
Schindler, Donald W. MacArdle, ed., copyright © 1966,
by permission of The University of North Carolina Press.

A quotation from *Music in London,* by George Bernard Shaw, is
reprinted by permission of The Society of Authors as agents
for the Estate of George Bernard Shaw.

Quotations from *Beethoven: Impressions of Contemporaries,*
O. G. Sonneck, ed., copyright © 1926 by G. Schirmer, Inc.,
reprinted by permission.

Quotations from *The Life of Beethoven* (2 vols.) by Alexander
Wheelock Thayer, Elliot Forbes, ed., copyright © 1964 by
Princeton University Press (rev. edn., 1967). Reprinted by
permission of Princeton University Press.

Quotations from *Rossini: a Biography,*
by Herbert Weinstock. Alfred A. Knopf, 1968. By courtesy
of The University of Chicago Press.

Published by Funk & Wagnalls,
a Division of Reader's Digest Books, Inc.

Printed in the United States of America

Second Printing

The last of the four portraits W. J. Mähler painted of Beethoven, who was then forty-five years old (Society of Friends of Music, Vienna).

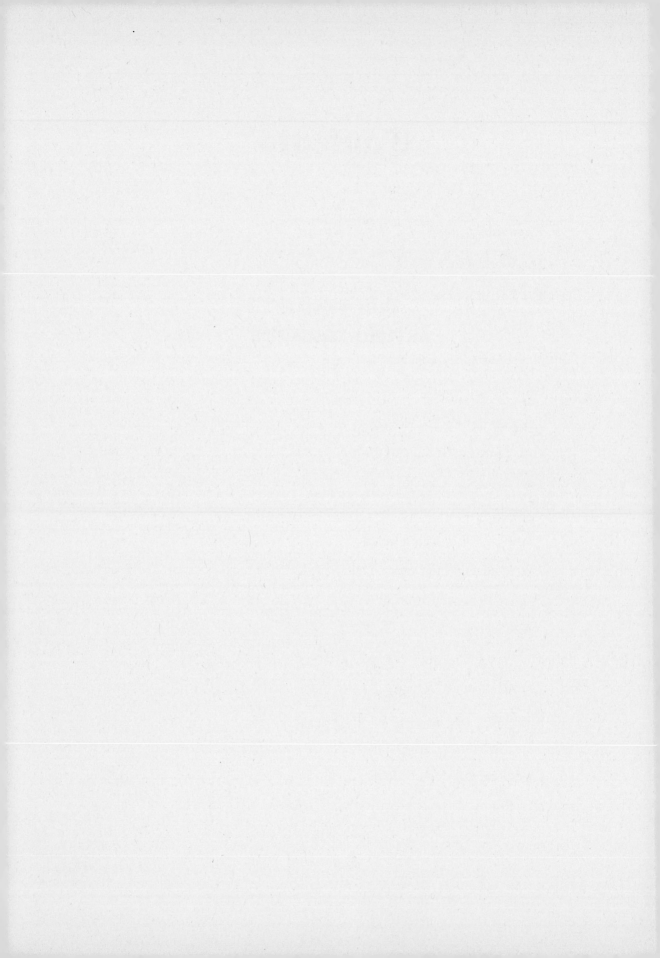

Contents

CONTENTS

Illustrations

ILLUSTRATIONS

A Note of Thanks

Thanks are due to various experts who have helped me with information on technical, medical, and historical points. I have acknowledged their contributions in footnotes throughout the book. I am indebted for general help to William Birnie, Gorton Carruth, Professor Elliot Forbes of Harvard University, Charles Gerhardt, Dr. Karl-Heinz Köhler of the Deutsche Staatsbibliothek in Berlin, Heinrich Kralik, Richard Lehman, Professor Paul Nettl of Indiana University, Dr. Joseph Schmidt-Görg, director of the Beethoven House in Bonn, Kenneth Sneider, Harold Spivacke, chief of the Music Division of the Library of Congress, and Robert Werner. My thanks go to Ted Hart, who prepared the index.

I want to record a special word of gratitude to Walter Hitesman, who in the first place prompted me to write the book and then took the most sympathetic interest in its progress. He made many valuable editorial suggestions, representing the point of view of the general reader.

G. R. M.

Foreword

The tourist who, like Siegfried, decides to undertake a Rhine journey will probably include Bonn in his itinerary, if only because the city lies near the Cologne Cathedral. There is not a great deal to see in that unwilling capital of West Germany: a splendid view of the Rhine, the well-preserved Market Place, the University, the modern government buildings. And there is the Beethoven House. Though, as with Shakespeare's native cottage, the birthplace of Ludwig van Beethoven has been disputed, it is now fairly well established that the Beethoven House was indeed the location where the composer saw the light of day.

The house now serves as a museum. The tourist can amble freely through the rooms and admire such relics as Beethoven's piano, his ear trumpets, the manuscript of the *Pastoral Symphony,* the partial manuscript of the *Moonlight Sonata,* many contemporary portraits, and the little roof chamber where the baby was born. If the visitor is a serious student, he may be shown the archive; it houses the best collection of Beethoven memorabilia, documents, and autographs in the world. The library contains about 3000 books and 8200 newspaper and magazine articles, monographs, and miscellaneous publications. Dr. Hans Schmidt, curator of the Beethoven Archive, believes that these figures would have to be augmented by 10 to 20 percent to arrive at the total number of books and essays published.

With that many books written about Beethoven, what need is there for another one? What is the purpose of a new biography of a man about whom so many have said so much?

Let me detail the reasons:

Curiously—and paradoxically—there exists no biography in English written later than the early 1940's.* A small book by John N. Burk, *The Life and*

---

* Manuel Komroff's *Beethoven and the World of Music,* published in 1961, can be regarded only as an essay.

Works of Beethoven, appeared in 1943 and attempted—not without success—to give in some four hundred pages a summary view not only of the life but also of the music. Of necessity it had to rush through Beethoven's life at a breathless pace.

Since then, some new facts have been discovered, such as the correspondence with Josephine Brunsvik. Since then, too, Emily Anderson's complete edition of Beethoven's letters has been published, a feat of scholarship which enables the biographer to correct errors and misconstruction.

A more important reason than fresh facts is fresh interpretation.

Writing a biography is a little like the performance of music: what you get is not the music itself but somebody's interpretation of the notes. The music, or the subject, passes through the brain and heart of the executant artist, or the writer. I see Beethoven neither as an isolated nor as a wholly instinctive genius but as a man who grew from the soil of his times and stood deep in the cultural, political, and social streams that swirled around him. He and Goethe were the two greatest creators living when the 18th turned into the 19th century and Napoleon tore up Europe. Both lived in the world, though in very different ways. Neither Goethe nor Beethoven is imaginable without Voltaire or Rousseau or the early German Romantics. That Beethoven withdrew from the world in his last years does not invalidate the belief that he drank the fructifying liquor the world had offered him.

I have attempted to show Beethoven in the cocoon of his times and trace the progress of chrysalis into genius, paying attention to his immediate predecessors and his contemporaries and their ideas. During his lifetime the world changed more significantly than perhaps in any other fifty-year period, except the period in which we are living. When he was eighteen, the French Revolution began. When he was twenty-two, the Reign of Terror in France made Europe tremble. When he was twenty-seven, Napoleon conquered Egypt. When he was thirty-two, Fulton operated his first steamship. When he was forty-four, the Congress of Vienna redrew the map. When he was in his fifties the Monroe Doctrine was proclaimed, the first railroad began to chug in England, and the Industrial Revolution was hurrying on apace. I have stressed both the economic pressures and the spiritual inspirations to which he was subjected; they were nonmusical, but they came out music. Modern man, or much of him, was formed in the period in which Beethoven lived. He is relevant to modern man, though he stands above time.

The book tries to give a synthesis of most of what is known of Beethoven's life, as of today. No one can claim that he has read everything written about Beethoven. I haven't. We do not, as in the lives of Bach or Mozart, suffer from a paucity of material. We suffer from an abundance, from too many recollections, too many tales, too many impressions, some of which are idolatrous and some of which are theatrical. Beethoven was vastly famous; he was a legend even in his lifetime.

From contemporary evidence I have selected what seemed to me to sound with the ring of truth. In this process a few anecdotes have fallen by the wayside. Quite a few names have been eliminated, so as not to encumber the biography with a confusing cast of characters many of whom appeared in subsidiary roles only.

Are there any new findings here, any unpublished data? At the beginning of the project it seemed improbable that such could be unearthed. Beethoven research is a field which has been plowed for almost one hundred and thirty years, every furrow being turned a dozen times. Making a major "discovery" about Beethoven's life is as unlikely as finding an antique Greek vase lying loose in the Parthenon. Yet the attempt was made.

A team was put together under the direction of H.C. Robbins Landon, the eminent Haydn scholar, who lives in Vienna and who knows the answer to the question so important in research: Where do you look? He was assisted by Else Radant, an Austrian historian, and Christine Swenoha. I want to pay particular tribute to the excellence of their work. It resulted in:

1. Facts about Beethoven's patrons, such as Lobkowitz and Lichnowsky; if this book contains new information about these important men, it is due to the ingenuity of the Vienna research team.

2. A re-examination of the documents of the Erdödy case.

3. One or two hitherto little-known accounts of Beethoven's early Vienna days.

4. More than seventy unpublished letters by Georg August von Griesinger, Saxon chargé d'affaires in Vienna and friend of Haydn and Beethoven.

5. The diary of Joseph Carl Rosenbaum, a garrulous citizen of Vienna, married to an opera singer and therefore a participant in the musical life in Vienna. His view of Beethoven was less than adulatory, and his diary serves as a wholesome astringent.

6. The exhuming of a Police Register in Karlsbad, which will be discussed in the section dealing with the "Immortal Beloved."

7. A combing of the Vienna newspaper files from 1793 to 1827, par-

ticularly the *Wiener Zeitung,* extracting what seemed pertinent to Beethoven's career.

Yet, however enjoyable the finding of new data may be, it is the old facts, the compiled testimony of many years, which must furnish the raw material from which a biography of a man as celebrated as Beethoven is constructed. A biography is not only written; it is cribbed from this and that.

The great source book is Alexander Wheelock Thayer's *Life of Beethoven,* a painstaking labor of love to which he devoted his life and which he never managed to finish. Thayer (1817–1897), an American, wrote it in English, but it was first published in German, translated by H. Deiters (5 volumes, the first of which appeared in 1866 and the last in 1908). Volumes 4 and 5 were edited by Hugo Riemann, who also revised the other volumes. The English edition was edited by the music critic and scholar, H. E. Krehbiel, and was published in New York through a grant given by the Beethoven Association in 1921. In all of these editions, the later life, having remained unwritten by Thayer, was reconstructed by the various editors from Thayer's voluminous notes. These notes have been lost.

A new edition of Thayer's *Life* in two volumes was published in 1964, revised and edited by Elliot Forbes. Though, as Mr. Forbes points out, Thayer erred here and there, for the most part his accuracy was remarkable and the work remains the mainstay of the biographical canon. However, because Thayer set facts down in chronological order, without regard to continuity of subject, it is more of a reference than a reading book.

Thayer, in addition to interviewing many persons who had known Beethoven, had at his disposal a quantity of source material. By the middle of the 19th century many accounts had been published. Thus he drew on recollections set down by Wegeler and Ries (*Biographische Notizen über Ludwig van Beethoven*), by Gerhard Breuning (*Aus dem Schwarzspanierhause*), Reichardt, Czerny, Moscheles, Seyfried, Grillparzer, Hummel, Treitschke, Varnhagen, Röckel, etc. In reusing this material, I have, wherever possible, consulted the original source.

Then there is Anton Schindler, Beethoven's fanciful famulus. Schindler's biography, first published in 1840 and then thoroughly revised for a third edition in 1860, has recently been reissued under the title *Beethoven As I Knew Him,* excellently edited by Donald W. MacArdle. Everybody who has tried to learn something about Beethoven knows that in reading Schindler he must take along a number of grains of salt.

A fine source book dealing with Beethoven's youth in Bonn is Ludwig Schiedermair's *Der junge Beethoven* (*The Young Beethoven*), unfortunately unavailable in English. I owe a debt to this book for the facts about Beethoven's Bonn period.

I have mentioned Emily Anderson. Beethoven's letters, like Mozart's letters, have been issued in a complete edition in English, translated and edited and annotated by her (*The Letters of Beethoven,* 3 volumes, 1961). It would be difficult to find a more knowledgeable or a more sympathetic editor than Miss Anderson. While in many cases I have consulted the original German texts as given in a five-volume compilation edited by Alfred Kalischer, I have used Miss Anderson's translation in virtually every quotation. Since I have often cited only salient passages from a letter, I have marked the number Miss Anderson assigned to it, should the reader want to read the entire letter.

I am grateful for the help extended by several libraries and archives, particularly the excellent Lincoln Center Branch of the New York Public Library. Other sources consulted were the British Museum, the Austrian National Library, the Austrian State Archive, the Library of the University of the Deutsche Demokratische Republik in Berlin, the Library of Congress in Washington, and the Society of the Friends of Music in Vienna.

The bibliography will show the indebtedness of the book to many scholars, men such as Ley, Frimmel,* Unger, Kalischer, Grove, Schmidt-Görg, Kerst, MacArdle, Nettl, Nottebohm, Nohl, Schünemann, Forster, and others. I have profited by two books, essays rather than biographies, Ernest Newman's *The Unconscious Beethoven* and J. W. N. Sullivan's *Beethoven, His Spiritual Development.* Though I disagree with some details of the former and the premise of the latter, I consider both books stimulating and Newman's book instructive even when he is being caustic. Certain other biographies I find too rich for my diet; they could be characterized as dithyrambs. The dictionary defines a dithyramb as "a passionate choric hymn . . . a highly emotional or rhapsodic speech or piece of writing." To that group belongs Emil Ludwig's biography—he calls Beethoven "the conqueror"—or Robert Haven Schauffler's —he calls Beethoven "the man who freed music"—or that of Romain Rolland, who saw him as "the great bull with its fierce eye . . . whose roar is heard above the time."

I wanted to give an idea of Beethoven's earnings and expenditures, the

---

* Theodor Frimmel's *Beethoven Handbuch* (2 vols., Leipzig, 1926) is a useful fact book, as is Paul Nettl's *Beethoven Handbook* (New York, 1967).

fees he was paid for his compositions and the price he had to pay for his over-coat, in terms which would be understandable to today's reader. This proved a complex problem. Professor Eduard Holzmair was consulted. He is an expert on Austrian currency questions and was director of the *Kunsthistorische* Museum in Vienna as well as director of the Vienna Coin Cabinet. I quote parts of his analysis:

"In former times the experts interpreted the value of money only according to the amount of precious metal contained in the coins under discussion, without taking into account variations of cost-of-living and of wages. It is true that today these two factors are considered indispensable for a judgment of purchasing power; yet the extent of our present knowledge permits us only general conclusions which can apply only approximately to specific cases.

"Calculations affecting Beethoven are *a priori* complicated by the fact that in his later life there existed little stability in Austrian currency. Because of the French wars, which pressed heavily on Austrian finances, the Austrian money unit, the originally stable 'Convention Gulden' (*Konventionsgulden*), was subjected to devaluation in the year of the state's bankruptcy, 1811. The paper money then issued stood in a ratio of five to one to the previous currency. Nevertheless, a further devaluation took place. Finally, in the year 1816, money became stable: 100 gulden Convention Currency were equated with 250 gulden of so-called '*Wiener Währung*' (Vienna currency). Therefore one first has to examine whether the sums mentioned refer to a time before or after the five-to-one ratio, and then one has to be aware of the co-existence of the Convention Currency (*Conventions-münze,* abbreviated as C.M.*) and *Wiener Währung* (W.W.**).

"Contrary to general impression, a florin is not the same as a ducat. The old florin (meaning a gold coin from Florence) was originally equivalent to the Venetian ducat (from *Ducatus,* the dukedom of Venice). But in Beethoven's time, what we are dealing with is a silver gulden which was called a florin and usually abbreviated as *fl.*

"This gulden was divided into sixty kreuzer until the end of the Convention Currency in 1857, that is, long past Beethoven's death. A groschen was three kreuzer.

"In Beethoven's later years, a kreuzer (C.M.) bought a pound of black

---

* Emily Anderson abbreviates this as A.C. (Assimilated coinage).
** Emily Anderson abbreviates this as V.C. (Viennese currency).

bread, which would cost today in Austria approximately two and a half shillings. That corresponds to ten cents. This calculation is perhaps on the conservative side, considering the higher level of prices in the U.S.A."

There was a great deal more to this analysis, but for the purpose of the book, Professor Holzmair suggested the following simplification:

	Before 1811	Present Equivalent
Austrian	1 gulden or florin = 60 kreuzer =	$ 6.00
"	1 groschen = 3 kreuzer =	.30
"	1 kreuzer =	.10
German	1 Reichsthaler =	9.00
"	1 Rheinthaler =	12.00
European	1 ducat (gold) =	25.00

The Pistole, louis d'or, friedrich d'or, and carolin were European (gold) coins which occur in Beethoven's biography only in isolated instances. They had "approximately the value of a double ducat, about $50."

After 1811

1 gulden (W.W.) or florin (W.W.) = 60 kreuzer = $1.00 to $1.25

1 groschen (W.W.) = 3 kreuzer =   .06 to .07

German and European (gold) currency did not depreciate to the extent Austrian did, though there was some inflation, confusion and instability.

After 1816

1 gulden or florin, C.M. = 2.5 gulden or florin, W.W. = $5.00 to $6.00

(Other denominations proportionate)

When I give equivalents in today's financial idiom, I use these figures. However, at best we are dealing with approximations.

This is not a book of musical analysis. I have not discussed the compositions musicologically. I have not attempted to define the characteristics of his style. Nor, on the other hand, have I tried to offer "descriptions" of the music. Can one describe music? Admittedly, I have had severely to restrain myself not to dilate on the great works. The temptation was there—but I am neither able to impart special revelations about them nor do I think that most nontechnical musical discussions are worth very much. The effort to apply word images to music usually results in tropes.

This, then, is a book about the man who composed the music. It is written for readers who enjoy and admire that music but have no professional relationship to it or technical knowledge of it. There are no musical quotations. It is

FOREWORD

written with the hope that it will help to illumine the artist as a human being. That is challenge enough, to try to paint the picture of the man, with the chiaroscuro of its elements. My reward would be if the reader were to feel, in Marlowe's words, "Well hast thou pourtray'd . . . the face and personage of a wondrous man."

GEORGE R. MAREK

New York, June 1969

ABBREVIATIONS OF THE MOST FREQUENTLY USED SOURCES:

Thayer's *Life of Beethoven* . . . T
Quotations used by Thayer . . . TQ
Emily Anderson: *Letters* . . . A
(followed by the number of the letter)
Schindler, any of several editions . S

BEETHOVEN: BIOGRAPHY OF A GENIUS

... He who lies here was possessed. Seeking one goal, caring only for one result, suffering and sacrificing for one purpose, thus did this man go through life ...

If there are some of us who can still feel a sense of total dedication in these fractured times, let us meet at his grave. Has it not always been the task of the poets and heroes, the bards and the divinely enlightened, to raise up poor and confused men, so that they may be mindful both of their origin and their destiny?

From a speech by Grillparzer
on the occasion of the unveiling
of a monument to Beethoven,
autumn, 1827.

Voltaire, Architect of the Enlightenment. "His spirit moved like a flame over the continent and the century" (Durant). Mozart called him a "godless arch-scoundrel," but Beethoven admired him. This statue, by French sculptor Houdon, graces the Comédie Française (Archives Photographiques, Paris).

CHAPTER 1

THE WORLD
WHEN BEETHOVEN WAS BORN

··∘[I]∘··

The second half of the 18th century was the Age of Curiosity. Never had so many minds questioned old beliefs, challenged accepted concepts, dug into the structure of society to find where were the rotted beams, explored remote geography, measured the movement of the stars, sifted chemical elements, doubted the tenets of organized religion, probed the bitter problems of politics, visited sickrooms to learn the nature of unexplained diseases, speculated over man's fate in the physical world while pondering the world which lies beyond the physical. There was a gigantic housecleaning. Windows were opened, rugs were rolled up, and men looked into every corner to clean away mental dust.

Should the power of the Church be curtailed? Should the Church be abolished altogether? When did obedience to the head of state, to king or emperor, cease being obedience and become slavery? Why did we need air to breathe, and what was the nature of this substance? How far could tolerance, especially religious tolerance, be allowed without undermining the security of society? Could words be exactly defined? Could new and more accurate ways of measuring time be invented? Could government exist without the consent of the governed? How could smallpox be curbed? Was it possible to construct new machines by which textiles could be woven? How could steam be harnessed for the benefit of industry? What could be done to reform the abuses of the clergy? Was there a God? Were serfs necessary to produce sufficient food? Could legal trials, different for the commoner than for the aristocrat, be equalized? What were the injustices of taxation? Was it possible for Protestantism and Catholicism to coexist? Could Reason become the chief guide to man's actions? Was it allowable to examine Biblical texts critically? What was the function of art, and what

3

was the artist's role in society? Was it possible to compile a record of all of man's knowledge in one gigantic compendium?

Everywhere in the European world, from Edinburgh to St. Petersburg, the questions flew. Millions of words filled the air, thousands of speeches, impassioned, eloquent, sometimes piquantly satirical, more often deadly serious, were hurled from parliaments and pulpits; tens of thousands of pamphlets, treatises, monographs, and books choked the printing presses.

The philosophic movement which began early in the century was called the Enlightenment. Its symbol was an embracing question mark. One of its prime movers was the Scottish philosopher David Hume, who died six years after Beethoven was born. In such works as *Inquiry Concerning Human Understanding* Hume challenged religion, challenged the concept of "natural law"—a concept he felt was merely a convenient formula to summarize the sequence of cause and effect—and assigned leading roles to human reason and human experience. He doubted whether a philosophical knowledge of God was possible. With this doubt began the triumphal march of Reason.

The brightest star of the Enlightenment, a man who dominated world thought, a brilliant personality, brilliant writer, brilliant fighter, without whom the modern world is unthinkable, was Voltaire. Poet, dramatist, author of numerous "romances," pamphleteer, preacher, encyclopedist, friend and foe of sovereigns, a man who was ugly, vain, ruthless, impish, with an insatiable appetite for fame and an equally insatiable appetite for a woman's caresses; yet often kind, considerate, courageous—he was the architect of the great intellectual change. Ideas, wit, aphorisms, slogans, epigrams poured from him as water from a fountain and in a style as clear as water. He corresponded with the leading minds of his age.* Though a hypochondriac and beset by fear of death, he lived to the ripe old age of eighty-four and worked to his last day. Wherever he was, there was the center of civilization. He worked in France, in England, in Switzerland, and in Prussia with his patron and admirer, Frederick the Great. He scorned equally the arrogant infallibility of kings and the myths and mysteries of the Church. He defended the family of the unjustly executed Protestant Jean Calas and in doing so he uttered the battle cry, *"Ecrasez l'infâme!"* (Crush infamy!) Around this battle cry, repeated by him a hundred times and often used by him as his signature, the philosophers rallied.

---

* His letters, a complete edition of which is even now being prepared in France, fill over a hundred thick volumes.

THE WORLD WHEN BEETHOVEN WAS BORN

Philosophers were everywhere, but it was primarily in France that the *philosophes* (as they called themselves) became a formidable force, after two centuries in which the Church had led the people and, at its worst, had become guilty of bigotry, simony, intransigence, and massacre (St. Bartholomew's Day, 1572). Second in importance only to Voltaire, Denis Diderot, enlisting most of the important writers of his time, published the *Encyclopédie,* an extraordinary treasure chest of man's knowledge. Though this work was threatened by a rigid censorship, though authors were menaced with imprisonment, the questioning could not be silenced. In Germany—a politically fractioned country, trailing behind the development of France and England—the Enlightenment produced the great Immanuel Kant. Building on Hume and Voltaire (with whom he often disagreed), Kant received his professorship in logic and metaphysics the year that Beethoven was born; eleven years later he published the *Critique of Pure Reason* and four years after postulated the Categorical Imperative: "Act as if the maxim from which you act were to become through your will a universal law of nature." It is doubtful that any but a handful of thinkers understood Kant (or understand him today); his is a convoluted style. Beethoven did; at any rate, there is an entry in his hand in one of the Conversation Books: "The moral law in us and the starry heavens above us. Kant!!!" It is a quotation from the *Critique of Practical Reason* (1788). And we know that at least one of Kant's books was found in Beethoven's library.

The ubiquitous curiosity of the age produced two moods: one of ironic pessimism and one of high optimism. Both moods were expressed by Voltaire. On All Saints' Day, November 1, 1755, a terrible earthquake occurred in Lisbon. In six minutes 15,000 people were killed: most of them were those who attended church. All Europe was shocked. Why had punishment been meted out to the pious, particularly? Voltaire pondered over it; the year following he wrote his finest poem, "On the Lisbon Disaster," and three years later he published his masterpiece, *Candide, ou l'optimisme.* There, in Voltaire's most limpid style, he turns his irony on the belief that this is "the best of all possible worlds." The book leaped through Europe: It is the work by which Voltaire is best remembered; it goaded people into throwing the itching powder of doubt on doctrines. Yet late in life, after all his battles, he was the spokesman for the optimism of the age:

> Well-constituted minds are now very numerous; they are at the head of
> nations; they influence public manners; and year by year the fanaticism that

overspread the earth is receding in its detestable usurpations. . . . If religion no longer gives birth to civil wars, it is to philosophy alone that we are indebted; theological disputes begin to be regarded in much the same manner as the quarrels of Punch and Judy at the fair. A usurpation odious and injurious, founded upon fraud on one side and stupidity on the other, is being at every instant undermined by reason, which is establishing its reign.*

This was written the year after Beethoven's birth. Alas, the victory which Voltaire hailed was a short-lived one, if it ever really existed! Fanaticism and fraud were to attack again and soon enough. But the point is that there *was* optimism in the world—and Beethoven was to believe in it—and that the Age of Curiosity brought about the Age of Change, in which an optimistic belief reigned that through Reason human beings could mold their fate and better their lot. After enough questions had been asked, some answers were given. The change led to a new attitude of man toward himself and toward those who governed him. It led, sometimes by paths which were not clearly marked and with discouraging detours, to the two culminating events of the 18th century, the American Revolution, which ended in 1782, and the French Revolution, which began in 1789. Both revolutions, unequal in bloodiness, unequal in their final result, are yet related actions, philosophically sired by the Enlightenment. (Benjamin Franklin was an avid student of Voltaire's writings.)

Diderot lived long enough to learn of the exciting events across the sea, the American Revolution. When he died in 1784, Beethoven was fourteen years old. Diderot was sitting at dinner; his wife asked him a question, and when he did not answer she looked at him and saw that he was dead. It was perhaps the only question which the philosopher left unanswered. He was a warmhearted and generous man; yet he too combined belief and disbelief. "The first step toward philosophy is incredulity," he said.

It was this incredulity, this unwillingness to take things for granted, this zest for digging, that was responsible for discoveries and inventions in fields other than those of abstract ideas. Joseph Louis Lagrange, the greatest thinker among the 18th-century mathematicians, formulated the metric system and explained Jupiter's satellites as well as the phenomenon of the periodicity of the visible portions of the moon. Benjamin Franklin conducted his experiments in electricity, and the French philosopher d'Alembert paid this tribute to him: "He snatched the lightning from the sky and the scepter from the tyrants." Joseph

---

* From the article on God, in the *Philosophic Dictionary*.

6

Priestley announced to the Royal Scientific Society of England his discovery of oxygen, clearing the way for Lavoisier to set down the principles of modern chemistry. William Herschel, who could spare for astronomy, he said, only the time that was left him from his work as a musician, discovered Uranus. Captain James Cook, sailing in the *Endeavor,* journeyed to remote islands, charted the coasts of New Zealand and eastern Australia, penetrated to Botany Bay (in 1770, the year of Beethoven's birth), went to the Bering Strait, and discovered the Hawaiian Islands. James Bruce traced the Blue Nile to its confluence with the White Nile.

John Kay, even before the middle of the century, invented the "flying shuttle," which made it possible to weave cloth in any desired width, and James Hargreaves invented the spinning jenny, which spun many threads simultaneously. The old problem of harnessing steam was newly attacked; James Watt suggested a solution that led to new machines that would furnish power and locomotion.

While inventors and philosophers looked to man's future, and scholars charted man's present knowledge—the first edition of the *Encyclopaedia Britannica* appeared in 1771 in three volumes—archaeologists journeyed into the past. Herculaneum and Pompeii had been discovered early in the century; now, in 1752, a marvelous Greek temple at Paestum was stripped of its overgrowth. This evoked a new interest in the antique, almost as fervent as that of the Renaissance. J. J. Winckelmann wrote the *History of Ancient Art,* and Piranesi etched the ancient monuments. Six years after Beethoven's birth there appeared the first volume of Edward Gibbon's *Decline and Fall of the Roman Empire.* Inquiry was everywhere!

Yet we must not sketch too bright a picture of the Age of Enlightenment. Reason did not illumine all minds, and enlightenment did not come quickly to the hidebound. Time does not proceed as a play does. The close of an act of history is not sudden. There was no curtain which fell on bigotry and the fear of hell's fires, to rise suddenly on a new age in which human beings were reasonable. Nine out of ten people who lived a difficult, dirt-ridden, and small-scale existence could not see the brighter light through the coated windows of their hut. It is true that after the French Revolution life speeded up in progress, though in cruelty as well. All the same, to the little man change could not be quickly apparent. Nor was it apparent to those who did not want to see: to the prince, the castle owner, the general, or the bishop. They felt that one could smile at the *philosophes,* that the noise would eventually die down, and that sooner or later life would resume its "natural" course, with the natural privileges accorded to the well-born preserved.

So the poor remained very poor and the rich very rich; so there were years of starvation and there were bloody wars, of which the Seven Years' War (1756–63) was not the least bloody. Serfs labored on land which belonged to an absent duke, and tenant farmers were reduced almost to serfdom. There were no industrial work laws, no minimum hours, no prohibition of child labor, and attempts at strikes were cruelly punished. Monarchies were absolute. When Diderot predicted, the year of his death, that soon belief in God and submission to kings would be everywhere at an end, he was wrong on both counts. Most people still sought solace in God. Voltaire wrote: "I want my lawyer, my tailor and my wife to believe in God; so, I imagine, I shall be less robbed and less deceived." He himself pronounced the famous sentence, "If God did not exist, it would be necessary to invent him."

Yet if you were fortunate enough to have been born in the right family and knew where to look—and where *not* to look—you could live a life wrapped in dazzling glitter and shining decoration. The simplest functions of life were ornamented, and art was abundant. Secular art was lighthearted and graceful, much of it allusive and clever. A painting such as Watteau's "The Embarkation for Cythera" is a perfect example of what this aristocratic art could produce. So are the paintings of Canaletto, Guardi, and Bellotto, which supplied the demand for travel souvenirs by those who made European tours. Boucher, Fragonard, and a dozen other painters told lovers' tales in lambent colors. The rococo was a riot of joy, eventually to be swept away by the Revolution. Today we marvel at the patience, the skill, and the eyesight which could be commandeered to create the inlaid clocks, the ormolu furniture, the exquisite porcelain, the intricate lace, the Aubusson tapestries, the Dresden figurines, the elaborate silver candlesticks, the jewelry as daedal as a woman's reasoning, the gold snuffboxes and the pearl-studded pillboxes, which were produced in mad profusion. This passion for beauty—or for conspicuous display—reached unbelievable extravagance. The play of the sexes was given new titillation by expensive ornamentation. The sheets of the Duchesse de la Ferté cost 40,000 crowns (more than $240,000 in today's equivalent). Ladies' dresses were of a costliness and elaborateness which virtually bankrupted many a husband and made dressing for a state occasion a building process that took several hours. Around 1750, hoop skirts were worn. The priests denounced them because they afforded a glimpse of a limb sheathed in lace, but women insisted on them because they could make a dramatic entrance wearing them and they flattered the figure even when the lady was pregnant. Hoop skirts took up so much room that Handel, for the performance of the *Messiah,* desired ladies to come without their hoops and gentlemen without their swords. This increased the attendance from 600 to more than 700.

As Paris was the intellectual capital of Europe, so was it the capital of fashion. Men wore velvet coats, a vest open at the throat, shirts of the finest silk, and sleeves terminating in ornate ruffles. Knee breeches (*culottes*) were of loud and gay colors, men's stockings of white silk. Among courtiers the fashion was to wear shoes with red heels. Practically everybody carried a sword and often a cane, except that the wearing of a sword was forbidden to servants, apprentices, and musicians.

Men wore wigs. Hair was powdered and curled and was worn long at the beginning of the Enlightenment, to become shorter and more simply dressed as the years proceeded. When Beethoven grew up, wigs were no longer worn. As a young man appearing as a virtuoso before the public, he spent at the coiffeur the time necessary to have his locks curled. Later he did not. Decidedly he did not!

Plainer people dressed simply, well-to-do merchants in sturdy coats and culottes of dark colors. Both sexes made liberal use of perfume. Aristocratic women were not only heavily rouged but wore beauty spots called *mouches* (flies), cut into the shape of stars, hearts, teardrops, and then placed on interesting parts of their visible anatomy.

The morals of the age were probably no better nor worse than those of preceding or subsequent ages. But the game which ends in bed was spoken of with a new freedom of language. The Enlightenment loosened the tongue of literature. The Abbé Prévost published anonymously in Paris in 1731 *The Adventures of the Chevalier des Grieux and of Manon Lescaut,* which was banned by the censors and at once leaped to popularity. This romance, telling the tale of a man's degradation for the love of a wanton woman, was followed by an avalanche of similar stories. They were mild enough compared to Choderlos de Laclos' *Dangerous Acquaintances* (1782), one of the most brilliant but surely one of the most immoral books of French literature. Nor may we forget that John Cleland's *Memoirs of a Woman of Pleasure,* now better known as *Fanny Hill,* belongs to the era (1749).

Literature was not of course limited to the lascivious. It preserved its privilege of being sentimental, though it did take a turn toward satirizing the foibles of society, and it developed a new freedom not only of language but of form. In

1767 Sterne completed *Tristram Shandy,* an uncorseted masterpiece; eight years later Sheridan's *The Rivals* became the hit of the London season. Oliver Goldsmith belonged to Dr. Samuel Johnson's circle of wit, the Literary Club; his *Vicar of Wakefield* is a moral and sentimental tale which became especially popular in sentimental Germany. It was read by the Breuning family, whose house the young Beethoven frequented. Beethoven might have read it.

Love marriages, with or without a dowry, became more frequent, but in the main young girls of good family were still kept in a convent until they became nubile, and parents decided who was to marry whom. Prostitution was widespread, and one of the scourges of the age was syphilis, against which the worldly Chesterfield warned his son. It was, he said, better to lose a mistress than to lose one's nose.

The populace had something to gaze at in the elaborate fireworks, water marvels, and the *camera obscura.* Chess, checkers, dominoes, billiards (which Mozart played enthusiastically) were popular, but card playing much more so. An opera house in Munich was financed by a tax on playing cards. Gambling was pursued by all classes of society, the only difference being the size of the stake. Both France and England and later the United States had a national lottery.

The main meal of the day was taken at three, supper at nine.* In the regions where wine was plentiful, breakfast often included a glass—or two or three—of wine. But coffee now became popular, being sold at the apothecary shops. The coffee houses, where philosophers disputed, where men of mind exchanged views and men without mind exchanged gossip, became numerous. Paris had 600 of them in 1750 and London over 3000.

The problem of man's physical well-being was as eagerly examined in the Enlightenment as was the problem of man's spiritual health. Yet medicine could not boast of exceptional progress during the last half of the 18th century. In our time medical knowledge probably increases faster in six months than it then did in sixty years. The rate of death in childbirth and among infants was about three out of five. One was lucky to live to the ripe old age of forty. True, the bubonic plague had been stamped out in most parts of Europe, but there were still plagues of cholera and frequent epidemics of typhoid fever. Diphtheria and whooping cough killed many children. Aside from syphilis, the dread disease of the age was smallpox. It was probably the widest-spread of all

---

* In Paris and London. Meal hours in Vienna were somewhat earlier.

afflictions. Beethoven suffered an attack of it, though a relatively light one. Voltaire calculated that out of every hundred persons at least sixty contracted smallpox. In the year Beethoven was born, an epidemic raged in London. An English surgeon, Edward Jenner, observed that dairy maids who had contracted cowpox rarely caught the far more serious smallpox. He hit upon the idea of immunizing people to smallpox by inoculating them with a vaccine made from a pox-infected cow. Many English physicians thought it was a mad idea, and an English clergyman preached against what he called "a sinful practice." But there were enough prominent persons—including Benjamin Franklin, who supported the inoculation movement in Philadelphia—later to enable Jenner and other physicians to proceed.

During the Enlightenment, surgery became a respectable profession, the surgeon becoming separated from the barber. The best surgeons were French. At that, their knowledge did not nearly reach the level of skill practiced in ancient Egypt, and bloodletting was still the standard remedy for practically every disturbance of heart, liver, or kidney. Leeches were still in wide use.

Medicine, as in every period of history, had its charlatans. The most famous was Franz Anton Mesmer, who preached that diseases could be drawn from the body by magnets and, having won an audience, then proceeded to demonstrate that an occult healing force lay within his own person. Our expression "to mesmerize" is a recollection of this curious faker. A further tribute was paid to him by Mozart in *Così fan tutte,* where the maid, disguised as a doctor, reawakens the lovers with a magnet.

The sway of Reason stamped out the belief in witchcraft. By 1790, persecution of witches, once so prevalent, virtually disappeared. Yet Reason could not prevent hundreds of superstitions. People were still looking for the Philosopher's Stone, fortunetellers were consulted, astrologers flourished, and chemists still promised to turn base metal into gold.

The age was particularly successful in widening geographical horizons. Men explored and colonized. People traveled with new zest, undeterred by difficulties, so that a comfort-loving young man like Boswell had himself transported over the Alps in a sedan chair. Highways were now safer, but the inns were often filthy; if located in strategic spots, they treated their customers with the same high-handedness that the innkeeper Hobson did in the 16th century when he gave travelers no choice whatever in the selection of horses (Hobson's choice). Those who could not afford a private equipage traveled by hired or public coaches. Some of these carried the mail—there was a regular postal service—and it was more expensive to book a sheltered place inside than to sit next to the coachman. Travel was of course slow, particularly because one was held up at many local frontiers, each little dukedom bustling with its customs officers. A letter posted in Vienna took about fourteen days to reach London. It took ten days to travel from Bonn to Vienna, if one traveled fast.

·∘[2]∘·

How was music performed and what was the position of the musician in late 18th-century society? In the early part of the century the Church furnished the chief inspiration for serious music: masses, requiems, hymns, organ preludes, Te Deums, oratorios, passions, and cantatas poured from a hundred pens.* There stood the towering figures of Bach and Handel. Bach built a mighty monument, vigorous in belief, cloud-capped in beauty. England's most famous church composition of the middle century (most famous still today) was Handel's *Messiah,* first performed in Dublin on April 13, 1742. Handel in his oratorios combined piety with a dramatic, indeed an almost theatrical, instinct. Audiences listening to this music could be religiously uplifted and at the same time enjoy an exciting show. Solemn music, yes, but not "lugubrious" nor "gloomy." Handel knew the combination. Beethoven on his deathbed said of Handel, "We can still learn from him."

As Reason gained ascendancy, the demand for secular music increased. One needed, so to speak, music to go with the painting of the two lovers toying in a garden swing or with that blue-white-and-gold Sèvres cup. Music turned toward the world. Most "artful" music still belonged to the well-born or at least the well-to-do. The farmer might sing at a harvest festival. There was merry music when the baker got married. There was dancing everywhere. But for chamber and concert music one had to be invited to the houses of the well-born. There the host himself—or the hostess—took up a violin or sat down at the harpsichord. To be able to play an instrument was an integral part of a nobleman's education. Empress Maria Theresa and all her children made music. Frederick the Great played the flute. Marie Antoinette played the harpsichord and sang prettily. There were hardly any "public performances" in the sense in which we now understand the term—that is, for a ticket-buying public. Except the opera!

---

* Voltaire, who had something to say about everything, scoffed at all that holy music: "The Most High has a decided taste for vocal music, provided it be lugubrious and gloomy enough" (*Philosophic Dictionary*).

By far the most popular form of musical entertainment was the opera. Court and society were mad for it. The Italians held the monopoly. At German courts Italian opera, sung in Italian, was the thing to hear, though one German composer, Johann Adolph Hasse, imitated Italian opera so successfully that he was known as *Il caro Sassone,* the beloved Saxon. France did produce one or two fine opera composers, such as Rameau; and in England, in the early part of the century, Handel stirred clamorous enthusiasm with a long series of opera productions, all with Italian singers and usually based on antique subjects (*Xerxes, Giulio Cesare,* etc.). By 1770, the date of Beethoven's birth, Mozart, fourteen years old, had tried his prentice hand at several minor operas in the Italian style. Still, most of Europe's popular operas were imports from Naples and Venice. Thousands of operas were produced, a composer usually pumping out a score in a month or six weeks, then forgetting about it.* Composers did little more than write out a blueprint of the score, giving a general idea of melody and harmony, to be filled out on the spur of the moment by the singer.

The singer was not merely a vocal athlete. He was almost a composer in his own right. He improvised. His vocal traceries, his intricate elaborations, had originality, grace, and beauty. Fleeting though the art was and insubstantial, it was an art, an art practiced not only by normal men and women but by a creature neither man nor woman. In the late 17th and most of the 18th century, boys with promising voices were operated on to produce *castrati,*** artificial male sopranos or contraltos. These epicene voices were as malleable as rich clay. To hear this superhuman chant, people flocked to the opera houses, and after a particularly well-executed aria, a few spectators climbed to the stage to give vent to their enthusiasm. Performances lasted from four to six hours. You grew hungry during the performance. If you did, you had only to beckon to one of the several hawkers who wended their way through the audience and who sold candied chestnuts, oranges, apples, and pear compote. If a singer performed badly, these fruits could be hurled at him.

The audience listened with passion to the notes that were held for unbelievable lengths, to the trills that were trilled so that each note was as exactly equivalent to the next as the ticking of a watch, to the runs of notes, now legato, now of pinpoint staccato, which played around the melody. When the singing

---

* Piccini, a contemporary of Gluck, composed 139 operas!
** The most famous of the 18th-century castrati was Farinelli. He spent twenty-five years of his life at the Spanish court of Philip V. The king was prone to attacks of melancholia, and Farinelli sang to him every single evening the same four songs and nothing else.

stopped, they discussed the merits of favorite singers, their probable earnings, their voyages to the leading opera houses of the Continent and of England, and their marital and extramarital affairs. The feuds between singers were fought not only by those directly involved but also by their public. The men who stood during the performance used their fists; the gentlemen who sat during the performance used the rapier.*

One does not have to be a historian of the theater to be able to predict what occurs when the actor or the singer becomes all-powerful. Sooner or later such a theater goes to pieces. What happened in Italy happened to the English stage at about this time. As Margaret Barton has pointed out in her biography of Garrick, the actors tampered with Shakespeare's plays. They thought nothing of giving *King Lear* a happy ending. *Macbeth's* witches became comic characters. During performances actors conversed with friends in the audience, and if in ill humor they ostentatiously spat on the stage. Every so often a young drunk climbed onto the stage to kiss the leading lady.

In Italy the operatic theater sank to a vaudeville of improvisation—and the operatic composer became a discouraged servant. What was the use of creating anything careful, of taking trouble with an opera, when the singers paid little heed to your work and when the public cared less? It is a sentimental notion that an artist can create his work independent of his time, that he can rise completely above contemporary conditions, heedless of the consumers of his wares. The artist needs his public. To a certain extent even the great artist gives the public what the public wants. Rather, he gives the public more than it wants. He builds on the known, adding the unknown, the new, the daring, to his structure. But he must have some basis to build on. His work cannot float in a dissociated ether. The art that we call timeless was anchored in its time. It bore some relation to the everyday world, the comfortable or disconsolate world in which lived those people who cooked the artist's dinner, who cleaned his room, and who paid him his money. During a period when people do not care what goes into a book, you will find few good authors. When you find a period in which paintings are out of fashion, you will find few first-rate painters. And if this is true of all art, it is especially true of the art of music and more especially true of the theater. Less than books or paintings or sculpture can music or a play or an opera live the sheltered life. It must live with its audience.

---

* We are describing conditions in England particularly, where audiences contained a higher percentage of "commoners."

Italian opera left to the ministrations of the singers not only became questionable music but lost the sense of the theater. As early as 1720 a satiric writer, Marcello by name, published a report on operatic conditions in which he made fun of these conditions by pretending to offer good advice to all those who took part in an opera performance. The opera composer, he writes,

> will hurry or slow down the pace of an aria, according to the caprice of the singers, and will conceal the displeasure which their insolence causes him by the reflection that his reputation, his solvency, and all his interest are in their hands. ... The director will see that all the best songs go to the prima donna, and if it becomes necessary to shorten the opera he will never allow her arias to be cut, but rather other entire scenes. [If a singer] has a scene with another actor, whom he is supposed to address when singing an air, he will take care to pay no attention to him, but will bow to the spectators in the loges, smile at the orchestra and the other players, in order that the audience may clearly understand that he is the *Signor Alipi Forconi, Musico,* and not the Prince Zoroaster, whom he is representing ...
>
> All the while the ritornello [the purely instrumental portion] of his air is being played the singer should walk about the stage, take snuff, complain to his friends that he is in bad voice, that he has a cold, etc., and while singing his aria he shall take care to remember that at the cadence he may pause as long as he pleases, and make runs, decorations, and ornaments according to his fancy; during which time the leader of the orchestra shall leave his place at the harpsichord, take a pinch of snuff, and wait until it shall please the singer to finish.

In serious opera the subjects were classical-allegorical-mythological. Comic operas were a little more inventive, a little less stilted. Essentially both kinds of opera were parades of arias. Between the arias people played chess; a visitor to Rome reported that "chess serves to fill out the boredom of the recitatives and the music serves to check too great a passion for chess." * I do not know what ambidextrous mind first reasoned that if people liked opera and liked gambling, then why not give them both at the same time and make doubly sure of their patronage? It is a fact that in the late 18th century most of Italy's opera houses were run in connection with a gambling casino. If the performance did not please you, you could get to the gaming tables without having to step out in the rain.

---

* Quoted by D. Grout, *A Short History of Opera,* and by Alberto Ghislanzoni, *Il Problema dell'Opera.*

Early in the century, Addison had complained against the absorbing popularity of Italian opera and had predicted that "our great Grand-children will be very curious to know the Reason why their Forefathers used to sit together like an Audience of Foreigners in their own Country, and to hear whole Plays acted before them in a Tongue which they did not understand." His diatribe is a little suspect: he himself was the author of an unsuccessful opera libretto. At any rate, it did not do much good—Italian opera continued to hold the European musical fort until the early part of the 19th century. Indeed, even in Germany, France, or England it has never been defeated. The best of it is too good for defeat.

While imported opera held sway in France as well, a native school of operatic composers did arise. French opera reflected the Enlightenment in its insistence on form, smoothly gleaming. It reflected the pictorial arts in the rococo of its ornamentation. It reflected French grace by the important role given to the ballet. The least consequential part of French opera was its drama. There was little connection between it and the music. The death of Hector could be set to a carefree tune.

One man rebelled against the practice of setting any plot to any music. He was not French at all; rather he was French only by expediency. Yet it was he who worked a profound influence not only on the French stage but on Mozart and Beethoven. This was Gluck.

Christoph Willibald Freiherr von Gluck was born in Bohemia and found his early employment in Vienna. For Vienna he produced a quantity of the usual Italian operas. At Vienna he met Metastasio, the obliging poet who furnished operatic librettos for many of the composers of the time. Nothing in Gluck's early career presaged the power and originality which the composer was to summon later. But then he came under the spell of the new ideals which were flowing through the world, and he was fortunate enough to meet a fine poet, Calzabigi, to help him make opera more "reasonable." The first product of this new collaboration was *Orfeo ed Euridice.* Here indeed was something new, though the subject was not only old but by coincidence the very same subject which had served the first Italian opera. The libretto was new in that it stripped away all that was superfluous or merely showy. The austere story is now austerely told. Euridice has already died before the curtain rises, and the first scene consists of a lament by Orfeo, joined by the chorus. What is true of the libretto is true of the music. Here are no unnecessary ornamentation, no stagey tricks. How beautiful it all is! And how fresh it must have seemed to contemporary audiences! The scene of the Furies, whose repeated cries soften before Orfeo's song and, being unable to resist the power of music, ebb away in a long sigh—that scene retains more dramatic power than the whole frantic song contest in *Tannhäuser,* which is also meant to prove that music hath charms.

Orfeo was a success in Vienna, where it was first performed in 1762, as well as in Paris twelve years later, where it was given with a French libretto and the added ballet music without which no Parisian production was possible. His next important work, *Alceste,* was welcomed with equal fervor. When the score was published, it was furnished with a preface in which Gluck put into words his ideas for the reform of opera. This famous document contained few thoughts which had not been expressed by the operatic composer before and no principle which by that time had not been recognized as valid. Gluck and his poet inveighed against the tyranny and caprices of the opera singers. They pointed out how weak were musical formulas applied to the text without regard to the meaning of the words. And they avowed that they had striven to restrict music to its true task of serving poetry, by expressing the situations of the story without interrupting the action or smothering it under superfluous ornaments. As has been pointed out many times, Gluck's manifesto foreshadowed the more elaborate theories of Wagner. In neither case did practice follow theory. Of neither composer's music could it be said that it merely served the poetry. Gluck is alive because of his music and not because of Calzabigi's words; Wagner is alive because of his music and often in spite of his poetry. At any rate, Gluck's declared loyalty to dramatic situation and textual meaning did serve to free opera from a style heavily artificial and excessively pretty. His ideas blended with the stream of the Enlightenment and its demand for clarity. Beethoven admired him.

·⦗ 3 ⦘·

As to nonoperatic music, we have noted that few composers and few executant artists were bold enough to show themselves in public recitals. Professional musicians would entertain in a palace, to the delight of a select few but as likely to the casual approval of guests stuffed with an opulent dinner and eager to resume gossip. The art particularly relished was that of improvisation. The artist would state a theme or somebody would suggest a theme to him, and he would then show his skill at composing on the spot by surrounding the theme with elaborate ornamentation, furnishing it with changing harmonies, chasing the theme through diverse adventures, now gay, now melancholy, shortening and lengthening the theme, playing hide-and-seek with it, and in short combining moody delight with the amazement which the cunningly intricate produces. Organists and harpsichordists were expected to be as adept at improvisation as singers were. Domenico and Alessandro Scarlatti gave recitals for audiences of perfumed ladies and gentlemen, improvising on the harpsichord. So did a child prodigy named Wolfgang Amadeus Mozart, who traveled with his father to the courts of Europe. A bishop and a dean at Augsburg threw themes at him for hours, and Mozart extemporized them into fugues.

When Beethoven was born, the greatest of the 18th-century composers, Johann Sebastian Bach, had been dead twenty years. He had served both clergyman and nobleman, had lived out a relatively modest life, had died in the provincial town of Leipzig, far from the main stream of the Enlightenment, and was now revered only by a few professional musicians who comprehended in some measure his true stature. Beethoven was to be one of these. If Bach was remembered, he was remembered more as a teacher; for pedagogic purposes he had composed forty-eight preludes and fugues—*The Well-tempered Clavier*—two for each major and minor key. Bach had taught his pupils a new playing technique, employing the full use of all the fingers of each hand. Up to then players had seldom used more than the middle three fingers and had tended to keep the hand flat. Bach asked his pupils to curve the hand. Without this innovation, Beethoven's playing could not have been possible.

The Bach who was famous was Karl Philipp Emanuel Bach, Johann Sebastian's second son of his first marriage. He thought his father's music rather old-fashioned and was in his own right a bold and progressive composer. For twenty-seven years he served Frederick the Great as Court musician.

What ever orchestras existed were constituted to serve the opera, the musicians being supported usually by the Court. An exception to this was to be found in Leipzig, where there evolved a body of players who met regularly and gave concerts for the prosperous businessmen in a hall called "Drapers Hall," the Leipzig *Gewandhaus*. This is the oldest regular concert series. But most musicians who met to play together "in concert" did so because they were employed by some potentate to entertain himself and his guests.

A musician was considered a servant. If he was employed by the Church, his standing was that of a humble artisan, one who carved notes instead of wood, but one who scarcely aspired to the intellectual pretension of a priest. If he was secularly employed, his standing was a little above that of the scullery maid and a little below that of the gardener or the gamekeeper. The French Court composer had the official title of *valet de chambre*. He dressed in uniform and ate with the servants. A music-loving employer, such as Prince Esterházy, at whose palace Haydn functioned, engaged his servants, his lackeys and cooks and coachmen, with an eye to their musical abilities. Haydn's orchestra consisted at least in part of the domestic staff.*

Yet, in the Age of Curiosity, questions were asked and changes sought even in the art of music, an art perhaps more conservative than other arts, anchored in tradition, less prone to violent changes, being only tenuously touched by social and political issues. Musicians began to ask how music could capture a wider audience, how it could be transplanted from the chamber to the hall, out of the salon into the auditorium, out of the Court opera into a theatrical entertainment which would please new groups in search of diversion. Composers knew that music needed to give out more sound and a warmer sound. To attract new listeners, delicacy had to be sacrificed for impact. Symptomatic of this tendency was the development of the harpsichord into the instrument which could play loud and soft, the forte-piano.** Dynamic range became wider. Orchestras became more fully manned. The symphony was born.

Haydn was a young man of thirty-eight when Beethoven was born, and had been in Esterházy's employ for nine years. He had already produced some forty symphonies, most of them essentially chamber music, yet gradually growing in sound and emotional force. Haydn did not invent the symphonic form; yet as a musician of the Enlightenment he clarified it and vastly enlarged it. Living to a venerable age (seventy-seven), he had the satisfaction of witnessing the triumph of the form with great audiences, particularly in England, where the process of popularization sped faster than on the Continent. Drama and wit, melancholy

---

* He ranked as a "household officer," a euphemistic term for servant. His employment contract with Prince Paul Anton Esterházy specified that "he will conduct himself as befits a loyal and self-respecting officer in a princely household, soberly, without harshness to the musicians under him. . . ." He was to appear in uniform, in clean white stockings and linen, with hair powdered and either in a pigtail or a bag. He was to present himself in the antechamber every morning and afternoon to receive his orders.

** In the harpsichord (and its various related forms such as a virginal or a spinet) the strings were plucked by quills. In the clavichord, tones were produced by pressure by small pieces of metal. In the piano, first called a forte-piano, they were similarly produced, except that leather and felt were soon substituted for metal. The forte-piano soon came to be known in English as the pianoforte, and in German at the Clavier, or the Klavier, or the Hammerklavier. "Clavier" originally (late 17th and 18th century) meant *any* keyboard instrument. The cembalo or clavicembalo were simply Italian terms for the harpsichord, but were used frequently in German nomenclature. Beethoven was called in an official document a cembalist, meaning that he played the harpsichord (see page 46).

and charm, all set forth with irresistible directness—these Haydn poured into the symphony.

Mozart's genius was nourished by the Enlightenment—his style being formed by the cool Classicism of the age—but short as his life was, he went far beyond the frontiers of the epoch. When Beethoven was born, Mozart had already astonished the world. Indeed, he astonished the world more as a child than later as a man, when it should have been more astonished. In 1770 the boy and his father spent much time in Italy. In Rome, during Holy Week, he heard Allegri's *Miserere* in the Sistine Chapel: this elaborate composition was the exclusive property of the Vatican Choir and no one was allowed to copy it. Mozart, after a single hearing, wrote the whole thing down from memory. He received the "Order of the Golden Spur" from the Pope. He could call himself "Chevalier de Mozart"—but he never took the title seriously. In Naples he was suspected of black magic, the Neapolitans not being *that* enlightened, and he had to prove to them that he could play as well without as with the ring which he wore and which was supposed to contain the source of his musical sorcery.

·◦[4]◦·

Beethoven was born at an unsleepy time of man's history. People were shaken awake by the alarm clock of philosophy and they were kept awake by the barbs and digs and dissatisfactions of probing minds. Beethoven's father and mother must have felt the speeded-up rhythm of change, must have been conscious of the incessant questions which flew through the air, even though the parents were geographically—and intellectually—far removed from searching Paris or enlightened London. One need not have been an intellectual to be drawn into the whirlpool stirred by the philosophers. We have no means of knowing whether the young Beethoven read *Candide,* but surely he must have heard of its wicked author. His schoolmates must have bandied about the heady new slogans, must have welcomed the promise of revolution, and must have enjoyed slamming to and fro the old-established authorities of church and state in a game of mental badminton.

The time was receptive. It was ready to welcome a genius who broke precedent. We take nothing away from Beethoven's achievement when we say that his entrance on the scene was well timed. The *Zeitgeist* must be taken into account. Beethoven was fortified in courage by the new courage in the world around him, a courage which was a product of the Enlightenment. The triumph of philosophy stimulated him to think philosophically. Obviously, he did not think in words or in formulated precepts. He thought in sound. Like the minds which challenged bigotry, he challenged music. He questioned. He searched.

The Enlightenment, however, was only the dock from which his ship sailed. It was the base from which he loaded the mental provisions for the initial stages of his journey. Later in life he was supposed to have said that "music was a higher revelation than philosophy." Before he could utter such proud words, he was to be deeply influenced by another spiritual movement which developed almost contemporaneously with the Enlightenment and which ran counter to the sway of Reason. That movement—and its prophet, Rousseau—we shall consider in due course. Suffice it to note here that both Reason and its antidote formed the composer of the *Eroica*.

Beethoven's birthplace in Bonn as it looks today (Beethoven House, Bonn).

CHAPTER 2

THE LIFE
OF A SMALL TOWN

Bonn was a small town. It pretended to the graces of a Paris, to the self-importance of a Berlin, and to the ceremonial splendor of a papal Rome. It succeeded in being none of these. It was really just a provincial town which gave itself airs because it was the seat of a prince of the Church and the capital of a small land called the "Electorate of Cologne" (*Kurköln*). The Electorate was one of the many states which made up the still mighty Holy Roman Empire.

There was no Germany in the 18th century. There were more than twenty million German-speaking people who were divided into 300 large or small states, all suffused with a sense of destiny and often inimical to the neighbor who spoke the same language. The German nation was further divided by the split between Protestantism and Catholicism. Each state was governed by a king or a prince or a grand-duke or a local sovereign, by whatever title he was called, and had its own coinage, its own police, its own army, its national dress, its special vainglory, and its guarded border at which the traveler had to come to a halt. Sixty-three of the principalities—and these included the Electorate of Cologne—were ruled by a member of the Church, an archbishop, a bishop, or an abbot. In them people lived under the sign of the crozier. There were fifty-one so-called Free Cities—these included such important cities as Hamburg, Nürnberg, and Frankfurt-am-Main—which enjoyed independent constitutions, but were loosely subject to the rule of the head of the Holy Roman Empire.

That Holy Roman Empire! It bound together temporal and churchly power so that Catholicism might remain invulnerable. It had endured for seven centuries, had weathered wars, papal schism, royal intrigue, and had even outlived the onslaught of the Reformation. It was governed by a monarch, with powers vested in him by the Pope.

When Beethoven was born, the ruler of the empire was the Emperor of Austria, Joseph II (1765–90), the son of Maria Theresa.* Administered from Vienna, with the Pope looking over Joseph's shoulder, the sprawling empire extended as far east as Hungary, as far south as Carniola (which is now part of Yugoslavia), as far west as Belgium, and north to the Baltic Sea. Voltaire said that the Holy Roman Empire was neither holy nor Roman nor an empire. The Enlightenment hastened the hardening of its arteries. There were signs that it was soon to slump of old age. As yet it held. In another thirty-odd years it was to disintegrate.

The term "Electorate" may need an explanation to us who are used to elections by popular vote. The Elector was elected by a committee of members of the highest aristocracy, usually of royal houses, and their choice had then to be confirmed by both the Pope and the Emperor of the Holy Roman Empire. No consideration was given to the wishes or the needs of the people to be governed. Choice of the elected sovereign was largely a political ploy, an award handed on a golden platter, a gift often given to the younger son of a royal house who, being the younger, could not succeed to the title of king. It was a game of ticktacktoe to fill spaces, so that the Habsburgs and the Wittelsbachs could rely on connecting lines. The security of the dynasty was the important consideration: nepotism was everywhere. The princes who wore the bishop's robe were quite as worldly as those who wore a uniform: they were quite as devoted to personal aggrandizement and quite as fond of fun and games. The best-governed German states were not the Electorates but the Free Cities. Lady Mary Montagu, the much-traveled wife of a British diplomat, whose letters form one of our valuable sources of knowledge of life in the 18th century, wrote to her daughter that the free towns had "an air of commerce and plenty," while those under the government of absolute princes "were not nearly as well off, displaying a sort of shabby finery, a number of dirty people of quality tawdered out; narrow, nasty streets out of repair, wretchedly thin of inhabitants, and above half of the common sort asking alms." Perhaps Lady Mary was exaggerating a bit.

Cologne, though it was allied with and carried the name of the state, was a

---

* In 1770 he was co-regent of Austria with his mother. He became sole regent after Maria Theresa's death in 1780.

Free City. Centuries ago the Archbishop of Cologne had been thrown out of the city, and Bonn had become the capital of the Electorate.

Bonn was a pleasant city, very old, very rich in tradition. It is situated on the western bank of the Rhine. The river—Germany's "holy river"—offered both delight and threat to the city. Outside the walls, one promenaded on the banks of the Rhine and watched the sailing ships going by or the loaded barges passing, drawn by horses along the banks. In good weather the Rhine looks green and smooth and inviting, and though it flows rapidly, it seems to be calming down after its twist around the dangerous rock of St. Goar, a huge and sparsely vegetated rock on which legend has placed that famous and beautiful and destructive siren, the Lorelei. In bad weather, when the Rhine carried the melted Alpine snows downstream, it could menace the city: it boiled over its banks and, turning an ugly brown, flooded the low-lying streets of Bonn, leaving dirt and devastation as residue of its anger. Across the Rhine are the "Seven Mountains," a chain of craggy hills, their sides warmed by thick forests and neat vineyards. The most famous of these mountains is the "Dragon's Rock" (*Drachenfels*), and the best wine, "Dragon's Blood," is produced there. The quarries in the mountains provided the stone for palaces and churches, including Cologne Cathedral. The woods offered secret trysting places for lovers and sunny spots for Sunday picnics.

In Beethoven's time some of the medieval city walls were still standing, topped by the Bastion *"Alter Zoll,"* where the customs (*Zoll*) were exacted. The farmers brought their produce to the market, a triangular place in the center of the city, on one side of which a handsome city hall was erected in 1748. In the market the noise was loudest; the children played hide-and-seek among the carts. The poor sections of Bonn were unpaved and dirty, with jerry-built houses, and outhouses plainly visible. At that, many people performed their natural functions right in the streets; there exists an official document, dated 1786, complaining of the practice and the "intolerable stink." * Offal was thrown into the streets, and chickens and pigs walked around freely.

All the same, there were enough good houses and open streets to give Bonn a comfortable aspect. One could escape the noise and the smells. The little city was speckled with gardens and dotted with inns, each of which displayed a patch of green. Trees were as numerous then as street lanterns a century later.

---

* Quoted in Ludwig Schiedermair, *Der Junge Beethoven,* 1925.

When one got near the Electoral Palace, one could enjoy an undisturbed panorama of flowers, formal lawns, and lanes lined with poplar trees. The Residence itself was a vast squarish structure, imposing but hardly an architectural triumph. Italian and French styles were mixed, as if the Electors weren't sure whether they wanted another Versailles or another Palazzo Vecchio. But whatever the building turned out to be, imposing it is and a testimony to the chest expansion of the Electors. (Today the building houses Bonn University.)

Many, if not most, of the 10,000 inhabitants of Bonn stood in direct or indirect relationship to the Palace. The saying was that "Bonn was fed from the Elector's kitchen." The Elector's personnel was a detailed organization: in addition to the soldiers, the private guard, the hunters, the architects, the gardeners, the lackeys, the window cleaners, the painters, the trumpeters, the fencing masters, etc., the staff ranged from "Chief-Keeper-of-the-Silver" (*Obersilberkämmerling*) to the "Fowl-plucker," (*Hühner-Pflücker*) and the "Pastry-Baker-Assistants" (*Zuckerbäckergehilfen*).* Then there were those engaged in the actual business of government, each with a high-sounding title, the fifty-three Privy Councilors, the judges of the ecclesiastic and secular courts, the Finance Commission, the War Department, and so on, in cumbersome complexity.

The people of Bonn were lighter-hearted and quicker-witted than their German neighbors to the north. The Palace set the example. Or perhaps it was the Rhine wine, so cheap and plentiful. Or perhaps there was a slight French strain in the populace. Bonn had been invaded several times by the French. In the documents of the period one finds French words straying among the German sentences: *"fêtes," "chaise," "consideration."* Among the young people of Bonn—and some of the older citizens as well—dancing was the popular diversion. In the town's hotel—the "English Yard" (*Hof von England*)— which catered to the quality and where "no gentleman was admitted with his cane or rapier," there was dancing twice a day: at 5 P.M. the "Health Balls" and at 10 the "Night Balls." Plainer people danced in the inns and their gardens.

Electors came and went, and like all rulers they were of varying quality. Clemens August, who reigned in the first half of the century, was a vain man—when he became archbishop he feared he might have to cut his beautiful

---

* The Bonn Court imitated the French Court, as did every other Western-European Court. In 1774 (four years after Beethoven's birth) Louis XVI employed at Versailles 295 cooks, 56 hunters, 47 musicians, 8 architects, along with couriers, guards, private chaplains, physicians, etc.

long hair—who let no occasion go by to show off the opulence of his person. He was a grandiose builder; the Residence was completed under his reign, to be furnished with precious furniture, extravagantly large mirrors, sumptuous chandeliers, and all the appurtenances of a royal seat in France. For summer residences and hunting lodges, for *maisons de plaisance* and *retiros* and rococo chapels, no expense was too great. His amusements were costly as well: sleighing parties, masquerades, operas, dramas, ballets. "His theater and opera alone," writes one historian, "cost him 50,000 thalers annually ($200,000) and the magnificence of his masked balls, twice a week in winter, is proof sufficient that no small sums were lavished upon them." * No wonder he left the finances of the Electorate in precarious shape. And this in spite of his skill in pressing subsidies from the coffers of France, Austria, and the Dutch. They all wooed the Electorate because of its strategically valuable position on the Rhine. Fortunately, Clemens August counted music among his diversions: he became the employer of Beethoven's grandfather and father.

In 1761 Clemens August was succeeded by Maximilian Friedrich, a merry little man, and like his predecessor very fond of women. The business of governing he left more or less to his minister, Baron Kaspar Anton von Belderbusch, a Machiavellian and ambitious diplomat. Belderbusch and Maximilian Friedrich shared the same mistress—an abbess, of all people!—the Abbess of Vilich, who must have been a wily wench indeed to satisfy both men. Maximilian Friedrich, too, was fond of music, of opera, and the theater. He turned one of the largest of the Palace's rooms into a concert hall and constructed a theater beneath it; in both of these grandfather and father Beethoven officiated. Pomp and ostentation were necessary stimulants to Maximilian Friedrich too. Life seemed boring without a parade of show. Still, the administration of the new Elector and his minister had its good side: princely extravagance was curbed somewhat, the financial situation of Bonn was improved, a threatening famine in 1771 quickly relieved by the importation of food, a poorhouse opened, jurisprudence speeded, and a scientific academy established. An observer in 1780 wrote that the present government was "the most enlightened and active of the ecclesiastic governments in Germany."

After twenty-three years, Maximilian Friedrich was succeeded by a member of the house of Habsburg, Maximilian Franz. Before we glance at him, who was

---

* Dr. Leonhard Enner, quoted by Alexander Wheelock Thayer, in *The Life of Beethoven,* Elliot Forbes, ed., 1964.

to be the last of the Electors and was to have some influence on the career of the young Beethoven, we should retrace our steps to inquire how it came about that a family with so pronounced a foreign name as van Beethoven, a name obviously Flemish, came to live and work in a German town on the Rhine.

Facts about Beethoven's grandfather and father are sparse. There are anecdotes, there is tradition; but most of it is the kind of recollection that springs to the fore after one member of a family has proved to be famous. Then somebody asserts, "I knew him as a child, I knew his father." Such remembrance must be doubted; not only has it become inexact in the intervening years but fame itself has brushed it with color.

The scholars who burrow in mildewed archives have found evidence of existing Beethovens as far back as the 13th century. The name turns up in chronicles of Flemish cities, in parts of northern France, in Mechlin and Antwerp.* Two theories about the derivation of the name are advanced: one that it means from (van) the Beet-Garden (Hof) — in other words, that the name was given to a gardener who cultivated beets. The other is this: There was a place in Belgium named *Betouwe;* the *"ouwe"* stands for "land," and *"bet"* is the root of "better." The name would then signify somebody who improved the soil. It is certain only that the "van" is not the equivalent of the German "von," denoting a member of the nobility.

A single tragic story about the early Beethovens has come down to us. It concerns the wife of an Arnold van Beethoven who was burned at the stake for witchcraft in 1595.

The grandfather's father, Michael van Beethoven, was a baker, as was his wife, Marie Louise. We know that Ludwig (originally Louis) van Beethoven, the grandfather, was baptized in the Church of St. Catherine in Mechlin and that he left home to be employed in St. Peter's Church in Louvain, where he eventually became choirmaster. After that he worked at the Church of St. Lumbert in Liége. There, tradition has it, Clemens August heard him and summoned him to the Court Chapel in Bonn (March, 1733) as a singer, at a yearly salary of four hundred florins ($2500).** The salary was a not inconsiderable one, particularly for a young man of twenty, and attests either to the generosity of the Elector or to the ability of his protégé, or both. At such a

---

* The spelling of the name was as erratic as the spelling of Shakespeare's name: Biethoffen, Piethoffen, Betthoffen, Biethofen, Bethoven, Bethof.

** Kant's salary as professor at the University of Königsberg was at the start 167 Prussian Thaler (about $1600).

salary one could afford to get married, and marry he did less than six months after his appointment. The girl of his choice, Maria Josepha Poll, was nineteen. She seems to have come from a good family. Her life rolled on with the usual fate of the small-town, middle-class, 18th-century housewife: bear children— and see them die. A year after she got married, a girl was born who lived only a little over a year. The baby was followed by a son, of whom nothing is known except a baptismal certificate. After a lapse of some four years, the Beethovens again became parents. This son, Johann, lived to be the composer's father.

The grandfather slowly rose in importance. In 1761 he became the official Kapellmeister to the Elector and is listed in the Court Calendar of the same year as one of the twenty-eight *hommes de chambres honoraires,* a distinction which hints at the respect accorded him by the Palace. Why was the Kapellmeister an important functionary? Why did the Elector spend money to maintain a "Court Band" (*Hofkapelle*) of some thirty or forty members? The Court records meticulously list the members of this band, these vocalists, violinists, viola players, cellists, oboists, and bassoon players, not counting the occasional trumpeter or drummer who could be pressed into service from the military band. Names of diverse nationalities appear, a Passavanti with a Kicheler, a Touchemoulin with a Belserotzky.

A complex of musicians in a sovereign's employment was considered his standard equipment, as necessary to him as the troupe of cooks or his regiment of private soldiers. Even the least important duke in some faraway and forested Bohemian province kept his own little musical retinue, the performers decently periwigged and uniformed, ready to execute his grace's wishes. When one duke visited another he often brought his musicians along. Music was needed not only to while away winter nights but to impress the important visitor with the Court's culture and wealth.

Bonn had a good musical service of long tradition. No genius worked there to shed luster and turn the town into a famed music center. But there was competence, there was variety. The inventory of the music library shows that the works of many composers were available, composers popular in the '70's, such as Dittersdorf, Stamitz, Cannabich, as well as the early compositions of Haydn and Gluck. An 18th-century engraving * shows us what Court concerts must have been like. In a large and airy room of state the musicians playing the lighter instruments are lined up, standing in two facing rows before two troughs

---

* In the Bertarelli collection in Milan.

which serve as music stands. The heavier instruments, contrabass, timpani, French horn, etc., form another row at a right angle. The harpsichordist sits somewhere near the center, while vocalists (two men and two children) are clustered directly in the center. The audience, a sparse one, sits on stately chairs. A casual atmosphere prevails: a nobleman and his lady are promenading around the room, a mother or nurse carries a prettily dressed little child in her arms, two men who have just entered are continuing a discussion, and one man, obviously bored with the proceedings, is leaning out of the window.

In Bonn's Court Theater plays and operas were performed. The operas, as we have mentioned, were chiefly Italian and chiefly comic little *divertissements, buffo* pieces by Galuppi and Piccini, with now and then a French *opéra comique* to vary the diet. Opera performances were festive occasions, operas were often sumptuously staged, with resident singers supplemented by artists imported for the occasion.

How did Grandfather Beethoven function? As Kapellmeister he was responsible for both the music to be heard at church service and the music to be played at banquets, at serenades, at spoken theatrical performances, at the ballet, and probably also at masked balls. He had to examine candidates for admission to the Electoral musical service. He was, as the documents show, responsible for keeping the peace among the musicians in the Elector's employ, a discipline not entirely easy to enforce. He complained to Maximilian Friedrich that a certain singer—Schwachhoverin was the lady's name—behaved "impertinently in the presence of the Court musicians" and told him that "she would not accept his command." He asked for satisfaction for such a "public affront"; otherwise his authority would be undermined. The Elector immediately supported him.

He must have been a valuable employee: even after he became Kapellmeister he continued to sing leading bass parts. Possibly such doubling was part of Maximilian Friedrich's economy program. How busy he must have been, on state occasions especially, appears from the Court Calendar of May 13, 1767, the Elector's birthday:

1. Early in the morning three rounds from the cannon on the city walls;
2. The court and public graciously permitted to kiss His Transparency's hand;
3. Solemn high mass with salvos of artillery;
4. Grand dinner in public, at which both papal nuncios, the foreign ministers and the nobility were the guests; and the eating was accompanied by "exquisite table-music";
5. After dinner "a numerously attended assembly";

6. "A serenata composed especially for this most joyful day" and
7. Supper of 130 covers;
8. Bal masqué until 5 A.M.

The high mass, the table music, the serenade, the Italian opera (in which Ludwig's son, "Giovanni van Beethoven," sang a part), and possibly the *bal masqué* were tasks entrusted to Ludwig. It was fortunate that the Elector's birthday occurred but once a year!

What was Grandfather Beethoven like? The little evidence we can piece together indicates that he was a man conscious of his worth. The official Court painter—one Radoux—did his portrait, which fact alone suggests that Ludwig van Beethoven the elder had attained a certain importance.* The portrait shows him richly gowned in the manner in which Franz Hals might have painted a worthy alderman. But how are we to know whether the painter was painting the truth or imitating Hals? What it does show is the face of a solid citizen, a round, well-fed face, with nothing remarkable about it except the eyes, which are exceptionally large, stern, and strong. Grandfather lived for a time in the house of a baker's family, Fischer by name; the youngest son, Gottfried, born in 1780 (he was therefore ten years younger than the composer), late in life was persuaded to set down his reminiscences. By that time the composer was dead and world-famous; a statue had already been erected to him in Bonn. Fischer, who was no professional writer and whose command of German was rudimentary, produced some suspect along with believable recollections. He could not have known the grandfather personally, but he or a member of his family saw the rooms in which grandfather had lived. He wrote that "everything was so beautiful and proper and well arranged, with valuables, all six rooms were provided with beautiful furniture, many paintings and cupboards, a cupboard of silver service, a cupboard with fine gilded porcelain and glass, an assortment of the most beautiful linen which could be drawn through a ring; everything from the smallest article sparkled like silver." **

Personal evidence seems nonexistent. If he composed music—which he undoubtedly did—nothing remains of it. No personal letter is extant: what written material there is consists of petitions or recommendations to the Elector,

---

* A copy of the portrait can be seen in the Beethoven House in Bonn.
** Thayer tried to buy the Fischer manuscript but refused to pay what he thought an exorbitant price for it. It was later bought by the city of Bonn.

penned in a language which scraped the ground and contained such superscriptions as

Most Reverend Archbishop and Elector
Most Gracious Lord Lord *

and such signatures as

Humbly recommending myself to your Electoral Grace's continued favor and grace, and expiring in profoundest submission, I am
Your Electoral Grace's
most humble
Ludwig van Beethoven
Cappell Meister

To maintain such a household as Fischer described, the Kapellmeister supplemented his income by engaging in the wine trade. No doubt he did well. Yet his home life could not have been unclouded: his wife, Josepha, began to drink. We can only guess why she fell a victim to alcohol. Could the deaths of the children have driven her to it? Was the wine too readily available in the wine merchant's house? Was there strife between husband and wife? Was he too stern a domestic taskmaster? We know only that at the time of her husband's death she was immured in a cloister, and had been there for some time.

The son who lived, Johann, was born about 1740. It was a foregone conclusion that he, too, would become a musician. His father taught him, and when Johann was twenty-two years old, Ludwig "humbly" petitioned the Elector, stating that "Johannes van Beethoven" had "for 13 years sung soprano, contralto and tenor in every emergency that has arisen" and was "also capable on the violin" and that therefore it was time now to reward him with a regular appointment. The Elector agreed: Johann's starting salary was 100 fl. ($625). Though the stipend was soon augmented by a few florins, it remained a meager sum. This may indicate that Johann was considered an unimportant employee—or that the Elector had become parsimonious. At any rate, Johann seems to have discharged his duties punctiliously.

Three and a half years after his appointment, Johann married. His bride was

---

* The repetition Lord Lord (*Herr Herr*) is part of the 18th-century formula used to address men of exalted station. It was occasionally used by Beethoven in dedications.

Maria Magdalena Keverich. The bride's father, Heinrich Keverich, held the position of "Overseer of Cooking" in one of the Electoral summer palaces, the palace of Ehrenbreitstein, second in grandeur only to the Palace in Bonn. Johann was twenty-six, his bride was twenty-one. She was "slim and beautiful." * Young as she was, she was no stranger to sorrow. At the age of seventeen she had been married. She bore her first husband one son, who lived a scant five weeks. Two years later her husband died, leaving Maria Magdalena a widow before she had seen her nineteenth birthday. Once again we must note that family life in the 18th century began early, that death of children was a common occurrence, and that women became old and spent in middle age.

Grandfather Beethoven was not pleased. He felt that his son had married beneath his station. He did not approve of Johann's marrying the daughter of a cook, a girl who had "once worked as a chambermaid." He had expected better. If his son proved to be obdurate, Ludwig wanted to have nothing to do with the wedding. Let him get the ceremony over with. As for himself, he did not want to live with the young couple. They could have his quarters; he would move out. The grandfather did change lodgings. Perhaps he did object to the wedding. But it is untrue that Maria Magdalena came from a lowly family. In fact, the Keveriches were equivalent in social standing to the Beethovens. Nor is it true —as even Thayer assumed—that she was an unschooled, uneducated girl. Fischer speaks of her "good education and culture," and says that "she was able to converse with the high and the lowly in a manner which was fine, adroit, and modest; therefore she was much loved and esteemed." Grandfather Ludwig, even if he did not like her, seems to have learned to make the best of the bargain.

No clear picture emerges of the woman who was to become Beethoven's mother. One contemporary, Franz Gerhard Wegeler—a man whom we will meet more than once in the story of Beethoven's life—spoke of her gentleness and the kindness with which she treated her family. Cäcilia Fischer, Gottfried's sister, could not recall that she had ever seen her laugh. Yet her brother, in the manuscript from which we have already quoted, remembered:

> The name day and birthday of Mme. van Beethoven was splendidly celebrated
> every year. . . . A canopy was constructed in the room in which hung the portrait

---

* That is a contemporary description. No authentic portrait of her or her husband has survived. Probably none was painted. The portraits shown in the Beethoven House in Bonn are not genuine, according to most authorities.

of Grandfather Herr Hofkapellmeister Ludwig van Beethoven. It was adorned with pretty decorations and beautiful flowers, little laurel trees, and leafy branches. The night before, Mme. van Beethoven was requested to go to bed early; at ten o'clock everybody entered silently and everything was made ready. Now the festivities began. Mme. van B. was awakened, she had to get dressed, she was escorted into the room and made to sit down underneath the canopy on a beautiful, elaborate chair. Now the marvelous music began: it was heard in the whole neighborhood, and all the people who had been ready to go to sleep became wide awake and gay once more. After the music was over, refreshments were served. Everyone ate and drank. Presently the mood grew very lively. People wanted to dance, and in order not to create any tumult, they took their shoes off and danced in their stockings.

This does not sound like a household of unmitigated gloom. Though life was difficult, it was not joyless. Though Beethoven's parents were people of small importance, they were not clods.

In Beethoven fiction Johann plays the part of the villain. He has been depicted as a cruel father, as an exploiter of his son's talent, as a dissolute drunkard. He has been invidiously compared to Leopold Mozart who, whatever his faults, guided Wolfgang Amadeus well. He has even been accused of being one of Belderbusch's spies; cited is a document of doubtful veracity in which are listed "informers and spies" who "can be bought for a cheap price." Johann is on the list. The more his character has been blackened, the more wondrous appear Beethoven's triumphs. This makes for sentimental biography, but it cannot be the whole truth. The evidence is too conflicting. It is true that Wegeler spoke of him as "undistinguished intellectually and morally" and "prone toward drinking." And Fischer wrote that "the tasting of wine was one of his early accomplishments." Yet how could a drunkard have continued to hold a position as a member of the Court, each member of which was strictly supervised and whose behavior was frequently reported in documents which read like a report card? One of these reports, dated 1784, has survived. It reviews the ability of each musician and says of Johann van Beethoven that he was "of seemly behavior." He never did attain the position which his father had held. He never did become Kapellmeister. Yet he continued to function as an Electoral *Musicus*. This he could not have done had he reeled in the streets of Bonn. To earn extra money he gave music lessons to the children of the well-to-do in Bonn, the sons and daughters of foreign ambassadors and of the "ladies and gentlemen of the aristocracy." Would these parents have entrusted their tender offspring to a wine-bibbing nonentity? Several of the parents were so well pleased with Johann that they sent gifts to him. The customary gift was wine. But, says Fischer, though he could order as much wine as he wanted, "he did not take advantage of the opportunity."

That he was a weak man and mediocre in talent we may believe. He longed to get away from Bonn into the greater world, but did not have the strength to do so and contented himself with making excursions into the surrounding country. Old Ludwig was supposed to have nicknamed his son *Johannes der Läufer* (John the Runner), a pun on *Johannes der Täufer* (John the Baptist). It is probable that he had inherited from his mother a tendency to drink. But it is equally probable that he did not go to pieces, did not really succumb to his vice, until Maria Magdalena died (at the age of forty, of consumption). Then he lost his hold on life.

Similarly, the meanness of the home has been sentimentally exaggerated. Though one official memorandum lists Johann as "very poor," the family was neither friendless nor in actual want. Around grandfather and father Beethoven quite a few friends gathered, all in one way or another in the service of the Court. If at that time you had strolled down the Bonngasse, you would have been able to pay your respects to a musical family by the name of Ries, whose young son Ferdinand was later to be of great service to the composer. You could also have met Nikolaus Simrock, who was appointed "Court Hornist . . . in the cabinet and at table" and who later in life founded a publishing firm which was to publish several of Beethoven's compositions. Almost opposite the Kapellmeister's lodging was house No. 515. The ground floor of this house was occupied by a lacemaker and a dealer in lace named Clasen; a little later the second story was leased by the Salomons. Philip Salomon was in the Elector's employ. So was his daughter. So was his son, Johann Peter,* who eventually took up residence in London, where he became a highly successful concert manager and conductor: he induced Haydn to write some of his finest symphonies for London, the "Salomon symphonies." In the rear of the Clasen house, on the second story, there was a lodging to let. There Johann Beethoven and his wife set up housekeeping. The apartment consisted of a kitchen and three rooms. It was a humble enough home, but it was not a pauper's dwelling.

The first son born to Johann and Maria Magdalena was a Ludwig Maria van Beethoven. The baby lived six days. A year and a half later another son came

---

* By the time Beethoven was born, Johann Peter had become concertmaster of the orchestra of Prince Heinrich of Prussia.

into the world. This was the composer. Five more children were to spring from the union. Of the five, only two survived infancy. They were Caspar Anton Carl, four years Beethoven's junior * and Nikolaus Johann, six years younger. Of the later children two were girls, one living only four days, the other dying a year and a half after her birth, and one was a boy who lived but two and a half years. Seven pregnancies, four funerals. Seven hopes, four griefs. Death becomes a statistic, until one imagines how copious were the tears shed by Maria Magdalena and Johann. Of the three children who grew up, one was a mediocrity, one became wealthy — and one a genius.

The date of Beethoven's birth has never been ascertained. All we have is his baptismal certificate, dated December 17, 1770. Since it was the custom in the Rhenish Catholic cities not to postpone baptism beyond twenty-four hours after the birth of a child, it is probable that Beethoven was born on December 16. The year is certain, though for a long time Beethoven believed that he was two years younger than he actually was. It was 1770, the year in which the Dauphin of France married Marie Antoinette, Paul D'Holbach published his famous work which attacked Christianity, *The System of Nature,* and Gainsborough painted "The Blue Boy."

---

* Belderbusch and the Abbess were chosen by Johann as the godparents. They consented, an indication that Johann was not quite the nonentity he is often pictured to be.

*Grandfather Ludwig Beethoven, painted by A. Radoux. The composer
had this painting forwarded to him in Vienna (Courtesy, Sen. Otto Reichert, Germany).*

CHAPTER 3

BOYHOOD

The boy was looking out of the window, his head cradled in his hands. His mien was serious, his glance rigid. Cäcilia Fischer came along the courtyard and saw him. "How are you, Ludwig?" she shouted up to him. No answer. She said, "Foul weather seems to be with you." No answer. She said, "Well, no answer is an answer too." Suddenly the boy exclaimed, "Oh, please, no, no, forgive me! I was busy with such a beautiful, deep thought I couldn't bear to be disturbed."

This is one of a few vignettes which have survived. It rings true. But how can one be sure? Nor can any one anecdote flesh out the portrait of the boy Beethoven. The boy, like the man, was contradictory—and contradictory were the impressions received by the people around him.

He was a merry boy, quite ready for pranks. He played with the other children in the garden of the Palace. He loved to be carried piggyback. He sneaked into the henhouse and stole some eggs. Good-natured Frau Fischer caught him at it. She called him a fox. The fox steals eggs. He said, "I am more of a music fox (*Notenfuchs*) than an egg fox."

No, he was an exceptionally serious boy. He was "shy and taciturn," he was "enclosed in himself," he was "peevish with people." He loved to turn the iron handle of the window shutters and listen to the musical noise the handle produced. He was always maneuvering around the clavier and trying to improvise, to the annoyance of Johann, who said that he had first to learn how to play before he could compose. His father took his little hand and guided the fingers in accompaniment of simple songs. Then he was set to work in earnest and stood before the clavier and wept. He wept, probably because he could not master the instrument quickly enough. He was ill cared for and often dirty.

Cäcilia said, "Why do you look dirty? You should make yourself proper." *
He answered, "When I grow up, nobody will worry about it."

Merry or sad, smiling or sullen, a carefree boy or one who early carried the heavy load of talent on his back—perhaps he was all of these.

In later years Beethoven said that he loved his grandfather. The portrait by Radoux was one of the few mementos he had forwarded to him when he moved to Vienna. But the grandfather died when Ludwig was but three years old. How full a recollection could Beethoven have retained of him? His mother, too, Beethoven remembered with tenderness. Of his father he said nothing. What were Johann's feelings for the boy? Fischer recounts that on Sunday evenings, when Johann used to visit them, he would say, "My son Ludwig is my only joy . . . My Ludwig, my Ludwig. I know that some day he'll be a great man of the world. Those of you who are here today and will still be alive, remember my words!" Yet he seems to have treated the boy who was "his only joy" with severity. That at least is the impression one receives from the few recollections time has not destroyed. There was—one guesses, and it *is* more or less a guess—little ease in the father-son relationship. If Johann loved the boy, his love was laced with calculation. A show of talent was a promise of money. In later years Beethoven's need for love was great. Was it because he was kept on insufficient rations of affection in his youth?

Yet doubt lingers that Johann was unrelievedly "brutal and tyrannical." **
There are traces of contrary evidence, and I am inclined to agree with the view of Adolph Bernhard Marx, one of the early biographers, who describes Johann as unstable, "originally good-natured," then "irascible as musicians are wont to be and oppressed and goaded by constant want," but not out-and-out hard and harsh.*** His mother, Beethoven recalled, loved him. But how much time or care could this woman—beset with household chores and frequent pregnancies —lavish on him?

Indifferent to the child's needs, the father concentrated his efforts on developing him as a performing musician and therefore as a source of income. Beethoven was not the miraculous child prodigy that Mozart was, nor did Johann possess much of the intelligence and carefulness that Leopold Mozart lavished on his children and that helped their early development. Still, musical talent

---

* She used the French-derived word *"propper."*
** Édouard Herriot, *The Life and Times of Beethoven,* 1935.
*** *Ludwig van Beethoven Leben und Schaffen,* 1863.

showed itself early—it nearly always does—and Ludwig made enough progress on the clavier for the father to exhibit him in a little concert in Cologne:

AVERTISSEMENT

Today, March 26, 1778, in the musical Academy-room in the Sternengass the Electoral Court Tenorist, BEETHOVEN, will have the honor to produce two of his scholars; namely, Mdlle. Averdonc, Court Contraltist, and his little son of six years. The former will have the honor to present various beautiful arias, the latter various clavier concertos and trios, in which he flatters himself that he will give complete enjoyment to all the members of august society, the more since both have had the honor of playing to the greatest delight of the entire Court.

Beginning at five o'clock in the evening.

Ladies and gentlemen who have not subscribed will be charged a gulden. Tickets may be had at the aforesaid Akademiesaal, also of Hr. Claren auf der Bach in Mühlenstein.

Two things are noteworthy about this *avertissement*. First, why was it inserted the day of the concert and not before? Could the "members of august society" not plan a day or two ahead? Second, the boy's age is given as six. He was actually seven years and three months old. Much has been made of Johann's lie. If it was a lie, not a mistake, it was an innocuous and traditional one. No father tells the right age of a child prodigy.

Unfortunately, we know nothing of the results of the concert, nor what Beethoven played, nor whether the august society deigned to show. A gulden was not a modest price to charge for a concert by beginners. (The equivalent of about two dollars today.)

Where and how long did Ludwig attend school? Again, there are no documents to instruct us. School attendance was compulsory, though as yet there were no state-endowed public schools in Bonn. The first of these was established in 1786, when Ludwig was sixteen. Then Maximilian Franz, acting on the pressure of the Enlightenment, opened a "Normal School of the Electorate of Cologne." Before that schools were private institutions or run by ecclesiastic chapters, such as the Jesuits or the Minorites. It is probable that Ludwig began school attendance when he was six and ended it when he was eleven—the usual period for elementary instruction. Aside from the three R's, the curriculum included Religion, Choral Singing, and beginners' Latin.

Beethoven's early letters show that he learned a decent handwriting. He used the Teutonic script * with the long S and H. His spelling, however, was atrocious and became more so as he grew older. The handwriting, too, became wild and erratic, so that the later manuscripts are often almost illegible. He learned enough Latin to be able to understand the Latin texts he set to music. He probably picked up his French in the streets of Bonn and later in the houses of the Viennese nobility, where it was spoken almost as much as German. Beethoven's French was quaint, to put it mildly. He knew Italian, though he did not speak it fluently. Italian was the language of music; no musician could do without it.

Arithmetic remained an impenetrable subject to him. The giant mind could not comprehend its plainest rules. He could add a little, and late in life his nephew tried to teach him the multiplication tables. In vain.

While Ludwig was a boy at school, the family changed lodgings three or four times. This is significant in light of Beethoven's later habit, a habit which amounted to a compulsion, of changing his dwelling frequently. Thayer suggests that Johann moved to a better address, anticipating that after grandfather's death he would be appointed Kapellmeister. His hope being dashed, he had to seek a cheaper place in the lower part of Bonn. Even if this were true, it would not account for all the moves, made with bag and baggage and babies, by the restless and insecure father. Beethoven inherited the restlessness.

Wherever the family's home, Johann's colleagues came to visit; the child must have heard many a conversation about music, many a morsel of gossip concerning the current composers, and a heap of technical discussion touching the church service and operatic problems. Musicians are inveterate talkers.

Music and always music, music for breakfast and music in the evening—it was the only road open to Ludwig, and he was placed on it as soon as the first signs of talent appeared. It is curious that neither of the brothers, Carl or Johann, showed exceptional musical ability. How disappointed the father must have been! ** When Ludwig was nine, he began to receive instructions more extensive than those provided by his father. His teacher was an old man, a friend of the grandfather, who for long years had served as the Court Organist; his name was Gilles van den Eeden. The name suggests that he, like the Beethovens, was of Flemish extraction, and perhaps for that reason Eeden felt

---

* He changed to the Latin script after 1817.
** Carl was for a brief time trained for music. Johann was apprenticed to an apothecary.

close to the Beethovens. Tradition has it that the teacher took the pupil without pay. His second teacher, Tobias Friedrich Pfeifer, was an unsteady but gifted vagabond, one of those personalities forever poised for flight, alighting here or there to astonish, impress, and irritate, then disappearing to leave puzzlement behind. He was employed as a "tenorist" in the theatrical troupe performing at Court. He was young and handsome and reckless, was taken in by the Beethovens as a boarder, and became a drinking companion of Johann. Fischer recalled him vividly:

> One morning he threw his barber Triputt down the stairs. One would have thought the fellow broke his neck and leg ... Barber Triputt screamed that he (Pfeifer) was an idiot, let his hair be dressed by whomever he pleased ... no matter how one tried, Pfeifer was never satisfied ... The Beethovens kept mum. Beethoven took another barber, by the name of Heuseler.
> Herr Direktor Pfeifer was taken ill in Beethoven's house. The Beethovens tried everything they could to help him and care for him. He was worth it ... Beethoven's maid complained that Pfeifer's illness gave her extra work.* Before and after Pfeifer's illness, late at night when everybody was getting ready for bed, he ordered the maid to make him coffee or sent her to fetch him wine, beer and spirits. Then he drank everything together, yet it had no effect on him. One couldn't say he was ever drunk, he was always clear-headed and peaceful ...

Pfeifer disappeared from Bonn after less than a year. It is in connection with him that a pathetic little story has become famous: "Often" when Pfeifer and Johann returned from a winehouse as late as eleven or twelve at night, Johann awakened the sleeping child, and Pfeifer sat him down at the clavier, giving him instruction till the early morning hours. There are some grounds for suspecting the story; it was related by one man only, who obviously wasn't there, and sounds too pitiless to have happened "often."

Ludwig had other teachers as well. The most significant of these was the composer Christian Gottlob Neefe. He was an unspectacular, thin little man, conscientious and quiet, yet possessing a hunger to learn, to know, to understand the new ideas which swirled through Europe. Influenced by the Enlightenment, he was "no friend of ceremony or etiquette" and "hated bad rulers more than bandits." That is what he said, and we may believe him. He was no genius but he possessed a decent enough talent; that talent included writing as

---

* Poor though they were, the Beethovens had a servant. With three children in the house (in 1779), one 9, one 5, and one 3 years old, the servant could hardly have had a sinecure.

well as composing. He wrote the biography of an actress, a good deal of sentimental poetry, and a number of critical articles. He composed organ pieces, piano sonatas, songs, concertos, and at least eight comic operas. He loved the theater, spoken or sung, and was familiar with the latest pieces of entertainment from Italy as well as their German imitations. Yet his taste was comprehensive enough to include the music of Johann Sebastian Bach, whom he praised with eloquence. Of Karl Philipp Emanuel Bach he wrote, "If you are able to play Bach well, you can play practically any composer." And he set down instructions on how to play Bach's music. Perhaps it is to this teacher that we may trace Beethoven's phenomenal virtuosity in playing the piano.

Neefe had come to Bonn with a theatrical group, the "Grossmann-Hellmuth Society," for which he served as music director.* Two years later (in 1781), he entered the service of the Elector, first as assistant to van den Eeden. After van den Eeden's death the following year, Neefe was promoted to chief Court Organist and shortly after to Kapellmeister. Since he directed both the sacred and the secular music, it is interesting to note that he was a Calvinist, though he did bring up his children in the Catholic faith. Not only that, he was most probably a Freemason. A "heretic" served Catholic music at a Catholic court—so far had tolerance progressed. Voltaire would have approved.

One is tempted to overestimate this agreeable man with the euphonious name and generous enthusiasm. His was not a searching mind; a certain naïveté peeps through his letters and essays. His compositions are no more than competent, barring a few songs which display the innocent charm of German folk songs. Nevertheless, Beethoven could hardly have had a better teacher. He himself acknowledged this some years afterward. He came under Neefe's tutelage when he was about eleven. Neefe was then thirty-three years old, presumably not too old to remember a young boy's eagerness. How long Beethoven remained with Neefe is uncertain. But we do know that while the boy was studying under Neefe, he took instruction from other musicians. What musician then living near the Bonngasse would not in later years claim to have added his measure to Beethoven's knowledge? We hear of a Franz Rovantini, who taught him violin playing; a Franciscan friar, Willibald Koch; a Father Hansmann; and a Zensen, who was the organist at the Münsterkirche.

Whatever their contributions, it was Neefe who gave him most. Presently, in a year or so, Neefe afforded Beethoven the opportunity to assist him in his

---

* He wrote the biography of Grossmann's wife, a book that Goethe's mother enjoyed.

duties, no doubt to lighten his own work. Even before that, Beethoven substituted at the 6 A.M. service of the Electoral Chapel. Obviously this early service was the least desirable, and the boy made it possible for the organist to snatch an extra hour of sleep. The distance from the Beethoven dwelling to the chapel was about a seven-minute walk. We can imagine the boy getting up before daybreak, hurrying to his post and seating himself at the organ, his feet groping for the pedals—his hands, as yet small, stretching for the three keyboards.* The service over, he may have spent the rest of the day with Neefe, being inducted into the laws of canon and counterpoint, thorough-bass and modulation. It was not a lazy life; but those who learn the trade of music are used to hard work, and those in whom talent stirs are used to fierce concentration.

Neefe himself was an indefatigable worker, as the sheer volume of his compositions and his writings shows. Yet, and even though his reputation spread beyond the borders of the Electorate, he was not sheltered from the political winds. What man working for a court is safe? His career in Bonn was not a smooth one. Maximilian Friedrich protected him, but when this Elector died and the new one, Maximilian Franz, came on the scene, Neefe was in trouble. A change of "management" brings about a new inquiry into the organization and not infrequently a change in personnel, made just for the sake of change. Maximilian Franz—of whom more in the next chapter—demanded and received a complete review of the entire governmental organization, including the music staff. Thirty-seven musicians were reviewed and judged for ability and deportment. Among these reviews we find:

8. Johan Betthoven has a rather stale voice, has long been in the service, very poor, of decent behavior, and married.
13. Christian Neffe, the organist. In my humble opinion, could well be dismissed, because he is not particularly skillful on the organ. Moreover, is a foreigner, of no *meritten* whatever, and of Calvinist religion.
14. Ludwig Betthoven, a son of the Betthoven *sub.* No. 8. Has no salary, but during the absence of the Kapellmeister Lucchesy ** he functioned at the organ; is capable, still young, of good quiet deportment, and poor.

---

* The organ of Bonn's Minorite Church, now called "Beethoven's organ," has been preserved. It is a fairly small one, yet too large for a small boy to operate easily. Beethoven made a note of the pedal measurements of this organ and took the note with him to Vienna. The organ is now in the Beethoven House in Bonn.
** Another Court musician, in a position similar to Neefe's.

A further report, dealing with expense reduction, stated:

> *Item.* If Neffe were to be dismissed another organist would have to be appointed, who, if he were to be used only in the chapel, could be had for 150 florins, the same is small, young, and a son of one of the court *musici,* and in case of need has filled the place for nearly a year very well.

So whoever it was who wrote this report—obviously an official whom the new Elector must have thought capable of making recommendations—suggested that a boy thirteen years old could take the place of a musician of Neefe's reputation. Maximilian Franz compromised: Neefe was not dismissed, but his salary was cut in half. Beethoven was employed soon after as a second organist at a salary of 150 florins (about $1000). Neefe had been receiving 400. Thus the Elector now had two employees for less than the cost of one.

We can imagine Neefe's indignation. He immediately looked around for another post. He did not find one quickly, and fortunately, as Maximilian Franz became acquainted with Neefe's capability and as he began to develop the musical and theatrical life of his new home, he rescinded niggardly expense reduction: early in 1785 he restored Neefe's former salary.

Nevertheless, the circumstance of the pupil's becoming a competitor to the teacher must have been a ticklish one. Neefe does not seem to have held the awkward situation against Beethoven. Far from it—the relationship continued as cordial as ever; the teacher had early discovered the exceptional quality of his pupil. He gave Ludwig every chance for practical as well as theoretical development. About two years previously (1782) Neefe had appointed the twelve-year-old boy "cembalist in the orchestra," though the appointment was a temporary one. It was not an inconsequential post, because the cembalist (harpsichordist) guided the rehearsals and served as one of the key members in performance.

When we speak of young Beethoven's holding this or that post, we must not exaggerate the importance of the appointment, though the titles may sound impressive. Ludwig was no more than a teen-age apprentice. That he was good enough to be paid for his work was decided just before Maximilian Franz's accession in 1784. Ludwig petitioned Maximilian Friedrich for a salaried appointment. (The petition has not been discovered.) The "High Lord Steward" supported it:

Most Reverend Archbishop and Elector.
Most Gracious Lord, Lord.

Your Electoral Grace has graciously been pleased to demand a dutiful report from me on the petition of Ludwig van Betthoven to Your Grace under date of the 15th inst.

Obediently and without delay [I report] that suppliant's father was for 29 years, his grandfather for 46, in the service of Your Most Reverend Electoral Grace and Your Electoral Grace's predecessors; that the suppliant has been amply proved and found capable to play the court organ as he has done in the frequent absence of Organist Neefe, also at rehearsals of the plays and elsewhere and will continue to do so in the future; that Your Grace has graciously provided for his care and subsistence (his father no longer being able to do so). It is therefore my humble and non-committal judgment that for these reasons the suppliant well deserves to have graciously bestowed upon him the position of assistant at the court organ and a small increase of remuneration.* Commending myself to the good will of Your Most Reverend Electoral Grace I am in deepest submission Your Most Reverend Grace's

most humble and truly obedient servant
Sigismund Altergraff zu
Salm und Reifferscheid.

Six days later the petition was endorsed, indicating the action taken:

High Lord Steward Count v. Salm, referring to the petition of *Ludwig van Betthofen* to become assistant to court organist Neefe, is of the humble opinion that the grace ought to be bestowed upon him, also that a small increase to his present support be granted.*
    Ad. sup.
        Ludwig van Betthoven
        On the obedient report the suppliant's submissive prayer, rests.

Bonn, February 29, 1784.

It is impossible to give in an English translation the stilted and curlicued 18th-century tone of the German original. It is a typical governmental document of the times, so freighted with polite and "humble" formulas that its precise meaning becomes obscure. Schiedermair concludes from the last two words of the report that the petition was refused.** Thayer concludes the

---

* It is virtually certain that the boy had not received *any* regular remuneration previously. Was this phrasing merely a polite way of stating the case?
** Schiedermair, *op. cit.*

opposite. The words are *"auszuwerfen sey."* This could mean "to throw out." It could also mean, according to the dictionary: "to fix" (a salary) or "to grant" (an annuity). Elliot Forbes writes that Thayer's interpretation "seems the more likely." My own knowledge of 18th-century German, as well as the logic of subsequent events, inclines me toward Thayer's view.

A few months before the petition, the young Beethoven had three "Sonatas for Klavier" published, with a fulsome dedication to the Elector. These were among the first pieces "composed by Ludwig van Beethoven, aged eleven years." (He was of course thirteen, not eleven.) Thayer writes:

> The necessity of the case, the warm recommendation of Salm-Reifferscheid, very probably, too, the Elector's own knowledge of the fitness of the candidate, and perhaps the flattery in the dedication of the sonatas—for these were the days when dedications were but half-disguised petitions for favor—were sufficient inducements to His Transparency at length to confirm the young organist in the position which Neefe's kindness had now for nearly two years given him. (T).*

As to the flattery, it seems to me that Maximilian Friedrich, old and wise in the way of the world and its artists, could hardly have been swayed by one more dedication—he must have received a heap of them in the course of his reign—and one from a mere youngster. Neefe's sponsorship, however, was a more consequential recommendation. He had expressed it publicly the preceding winter in one of the reports about musical doings which he wrote for a periodical, Cramer's *Magazin der Musik*.

> Louis van Betthoven, son of the tenor singer mentioned, a boy of eleven years and of most promising talent. He plays the clavier very skillfully and with power, reads at sight very well, and—to put it succinctly—he plays chiefly *The Well-tempered Clavier* of Sebastian Bach, which Herr Neefe put into his hands. Whoever knows this collection of preludes and fugues in all the keys—which might almost be called the *non plus ultra* of our art—will know what this means. So far as his duties permitted, Herr Neefe has also given him instruction in thorough-bass. He is now training him in composition and for his encouragement has had nine variations ** for the pianoforte, written by him on a

---

* See page xix for abbreviations of frequently quoted sources.
** The Variations to which Neefe refers were published with a dedication in French, *"par un jeune amateur Louis van Beethoven, agé de dix ans."* Dedications and titles in French were often used by German artists, an innocent bit of snobbishness.

March — by Ernst Christoph Dressler — engraved at Mannheim. This youthful genius is deserving of help to enable him to travel. He would surely become a second Wolfgang Amadeus Mozart were he to continue as he has begun.

Though this article may contain a bit of self-advertisement, it can only increase our respect for Neefe. A warmhearted mentor he must have been!

Beethoven now had his first paid position. Yet he did not! Before the employment contract could become operative, two events occurred to unsettle life in Bonn. In February, the same month in which the above memoranda were written, the Rhine inundated the city. The residents of the lower town had to flee, damage was extensive, terror spread. Fischer relates that Beethoven's mother acted courageously, trying to calm the neighbors, but at last she too had to make her escape. The town had hardly recovered from the shock when Maximilian Friedrich died, on April 15, 1784. The theatrical company was dismissed, nobody gave much thought to music; courtiers and Court musicians waited around for the successor's wishes.

We have seen that the successor shrewdly decided to employ both Neefe and Beethoven. In June, Beethoven's name appears in a list of the salaried members "of the Court Chapel and Music." There it is — at 150 florins.

Ludwig was thirteen and a half years old. In terms of the musical *Wunderkind* he was not so young; at that age Mozart had finished two little operas (*La finta semplice* and *Bastien und Bastienne*), several masses, several symphonies. At that age Mendelssohn was to become sufficiently famous to be taken to the old Goethe.*

What did the new assistant organist look like? He was described as "a boy powerfully, almost clumsily built." In the Fischer reminiscences he is pictured as "short of stature, broad shoulders, short neck, large head, round nose, dark brown complexion; he always bent forward slightly when he walked. In the house he was called *der Spagnol* (the Spaniard)." His forehead was remarkably full and round; this can be seen in the silhouette that was drawn of him when he was about sixteen. Little else can be deduced from the drawing: it is the conventional 18th-century picture, showing its subject with wig, queue, and jabot, all courtly and polite.

For official state occasions he wore a uniform which is described in the Fischer manuscript: "Sea-green dresscoat, green short buckled trousers, silk

---

* Actually the visit was made when Mendelssohn was twelve, Goethe seventy-two.

stockings white or black, a waistcoat of white flowered silk with flap pockets and piping of real gold, hair curled and with a pigtail, a collapsible hat carried under the left arm, a sword * with a silver strap at the left side." Of course, this elegant wardrobe was furnished by the Court. Wearing it, Beethoven must have looked very different from the boy who a few years earlier had not been *"propper."*

He did not altogether escape the illness which took so gruesome a toll of the people of the 18th century. Smallpox, if it did not exact death, often disfigured. Epidemics raged through Europe during the years of Beethoven's early child-hood. Emperor Joseph II's wife, only three years married and pregnant with her second child, caught the disease. Joseph, immune because he had had it as a child, watched her die, a girl of twenty-one. Joseph's sister, the Archduchess Maria-Josepha, perished from smallpox just before her planned marriage to King Ferdinand of Naples. Gluck, Haydn, Mozart ** had contracted it and recovered. Beethoven got off lucky; the disease left some scars but did not disfigure him. What other illnesses the boy underwent we do not know, though there is a theory that in his teens he caught an infection of the typhoid variety.

Before leaving the child Beethoven, we ought to mention some of what might be called the Beethoven Apocrypha. The most preposterous of these legends is the tale, seriously propounded, that he was the illegitimate son of King Frederick the Great. The assertion ran through seven editions of the Brockhaus *Conversations Lexikon,* the German counterpart of the *Encyclopaedia Britannica.* Beethoven knew about it. According to Schindler, he was "deeply mortified" and asked his old friend Wegeler's help in making known to the world "the integrity of his parents, especially of his mother." Schindler claims the credit for causing the publishers to withdraw the falsehood from the eighth edition. Aside from any question of the "integrity" of Frau Beethoven, the fact is that Frederick had not been in Bonn before Beethoven's birth and Beethoven's mother never once left Bonn after her marriage.

Another popular story is the tale of the spider: when the boy was practicing his violin, a spider descended from the ceiling and alighted on the instrument. His mother saw the spider and killed it, whereupon Ludwig smashed his violin

---

* I have mentioned that musicians were not allowed to carry swords. Court employees were the exception.

** Leopold Mozart was advised in Paris in 1764 to have his children vaccinated. He wrote: "I prefer to leave it all in God's hands; let Him and His divine mercy dispose as He will of the life of this wonder of nature." Three years later Wolfgang fell ill. Then his sister caught it.

to bits. Schindler tells the story, though he admits that Beethoven in later years could not remember any such incident. Undoubtedly untrue.

When the boy was eleven, he was invited to go to Holland. He went there not for a holiday but with the hope of playing in public. His father could not leave Bonn, so he and his mother set out, traveling by the Rhine boat. She said afterward that the weather was so cold that she had to keep Ludwig's feet in her lap to prevent them from being frostbitten. The story springs from the Fischer manuscript; recently some confirmation has turned up. So the Holland trip probably did take place. Whether Ludwig actually gave a concert in Holland we do not know. On his return, when he was asked how he had fared, he replied, "The Dutch are penny-pinchers. I will never go to Holland again." He never did. But then, he never traveled much anywhere, even when a generous reward awaited him at journey's end.

Wegeler is the authority for an incident in which the young organist appears as a prankster. He was to accompany one of the Court singers in a church service. The singer's name was Ferdinand Heller,* and he prided himself on his ability to sing in tune, however complicated the accompaniment. Beethoven asked him if he would mind an attempt to confuse him. Heller gave his consent, perhaps without thinking. Beethoven maneuvered the accompaniment so extravagantly that Heller became unsaddled and could not find his way in the closing cadence. Now very angry, he complained to the Elector, who must have smiled at the "temperament" of his artists, then reproved Beethoven gently and recommended that he return to "simpler accompaniment." Would a recent employee dare such a liberty? Yet the unlikely anecdote is likely to be true. Schindler says that Beethoven remembered the incident and remembered that he "was most graciously reproached and forbidden to play any more such clever practical jokes in the future."

Every biographer who attempts to reconstruct Beethoven's youth owes a debt to the scholar Dr. Ludwig Schiedermair. Living in Bonn and teaching at the University, he spent many years unearthing every scrap of contemporary documents. Building on the work that Thayer and a dozen others had done before him, he published, in 1925, his book, *The Young Beethoven.* It is a detailed account of what there is. But there isn't much. After one has combed the book and noted this or that small additional find, the biographical archaeologist must

---

* He was No. 9 in the report mentioned on page 45: "A good musician. The voice now weakening. Of good behavior and married. He composes."

confess that the diggings show a meager result. The fact remains that we know little of Beethoven the boy. Not a single letter written before he was seventeen has been preserved. We have a few early compositions—the Dressler Variations, a small piano concerto, a song or two, three clavier quartets—but these presage little of the greatness that was to follow.*

We must, then, largely conjecture the figure of the fourteen-year-old organist, swarthy and dark-haired, serious but not without a modicum of fun in him, awkward in body but already sure of himself as a performing musician, walking with "a stooping gait" from work to study, overworked and perhaps undernourished, at ease with Neefe, not at ease with his father, small member of a Court society whose spirits were rising, trying his prentice hand at composing in the manner of the workshop, timidly beginning to reach for new expression, but always absorbing, gulping, ingesting, listening not only to the sounds of his profession, listening to and assimilating as well the cultural, literary, and sociological ideas which now alighted on the Rhine.

"Geniuses are commonly believed to excel other men in their power of sustained attention . . . But it is their genius making them attentive, not their attention making geniuses of them," wrote William James.** What was it that Beethoven paid attention to? We shall understand his development better if, having heard the anecdotes, we look around at his environment. It was a new environment in old Bonn, shaping Beethoven's mind with strong fingers.

---

* Mozart—finally perhaps a greater enigma—is clearer to us in the early stages. He began earlier, and early became a celebrity. Not only that, Leopold Mozart, being a literate man and being much away from home, sent copious letters to Salzburg which dwell on his "wonder of nature."
** *Psychology, Briefer Course, XIII,* 1892.

CHAPTER 4

NEW PRINCE, NEW FRIENDS, NEW IDEAS

··◦][I][◦··

Who was to be Maximilian Friedrich's successor as Elector of Cologne? The question had long been carefully considered. More than considered: it had been discussed in secret council, a plan had been drawn, the *quid pro quo* priced.

The problem was one of equal importance to the Emperor of the Holy Roman Empire and to the Emperor of Austria, who happened to be one and the same person. Joseph II knew that Catholicism needed buttressing in the west of the empire, because most of the agnostic assaults were moving West to East. West to East also flowed the new ideas, which enunciated, in voices becoming ever clearer, that "government must be by consent of the governed." * That was a proposition which a Habsburg Emperor could hardly stomach.

Not that Joseph II was inimical to new ideas. Quite the contrary, he was an impassioned reformer, a do-gooder with crown and scepter, acting as soon as he became Emperor "like a fanatically tidy housekeeper moving into an ancestral home that hadn't been dusted in a hundred years." ** Like his mother, Maria Theresa, he was a good Catholic and understood the political and stabilizing value of the faith. Yet, while piously making the sign of the cross, he labored for Church reform and religious tolerance and social amelioration the whole livelong day, exhausting his seven or eight secretaries with dictating new decrees, new laws, new pronouncements. He was a benevolent but impatient chief of state, forcing progress on people whether they liked it or not. He was genuinely concerned with the welfare of his subjects, as long as such welfare was to be achieved according to his ideas and his plan. He strove for nothing

---

* Rousseau, *Social Contract.*
** Dorothy McGuigan, *The Habsburgs,* 1966.

Maximilian Franz, Elector of Bonn. Brought up in Vienna, music-loving and liberal-minded, he took a real interest in the young Beethoven (Bonn City Archives).

less than the abolishment of feudal, hereditary, and clerical privileges. He stretched a hand toward the fat possessions of the Church, wanting to use them for the relief of the poor. He worried the Pope enough for the Pope to come to visit him. It proved an extraordinary visit. The two men got along famously. He offered Pius VI royal gifts; as soon as the Pope's back was turned, Joseph closed one of the wealthiest monasteries. His most famous law, "The Patent of Tolerance" (1781 and 1782), permitted the Jews to stop wearing the yellow band by which they had been forced to identify themselves. Torture to elicit confession was declared illegal; eventually he abolished the death penalty. He outlawed serfdom and enabled tenant farmers to buy their own lands from the nobles at reasonable prices. He left no part of Austrian social life, however trivial, undisturbed: girls in coeducational schools were forbidden to wear corsets to flatter their figures; peasants could, for the first time, marry whom they wished; houses had to be numbered; the famous German gingerbread cookie, called *Lebkuchen,* could no longer be baked since it was bad for the digestion; the dead were not to be buried in expensive coffins. In fact, no coffins were to be used at all: just a plain sack. That was too much: the people protested violently, and Joseph had to annul the decree, to his bitter disappointment.* He opened Vienna's parks and gardens to the public, built orphanages and poorhouses, and established the General Hospital (*Algemeines Kranken-haus*) of Vienna, which until Hitler's day remained one of the models of the world. He walked among his people like a Harun-al-Rashid, listening to their talk. Yet he vastly overestimated their ability to understand the reforms and he underestimated the powers of the entrenched, of clergy and nobility. The sum of his achievement could not be measured while he lived. To his contemporaries it often appeared that by running so fast he got nowhere.

This his youngest brother believed. So did most of his councilors. It was better to reform mildly than to disturb wildly. In the West particularly, the *status quo* needed to be changed, but only a little—so that it might continue. In the Electorate the Church was under attack from young people. A few concessions to the progressive and young could not hurt and would in fact help to preserve the power of the clerics. Politically too it was important to have a bastion in the West, a fortress to fly the flag of Austria. The Cologne Electorate lay between Prussia and France. Neither was a friend of Austria; neither Prussia nor France could be trusted. It was most desirable to have a Habsburg sitting on

---

* Facts taken from Saul Padover, *The Revolutionary Emperor, Joseph II.*

the throne of Cologne, protecting the interests both of the Roman Empire and of Austria and, so to speak, letting the Rhine flow into the Danube.

But which Habsburg? Who was the right man for the position? A conservative ruler, but not a regressive one, was wanted. Joseph's brother, Archduke Maximilian Franz, seemed a likely choice. He was intelligent in mind and lumpish in body; he had sustained an injury to his knee and was therefore unfit to lead troops. The bishop's miter would become him more than the general's cap. Maximilian Franz was pushed into a Church career. Being a Habsburg, it was not difficult for him to rise quickly to the office of bishop. Belderbusch became involved: he saw himself as "Kingmaker" and thought it prudent (or profitable) to espouse the Habsburg cause. When Maximilian Friedrich died in 1784, Maximilian Franz, aged twenty-eight, was speedily "elected"—it had all been prepared beforehand—and made his way to Bonn, entering with due pomp and circumstance. An Austrian on the Rhine? The inhabitants of Bonn must have wondered and speculated. There was nothing they could do about it; there he was, ensconced in the Palace. How would he govern, how would he get along with these people whose dialect was so markedly different from Viennese?

Perhaps Joseph did not expect much from his youngest brother. He was wrong. Maximilian Franz brought new life and spirit to Bonn. From not very promising beginnings he developed into a remarkable man and a remarkable ruler. He had learned positively and negatively from his older brother, and he applied to his regime the principle of moderate change. He avoided irritating France, gained a measure of independence from Rome, improved the government's judicial and financial functions, and declared that he would choose the servants of the state by their ability and not by their birth. The sinecures and privileges of the nobility were to be abrogated, but not too drastically. Room was to be made for youth.

He himself behaved modestly and was an accessible sovereign. He personally opened letters and petitions addressed to him. Anybody could get an audience. He listened and made up his mind. We have seen that he used his own judgment when Neefe's case was presented to him. Once he saw a peasant woman struggling to lift a heavy basket in the market square; he graciously lifted it for her. The story may be apocryphal: the fact that it was told in Bonn indicates the Elector's popularity. At five o'clock in the morning he used to wander through the city clad in a dirty white cloak. His main personal weakness was gluttony, though he drank only water. Eventually he became so fat that a special curved segment had to be cut out of the dining table so that he might sit comfortably near it and gorge himself.

For our purpose, which is the tracing of the influences on the young Beethoven, his most important achievement was the lift he gave to education in all forms, theater and music included. Here he was ambitious. A scant two years after his election, he opened the Bonn University, which he dedicated as a "monument to enlightenment." If the faculty gathered there was not a collection of celebrities, it was nonetheless a stimulating group, presenting a rainbow of thought. The new philosophy of Kant was taught, provoking much discussion. Jurisprudence was presented by a man who was a friend of Schiller and who now and then interrupted his lectures to recite one or another of Schiller's poems, to the great delight of the auditors. The study of medicine was significantly enlarged. A professor of Greek and literature preached revolution with fanatic zeal. His name was Eulogius Schneider; some years later a guillotine erected in Strassburg cut short his life. Beethoven attended some lectures in philosophy. His name is registered among the "candidates," meaning nonmatriculated students.

The books the students needed were available in the Court Library. Karl Wilhelm Humboldt, who was later to become the great reformer of the Prussian educational system, visited Bonn and observed that the books of such "radical" philosophers as Moses Mendelssohn * and Kant were in the Library. In the bookstores the works of both the new German authors and of the French apostles of the Enlightenment were freely available. Voltaire was read, damned, and idolized, even as in Paris. Rousseau, whose *Émile* and *La nouvelle Héloïse* had appeared twenty, and whose *Confessions,* ten years earlier, now became an author of the day, widely quoted.

Maximilian Franz had been brought up in Vienna, the head of Europe's largest empire, and its representational symbol. As such, the city was perpetually dressed up in gala uniform. Its people, gay gourmandizers of life, enjoyed the glitter and the glamour. Schiller described Vienna as the city of continuous Sunday, the roasting spit turning constantly over the fire. Entertainment was as important to the Viennese as to the ancient Romans. They were mad about the theater, mad about the opera, and mad about music, provided it was not too cerebral. Though Joseph II was too wrapped up in bettering the world to think

---

* Grandfather of Felix and friend of Lessing. Inspired by him, Lessing wrote the great play of tolerance, *Nathan the Wise.*

much about the arts and too parsimonious to spend money to support talent, his mother had found much pleasure and respite from her cares through music, and he had inherited this inclination. It was true of his brother as well. Maximilian Franz came to Bonn with an artistic tradition and education behind him.

His love for music was a genuine one. He knew Mozart well and appreciated him.* He had recommended him as teacher to the Princess of Württemberg. But Joseph had told the Princess to take Salieri, no one else, for the Emperor "cares for no one but Salieri," as Mozart remarked bitterly. When Mozart wanted to marry his Constanze and tried to convince his father that he was, or would soon be, in a position to support a wife, he wrote in a letter to him, on January 23, 1782, that Maximilian Franz could be counted on for opportunities:

> Now of him I say that he thinks the world of me. He shoves me forward on every occasion, and I might almost say with certainty that if at this moment he were Elector of Cologne, I should be his Kapellmeister. It is, indeed, a pity that these great gentlemen refuse to make arrangements beforehand.** I could easily extract a simple promise from him, but of what use would that be to me now? Cash would be more acceptable.***

Two months previously, Mozart had played at Court at Maximilian's invitation:

> Yesterday at three o'clock in the afternoon the Archduke Maximilian sent for me. When I went in, he was standing near the stove in the first room and was waiting for me. He came up to me at once and asked me if I had anything particular to do that day. I replied: "Nothing whatever, your Royal Highness; and if I had, I should still consider it a favour to be allowed to wait on your Royal Highness." "No, no," he said, "I refuse to inconvenience anyone." He then told me that he was intending to give a concert that very evening to the visitors from Württemberg and suggested that I should play and accompany the arias, adding that I was to come back at six o'clock when all the guests would be assembled. So I played there yesterday.****

---

* The question arises why, when the time came, Mozart was not called to Bonn. Maximilian Franz may have done so, but just then Mozart was again in hopes of obtaining an official position in Vienna and, besides, was deeply immersed in the composition of *Figaro*. At any rate, Mozart probably would not have wanted to move from the imperial metropolis to a provincial town.
** Note that Mozart knew about the Cologne plan two years before it came to pass.
*** Emily Anderson (ed.), *Letters of Mozart and His Family*, 1938.
**** *Ibid.*

This favor did not prevent Mozart, who had a sharp eye and a sharp tongue, from making fun of Maximilian Franz:

> Before he became a priest, he was far more witty and intelligent and talked less, but more sensibly. You should see him now! Stupidity oozes out of his eyes. He talks and holds forth incessantly and always in falsetto—and he has started a goiter. In short, the fellow seems to have changed completely.*

That the Elector loved music and respected musicians is further evidenced in his treatment of Haydn.** With Johann Peter Salomon, Haydn came to Bonn for the Christmas holidays of 1790. The two men were on their way to London. They interrupted their journey, possibly to gratify a wish expressed by the Elector.

> On Sunday (Dec. 26th) Salomon conducted Haydn to the Court Chapel to listen to a Mass. Hardly had the two entered the church and chosen suitable seats when the high Mass began. The first chords announced a product of Haydn's muse. Our Haydn looked upon it as an accidental occurrence which, however, might have been planned in order to give him pleasure and to flatter him. At any rate, he was decidedly pleased to hear his own work. Toward the close of the Mass, a person approached him and invited him to repair to the Oratory, where he was expected. Haydn went there and was not a little surprised to find that the Elector had had him summoned. The Elector at once took Haydn's hand and presented him to his virtuosi with the words, "I will now make you acquainted with the Haydn whom you revere so highly." The Elector gave both parties time to become acquainted. And then, to give Haydn a convincing proof of his esteem, he invited him to dinner. This unexpected invitation put Haydn into some embarrassment, for he and Salomon had arranged a modest little dinner in their lodgings and it was now too late to make a change. Haydn was therefore forced to excuse himself, and the Elector accepted the excuse as valid. Then Haydn took his leave and repaired to his lodgings, where he was surprised by a further unexpected proof of the Elector's good will: by a secret order the little dinner had been metamorphosed into a banquet for twelve persons, to which the most skillful musicians had been invited.

Was Beethoven among the "most skillful musicians"?

As to the Elector's interest in the theater, he brought with him the enthusiasm which he had felt when, in his early twenties, he had sat at resplendent

---

* *Ibid.*
** Based on Haydn's own testimony in A. C. Dies, *Biographische Nachrichten von Joseph Haydn.*

nights in the theater of Schönbrunn Palace. He began to develop the "National Theater of Bonn," which his predecessor had brought to a degree of competence, into a fine repertory group. As a music lover and as a Viennese, he turned the National Theater toward the cultivation of opera. At first he proceeded slowly, knowing that some of the Rhenish Church dignitaries frowned on "Viennese frivolity." Gradually, however, he had his way. At first he imported various companies.* At the beginning of 1789 he opened, with his own troupe, the new Court Theater, which was the old theater refurbished and reconstructed to accommodate three tiers of loges, so that the "ladies and gentlemen of august society" could be seen by everybody. The director of the opera was Joseph Reicha; the "Stage-director of Comic Opera" and official cembalist was Neefe; the orchestra consisted of players from the "Electoral Instrument Body." Beethoven was there, playing the viola.

The repertoire of the Opera House became rich and varied. Beethoven not only heard but must have taken part in operas by the Italians—Paisiello and Salieri and Cimarosa—and the German "Plays with Singing" (*Singspiele*), such as Dittersdorf's new and immediately popular *Doctor and Apothecary*. Here too Beethoven must have first marveled at the operas of the man whom, Neefe said, he might someday equal. What impression did *Don Giovanni* and *The Marriage of Figaro* first make on him?

Not only the opera but music-making in general became more expert. The Elector made strenuous use of his musicians at home and abroad. He took them along when he went on state visits. For one of these visits—to Mergentheim in October, 1791—we have a description of the talent brought from Bonn. It was written by C. L. Junker, chaplain, author, and a respected, competent observer of the musical scene.** He spent, he writes, "two of the happiest days of my life" with those "excellent artists." First he heard "dinner music," which, unlike the usual program that accompanied eating, was substantial enough to include the Overture to *Don Giovanni*. Soon after, he went to the opera, Paisiello's *King Theodor,* which he enjoyed but mildly. The next morning he attended the rehearsal for the gala "Court Concert," which was scheduled for 6 P.M. The program was a long one and included a Mozart symphony (which symphony Herr Junker does not say). He admired the orchestra's expressiveness: "Such exact observance of *piano* and *forte* and *rinforzando,* such a swelling and

---

* For the Carnival season of 1785, the well-known Böhm Theater Troupe was engaged. They brought Gluck's *Orfeo* and *Alceste* to Bonn.
** It appeared in *Bossler's Musikalische Korrespondenz,* November 23, 1791.

gradual increase of tone, followed by its diminution, ranging from the highest volume to the softest tone—this could only have been heard in its day in Mannheim." * He found the musicians "people of elegant distinction and fine decorum." They made a splendid sight in their red-and-gold uniforms. He described how in the concert the audience pressed around them so that they could hardly play; they were perspiring visibly but bore the discomfort with good humor.

Junker's greatest thrill came from listening to a young pianist:

I heard also one of the greatest pianists, the dear good Bethofen, some compositions by whom had appeared in the Speier *Blumenlese* in 1783, things which he had written in his eleventh year. True he did not perform in public, possibly because the instrument here was not to his liking. It is one made by Spath; in Bonn he is accustomed to play upon a piano by Steiner. But, what was infinitely preferable to me, I heard him improvise, and I was even invited to propose a theme for him to vary. The virtuosity of this amiable, soft-spoken man may in my view be safely judged by his almost inexhaustible wealth of ideas, the altogether individual style of expression in his playing, and the marvelous facility with which he plays. I cannot imagine anything which is lacking in him which constitutes the greatness of an artist. I have heard Vogler ** play the piano—I cannot judge his organ playing, not having heard him play on that instrument—I have heard him often, heard him for hours, and have always admired his great talent. But Bethofen, in addition to his facility, plays with greater variety, greater expression, more weight, more appeal. He goes more to the heart, equally great therefore as an *adagio* and *allegro* player. Even the members of this excellent orchestra are without exception his admirers; they are all ears when he plays. He himself is modest and free from all pretensions. He confessed to me however that upon the journeys which the Elector had enabled him to make, he had seldom found in the playing of the most famous virtuosi the quality which he thought he had the right to expect. His playing differs so markedly from the usual ways of treating the instrument that it impresses one with the thought that he wanted to find a path of his own discovery so that in the end he might attain the height of perfection on which he now stands.

Had I acceded to the pressing entreaties of my friend Bethofen which Herr Winneberger [Kapellmeister in the city of Wallenstein] supported, and remained another day at Mergentheim, I have no doubt that Herr Bethofen would

---

* Mannheim boasted of an exceptionally fine orchestra.
** The Abbé Georg Joseph Vogler was a pianist who was an early forerunner of the Lisztian manner. Composers such as Weber and Meyerbeer held him in high esteem; others thought him a charlatan, with his monster concerts, his posing, his extraordinary self-praise, and his arrogance.

have played for me for hours; and the day spent in the society of these two great artists would have proved for me a day of highest bliss.

Let us remember that the year was 1791, that Beethoven was nearly twenty-one, that he was no longer a boy, and that he had gained at least some local fame. We have given Herr Junker's panegyric out of chronological order because it throws a light not only on Beethoven but on the musical conditions created by Maximilian Franz. Whatever his shortcomings, he was a superb organizer of artistic and intellectual life. Wegeler wrote in his old age that this was a beautiful and in many ways an active period in Bonn. The point could be further proved were we to follow the careers of several of the young men who grew up in Bonn at that time and who later became distinguished scientists, writers, artists, and jurists. Maximilian Franz has been blamed for not suffi-ciently and quickly appreciating the greatness of his Court musician. But of greatness, except perhaps as a performer, there was as yet only an uncertain sign. The strong, straight, life-filled tree into which Beethoven grew began with a tiny sprout.

Be that as it may, surely some of Beethoven's grasp of the world of ideas, his intellectual breadth, can be traced to the influences of Maximilian Franz's admin-istration, and the opportunities offered by that sovereign's artistic interests.

·≈[2]≈·

Before resuming the account of Beethoven's career, we ought to round off our picture of Joseph's brother. His was not a fortunate fate. France, after the idealism of the French Revolution had broken into pieces, after the cap of liberty had been dropped in the mud and internal dissension had set leader against leader, now faced the enmity of most of Europe, an enmity fed by general and specific fears. Who was the next sovereign to be imprisoned, where was the next mob going to storm a traditional citadel, on whose neck was the guillotine to fall next? Crowned heads believed that all crowns, that the idea of the Crown itself, would melt in a fiery furnace if they did not come to the aid of Louis XVI. He had fled, been overtaken and captured, and by June, 1791, was in custody in Paris. But putting the King under lock and key did not prevent France's condition from getting more and more out of hand. More blood flowed, the jockeying for power increased—and the supply of food decreased. A war would unite the country. A war was necessary. A war would wipe out internal factions. Such has always been the desperate gamble of those who cannot cope with the problem of supplying sufficient bread and work to their countrymen.

Austria and Prussia, ill-met by moonlight, scotched their old antagonism. The War of the First Coalition began on April 20, 1792. This was a war of violent swings, and the Electorate of Cologne was exposed to both sides. At first the Austrian and Prussian troops invaded France. Within two months the French repulsed them and were crossing the Rhine. Mainz fell, the whole left bank of the river was left bare to the invader. Maximilian Franz beat a hasty retreat on October 22. Immediately after, the Prussians, victorious at Koblenz, chased the French troops away, while in Paris the Jacobins, under Danton, wrested the power from the Girondins. Maximilian Franz returned to Bonn—but not for long. By December the French had occupied the Austrian Netherlands and were threatening to come upstream. Once more the Elector moved, this time to Münster. By March, 1793, after Louis XVI had been executed, Britain, "Holland," Spain, and Sardinia entered the Coalition, and the French were driven from the Netherlands. Once more, in April, Maximilian Franz returned to Bonn; from there he must have watched with a mixture of horror and satisfaction the grim developments: in April dictatorial powers were accorded to Danton, the Reign of Terror began in June, in July Charlotte Corday murdered Jean Marat, in October Christianity in France was officially abolished, and in the same month Maximilian Franz learned that his sister, Marie Antoinette, had been guillotined.*

France mustered all its forces, every man capable of bearing arms was conscripted, a new military leader by the name of Napoleon arose to capture Toulon from British forces, and on December 26 the French forced the allies to retreat across the Rhine. The next spring Danton and Camille Desmoulins were executed, in July Robespierre and Saint-Just lost their lives, while the armies under the Tricolor took new courage. Again Maximilian Franz was forced to leave Bonn, this time forever. He lived out his life—he had but seven more years to live—in various palaces, and died sad and obese and unimportant. He would be remembered only by professors of history and would be undistinguishable to the layman from most of the Maximilians and Franzs who dot the Habsburgs' history, were it not for the fact that he aided a musician named Beethoven.

---

* However, Maximilian Franz did not love his sister. He had visited her in Paris at the height of her glory and had caused her much embarrassment by his unpolished and awkward behavior. He had not forgiven her for showing her vexation.

NEW PRINCE, NEW FRIENDS, NEW IDEAS

·≡[3]≡·

Let us now detail another important and fortunate influence on the young Beethoven. This was the coming into his life of the Breuning family.

Emanuel Joseph von Breuning was one of Bonn's most promising young men. At the early age of twenty he had become Court Councilor, a remarkable achievement, and was well advanced in an important career in the government. He had married Hélène von Kerich, the daughter of Stephan von Kerich, private physician to the Elector. The marriage was a most happy one. Both were of high intellect, easy manners, easy sociability, and good humor. And they were very well-to-do. They lived in a handsome large house on the Münsterplatz. Gradually that house became the meeting place of Bonn's best people—artists, musicians, writers, university professors, political leaders.

Then suddenly the career of the Court Councilor was cut short. On a bitter cold January night in 1777, a fire broke out in the Palace, and nothing could stem the fury of the flames. The town was aroused, and there was pandemonium. One of the Court musicians, Passavanti, ran screaming from the building and sobbed, *"O mio povero contra-basso, che ho portato sul dosso mio da Venezia!"** Breuning was one of the few who kept their heads. Gathering a group of courageous volunteers around him, he dashed into the building again and again, saving the most important documents. He had successfully darted in and out several times when a wall caved in and buried him under its stones. He died instantly. He left three little children and a wife who was only twenty-seven and several months pregnant.

Hélène von Breuning did the unexpected. Instead of quietly wearing her widow's weeds, she determined that the emptiness of death would be best annulled by the fullness of life. She would not flee from life: on the contrary, for her children's sake, as for her own sake, she would continue to take part in all that was worth while in Bonn's activities. What she and her husband had begun together she would now try to produce alone, the ambience of busy happiness. She filled the house with gaiety. Holding her handsome head high, she presided as the mistress of a home where men of opposite opinions could discuss and argue, she herself acting as a charming moderator. The result was bustle, noise, and laughter. Illustrious visitors were delighted if they could wangle an invitation to the Münsterplatz. Her children were encouraged to invite other children to the house. Aristocratic though she was, Hélène was

---

* "Oh my poor double-bass which I carried on my back from Venice!"

remarkably free of snobbishness. In an age in which university students from noble houses still sat on separate benches from the commoners, she offered an equal place at her table to all she liked.

So it came about that a poor young student, Franz Gerhard Wegeler, was introduced into the family. Eventually he became a distinguished physician and professor of medicine at Bonn University. He married the daughter of the family and was one of the few whose friendship with Beethoven weathered all of the composer's storms—or nearly all. To him we are indebted for a great deal of generally trustworthy biographical knowledge.

All of the Breuning children, to a greater or lesser degree, touched Beethoven's life. Eleonore Brigitte (called Lorchen), who was to marry Wegeler, was six years old when her father perished. Of course she was the darling of the house, pretty, vivacious, teasing—and teased by her brothers.

Christoph was four. He later studied jurisprudence, became municipal Councilor in Bonn, then President of the City Council, and finally Privy Councilor in Berlin. He died in the same year as his sister, 1841, thus outliving Beethoven by fourteen years.

Stephan was three years old. He later studied law, and, just before Maximilian Franz had to leave Bonn, was appointed to an office in the Teutonic Order, probably at the Elector's instigation. In the spring of 1801 he went to Vienna, where he renewed his acquaintance with the composer and became one of Beethoven's staunchest friends. They had studied the violin together. He rose to an important position in the Court War Council of Vienna. He married twice; from the second marriage sprang Gerhard von Breuning, born in 1813, who in the last year of Beethoven's life was the composer's almost constant little companion.

Lorenz (called Lenz), the posthumous baby, studied medicine, left Bonn during the War of Coalition—as did most others who could afford to—and lived in Vienna for three years. He then returned to Bonn and died in 1798, only twenty-one years old.

Hélène von Breuning never remarried. After the death of her husband, her brother, Abraham von Kerich, canon of Bonn, moved into the house. So did Breuning's brother, Lorenz, who also was a canon, and who helped Hélène tutor the fatherless children. That the love which enveloped the four children and the joy which pervaded the house were wise investments is proved by their later history: all of them—except Lenz because of his early death—became distinguished and successful human beings.

Wegeler claimed the credit for introducing Beethoven into this household. Most authorities fix the date at 1784. Beethoven was therefore fourteen. The children needed a piano teacher, and Wegeler recommended Beethoven. Hélène could of course have employed somebody more experienced. Perhaps she was impressed by the boy or perhaps she wanted a teacher not much older than the children who were to be instructed.* Soon enough Ludwig was considered a part of the family, a child of the house. Not only did he spend whatever free time he had during the day, but he slept there many a night. Wegeler relates that "he felt free there. He moved with ease. All circumstances worked together to make him feel cheerful and to develop his spirit."

It was here in this house on the Münsterplatz that Beethoven came to lay the strong foundation of his culture. His mind, trained, concentrated, focused, and burning on one subject only, now began to open to other worlds, the world of the word especially. The "classics" were read, poetry was recited, the new romantic literature avidly devoured. The children and the grown-ups shed tears over Goethe's *The Sorrows of Young Werther.*

The boy was not invariably an easy companion. He did not particularly enjoy giving lessons. Hélène, remembered Wegeler, got him an assignment to teach the Austrian ambassador, who lived in a house opposite hers. She watched him "creeping like snail" to the door, then turn, run back, and promise her that tomorrow he would give *two* lessons; today he simply couldn't.**

When Beethoven was behaving strangely or obstreperously, Hélène used to smile and say, "He has his *raptus* again." Beethoven never forgot the expression, nor did he ever forget the affection and understanding he met in the Breuning home. "In his later days he still called the members of this family his guardian angel of that time and remembered with pleasure the many reprimands which he had received from the lady of the house. 'She understood,' said he, 'how to keep insects off the flower.' " ***

One of the men he met at the Breuning household was Count Ferdinand Ernst Gabriel Waldstein und Wartemberg von Dux, Knight of the Teutonic Order. This floridly named man, a scion of one of the highest Austrian aristocratic families, had come to Bonn at Maximilian Franz's invitation. The Elector

---

* Eleonore was thirteen, Christoph eleven, Stephan ten.
** Schindler, on the other hand, spoke in after years to a "Frau von Bevervorde" from Bonn, who assured him that she had no complaints to make of the regularity of Beethoven's instruction. But then, she was a very pretty girl.
*** Anton Felix Schindler, Donald W. MacArdle, ed., *Beethoven As I Knew Him,* 1966.

liked him; he was his "constant companion." Proust might have used him for one of his characters. Waldstein was handsome, erudite, mercurial, of exquisite bearing, a witty dinner guest, a charming raconteur, the cynosure of Court festivities. He was a passionate champion of the Enlightenment. Yet with his supranational views he combined a stubborn narrow-minded chauvinism for Austria and a blind hatred of the French, so that he got into serious difficulty with his friend Maximilian Franz during the war. Maximilian Franz, who tried to stay neutral, rather preferred the French. In the early days Waldstein helped the Elector develop the musical life of Bonn. He himself was a fine pianist and fancied himself as a composer. Like Maximilian Franz, he was a great admirer of Mozart.

Early he recognized some of Beethoven's quality. He commissioned Beethoven to write a composition which Waldstein then gave out as his own. It was a ballet, the *Ritterballet,* and it was performed in 1791 at the Bonn Palace during the Mardi Gras.

Wegeler believed that it was Waldstein who suggested to the Elector that Beethoven be employed as Court musician, and that it was he who saw to it that Beethoven be discreetly granted some small financial aid. We shall see that it was he who predicted early that Beethoven's name would shine as brightly in the firmament as those of Mozart and Haydn.

There was a darker side to Waldstein's character: careless and imprudent, impatient and reckless, he was a gambler and a speculator. He ventured into dubious business dealings and get-rich-quick schemes and became the victim of swindlers. The lordly name of Waldstein was then besmirched and dragged into the mire. In 1816 he was forced to petition for bankruptcy. He died seven years later, a pauper.

Beethoven at some time or other quarreled with him. The cause of the estrangement might have lain in Waldstein's doubtful probity. Who can ascribe causes to Beethoven's quarrels—so often causeless—with his well-wishers? Yet now the name remains cleansed and will remain illustrious as long as we care about music, the sonata which Beethoven composed in 1805 and which bears Waldstein's name being one of the crown jewels of piano literature.

As his own home darkened, Beethoven sought more and more stimulations in other places; one of these was a tavern located in the Market Square, the Zehrgarten, and run by the widow Koch. The inn served as a meeting place for Bonn's men of intellect, the same men who would on other evenings be invited to the Breunings. But there was a further attraction, the daughter of the widow

Koch, Babette. She was the belle of Bonn. Wegeler waxed rhapsodic about her: "an intimate friend of Eleonore von Breuning's, a lady who of all the members of the female sex whom I have met in my rather active and very long life came nearest to the ideal of the perfect woman." * She seems not to have made a devastating impression on Beethoven, though he mentioned her in a letter sent from Vienna.

··∘ɔ[4]ɕ··

Shall we then, in summary fashion, review the influences which nurtured the young Beethoven and which prepared the process by which he transformed himself from musician to master, from talent to genius?

First and foremost there was opportunity. Music was all around him. Maximilian Franz not only needed it for courtly purpose but truly loved it. The chaste old Organ Preludes; the stately church rituals of Catholicism; the edifice built by Bach; the wonder of Haydn; the marvel of Mozart; the lighthearted fripperies of Italian comic operas and German *Singspiele,* nine-day wonders which came and went; a few of the fascinating products of that German genius in London, Handel, who though now some thirty years dead was still little known in Germany; the military marches played by the Electoral band; the casual music which accompanied a banquet; the folk songs of his people—not only did Beethoven hear all these, but he experienced many of them "from inside," by playing them.

He grew up when the art of improvisation was still at its height; he was to become and continue to be a supreme practitioner of the art after it had fallen into decline. Because he was—and had to be—a musician-of-all-work, he acquired wide practical knowledge of the instruments of the orchestra. Organist, violinist, violist, cembalist, he was all of these, and in addition had a good working knowledge of wind and brass instruments.

The second piece of good fortune he enjoyed was the intellectual climate of his home town and his period. The modern world was being born. Dissent and pain were there, but also the exhilaration of change, the stimulation of daring ideas. At the Breunings', at the university, at the tavern, people talked and prodded one another into thinking. If anything is characteristic of the Age of Enlightenment, it is its prodigality with words. Conversation was a passion. It was real conversation, a dialogue of give and take, the art of listening and the

---

* Franz Wegeler and Ferdinand Ries, *Biographische Notizen über Ludwig van Beethoven,* 1838.

art of speaking having been honed to a fine edge in Paris. The Rhinelanders talked, at dinner table or while taking the long walking tours so beloved by the Germans, or when sailing up and down the Rhine in their boats, the talk made more fluid by wine. They had indeed learned from the French the delights of discoursing.

Third, it was in Bonn that books were opened for him. He began to read; all his life he continued to read. His taste became wide and international. We know that the study of the ancient authors was cultivated in the Breuning household and that Beethoven became intimately familiar with the epics of Homer, the *Lives* of Plutarch, and the poetry of Virgil. Poetry was not only read in the Breuning home; the children wrote quite a bit of poetry themselves. Both Christoph and Stephan "made essays in poetry" and not without success.

Beethoven's knowledge and appreciation of literature must be emphasized. Too often Beethoven is depicted as an uneducated, unlearned man, or at least a man to whom education meant little, an almost unconscious genius, a vessel for music, isolated in the realm of tone, not sentient of other arts or of achievements other than music, miraculously bringing forth his music without being "handicapped" by general interests. These claims, the claims of monomaniacal occupation and lack of general culture, are not valid. The wonder of him is major enough without turning Beethoven into a hermit. No, he was a widely read, knowledgeable man, his interests embracing a large territory. Yet even J. W. N. Sullivan, who says many perceptive things,* falls into the error of believing that Beethoven "was not an educated man." ... "The low standard of education he achieved seems to have been as much due to his lack of plasticity as to his lack of opportunities. He was not an educable man. He accepted none of the schemes of thought or conduct current in his time; it is doubtful whether he was even fully aware of their existence." Nothing could be more fallacious.

The reason one may get the impression that Beethoven was in no degree literate lies in his inability to express himself in words. In that he differed from many other non-literary artists, from Michelangelo and Piero della Francesca, from Weber and Tchaikovsky, even from Mozart, whose letters, while not "intellectual," show the liveliest humor and keen observation; even from Haydn, who at least had the gift of repartee. Beethoven's letters—those which were not polished by one of his brothers or by Schindler or by some other friend —sound as if they were written by a man sitting disheveled at a disorderly desk

---

* In *Beethoven: His Spiritual Development*, 1927.

and wielding a spluttering pen. Sentences are broken, the vocabulary is crude, of grammar there is little trace. Despite his bad writing and brutal syntax, he achieves conviction even here, when he is overwhelmed by his suffering, or when he is in love, or when he is angry at the putative perfidy of his friends.

These tattered phrases torn from a clothesline, these squeaky stammerings should not fool us. Though he could not use words, he was highly susceptible to them as conveyors of ideas, as carriers of beauty, as informing messengers. The sound of poetry and the thoughts bound into books were absorbed by him to help form a huge mind. His artistry was enriched by other artistry, in and away from music. The process began during his early days in Bonn, when—poor but already self-assured—he had the luck to be well led to the Piraean spring.

He drank from it slowly. The time of preparation was not alone one of learning music but one of forming the whole artist. Beethoven was twenty-four before he published a composition he thought good enough to mark "Opus One" (three Piano Trios).

*Travel by stagecoach in the early nineteenth century. Uncomfortable,
but one saw the countryside. From a contemporary lithograph (Collection Viollet, Paris).*

CHAPTER 5

HEAD OF THE FAMILY

··ᴈ[I]ᴄ··

𝔚hen Beethoven was almost seventeen, he went on a journey to Vienna. Neefe, it will be remembered, had said that the young genius ought to be given the opportunity to travel. Somebody gave him this opportunity. The fact alone seems prosaic, but its implications are not. To travel as far as from Bonn to Vienna was a costly affair, even if one used the cheapest means, the public stagecoach, and stopped at the rudest inns. Beethoven could not have paid for this out of his own pocket. Aside from the expense, few musicians employed in steady service would be allowed to absent themselves for "educational purposes." Father Johann was never given such a chance, much as he might have desired it. Even Neefe stuck pretty close to Bonn as long as he filled an official position. In 1787 Maximilian Franz was in the thick of building his artistic organization. That he gave Beethoven permission to go implies that he believed his employee worthy of the chance for development.

Who defrayed the cost of the journey? The Breunings? Waldstein? * It is probable, though no proof exists, that it was Maximilian Franz who supplied the travel funds. Perhaps Waldstein advised him to do so, saying that it would be a good idea to send the promising youth to the "capital of music," their home town, and to arrange for him to meet and receive instruction from their admired Mozart.

We find then that on April 1, 1787, a "Herr Peethofen musikus von Bonn bei Kölln" had arrived in the city of Munich.** A scholar has calculated that if he were in Munich by April 1, Beethoven must have left Bonn about March 20 and reached Vienna on April 7, the journey consuming a little more than two

---

* Wegeler wrote to Schindler in 1839 that it was Waldstein who supplied the travel funds.
** From the midweek report of visitors in the *Münchener Zeitung*.

weeks.* Conversely, there is an entry in the same newspaper on April 25 stating that Herr Peethofen was staying at an inn in Munich called Zum Schwarzen Adler (At the Black Eagle). This suggests that Beethoven left Vienna on his return journey on April 20. His whole sojourn in the imperial city lasted less than two weeks. The fact that the local paper took note of his arrival indicates that he did not travel like a poor, wandering student. The inn he stayed at—a large one, near the Cathedral—was undoubtedly not Munich's best hostelry; neither was it the worst.

He did not, of course, go to Vienna with the object of staying for a brief time only. He was there to study and learn and he expected to stay sufficiently long to accomplish his purpose. As to the people he met—Schindler quoted somebody or other as saying that Beethoven was deeply impressed by only two persons, the Emperor Joseph and Mozart. Did he actually meet the Emperor? It seems doubtful, even had Beethoven been supplied with a letter of presentation from Maximilian Franz. Joseph remained in the city for only four days after Beethoven's arrival, setting out on April 11 for Kiev to call on Catherine the Great.** It is improbable that he had time to grant an audience to an obscure musician, however well recommended, though Beethoven might have seen him at an official function.

Beethoven did see Mozart. It was not a propitious time for forming anything but the most superficial contact with Mozart, who had just returned from Prague, was worried about his father's poor health (his father died on May 28), and was deeply immersed in executing the commission which Prague had bestowed on him after the success of *Figaro,* the composition of *Don Giovanni.* He was worried about finances as well; at the end of April he moved to a cheaper house.*** Mozart's and Beethoven's meeting—the two met only during Beethoven's first brief visit; when he returned to Vienna, Mozart was dead— has been described, pardonably, with a good deal of sentimental exaggeration. A reasonable version is given by Otto Jahn: ****

> Beethoven, who as a youth of great promise came to Vienna in the spring of 1787 but was obliged to return to Bonn after a brief sojourn, was taken to

---

* He traveled slowly. His second journey to Vienna, made during war conditions, was completed in ten days or less.

** She was making a triumphal tour of South Russia accompanied by Potemkin. A Russo-Austrian alliance against the Turks was discussed on this occasion and formalized the following year.

*** Landstrasse No. 224. Beethoven lived at Landstrasse 323 when he was working on the Ninth Symphony. Both locations are far removed from the center of the city.

**** In *W. A. Mozart,* 1905.

Mozart and at the musician's request played something for him which he, taking it for granted was a show-piece prepared for the occasion, praised in a rather cool manner. Beethoven, observing this, begged Mozart to give him a theme for improvisation. He always played admirably when excited, and now he was inspired, too, by the presence of the master whom he reverenced greatly; he played in such a style that Mozart, whose attention and interest grew more and more, finally went silently to some friends who were sitting in an adjoining room, and said, vivaciously, "Keep your eyes on him; some day he will give the world something to talk about."

Beethoven may have taken a few casual lessons from Mozart. And that is all we know of this visit. Suddenly he was called back to Bonn by disturbing news of his mother's failing health.

On his return journey he stopped in Augsburg. There he called on the advocate Dr. Joseph Wilhelm von Schaden, whose wife, Nanette, was a pianist of great skill as well as a fine singer. Beethoven probably had made their acquaintance in Bonn. They were hospitable to the young traveler. Beethoven, having run out of funds, borrowed a sum of money from them.* He returned to Bonn early in May and wrote to Dr. Schaden in September. It is the earliest letter of his that has been preserved.

BONN, September 15, 1787

Most nobly born and especially beloved friend!

I can easily imagine what you must think of me. That you have well founded reasons not to think favourably of me I cannot deny. However, before apologizing I will first mention the reasons which lead me to hope that my apologies will be accepted. I must confess that as soon as I left Augsburg my good spirits and my health too began to decline. For the nearer I came to my native town, the more frequently did I receive from my father letters urging me to travel more quickly than usual, because my mother was not in very good health. So I made as much haste as I could, the more so as I myself began to feel ill. My yearning to see my ailing mother once more swept all obstacles aside so far as I was concerned, and enabled me to overcome the greatest difficulties. I found my mother still alive, but in the most wretched condition. She was suffering from consumption and in the end she died about seven weeks ago after enduring great pain and agony. She was such a good, kind mother to me and indeed my best friend. Oh! who was happier than I, when I could still utter the sweet name of mother and it was heard and answered; and to whom can I say it now? To the dumb likenesses of her which my imagination fashions for me? Since my

---

* The amount was three carolins, about $150 today.

return to Bonn I have as yet enjoyed very few happy hours. For the whole time I have been plagued by a tightness in the chest [my own translation]; and I am inclined to fear that this malady may even turn to consumption. Furthermore, I have been suffering from melancholia, which in my case is almost as great a torture as my illness. Well, just put yourself in my place; and, if you do, I shall hope for your forgiveness for my long silence. It was extraordinarily kind and friendly of you to lend me three carolins when I was at Augsburg. But I must beg you to bear with me a little longer. For my journey has cost me a good deal and I cannot hope for any compensation here, not even in the smallest way. Fortune does not favour me here at Bonn.

You must forgive me for taking up so much of your time with my chatter, but it has all been very necessary for the purpose of my apology.

I beg you not to refuse from now on your esteemed friendship to me whose most earnest desire is to deserve it, if only to a small extent.

With the greatest respect I remain

your most obedient servant and friend
L. V. BEETHOVEN
Church Organist to the Elector of Cologne.   (A-1).*

(It is impossible to convey in translation the flavor of Beethoven's German —hardly any punctuation, sentences running together, capricious spelling.)

It is a sad letter, but it was written under sad circumstances, and perhaps Beethoven was underscoring his griefs as an apology for not repaying the debt. It was certainly not true that he could not earn anything in Bonn. The "tightness in the chest" (*"Engbrüstigkeit"*) has been variously interpreted. Thayer and Emily Anderson translate it as "asthma." That Beethoven was inclined to be a hypochondriac is shown by considerable later evidence. Perhaps, too, the fact that his mother died of tuberculosis made him talk of consumption. Nothing was wrong with Beethoven's lungs, nor did he ever suffer from asthma.**

Yet, discounting possible youthful exaggeration in the description of his melancholy condition, one must pity not only the family but the son who was plunged into a sea of troubles. His mother died on July 17 at the age of forty. Some time before her death, Johann, in a petition which has not been preserved,

---

* Emily Anderson, ed., *The Letters of Beethoven*, 1961.
** Much later in life Beethoven complained of respiratory ailments. In July, 1816, he mentions a bad "condition of his chest"; a year later he writes that his doctor "has finally pronounced my condition to be caused by a disease of the lungs," but adds that he mistrusts his doctor. Later he tells his friends of various "colds" and "rheumatic conditions." Nevertheless, he himself never again mentions asthma or tuberculosis. The autopsy revealed that his lungs and chest cavity were perfectly sound.

described the straitened circumstances of his life and asked for the Elector's help. A summary of the document was given in a volume preserved in the Bonn archives called *Secret Government Protocols:*

Your Elec. Highness has taken possession of this petition.	Court Musician makes obedient representation that he has got into a very unfortunate state because of the long-continued sickness of his wife and has already been compelled to sell a portion of his effects and pawn others and that he no longer knows what to do for his sick wife and many children. He prays for the benefaction of an advance of 200 rthlrs.* on his salary.

We do not know whether the Elector granted the petition. We do know that Franz Ries, the Court musician who was a friend of the family and under whose tutelage Beethoven studied the violin, aided the Beethovens generously, then and later. Franz had a son Ferdinand, born in 1784, who became one of Beethoven's pupils and closest friends. Ferdinand was co-author (with Wegeler) of a book of reminiscences, *Biographische Notizen über Ludwig van Beethoven,* from which we have already quoted.

Once more we turn to the Fischer manuscript: "After her death, Herr Johann von Beethoven sold her wardrobe to a peddler. Thus it happened that her clothes were displayed in the marketplace. Cäcilia came by, saw the pretty clothes, which she recognized. She asked and received the reply: 'From the dead Mme. von Beethoven.' She became very sad and brought the news to her parents."

A further tragedy was in store, for, as usual, troubles did not come single spies. The little sister, Maria Margarethe, died on November 25, a year and a half old.

So it was to a house of mourning that the young Beethoven returned. Grief and poverty surrounded him. Johann succumbed, seeking forgetfulness in alcohol. A well-authenticated incident sheds light on the shame to which Ludwig must have been subjected. Johann, drunk and probably disorderly, got into trouble with the police, and Ludwig had to make a desperate effort to rescue his father when he was threatened with arrest. Beethoven had to shoulder the entire responsibility for the support of himself, his father, and his two brothers. He became the head of the family and petitioned the Elector to continue the father's salary though the father was unable to discharge his duties, and to let

---

* 200 Reichsthalers: about $2000 today.

him, Ludwig, administer the money. The petition has disappeared, but the decision, in the Memorandum of November 20, 1789, is clear:

> Ad Sup.
> Of the Organist L. van Beethoven
> His Electoral Highness having most graciously granted the stated prayer of the supplicant and dispensed henceforth altogether with the services of the father of the abovementioned, who is to withdraw to a small city in the Electorate, he graciously commands that he be paid, in accordance with his wish, only one hundred Reichsthaler of his hitherto annual salary and that beginning with the New Year the other hundred thaler be paid to his petitioning son, in addition to the salary which he now draws and the three measures of grain needed for the support of his brothers.* The aforementioned supplicant is to be informed of this decision, after which the Electoral Court Chamber is to do the necessary, and whoever it may concern is to respect this decision. Document X.

This was a generous decision. It is probable that the banishment of Johann was not seriously meant, the words being written into the document merely as a warning. Johann did not have to "withdraw to a small city," but lived out his life in Bonn itself. It was a half-lived life, and perhaps he himself never recognized his failure as a musician, his failure as a father. All the same, the descent into oblivion of the Court musician, the son of a man who once held the important position of Kapellmeister, must have been a dark progression for Ludwig to watch. Having the father around, now morose, now boisterous, must have represented to the son a load which chafed his daily life, a nervous responsibility which work could not lighten nor small triumphs erase from consciousness.

Nevertheless, Beethoven composed music during his last four years in Bonn. Genius must create, as the root of a tree splits a marble floor asunder because it must grow. The musical output which remains is small change: a quantity of piano and chamber music, sets of variations, a few songs. Among these there was a song entitled "Color of Fire" (*Feuerfarb'*), which he composed to a poem by Schiller and which a friend sent to Schiller's wife, Charlotte, with a note stating that this was written by a young composer "whose musical talents are universally praised" and who had it in mind to set Schiller's poem "Ode to

---

* The "three measures of grain" is a throwback to older contracts, which awarded, as part of the stipend, so-and-so many fagots of wood or ells of cloth or, in Haydn's case, a food allowance of half a florin a day "in lieu of taking his meals at the officers' table."

Joy" to music. Several songs are sweet, simple, sad, such as "Elegy on the Death of a Poodle," or lightly amorous, such as "The Test of Kissing."

Joseph II died on February 20, 1790, the news of his death reaching Bonn on the twenty-fourth. A memorial service was planned, and Professor Eulogius Schneider proposed that it include a musical tribute. He had in his possession a poem which only needed to be set to music by one of the Bonn musicians. That is how Beethoven came to compose the Cantata on the Death of Joseph II. For some reason, possibly because the parts for the wind instruments were difficult, it was not performed on that occasion, nor did Beethoven publish it. He lost the manuscript; it turned up in an auction sale in 1813. The composer Johann Nepomuk Hummel purchased it at the auction, along with a cantata on the crowning of Joseph's brother, Leopold II, which Beethoven composed at the same time. After Hummel's death, the two manuscripts found their way from his estate into a secondhand bookshop in Leipzig; there they gathered dust for years until they were found and bought in 1884 by the collector Armin Friedmann of Vienna. It was the critic Eduard Hanslick who gave Vienna the news of this rediscovery, and the *Joseph Cantata* was performed in Vienna in November of that year. Hanslick showed the score to Brahms, who wrote, "Even if there were no name on the title page, none other could be conjectured—it is Beethoven through and through!"

The two cantatas * are Beethoven's two most important compositions dating from the Bonn period, though we cannot be sure what works he took to Vienna with him to be reshaped in the alembic of his mind. Nor can we be sure what youthful works he lost. Beethoven, unmethodical even then, often treated the notepaper he had covered as if the sheets were yesterday's newspaper.

Whatever the quantity was, Beethoven had not yet found his quality. His work was still traditional: clear, clean products of the 18th-century Enlightenment, so to speak music of Reason, politely organized, light, pleasant, but hardly profound pieces, with echoes of Neefe, Haydn, and distant echoes of Mozart, many of them destined for his own use as a virtuoso. Here and there one hears an astonishing turn of phrase, a shudder of impatience, which presage the true Beethoven. Yet with all due respect to Brahms, one could *not* be certain who wrote this music if the title page were missing. That they were, in spite of limitations, notes of promise was quickly recognized by the musical circles of

---

* Some musicologists have found portents of the Ninth Symphony in the *Joseph Cantata,* and of *Fidelio* in the *Leopold Cantata.*

Bonn. How else would it have been possible for Waldstein, Neefe, and others to make such generous predictions of Beethoven's future?

·◦[2]◦·

That future could not lie in Bonn. In 1792 the war began, the clouds were hovering over the Electorate, the rounds of masked balls and operas gave way to rounds of artillery practice, chamber music could no longer compete with the brassy sounds of the military band. Beethoven must have longed to go away, away from his debilitated father and the smell of funerals.

Once more Vienna was his goal, as no other city offered so concentrated an opportunity to learn and be inspired. Again, who made it possible for Beethoven not only to leave Bonn but to be assured that when he got to Vienna he would have something to live on? It was probably Maximilian Franz. Beethoven was to go to Vienna to study with Haydn; this idea might well have been discussed on the occasion of a second visit by Haydn to Bonn.

By autumn the war with France was in full swing. Bonn was overrun with refugees, and nobody knew what bloody horror the next day might bring. Maximilian Franz, who had fled from Bonn and then returned, was occupied with other tasks than the pleasant one of developing the musical life of Bonn, and not only could he spare a musician but—without giving him too much credit for clairvoyance—he might even have felt that a young man with talent as promising as Beethoven's ought to be shipped off to safety.

Neefe knew of the plan and duly recorded in the *Berliner Musik Zeitung* early in 1793 that "Ludwig van Beethoven, assistant Court Organist and unquestionably now one of the foremost piano-forte players, went to Vienna at the expense of our Elector to visit Haydn in order to perfect himself under his direction more fully in the art of composition."

His farewell was as gay as farewells usually are when they are tendered to a young man with a future. His friends got together and bought an autograph album, a handsome little book which Beethoven, who lost so many souvenirs of his life, preserved. Names now forgotten can be read there, wishing him godspeed, several of them quoting some edifying sentiment as was the custom of the time.* His fellow musicians in the orchestra did not write; they might have been away, or they might have been envious. I find it significant—though nothing has been made of this by Beethoven biographers—that there is no

---

* There are fifteen entries, including three from the Koch family.

message from his father. The most interesting inscription is that of Waldstein, which proves that Waldstein's opinion of Beethoven was no less firm than Neefe's:

Dear Beethoven! You are going to Vienna in fulfillment of your long frustrated wishes. The Genius of Mozart is mourning and weeping over the death of her pupil. She found a refuge but no occupation with the inexhaustible Haydn; through him she wishes to form a union with another. With the help of assiduous labor you shall receive *Mozart's spirit from Haydn's hands.*

Your true friend
WALDSTEIN.

Bonn, October 29th, 1792

The last people on whom he called were the Breunings. Eleonore's contribution was an impersonal enough quotation from the then popular poet Herder —"Friendship with one who is good lengthens like the evening shadow until the sun of life sinks." And she signed it "Your true friend."

It is, however, not the only sign of life we have from the charming Lorchen, and it is quite possible, indeed probable, that a strong attraction existed between the two. She gave Beethoven her silhouette, one of those shadow profiles cut from black paper which were then the rage, and he preserved this memento all his life, writing a year before he died to Wegeler, "So you see how precious even now are all the dear good memories of my youth." Two letters from Beethoven to Eleonore, written during his first years in Vienna, show that the two had quarreled before his departure from Bonn. In the first letter he addresses her as "adorable Eleonore."

November 2nd, 1793

Adorable Eleonore!
My Dearest Friend!
I have been almost a whole year in this capital and only now are you receiving a letter from me. But certainly you have been constantly and most vividly in my thoughts; and very often I have conversed in spirit with you and your dear family, though frequently not as calmly as I should have wished. For whenever I did so I was always reminded of that unfortunate quarrel; and my conduct at that time seemed to me really detestable. But what was done could not be undone. Oh, I would give a great deal to be able to blot out of my life my behaviour at that time, a behaviour which did me so little honour and which was so inconsistent with my usual character. ... So now let us draw a curtain over the whole affair and just learn from it the lesson that when two friends

81

begin to quarrel it is always better to have no mediator but to let each one make a direct appeal to the other.

You are about to receive a dedication from me. I only wish that the work were greater and more worthy of you. But people in Vienna have been pestering me to publish this little work. So I have taken this opportunity of giving you, my adorable Eleonore, a proof of my regard and friendship for you and of my constant remembrance of your home. Please accept this trifle and bear in mind that it comes from a friend who admires you. Oh, if it only gives you pleasure, then my wishes are wholly fulfilled. Let it be a small token to recall the time when I spent so many and such blissful hours in your home. Perhaps it will continue to remind you of me until I return to Bonn, although indeed that will not be for some time. But oh! my beloved friend, how happy our meeting will be! For you will then find me a much more cheerful person; and you will see that time and more favourable circumstances have smoothed out the wrinkles produced by my earlier unpleasant experiences. . . .

I am venturing to make one more request, which is, that I should very much like to be the fortunate possessor of another waistcoat of angora wool knitted by you, my beloved friend. Do forgive your friend's presumption, which is prompted solely by his great preference for everything worked by your hands. And now I must tell you a secret, namely, that there is a touch of vanity fundamentally connected with my request. For I want to be able to say that I have received a present from one of the best and most adorable girls at Bonn. I still have, of course, the waistcoat which you very kindly gave me there. But it is now so out of fashion that I can only keep it in my wardrobe as a very precious token from you.   (A-7).

The second letter (written probably in June 1794; only a fragment is extant) proves that the adorable Eleonore complied with the request:

The beautiful neckcloth, your own handiwork, came as a very great surprise to me. And though its arrival afforded me much pleasure, yet it aroused melancholy feelings in me. It awakened memories of things long past; and moreover, your generous behaviour to me made me feel ashamed. Indeed I hardly believed that you could still think me worth remembering. Oh, if you could have witnessed what I felt yesterday on the arrival of your gift, you would certainly not think that I exaggerate when I tell you that your remembrance made me tearful and very sorrowful. . . .   (A-9).

They were never to meet again. At the end of his life she wrote to him and he to her. He had not forgotten her. She had not forgotten him.

··❧[3]❧··

Armed with good wishes, then, and no doubt carrying in his trunk a number of musical sketches, Beethoven set out, probably at six o'clock in the morning of November 2, 1792. He had a memorandum book with him in which he kept a record of his travel expenses. Somewhere he teamed up with a travel companion, whose identity has never been discovered, who shared expenses with him and whose handwriting appears in the little notebook. The trifling sums are recorded alternately by the companion and by Beethoven, obviously to settle accounts at the end of the trip. These included tips—which Beethoven in one entry calls "grease-money"—tolls, the price paid for the post chaise,* and a number of meals. No expenses are recorded for lodging; it may be assumed that each went separately to an inn of his choice. Beethoven notes that at or near Koblenz he gave the postilion a tip of "one small thaler, because the fellow drove us like the Devil, at the risk of a beating, right through the Hessian army." This army marched from Koblenz on November 5 to fight the French and was assembling there a few days before. Driving on a road choked with troops was no easy matter, yet Beethoven and his companion got through safely.

The little expense account has something good-naturedly humorous about it. If we put it in evidence along with the good wishes from his friends, we cannot reconcile ourselves to the picture of Beethoven as the sullen and withdrawn young man which some biographers have sketched. No, at the age of twenty-one the man who traveled to Vienna for further instruction in composition, though quite the master as a "foremost piano-forte player," was more likely somebody who journeyed with zest, who was open, cheerful, positive, eager for new knowledge and impressions, and above all filled with ambition. His first successes in the city on the Danube confirm this image.

---

* More expensive, because it was faster, than the stagecoach taken on his previous journey.

View of Vienna from the palace of Prince Kinsky. Aquarelle by B. Wigaud.

CHAPTER 6

THE CITY ON THE DANUBE

The traveler from Bonn would approach Vienna on the road which leads along the Danube and which unrolls as satisfying and exhilarating a panorama as is to be seen anywhere in Europe. The prospect before him changes continuously, woods dark enough to serve as settings for a fairy tale, huddled hamlets, fields dotted with cornflowers and poppies, high cliffs on the top of which are placed, as if to spite nature, comfortable cloisters such as the beautiful one at Melk and uncomfortable fortresses such as the one at Dürnstein, where Richard the Lion-Hearted once lay imprisoned. Through it all flows the river, now turbulent, now broad and lazy, now gray, now green, now silver, but very seldom blue. Even in the winter, with the raw wind chafing the river's surface, the valley—it is called the *Wachau*—refreshes a weary man, the more so as he knows that he will soon be reaching journey's end. Before the end, after the Danube bends around the Leopoldsberg and divides into several branches, the traveler in Beethoven's day had to stop at the "Customs Office of the Vienna City Police" to have his papers scrutinized and his belongings examined.* That nuisance being over, he was sent on his way to the "Emperor City," the *Kaiserstadt.*

In those days Vienna presented itself as if it had been placed on a platter for display. The city itself—what is now the inner city, the First District—lay on a higher ground than the immediate surroundings. As you came to it, you first traversed an open space called the Glacis, which originally held a moat; then you confronted the tall circular wall, built against the onslaught of the Turks,

---

* Mozart as a child so enchanted a customs official here by playing a minuet on the violin that the official let his harpsichord pass without duty.

which ringed the city (the famous Ringstrasse now occupies its site). The wall had a number of gates and bastions in which people lived. The top of the wall served as a popular promenade.

Outside the *Bastei* and the Glacis lay the *Vorstädte.* They were more than suburbs and less than independent villages; each was a district with its own individuality and trade and local lore, several of them speaking a dialect of their own. The *Vorstädte,* as well, were surrounded by a protective wall, "The Wall of the Linien." Beyond, there was pure country, fields and vineyards, and the mountains began in earnest. Tame and gentle, the near ones—such as the Kahlenberg or the Leopoldsberg—seemed to be merely attendants on the snow-covered potentates of mountains farther off, but near enough to be seen from Vienna on a clear day. Everywhere, within easy travel distance by coach, was the forest, the *Wienerwald.* There was no forest like it; so inviting was it, so hospitable, so green and gracious, that it seemed expressly made for the delectation of the city's people. Its birds and rabbits, its flowers and trees seemed to have been taught a lesson in Viennese insouciance and gaiety.*

Beethoven reached Vienna on November 10, 1792 (probably). The day was gray but not cold;** it invited walking. No doubt he looked for lodging first. Then, being an enthusiastic walker, he may have gone out to observe the city in which he was to stay for a period. He had not as yet any intention of making Vienna his permanent home. Far from it, he was there for instruction and for displaying his art as a pianist and would then return to his family and his sovereign.

The city he saw had 200,000 inhabitants and was therefore twenty times the size of Bonn. We do not know where he lodged the first few nights; Thayer says in an "attic-room" but gives no further particulars. Probably it was a modest enough quarter, and he soon moved out. As he walked in the inner city he must have marveled and been awed. The center of Vienna was, and is, the Church of St. Stephen (*Stefanskirche*). Huge as it is and splendid in Gothic intricacy, it was never finished. Only one of its spires reaches into the sky, like the center pole of a carrousel around which the city turns. Two main streets lead away

---

* We speak of 1792! Today, with the automobile roads crossing it, the forest has lost much of its magic. Alas!

** According to the excellent record kept by the Vienna Observatory. Parenthetically (having nothing to do with our story), the weather on December 6, 1791, the day of Mozart's funeral, was "mild and hazy," according to the same authority. So the story that the mourners, few as they were, did not follow the coffin because there was a terrible snowstorm (or rainstorm, in some accounts) looks like a fable. The musicologist Nicholas Slonimsky has pointed this out.

from the church, the Kärntnerstrasse and the Graben, where stands the overornate, overgilded "Pest-Column," erected in 1693 in thanks for Vienna's liberation from an epidemic: these were, and still are, the elegant shopping streets.

A few paces from the Kärntnerstrasse one comes upon the *Neuer Markt,* an Italianate piazza in the center of which stands the marvelous baroque "Donner Fountain," so called because it was designed by Raphael Donner. Its figures represent Austrian rivers; a few nude *putti* play around them. Maria Theresa objected to their nakedness and they were removed, to be put back into place in 1801.* The piazza was occasionally used by the Court for sleigh rides. A last and particularly sumptuous sleigh festival was held during the Vienna Congress in 1815. On one side of the piazza was the *Mehlgrube* ("Flour Cave"), a building of flats and a ballroom—the present site of the Hotel Ambassador. Mozart had used it for recitals and Beethoven was to use it.

Near the Graben lies the *Kohlmarkt,* formerly a market. There Beethoven may have looked into the shop window of "Artaria and Comp., art dealers." On that day they were advertising the newly published—it was, in fact, not quite ready—piano score of *The Magic Flute,* an opera then a year old. It cost 4 florins, 30 kreuzer—expensive indeed (about $25). Mozart's funeral (third class) had cost only about twice as much. From Artaria's place of business a five-minute walk would have brought Beethoven to the seat of the Habsburgs, the *Hofburg.* This was the focal point from which emanated the laws which ruled Austria and the Holy Roman Empire. The *Hofburg,* architecturally not one of Vienna's most successful buildings, is huge, stern, and cold in exterior. Inside, in the representational rooms, the contrast was striking: all was pomp and circumstance, all was gold and mirror and polished candelabra and gleaming parquet floors; porcelain stoves, which seemed to have been shaped by a pastry cook, standing obediently in the corner; tapestries on exotic and erotic themes warming the walls; busy action on every ceiling with blue, white, and gold decorations crisscrossing one another, and angels flying in all directions.

The *Hofburg* is a complex of palaces, the finest edifice being Fischer von Erlach's Imperial Library. Much of the beauty of 18th-century Vienna is due to this great architect's work. Vienna owes him what Rome owes to Bernini. Near the library stands the palace of Prince Lobkowitz, an obese building which von Erlach had graced with a charming portal. Contiguous with the *Hofburg* is Erlach's Spanish Riding School, housing improbably beautiful horses, every one

---

* The present ones are bronze copies. The originals are in the Baroque Museum in the Belvedere.

a ballet dancer. Going diagonally away from the *Hofburg* one walks down the narrow Herrengasse. This, the "street of gentlemen," was where many of Vienna's bluebloods, princes, counts, and barons had settled, and Beethoven was to become well acquainted with the street. The density of stone and glass there was almost oppressive. As one got away a little from the core of the inner city, the palaces seemed to become lighter and were relieved by the green of parks and gardens. The Liechtenstein Palace with its marvelous collection of paintings (now in Vaduz, Liechtenstein) stood in a park of its own. The most spectacular of the city palaces is the Belvedere, which Prince Eugen of Savoy, an Italian who was brought up at Versailles, had built for himself. The site was a long steep slope affording a panorama of the city from its highest ridge. On this ridge the architect Johann Lucas von Hildebrandt placed the upper Belvedere, the building used for receptions and masked balls. A terraced garden ambles down to the lower building, the garden being extravagantly populated with marble figures, sphinxes, fauns, tritons; in the center a fountain plays; the flower beds are framed by maple and yew hedges clipped and twisted into innocent mazes. It all looks as if it had been invented by Fragonard. But it was Canaletto's nephew, Bernardo Bellotto—whom the Viennese insisted on calling Canaletto—who painted it, along with many other Viennese scenes and sights, thus bequeathing us an exact knowledge of the Vienna of the 18th century.*

At the time Beethoven reached Vienna the occupant of the *Hofburg* was the newly crowned Franz II. He was the great Joseph's nephew and had become Emperor through the accident of two deaths. Two years before, in 1790, Joseph had sickened and died, a disappointed, disillusioned, sorrowful man who wished for his epitaph the sad words, "Here lies Joseph II, who failed in all he undertook." In the last week of his life he had sent frequent messages to his brother Leopold, who ruled Tuscany, urging him to hurry to Vienna. Leopold was next in line of succession, but he was in no hurry to assume the burden of the crown. From Tuscany Leopold wrote to his son Franz, instructing him to lock up all the offices in the *Hofburg* as soon as Joseph was dead and to prepare a detailed confidential report on the ability and loyalty of all government officials. The funeral and all the painful formalities were to be got over with before Leopold would arrive. Such ceremonies were too much for his "very sensitive nerves." When he finally did come, he was met by Franz, Franz's

---

* Most of these paintings are now in the *Kunsthistorische Museum* in Vienna.

mother, and Franz's thirteen brothers and sisters, one of whom was the Arch-duke Rudolph, who was to play so important a part in Beethoven's life. There was a great family reunion in the *Hofburg,* but soon Leopold had little time to give to his family. Austria was seething with disorder. The people were rebel-ling against Joseph's puritanical and drastic measures. Leopold galloped from one end of the realm to the other, at first emasculating then revoking altogether his brother's more unpopular measures. To quote Dorothy McGuigan again, "It was clear to him, as it had never been to Joseph, that the whole bottle of medicine could not be forced down the patient's throat at once." He had to worry as well about what was happening in Paris. Marie Antoinette implored him to help her. Leopold was not sure he wanted to become embroiled. He wrote her: "We have a sister, the Queen of France. But the Holy Empire has no sister. Austria has no sister. I can only act for the interests of my people, not for family interests." Then he changed his mind. Before he could do anything about it, he suddenly died, in March, 1792, probably of pneumonia. Marie Antoinette was sure he had been poisoned by French agents.

So Leopold was dead after a reign of little more than a year. His son Franz, next in line of succession, took up the crown. Franz was destined to become Napoleon's adversary, to live under the shadow of a war that was to last twenty-two years, to become a father-image to Austria, to see the end of the Holy Roman Empire, to have Haydn compose the Austrian National Anthem for him—*Gott erhalte Franz, den Kaiser* ("God preserve Franz, the Emper-or") —and to outlive Beethoven by eight years.

It is probable that Beethoven, in his peregrination around the city, halted at a coffee house and read the newspaper, the *Wiener Zeitung.* The Vienna coffee houses were the clubs of the plain people, with particular coffee houses soon catering to particular groups, the wool merchants, the cavalry officers, the poets, the minor Court officials, etc. All of the coffee houses supplied news-papers. Beethoven loved to read the papers. On the day of his arrival, Novem-ber 10, 1792, he could have read in the *Wiener Zeitung* disquieting foreign news:

ROME, Oct. 18. Several indications have heightened the fear of a French attack on Rome and have caused the Pope to buttress the defense fortifications along the coast.

PARIS, Oct. 22. A deposition by the government of Constantinople was submitted to the National Convention. It is desired that Ambassador Semonville be replaced by another choice, since he is accused of unseemly behavior. The council immediately took the necessary step to reprove the Turkish government and to revenge the insult to Citizen Semonville.

PARIS, Oct. 21. Thirteen émigrés who were captured were nearly lynched, but the municipality succeeded in dispersing the mob in front of the prison. Nine of the prisoners had to be executed.

PARIS (no date). Labor disputes have begun. Laborers no longer wish to be paid by piecework but per diem. There were stormy discussions with the famous Marat.

KOBLENZ, Oct. 26. The greater part of the French army has retreated to Bingen. Frankfurt is partially liberated but detachments of cavalry are filtering through Hessen. Arnsburg was damaged by fire. So many Hessian and Prussian troops are expected in Koblenz that twelve to fifteen men have to be quartered in every house.

Beethoven must have read this with a sigh of relief, since he had just come through Koblenz.*

As Beethoven called on Haydn and on those for whom he had letters of introduction, he was instantly marked as a "foreigner," for his Rhenish German was practically a foreign language to the Viennese. If he stopped to ask directions of a man in the street, he might not have been understood. But Vienna was used to foreigners, being almost as much of a melting pot as New York and drawing its citizens from Italy and Hungary, Bohemia and Serbia, Poland, and Russia. The Viennese dialect itself is a melting-pot language, in which Italian, French, Czech, and even old Latin expressions keep careless company with German.**

We have spoken so far only of the palatial side of the city. It was a different city for those who spoke low Viennese, such as the workmen and the tradesmen. They lived in narrow, dark streets, or in hovels on the outskirts, or in ugly tenement-like buildings which had recently been constructed. The people were regulated and legislated to within an inch of their little lives. Vienna's health record was not good, mortality rates for tuberculosis, dysentery, and typhus being high. Yet in spite of all their troubles, or perhaps because of them, the Viennese developed a unique character of their own, a character which mixed butter with a dash of paprika and a heaping spoonful of sugar. They were patriots but scoffed at the flag. They were sentimentalists but wouldn't be

---

* News traveled slowly: news items from October 10 to 26 were published on November 10.
** Hofmannsthal re-creates this language superbly in *Der Rosenkavalier*. A familiar "Hello" and "Good-bye" in Vienna is *"Servus"* from the Latin—"Your servant."

caught shedding tears. They took the cash and let the credit go. They loved Franz, but flirted with the egalitarian ideas of the Revolution. They adored their city, but anybody with an idea which would benefit the common weal had a devil of a time to get them to work together. They were realists who succumbed to charlatans and fakers. Above all they made fun of themselves. Nearly everything was a joke. Only three things were to be taken seriously: food, music, and the theater.

Meals were elaborate occasions in the wealthy homes. Dinner parties were usually set for three o'clock, and guests were invited by printed invitations. If a prince arrived, the porter rang the bell three times; for a count, twice. Two servants, richly liveried, received each guest. One opened the door, the other took the outer wraps and accompanied him or her through a series of rooms to the reception room of the hostess, who remained seated and greeted the guest "with a slight nod." To friends she extended her hand for a kiss. It was strictly forbidden to invite thirteen. A traveler reports the number of courses as "three without counting the soup." Three? Well, the first course was usually hors d'oeuvres of various kinds, plus an assortment of sausages, plus boiled beef, plus puddings, plus fish. The second course consisted of game: pheasant or quail. The third was a *Mehlspeise,* a warm pastry. There was a wide choice of wine. Most preferred a light Rhine wine or a Hungarian wine watered. Champagne was drunk with the dessert, followed by a glass of Tokay. It was polite to eat rapidly. Only those guests who were specifically asked to remain for the evening could remain, to play cards or billiards or listen to music. The others waddled away.

But even the simpler people of Vienna ate well when they did have a little money. Their main repast was taken around noon. Their meals were replete with sweets, and they concocted such miracles as *Palatschinken* (pancakes filled with jam or cheese) and *Kaiserschmarrn* (The Kaiser's trifle, another pastry). These and the new wine induced the characteristic for which the Viennese are famous: *Gemütlichkeit.* It is a quality which disappears rapidly when trouble or hatred rears its head!

To music and the theater they paid a constant tribute even when they did not have enough to eat. Ilsa Barea * writes that in the early days of Beethoven's sojourn the Viennese "to whom music was accessible, and they were the overwhelming majority ... found release from self-doubts and resentments in

---

* In her superb book, *Vienna, Legend and Reality,* 1966.

91

the serenity of Haydn ... the perfection of Mozart." Music played an immense role during and after the Napoleonic wars. "The other escape route was the theater."

Beethoven must soon have inquired where the halls or rooms or theaters were in which he could display his skill. There were as yet no concert halls as such. Music was played in the palaces, in the homes of patrons, in the ballrooms, in assembly halls, in a park called the Augarten, or occasionally in one of the theaters.

During the 18th century, theaters were built of wood; in spite of all precautions, sooner or later, usually sooner, they burned to the ground. Early in the century, however, a theater built of brick and mortar, financed by the City Council, was opened. It was located near the Kärntnerstrasse, about where the Hotel Sacher is. This solid theater lasted for some fifty years. One night, when Gluck's ballet *Don Juan or the Stone Guest* was being given, the hellfire which engulfs Don Juan at the end started a real fire, fortunately after the audience had left. The entire theater was reduced to ashes and rubble, brick and mortar notwithstanding. The cashier, who tried to save the receipts, lost his life, along with his wife, who attempted to rescue him. Immediately rebuilding was begun. The new version became a famous house, the predecessor of Vienna's Imperial-Royal * Court Opera.

Near the *Hofburg* stood a ballroom, the *Hofballhaus,* which, renovated and newly equipped, became the "Theater near the Burg." This eventually became the "Burgtheater," one of the most elegant, beautiful, and meritorious theaters of the world. There a new style of acting was developed; there the drama of all nations was presented; there the purest German was spoken. It was the Mecca of all actors. To be an official member of the Burgtheater meant that the actor had reached the top of his profession. Though later the house was exclusively devoted to the spoken drama, in the beginning it served opera and ballet as well. Gluck's *Orfeo, Alceste,* and *Paris and Helen,* Mozart's *The Abduction from the Seraglio, The Marriage of Figaro,* and *Così fan tutte* were first performed there, and *Don Giovanni* in its Vienna version was given there after its Prague premiere. In Maria Theresa's time the Burgtheater served the Court almost exclusively—a private passage for her use led from her apartments to the theater—but when Beethoven became acquainted with it, it had become a theater for the citizens, or at least for the more prosperous citizens.

---

* The "K.K." one sees in the old documents means *Kaiserlich-Königlich,* "Imperial Royal."

In spring and summer when the Court repaired to Schönbrunn Palace, performances were given in its little gingerbread theater, an exquisite imitation of the Versailles theater. However, it lacked a Molière!

The plain people in a Sunday mood went to the theaters in the suburbs. What they wanted most was a good belly laugh. Slapstick farces in Viennese dialect, comedies with inane plots and plenty of *double-entendres,* satirical plays mocking the Austrian soldier, parodies, and knockabout burlesques—this fare was to be had in abundance in theaters in the Josefstadt or the Leopoldstadt.

In the district of Wieden—very near the majestic church of St. Charles * with its enormous cupola which had not as yet acquired the golden-green patina which it now possesses—stood an ugly, shapeless building called the *Freihaus.* ** There poor people lived—clerks, tradesmen, artisans, functionaries— often in one room and a kitchen. On the ground floor were cheap shops and repair shops, and stairs and passages were dank and airless, the courtyards noisy and strewn with offal. In front of the building was an outdoor fruit and vege- table market. Under huge umbrellas stood formidable harridans hawking the wares: these were the famous *Naschmarktweiber.* If the passer-by did not stop to purchase a few apples, he was loudly berated by a chorus of these women, shouting the Viennese equivalent of billingsgate. The *Freihaus* had its own theater; Joseph II had licensed it, stipulating that all the performances were to be given in German. Joseph thought it would benefit the Viennese to be given entertainment other than Italian operas or foreign harlequinades.

Emanuel Schikaneder took over the direction of the *Freihaus* Theater in 1787. He was an actor, actor-manager, promoter, producer, stage designer and poet of sorts, shaking libretti and comedies in verse or prose out of his sleeves. He was an extravagant, irresponsible, capricious Jack-of-all-trades of the thea- ter, but he was so enthusiastic and so persuasive that few could resist him. To help his theater he persuaded his brother-Freemason Mozart to collaborate on an "easy" comedy with music. He proposed to throw into it all the sure-fire ingredients he knew: magic effects, moral preaching, an evil spirit or two, a comic little Moor, the old trick of juxtaposing the idealistic prince and his down-to-earth servant, trial by fire and water, two pairs of lovers, and for himself the best part, a part where he could sing and improvise jokes. This was *The Magic Flute,* and Schikaneder's role was the birdcatcher Papageno, attend-

---

* Again, designed by Fischer von Erlach. He did not live to complete the *Karlskirche.* His son finished it after his designs.
** Part of the building was still standing after World War II.

ant to Prince Tamino. The work had its first performance at the *Freihaus* on September 30, 1791. It soon scored a triumph, though too late to do Mozart much good. Twenty-four performances were given by the end of the year. Shortly after Beethoven's arrival in Vienna the following November, Schikaneder announced "the one hundredth performance" of the *Flute*.* Schikaneder made a great deal of money from *The Magic Flute*—all of which he later lost—and he now became ambitious to head a theater more worthy of his talents, more splendid and more accessible. In 1786 Joseph had awarded him a permit to build, and Leopold endorsed the permit. Yet it took Schikaneder many years to obtain the financial assistance, clear the legal entanglements, and overcome the intrigues which beset any public enterprise in Vienna. The site he chose was in a near suburb, on the bank of the river Wien. When the Theater-an-der-Wien finally opened in 1801, built in the fashionable new Empire style, all Vienna marveled. It was the largest theater in Vienna, with a capacity of 1500, gaily decorated in bright blue and silver and equipped with the latest technical apparatus needed for producing Schikaneder's beloved magic effects. The curtain of the theater showed an elaborate painting—symbolic, but bad art—a landscape with temples, a stately Sarastro and a Tamino fleeing from the serpent. Over the entrance Schikaneder paid tribute to himself by having himself pictured as Papageno. The financial "angel" of this theater was a wealthy stagestruck merchant called Bartholomäus Zitterbarth.** He and Schikaneder did not get on too well. After three years Schikaneder was forced to sell his share and rights in the theater to Zitterbarth. But money is one thing, ability another, and Zitterbarth soon had to call Schikaneder back as manager. Whereupon Schikaneder delightedly proceeded to squander Zitterbarth's money on ever more elaborate productions. He ranged over an amazingly wide repertoire: a score of his own comedies and farces, sentimental German tragedies, French operas, but also Mozart operas and *Hamlet*.

Schikaneder died in 1812, insane and penniless. Like Mozart, he was buried in a mass grave. In the history of music he remains unforgotten not only because he worked with Mozart but because he aided Beethoven, putting the Theater-an-der-Wien at his disposal. Several of Beethoven's works were first performed there. After World War II, when the Vienna Opera House had been made

---

* He exaggerated a little; there were closer to sixty.
** The improbable name sounds as if it came from a Viennese allegorical play; it means Tremblebeard.

unusable by an incendiary bomb, opera performances were temporarily housed in the Theater-an-der-Wien. Later, when the Opera House was rebuilt, the fate of the Theater-an-der-Wien, now obsolete, was discussed by the City Council. The fact that Beethoven once stood there conducting his first symphonies, as much as any other consideration, prompted the decision in 1962 to preserve and restore the historic theater.*

As curious a personality as Schikaneder was Count Joseph Deym. He knew Schikaneder and was on friendly terms with Mozart and his wife. He had to flee from Vienna by order of Maria Theresa, because as a minor he had become involved in a duel, and the stern Empress would have none of such youthful nonsense. In 1790 he at last returned to Vienna under an alias, calling himself plain Herr Müller, which didn't fool anybody, certainly not the "Morals Police," but put a tolerable face on the affair. Abroad Deym had learned the craft of sculpting effigies in wax or plaster and he now opened a Viennese version of Madame Tussaud's Museum. One of the exhibits was a crypt in which lay the wax figure of Joseph II. As you entered it, you heard a dirge played on a mechanical organ-cylinder, called the *Orgelwalze.* Deym had commissioned Mozart to compose this dirge.

When the dead Mozart was laid out on his bed, Count Deym appeared and made a wax mask of his features. He got hold of a set of Mozart's clothes and then invited his customers to come and see Mozart "as he lived." Ilsa Barea has given us the point of the anecdote: had Mozart not been a popular local celebrity, had the Viennese public—a large public—not cared about music, Count Deym would hardly have bothered. "The point is that the ordinary Viennese citizen did know of a marvelous musician called Mozart, even if he hardly knew his music; with the result that Count Deym could cash in on it in a grotesquely macabre fashion. There was no unbridgeable gulf between the well-educated connoisseurs, the well-bred patrons and fastidious musicians on the one hand, and the many, the very many, who merely enjoyed melody on the other. This was one of the legacies the eighteenth century left to the nineteenth in Vienna." **

Such was the city which Beethoven was never to leave permanently, a city of palaces and parks; of ill-lit sour-smelling little rooms and sunlit suburban

---

* Some other famous works connected with the Theater-an-der-Wien were Kleist's *Käthchen von Heilbronn,* Grillparzer's *Ahnfrau,* almost all of Nestroy's farces, Johann Strauss's *Die Fledermaus,* Lehar's *The Merry Widow.*
** Ilsa Barea, *op. cit.*

houses; of representational buildings designed by a great baroque architect and quite a few buildings designed by hobbling imitators; of churches which better induced pageantry than worship; of quiet, restful places near the river, and muddy side streets where prostitutes prowled; of a university which became one of Europe's leading institutions of learning and which even then, in spite of censorship and chicanery, managed to expose its students to Leibnitz, Kant, Hume, and Voltaire.

Perhaps most of what has just been said could be said of other metropolises as well. What gave Vienna its own special character was the people's pleasure in and concern with music and the theater. The Vienna of the late 18th and early 19th century excelled only in minor pictorial arts, such as the fabrication of exquisite porcelain. Nor did any first-rate painter arise there, or great writer or poet.* But musical talent, in the instrumental and orchestral fields or in the theater in operas and *Singspiele,* was as concentrated there as pictorial genius was in the Florence of the 15th century. The audience nourished the composer —and vice versa. Most of the composers, the Weigls and Salieris and Gyro-wetzes, are now mere names known only to the musical historian, but in their day they were lively and celebrated personalities, and their contributions formed a firmly packed foundation on which Beethoven could build.

True, there was no logic to Vienna's taste. The Viennese let Mozart perish in penury, though they heaped honors on Haydn. They gobbled up jelly-rolls of Italian operas,** but swallowed yard-long fugues without a murmur. They paraded to brassy marches, but sat in sensitive silence when a string quartet played. They clapped for childish comedies with music, but they responded as well to *The Magic Flute*—and not only to Papageno's prancing, but to the nobility of the Overture. They sang sentimental songs, some of them mawkish, but they loved, as well, the pure, light-filled melody which Gluck set in the Elysian fields.

Enthusiasm was genuine and widespread. True understanding of music, if not ubiquitous, was not a rarity. When Beethoven began his ascent, many could climb with him. Many wanted to.

---

* Grillparzer was not a great poet. He was a fine dramatist, but still not of the quality of a Lessing or Schiller, with whom the Austrians like to compare him.

** Thayer calculated that in the thirteen-month period ending December 15, 1792, there had taken place in the two Court Theaters 180 performances of Italian operas and 163 of ballet. This, though the theaters were closed between March 1 and May 24, almost three months, the period being one of mourning for the death of Leopold.

Count Moritz von Fries and his family. The oil painting was done
by Gerard, one of Beethoven's early admirers (Austrian National Library, Vienna).

CHAPTER 7

FIRST YEARS IN VIENNA AND GROWING FAME

·❧[1]❧·

For a while Beethoven continued in his conscientious vein, trying to make ends meet on his small stipend and keeping track of his little expenditures. In the memorandum book we find a record of sums spent for rent, the hiring of a piano, meals "with wine," money for a cleaning woman, wood, coffee, overcoat, boots, shoes, writing desk, etc. The book shows as well how careful he was about his appearance, which was to prepare him to meet the important people: he went to the wigmaker, he spent a ducat ($25) for fine black silk stockings, and one florin, forty kreuzer, ($10) for coarser winter silk stockings. He worried about insufficient funds: he had counted on a hundred ducats from the Elector, yet only twenty-five were waiting for him.

Hardly had he got his bearings in Vienna when the news reached him that his father had died. Johann died on December 18, 1792, a little more than a month after Beethoven's arrival. No one seems to have mourned him; the cold death notice, "1792, Dec. 18, obiit Johannes Beethoff," is all we have. No word from the sons, no word from Johann's fellow musicians. Maximilian Franz cracked a cruel joke, stating that "the revenues from the liquor excise" would undoubtedly suffer because of Johann's death.

The big question which now confronted Beethoven was: would at least half of his father's pension, which he had administered and which was to help support himself and his younger brothers, be continued? Where was the document which spelled out this arrangement? To his horror, Beethoven discovered that it had disappeared. Therefore, and probably on the advice of Franz Ries, who continued to act as a friend of the family and to counsel him, Beethoven sent a petition to the Elector in which he reminded him that Maximilian Franz had graciously decreed to set aside a hundred thalers of Johann's pension so that he, Ludwig, could "clothe, nourish, and educate my two young brothers and also discharge our father's debts." Though the amount had been paid regularly, Beethoven had never presented to the Bonn Revenue Exchequer the document which specified the grant. This was done out of consideration for his father's feelings and at his father's urgent plea. Had the document become an official exhibit, had it been published in a Court publication, it would have appeared to the eyes of Johann's fellow townsmen that he was "incapable of caring for his family." Therefore Johann himself had continued to draw his full salary but had conscientiously handed over the hundred thalers to Ludwig. How great was his shock now to learn that Johann had done away with the Elector's document. Therefore Ludwig had no proof; he was constrained to "pray your Electoral Highness for a gracious renewal of this decree"—in other words, to continue to let him have the hundred thalers and to direct the Exchequer to pay the sum over to himself.

We may imagine with what anxiety Beethoven in Vienna, not as yet able to earn money, awaited the decision. How relieved he must have been when, on May 3, 1793, the Privy Council granted the request and added that he was "further to receive the three measures of grain graciously bestowed upon him for the education of his brothers." The Electoral assistance did not last long. Beethoven received payments until March, 1794, a little less than a year. Shortly after that, Maximilian Franz's reign came to an end—and in 1797 the whole proud Cologne Electorate was no more, the territory having been annexed by France. By that time, as we shall see, Beethoven was no longer dependent on Maximilian Franz's subsidy.

···◦[2]◦···

Undoubtedly one of the first calls Beethoven made was on Haydn. Haydn enjoyed a unique position in Vienna: he was not only a composer of whom the city was proud but he was beloved and popular as a man. Because of his successes abroad, he was considered a worthy representative of Vienna; his statesmanship was leavened by his humor, and this combination appealed to the Viennese. He who had in his early days been a revolutionary was now, at the age of sixty, on the way to becoming a "classic." Beethoven was not easily awed by anybody, but he must have approached the older man with some trepidation. Their acquaintance, briefly begun in Bonn, developed into a personal relationship which, if not profound, was cordial. Haydn recognized that this swarthy, earnest youth was somebody exceptional.

FIRST YEARS IN VIENNA AND GROWING FAME

Instruction began. Its object was in the main to teach Beethoven the art of counterpoint. The Beethoven scholar Gustav Nottebohm made a study * of all the exercises which Beethoven composed under Haydn's direction. They were based upon six plain chants, Haydn using a textbook, Fux's *Gradus ad Parnassum.*** No fewer than 245 such studies are extant, and nobody knows how many there were originally, some of the sheets having undoubtedly been lost. Only forty-two of these exercises have changes or indications of corrections in Haydn's handwriting. It is apparent that Haydn was not overly exacting as a teacher. How could he have been? The demands on his time were great, and he was just then preparing for his second visit to London, a visit of great consequence to him. Haydn actually left Vienna on January 19, 1794, which would be the latest date for the end of Beethoven's studies with him. Nor can it be assumed that a great creator is necessarily a good teacher. Nor was the pupil particularly tractable, harboring ideas of his own from the first.

Still, 245 exercises suggest with what eagerness Beethoven threw himself into learning the tools, the formulas, the traditions of his profession. Further proof is furnished by the other teachers whom he sought out as soon as he realized that Haydn did not give him enough. Beethoven dug deep. His probing into music of past and present, begun as a young organist in Bonn, partook of the restlessness of the explorer and the skepticism of the scientist. Like a Leonardo laboring in Verrocchio's workshop and learning to paint so much like Verrocchio that the attribution of at least one picture to one or the other remains doubtful, Beethoven learned to compose like his predecessors before he composed like Beethoven. He never kicked the old aside; he carried it with him onto new paths. Tradition was in his bloodstream: such a man can make the most powerful of rebels.

Whatever Haydn's contributions were, and Beethoven later and rather peevishly said that he learned little from him, the two men remained on reasonably good terms. The account book mentions Haydn a few times: "Haidn 8 groschen" ($2.40) on December 12; then the following October, "22 kreuzer chocolate for Haidn and me" ($2.20); "Coffee 6 kreuzer for Haidn and me" (60¢). In return the older man must on several occasions have stood treat for chocolate or coffee. The "Haidn 8 groschen" is usually interpreted as a fee for a lesson. I doubt this. It seems unlikely that Haydn would charge so little

---

* *Beethovens Studien,* 1873.
** Johann Joseph Fux (1660–1741) was a "master of counterpoint" and an eminent theoretician.

(about two dollars in today's equivalent); it is more likely that the entry refers to a meal they had taken together.

Only about thirty years ago a letter by Haydn was discovered which throws further light on the relationship between the two men. Only the signature is in Haydn's handwriting. On November 23, 1793, Haydn wrote to Maximilian Franz and sent him "in all humility" a few pieces of music, including a quintet, an oboe concerto, a set of variations, and a fugue composed by his "dear pupil Beethoven, who was so graciously entrusted to me. . . . On the basis of these pieces, expert and amateur alike cannot but admit that Beethoven will in time become one of the greatest musical artists in Europe, and I shall be proud to call myself his teacher. I only wish that he might remain with me for some time yet." Haydn then writes of the difficulties Beethoven experiences to make ends meet. He knows about the allowance which Maximilian Franz has awarded him. But that allowance is insufficient to cover his expenses, and Haydn himself, "in order to prevent him from falling into the hands of usurers," has guaranteed some loans of Beethoven's and lent him 500 florins. Haydn assured Maximilian Franz that not one kreuzer had been spent unnecessarily. He asked that His Highness consider increasing the allowance to 1000 florins for the following year. He assured the Elector that Beethoven would not squander this sum, "being utterly devoted to his art."

On the same day, Beethoven wrote the Elector: "I have employed this year all the powers of my soul for the benefit of music in order to be able during the coming year to send Your Electoral Highness something that will reflect your magnanimous treatment of me and your sublime character in general more clearly than what is being sent to Your Electoral Excellency by Herr Haiden." Was Beethoven apologizing? This letter, too, is written by another hand; only the signature is Beethoven's. The letter was probably enclosed with Haydn's. Both letters must have reached the Elector at an unfortunate time, at the very moment when the war was going particularly badly. A few days afterward (December 26) France forced the allies to retreat across the Rhine.

We do not know what the Elector replied to Beethoven; only the reply to Haydn has survived.* The Elector administered a sharp rebuke to both men, perhaps because he was in ill humor—little wonder if he was!—or because he was offended by the obvious "collusion." He replied that with the exception of

---

* It is a rough draft by another hand, with corrections in the Elector's handwriting and dated December 23, three days before the French victory.

the fugue, all the music sent him was composed and performed in Bonn before Beethoven departed for Vienna. He could hardly consider the submitted work to be evidence of progress. It was true, he wrote, that Beethoven's allowance was a mere 500 florins; yet his salary of 400 florins had been continued to be paid to him, and on nine hundred florins one ought to be able to get along. "I cannot therefore see why he is as much in arrears in his finances as you say. I am wondering therefore whether he had not better come back here in order to resume his work. For I very much doubt that he has made any important progress in composition and in the development of his musical taste during his present stay, and I fear that, as in the case of his first journey to Vienna, he will bring back nothing but debts." That was that. A resounding slap in the face. It must have made Beethoven realize that not much more could be expected from his harassed Bonn patron. He had better seek success in Vienna.

Among Beethoven's early acquaintances in Vienna was the Abbé Joseph Gelinek. He was one of the most successful of the pianists in a city which had no dearth of pianists. Otto Jahn, Mozart's biographer, tells the story that Carl Czerny's father once met Gelinek hurrying to an appointment. "Where are you going?" he asked. "I have been requested to measure myself with a young pianist who has just arrived—and I will work him over properly." A few days later he met him again. "What happened?" "Ah, he is not a man, he is a devil! He will play me and all of us to death. And how he improvises!"

It was in Gelinek's home that Johann Schenk heard Beethoven play. Schenk was a composer, teacher, expert theorist, and author of a little opera, *The Village Barber,* which held its own on the German stage for many years. Beethoven confided to him that Haydn's instruction did not satisfy him, and Schenk offered further instruction with the understanding that he would give the lessons without payment and that their cooperation would have to be kept secret. He recommended that Beethoven copy every exercise twice; otherwise Haydn would recognize the handwriting of a stranger on the sheets submitted to him. Such is the story Schenk tells in his autobiography, which was written many years later, in 1830, by a man in his seventies and may contain some sentimental exaggerations. In the same manuscript * Schenk speaks of the impression which Beethoven's piano playing made on him:

> Thus I saw the composer, now so famous, for the first time and heard him play. After the customary courtesies he offered to improvise on the pianoforte. He

---

* Emily Anderson has ascertained that the manuscript is in the Benedictine Abbey in Gottweig.

asked me to sit beside him. Having struck a few chords and tossed off a few figures as if they were of no significance, the creative genius gradually unveiled his profound psychological pictures. My ear was continually charmed by the beauty of the many and varied motives which he wove with wonderful clarity and loveliness into each other, and I surrendered my heart to the impressions made upon it while he gave himself wholly up to his creative imagination, and anon, leaving the field of mere tonal charm, boldly stormed the most distant keys in order to give expression to violent passions.... (TQ).

Another of Beethoven's teachers was Johann Georg Albrechtsberger, the panjandrum of Vienna's church music, who had just been appointed Kapellmeister at St. Stephen's Church. Albrechtsberger took Beethoven through the paces from the simplest problems on, as if his pupil were an absolute beginner. It is charming to find that in one exercise, in which Beethoven wrote an unprepared seventh chord with a suspension, Beethoven wrote in the margin, "Is this permitted?"

Still another of Beethoven's teachers, though on a more informal basis, was Antonio Salieri, the Imperial Kapellmeister and director of the opera house. Salieri, born in Legnago, had come to Vienna when he was but sixteen and had gradually won great popularity with the Viennese operagoing public. He turned out a whole slew of comic operas, which were more to the taste of the Viennese than Mozart's problem pieces. Certainly Salieri was more to the Emperor's taste than Mozart. Some years before (1786), Salieri and Mozart had appeared together on a double bill in Schönbrunn, in which Mozart's contribution to a gala evening in honor of the governor-general of the Netherlands was *Der Schauspieldirektor* (The Impresario), and Salieri's was *Prima la musica, poi le parole* (First the Music, Then the Words), the libretto of which eventually formed the basis of Richard Strauss's *Capriccio*. Today, if Salieri is remembered at all, he is remembered because he was Mozart's competitor.

The rivalry between Mozart and Salieri gave rise to the rumor that Salieri had poisoned Mozart, and Rimsky-Korsakov fashioned a little opera on that theme. Not the slightest evidence exists that the accusation is true, though Salieri was supposed to have confessed the deed in delirium on his deathbed, in 1825. The story was told to Beethoven, who did not believe a word of it. No doubt Salieri was a diplomat and perhaps even a bit of an intrigant, who knew how to make the right moves with the people who counted. But a murderer? He treated Beethoven with great kindness and inducted him into the art of writing for the voice. As an Italian, Salieri knew that art. Then and later Beethoven showed him some of his Italian songs, which Salieri corrected for verbal accent.

Beethoven and Salieri kept up friendly relations for many years, and the composer dedicated three violin sonatas to him (Opus 12). The pianist Moscheles, who was in Vienna in 1809, called on Salieri and found a note on his table which read, "The pupil Beethoven was here!"

Haydn, Schenk, Albrechtsberger, Salieri—Beethoven absorbed all they had to give without becoming confused by the teaching. Even then, said those who knew him, he was "headstrong." His self-assurance buttressed his gifts and may well have impressed those who, through birth or wealth, were not easily impressed.

·◦≋[3]≋◦·

These extraordinary personalities, men and women with whom Beethoven early became acquainted, helped him, admired and encouraged him. They made it possible for the young virtuoso and composer to gain almost immediate fame, a fame so quickly won that the case is exceptional in musical history. The talent was there, but so were men to recognize it. Beethoven, though he acknowledged the fact but intermittently, was beholden to the intelligence and sensitivity of a number of aristocrats living in Vienna, some recently settled there, some to the manner born. In the days when Europe was rocked by the shock waves of the French Revolution, Vienna was a comparatively safe abode for a rich man. It was, as well, the right spot to be in if one needed favors or appointments from the Emperor. Besides, no city offered possibilities for a more pleasant existence—again, if one had money. As Vienna itself was a melting pot, so were the nobles living there scions of families of diverse origin, from Italy, France, Russia, Bohemia, Moravia, Hungary, Silesia, the Netherlands, Poland, and so on. The names suggest a cosmopolitan congregation: Lichnowsky, Rasoumovsky, Zmeskall, Esterházy, van Swieten, Guicciardi, Schwarzenberg, Auersperg, Trautmannsdorf. Most of these were lovers of music. It was fashionable to know performers and composers personally, treating them with tolerant kindliness mixed—at least before Beethoven—with a bit of condescension, and shrugging over their idiosyncrasies. We are speaking of the successful composers and performers, or such as promised to be successful. Several of the noble families regularly employed a group of musicians, ranging from a quartet to a chamber orchestra.

Music, then, was part of the life of the nobleman who, after paying his respects to the Emperor, conferring with the manager of his estates, exercising himself and his favorite horse and haggling over the price of a clock brought from Paris, still saw the day stretch out before him. Music represented diversion for him and his guests. There was a need for diversion: one could not hunt all the time and one could not attend a ball every night. To a few of the counts and princes, however, music meant more than a diversion; to them it was one of the rewards of life.

The Emperor himself was musical, and though much occupied and much besieged, spent a good portion of his time with music. He preferred easy, non-problematic music. Solving problems was not his *forte*. Franz was an indolent man—"When I see you enter my study," he once said to Count Kobenzl, "I shudder at the thought of all the business you bring with you"— who wanted to be left alone to putter in his workshop. He liked to design seals and press them on sealing wax, and he loved to cook candy on the stove. But the world would not let him alone. Still, he never abandoned listening and playing. At court, orchestral concerts were given: Franz played in the violin section. When Franz was at his summer place at Laxenburg, Salieri sometimes conducted. When Franz traveled, he took with him his own string quartet, journeying as far as Paris in 1815, and of course he took the part of the *first* violin. Even the disastrous defeats which Franz suffered before Napoleon was finally caged—the Viennese used to whisper Caesar's statement paraphrased for Franz: *"Venit, videt, perdit"* ("He comes, he sees, he loses")—did not dampen his musical enthusiasm.

Beethoven was astute enough to take advantage of musical opportunities. Very soon after his arrival he moved to the ground floor of a house on a good street, the Alserstrasse. Prince Karl Lichnowsky lived there.* Living in a princely abode did not mean that Beethoven had suddenly become affluent. Some of the palaces belonging to the nobility took in tenants, as only the main floor, one flight up, the *piano nobile,* was occupied by the owner, while other floors were rented more or less expensively. It was possible for an indigent artisan to rent for very little a stuffy room under the roof. Nor was the street floor the most desirable location. The result of Beethoven's move was that very soon Prince Lichnowsky took such a liking to him that he moved him from the street floor and invited him to live in his own lodgings. Beethoven stayed in Lichnowsky's house until May, 1795, a period of over two years.

---

* The house is no longer in existence; the site is now No. 30 Alserstrasse (District IX).

A remarkable man, Lichnowsky! He looks in his portraits like the picture-book idea of the aristocrat: long face, Roman nose, the thinning hair carefully combed to frame a high forehead, the jowls turning to fat, the eyes looking with some arrogance upon the world but showing as well intense intelligence. He was highly educated, highly knowledgeable in several fields,* his real passion being music, of which he possessed a deep understanding. He was immensely rich, deriving his fortune from large estates in Silesia. On one of his journeys to his estates, he had taken Mozart along, whose pupil and friend he was, traveling as far as Leipzig, Dresden, and Berlin, where he had business with the Prussian King, Frederick William II. He wanted the king to know Mozart, but nothing much came of it. (From that journey Mozart wrote his wife one of the most frankly erotic love letters ever penned.)

The prince was a more than competent pianist. He was able to study Beethoven's new piano sonatas and play them so that Beethoven could become convinced that they were practical for execution. Many of Beethoven's compositions were tried out in the prince's home. Lichnowsky had a younger brother, Count Moritz, who was even more talented than Karl and became very much attached to Beethoven, remaining loyal to him through thick and thin.

It was an exceptional family altogether. Prince Karl was married to Countess Christiane Thun. She, too, was an accomplished musician. She was one of three beautiful girls who were known in Vienna as "The Three Graces." Her father, Count Joseph Thun, was a great philanthropist. He was, however, highly eccentric; he had come in contact with the famous physician Lavater, and afterward he believed that he could heal diseases through the power of his right hand. The mother of Christiane was the Countess Wilhelmine Thun. She too befriended Mozart so warmly the Mozart wrote to his father:** "I have lunched twice with Countess Thun and go there almost every day. She is the most charming and most lovable lady I have ever met; and I am very high in her favor." The countess was known far and wide for her gracious hospitality, and such men as the famous Dr. Charles Burney—who traveled throughout Europe and reported on musical conditions—praised her. Knowing that she was a desirable woman, she could get what she wanted with a flutter of her eyes. What she usually wanted was something good for her family—or for music. What a mother-in-law to have!

As to the beautiful Princess Christiane, wife of Karl Lichnowsky, we possess

---

* For example, he was a student of Voltaire and translated Voltaire's play *Zaïre* into German verse.
** Letter of March 24–28, 1781.

some astonishing testimony from a member of her circle, the Countess Lulu Thürheim.* She describes ** the extraordinary princess as a product of the Enlightenment, a woman who was able to understand abstruse questions easily and discuss philosophical subjects lucidly. She was a master of dialectics, schooled in the "sophism of imagination." She was paradoxical, "combining a good heart and Christian forbearance with violent prejudices" against persons she disliked, whose social position she did not scruple to annihilate.

By nature she was a frigid woman, writes Countess Thürheim, and she felt guilty because she was frigid. She did not love Karl, which did not stop her from pursuing him constantly. One day she maneuvered to have him bidden to a house of ill repute, where she met him, her own husband, in disguise.*** Later she took it into her head that a young child around the house was her husband's illegitimate daughter. Protest as he would that he had nothing to do with it (or, as Countess Thürheim writes, "very little," whatever that may mean), she insisted on adopting the child and giving her as good an education as that received by her own daughter. But her son she entrusted "to the hands of miserable people," justifying herself by saying that Karl had ordered it so and that she "did not have the right to oppose the wishes of her husband, whom she loved so little." Nevertheless, she was never untrue to her husband. He would willingly have forgiven her that, writes the countess, because he himself was a "cynical lecher." Was this so? Was there a Stygian side to Lichnowsky, who appears in Beethoven's life as a bright and generous patron? Did Karl Lichnowsky seek in music a consolation for a happiness which was not vouchsafed to him through his wife and children?

Beethoven must early have got a glimpse of the other side of the curtain. The enlightened patrons of music and the patrons of bordellos were occasionally the same men. Along with philosophical maturity and intellectual pursuit went Casanova-like expeditions to various beds. The amorous round-dance was on, and nobody minded so long as the noise wasn't obtrusive. Perhaps Beethoven's moral stiffness in later years was rooted in early observation of the opposite.

At the Lichnowskys' there was chamber music every Friday morning. In other houses, chamber music sessions were sometimes held at strange hours.

---

* Her sister became the second wife of Prince Rasoumovsky, whose first wife was Christiane's sister. Perhaps we should discount her description of Christiane on the grounds of jealousy toward a predecessor's relative. On the other hand, it is not likely that Lulu would have dared to print revelations which could have been exposed as lies.
** In her book, *My Life, Memoirs From Austria's Great World, 1788–1819.*
*** It sounds like the plot of *Die Fledermaus.*

Jean Jacques Rousseau. He "threw enchantment over passion," wrote Byron. "He only felt," said David Hume. What he felt and preached inspired such men as Goethe, Constable, Wordsworth, Beethoven (Metropolitan Museum, gift of Edith Root Grant, E. W. Root, and Elihu Root, Jr., 1937).

Maximilian Friedrich, for twenty-three years Elector and Archbishop of Cologne. He was a merry man, fond of the theater and of music. He employed Beethoven's father; it was during his reign that Beethoven was born (Bonn City Archives).

View of Electoral Palace at Bonn, from a contemporary drawing. Beyond were the fields, gardens, and woods where the child Beethoven could roam. Parts of the building still stand and now house Bonn University (Beethoven House, Bonn).

Left: Christian Gottlob Neefe, composer, organist, all-around musician, as well as author. He was a man of enlightened views. Neefe was Beethoven's first important teacher, and in after years Beethoven bore him grateful remembrance (Beethoven House, Bonn). Right: Beethoven at the age of sixteen. A typical silhouette of the period, no doubt somewhat flattering. This is the earliest known picture of Beethoven (Beethoven House, Bonn). Below: An eighteenth-century concert in an aristocratic palace. The drawing gives an idea of what these informal music-making occasions must have been like (Civica Raccolta, Milan).

Right: Count Ferdinand Ernst von Waldstein, scion of one of the highest aristocratic Austrian families. One of Beethoven's earliest patrons. This portrait (unsigned) was found in the castle of Dux (Duchov), Czechoslovakia. Far right: The Breuning family residence, Münsterplatz, Bonn. Here the boy Beethoven was treated like a son and formed friendships, some of which lasted all of his life (Bonn City Archives). Below: the Breuning family, silhouette by an unknown artist. Left to right: Hélène Breuning, 32 years old; Eleonore, 11; Christoph, 9; Lorenz, 5; Hélène's brother-in-law, 44; Stephan, 8 (Beethoven House, Bonn).

Joseph Haydn, painted by John Hoppner in 1791, the year before Beethoven sought him out in Vienna (By permission: British Royal Family and A. C. Cooper, Ltd., copyright reserved).

We read with astonishment of one series from six to eight in the morning! Lichnowsky's group of four included the violinist Ignaz Schuppanzigh, who became one of Beethoven's intimate friends, and a genial amateur cellist, Nikolaus von Zmeskall, of whom more in a moment. After the concerts, the musicians generally stayed to eat and to mingle with the guests and other artists.

Wegeler came to Vienna about a year after Beethoven's arrival and stayed for two years. He too became a part of the Lichnowsky circle and reported that even in the early days Beethoven's behavior revealed so antic a disposition that Lichnowsky had to summon all his diplomatic tact to shield him. Why did these men, accustomed to bows and scrapes, to being flattered and catered to, tolerate Beethoven's undandified manners, his bellicose moods, which though comparatively restrained in the first years were yet frequent enough to tempt an ordinary man to send the fellow packing? It seems almost as if they could foretell the future. Who would take an equivocal stranger into his home, no matter how recommended, if he did not see or feel behind the exterior the greatness of the guest? There are two answers: their passion for music was an honest passion. They might sometimes have failed to pay the piper, but they loved the piping. And Beethoven fascinated them, not only as an artist but as a personality. "I remember very well," wrote one of Vienna's pianists, "how Haydn as well as Salieri sat in the small music-room [of the Lichnowskys] on a side-sofa, both of them most carefully dressed in the older fashion, with a chignon, shoes and silk stockings, while Beethoven used to appear in the Rhenish fashion, freer, not to say carelessly dressed." * Beethoven was a new apparition, strong, earnest, free, exuding talent from eyes and fingertips. There was no escaping this fiery youth, even before he sat down at the piano.

He did not willingly do so. Wegeler relates ** that a trick was occasionally played on the recalcitrant musician. Engaged in conversation, the others occupied all the chairs in the room, so that Beethoven, if he wished to continue the discourse, had to sit on the chair before the piano. "Soon, still turned away from the instrument, he aimlessly struck a few chords out of which gradually grew the most beautiful melodies. Oh, why did I not understand more of music! Several times I put ruled paper upon the desk as if without intention, in order to get a manuscript of his; he wrote upon it but then folded it up and put it in his pocket! Concerning his playing I was permitted to say but little, and that only

---

* Quoted by Karl Kobald in *Beethoven,* 1964.
** Wegeler and Ries, *op. cit.*

in passing. He would then go away entirely changed in mood and always come back again gladly. The antipathy [toward performing] remained, however, and was frequently the cause of differences between Beethoven and his friends."

Wegeler, too, is the author of the famous anecdote that the prince gave orders that his serving man was to respond to Beethoven's ring first, should it happen that both the prince and Beethoven rang for him at the same time. Beethoven overheard what the prince said and the same day went out and engaged a servant for himself. Similarly, at one time Beethoven conceived a whim to ride horseback, whereupon the prince offered him the choice of his stable. Beethoven bought himself his own horse—and then promptly forgot that he owned one and never rode again. The prince's dinner hour was fixed for four o'clock; he expected everybody to appear punctually. That kind of regimentation did not suit Beethoven. "Must I then be home at half-past three, put on my good clothes and shave?" So he frequently went to a tavern and paid for his own meals.

When Beethoven's salary from the Elector stopped, it was Lichnowsky who set aside a not inconsiderable fixed yearly sum of 600 thalers ($5100 to $7200) for Beethoven's use as long as he remained without a suitable post. The prince also paid the cost of publishing Beethoven's Opus 1 (Three Trios). When Beethoven took up his own lodgings, the prince continued to act with rare tact. Let Schindler tell the story:

> The prince was in the habit of frequently visiting his favorite in his workshop. In accordance with a mutual understanding, no notice was to be taken of his presence, so that the master might not be disturbed. After the morning greeting the prince was in the habit of looking through any piece of music that chanced to be at hand, watching the master at his work for a while and then leaving the room with a friendly "adieu." Nevertheless, these visits disturbed Beethoven, who occasionally locked the door. Unvexed, the prince would walk down the three flights of stairs. As the sartorial servant * sat in the anteroom, His Serene Highness would join him and wait until the door opened and he could speak a friendly greeting to the Prince of Music. (S).

Nikolaus Zmeskall von Domanovecz was a Hungarian, eleven years older than Beethoven. He outlived Beethoven by six years. He spent nearly all his life in Vienna, being secretary of the Hungarian Chancellery. He was a man of property who owned vineyards in Hungary. He never married, and once the

---

* He was a tailor in addition to being Beethoven's servant.

friendship was formed, he devoted himself with fanatic zeal to Beethoven. He introduced him to the right circles, boasted of his friendship, ran Beethoven's errands, was ever ready to join Beethoven in a walk or to meet him at The White Swan, a restaurant the composer liked, and was an unfailing auditor at the premieres of Beethoven's works, even though in later years he suffered so grievously from gout that he could hardly walk. He, too, arranged chamber concerts in his home—"Private-Morning-Concerts" he called them—to allow Beethoven to present his newest compositions.

Right from the start he saved every letter, every scrap of paper, every communication, every discarded sheet of notepaper that he could lay his hands on.* There was something of the hangdog about this grave man, a Saint Bernard who obeyed his master at once. Beethoven treated him with more than a little condescension, though he was truly fond of him. On him he vented some of the complicated sobriquets with which he loved to come forth. He called him "Beloved Conte di Musica," "Baron Muckdriver," "Commander of Rotten For-tresses," "Not Music Count—but Gulp-Count" (*Fressgraf*), and "Burgundian," because Zmeskall loved to eat and drink.

Zmeskall wore glasses; so did Beethoven for a time. Beethoven teased Zmes-kall about the "*faiblesse de vos yeux*" and wrote a duet for viola and cello called "Duet with Obbligato for Two Spectacles."** Since Beethoven himself was too clumsy to sharpen the goose quills with which he wrote, he asked Zmeskall to do this for him:

> Best of Music Counts! I beg of you to send me one or a few pens of which I am really in great need. As soon as I learn where really good and admirable pens are to be found I will buy some of them. I hope to see you at the *Swan* today.
> Adieu, most precious Music Count

> His Highness von Z. is commanded to hasten a bit with the plucking of a few of his quills (among them, no doubt, some not his own). It is hoped that they may not be too tightly grown in. As soon as you have done all that we shall ask, we shall be, with excellent esteem your
>
> F_____
> BEETHOVEN (TQ).***

---

* These papers are now in the National Library in Vienna.
** The manuscript is in the British Museum. Zmeskall, who was a cellist, probably performed the work with Beethoven playing the viola.
*** I prefer Thayer's translation of these notes to Anderson's.

He made him bestir himself to look for a servant, then and in later years:

Most noble Sir and, mark you, Holder of the Grand Cross of Violoncellity!
If your servant is a good fellow and knows of a good one for me, then you
would do me a great kindness if you would tell your good fellow to find a good
fellow for me also—But in any case I should like to have one who is married;
for greater orderliness, though perhaps not greater honesty, can be expected
from a married servant—My present beast of a servant is leaving at the end of
this month. (A-430).

The patron who earned the most secure immortality was Count (later
Prince) Andrei Kirillowitsch Rasoumovsky. The Rasoumovskys owed their
eminence to a special talent. Two brothers by the name of Razum, exceptionally handsome and strong men, born in a little village in the Ukraine, became
the lovers of two Imperial Russian princesses, who later became the Empresses
Elizabeth Petrovna and Catherine II. The brothers satisfied the two ladies so
well that they were elevated to the aristocracy, and the Empresses provided
them with wives from noble families. This made the affair legitimate all
around. The children of these marriages proved to be able men; Count Alexander, the fourth son of the younger Razum, had entered the diplomatic service,
had represented Russia in several cities, from Venice to Stockholm, had become
very wealthy indeed, and had inherited from his father his skill with women.
His liaisons with ladies of high aristocracy were well known and envied. The
Queen of Naples, a lustful creature, had been his mistress. Now he had become
Russian ambassador to Austria and had married Elizabeth, Countess Thun, the
elder sister of Karl Lichnowsky's wife. His new palace in the Landstrasse was to
become one of the showplaces of Vienna.* Surrounded by a huge garden, the
house itself was a rich museum; among the rooms bursting with art collections,
the most sensational was the Canova Hall, filled with statues by the sculptor
Antonio Canova, who was just then becoming the rage of Vienna.** The
palace also contained a magnificent library.

Looking at his portrait, with the virile face, a smile on his lips which suggests
more self-satisfaction than mirth, his expressive hands, his romantic uniform
with a furred cloak draped over straight shoulders, one can understand the

---

* It was built between 1803 and 1807.
** Later in a garden near the *Hofburg* an imitation Greek temple was constructed to house Canova's
powerful *Theseus* group. It now looks down on the visitor from the top of the stairs of the
Kunsthistorische Museum.

fascination which must have emanated from him. Like his brothers-in-law the Lichnowskys, he was an expert musician, a violinist who took part in the playing of Haydn's quartets, the proper rendition of which he was supposed to have learned from Haydn himself. Later he engaged a permanent professional quartet with, Schindler says, "a lifetime contract, the first and only example of its kind in Austria," the leader of which was Schuppanzigh and which, as the Rasoumovsky Quartet, gained European fame. Seyfried * wrote:

> The musicians of this quartet were put entirely at Beethoven's disposal. He was as much at home in Rasoumovsky's palace as a hen in her coop. Everything he wrote was taken warm from the nest and tried out in the frying pan. Every note was played precisely as he wanted it played, with such devotion, such love, such obedience, such piety as could be inspired only by a passionate admiration of his great genius. And it was precisely the delving into the most secret depths of the music, the total comprehension of the spirit of the work, that enabled this quartet to gain, through the playing of Beethoven's music, its universal fame.

The stamp of approval was placed on Beethoven by another high authority, if not the highest: this was the formidable Gottfried Freiherr van Swieten. He was the son of Maria Theresa's stern and stiff physician, and he himself was stern and stiff, impressive in learning, imposing in demeanor, looking with disdain upon all who did not quite share his wide knowledge of art. His taste was only for the most exalted. He had no patience with lesser stuff. He was one of the few who valued Handel and Bach. In his youth he had been active at the court of Frederick the Great, had known Karl Philipp Emanuel Bach, and under his direction had composed several symphonies—of which Haydn did not think much, though the composer and the amateur were good friends. It was van Swieten who adapted from an English text the words for Haydn's *Creation*. Then he undertook so successful a propaganda for the work that when the first performance was announced the people stormed the theater, trampling over the fruits and vegetables displayed in the New Market. The vendors threatened reprisals; van Swieten paid for the damage. When Beethoven met him, van Swieten was about sixty years old and was looked upon as patriarch of music in Vienna. The Year Book which recorded musical events in Vienna and Prague

---

* Ignaz von Seyfried was Schikaneder's Kapellmeister for thirty-one years and became an admirer of Beethoven. The quotation is from an article on Schuppanzigh which he wrote for the *Universal Lexicon of Music*. (Of Rasoumovsky's tragic fate in later years we shall have to speak in its chronological place. See page 481.)

in 1796 speaks of him as the arbiter of fashion. When he attended a concert, all the "semi-connoisseurs" never took their eyes off him, trying to read in his expression his opinion of the music played. If at a concert somebody dared to whisper, His Excellency, who usually sat in the first row of seats, would rise solemnly to his great height, turn his face toward the culprit, fix a long and stern gaze upon him, and then slowly resume his chair. It was always effective.

Van Swieten was an organizer. He was director of the Imperial Library, the treasures of which he augmented by keen purchases. He organized an association of his music-loving friends, among them Liechtenstein, Esterházy, Schwarzenberg, Auersperg, Kinsky. He was permanent secretary of this association and arranged concerts at the members' palaces as well as in his own house and occasionally in the great hall of the Imperial Royal Library. Performances were given at midday to an audience of invited guests. Van Swieten was insatiable in his appetite for music.

After a musical performance in his house he made Beethoven stay, long after the other guests had departed, to play fugues by Bach, taxing though the preceeding program had been. Schindler kept a note which van Swieten addressed to Beethoven, inviting him to his home "at half-past eight, with your nightcap in your bag. Give me an immediate answer." No doubt Beethoven came—and stayed deep into the night.

Prince Franz Joseph Lobkowitz, "Knight of the Golden Fleece," was a young man of twenty when Beethoven came to Vienna. Countess Thürheim described him as "good-hearted as a child and the greatest fool for music one can imagine. In his castle in Eisenberg one artist held the door open for the other and they ate without stopping." One of his legs was shorter than the other, but that did not prevent him from being busy all the time. He too was an amateur musician of considerable accomplishment. His palace in Vienna was called by Kapellmeister Reichardt "the true residence and academy of music." This residence was always open; often several rehearsals of music were going on at the same time in several rooms. Lobkowitz could not do enough for the arts; his passion for music and theater swept away his prudence. Large as his fortune was, with the devaluation of money caused by Austrian defeats and his attempts to support theatrical ventures, Lobkowitz reduced himself to bankruptcy in twenty years, though subsequently he did recover some of his fortune. He and Lichnowsky and later the Archduke Rudolph formed the triumvirate who surrounded Beethoven with admiration and support. Beethoven felt closest to

Lichnowsky and Lobkowitz. With Lobkowitz, too, he quarreled; against him, too, he raged.

Prince Lichnowsky introduced Beethoven to Count Johann Georg von Browne-Camus. Little is known of him, except that he seems to have been of a frivolous and unstable temperament, a strange man, described by his tutor, Johannes Büel, who later became acquainted with Beethoven, as "full of excellent talents and beautiful qualities of heart and spirit on the one hand, and on the other full of weakness and depravity." (TQ).

The fact that Beethoven dedicated several compositions (among them Op. 9, 22, 48) to Browne indicates that he received tangible support from him. The dedication of Op. 9 (Three String Trios) reads: "L'auteur auroit la satisfaction tant désirée de présenter au premier Mécene de sa muse la meilleure de ces oeuvres." * "The first Maecenas of his Muse," Count Browne, gave Beethoven a horse as a gift. Ferdinand Ries, whom Beethoven recommended as piano teacher to the count's family, remembered:

> He rode the animal a few times, soon after forgot all about it and, worse than that, its food also. His servant, who soon noticed this, began to hire out the horse for his own benefit and, in order not to attract the attention of Beethoven to the fact, for a long time withheld from him all bills for fodder. At length, however, to Beethoven's great amazement, he handed in a very large one, which recalled to him at once his horse and his neglectfulness. (TQ).

One of the most attractive members of Viennese nobility was Count Moritz von Fries. He was, perhaps more than any of the others, a true disciple of the Enlightenment. He traveled far and wide—Goethe mentions him in his account of the Italian journey—lived for a time in Paris and had himself painted by Vigée-Lebrun and then, with his wife and baby, by Gérard. The Gérard portrait shows an almost improbably handsome couple, both dressed in the *Empire* style, the countess, who was one of Vienna's most gloriously beautiful women, in deep décolletage. Goethe praised the painting.

Fries's palace on the Josefsplatz was built by the same architect who had designed the *Gloriette* in Schönbrunn; it contained a private theater, on the curtain of which were inscribed the words, GAYETÉ ET INDULGENCE, a typical slogan of the Enlightenment.

---

* "It would give the author much satisfaction to present to the first Maecenas of his Muse the best of his works."

In this palace Beethoven fought a "duel." The anecdote is given here, though the incident belongs to a later period (April or May, 1800), because it further illustrates the kind of musical entertainment offered in the palaces—and Beethoven's behavior. It concerns a famous pianist, Daniel Steibelt, who had come from Paris. Ferdinand Ries is the narrator:

> When Steibelt came to Vienna with his great name, some of Beethoven's friends grew alarmed lest he do injury to the latter's reputation. Steibelt did not visit him; they met for the first time one evening at the house of Count Fries, where Beethoven produced his new Trio in B-flat major for Pianoforte, Clarinet, and Violoncello (Op. 11) for the first time.* There is no opportunity for particular display on the part of the pianist in this Trio. Steibelt listened to it with a sort of condescension, uttered a few compliments to Beethoven, and felt sure of his victory. He played a quintet of his own composition, improvised, and made a good deal of effect with his tremolos, which were then something entirely new. Beethoven could not be induced to play again. Eight days later there was again a concert at Count Fries's; Steibelt again played a quintet which had a good deal of success. He also played an improvisation (which had, obviously, been carefully prepared) and chose the same theme on which Beethoven had written variations in his Trio. This incensed the admirers of Beethoven and him; he had to go to the pianoforte and improvise. He went in his usual (I might say, ill-bred) manner to the instrument as if half-pushed, picked up the violoncello part of Steibelt's quintet in passing, placed it (intentionally?) upon the stand upside down and with one finger drummed a theme out of the first few measures. Insulted and angered he improvised in such a manner that Steibelt left the room before he finished, would never again meet him and, indeed, made it a condition that Beethoven should not be invited before accepting an offer. (TQ).

To Fries, too, Beethoven dedicated a number of compositions. The fact that the Seventh Symphony is one of these proves that the relationship lasted many years.

This by no means exhausts the catalogue of patrons in high places. Yet these were the most immediate in furthering the composer's career. Schindler hinted that Beethoven was so quickly received into the palaces because their owners believed him to be of noble birth, the "van" facilitating his entry. Without discounting prevalent class distinction, without minimizing the distance which

---

* A mistake. The Trio had been performed two years before.

separated commoner from nobleman, being aware even that lawsuits by one were tried in different courts from the other, one must doubt the statement. The owners of the palaces were not fooled that easily. Any man-of-the-world or even a major-domo could hardly have mistaken the origins of the Rhenish visitor, however proudly he bore himself.

Lest we convey too favorable a picture of the musical knowledge and expertness of Vienna's elite, we ought to append an incident related by that indispensable chronicler, Ries:

> Count Browne made a rather long sojourn about this time (about 1802) in Baden near Vienna, where I was called upon frequently to play Beethoven's music in the evening in the presence of enthusiastic Beethovenians, sometimes from notes, sometimes by heart. Here I had an opportunity to learn how in the majority of cases a *name* alone is sufficient to characterize everything in a composition as beautiful and excellent, or mediocre and bad. One day, weary of playing without notes, I improvised a march without a thought as to its merit or any ulterior purpose. An old countess who actually tormented Beethoven with her devotion went into ecstasies over it, thinking it was a new composition of his, which I, in order to make sport of her and the other enthusiasts, affirmed only too quickly. Unhappily Beethoven came to Baden the next day. He had scarcely entered Count Browne's room in the evening when the old countess began to speak of his most admirable and glorious march. Imagine my embarrassment! Knowing well that Beethoven could not tolerate the old countess, I hurriedly drew him aside and whispered to him that I had merely meant to make sport of her foolishness. To my good fortune he accepted the explanation in good part, but my embarrassment grew when I was called upon to repeat the march, which turned out worse since Beethoven stood at my side. He was overwhelmed with praise on all sides and his genius lauded, he listening in a perturbed manner and with growing rage until he found relief in a roar of laughter. Later he remarked to me: "You see, my dear Ries, these are the great cognoscenti, who wish to judge every composition so correctly and severely. Only give them the name of their favorite; they will need nothing more." (TQ).

·≈[4]≈·

If, then, substantial aid to music and musicians was available, if the men in high places were ready to act as Maecenases, did a composer, did Beethoven, have an easy time in making his way? If it was all that easy, how did it happen that Mozart died penniless and that in the last year or so of his life he needed desperately and repeatedly to borrow money from a well-to-do but certainly not aristocratic friend, Michael Puchberg? How did a composer make a living? How were musicians compensated?

First, if he was a virtuoso of reputation, an artist trailing clouds of glory, he played at the houses of noblemen. He "entertained." Beethoven's early reputation and income were derived from his virtuosity as a pianist. As such he was in demand before he could be estimated as a composer. Remuneration for his appearances was left entirely to the discretion of the host. The money was discreetly handed over, as a gift, often by one of the staff. A nobleman did not usually soil his hands by handling cash, though Mozart relates how Prince Lichnowsky, on the voyage previously mentioned, stepped outside the inn where they stayed to negotiate personally for the price of horses for the next lap and later, running out of cash, borrowed from him. The fee was presented in a sealed envelope or in a decorative little box. The pretense of not paying a stipulated fee was punctiliously observed; * the artist did not open the envelope till he got home. (Well, perhaps he peeked, in the anteroom.)

Artists maneuvered to be invited to Court. A sovereign's approval, even if he were only the head of a small duchy, counted for much. Mozart was frequently so invited. This was the highest honor that could be paid, but the practical results were often disappointingly slim: a ring of doubtful value, a snuffbox, a decoration, a medallion, or merely a pat on the back from the royal hand. From Frederick William II Beethoven received a gold snuffbox filled with louis d'or. "Not an ordinary snuffbox," said Beethoven, "but such a one as might have been customarily given to an ambassador."

Second, composers who played an instrument—and virtually all of them did —undertook concert tours. These were not organized—whatever impresarios there were confined themselves to one city and operated mostly in the opera house—or rather they were organized by the artists themselves. Had they sufficient fame in Leipzig or Prague so that the announcement of their coming would attract an audience? This was their hope; in that hope they braved the discomfort and expense of travel.

The third earning possibility was the outright sale of a new work. Patrons were expected to buy these. "Outright" means that the patron had the exclusive use of it for a period of time, after which by agreement the work reverted to the composer to be sold again in whatever way he could.

---

* How long such pretentious customs drag through the years! When I was a boy in Vienna, one always handed the doctor his fee in a sealed envelope. The doctor rarely sent a bill.

New works could be sold also to music publishers. During Beethoven's early years, music-publishing houses began to spring up in greater number than in Mozart's day. Most of these publishing firms were run in connection with a retail store, where sheet music, scores, art prints, and books were for sale. Beethoven's music was bid for and published by a dozen different houses. Some of these publishers were personal friends of his, such as Simrock in Bonn. The sale of the compositions was usually limited to the territory in which the publisher operated. Thus it was possible for Beethoven to sell the same work to one publisher in Austria, to another in Prussia, to still another in France. The publisher engraved the piece of music more or less carefully—according to Beethoven not nearly carefully enough: he was forever complaining of typographical errors—printed it, and offered the sheet music for general sale.

It was also possible for the composer to purchase a quantity of the music at a wholesale price and to sell it himself at retail. A composer would solicit "subscriptions" in advance of the publication of the work. Beethoven counted a number of the nobility among his subscribers. A subscriber obligated himself to take a specified number of copies. To clarify how the subscription plan worked, we cite two advertisements which appeared in the *Wiener Zeitung* of 1795:

> May 16. *Advance Notice.* Three great Trios for the Piano Forte, Violin, and Bass, by Ludwig van Beethoven, which will appear within six weeks engraved by Artaria, can be reserved at the author's in exchange for a reservation certificate. The price of a complete copy is one ducat. The names of the subscribers will be published, and they enjoy the advantage of obtaining this work, which will be available to others only two months later and perhaps at a higher price. In Vienna subscribers may apply at the author's in the Ogylfischen House in the Kreuzgasse behind the Church of the Minorites, No. 35, first floor.

> August 29. *Notice.* Since all the subscribers to the Trios of Ludwig van Beethoven have received their copies, be it announced that exactly similar copies are to be had for one month at the author's and at the subscription price of one ducat. He resides in the Kreuzgasse, . . .

Fourth, a composer brought his works forward by playing or conducting them himself at public concerts. Occasionally he did this at "benefit concerts," the beneficiary being himself. He paid for the advertisements, hired the hall and the musicians. In Beethoven's lifetime public concerts gradually became a little more frequent, plain people more often purchased tickets, and once in a while the baron sat next to the businessman.

Fifth, if a composer was able to write operas, he could offer these to one of many opera houses. More often, he would be commissioned to write an opera by the director of the opera house. He was paid a one-time fee for it, a fee for the first performance. After that, the opera belonged to the theater, which did not have to pay any further remuneration. Thus Mozart got 450 florins (about $2,700) for *Don Giovanni* in Prague and, as an exceptional measure, 225 additional for the Vienna performance of the same opera, for which he composed some additional numbers.*

There were no effective copyright laws which protected the composer. Once the work was paid for, whether by prince or by publisher, that was the end of it. The composer himself, or friend or adviser, was therefore obliged to make the best possible arrangement for the initial fee. At the beginning, Beethoven handled these transactions himself; later his brothers Carl or Johann (Carl but briefly) sometimes acted as his agent, as did an intimate friend or two.

Sixth, a composer could be commissioned for a special work to serve a virtuoso. Beethoven rarely accepted such a commission, but did compose his Violin Concerto for Franz Clement, just as years later Berlioz wrote *Harold in Italy* for Paganini, who wanted a concerto for the viola.

Seventh, a composer could take pupils. Beethoven had a few. He must have been the most unsystematic of teachers, impatient and unpunctual. His most illustrious pupil was Archduke Rudolph, and we shall have occasion to observe the unsteady course of their relations. One of his pupils, the Countess Babette Keglevics, to whom he dedicated the Piano Sonata Opus 7, told her nephew that Beethoven, who lived across the street from her, once appeared in a "dressing robe, slippers and tasseled nightcap" to give her a lesson.

A charming anecdote belonging to Beethoven's early years in Vienna illustrates Beethoven's reluctance to teach and his ability to help himself. It is to be found in the diaries of one Carl Friedrich Kübeck.** He later became "Freiherr von Kübau":

My aunt, who lived in the Bürgerspital, frequently visited a family living on the floor above. The family's name is M....r. The father once enjoyed a great reputation as an actor but is now well advanced in years. It seemed to me as if he was still continuously

---

* Lorenzo Da Ponte, librettist of *Don Giovanni,* got about 200 florins in Prague and 100 in Vienna.
** Edited by his son Max in 1909.

"onstage." [The reference is to Johann Heinrich Müller, a famous actor employed at the Court Theater from 1763 on, and pensioned in 1801. He was, at the time of this incident, only fifty-eight years old.]

He has two sons, one of whom, as I was told, is a mediocre actor while the other is altogether stupid. He also has two daughters, one of whom is pretty and married; the other has a nose which is a little too large, but she is very lively.

Much music is played in that house ... They have a new instrument, a forte-piano made by Herr Walther ... My aunt let it be known that I knew how to play ... I played a few easy pieces at sight but quite indifferently, because the instrument was unfamiliar to me ... The next time I came, I found there the Hero of Music, Herr van Beethoven, a small man with a shock of unruly hair, not powdered, which seemed curious; a face which was disfigured by pockmarks, small twinkling eyes, his limbs constantly in motion. He sat down at the forte-piano and for half an hour he transported us into raptures. Nina M...r, the mischievous daughter of the artistic father, took it into her head to tease me and presented me to the great master as a "young artist recently arrived from the provinces."... Beethoven looked at me with sympathy, and his glance, which was usually so wild, quite obviously expressed that he understood my embarrassment. He scolded Nina for her joke and said, "Well, we will see whether this young man has any talent for music. But not today. Come tomorrow—I will chase everybody out of the room and we will try it all by ourselves."

I went. It was the 5th of April, 1796 ... He made me play for about an hour—all kinds of things. When I had finished he said to me, "My friend, you have no special talent for music. Do not waste much time on it. However, you have acquired a certain facility and you have obviously been taught in a strict school.... I can make use of you and help you at the same time. I am giving lessons to a young person several times a week. I cannot do it more frequently, yet it is insufficient to enable her to make progress. If you want to give her lessons every day and teach her those pieces the artistic execution of which I myself will teach you, I will recommend you to her."

I accepted the proposition with pleasure. On the 8th of April Beethoven bade me come to him and took me to the place to introduce me.... It was a family consisting of father, daughter and a governess. They are from Venice. The father has some kind of secret business with the government and that is why he is in Vienna. He is a widower and they address him as Marchese. His name is M...n [not identified]. His nose is a veritable promontory, besmudged with tobacco. He speaks no German and a kind of Latin I can hardly understand. His daughter is addressed as Contessina. Her real name is Julie but they call her Litta. She is thirteen years old, has black eyes, a pale complexion ... and never have I seen such a beautiful girl. She speaks very broken German. ... The governess is a Frenchwoman, Mamselle Marie Vedel, speaks French, Italian, English and fluent German.... The Marchese handed me over to the governess, who told me on behalf of Herr von Beethoven that I was to come daily from five to six P.M. and that I was to follow exactly all the instructions of Herr Van Beethoven and I was to receive twenty florins monthly. [$120 a month, for one lesson a day—exceptionally good pay.]

... I would have liked to kiss Beethoven's hands but he refused all thanks....

On the tenth of March (1797) the governess told me that the Marchese would not remain in Vienna ... because of the present political conditions. He was fleeing to Prague. He had instructed her to pay me my salary for the month of March ... Beethoven ... had already stopped coming in January. He was involved in other things and gave lessons only as a favor. ...

So much for the substitute teacher. Four years later he met Beethoven again:

Feb. 10, 1801. How very surprised was I when I met Beethoven this morning! ... He came running toward me with his big, decisive steps. He let me know how glad he was to see me again. We spoke of this and that ... then he alighted on his favorite topic, politics. It bored me very much. We parted. ...

Finally, some musicians found a source of income in official positions, few in number and hotly contested. These were either ecclesiastic, as official composer to a church, or secular, as director or Kapellmeister of an opera house, or with a Court institute. Mozart tried all his life to obtain an official position; the nearest he came to it was a pittance granted him by Joseph II, of which he said, "Too much for what I do, too little for what I could do." Beethoven never obtained an official position.

It is apparent that the income of a composer—at best not easily gained—not only depended on his skill as an artist but his skill as a self-promoting business-man. Mozart was maladroit as a businessman. He had many influential friends; he was respected and beloved. He did earn money even after he ceased being a well-recompensed child prodigy. But he spent money imprudently and was sometimes embroiled in unfortunate financial speculations. Nor was Constanze, his wife, a careful manager. Beethoven very soon acquired a sense of what he was worth. He insisted on the dignity of labor being paid for. He hardly ever courted easy popularity or "composed for money"—the exceptions will be noted —but he was able enough to extract reasonable compensation for his work. "There ought to be in the world a *market for art*," he wrote in 1801 to the Leipzig publisher Anton Hoffmeister, "where the artist would only have to bring his works and take as much money as he needed. But, as it is, an artist has to be to a certain extent a businessman as well, and how he can manage to be that—Good Heavens—again I call it a *tiresome business*. . . ." (A-44). Beethoven did manage it, to a certain extent.

There was, however, more to it than that. Not only was Beethoven made of sterner stuff, but new influences were at work which gave a new role to the artist in society.

Still, a Schubert could virtually starve, though his music was by no means unknown to his contemporaries. To be sure, he too had no business sense whatever, his modesty being so great that he preferred once to go to the performance of a new play by Grillparzer on an evening when one of his own works was being played for the first time, a rare enough event. Here too the absence of copyright protection allowed people to sing and perform *Der Erlkönig* and *Die Forelle* without Schubert's earning a kreuzer.

An understanding of Beethoven's position in Vienna necessitates acknowledgment of his earning power. For many years his earning power was considerable—speaking of course in contemporary terms and forgetting any judgment as to what his music was *really* worth! That he became poorer in his last years was a misfortune due partly to himself, partly to the death or impoverishment of the very men who had helped him, and partly to economic depressions.

It is important that we do not think of Beethoven in his twenties and thirties as starving in a garret. Such would be far from the truth and would make his "self-assured" behavior ridiculous rather than forthright. He soon earned enough to make it possible for his two brothers to leave war-torn Bonn and come to Vienna, Carl in 1794, Johann in 1795. Carl at first became a music teacher, and is supposed to have had some moderate success in obtaining pupils, his success being due no doubt to the name of Beethoven. Later he became a government official, holding various minor posts. Johann obtained a position in an apothecary's shop. Ludwig at first offered him financial assistance, but soon enough Johann, who had a very good head for business, was getting along fine. Carl was described by Czerny as small of stature, redheaded, and ugly. Johann was a tall thin man, dark-haired, near-sighted, not bad-looking, and a fop.

··<[5]>··

Beethoven made his first public appearance as a piano virtuoso and composer on March 29 and 30, 1795, at the two annual concerts in the Burgtheater which were given for the benefit of the widows and orphans of the Society of Musicians (*Tonkünstlergesellschaft*). It was "A Grand Musical Academy," employing, as the program stated in German and Italian, "more than one hundred and fifty participants." It opened with a symphony by Antonio Cardellieri, a young man who was a pupil of Salieri, and closed with an oratorio, *Gioas,*

Re di Giuda (Gioas, King of Judea), by the same composer. In between came "a new concerto for the piano-forte, played and invented by Maestro Herr Ludwig von Beethoven" [not van, but *von*]. The concerto is now known as the Second Piano Concerto. Though this, Beethoven's first contact with a general public, must have been an important occasion—or perhaps *because* it was such an occasion—Beethoven could not bring himself to finish composing the concerto on time. Wegeler reports:

> Not until the afternoon of the second day before the concert did he write the rondo, and then while suffering from a pretty severe colic which frequently afflicted him. I relieved him with simple remedies so far as I could. In the anteroom sat copyists to whom he handed sheet after sheet as soon as it was finished. ... At the first rehearsal, which took place the next day in Beethoven's room, the piano-forte was found to be half a tone lower than the wind-instruments. Without a moment's delay Beethoven had the wind-instruments and the others tune to B-flat instead of A and played his part in C-sharp.*

A few days later, on April 1, there appeared in the *Wiener Zeitung,* the leading newspaper, a brief report to the effect that "the famous Herr Ludwig von Beethoven reaped wholehearted approval of the public." Let us remember, however, that it was a charity concert and would hardly have been commented on with uncharitable words. No doubt Beethoven, perhaps still a little pale from his colic attack, did play superbly.

In the second concert, Beethoven "improvised on the pianoforte." The day after, on March 31, Constanze Mozart had arranged a performance of excerpts from her husband's opera *La Clemenza di Tito* in the Burgtheater. The advertisement announcing this performance states that "Herr Ludwig van Beethoven will play a concerto of Mozart's composition on the pianoforte." Thayer suggests that the concerto was Mozart's D Minor, which Beethoven loved especially and for which he wrote cadenzas.

The next news comes in connection with the annual ball given by The Society of Pictorial Artists. It was held in the Redoutensaal and was considered one of the most desirable and elegant of Vienna's social affairs. Leading composers were glad to contribute their talents; Haydn had composed a set of dances for these balls, as had Dittersdorf and others. Now Beethoven was

---

* Wegeler confused two compositions. The concerto which Beethoven played was not that in C, Opus 15, which is now known as Concerto No. 1, but was actually composed later. But the point of the anecdote remains valid.

invited to participate, a proof of his growing fame. He shared the distinction with the Imperial Royal Kapellmeister Süssmayr, the friend of Mozart who had completed the *Requiem* after Mozart's death. Beethoven's *Twelve German Dances and Twelve Minuets* must have added to the success of the night of November 22, 1795. A little gaiety was badly needed just then. Three days later the Austrian army in Piedmont was roundly trounced by General Schérer.

About three weeks later—December 18—at the very height of the pre-Christmas season, Beethoven made his second public appearance as a composer and virtuoso. The scene was again the Redoutensaal and the concert starred the indefatigable Haydn. Two singers sang something or other. Haydn conducted three "grand symphonies not yet heard here which the Kapellmeister composed during his last sojourn in London"; and Beethoven played a concerto "of his composing." Thus the advertisement which appeared in the *Wiener Zeitung*. The concerto was probably No. 2, heard in the spring. Musical events were so rarely considered newsworthy that even a concert in which Haydn and Beethoven played together was passed over in silence. The newspapers had more important matters to report: negotiations for an armistice with France were in progress.*

We know more about the fate of his Opus 1, the Three Piano Trios. Their introduction took place on a gala evening at Prince Lichnowsky's the preceding year, with many of Beethoven's fellow artists and Lichnowsky's friends invited. Haydn was the guest of honor, and everyone was eager for his opinion. He liked two of the three, but advised Beethoven not to publish the third, in C Minor. Quoting Ries:

> This astonished Beethoven, inasmuch as he considered the third the best of the Trios, as it is still the one which gives the greatest pleasure and makes the greatest effect. Consequently, Haydn's remark left a bad impression on Beethoven and led him to think that Haydn was envious, jealous, and ill-disposed toward him. I confess that when Beethoven told me of this I gave it little credence. I therefore took occasion to ask Haydn himself about it. His answer, however, confirmed Beethoven's statement; he said he had not believed that this Trio would be so quickly and easily understood and so favorably received by the public.**

* The truce was not to last long: General Bonaparte was only too anxious to make a name for himself.
** Wegeler and Ries, *op. cit.*

In a few months the Trios had become well known and admired by musicians. But Beethoven did not yet think them fit for publication. He revised them, working on them probably during 1794 and the early months of 1795, and at last approached Lichnowsky to inquire whether he would be willing to pay for some or all of the cost of having them engraved. Lichnowsky was willing. In the *Wiener Zeitung* of May 9, 13, and 16, 1794, an advertisement offering subscriptions to these three Trios appeared. Artaria and Company published the work and appended a printed list of subscribers. This gives 123 names, mostly of music lovers in high places, subscribing to 241 copies. Beethoven paid the publisher one gulden per copy, and the subscription price was one ducat. Since the difference between a gulden and a ducat is about $19 in today's money, Beethoven realized a decent profit, if indeed he sold all of the 241 copies.

The Trios must have been a success with the music-buying public. It appears so from the fact that the publishers were willing to promote Beethoven's next work, the three Piano Sonatas, Opus 2. The advertisement in the *Wiener Zeitung:*

> March 9, 1796. NEW MUSIC. Artaria and Company. Three Sonatas for the Fortepiano by Hrn. Ludwig van Beethoven, Opera 2. Since the previous work of this author, the three clavier trios, Opera 1, which is now in the hands of the public, has been received with so much approbation, it is probable that the same will be accorded to the present work, the more so because in addition to the intrinsic worth of the comprsition [*sic*] one can experience from it not only the force which Herr v. Beethoven possesses as a pianist but also the delicacy with which he knows how to treat the instrument. All possible care has been expended on the beauty and correctness of the edition. The price is 3 florins.

Beethoven, then, was busy composing, busier playing here and there, accepting a pupil, filled with hope, with the belief in Fortune's favor, with such confidence in himself that Haydn called him "the Great Mogul." In 1796 he undertook a concert tour of some five months' duration, which brought him to Prague, Dresden, Leipzig, and Berlin. He went to Prague in the company of Prince Lichnowsky, as Mozart had done before him. In Dresden he enchanted everybody, and the Elector of Saxony retained him for a full evening so that he might play for him alone. Then he presented him with a golden snuffbox. In Berlin he played several times at the Court of Frederick William II and was generously compensated.

The first of Beethoven's profound and glorious works still lay within the recess of his mind. In a sense, but only in a sense, the compositions of his first years in Vienna were still exercises. They were attempts to find, define, and shape the substance of what he wanted to express. If Michelangelo really did say that every block of marble contained a sculpture and that the artist merely needed to learn what to chip away, it can be said of Beethoven that all of him consisted of music and that he had to learn to chip away the inconsequential and the conventional, so that he might bring forth his "Pietà" and his "Moses."

That the music of Haydn and Mozart helped to form his own was natural to a composer who worked in the city where, and at the time when, these two names were revered. But Beethoven neither imitated them nor plundered them. Nor did he, in certain respects, surpass them—certainly not Mozart. We are not concerned here with "better-best" comparisons. Of course he did learn from Haydn and Mozart. Yet almost from the very start of his Vienna period—after the early Bonn compositions—Beethoven composed like Beethoven, and no amount of stylistic detective work will prove otherwise. The Beethoven of the *Pastoral* is a different Beethoven from the one who wrote the First Piano Sonata, as the Beethoven of the Quartet Op. 131 is a different Beethoven from the one who wrote the *Pastoral.* Yet they are all one genius, and even the first Beethoven, tentative though some of the new ideas may still be, decorously promenading in the garden of the Enlightenment, is true to himself. In turning a phrase here or there he may still be the debtor of his great godparents; this or that transition may still be presented with 18th-century courtliness, but the essence of his thought, the substance of his expression are his own. Even his early Piano Concerto No. 1 is a "rebellious" work. A rebel need not be rambunctious.

If this seems obvious, if this is saying that Queen Anne is dead, let us remember that it is frequently stated that the early works are "Haydnesque" or "Mozartian." For example, take those Piano Trios Opus 1: the first has "Mozartian themes and clarity," the second "owing more to Haydn, especially in the slow movement and the finale," and only the third—the one Haydn did not like—"unmistakably Beethoven." * As to the First Piano Sonata, the same author says: "Structurally there is little in the Sonata No. 1 in F minor that might not have been done by Haydn or Mozart" and then adds "but in feeling the

---

* Marion M. Scott, *Beethoven,* 1934.

difference is immense." I quite agree with Paul Henry Lang: "Equally untrue and unscientific is the attitude often encountered wherein the forms of these earlier works are held to be still the traditional ones used by Haydn and Mozart, only their content being different." * To put it in other words: superficially the music sounds like that of his predecessors. Once one listens more closely, one hears the new voice, though not as yet speaking with its own full eloquence.

In his first years in Vienna he composed a quantity of small works, and works for small ensembles—trios, quintets, sextets, serenades—suitable for being performed at the Lichnowskys' or the van Swietens'. He composed a number of songs, some good, some not so good, among them the beautiful "Adelaide" (1795 or '96). He composed the first two Piano Concertos, No. 2 in 1795 (as we have seen), which is a fairly conventional work; Beethoven himself, though he revised it later, said, "I do not give it out as one of my best." No. 1 followed two years after. Beethoven played both concertos at his own concerts when he journeyed again to Prague in 1798.

He was captivated by the challenge and possibilities of the Variation form. His interest was a reflection of his skill at improvisation. Variations were, so to speak, improvisations set down on paper. He often used popular melodies for his themes; his audiences would recognize them and could follow what he did with them. This made the compositions more marketable. He helped himself to tunes by Paisiello, Dittersdorf, Mozart, Grétry, Handel, Süssmayr, Winter, Salieri, and to a Russian dance tune by Wranitzky. These variations are playthings, and only much later was he to develop the form to grandeur.

Had one, in the last years of the 18th century, drawn an estimate of current music, one could have recognized that this young composer, a man in his twenties, was an important and highly original new talent. His knowledgeable friends recognized him as such. Not everybody did, of course. As late as 1809 one L. A. C. Bombet ** wrote: "Cimarosa, Haydn, and Mozart have but just quitted the scene of the world. Their immortal works are still performed, but soon they will be laid aside: other musicians will be in fashion, and we shall fall all together into the darkness of mediocrity." *** The translator (the book was

---

* From *Music in Western Civilization,* 1941. His chapter on Beethoven is very worth reading.
** "Bombet" was a pseudonym for Stendhal, who wrote on musical subjects, occasionally substituting invention for facts.
*** From his book, *The Lives of Haydn and Mozart With Observations on Metastasio and on the Present State of Music in France and Italy.*

written in French) appends to this an angry note: "We by no means coincide in this opinion with our author; on the contrary, we consider the modern music to be formed upon principles, which will ever preserve it from the oblivion which he apprehends. . . . Nor can we imagine the art is on the decline, while so great a genius as Beethoven lives. This author, though less perfect in other respects than Haydn, exceeds him in power of imagination; and, from recent specimens of his unbounded fancy, it is to be expected that he will extend the art in a way never contemplated even by Haydn or Mozart."

Yes, the expectation was aroused, though one could hardly foresee how richly it was to be fulfilled. When Beethoven was not quite twenty-eight, he finished three Piano Sonatas, Op. 10. For the third of these, No. 7 in D, he wrote a slow movement marked *Largo e mesto* (Slow and sad). What a revelation it is! How full of wonder! Here one enters another world, an undiscovered country. Here, indeed, is "unbounded fancy" bred in a new style. Beethoven muses, ponders, dreams, meditates—and what he meditates on must be "the troubled heart of man," as Vladimir Horowitz, who played the sonata beautifully, has said.* Beethoven takes his time: the movement is the slowest of all his slow movements, save the *Lento* of the last quartet. There seems to be no "form"; it just goes on and on—and we have the illusion that we have come to understand what there is in us that is more than mortal. The intensity of its feeling is almost too much to bear. Yet it is never despairing; one thinks of Hamlet, "The readiness is all."

No outer cause was responsible for this composition. As far as we know, and we know fairly well, nothing disastrous happened to Beethoven, no misfortune swooped down on him. On the contrary, in the years of 1796 to 1798 he was particularly successful and often cheerful. No sign of deafness had appeared before 1798. A better explanation lies in an inner cause: Beethoven had come under the influence of the Romantic concept. He responded to it, as his contemporary artists and those who were to come after him for almost a century, responded to it. Just a little prematurely by the calendar he stepped from the 18th to the 19th century. His thinking and feeling which had embraced the Enlightenment now embraced its opposite.

Isaiah Berlin has said that the assumption which the Romantics brought into the world was "that the answers to the great questions are not to be discovered so much as to be invented." Truth was not to be arrived at by "rational

---

* Interview with Samuel Chotzinoff about recording.

examination or some more mysterious procedure," not by "obtaining illumination from pre-existent models or truths," but by "the unique expression of an individual and therefore unique creative activity." *

Beethoven became—obviously without setting up any formal precepts or doctrines—the propulsive force of Romantic music. He invented answers.

---

* From the Preface to *The Mind of the European Romantics* by H. G. Schenk, 1966.

Extremes of Romanticism: the weird and sexual, exemplified by Fuseli's "The Night-mare," (Detroit Institute of Arts); and the innocent and sylvan, by Constable's "Salisbury Cathedral" (Metropolitan Museum, bequest of Mary Stillman Harkness).

CHAPTER 8

THE ROMANTIC CHANGE

·◦[I]◦·

Reason was not enough. The Enlightenment had lighted a strong candle, it had chased away ghosts, had made men debouch from a murky half-light into noonday brightness, had put the courage to doubt into many brains, had proved that man could be guided by logic, had taken the edge off some old fears, both the fear of a priest's harangue and the fear of a king's frown. Two major revolutions had changed some of the world. But it still was not enough.

The wide swing of the pendulum now forced a counter-swing. It was inevitable: reason could not satisfy all the demands of life. Shadow is as necessary as light, mystery as desired as clarity. Try as they would, the philosophers could not explain all of man by organized thought. Systems left out the unsystematic; neither unreasonable love nor unreasonable hate could be downed or docketed. Hearts still needed to be warmed by illogical fire. Men still longed for the miracle.

People were beginning to tire of the cold cynicism which was a by-product of the sway of Reason. One could have a good time with the cynic, but one could not become friends with him.* The age began to mock its own achievements. Here is a bit of dialogue from Beaumarchais' play, *The Barber of Seville:*

ROSINA: You are always insulting our poor century.
DR. BARTOLO: I beg your pardon! But what has it produced that it should be praised? Stupidities of all sorts: Liberty of Thought, Sexual Attraction, Electricity, Magnetism, Tolerance, Vaccination, Quinine....

---

* Mozart and Da Ponte gave us a portrait of the 18th-century cynic in the person of Don Alfonso in *Così fan tutte.*

The time was ripe for romantic thinkers and romantic artists. These appeared in profusion at the beginning of the 19th century. But the man who set the Romantic movement in motion came earlier, fighting Voltaire in his own time and on his own ground. That man was Jean-Jacques Rousseau (1712–1778). Fortunately for civilization's development, his mind was as philosophically stimulating as Voltaire's was.

The art of the Enlightenment—and at no time, even at the time of the greatest passion for Reason, were people willing to dispense with art—was a bright, accessible art. It is exemplified in painting by the razor-sharp lines of Ingres, in drama by Beaumarchais' *Marriage of Figaro,* in poetry by Pope, the "prince of rhyme," whose *The Rape of the Lock* is an elegant, ornamented, exquisitely polished piece of work. Music, too, was elegant, ornamented, exquisitely polished, seeking the perfect balance between form and content, often with more attention to the former than the latter. More important than emotion was "beauty," though nobody could define what beauty was. Music favored the *galant,* melodies singing and dancing, harmonies piquant, tempo prevailingly winged.

The most successful composers created music which lightly touched the sensibilities. In Vienna one talked of *Empfindsamkeit* (sensitivity), in Paris, of *sensibilité,* in Naples of *dolcezza.*

Above the hundreds of composers producing merely pleasant or "precious" work stood the very few whose genius was great enough to create music of deep emotion while keeping within a formal framework. We call their work the "Classic" school. The label means little, for who could tag Gluck, Haydn, or Mozart? Mozart's *Figaro* is both Classic *and* Romantic, and incomparable on both counts. In *Don Giovanni,* one of the greatest and most mysterious creations art has produced, the romantic content—a content dark and profound— pervades the entire work and is sometimes at odds with its enlightened Classicism. No wonder that the Viennese at first considered it almost incomprehensible, confused, and ugly in its dissonances. *Don Giovanni* was difficult for an audience brought up on rococo music to appreciate—though it did have a great success in Prague—because it contained thoughts too shadowy for the day. *The Magic Flute* was easier because Schikaneder's libretto was funny—then!—and its lofty morality straightforward.

These works, as well as Mozart's last symphonies, his later chamber music, and Haydn's final symphonies and chamber music are brushed by a new spirit. But it remained for Beethoven to think about music in a markedly new way and to create the great change. In this he was aided by the great change in all art, involving a new attitude of the artist toward himself and his mission.

When Beethoven came on the scene, he had absorbed in himself all that the Enlightenment could teach him. Like the young Goethe, Beethoven, wearing his morning face, was a pupil of 18th-century thought. In his "student" efforts and very early works, content, however new, was still contained in the Classic mold, without his kicking over the traces. Soon, however, he came under the influence of the new movement which, though world-wide, found its strongest and most important expression in the German lands.

As I have mentioned, the progenitor of the Romantic concept, the one man most responsible for raising the lock on the dam and releasing the stream which was at first to mix with and then to swamp the Enlightenment, was Voltaire's great enemy, Rousseau. It took longer for his beliefs to gain acceptance than it did for the teachings of the *philosophes*. But when Rousseau did prevail, he suffused 19th-century literature, painting, and music. This arrogant man who raised the worship of himself almost to veneration—"He believed he was unique," writes one of his most recent biographers, Jean Guéhenno, "and for this reason answerable only to his own jurisdiction"—was yet so honest with himself, so self-castigating, that he could confess to shame and "crime": as a youngster, he wrote, when he earned his living as a footman, he had stolen a piece of ribbon and let another servant take the blame. His mistress bore him five children, and one after another Rousseau had them callously shipped off to a hospital for foundlings. When questioned about his action, he lied, but he recorded the truth for posterity.

Rousseau's philosophy was quite at variance with his character. He believed that man was born good, and that civilization suborned his true nature. Government, society, codified law were of little value. Only those laws were serviceable which an individual gives to himself. The quintessence of Rousseau's thought was the concept of man's individual worth, a worth inborn. "Everything is good as it emerges from the hands of the Creator; everything is spoiled in the hands of mankind" (*Émile*). In order for man to develop his worth, he must forget so-called "civilization," he must go back to a natural state. A true civilizing process will develop best by direct contact with nature. Education, to be worth anything, must be natural self-activity. As to this much-vaunted Reason—not all problems can be reasoned out, nor should they be. Emotion is an important ingredient of a truly civilized man, feeling is as valid as thinking, the state of dreams as valuable a state as the state of consciousness. Occasionally, said

Rousseau, amid the artificialities of life within a complex citified society, Reason was a legitimate guide. But in a crisis and in the fundamental problems of belief and conduct, our feelings serve us more reliably than Reason. Being a revolutionary zealot, he exaggerated, of course, and called a thinking man a "depraved animal." In *La Nouvelle Héloïse* Rousseau wrote at length about the superiority of sentiment to intellect. Similarly, in the *Confessions,* he stated that Reason would of course deny God and immortality. But our feelings favored them. Why should we not follow our feelings?

In postulating this, Rousseau gave artists two cues: one, express yourself, express your feelings; two, delve into the unconscious, dredge the mystery within you. He told them how to accomplish this: the creator should not be at home in society but must seek solitude far from salons and cities, walk the fields and the forests lost in a reverie. Only thus can he come to express what arises from his own soul. Here lies the great difference between Classicism and Romanticism.

As J. B. Priestley summarized it, "The classical depends upon the conscious mind, the romantic upon the unconscious." * To define it differently—and perhaps to oversimplify it: Classicism deals with the world, Romanticism deals with the soul of the artist.

Priestley went on to say:

> It is not a matter of vague influences but of direct inspiration: the Romantics, first, in Germany, then in England, later in France and elsewhere, discovered in him their prophet. No doubt the Age of Reason, decaying to make room for its opposite, would sooner or later have been succeeded by an Age of Romance, even if there had been no Rousseau, but he hurried on the process of transformation; he was the catalyst.

It was in this sense, the sense of personal fulfillment, that Rousseau pronounced his famous protest: "Man is born free; and everywhere he is enchained." These chains which education and society have forged were now to be rent asunder.

The new creed led to a new romantic attitude toward sexual love. Rousseau's erotic dreams, expressed in the *Confessions* so frankly that they shocked his contemporaries, who were used to eroticism, apostrophize the ecstatic relationship between man and woman. Love was a torment, a never-to-be satisfied

---

* In his *Literature and Western Man,* 1960.

longing, a continuous hunger, an affair of nighttime with no considerations of day—of children or income or advancement—being permitted to enter into it. From ecstasy and torment sprang romantic melancholy.

All this was of the greatest importance to the direction of the arts, music included. Incidentally, Rousseau, like Voltaire, had something to say about everything. He even had the audacity to declare himself a musician and to produce an opera, *Le Devin du village* (*The Village Soothsayer*). Curiously enough, the little opera had a great success and influenced Mozart in his *Bastien and Bastienne.* Because he hated the artificiality of French music, Rousseau warmly defended Gluck and attacked an Italian company which, in 1752, performed Pergolesi's *La Serva Padrona* (*The Servant as Mistress*). A great fracas resulted, pointless polemics being bandied back and forth, in which such men as Diderot and D'Alembert shouted loudly. This became known as "The War of the Buffoons."

·❧[2]❧·

Suddenly and almost miraculously the Romantic movement was born in Germany. As late as 1780 Frederick the Great, in a letter to D'Alembert, had written: "The Germans up to now know nothing except to eat, drink, make love, and fight." To be sure, Frederick was a Francophile and was prejudiced. But there was a point to what he said, and there was a point to his complaining that "We have no good writers whatever: perhaps they will arise when I am walking in the Elysian Fields." But now one of those phenomena of growth and proliferation occurred which one finds occasionally in the history of civilization. Who can explain it? Rousseau's philosophy made a direct appeal to the Germans. The German soul (if one can speak of the soul of a people) is peculiarly subject to violent swings: it soars to a starry idealism, only to plunge suddenly into a fetid mire of chauvinism and cruelty. A German can be a poet at one moment, a bully the next. Now Germany entered its finest phase. It burst into bloom. In a relatively short time, German thought spun a marvelous panoply which covered the land, and under the protection of which not only literature but other arts developed with astonishing vigor. Many hands wove the panoply. Never before or since did so many German writers produce so many fine poems, novels, confessions, tragedies, comedies, reflections, translations, treatises, and maxims as in those sixty years of the Romantic movement, which began about 1770 and lasted until about 1830, paralleling almost exactly Beethoven's lifetime.

THE ROMANTIC CHANGE

It began with the famous *Sturm und Drang,** "Storm and Stress," a literary movement which was more of a young man's bushy-haired protest than a movement of lasting achievement. All the conventions of classical form, politeness, and restraint were now to be declared taboo. Rules were hateful. Away with classic tragedy of measured verse, away with Racine and Corneille! Let us go back for inspiration to primitive man, to folk-myth, legend, saga! The proper study of mankind was to be simple man with his primordial instincts. Let us write about these instincts with sprawling license!

From these precepts came the Romantic school. The excesses fell away and there sprang up a host of writers of quality, among them Herder, the two brothers Schlegel, Tieck, the poet Novalis, whose *Hymns to the Night* were hymns to the dark unconscious and who created the mystic "blue flower," the flower none could pluck: it became the symbol of Romanticism. Such writers as Jean Paul Richter and the half-mad poet Hölderlin felt close to the English romantics and they to them. E. T. A. Hoffmann spun frightening fairy tales and horror stories—he is often compared to Edgar Allan Poe. All these writers were conscious of music and attempted to form their styles on musical principles. That was part and parcel of the mystic-romantic spirit. Hoffmann, besides being a writer, was a musician, an admirer of Beethoven, and believed that "music is the only truly romantic art." Hölderlin deplored that he had to deal with words: music was so much richer an expression. The peeling away of the skin of the everyday, exposing the eternal—what other art could accomplish this so well?

The eternal—the Romantics sought it over and over again by searching the shadowed deep layers of their minds and by searching the past, especially as it was handed down in anonymous art. They fell for one of the most curious hoaxes of literature. From England came a collection of ballads and folk songs, purporting to be ancient Gaelic poems collected by and attributed to a martial bard called Ossian. Dr. Johnson and Hume saw through the fraud. These were not ancient poems; they were poems by a young Scottish schoolmaster, James Macpherson, written in the new rhapsodic style. They were welcomed with the greatest seriousness in Germany. Beethoven read Ossian.**

The Romantics also discovered Shakespeare. He had previously been consid-

---

* The name comes from an unimportant play by Klinger.
** So did Napoleon. Talleyrand, praising Napoleon, told the Directorate that Napoleon loved Ossian's poetry because it removed one from the earth. Madame de Staël commented that the earth would not wish for anything better than to have him removed from it.

ered by most as little more than a rough-hewn, ill-mannered poet. Voltaire, who could not understand him at all, called him a "drunken savage." Now he was freshly and superbly translated into German and soon was considered the national property of the Germans—"Better in German than in English," an opinion which some Germans still hold today. Hamlet became the glass of fashion and the mold of form to the Romantics. Portia became a *Fräulein.* Beethoven read Shakespeare enthusiastically.

This turning away from the classical and this enthusiasm for Shakespeare began early. In the little satiric opera, *The Impresario,* to which I have previously referred, the librettist, Gottlob Stephanie, discusses current theatrical conditions:

> THE IMPRESARIO: Corneille, Racine, Voltaire, the Fathers of true Tragedy, are now thrown into the ash-can. Their plays, the touchstones of the tragic actor, are declared useless. Shakespearianism has us in its thrall. Heroic and state actions are the pieces we now parade. A tragedy without a comic character, without a mad fool, without a thunderstorm, and without ghosts, is judged to be dreary stuff. The audience yawns and the box-office till remains empty.

Yes, the Romantics needed the thunderstorm, the ghost, and the mad fool who spoke wisdom.

Another poet who influenced the Romantic development was Friedrich Gottlieb Klopstock. How famous he was! They knelt before him as a high priest of noble verse! Though he added richness to the German language, he was a pompous poet. His major work, the epic poem *The Messiah,* comprised nearly 20,000 hexameters, more than the *Iliad* and the *Odyssey* put together. Today Klopstock is an indigestible loaf to swallow; even in his own day Lessing wrote:

> Who is not going to praise Klopstock?
> But is everybody going to read him? No.
> We would like to be considered less lofty
> And to be read more.

Beethoven did read him and did consider him lofty. That is, until he began the perusal of Goethe. Beethoven said that Goethe turned him away from

Klopstock. He understood the difference between the former's pedestrian gait and Goethe's winged flight.

The three greatest geniuses of German Romantic literature were Lessing, Schiller, and Goethe. All three were first nourished by the Enlightenment, then turned away from it. Lessing thought deeply about the nature of beauty, which he tried to define in his famous essay on Laocoön. His masterpiece, the drama *Nathan der Weise* (*Nathan the Wise*), is a romantic plea for universal brotherhood. In its pivotal scene the Sultan, in order to trap the Jew (Nathan), asks him the question: "Which of the three religions is the true religion, Christianity, Judaism, or Mohammedanism?" Nathan answers with the parable of the three rings. A father owns a precious ring which contains the magic property of making its bearer beloved by all men. He has three sons, whom he loves equally, and he cannot decide to which of the three to bequeath the ring. So he commissions a goldsmith to make two copies of the ring; the goldsmith succeeds so perfectly that even the father cannot tell the rings apart. On his deathbed he tells each son that he is the possessor of the true ring. After the father's death, the sons quarrel bitterly, each claiming to be the real inheritor. They take their case before a judge, who rules: it is impossible to know which is the true ring. There is but one way in which each of you can prove that he is indeed the legitimate possessor: by his actions. Let your conduct be one of love toward all mankind, of tolerance, wisdom, forbearance—and your ring will come to be the one which will work the magic.

Schiller restated the theme of universal embrace in the "Ode to Joy." Schiller was the very incarnation of all that was idealistic in the German romantic mind. He began as a disciple of the Storm and Stress movement, with such plays as *Die Räuber* (*The Robbers*) and *Kabale und Liebe* (*Intrigue and Love*). He went on to write beautifully idealistic poetry and historical dramas, in which, to be sure, he twisted historical facts to his poetic purpose: such tragedies as *Maria Stuart, The Maid of Orléans, William Tell,* and *Don Carlos,* perhaps his greatest play, in which Schiller's spokesman, the Marquis of Posa, asks Philip for "liberty of thought." Beethoven was fond of quoting *Don Carlos.*

It would be wrong to consider the Romantic Movement a German possession. It spread everywhere, as the Enlightenment had spread everywhere. Coleridge and Wordsworth (Wordsworth was born in the same year as Beethoven) were Romantic poets, the first expressing, among his variegated verses, dreams of Kubla Khan, the other expressing a love for nature which he surely derived from Rousseau. In the pictorial arts the movement influenced Gainsborough

and Lawrence, some of whose portraits still belong to the Age of Enlightenment, but whose landscapes are steeped in Romanticism and are the forerunners
of Constable (another contemporary of Beethoven), the poet of the wet English sky, clouds, and fields. In France it led to Géricault's "The Raft of the
Medusa" (1818), the wild and accusatory painting which became the declaration around which the young painters rallied, among them his pupil Delacroix,
who painted the exotic and oriental and passionate *Death of Sardanapalus* in
the year Beethoven died. It led to Corot's Roman landscapes, in the 1820's. In
Spain it helped Goya find new expressions for his genius. In Germany, Caspar
David Friedrich—still another contemporary of Beethoven—painted moonlight and twisted trees. Over and over again artists speculated on man's relationship to nature. They wandered o'er hill, o'er dale.

The change from Enlightenment to Romanticism is more profound than a
change in attitude toward nature, toward dreams, or toward love. Romanticism
assigned a new role to the artist, gave him a new reason for being, and allowed
him a new way of thinking about himself, a way which may have finally led to
excessive arrogance—at least in some artists—but which for many years aided
art by turning the artist into a privileged being in the eyes of society—and in his
own eyes. No longer was he a mere craftsman; now he was a "genius" to be
approached on tiptoe. No longer did he merely execute commissions; now,
though he continued to sell his wares to patrons, he also wrote or composed or
painted "for himself." Now he expressed the state of his mind and soul. Now he
was allowed eccentricities which in former times he would hardly have dared to
arrogate to himself.

Because the artist enjoyed greater freedom, he widened the horizon of art and
increased its power. In the change, art lost some of its elegance, some of its
formal "perfection," and some of its detachment. It laid its hand on the nude
and trembling body, there where the heart beats. It became more deeply
concerned with, more deeply embroiled in, pain and suffering. Art has always
been concerned with pain and suffering, ever since Euripides wrote *The Trojans*
or the Greek sculptors hewed the sepulchral reliefs. Now the expression of
suffering became more intense and unbridled, the range more encompassing,
the "language" bolder. Sinews were exposed, the face showed its distortion, the
tears flowed. It was a form of popularization which transported art into the
thick of people's lives.

Even music changed, the art which seemingly has the least connection with
everyday life. There is a difference in both the outer and the inner attitude taken

by Mozart and by Beethoven. Obviously it is dangerous to draw inflexible lines or to categorize strictly. It is presumptuous to classify an artist who was able to command so many shades of emotion and feeling, from the impudent to the tragic, as Mozart could. Mozart could do it within the compass of 18th-century style. And in the last analysis, any artist of whatever period expresses *himself,* no other course being open to him. Still, I think it is legitimate to say that while Mozart expressed the world around him, Beethoven expressed what was going on in himself. Mozart's attitude was the attitude of a craftsman; that he happened to be a genius does not change the fact. Beethoven's attitude was a Rousseauean attitude: he saw himself as a creator set apart from ordinary mankind. That Beethoven sometimes worked only as a craftsman does not change the fact.

Beethoven had something in common with Goethe, though as men they could not have been more different. Goethe, too, was an artist conscious of his own self. "I have always striven to improve myself, to raise the standard of my personality," he said. The perimeter of his art was marvelously wide, but all of it emanated from a core of occupation with his own self. All the world was a stage to him, and he its chief actor. His mind was so inquisitive and so receptive that virtually nothing in philosophy, in pictorial arts, in botany, anthropology, optics, philology, sociology, literature, and practical politics failed to interest him. He had one failing: he was not really musical. He was interested in music but he could not really comprehend either Mozart or Beethoven. He was as awkward with music as Beethoven was with words.

Like a well-tailored and well-groomed Colossus, he bestrode the worlds of the Enlightenment and Romanticism—and then stepped beyond them. Again we must say that one cannot label Goethe, any more than one can label Beethoven. As a young poet he was much influenced by the fashionable lawlessness of the *Sturm und Drang* movement. He was then, as he remained always, a passionate admirer of Shakespeare. His youthful play, *Götz von Berlichingen,* is a *Sturm und Drang* product, imitating Shakespeare in freedom of form and expression—without of course coming close to Shakespeare's greatness. When he sent the first draft of *Götz* to his friend Herder, Herder remarked, "Shakespeare has ruined you."

His youthful novel, *The Sorrows of Young Werther,* was as important to the Romantic movement as Rousseau's *Héloïse. Werther* leaped through Europe. A flood of tears was released. Young men dressed à la Werther—blue coat, yellow trousers, jackboots—and mooned over unrequited love. Enough of them committed suicide to force Goethe to add a cautionary introduction to the second edition. *Werther* explores the morbidity of adolescence, Werther himself being completely obsessed by his own feelings. Goethe, this chameleon of a genius, then turned around and produced works totally at variance with the Romantic style: *Iphigénie,* for example, is a cool and perfectly shaped product of Classicism.

His poetry is among the most beautiful and most magical of any language, but of course it has the limitation inherent in poetry, that of being untranslatable. Thus only German-speaking people can appreciate that this nonmusical man wrote verse which sings with profound musicality. Goethe and Heine are the two poets who have been set to music more often than any other, even than Shakespeare. Goethe's melodiousness delighted and inspired Beethoven; he turned to Goethe at many hours.

The work which occupied Goethe virtually all his working life—and he lived eighty-three years, always developing his genius—is *Faust.* Peter Gay has called it "The play that everyone half knows." Its first part, with all the richness of thought and expression, is relatively simple. Part II is no longer "practical" either in the theater or as poetic form. It wanders all over the place, all over man's thought. In the end Faust's guilt is expiated through love, the "eternal feminine." All of us believe that we have something of Faust in us. Surely Beethoven's was a Faustian nature.

Goethe scorned narrow patriotism and national cultural complacency. He remained a citizen of the world, even during the Napoleonic Wars.* "There is no patriotic art and no patriotic scholarship," we read in *Maxims and Reflections.* "Both belong, like everything else of great value, to the whole of mankind. Art and scholarship can be promoted only by the free and general intercourse of all contemporaries building on what has come down to them from the past." Shortly before Beethoven's death, in a long letter to Carlyle, Goethe once again spoke of worldwide understanding and progress and tolerance. His influence was so important that for a time the Germans became supra-national, though the period was brief enough. The time became known as the *Goethezeit.*

The historian Hans Kohn summarized Goethe:

---

* This was not true of all the German Romantics. Schiller, however, stood near Goethe. He makes Posa, the true hero of *Don Carlos,* "the deputy of all mankind" . . . "his passion was the world and future generations."

He was aware as any twentieth century writer of the dark abyss in the human heart and the follies and tragedies of history. Yet this knowledge did not make him despair. He was born in the age of Voltaire, the age of confidence in reason. His youth was overshadowed by the passionate sentimentality of Rousseau and Werther, his manhood was lived amid the turmoil of the French Revolution and of the Napoleonic Wars, when the old order crumbled and man was at the mercy of elemental forces. He did not live the sheltered life of the ivory tower. From his early student days in Weimar he experienced the deepest joys and sorrows of life. He did not remain a spectator but participated in a way few men have in as many of the active and creative pursuits as human limitations allow.*

This "favorite of the gods" (*Liebling der Götter*), as Goethe once called himself, was one of the few contemporary figures whom Beethoven admired. "Admiration" is too weak a word. Beethoven almost worshiped Goethe. Over and over again the composer attempted to enter into a meaningful relationship with the poet, and it must have grieved Beethoven that Goethe, too successful, too busy, and too self-centered, never really reciprocated the feeling, though always remaining polite.

It is important in our understanding of Beethoven to acknowledge Goethe's influence on him. That influence went farther than the sharing of the belief that it was the artist's task to express both the turmoil and the peace within his own self and to search for his own perfection. Beethoven also adopted Goethe's belief in a pitiless fate — "fate" used in the sense of the Greek dramatists — in a demonic force which could ride roughshod over man's reason. He believed both in the desirability of action — "in the beginning was the deed," says Faust — and in the necessity for resignation: "Renounce you must, you must renounce." Let action and resignation impinge on each other and you have struggle, you have suffering. Neither easy optimism nor lazy pessimism is possible. Art must show the struggle, as well as the beauty, of existence, if it is to penetrate into the bloodstream and help human beings to live life more intensely. Beethoven created such art.

---

* From *The Mind of Germany*, 1960.

*Miniature of Beethoven (1803) by Christian Horneman. Beethoven sent it to
his friend Stephan von Breuning as a token of reconciliation after a quarrel (Beethoven House, Bonn).*

CHAPTER 9

BEETHOVEN
AS A YOUNG MAN

Anybody who has read the last page and knows how the story ends must feel a heaviness in his heart as he contemplates Beethoven's life. If he is among the millions who are inspirited by his music, he remembers Beethoven's suffering with a special poignancy, the picture of the deaf old man with his unkempt hair and burning eyes exercising a special appeal to the imagination. How malevolent his fate seems, how senseless, how cruel! A deaf composer—how terrible! To be sure, his lot was not so final as that of a painter who has lost his eyesight. A blind painter can no longer paint; a deaf musician can continue to compose. A musician can hear music without hearing; in his mind he knows what those silent signs on the ruled paper will sound like when they come to life in performance. All the same, for a musician no longer to be able to hear sounds performed is to be deprived of the complete experience of his own work, to be cheated of much of the joy of his achievement. As a creator the deaf Beethoven was like a gardener who can still see the flowers but can no longer scent their perfume. As a human being the man who could not hear stood behind a wall he could not scale, however many hands stretched out to help him.

What is more natural, therefore, than that we should ascribe Beethoven's negative characteristics—his suspiciousness, his quarrelsomeness, his sickly sensitivity, his slovenly habits, his attacks of arrogance, his unpunctuality—that we should ascribe these traits which grew more pronounced as he grew older, to that dark isolation of silence which surrounded him? The deafness explains the defects.

But does it? The more one studies this genius who was a spotted man, the more one weighs the delight of his mind against the dole of his failings, the more one comes to sense that deafness cannot furnish the whole explanation. The spots were there before his ears gave out.

Does misfortune change the chemical constituents of character? It may change the relative quantities within the compound. It may increase the mordant ingredients of the mixture, letting the strands of bitterness boil to the surface. The acid may become sharper. But it rarely puts into a personality elements of which no trace had been previously present.

If darkness was there before darkness fell; if even as a young man, young and successful, something pushed him to strike out at people, to look askance, to doubt their goodwill, to be "up in arms at the most trifling fancied slight to himself"; * if he could be rude to Lichnowsky, supercilious with Zmeskall, peremptory with Schuppanzigh; if he, who was so warmly welcomed in Vienna, could write to Eleonore that some of the Viennese pianists were his "sworn enemies" and he wanted to "revenge" himself on them: ** then we must conclude that neither deafness nor other slings and arrows can wholly account for Beethoven's faults.

An early example of that truculent streak which marred Beethoven's relationships with his friends, his suddenly taking umbrage only to regret his rashness afterward, is to be found in a letter to Franz Gerhard Wegeler, his friend from early youth. Wegeler, a tolerant and easygoing man but by no means a nonentity—what a sweet and gentle character he was! Sometime between 1794 and 1796 some quarrel split them apart and it is more than probable that the quarrel was of Beethoven's making. Beethoven, shaken to the core, regretted his action and wrote him: ***

> My Dearest and Most Excellent Friend!
> What a horrible picture you have shown me of myself! Oh, I admit that I do not deserve your friendship. You are so noble and well-meaning; and this is the first time that I dare not face you, for I have fallen far beneath you. Alas! for eight weeks now I have been a source of distress to my best and noblest friend. You believe that my goodness of heart has diminished. No, thank Heaven, for what made me behave to you like that was no deliberate, premeditated wickedness on my part, but my unpardonable thoughtlessness, which prevented me from seeing the whole affair in its true light.—Oh, how ashamed I feel both on your account

---

* Ernest Newman: *The Unconscious Beethoven*, 1927.
** Postscript to the second letter to Eleonore von Breuning, June, 1794.
*** The letter is not dated but is ascribed by Emily Anderson to those years.

and on mine—I hardly venture to beg you once more for your friendship—Ah, Wegeler, my sole consolation is that you have known me practically from childhood; and yet, oh do let me say this in my defense, I really was always good and ever tried to be upright and honorable in my actions. Otherwise how could you have loved me? Is it possible that in a short time I should suddenly have changed so dreadfully, so much to my disadvantage?—Impossible. And could those feelings for what is great and good suddenly be extinguished in me? No, Wegeler, my dear and most excellent friend. Oh, try once more to throw yourself unrestrainedly into the arms of your B[eethoven] and rely on the good qualities which you have always found in him. If you will do this, I guarantee that the new temple of sacred friendship which you will erect upon these qualities, will stand firmly and for ever, and that no misfortune, no tempest will be able to shake its foundations—firm—eternal—our friendship—forgiveness—oblivion—revival of our dying, declining friendship—Oh, Wegeler, do not reject this hand which I am offering you in reconciliation, but place your hand in mine—Oh, God—But I will say nothing more—I am coming to see you, to throw myself into your arms and to plead for the prodigal friend; and you will return to me, to your penitent Beethoven who loves you and will never forget you.

I have received your letter this very moment, as I have just come home— (A-15).

Discount if you will the hyperbolic language, language which springs from the early literature of Romanticism and sounds as if it might have come from *Werther*. Who would now write a letter and speak of "the new temple of sacred friendship" or "I am coming to see you, to throw myself into your arms and to plead for the prodigal friend"? Yet the style is unimportant. What is important is the quick sense of injury, followed by penitence. What is important—and what repeats itself all through Beethoven's life—is his protestation that his actions are "upright and honorable," while he thoughtlessly wounds a friend. Wegeler did accept the proffered hand: they remained friends, though they never saw each other again after Wegeler left Vienna in the summer of 1796. In a lighter vein, we can cite two little notes written (probably) to the composer Johann Nepomuk Hummel. They were written in 1799, either on the same day, or the second after but a day's interval.

Don't come to me any more! You are a false dog, and may the hangman do away with all false dogs. BEETHOVEN

Then—the weather vane veers 180 degrees:

Dear Little Ignaz of My Heart!
You are an honest fellow and I now realize that you were right. So come to me
this afternoon. You will find Schuppanzigh here too and we shall both blow you
up, cudgel you and shake you so that you will have a thoroughly good time.
Kisses from your Beethoven, also called dumpling.* (A-33 and 34).

What were the reasons for these raging swings, these tempests of suspicion,
these strident scoldings from a mind that could the next moment summon calm
nobility? A full explanation can never be offered. The mystery of a complex
personality can never be wholly unraveled and surely not that of a man as
complex as Beethoven. It is futile to stretch a dead man out on a psychoanalyst's
couch and spin Freudian theories about him.**

We can say reasonably that Beethoven emerged from a difficult childhood
and a humble home to a heady change of locale, to quick fame, and to adulation
as a performing musician. His background had not prepared him for consorting
with the titled. The turnabout—the change in surroundings, dress, manners,
financial condition, worldly atmosphere, acquisition of a coterie of admirers—
confused him. He may have covered up social insecurity by insisting that he
need not be overly civil, while insisting that others be civil to *him*. In his
dealings with the aristocracy, he took exaggerated care not to give the appearance of a flatterer and therefore occasionally fell into plain rudeness. He rather
overused the new freedom accorded to the artist. He felt himself to be powerful
and was aware of his power; those around him fed his sense of power. He even
drops remarks about using people for what he can get out of them and of
"power being the only true morality," remarks which are quickly contradicted
by his better thoughts and behavior.

His pride was enormous. Georg August Griesinger, Saxon minister to Vienna, said that "many people . . . called the young Beethoven arrogant and
immoderately proud." Griesinger told Ignaz Seyfried an anecdote which was
appended to a book by Seyfried.*** Though the anecdote has come down to us

---

* *Mehlschöberl* in the original. It is a Viennese pastry. In the first note he uses the form *Er*, third
person singular, a form used with servants and lower-class acquaintances. In the second note he uses
the familiar *Du*.
** Though that is precisely what has been done to Beethoven—in *Beethoven and His Nephew: A
Psychoanalytic Study of Their Relationship*, by Editha and Richard Sterba, M.D.—with the standard
psychoanalytical clichés being trotted out: Beethoven hated his mother and had homosexual
tendencies. "God bless us every one!" said Tiny Tim. No sensible biographer would accept either
finding on the basis of the evidence.
*** *Beethoven: Studies*, translated by Henry Hugh Pierson, 1853.

third-hand, Thayer thought that it could be taken as "substantially historical," and I give it here as Thayer transcribed it:

> When he [Griesinger] was still only an attaché, and Beethoven was little known except as a celebrated pianoforte player, both being still young, they happened to meet at the house of Prince Lobkowitz. In conversation with a gentleman present, Beethoven said in substance that he wished to be relieved from all bargain and sale of his works, and would gladly find someone willing to pay him a certain income for life, for which he should possess the exclusive right of publishing all he wrote; adding, "and I would not be idle in composition. I believe Goethe does this with Cotta, and, if I mistake not, Handel's London publisher held similar terms with him."
> "My dear young man," returned the other, "you must not complain; for you are neither a Goethe nor a Handel and it is not to be expected that you ever will be; for such masters will not be born again." Beethoven bit his lips, gave a most contemptuous glance at the speaker, and said no more. Lobkowitz endeavored to appease him, and in a subsequent conversation said:
> "My dear Beethoven, the gentleman did not intend to wound you. It is an established maxim, to which most men adhere, that the present generation cannot possibly produce such mighty spirits as the dead, who have already earned their fame."
> "So much the worse, Your Highness," returned Beethoven; "but with men who will not believe and trust in me because I am as yet unknown to universal fame, I cannot hold intercourse!"   (TQ).

His pride must have welled up as compensation for his experiences as a child, his observance of the way his father behaved, his reading and writing those formulas of "expiring in profoundest submission" and "humbly recommending myself to Your Transparency's grace," which had slithered around the Bonn Court. The French Revolution had exploded, Voltaire had been heeded, Beethoven was living on the same floor with a prince, quite a few "Transparencies" had been reduced to fugitives. In Vienna, the change was not so drastic as in Paris. The palaces were standing, the silver polished, the servants plentiful and willing. There was no topsy-turvydom. Yet even there, while Austria fought a war against the Revolution, the Revolution left its mark. Add to this the new creed of Romanticism, and one can trace the springs which fed the young composer's "immoderate" pride.

Yet these causes may be but partial ones. The true cause lay deeper. It is to be found in the immensity of the task of innovation which he was shortly to bring to music and with which he was then struggling. The giant step needed a giant's strength. It needed so tremendous an effort, so fearsome a strain, that the irritability, the quarrelsomeness, the peremptoriness, and even the arrogance were symptoms of nerves and a brain taxed to the limit. The innovator never has an easy time. Though Beethoven was, as we have said, "made of music," a vast amount of labor intervened between the first coming of his ideas—and ideas came to him day and night in an almost unceasing stream—and the final working out, the holding them fast on paper. Like a Sisyphus he kept pushing the load of ideas to a new, higher plane and there slashed and kneaded and vitalized their shape, searching for the one right expression. Everyone has noticed the inevitability of Beethoven's best music. It seems predestined. Whatever sketchbooks have been preserved show us how he arrived at this result by continuous revisions, by worrying the material, by chipping away at the superfluous marble. We know that he carried his ideas with him for years. He said that his memory was so good that he never forgot any of them.

His friends and pupils knew of the presence of the struggle of creation and innovation and often stood in awe of it. Ferdinand Ries relates that on one of their walks together in the country,

> Beethoven muttered and howled the whole time, without emitting any definite notes. When I asked him what he was doing he answered, "A theme for the last *allegro* of the sonata [the *Appassionata*] has occurred to me." When we reached the house he ran, without stopping to take off his hat, to the piano. I sat in a corner, and he soon forgot all about me. At last he got up; he was astonished to find me still there, and said, "I cannot give you a lesson today: I must go on working." *

The act of creation differs in severity with different artists, as much as does the act of giving birth with different women. One may conjecture that Mozart or Raphael or Renoir or Mendelssohn or Goethe had a relatively easy delivery, while Cézanne or Tolstoy or Brahms or Leonardo did not. Beethoven did not. I believe that his less attractive characteristics—present before the deafness—were due at least in part to the pain, and to the travail.**

This also may account for Beethoven's habit of procrastinating. It was hard

---

* Wegeler and Ries, *op. cit.*
** I am reminded of Flaubert's travail. To write the 400 pages of *Madame Bovary* he wrote 4000. In his letters one can read the struggle: "Sometimes, when I find I haven't written a single sentence after scribbling whole pages, I collapse on my couch and lie there dazed, bogged in a swamp of despair."

for him to let go, terribly hard to write *finis* to a composition. He procrastinated as well in letter writing—anyway, writing a letter was a chore to him—and in fulfilling ordinary social obligations. Johann Andreas Streicher, who became famous as one of the best makers of pianos, sent him in 1796 as a gift one of his new and excellent instruments. Such a gift gives us an idea of the esteem in which the young Beethoven was held. He acknowledged the gift two days later, writing with exuberance and gratitude.* He thought that this piano was actually too good for him "because it robs me of the freedom to produce my own tone." Yet when shortly afterward Streicher wanted a report on a pupil he had sent him, Beethoven replied tardily. He then apologized "humbly." It wasn't that he disliked the pupil; she was probably the highly talented Fräulein von Kissow, then thirteen years old, and Beethoven thought that "she will put to shame many of our commonplace but conceited organ-grinders." ** Incidentally, in the same letter he makes some remarks on the development of the piano which are important in the light of some of his later piano sonatas:

> There is no doubt that so far as the manner of playing it is concerned, the *pianoforte* is still the least studied and developed of all instruments; often one thinks that one is merely listening to a harp. And I am delighted, my dear fellow, that you are one of the few who realize and perceive that, provided one can feel the music, one can also make the pianoforte sing. I hope that the time will come when the harp and the pianoforte will be treated as two entirely different instruments. (A-18).

In replying tardily to Streicher, Beethoven was not being deliberately inconsiderate. He was just too preoccupied to give a prompt answer to a man who had sent him so munificent a gift and then had asked him for a simple favor.

The publishers and other people who ordered compositions from Beethoven were driven to distraction by his procrastination—just as the Dominican Friars of Santa Maria delle Grazie and Duke Ludovico were driven to distraction by Leonardo's inability to finish "The Last Supper." One feels the parallel with Beethoven: Leonardo, said a contemporary witness, would sometimes paint from sunrise till darkness, "never laying down the brush, but continuing to paint without eating or drinking. . . ."

---

* Letter from Pressburg, November 19, 1796. (A-17).
** In 1867 Ludwig Nohl published her reminiscences about Beethoven, the veracity of which seems doubtful.

Then three or four days would pass without his touching the work, yet each day he would spend several hours examining it and criticizing the figures to himself. I have also seen him, when the fancy took him, leave the Corte Vecchia when he was at work on the stupendous horse of clay, and go straight to the Grazie. There, climbing on the platform, he would take a brush and give a few touches to one of the figures: and then suddenly he would leave and go elsewhere.*

In both artists what we call procrastination, the inability to meet a due date, is a putting off because they are dissatisfied, because they can't stop searching for the "unattainable" better. Beethoven, that marvelous organizer of music, was the most disorganized of persons. A symptom of this is his frequent change of domicile. In his life in Vienna, from 1792 to his death in 1827, a period of thirty-five years, he occupied no fewer than thirty-three dwellings. But that does not tell the whole story. In the summer he went to at least one country place and some summers to more than one. If you add his summer residences, thirty-eight, to his winter residences, you arrive at the amazing total of seventy-one.** A few of these changes had practical causes: occasionally the landlord objected to the noise and the mess; occasionally Beethoven, having become so ubiquitously known a celebrity, had to flee from the stares of the curious. Nevertheless—and making due allowances for changes of mind and habit which we all experience—seventy-one domiciles indicate a deep-seated restlessness which contrasts strangely with his reluctance to travel. After he became completely deaf, we can understand that he did not want to expose himself to unfamiliar surroundings in strange cities. Before that—even after—he spoke of going to London, to Paris, to Kassel; he fooled himself into believing that he wanted to and might have "before now traveled over half the world" (1801). But he couldn't bring himself to move; he toyed with preparations—then countermanded them. He went almost nowhere, barring the couple of early tours. Yet while remaining in Vienna, he could not stay put, he could not find a home. Sometimes he paid for two residences, having signed two leases, only to move to a third.

A dwelling place was the cause of another quarrel with another friend of his youth. It was, of all friends least expected, Stephan von Breuning.*** The two bachelors decided to set up housekeeping together, on the theory that two young

---

* Matteo Bandello, around 1496.
** For summer residences he chose, besides many others, Baden twelve times, Heiligenstadt four times.
*** The incident, however, belongs to a later date, to 1804.

men could live as cheaply as one. Breuning had his own housekeeper and cook. The two friends dined together, and for a time they seemed to live in harmony and comfort. Then Beethoven discovered that, somehow or other, due notice had not been given to his previous landlord and that he was therefore liable to continue to pay rent for the previously occupied rooms. Beethoven just then had not quite recovered from an illness and was in a depressed state of mind. One day in July he brought up the question as to who was at fault for his having to pay two rents.

A violent quarrel ensued. Beethoven left the table, packed up, and forthwith moved to Baden, willing to pay for yet another lodging rather than remain in the same house with Breuning.

Ferdinand Ries, who tried to act as mediator, said that Breuning, too, had a temper and that he was particularly enraged at Beethoven's conduct because the incident occurred in the presence of Beethoven's brother Johann. However, Breuning took the first step toward a reconciliation, writing Beethoven a letter to the effect that they should let bygones be bygones. Beethoven, still weak, restless, bothered in Baden by bad weather and by the attentions of people, forcing him to "run away if I want to be alone," could not be placated. He expressed himself in a letter to Ries:

[BADEN, *c.* July 20, 1804]

Dear Ries,

As Breuning by his behavior has not scrupled to present to you and the caretaker my character from an aspect in which I appear to be a wretched, pitiable, and petty-minded fellow, I am asking you, first of all, to give my answer verbally to B[reuning]. But I am answering only one point, namely, the first one in his letter; and to this I am replying solely in order to justify my character in your estimation—Tell him therefore that I never intended to reproach him for his delay in giving notice and that, if B[reuning] had really been to blame for this, any harmonious relationship in the world is to me far too precious and valuable for me to offend any one of my friends for the sake of a few hundred gulden or even more. You yourself are aware that I reproached you, but only in jest, for being responsible for the notice having been given too late. I know for certain that you will remember this. Yet I had forgotten the whole affair—Well then, at table my brother began to talk about it and said that he thought that B[reuning] was to blame in the matter. I promptly denied this and said that *you* were to blame. I should have thought it was sufficiently obvious that I was not throwing the blame on B[reuning]. But on hearing my remark B in a rage jumped up and declared that he would like to send for the caretaker.

This unusual behavior to me on the part of that particular friend and companion of mine quite upset me. I too jumped up, knocked over my chair and walked off—and did not return. ... I want to show him in every way that I am not as petty as he is; and after this letter to you I am now writing to him on the same lines, although my resolve to break off our friendship is definite and final —

Your friend
BEETHOVEN (A-93).

"Definite and final"? No. Yet Beethoven's fury had not stormed itself out: four days after the first letter, Ries got a second missive:

BADEN, July 24, 1804

... No doubt you will have been surprised to hear about the Breuning affair. Believe me, my dear fellow! when I tell you that my sudden rage was merely an explosion resulting from several previous unpleasant incidents with him. I have the gift of being able to conceal and control my sensitivity about very many things. But if I happen to be irritated at a time when I am more liable to fly into a temper than usual, then I too erupt more violently than anyone else. ... And now our friendship is at an end! I have found only two friends in the world with whom I may say, I have never had a misunderstanding. But what fine men! One is dead,* the other is still alive.** Although for almost six years neither of us has had news of the other, yet I know that I hold the first place in his heart, just as he holds it in mine . . . Don't forget to see about rooms for me. All good wishes. Don't do too much tailoring.*** My best regards to the most beautiful of the beauties. Send me half a dozen sewing needles — For the life of me I should never have thought that I could be so lazy as I am here. If an outbreak of really hard work is going to follow then indeed something fine may be the result.

Vale.
BEETHOVEN (A-94).

He really believed that he had "the gift of being able to conceal and control my sensitivity about very many things."

Was the friendship, then, "at an end"? Not at all. By chance they met again in the autumn, and now Beethoven was all contrition. He sent Breuning a colored miniature done on ivory by Christian Horneman, the best of the portraits of him up to that date — though it was an idealized image which concealed the pockmarks and made the thirty-three-year-old composer look younger than his years and handsome. And he wrote him:

---

* Lorenz von Breuning, who had died in 1798.
** Karl Amenda, who had left Vienna in 1799.
*** Ries was living in the house of a tailor who had three beautiful daughters.

Behind this painting, my dear good St[ephan], let us *conceal* forever what *passed between us* for a time—I know that I have wounded *your heart;* but the emotion within me, which you must certainly have detected, has punished me sufficiently for doing so. It was not *malice* which was surging within me against you, no, for in that case I should no longer have been worthy of your friendship. It was passion, both *in your heart* and *in mine.*—But distrust of you began to stir within me—People interfered between us—people who are far from being worthy of *you* or of *me.*—Let me tell you that my portrait was always intended for you. You know, of course, that I always meant to give it to someone. To whom could I give it indeed with a warmer heart than to you, faithful, good and noble Steffen—Forgive me if I hurt you. I myself suffered just as much. When I no longer saw you beside me for such a long time, only then did I realize to the full how dear you were to *my* heart, how dear you will ever be.

Your

Surely you will rush to my *arms* as *trustfully* as you used to do—   (A-98).

We observe—in this and other instances—that Beethoven, when he could blame no one specifically, blamed anonymous enemies. It was "people" who "interfered between us," unworthy people, "they," "malicious folk" who caused the trouble.

Let us return to Griesinger, who was a friend of van Swieten and of Haydn. Griesinger's correspondence with the music publishers Breitkopf and Härtel offers a lively source of information of musical conditions in Vienna around the turn of the century, though (to my knowledge) it has not so far been used as a source in Beethoven biographies. Sometime in 1803 Breitkopf and Härtel sent Griesinger the text for an oratorio called *Polyhymnia,* by a minor poet, Christian Schreiber. They asked him to submit the poem to Haydn, because Haydn was thinking of composing a third major oratorio. Griesinger promptly complied with the request, but Haydn could not make up his mind. So Griesinger told Haydn that he knew that Beethoven was in search of "good poems" and that perhaps Beethoven would be glad to set the "Polymnia" (*sic*) to music. Possibly Griesinger said this to whet Haydn's appetite. At any rate:

This made a great impression, and "Papa" [Haydn] asked me (without mentioning any names) to show the poem to Beethoven and to get his opinion whether he would find it suitable for musical treatment, and whether he thought that by doing so one could reap honor from it. Papa's amenability will astonish you as much as it did me; but that is how it was! As you can easily imagine, I ran with the Polymnia immediately to Beethoven, and he promised to give me his judgment within eight days. Presumably Haydn will decide according to

Beethoven's pronouncement. His [Beethoven's] judgment is surely more competent than that of Swieten, whom Haydn usually consults in such cases. . . .*
[Later]:
The eight days in which Beethoven was to examine the said poem stretched
themselves into three weeks. His judgment of the Polymnia is the following:
The poem is well written but it does not contain enough action. The beginning
resembles the *Creation* by Van Swieten, being overly rich in description and
therefore a little monotonous. In the field of didactic poems Haydn, with the
Creation and the *Seasons,* had created masterpieces; no other composer could be
more skillful in this field. As far as he [Beethoven] was concerned, he felt that
oratorio texts such as those which Handel used were more suitable for musical
composition; at least he believed that he would succeed better with such. Would
I leave the Polymnia with him for yet a little while? Perhaps after reading the
poem several times he would not be able to resist setting it to music. Well, then,
I brought this report to Haydn, suppressing the last statement. But Haydn
complained mightily about the influence of the humid weather on his health;
even if he worked only half an hour a day he felt dizzy. He had to be careful,
otherwise he would suffer a stroke at the piano, etc., etc. However, he was very
happy that Beethoven's judgment about him was so friendly, for he was under
the impression that Beethoven was guilty of a great pride toward him [*denn
er beschuldigt diesen eines grossen Stolzes gegen ihn*].**

There we have it again: "great pride" and procrastination. The eight days
became three weeks and then Beethoven asked for more time. In the end,
neither composer used the poem.

Such then were some of the less admirable traits of this man. Other equivocal
characteristics, such as his dubious sense of business honesty and his meddling in
his brothers' affairs, will have to be more closely examined in their proper
biographical place.

It is not difficult to enumerate Beethoven's faults; it is easy to write biography
by bearing down on a man's shortcomings, just as it is easier to write a cutting
criticism than a laudatory one. The portrait must be corrected — in haste. We
must show that the man who had so violent a temper that once in a restaurant
he threw a dish of food at a waiter so that the gravy ran down the poor fellow's
face; that the same man who, being invited to a prince's house and noticing that
he was not seated at the same table as the prince at the supper which followed
the musical entertainment, grabbed his hat and stalked out in a huff, was also a

---

* Letter to Breitkopf and Härtel, December 14, 1803.
** Letter of January 4, 1804.

noble, courageous, warmhearted, and attractive human being, one who commanded not only admiration but affection.

The incident at the prince's table (the prince was Louis Ferdinand of Prussia, and the incident is related by Ries) illustrates the fact that one really could not remain angry at Beethoven. Far from resenting Beethoven's rudeness, Prince Louis invited him again a few days later and placed him at his side in the place of honor.

One of the salient characteristics of the young Beethoven, a characteristic he never lost, was the magnetism he exerted over young people. They flocked to him. It is natural that they understood his more advanced compositions more readily than the old guard, who had been brought up on Haydn. To many young people in Vienna—and to quite a few older ones, too, for that matter—he was a progressive, clearing old paths and blazing new trails. He was a representative of revolutionary thought and feeling. They understood his dedication to the task of widening the horizon of music. They came to him as both a musician and a man because he embodied emancipation. Here was an architect of daring, suitable to the new world that youth was trying to construct. He believed in the importance of the individual; that is just what the young people wanted to believe. Yet, aside from his role as an artist, as a man he attracted young people. Some of his patrons were older than he: Karl Lichnowsky, fourteen years older; Andrei Rasoumovsky, eighteen years older; and the elder statesman of the circle, van Swieten, was thirty-seven years older. Yet even among patrons he attracted the younger element: Lobkowitz was two years younger than Beethoven, Moritz Lichnowsky one year younger, Ferdinand Kinsky eleven years younger, Count Moritz von Fries seven years younger, Johann von Pasqualati (whom we have yet to meet) the same age as Fries; and the Archduke Rudolph, who was to become his pupil in the winter of 1803, eighteen years younger, so that the relationship began when Beethoven was thirty-three and the archduke a boy of fifteen.

As to the men with parentage less august, with whom the composer could be at ease—there, too, youth predominated. Ferdinand Ries was Beethoven's junior by fourteen years, Johann Nepomuk Hummel eight, and Carl Czerny twenty-one years younger. But the ever-useful Zmeskall, factotum-in-ordinary, was eleven years older. Ignaz Schuppanzigh, first the leader of the quartet at Prince Lichnowsky's and later wooed by Count Rasoumovsky to form the Rasoumovsky Quartet (one assumes at a higher salary), who proved as useful to Beethoven as Zmeskall, was six years younger than Beethoven. He was as frequently joshed by Beethoven as Zmeskall was: being very fat, he was soon called Falstaff, with many Beethovian variations on the theme of obesity.

The young men around Beethoven were of exceptional quality. One of these was Karl Amenda. He was born in Courland, in Latvia, was a year younger than Beethoven, learned music from his father, became an excellent violinist, and after studying at the University of Jena went to Vienna in the spring of 1798. There he became precentor to Prince Lobkowitz and later taught music to the family of Mozart's widow. Eventually he returned to his native country to pursue a theological career. A document exists which reports the friendship of the two young men: it is written "from oral tradition" in the third person, but Amenda probably wrote it:

Brief Account of the Friendly Relations between L.v. Beethoven and Karl Friedrich Amenda, afterward Provost at Talsen in Courland, written down from oral tradition:
After the completion of his theological studies K. F. Amenda goes to Vienna, where he several times meets Beethoven at the table d'hôte, attempts to enter into conversation with him, but without success, since Beeth. remains very *réservé*. After some time Amenda, who meanwhile had become music-teacher at the home of Mozart's widow, receives an invitation from a friendly family and there plays first violin in a quartet. While he was playing, somebody turned the pages for him, and when he turned about at the finish he was frightened to see Beethoven, who had taken the trouble to do this and now withdrew with a bow. The next day the extremely amiable host at the evening party appeared and cried out: "What have you done? You have captured Beethoven's heart! B. requests that you rejoice him with your company." ... From that time, the mutual visits became more and more numerous and the two took walks together, so that the people in the streets when they saw only one of them in the street at once called out: "Where is the other one?" ... B. complained that he could not get along on the violin. Asked by A. to try it, nevertheless, he played so fearfully that A. had to call out: "Have mercy—quit!" B. quit playing and the two laughed till they had to hold their sides. One evening B. improvised marvellously on the pianoforte and at the close A. said: "It is a great pity that such glorious music is born and lost in a moment." Whereupon B.: "There you are mistaken; I can repeat every extemporization"; whereupon he sat himself down and played it again without a change. B. was frequently embarrassed for money. Once he complained to A.; he had to pay rent and had no idea how he could do it. "That's easily remedied," said A. and gave him a theme (*"Freudvoll und Leidvoll"*) and locked him in his room with the remark that he must make a beginning on the variations within three hours. When A. returns he finds B. on the spot but ill-tempered. To the question whether or not he had begun B. handed over a paper with the remark: "There's your stuff!" (*"Da ist der Wisch!"*) A. takes the notes joyfully to B.'s landlord and tells him to take it to a publisher, who would pay him handsomely for it. The landlord hesitated at first but finally decided to do the errand and, returning joyfully, asks if other bits of paper like

that were to be had. But in order definitely to relieve such financial needs A. advised B. to make a trip to Italy. B. says he is willing but only on condition that A. go with him. A. agrees gladly and the trip is practically planned. Unfortunately news of a death calls A. back to his home. His brother has been killed in an accident and the duty of caring for the family devolves on him. With doubly oppressed heart A. takes leave of B. to return to his home in Courland. There he receives a letter from B. saying: "Since you cannot go along, I shall not go to Italy." Later the friends frequently exchanged thoughts by correspondence. (TQ).

Amenda was a handsome man, amiable and intellectual. Though their personal contact lasted but a year, Beethoven never forgot him. He dedicated his Quartet in F (Op. 18, No. 1) to Amenda, writing on the first-violin part that it was "A small memorial of our friendship." Later, in mid-1801, Beethoven confided to Amenda the fact of his growing deafness, as yet a secret.

The third-person document is cited by the Sterbas * as one indication that there was in Beethoven a "strong unconscious homosexual component." They suspect the two friends' being continuously together and bear down on such expressions as capturing "Beethoven's heart." They misunderstand custom and style of the period. What would they say to the following?

> My dearly Beloved:
> Heaven has tied our hearts in a knot which can never be untied. Only death can part us. Give me your hand, my fond one—and thus we reach life's goal. YOUR MALCHUS.

This is what Karl August von Malchus, secretary to the Austrian Legation in Bonn, a highly respected economist, and later finance minister to the King of Westphalia, wrote in the souvenir book when Beethoven departed from Bonn. Such treacle meant nothing; it was merely stylish, as "Good sweet honey lord" was stylish in Shakespeare's time.

Ferdinand, son of Franz Ries, we have mentioned a number of times. He was a brilliant musician who had emigrated from Bonn after the French invasion, when his father was reduced to straitened circumstances, knocked about different parts of Germany, reached Vienna in 1801, and had there become Beethoven's pupil. He was eventually to become a successful pianist, conductor, and composer, settling in London in 1813 and living there for eleven years. To him Beethoven showed his finer nature: when Ries arrived practically penniless in

---

* Editha and Richard Sterba, *op. cit.*

Vienna, Beethoven received him with great kindness, cared for him, advanced him loans of money which he subsequently converted into gifts, and allowed him to be the first to assume the title of "Pupil of Beethoven." In the *Notizen* Ries remembers their first meeting. He had brought along a letter from his father and handed it to Beethoven, who read it and said: "I cannot answer your father now, but write to him, [saying] I could not have forgotten how my mother died; thus he will be satisfied." (Father Ries helped Ludwig during the sad months which followed his mother's death.)

It was to young men such as Stephan von Breuning, Amenda, Wegeler, and Ries that Beethoven could unburden himself and for whom he could feel an affection untroubled by reservations caused by wealth or high station. All the same, it did help if his friends did not see him too frequently, if separation prevented their rubbing against each other and drawing Beethoven's sparks. It was in a sense lucky for Amenda to leave, for Ries to be in London, for Wegeler to move to Koblenz.

These young men joked and laughed and indulged in horseplay with Beethoven. Beethoven was far from gloomy. His constitution as a young man, in spite of not infrequent attacks of gastrointestinal disturbances, was robust and powerful. He was indefatigable; he could be ebullient, spluttering with life, drastic in drollery. He loved to laugh, and when he laughed it was a big, resounding laugh, a giant of a laugh that shook the flowers on the table and must have often fallen strangely on the ears of his courtly contemporaries. He did not have verbal wit; only in his music could he be witty. But how he loved puns! They pop up in the letters, displayed with childish glee. He must have repeated them in conversation, *Bach* for the composer and *brook, stechen* for *engrave* and *stab, Noten* and *Nöten, notes* and *needs*—forced or unforced, the more outrageous the better.

Yet Beethoven could be wanting in humor. Ries tells us that Beethoven played for him and another friend the *Andante* of his *Waldstein Sonata,* and being greatly urged he repeated it. Ries, passing Prince Lichnowsky's house on his way home, went in to tell the prince of the new and glorious composition of Beethoven's, and the prince persuaded him to play whatever he could remember of it. As Ries recalled more and more, the prince asked him to repeat it. So it happened that the prince too learned a portion of the sonata. The next day the prince called on Beethoven and said that he had composed something which was not at all bad and would Beethoven listen to it. Beethoven did not want to hear it; nevertheless the prince sat down and to the astonishment of the composer played a portion of the *Andante*. It was hardly a new joke—it had been played before in musical history. Beethoven took the matter seriously and became angry at Ries; he thought it a breach of trust.

His friends could not have been as faithful to him as they were had he not shown them what lay within him: sweetness of soul and nobility of mind. He could be a fascinating and often a charming companion. His friends have left us testimony to Beethoven's gaiety and ease of manner. He could even be a good host, on the rare occasions when his household was functioning smoothly and he was not quarreling with servants.

When he came to Vienna, he knew nothing at all of the fine art of cooking. He cared little about good food, his favorite dish being a mess of macaroni with plenty of cheese on top. He liked, too, the simplest kind of stew, and fish from the Danube. Ignaz Seyfried * reported that Beethoven liked a kind of bread soup cooked like mush,

> ... to which he looked forward with pleasure every Thursday. Together with it, ten sizable eggs had to be presented to him on a plate. Before they were stirred into the soup, he first separated and tested them by holding them against the light, then decapitated them with his own hand and anxiously sniffed them to see whether they were fresh. When fate decreed that some among them scented their straw, so to speak, the storm broke. In a voice of thunder the housekeeper was cited to court.**

He kept stracchino (an Italian cheese) and Verona salami in his room. He so often forgot about mealtime that he must have taken a bite when he got hungry. But once he did see himself in the role of a master chef, having become sufficiently impressed by the fuss the Viennese make about cooking; he invited his friends to a dinner he was to cook himself. Seyfried remembers:

> They found their host in a short evening jacket, a stately nightcap on his bristly shock of hair, and his loins girded with a blue kitchen apron, very busily engaged at the hearth.
> After waiting patiently for an hour and a half, while the turbulent demands of their stomachs were with increasing difficulty assuaged by cordial dialogue, the dinner was finally served. The soup recalled those charitable leavings distributed to beggars in the taverns; the beef was but half done and calculated to gratify

---

* He was six years younger than Beethoven, and his friendship with the composer dated from about 1800.
** O. G. Sonneck (ed.), *Beethoven: Impressions of Contemporaries*, 1926.

only an ostrich; the vegetables floated in a mixture of water and grease; and the roast seemed to have been smoked in the chimney. Nevertheless the giver of the feast did full justice to every dish. And the applause which he anticipated put him in so rosy a humor that he called himself "Cook Mehlschöberl," after a character in the burlesque, "The Merry Nuptials," and tried by his own example and by extravagant praise of the dainties which still remained to animate his continent guests. They, however, found it barely possible to choke down a few morsels, and stuck to good bread, fresh fruit, sweet pastry, and the unadulterated juice of the grape.*

Beethoven did like to drink, but there is no evidence that he drank to excess, as some biographers claim, tracing the habit to his father and grandmother. From time to time he took a glass of wine too many, but usually he drank but a small bottle with a meal, as is the European custom. Beethoven thought that wine was good for his health and he appreciated the gifts of wine which his admirers sent him. As a young man particularly he loved coffee, and he was very proud of making the coffee himself, counting the beans precisely, and serving it to his friends. It was good coffee.

In his youth he loved going to the theater and to the opera. He did not know how to play cards, nor did he participate in the popular social games, such as charades or forfeits. He never managed to learn to dance. His favorite social pastime—before he became deaf—was conversation. Aside from talking about music, he loved to discuss politics. His political ideas were hardly original, but he was what we would call today a democrat, an advocate of what Rousseau termed in his day "elective aristocracy"—that is, government by men popularly elected for their superior ability. He expressed his ideas with vehemence: with all his force he believed in the dignity of man (excepting only his own servants) and with equal fervor he embraced the cries of *liberté* and *égalité* of the French Revolution.** He was not so sure of *fraternité*. He admired the men of the American Revolution. Napoleon he at first held in great esteem—as did many European idealists—and "likened him to the greatest Roman consuls" (Ries). But his democratic principles did not prevent him from taking delight in royal decorations and medals. He wore them on all possible occasions. He grumbled about the Austrian government, but so did most other Viennese. The difference was that Beethoven said what he pleased in whatever public place he

---

* *Ibid.*
** This may have contributed to his appeal to young people.

happened to be and in anybody's presence and in a loud voice. The police never bothered him, perhaps because they thought him a harmless eccentric, perhaps because he was too great an ornament of the city to be molested.

He could be generous. When he learned that the only surviving child of Johann Sebastian Bach—Regine Susanna—was living in want, he volunteered to raise money for her, and that quickly, before "this brook has dried up and we can no longer supply it with water." * He could be equally gracious to other musicians in straitened circumstances.

One could never tell how he would react toward strangers. One day he would refuse to admit anyone; the next caller he would receive with courtesy. He reminds one of Rousseau,** whose life was even more tragic than that of Beethoven, persecuted as he often was, and suffering from an ignominious disease of the urinary tract. Rousseau fled society and morbidly isolated himself. Yet one visitor described his meeting with him:

> You have no idea how charming his society is, what true politeness there is in his manners, what a depth of serenity and cheerfulness in his talk. Did you not expect quite a different picture, and figure to yourself an eccentric creature, always grave and sometimes even abrupt? Ah, what a mistake! To an expression of great mildness he unites a glance of fire, and eyes the vivacity of which was never seen. When you handle any matter in which he has taken an interest, then his eyes, his lips, his hands—everything about him—speak. You would be quite wrong to picture in him an everlasting grumbler. Not at all; he laughs with those who laugh, he chats and jokes with children, he rallies his housekeeper.***

This, from time to time, could apply to Beethoven. He shared with Rousseau that deep love of nature, that genuine longing for the outdoors, that need to breathe fresh air, that desire to peer at flowers, touch trees, hear, as long as he could, the twittering of the birds, which Rousseau believed to be the true source of inspiration for the artist. It was fortunate for Beethoven that he lived in a city in which Nature wove her spell close by. Beethoven always was an early riser, five or six o'clock: he liked to work early in the morning. After breakfast he began his walk, tirelessly roaming through the fields beyond the Glacis or in the Vienna woods or along the Danube—sometimes until three o'clock in the

---

* Letter to Breitkopf and Härtel, April 22, 1801.
** Several of his contemporaries—Czerny and Baron de Trémont among them—likened Beethoven to Rousseau.
*** From John Morley, *Rousseau and His Era.*

afternoon, stopping here and there on a bench to rest. Then he would take his midday meal. In the summer, when he left Vienna behind him, he spent even longer hours outdoors.* Beethoven wrote of "the ecstasy of the woods . . . every tree said to me, 'Holy! Holy!'" He could have said with Thomas Jefferson, "There is not a sprig of grass that shoots uninteresting to me." In turn, the violet by a mossy stone, the telltale cuckoo, the chestnut trees "lavish of their long-hid gold" gave Beethoven the peaceful background against which his thoughts took shape.

As Wordsworth wrote in *Tintern Abbey:*

> Nature never did betray
> The heart that loved her.

It is not true that Beethoven was always careless of his appearance and personally unclean. The romantic biographers would have it that he never cared about what he wore or how he looked. They would depict him as a tattered Tom. Yet it is certain that he did not in his young days frequent the palaces looking like a vagrant. Here, as in almost every point at which we touch his personality, we find contradictions: sometimes he dressed carefully and enjoyed the fine linens, the silk handkerchiefs, the formal coats, and the carefully tied ascots which were then the mode; at other times, he dumped his clothes on the floor when he got undressed and dumped them on himself when he got dressed. The miniature which he sent to Breuning and three other portraits fashioned around that time show him to be anything but disheveled. On the other hand, Czerny, who was taken to him as a child of ten, which would have been in 1800 or 1801, recalls him as of rather frightening appearance:

I was about ten years old when Krumpholz [an old violinist] took me to see Beethoven. With what joy and terror I greeted the day on which I was to meet the admired master! Even now this moment is still vividly present in my memory. It was a winter's day when my father, Krumpholz, and I took our way from Leopoldstadt (where we were still

---

* Schindler gives a slightly different version of Beethoven's walking routine: "Beethoven rose every morning the year round at dawn and went directly to his desk. There he would work until two or three o'clock, his habitual dinner hour. In the course of the morning he would usually go out of doors once or twice, but would continue to work as he walked. These walks would seldom last more than an hour, and may be compared to a bee's excursions to gather honey. Beethoven would go out in every season, heeding neither cold nor heat. His afternoons were regularly spent in long walks. Late in the afternoon he would go to a favourite tavern to read the papers, unless he had already satisfied this need in a coffee-house."

living) to Vienna proper, to a street called *der tiefe Graben,* and climbed endless flights to the fifth and sixth story, where a rather untidy-looking servant announced us to Beethoven and then admitted us. The room presented a most disorderly appearance; papers and articles of clothing were scattered about everywhere, some trunks, bare walls, hardly a chair, save the wobbly one at the Walter forte-piano (then the best), and in this room was gathered a company of from six to eight persons, among them the two Wranitzky brothers,* Süssmayr, Schuppanzigh and one of Beethoven's brothers.

Beethoven himself wore a morning-coat of some long-haired, dark-gray material and trousers to match, so that he at once recalled to me the picture in Campe's ** "Robinson Crusoe," which I was reading at the time. His coal-black hair, cut *à la Titus,* bristled shaggily about his head. His beard—he had not been shaved for several days—made the lower part of his already brown face still darker. I also noticed with that visual quickness peculiar to children that he had cotton which seemed to have been steeped in a yellowish liquid, in his ears.

At that time, however, he did not give the least evidence of deafness. I was at once told to play something, and since I did not dare begin with one of his own compositions, played Mozart's great C major Concerto, the one beginning with chords. (K. 503) Beethoven soon gave me his attention, drew near my chair, and in those places where I had only accompanying passages played the orchestral melody with me, using his left hand. His hands were overgrown with hair and his fingers, especially at the ends, were very broad. The satisfaction he expressed gave me the courage to play his *Sonata pathétique,* which had just appeared, and, finally, his "Adelaide," which my father sang in his very passable tenor. When he had ended Beethoven turned to him and said: "The boy has talent. I will teach him myself and accept him as my pupil. Send him to me several times a week. First of all, however, get him a copy of Emanuel Bach's book on the true art of piano playing, for he must bring it with him the next times he comes."

Then all those present congratulated my father on this favorable verdict, Krumpholz in particular being quite delighted, and my father at once hurried off to hunt up Bach's book.***

However, in judging the accuracy of these reminiscences, we should take into account that they were written some forty years after the meeting. Reminiscences have a way of blending with later impressions.

Shaving was a major operation with Beethoven. Because he was awkward, his face often showed the nicks and cuts of the battle. He never enjoyed the equivalent of a modern bathroom nor the kind of toilet facilities available in a Lobkowitz palace. The maid brought him a tub of water every morning and he washed himself all over. Sometimes, when he was distracted by his thoughts, he

---

* Paul Wranitzky was first violinist at the Court Theater, later Kapellmeister.
** Campe rewrote "classics" for children.
*** O. G. Sonneck, *op. cit.*

let the water run onto the floor, no doubt to the delight of the landlord or the family living below him. Sometimes too, when his head was heated by his labor, he unceremoniously poured a jug of water over it.

He heaped his manuscripts in a corner and never allowed anyone to touch them. There they were, tempting for friends or visitors to steal. (Who knows how many *were* stolen!) When Beethoven was looking for a certain manuscript, he threw the papers all around the room, complaining bitterly that somebody had touched his possessions and why couldn't people leave things alone? His furniture was crude, the chairs rickety from abuse. He would spill the inkpot into the piano. He always had good pianos, but sometimes they were legless. A theory has been advanced that Beethoven composed while lying on the floor. A more reasonable supposition is that because of the frequent changes of lodging, with the pianos having to be carried up and down narrow staircases, it was easier to transport them without their legs. Beethoven owned at least a quartet of very fine pedigreed Italian instruments, all gifts of Prince Lichnowsky. These were a Joseph Guarnerius violin, a Nicholas Amati violin, a Vincenze Ruggieri viola, and an Andreas Guarnerius violoncello.

All his bodily movements were clumsy. Food spilled, dishes broke, glasses tumbled to the floor when Beethoven took hold of them. But the awkwardness was mostly a symptom of preoccupation, one so enveloping that he would go to a restaurant, consume his meal, and then leave without paying—in restaurants where he was known, this did not matter, for the proprietors trusted him —or go to a restaurant, sink into meditation, and then call for his bill without having ordered anything.

With all that, he was a fairly good businessman, though he protested he understood nothing of business. That is characteristic of many artists. Thayer wrote that "he showed no lack of a keen eye to profits." In his young years in Vienna, far from having financial worries, he was much in demand. He wrote to Wegeler:

June 29, 1801

> You want to know something about my present situation. Well, on the whole it is not at all bad. For since last year Lichnowsky who, although you may find it hard to believe what I say, was always, and still is my warmest friend (of course we have had some slight misunderstandings, but these have only strengthened our friendship), has disbursed for my benefit a fixed sum of 600 gulden on which I can draw until I obtain a suitable appointment. My compositions bring me in a good deal; and I may say that I am offered more commissions than it is

possible for me to carry out. Moreover for every composition I can count on six or seven publishers, and even more, if I want them; people no longer come to an arrangement with me, I state my price and they pay. So you see how pleasantly situated I am. For instance, I see a friend in need and it so happens that the state of my purse does not allow me to help him immediately; well then, I have only to sit down and compose and in a short time I can come to his aid— (A-51).

2

To form a portrait of Beethoven, we must do more than describe his looks and habits and his dealings with friends, patrons, publishers. We must go further than to detail "what Keats had for breakfast." Shall we attempt to gaze into his mind?

The best way to gaze into Beethoven's mind is to listen to his music. Yet a side path is open to exploration: what were the words and thoughts written by others which interested and stimulated him? Beethoven had a habit of copying out quotations from the books he read or underscoring passages which he liked. Among the books he owned were the Bible in French and Latin; *The Apocrypha;* the *Odyssey;* La Fontaine's *Fables;* Thomas à Kempis; complete editions of Goethe, Schiller, Klopstock, Herder, and Shakespeare; he read and reread Plutarch's *Lives,* Cicero's *Letters* (in Latin); Horace's *On the Art of Poetry;* Aristotle's *Politics;* Plato's *Republic;* the *Iliad;* works by Euripides, Ovid, Quintilian, Tacitus, Lucian, Xenophon (according to Schindler); several of Kant's philosophical writings, and a host of now forgotten poets. (Later he owned twenty (!) volumes of Campe's *Tales for Children,* which he obviously had bought for his nephew Karl.) Three days after his death, an artist, J. N. Hoechle, sketched Beethoven's study. The bookcase, with many books, is prominent. After Beethoven died, his library was dispersed, either through purchase at the auction * of his possessions or by friends who legitimately or illegitimately took the books as souvenirs.

There is no way of tracing *when* he read what he did read. So it is possible that we may ascribe favorite quotations to the period of his youth when in fact he did not come upon them until later on. Still, to group them together seems the practical way to present a survey. We know, at least, that Beethoven began the reading of the antique authors early and as a young man was reading

---

* It is possible, as Schindler suggests, that some books and music which Beethoven never owned were smuggled into the auction because material "from the master's library" would bring high prices. Such tricks were not beyond the practice of the time.

Shakespeare and Goethe. His copy of the *Odyssey* (published in 1781), leather bound, shows many coffee stains and wax-candle drippings, indicating that he read by night.

When we examine Beethoven's literary taste, we face again the usual contradiction. In a letter to Breitkopf and Härtel, November 2, 1809, he said:

> There is hardly any treatise which could be too learned *for me*. I have not the slightest pretension to what is properly called erudition. Yet from my childhood I have striven to understand *what the better and wiser people* of every age were driving at in their works. Shame on an artist who does not consider it his duty to achieve at least as much— (A-228).

And yet? Yet one of his favorite books was a work by Christoph Christian Sturm, *Observations on the Works of God in the Realm of Nature and Providence.* He owned two separate editions of this and marked forty-one passages. Sturm was a pastor from Hamburg who in two thick volumes penned a series of pseudo-philosophic preachments, one for every day of the year. His sentiments are insipid, his style hobbling, his conclusions vapid. Sturm mixes scientific facts (antiquated) with religious uplift. Typical subjects: "The Electric Fire," "The Hope of Spring," "Infinity of the Starry Sky," "Comparison of Human and Animal Senses," "Nature Is a School for the Heart," "Harmony and Patriotism of the Bees." Invariable conclusion: God has ordered everything for the best. One would guess that it would be the last sort of reading to appeal to Beethoven. What must have impressed him was Sturm's incessant exhortation that man must be in communion with Nature to "make God's acquaintance and in so doing find a foretaste of heaven." Beethoven was so enthusiastic about Sturm's *Observations* that occasionally in his wanderings in the outskirts of Vienna he used to talk to the priests in the little villages, propagandizing Sturm's work. The priest at Mödling, according to Schindler, answered him, "Our people need to know nothing more of celestial phenomena than that the sun, the moon, and the stars rise and set."

The man who read Kant could be satisfied with Sturm. The man who understood Plato could fall for a puerile hoax. He was informed that a lamp had been invented which would enable the blind to see. He got very excited and was bitterly disappointed when somebody told him it was all a joke.

Before we dismiss the Hamburg pastor, we may ask: Was Beethoven religious? Is that why he responded to Sturm's book? The answer depends on what we mean by "religious."

Beethoven was born a Catholic. He never became a practicing one. There is no record of his ever attending church service or observing the orthodoxy of his religion. He never went to confession, though he told his nephew to go. On his deathbed he did take the last sacrament, but generally he viewed priests with mistrust. No one ever reported that Beethoven genuflected or made the sign of the cross.

He said, "Religion and Figured Bass * are in themselves closed concepts about which one ought not to dispute." His lack of orthodoxy did not prevent him from composing religious works, although a case might be made for the assertion that such music shows a less direct, a less opulent, flow of inspiration than his other music. This in spite of the glories of the *Missa Solemnis.*

Schindler says that "his religious views were not so much based on church doctrine as on a sort of deism. Though he never elaborated a specific theory, he acknowledged God revealed in the world as well as the world in God." But Beethoven was not in a strict sense a Deist. The Deists believed that the existence of God could be proved rationally from the course of nature without enlisting the aid of miracles or supernatural phenomena. Beethoven was not interested in "proving" any tenet, any more than he wanted to "dispute." His creed may have been influenced by Herder, whom he read and who wrote ** that God had no personal form and was unknowable except through the order of the universe and the spiritual consciousness of man. Beethoven's, like Rousseau's belief, was a form of pantheism, of God in all things. Neither Beethoven nor Rousseau felt the necessity of explaining the inexplicable. In times of woe and disillusion, Beethoven often and touchingly used the word "God," calling on Him for peace or solace. He even wrote down short sentences pleading for divine support. Yet his belief was mystic, not conventionally religious. He certainly had little use for any go-between, be he priest or prophet. Nor did he expect the Creator to do his work for him. When the young composer Moscheles made a piano score of *Fidelio,* he wrote at the end of it, *"Fine* with God's help." Beethoven was not at home when Moscheles submitted the work. When Beethoven returned it, he had written underneath, "O Man, help yourself."

To return now to the inquiry into Beethoven's relationship with the words of famous men—the Beethoven scholar Ludwig Nohl accomplished late in the

---

* *Generalbass.* A system of shorthand for harmony, also called "thorough-bass."
** In *God, Some Conversations,* 1787.

19th century a yeoman piece of work. After searching the available sources, he grouped the quotations which Beethoven had either underscored or copied or the passages which he had dog-eared—in short, wherever he found evidence that Beethoven was interested in a particular passage—and eventually published his findings.*

Nohl tabulated more than fifty passages from the *Odyssey* and forty-three passages from Goethe's *West-Östlicher Divan (The Oriental Collection)*, a collection inspired by Eastern verse (particularly Persian). It contains some of Goethe's most recondite poetry. Goethe published this work in 1819: therefore Beethoven's study of it belongs to the later period in his life. Shakespeare is represented in the *Breviary* by thirty-one passages; the two plays which Beethoven seems not to have read are *Love's Labour's Lost* and *As You Like It*. One of his favorite plays seems to have been *The Merchant of Venice*. We may theorize that what appealed to him about this play was the famous discussion of music in Act V. He underscored the entire passage with special force. Direct and implied evidence indicates that Beethoven read these other works by Shakespeare: *Hamlet, The Tempest, Othello, Much Ado About Nothing, All's Well That Ends Well, The Winter's Tale,* and probably a few of the sonnets.

I give below a few of the marked quotations from Shakespeare, along with my own guesses (guesses they are, nothing more) as to the reasons why Beethoven selected them. Let me warn that no conclusions can be drawn from the absence of quotations from many famous plays. This simply means that the volumes containing these plays which were in Beethoven's possession can no longer be found. Once Schindler asked him the "meaning" of two sonatas, the D Minor Op. 31 and the *Appassionata*. It was no doubt a foolish question. Beethoven, who was "in a cheerful mood," replied, "Just read *The Tempest*." Perhaps Beethoven was putting Schindler on—the explanation explains nothing—but at least we know that he knew *The Tempest,* though his copy of the play has been lost.

A selection of *Odyssey* quotations follows. I have used the new translation by Richmond Lattimore. Beethoven read the standard translation by J. H. Voss, still in use when I was a student.**

---

* In a little book called *Beethoven's Breviary (Beethovens Brevier)*, 1901.
** I have omitted citations from German poets, as the originals may be unfamiliar to English-speaking readers. There are no English translations which give the true music of Goethe's lyric poetry; to write such would be beyond my ability.

·◦] FROM SHAKESPEARE [◦·

JESSICA: I am never merry when I hear sweet music.
LORENZO: The reason is, your spirits are attentive:
for do but note a wild and wanton herd
or race of youthful and unhandled colts,
fetching mad bounds, bellowing and neighing loud,
Which is the hot condition of their blood;
If they but hear perchance a trumpet sound,
Or any air of music touch their ears,
You shall perceive them make a mutual stand,
Their savage eyes turn'd to a modest gaze
By the sweet power of music: Therefore the poet
Did feign that Orpheus drew trees, stones, and
    floods;
Since nought so stockish, hard, and full of rage,
But music for the time doth change his nature.
The man that hath no music in himself,
Nor is not moved with concord of sweet sounds,
Is fit for treasons, stratagems, and spoils,
The motions of his spirit are dull as night,
And his affections dark as Erebus.
Let no such man be trusted.
    (*The Merchant of Venice,* Act V, Scene I)

It is not surprising that the beauty of these verses about music should have reached Beethoven; it has reached so many millions as to turn the end of the speech into a worn and carelessly quoted cliché. Perhaps, too, Shakespeare's using imagery from nature touched Beethoven; the "unhandled colts," "trees, stones, and floods."

GRATIANO: You have too much respect upon the
    world:
They lose it that do buy it with much care.
    (*The Merchant of Venice,* Act I, Scene I)

Beethoven was fond of moralizing sentiments. Occasionally he bandied them about; occasionally he pontificated, pronouncing maxims of conduct to which he did not always adhere. Moralizing, too, was a habit of his times. Goethe noted that Beethoven held the world in contempt.

NERISSA: ... superfluity comes sooner by white hairs; but competency lives longer.
    (*The Merchant of Venice,* Act I, Scene II)

Beethoven did not despise money and sought for "competency."

BASSANIO: Gratiano speaks an infinite deal of nothing, more than any man in all Venice.
(*The Merchant of Venice,* Act I, Scene I)

Beethoven made fun of the Viennese passion for talk and more talk. He called loquacious acquaintances "Papageno."

BRABANTIO: I had rather to adopt a child than get it.

This quotation may refer to nephew Karl. If so, it belongs to a later period. The entire scene of the father's grief must have found an echo in Beethoven's heart.

(*Othello,* Act I, Scene III)

PRINCE OF ARRAGON: O, that estates, degrees, and offices
Were not derived corruptly, and that clear honour
Were purchased by the merit of the wearer!
How many then should cover that stand bare!
How many be commanded that command!
(*The Merchant of Venice,* Act II, Scene IX)

Recognition of merit—this and other quotations, too, suggest that Beethoven was avid for such recognition. He wanted "honour" if "purchased by the merit of the wearer." It was part of his belief in the significance of the individual.

SALARINO: It is the most impenetrable cur
That ever kept with men.
(*The Merchant of Venice,* Act III, Scene III)

The only reference to Shylock. Beethoven, later in life, did occasionally have to borrow money.

BASSANIO: Every offence is not a hate at first.
(*The Merchant of Venice,* Act IV, Scene I)

Did Beethoven reprove himself for being quick to sense "hate" when an offense was slight or merely imagined?

ANTONIO: . . . the weakest kind of fruit
drops earliest to the ground.
(*The Merchant of Venice,* Act IV, Scene I)

There are several quotations touching the need for being strong. It was one of his dominant beliefs.

PORTIA: The quality of mercy is not strain'd;
It droppeth as the gentle rain from heaven
Upon the place beneath: it is twice bless'd;
It blesseth him that gives, and him that takes.
(*The Merchant of Venice,* Act IV, Scene I)

Was it the sentiment or the beauty of the poetry which appealed to him?

ANT.: For herein Fortune shows herself more kind
Than is her custom: it is still her use
To let the wretched man outlive his wealth,
To view with hollow eye and wrinkled brow
An age of poverty.
(*The Merchant of Venice,* Act IV, Scene I)

This and other quotations, as well as some of his conversation, indicate that Beethoven feared the specter of poverty in old age.

PORTIA: How far that little candle throws his beams!
So shines a good deed in a naughty world.
(*The Merchant of Venice,* Act V, Scene I)

Heavily underscored by Beethoven.

PORTIA: The brain may devise laws for the blood,
But a hot temper leaps o'er a cold decree.
(*The Merchant of Venice,* Act I, Scene II)

It is tempting to speculate at length on this and the *Romeo and Juliet* quotations. Let us postpone comment until we discuss Beethoven's love life. It is significant, I believe, that Beethoven underscored Romeo's words ("And what love can do," etc.) three times and marked the page with a dog-ear.

ROMEO: And what love can do, that dares love attempt.
(*Romeo and Juliet,* Act II, Scene II)

FRIAR: These violent delights have violent ends,
And in their triumph die, like fire and powder,
Which as they kiss consume. The sweetest honey
Is loathsome in his own deliciousness,
And in the taste confounds the appetite.
Therefore, love moderately; long love doth so;
Too swift arrives as tardy as too slow.
(*Romeo and Juliet,* Act II, Scene VI)

OTHELLO: If after every tempest come such calms,
May the winds blow till they have waken'd death!
And let the labouring bark climb hills of seas
Olympus-high, and duck again as low
As hell's from heaven!
(*Othello,* Act II, Scene I)

The turbulence of Nature ... and the calm of love, two themes which appear in his thoughts.

OTHELLO: Put out the light, and then — put out the light!
If I quench thee, thou flaming minister,
I can again thy former light restore,
Should I repent me; ...
(*Othello,* Act V, Scene II)

Only the first four words are underscored, but these heavily. He may have been thinking of death. Or he may have recognized and responded to the greatness of Othello's speech. The loftiness of this soliloquy is Beethovian.

BEETHOVEN AS A YOUNG MAN

·≡[FROM *THE ODYSSEY*]≡·

Then the thoughtful Telemachus said to her in answer:
"See, I will accurately answer all that you ask me.
My mother says indeed I am his. I for my part
do not know. Nobody really knows his own father.
But how I wish I could have been rather son to some
fortunate
man, whom old age overtook among his possessions.
But of mortal men, that man has proved the most
ill-fated
whose son they say I am: since you question me
on this matter."

(Book I)

Only the words in italics are marked in Beethoven's copy. I quote enough of the passage to indicate that he must have been thinking of his father, "ill-fated" man.

"People, surely, always give more applause to that
song
which is the latest to circulate among the listeners."

(Book I)

Nohl thinks this refers to Rossini, who was the rage of Vienna from 1815 on. It could apply equally well to other contemporary composers.

For few are the children who turn out to be equals
of their fathers,
and the greater number are worse; few are better
than their father is.

(Book II)

Was Beethoven thinking of his nephew?

And if some god batters me far out on the wine-blue
water,
I will endure it, keeping a stubborn spirit inside me,
for already I have suffered much and done much hard
work on the waves and in the fighting.

(Book V)

An expression of courage, possibly chosen when he was young. Schindler says it was one of his favorite quotations, as well as the one following. His "stubborn spirit" must have derived solace from it when he became deaf.

even for immortal gods that man has a claim on
their mercy
who comes to them as a wandering man, in the way
that I now
come to your current and to your knees after much
suffering.

(Book V)

This beautiful expression of man's suffering is not only underscored but the page is marked with a dog-ear.

"may the gods give you everything that your heart longs for;

may they grant you a husband and a house and sweet agreement

in all things, for nothing is better than this, more steadfast

than when two people, a man and his wife, keep a harmonious

household . . ."
(Book VI)

Beethoven, who longed for "a harmonious household," never achieved it.

Whoever it is of people you know who wear the greatest burden of misery, such are the ones whom I would equal for pain endured.
(Book VII)

Another plaint of suffering.

The herald came near, bringing with him the excellent singer

whom the Muse had loved greatly, and gave him both good and evil.

She reft him of his eyes, but she gave him the sweet singing art.
(Book VIII)

Obviously autobiographical. For "eyes" read "ears."

For with all peoples upon the earth singers are entitled to be cherished and to their share of respect, since the Muse has taught them

her own way, and since she loves all the company of singers.

He copied these verses and quoted them on the reverse of the title page of his choral composition, *Meeresstille und Glückliche Fahrt* (*Peaceful Sea and Happy Journey*). The poem is by Goethe. The dedication reads, "To the author of the poems, the immortal Goethe." (Published in 1815.)

So the famous singer sang his tale, but Odysseus melted, and from under his eyes the tears ran down drenching

his cheeks. . . .
(Book VIII)

Another tribute to the power of music.

Or could it then have been some companion, a brave man knowing

thoughts gracious toward you, since one who is your

companion, and has thoughts
honorable toward you, is of no less degree than a
    brother?
            (Book VIII)

Beethoven wrote a determined "Yes" next to the last verse. It indicates his need of friends.

"Wine sets even a thoughtful man to singing, or
sets him into softly laughing, sets him to dancing.
Sometimes it tosses out a word that was better un-
    spoken."
            (Book XIV)

He hardly ever succumbed to "mad wine." But there were one or two occasions——

Too much sleep is only a bore.
            (Book XV)

Nohl points out that there is an entry in his diary: "Always studied from half-past five till breakfast" (1815.)

So he spoke, and kissed his son, and the tears running
down his cheeks splashed on the ground. Until now,
    he was always unyielding.
            (Book XVI)

Probably refers to the nephew.

For Zeus of the wide brows takes away one half of
    the virtue
from a man, once the day of slavery closes upon him.
            (Book XVII)

Schindler says that Beethoven copied these verses and admired them very much. It is a confirmation of that sense of liberty which he felt so strongly.

my maidservants, those careless hussies ...
            (Book XIX)

No comment!

Human beings live for only a short time,
and when a man is harsh himself, and his mind
    knows harsh thoughts,
all men pray that sufferings will befall him hereafter
while he lives; and when he is dead all men make
    fun of him.
But when a man is blameless himself, and his
    thoughts are blameless,
the friends he has entertained carry his fame widely
to all mankind, and many are they who call him ex-
    cellent.
            (Book XIX)

He copied this passage in his diary (1818). Surely he wanted his friends to think well of him and "call him excellent."

These few scraps may give us an inkling of Beethoven's reactions to the books with which he lived. He rummaged not only among masterpieces stamped by time's approval; he explored as well contemporary and by no means conservative writings, the new poetry of such men as Müllner, Werner, Seume, Herder, and of course Schiller. As to the antique authors whom he admired, let us add one more quotation: he copied from Pliny a sentence which must have served him as a motto: "What more can one give a man than fame and praise and immortality?"

As a young man he achieved fame and was awarded praise; later he knew quite well that immortality would be vouchsafed to him. What impresses us, even in the young Beethoven, is the sureness with which he walked his way. Nobody could persuade him what to compose, let alone how. In music the democratic being seemed to have been an intransigent lord, a ruler of the realm, issuing royal commands. When he addressed Zmeskall as "Excellent *plenipo-tentiarius regni Beethovensis*" (Plenipotentiary of Beethoven's kingdom), it was of course a joke, but there was something behind this feeling of sovereignty which could make him confess to Amenda: "I regard him [Zmeskall] and S[chuppanzigh] merely as instruments on which to play when I feel inclined. But they can never be noble witnesses to the fullest extent of my inward and outward activities, nor can they ever truly share my life. I value them merely for what they do for me." * Note the allusion to *Hamlet* in the phrase, "instruments on which to play."

Yet he was not stupidly impervious to criticism. To Breitkopf and Härtel he wrote, in the same year: "As for myself, far be it from me to think that I have achieved a perfection which suffers no adverse criticism. But your reviewer's outcry against me was at first very mortifying. Yet when I began to compare myself with other composers, I could hardly bring myself to pay any attention to it but remained quite calm and said to myself, 'They don't know anything about music.' " (A-48).

He was both padishah and prankster. He thought it very funny to address Zmeskall as "Baron-ron-aron-ron," and to compose for Moritz Lichnowsky a musical setting of the words, "Count, dearest Count, most excellent sheep," rhyming *Graf* with *Schaf*.

He was not a joiner. He did not belong to any organization, though the Viennese loved to form this or that *Verein*. When he was quite young, he

---

* July 1, 1801. A-53.

probably was a Freemason. He composed a choral piece in Bonn in 1791 or 1792 to the words, "Who is a free man?" He revised this in 1795, under the title *Maurerfragen* (*Mason's Questions*), and still later made a third version to words by Wegeler, "What is the goal of a Mason?" He might have become a Freemason because it was the fashionable thing for a young liberal to do. He was in distinguished company: Mozart had been one, his friend Wegeler was one, so was Schikaneder, and so were Goethe and George Washington. But even that adherence to a "club" he soon ignored. He could not belong to a group. He was a man alone.

He was a man alone, even before "a cruel stroke of fate" forced him to be one.

CHAPTER 10

NAPOLEON,
WAR, DEAFNESS

··◦[1]◦··

I really believe he is Antichrist," Tolstoy has one of his characters, Anna Scherer, say of Napoleon in the first sentences of *War and Peace*. When Tolstoy wrote these words and expressed his fresh view of history, Napoleon had been dead some forty years and Tolstoy was not the only one to curse the man who had pulled down the girders of Europe, Egypt, and the Middle East, burying millions under the debris.

Antichrist? To many thousands who lived through the momentous years when the 18th century turned into the 19th, the young Napoleon was far from that: to them he was the standard-bearer of a new order, the apostle of the creed that only in a United Nations of Europe lay future hope, and the example of a man who had managed to break the ancient barriers of birth and rank. Because he ascended with aquiline speed from an obscure lieutenancy, lean, slovenly, poorly dressed with badly shined shoes, to full commander and then to Consul of France, he proved to young men born in huts or suburban streets that everybody could become somebody, that the marshal's baton lay in the foot-sol-dier's knapsack, and that the big chance existed even for those whose names did not sport a *von* or a *de*. The power of his personality was tremendous. While making war, he appeared as the "Prince of Peace" and declared that he would put an end to European dissension, that the peoples of the world would no longer have to witness "the terrible pictures of chaos, devastation and carnage" of war. What a glorious figure he was in the beginning! He seemed little short of a new Christ.

In the early years Napoleon still possessed some traces of idealism, though even then he was very much of a *poseur*. Obviously he was a genius at military strategy, but he was as well a genius at rhetoric, at sounding those round,

"The Coronation of Napoleon I" (detail) by J. David (The Louvre, Paris).

ringing, rolling phrases of promise. He was not yet Emperor, not yet the absolute Dictator, not yet a Pharaoh self-deified.

How could he be judged correctly in face of the forward moves he accomplished? He suppressed the last rising of the Royalists, in 1795, and saved the Republic for a new "progressive" governing body, the Directory. He instigated the improvement of the French Code of Laws. He promoted important reforms of the educational system. He posed as, and partly was, a disciple of Voltaire: "The more I read Voltaire the more I love him." He was opposed to the slave trade. He announced as France's mission the liberation of the subjugated minorities of the vast Austro-Hungarian Empire—and they *were* subjugated— the people to the south living in upper Italy, those in the Kingdom of Naples and those living far west of Vienna in the Netherlands. He proclaimed to the Italians that "the French were coming to break their chains." At that very moment he wrote from Italy to the Directory, "We will levy twenty million francs in war reparations on this country; it is one of the richest in the world." To his soldiers he said, "You are famished and nearly naked . . . I lead you into the most fertile plain in the world."

Austria was old and rich. Austria's generals were bewhiskered, a row of medals glistening on their elegant uniforms, their boots very well shined. The Habsburgs' thrones had to be defended, the Holy Roman Empire and the monarchy both had to be kept intact. The generals were going to do it in short order, they were going to flatten the upstart. Emperor Franz believed that the only way to govern the heterogeneous groups of his monarchy, and lead them to war, was strict paternalistic authoritarianism. There was to be no nonsense about democratic principles or liberty of opinion. Go and fight for the Habsburgs and don't ask questions! Franz clamped down a tight censorship on newspapers, stage plays, and books. He increased the internal police and espionage force. Government spies, called *Spitzel* ("snoopers") in Viennese slang, were everywhere. Intellectualism became suspect, informers plied their trade, the police kept dossiers on everybody prominent. Every piece of written material had to be approved before publication. If a drama contained the word "conspiracy" it could not be printed or performed, even if the play dealt with a conspiracy of the year 1000. Schiller's plays could not be performed: had not Schiller, echoing Rousseau, written, "Man is free, even when he is born in chains"? Dissent went underground, perhaps deeper in Austria than in any other European country except Spain. Compare this condition to the new regime in France: Napoleon recommended to the Directory that freedom of the press be declared. So it was, on March 19, 1796. That this freedom proved largely illusory, that the Directory itself was soon to be abolished, and that in a little more than three years—on December 24, 1799—Napoleon would become First Consul with practically unlimited power, only a Cassandra could foretell.

As it later appeared, the truth was that Napoleon's putative progressive ideas were "the ideas of a roguish merchant rather than a statesman," wrote H. G. Wells.* Wells goes on to say:

> His little imitative imagination was full of a deep cunning dream of being Caesar over again—as if this universe would ever tolerate anything of that sort over again! He was scheming to make himself a real emperor, with a crown upon his head and all his rivals and school-fellows and friends at his feet.

The first Italian campaign proved a triumph for Napoleon, a series of humiliations for Austria. His thrusts into Italy were swift, his leadership brilliant. At Arcola, when his troops could not manage to capture a bridge from the Austrians, he himself seized the tricolor and led them on. Never mind that he fell into the canal and had to be fished out. He won the battle anyway—on November 17, 1796. A few months afterward, now in possession of most of the Austrian holdings in northern Italy, he founded the vassal Ligurian Republic in Genoa on June 6, 1797. A month later, other republics were proclaimed, comprising such cities as Milan, Modena, Ferrara, and Bologna. On March 16, 1797, Napoleon forced the passage of the Tagliamento, and a few weeks after that he conquered the greater part of lower Austria. As he swept from victory to victory, he who was an assiduous reader of Plutarch's *Lives* saw himself more and more as a Roman hero and began to dream of a vast new Roman Empire.

The Austrians had to call a halt. They sued for peace. France agreed: on October 17, 1797, the peace treaty of Campo Formio was signed. It was a dishonorable agreement and proved eventually to be disastrous. Austria ceded parts of the Netherlands and Lombardy, granted free navigation on the Rhine to the French in return for a secret understanding eventually to annex certain South German territory. Napoleon and Franz together consented to the rape of the ancient republic of Venetia; Napoleon thus split Venice in two, securing the services of the Venetian fleet for France.**

---

* In *The Outline of History*, 1920.
** It was on that plain of Venetia that the Austro-Hungarian Empire was strangled to death in 1918: perhaps historic retribution does exist after all.

Having got the Austrians out of the way temporarily, he proceeded with his two next plans of conquest: one was the expedition against Egypt, the other the invasion of England. Though in 1798 his forces landed in Ireland, he never succeeded in breaching the island set in the silver sea, because it was protected by its marvelous fleet. Indeed, Horatio Nelson destroyed a large part of the French fleet in the Mediterranean, thus for a time seriously endangering Napoleon's Egyptian campaign. Then the British bungled too, and Napoleon occupied Alexandria. He fought the Battle of the Pyramids, and on July 21, 1798, became master of Egypt, advancing the next year into Syria.

The Second Coalition was formed—Britain, Russia, Austria, Turkey, Portugal, and Naples against France. The Peace of Campo Formio did not last long. War continued, and Bonaparte was ready to take on the whole Coalition, knowing that these partners were often more suspicious of one another than of their common enemy. Once more Italy became a battlefield, with the fortunes of war swinging in the balance, until on June 14, 1800, Napoleon defeated the Austrians decisively at the bloody Battle of Marengo.

··◦[2]◦··

Yet this battle was but a prelude to slaughter with fiercer orchestration. Fourteen years there were, during which soldiers' boots tramped through people's lives. Those fourteen years of Napoleon's apogee and destruction did not prevent Beethoven's genius from functioning and growing even though they did change the economic conditions and social ambience under which he lived.

At the beginning of the Napoleonic wars Vienna lay far from the turmoil. The Viennese, hardly a warlike people, continued to pursue the easy life, shutting out as long as they could the sound of the cannonades. That is, the rich people did. For the poor, life soon became almost unbearably difficult.

Vienna, always a crowded city, became overcrowded. Fugitives arrived from the outer provinces, among them a host of dukes and grand-dukes and barons and relatives of the Habsburgs, all with their numerous entourages. A housing shortage developed. By 1804, said a reporter for the journal *Elegante Welt,** a luxury apartment cost 200 florins ($1200) a month, and the cheapest back room fifteen florins ($90)! Laws were issued to freeze rents. The landlords quickly learned how to evade such regulations, and a black market flourished. Though a few large new apartment houses were built, the Viennese had to live

---

* Issue of March 10, 1804.

"under the roof, under the stairs, under the earth," and such places "where one needs artificial light the entire day." Halls and staircases were filthy, and one was surprised that they led to beautiful and clean apartments. Beethoven lived in 1799 in rooms at the St. Petersplatz, to which one had to ascend four flights of stairs. The location was good, in the center of the city; the apartment no doubt was costly, though not so expensive as if it had been on a lower floor. In the autumn he moved to a third-floor dwelling in the *Tiefen Graben,* again one in a good central location.

The sedan chairs of the 18th century had largely disappeared. By 1804 there were 900 *Fiaker* (horse-drawn cabs) and 300 coaches for hire available, in addition to the private equipages. Traffic was turbulent. It was remarkable, wrote the same reporter, that there were "no more than two or three accidents a year." The traffic moving over the granite pavements caused—reported a traveler, Wilhelm Fischer, in 1802—"terrible dust, which hovered in the air the whole summer and even during part of the winter. . . . It was like a dirty fog." No wonder Beethoven was anxious to escape to the country! Because this dust entered the lungs, tuberculosis was rampant. Fischer said that among the poor people every twenty-fifth person died before his time. Though hospitals were large, the largest one consisting of 111 rooms, they were filled. Treatments cost thirty kreuzer ($3) a day, a private room $6. Whoever brought a certificate of poverty signed by the local priest was treated for nothing. A sick servant was treated for a dollar a day, paid by the employer. In the maternity rooms, women were allowed to give birth while hiding their faces behind a heavy veil. They were not forced to reveal their identity, as long as they had with them a sealed envelope containing their name and address, to be used in case of death in childbirth. This practice made illegitimacy less embarrassing.

Because Napoleon exacted ever-increasing sums for reparations and because many fertile fields were destroyed by battles, the cost of food rose fantastically. In 1802 a pound of butter cost between twenty and thirty kreuzer ($2 to $3), beef 70 cents a pound, pork 90 cents to $1.10, and a kilo of bread 60 cents.

The government levied every possible tax the ministers could devise, including a tax on the gold and silver dishes a family had in its possession. That law merely caused the possessors of gold and silver vessels to melt them down and sell the metal, the result of which is that the museums and collections of Vienna, so rich in other treasures, show a remarkable lack of precious metal work of the Renaissance and the Baroque periods.

"The butter to be sacrificed because of the war always turns out to be the margarine of the poor," said Professor James Tobin of Yale.* Substitute "lard" for margarine and you have the situation in 1800. Those to whom the price of black bread matters are the first to have to cut it thinner. In the *Freihaus* the smell of cabbage became more pungent, but there was no shortage of perfume for those who lived in the Herrengasse.

It was the usual story: the poor got poorer and the rich got richer. Wild financial speculations began, and people studied the stock exchange as if they knew what they were studying. Manufacturers supplying the army with *matériel* cheated unmercifully while they lined their pockets with the gains of war; over and over again the Austrian generals complained of the poor stuff, tents or meat or shoes, which were sent to the men in the field. Currency became unstable, and people began to hoard silver and copper coins; around 1799 these coins disappeared from circulation and paper money had to be issued. The middle class was particularly severely hit. They tried to keep up a pretense of gentility, but the rate of suicides increased sharply. A pretty, marriageable daughter was an asset: she could be betrothed to one of the parvenus, with the understanding that the bridegroom was to support the whole family. Many who had money tried to buy their way out of military service or send a substitute. There was little hatred for the French until Napoleon came close to Vienna itself. Then everyone was hot for defending the city.

In spite of shame and shambles, laws and inflation, the Viennese lost neither their passion for amusement nor the habit of turning everything into a joke. The need for entertainment and "perpetual Sundays" became greater than ever, whether in the Wieden or the Prater or the *Hofburg*. With increasing frequency one saw the wounded and the crippled return, to be quickly hidden away. One surgeon, Dr. Sigmund Wolffsohn, in 1807 built the Apollo Dance Hall out of profits derived from his invention of artificial arms and legs. But most of the time the city shone as before. Mighty Austria was certain to win the war eventually against the Corsican, and in the meantime better to forget the temporary defeats. Forget them—by snatching all the gaiety one could.

After the death of his first wife, Emperor Franz had married again; the new Empress, Marie-Thérèse of Bourbon-Naples, was a pleasure-loving, good-natured little woman, and she spent whatever time she had left from her frequent pregnancies in inventing new diversions and entertainments. The carnival continued and so did the Redouten, the balls and plays and private concerts and

---

* In a speech to the Social Science Associations in Washington in December, 1967.

opera performances for the Court (Marie-Thérèse occasionally sang at these performances), the Chinese shadow plays, the magic tricks presented in a House of Whims, where bells rang unexpectedly and water doused the surprised visitor.* The Empress was on friendly terms with the singer Joseph Simoni, who took part in the concert of 1801 in which Beethoven appeared, and she shocked society by promenading in the Prater arm in arm with him.

A dance craze swept Vienna. The minuet expired, and in its stead came a new dance in a livelier three-quarter rhythm in which one glided without lifting the foot high and held one's partner in a close embrace, an embrace which the clerics stamped as "lascivious," leading to "the most indecent positions." Charles Burney, famous 18th-century chronicler of musical matters, wrote: "The verb *waltzen* . . . implies to roll, wallow, welter, tumble down, or roll in the dirt of mire." As early as 1797 the *Journal of Luxury and Fashion* reported that most of the girls "are most unwilling to sacrifice this Bacchanalian orgy to the strict prohibitions of their mothers." **

Yet if the time favored the frantically frivolous, it demanded as well the escape inward, the flight into a "better world" which art, and romantic art especially, offered to men and women capable of feeling and thinking. The Empress herself, the same Empress who in a carnival night would appear in seven different disguises, as pretzel vendor or harlequin, sang in private performances of Haydn's oratorios—Haydn said tactfully that she sang with taste but "a small voice"—and would later accept the dedication of Beethoven's famous Septet, Op. 20. Music offered the best escape route against the worries of the day. And the safest. What was censorable about music? The nobility and the intelligent public continued to cultivate it and to welcome composers, pianists, singers, conductors. Beethoven did not then suffer from the war.

---

* A tourist guidebook published in 1803 (*Guide du Voyageur à Vienne*) says of the two *Redouten* Halls: "The halls are open from 9 P.M. to 6 A.M. Formerly it was obligatory to enter masked, but for several years now those who do not wish to be bothered can content themselves with placing a little mask on their hat. . . . Entrance fee is 2 florins. Refreshments of all kinds are available. One can sup in private rooms which surround the grand halls. Two orchestras play minuets and waltzes, but few dance. The number of visitors increases as the end of the carnival approaches; when there are as few as a thousand the halls seem empty. When the number rises to three thousand the crowd is oppressive and the heat unbearable. Their Majesties frequently honor the *redoute* with their presence."

This same guidebook says under "Inns": "In none of the great cities of Europe are the inns as mediocre as they are in this capital, and that in every respect." Among the "most frequented" inns, "The Swan" is listed, indicating that Beethoven's favorite restaurant was a relatively good one.

** Quoted by Dr. Eduard Reeser in his *The History of the Waltz*, Stockholm.

Vigorous in mind and body, the young Beethoven proceeded from one composition to another, and almost with each his greatness grew in a nearly direct progression. As yet he concentrated on the more intimate forms of music, but some time in the last years of the century he worked on his first symphony. We do not know the exact dates of all his compositions; yet we can say that when he was twenty-six he completed the Piano Sonata No. 4 (in E-flat Major, Op. 7) and dedicated it to the Countess Babette von Keglevics, with whom he was supposed to be in love. It is a romantic work which ambles with easy grace; it was known in Beethoven's time by the sentimental title, *Die Verliebte*.

In 1797, the year which ended with the Peace of Campo Formio, the year when Coleridge wrote *Kubla Khan,* Turner painted *Millbank, Moonlight,* and Cherubini composed *Medea,* Beethoven worked on the three Piano Sonatas, Op. 10. In the next year followed the Piano Concerto No. 1. Three String Trios Op. 9, three Violin Sonatas Op. 12, and the revision of the Piano Concerto No. 2 belong to this period, as well as the Piano Sonata in C Minor, Op. 13, called by Beethoven himself *Sonate Pathétique.* Here we have a true product of the Age of Romanticism, with its highly charged introduction and its second movement as sad and yet as glowing as the parting scene in *Romeo and Juliet.* It was too new for some, too heady for others; young Moscheles, perfecting himself as a pianist, was warned against "such eccentric stuff." Yet it won great fame; no doubt the title helped, though there is nothing "pathetic" in the Tchaikovskian sense about it, the word here denoting "full of tenderness."

Around this time Beethoven began to concentrate on the form which he was to carry to its profoundest issue, the string quartet. Six of them, Op. 18, were finished by 1800. Before April of that year, he had completed the Septet, Op. 20, mentioned above. This achieved so wide a popularity that Beethoven eventually got sick of it. "He could not endure his Septet and grew angry because of the universal applause with which it was received," reported Czerny. As the 19th century dawned, he began to sketch out the Third Piano Concerto.*

He still brought these works forward for the delectation of exclusive circles, dedicated them to titled patrons, and used them for his own function as Palace virtuoso. Yet these compositions were beginning to be destined for a new age, an age in which aristocratic pride and ease could no longer be either as prideful or as easeful. The artist mirrors his time; he also prophesies the time to come.

---

* The compositions mentioned here are not a complete catalogue of his production of this period; they are the highlights.

He did introduce the first of the Nine in a public concert, a rare event in those war years. Those of us who take pleasure in finding on the road of history a few clearly legible milestones may find satisfaction in the date of the first presentation of the First Symphony: 1800. With it began the series of the greatest symphonic works created by the mind of man.

The concert took place on April 2, at the Burgtheater. It was Beethoven's first public appearance for his own benefit, and we can only guess as to its financial outcome. The probabilities are that it was reasonably profitable, two indications pointing toward that conclusion: first, the general reputation of Beethoven, of which he took legitimate advantage by advertising the concert in the *Wiener Zeitung* of March 26, well before the event; second, the fact that shortly after the first concert he gave a second. The program poster read:

> Today, Wednesday, April 2nd, 1800, Herr *Ludwig van Beethoven* will have the honor to give a grand concert for his benefit in the Royal Imperial Court Theatre beside the Burg. The pieces which will be performed are the following:
>
> 1. A grand symphony by the late Kapellmeister Mozart.
> 2. An aria from "The Creation" by the Princely Kapellmeister Herr Haydn, sung by Mlle. Saal.
> 3. A grand Concerto for the pianoforte, played and composed by Herr *Ludwig van Beethoven.*
> 4. A Septet, most humbly and obediently dedicated to Her Majesty the Empress, and composed by Herr *Ludwig van Beethoven* for four stringed and three wind instruments, played by Herren Schuppanzigh, Schreiber, Schindlecker, Bär, Nickel, Matauschek and Dietzel.
> 5. A Duet from Haydn's "Creation," sung by Herr and Mlle. Saal.
> 6. Herr *Ludwig van Beethoven* will improvise on the pianoforte.
> 7. A new grand symphony with complete orchestra, composed by Herr *Ludwig van Beethoven.*
>
> ———————
>
> Tickets for boxes and stalls are to be had of Herr van Beethoven at his lodgings in the Tiefen Graben, No. 241, third story, and of the boxkeeper.
>
> ———————
>
> Prices of admission are as usual.
>
> ———————
>
> The beginning is at half-past 6 o'clock

Note that Herr van Beethoven was his own ticket seller. How many people climbed to the third story where his lodging was to purchase admission? And did Beethoven himself hand out the tickets and make the change? What a curious farrago of a program! A Mozart symphony, two selections from *The Creation,* a Beethoven Piano Concerto (was it No. 1 or No. 2?), the Septet, the first "new grand symphony," and, in between, Beethoven improvising on the pianoforte. How long did the concert last? One cannot compute the length, knowing neither which symphony by Mozart was played nor how long Beethoven improvised. But it is a safe guess that if the audience assembled punctually at half-past six on that spring evening, they were not dismissed into the darkness of the Vienna streets until at least nine-thirty.

A report was published. A correspondent for the *Allgemeine Musikalische Zeitung* was present, though he took his time about reviewing the concert, the report not appearing until about six months later. He called the occasion "the most interesting concert in a long time," and thought the symphony contained "considerable art, novelty, and a wealth of ideas, though the wind instruments were overused." The performing orchestra was that of the opera house, and according to the same correspondent, it made a poor showing. Beethoven did not want the regular Italian conductor (Conti) to take the concert, but entrusted it to the Kapellmeister of the Court Orchestra, Paul Wranitzky.* The correspondent continued:

> The gentlemen refused to play under him. The faults of this orchestra, already criticized above, then became all the more evident since B's compositions are difficult to execute. When they were accompanying, the players did not bother to pay any attention to the soloist. As a result there was no delicacy at all in the accompaniments and no response to the musical feeling of the solo player. In the second part of the symphony they became so lax that despite all efforts on the part of the conductor no fire whatsoever could be got out of them, particularly from the wind-instruments. With such behavior what good is all the proficiency —which most of the members of this organization undeniably possess? How, under such circumstances, is even the most excellent composition to be effective? (TQ).

All the same, the First Symphony became quickly known, at least throughout Austria and Germany. There were, to be sure, some protesting voices raised. In

---

* He was also a composer; Goethe planned to have him compose a sequel to *The Magic Flute,* but the project came to nothing. Beethoven composed a set of Variations to one of his tunes.

Leipzig, in 1801, it was called "the outrageous effrontery of a young man"; and when it was given at the Paris Conservatory in 1810 it was scolded for its "prodigal use of the most barbaric dissonances."

It is a particularly endearing work. It is a whirl of good humor, full of audacious ideas, charming and lightly lyrical, its most original movement being the third. This is still called a Minuet, as was traditional in the older symphonies. Yet, as we have observed, the minuet as a dance had become passé, and what we have here is less of a stately dance than a glowing scherzo with which Beethoven "took a leap into a new world." (Lawrence Gilman)

Shortly after the first concert, Beethoven again appeared in public, this time in a concert given by a remarkable horn virtuoso, Johann Wenzel Stich, who used the professional name of Punto, a name which seems to fit a circus clown better than a musician but which is the Italian translation of the German word *Stich.* The concert was given on April 18, and it was announced that Beethoven was to compose a new horn sonata for it. Ries states that Beethoven did not begin this work until the day before the performance, though it was ready for the concert. The statement is incredible, yet it may be true. This concert too was reviewed by the *AMZ,* on July 2, 1800. The correspondent writes that the applause was so great that the sonata had immediately to be repeated. In May of that year the two artists performed again in Budapest.

Beethoven intended originally to dedicate his first symphony to his old employer, Maximilian Franz. It was sixteen years since Maximilian Franz had become the Elector of Bonn. On April 27, 1800, he returned to Vienna with a small retinue and took up his abode in a modest villa in the suburbs. But by the time the symphony was ready for publication, Maximilian Franz was dead, and Beethoven dedicated the work to van Swieten.

He offered the symphony, the Septet, the Piano Concerto No. 2, and the Piano Sonata Op. 22 to the Leipzig publisher, Anton Hoffmeister, for seventy ducats ($1750), a not inconsiderable price. Beethoven discussed his prices objectively and frankly. He wrote: "This sonata is a first rate piece, most beloved and worthy Brother!" So it was worth twenty ducats. The concerto was only worth ten, because, as he had already written, he did not consider it one of his best works. A symphony ought to be worth more than a sonata. On the other hand, it would have a smaller sale, so twenty ducats was a fair value. The whole lot would be seventy ducats; "how many thalers in gold that amounts to does not concern me, because I am a really poor businessman and arithmetician." Poor arithmetician? Yes. Poor businessman? No!

The third of Beethoven's public appearances of that period took place at the beginning of 1801. The war had resumed in 1799, Napoleon was victorious in his second Italian sortie, and at the end of 1800 his army was advancing against Austria proper. On December 3, the Austrians were once more defeated at Hohenlinden. The metropolis itself was being threatened.

Now the stream of the wounded increased. Funds for their succor were needed, and one means of raising funds was a series of public concerts. Two of these were given in the large Redoutensaal. One was a performance of Haydn's *Creation,* conducted by Haydn himself. The other was a gala program on January 30, 1801, in which both Haydn and Beethoven took part. This concert was arranged by Christine Gerhardi, a young woman of good society, cultured, talented, and an excellent singer. Indeed she was for a time one of the most popular amateur singers in Vienna, and it is probable that Haydn had her in mind for the soprano part when he composed *The Creation.* (She sang it at the first performance in the Burgtheater.) She lived near Vienna's General Hospital, very near where Beethoven first dwelt with Lichnowsky. The director of the hospital was Professor Johann Peter Frank; she met his son Joseph. Beethoven knew both of them, and sometimes accompanied Christine when she sang at the musical soirées at the home of Professor Frank. Joseph Frank and Christine Gerhardi fell in love and were married in 1798. Christine was a great admirer of Beethoven, as we can judge from a letter he wrote her in answer to some extravagant verses which "caused me some embarrassment."

At the concert Christine, now Mme. Frank, sang, and so did Magdalene Willmann (of whom we shall speak in the next chapter), and so did the court singer Simoni. The program was even more of a potpourri than the concert in 1800; there were arias, scenes from operas, sonatas, and symphonies; Haydn conducted two of his own symphonies and Beethoven performed once again with Punto. No doubt the concert was a social affair of great splendor and raised a sizable sum. But the *Wiener Zeitung,* announcing it, mentioned only one artist by name: "the famous amateur singer, Frau von Frank." This moved Beethoven to generous anger. He wrote to Christine, urging that in future concerts *all* the artists who were giving their talents should be made known to the public. They deserved this, and besides it was good business, because well-known names attract audiences, and a large audience, after all, was the chief object of such an affair.

Thayer says that whether Beethoven's "remonstrances produced any effect cannot now be ascertained." He seems to have overlooked—and this is rare with Thayer—a news story which appeared on February 7, 1801, in the *Wiener Zeitung,* about a week after the concert, and which gives credit where credit is due exactly as Beethoven wanted it:

> The recently announced musical academy for the benefit of the wounded of the I. R. Army took place on the 30th of January, to the greatest pleasure of all listeners. ... The noble instigator, Frau Christiana v. Frank, born Gerhardi, earned everybody's admiration through the rare excellence of her singing. Herr v. Bethoven [*sic*] played on the pianoforte a sonata authored by him which was accompanied by the horn of Herr Punto. Both completely fulfilled the expectations which the public has come to cherish for the art of these two masters. Frau Galvani and Herr Simoni contributed through their singing as well as Kapell-meister Paer and Conti through the guidance of the orchestra. Finally the great Haydn undertook the direction of two of his symphonies. ... The receipts came to the respectable sum of 9463 gulden, 11 kreuzer.*

These instances will suffice to show Beethoven as an active member of the musical life of the city. Yet the occasions were infrequent enough not to interfere with the solitude of creation.

He did meet new friends. One of these was the famous pianist John Baptist Cramer. Educated in England, he was considered in those years the foremost pianist of Europe. He came to Vienna in 1799 not to give concerts but to learn more about the styles of playing by Viennese pianists and to renew his friendship with Haydn, with whom he had been on good terms in England. Cramer and Beethoven almost immediately took to each other, and in the mastery of the piano one learned from the other.

Beethoven, says Ries, "had praise for but one as being distinguished—John Cramer." Cramer said, "No man in these days has heard extemporary playing unless he has heard Beethoven."

Many years later Thayer interviewed Cramer's widow, who told him:

> "At an Augarten Concert the two pianists were walking together and hearing a performance of Mozart's pianoforte Concerto in C minor (K. 491), Beethoven suddenly stood still and, directing his companion's attention to the exceedingly simple, but equally beautiful motive which is first introduced towards the end of the piece, exclaimed: 'Cramer, Cramer! we shall never be able to do anything like that!' As the theme was repeated and wrought up to the climax, Beethoven,

---

* It was indeed a respectable sum, about the equivalent of $53,000 in today's value.

swaying his body to and fro, marked the time and in every possible manner manifested a delight rising to enthusiasm." (T).

Beethoven's acquaintance with two other important personalities was directly due to the war. After the Treaty of Campo Formio had been signed, the French Directory (which essentially now meant Napoleon) made stiff demands on the Austrians as condition for a renewal of diplomatic relations. They wanted, for example, a national French Palace to be built in Vienna, a national French theater, and the right of jurisdiction over all French citizens living in Austrian lands. Emperor Franz refused. To negotiate the matter, Napoleon sent a handsome young general to Vienna. His name was Jean Baptiste Julius Bernadotte. He was six years older than Beethoven. He arrived in Vienna on February 5, 1798, with a retinue of officials and secretaries the oldest of whom was twenty-five. (Napoleon employed young men for diplomatic careers. Many of their Austrian counterparts were old fogies.)

The Empress was in an advanced stage of pregnancy and gave birth on the first of March. This delayed the ceremony of Bernadotte's presenting his credentials to the Emperor until the second of that month and his public audience until April 8. A foreign minister could neither make nor receive official calls until his reception in Court. Bernadotte occupied himself by living a busy unofficial life. He talked unofficially quite often to the Emperor and the Empress, as well as with many of the aristocracy and with musicians. Conversing in his soft southern French, he spoke of the Revolution and its champions and, most of all, of his idol Bonaparte. They listened fascinated, and he charmed many of the Viennese, even though he was under orders that he was not to recognize "under any pretext, and in the case of any person whatever, any other official rank than that of Citizen."

We may imagine how Lichnowsky or Lobkowitz liked being addressed as "Citizen," in a Vienna where even today everybody has a title and a bookkeeper is called *"Herr Direktor"* by the waiter, who is called *"Herr Ober."* Rasoumovsky disliked Bernadotte, and vice versa. Bernadotte wrote about Rasoumovsky in one of the confidential reports: "A person of broad education, insufferable arrogance, and undue egotism, capable of sacrificing everything, even his family, for the Royal cause." It was well known to the police that Bernadotte received Jacobins and Austrian partisans of the Revolution in his hotel. Just the same, when he went to Court he was petted and admired, and the ladies swooned over his tousled hair and fiery eyes.

The good relations between Bernadotte and the Court did not last long, for Bernadotte had the arrogance to order the French flag hoisted over the façade of his hotel. It was his answer to the announcement that a special festival in honor of the war volunteers of the preceding year was to be held. A mob gathered, jeering and flinging stones. Bernadotte, dressed in full uniform, appeared on the balcony, his hand on the hilt of his sword. "What is this rabble up to?" he screamed. "I shall kill at least six of you." The flag was pulled down and burned on April 13, 1798. The cavalry, stationed at Schönbrunn, was hastily summoned, and the mob was dispersed. Now Bernadotte insisted on immediate satisfaction, refused all orderly investigations, accused Schwarzenberg, Kinsky, Lobkowitz, and Rasoumovsky as being the secret instigators of the riot, and demanded his passport to leave for Paris. Napoleon sent a threatening dispatch: "... But if this influence or individual interests guided the Viennese Chancellery as they seem to have guided the operations of the police on the day of the 24th Germinal,* there would remain for the French nation only one course of action, and that would be to blot out a number of European powers, or to blot out the House of Austria itself." In the end, the scandal was forgotten over graver issues.

While Bernadotte was in Vienna, and while he was still in good standing, he made the acquaintance of Beethoven. They conversed quite often. In Bernadotte's retinue was a violinist two years younger than himself who had already achieved remarkable success. Rodolphe Kreutzer was professor at the Paris Conservatory, concertmaster at the Opéra, and played chamber music for Napoleon. Beethoven met him, they became friendly, Beethoven praising his modesty. Kreutzer had published a collection of French Revolutionary music with which Beethoven was familiar and which included the *Marseillaise,* the *Carmagnole,* and the *Chant du Départ.* Kreutzer must also have discussed the new French composers, Méhul and Cherubini, with citizen Beethoven. Later Beethoven dedicated his Sonata Op. 47 to him, now known as the *Kreutzer Sonata.*

Schindler says that it was Bernadotte ** who suggested to Beethoven the

---

* A date in the French Revolutionary calendar equivalent to about April 14.
** To follow to the end the career of this undiplomatic diplomat, let us note that Bernadotte became one of Napoleon's most trusted friends—for a time at least; the trust turned into suspicion later, as was Napoleon's way—that he was appointed Marshal of France in 1804, that he distinguished himself in the Battle of Wagram in 1809, that he was adopted in 1810 by King Charles XIII of Sweden and Norway with the intention of declaring him his successor, that he did in fact become King under the name of Charles XIV, and that he died long after Beethoven in 1844. In 1823 Beethoven wrote him a letter which recalled their being together in Vienna and which asked him to subscribe to the *Missa Solemnis.* Bernadotte did not do so.

idea of his composing a heroic symphony: "The suggestion was made by the General that Beethoven should honor the greatest hero of the age in a musical composition. The idea soon became a reality which the master, having battled with his political scruples, gave to the world under the title of *Sinfonia Eroica*."

Still another important new friend was Count Franz von Brunsvick. He and his two sisters, Therese and Josephine, entered into so significant a relationship with the composer that we shall postpone the telling of it to the next chapter.

·◦[4]◦·

Then, like a scratch which interrupts the sound of music, like a spiderweb into which one walks unaware, like an inexplicable shadow on a bright day, came the first symptoms of a disability which must in the beginning have mystified and puzzled and frightened Beethoven but which he might have considered as a passing affliction. What was the cause of these periods in which words around him became a babble, conversation unintelligible? How explain, how combat, these moments when sound moved into the distance? Music he could still hear, but sometimes even its sounds became truncated, the high tones disappearing. What was this ringing in his ear? Was this a temporary weakness? The doctors he consulted assured him that it was. Beethoven willingly believed them. Though he often enough exaggerated the ills that his flesh was heir to, though he sometimes magnified "the bad state of his nether region" (diarrhea) or "weakness of the chest" (more or less severe colds), he possessed the natural optimism of the strong human being. He thought he might be cured.

The first signs of his deafness appeared early, when he was but twenty-eight years old. They were signs only, as he wrote to Amenda three years later:

VIENNA, July 1, 1801

... How often would I like to have you here with me, for your B[eethoven] is leading a very unhappy life and is at variance with Nature and his Creator. Many times already I have cursed Him for exposing His creatures to the slightest hazard, so that the most beautiful blossom is thereby often crushed and destroyed. Let me tell you that my most prized possession, *my hearing,* has greatly deteriorated. When you were still with me, I already felt the symptoms; but I said nothing about them. Now they have become very much worse. We must wait and see whether my hearing can be restored. The symptoms are said to be caused by the condition of my abdomen.* So far as the latter is concerned, I

---

* "Abdomen" is Anderson's translation of the word *"Unterleib,"* "lower body," which Beethoven uses here and in the subsequent letter to Wegeler.

am almost quite cured. But that my hearing too will improve, I must hope, it is true, but I hardly think it possible, for diseases of that kind are the most difficult to cure.

Further in the same letter:

Yes, Amenda, if after six months my disease proves to be incurable, then I shall claim your sympathy, then you must give up everything and come to me. I shall then travel (when I am playing and composing, my affliction still hampers me least; it affects me most when I am in company) and you must be my companion. I am convinced that my luck will not forsake me. Why, at the moment I feel equal to anything. Since your departure I have been composing all types of music, except operas and sacred works. I feel sure you will not refuse my request; I know that you will help your friend to bear his troubles and his infirmity. My pianoforte playing too has considerably improved; and I hope that our tour will perhaps enable you to make your fortune as well; and then you will stay with me for ever—I have safely received all your letters. Although I have replied to them so seldom, yet you have always been present in my thoughts; and my heart beats just as tenderly for you as ever.—*I beg you to treat what I have told you about my hearing as a great secret to be entrusted to no one, whoever he may be—*   (A-53).

Two days before this letter, he had written to Wegeler. To him he gave further details, not only because Wegeler was the older and more intimate friend, but also because he was a physician and could hold an opinion about the treatment Beethoven was being given. He told Wegeler that when they would meet again he would notice that his friend Beethoven had become "a first-rate fellow; not only as an artist but also as a man you will find me better and more fully developed." But . . .

VIENNA, June 29, 1801

. . . But that jealous demon, my wretched health, has put a nasty spoke in my wheel; and it amounts to this, that for the last three years my hearing has become weaker and weaker. The trouble is supposed to have been caused by the condition of my abdomen which, as you know, was wretched even before I left Bonn, but has become worse in Vienna where I have been constantly afflicted with diarrhea and have been suffering in consequence from an extraordinary debility. Frank tried to *tone up* my constitution with strengthening medicines and my hearing with almond oil, but much good did it do me! His treatment had no effect, my deafness became even worse and my abdomen continued to be in the same state as before. Such was my condition until the autumn of last year; and sometimes I gave way to despair. Then a medical asinus advised me to take cold baths to improve my condition. A more sensible doctor, however, prescribed the usual tepid baths in the Danube. The result was miraculous; and my inside improved. But my deafness persisted or, I should say, became even worse. During the last winter I was truly wretched, for I had really dreadful attacks of colic and again relapsed completely into my former condition. And thus I remained until about four weeks ago when I went to see *Vering*. For I began to think that my condition demanded the attention of a surgeon as well; and in any case I had confidence in him. Well, he succeeded in checking almost completely this violent diarrhea. He prescribed tepid baths in the Danube, to which I had always to add a bottle of strengthening ingredients. He ordered no medicines until about four days ago when he prescribed pills for my stomach and an infusion for my ear. As a result I have been feeling, I may say, stronger and better; but my ears continue to hum and buzz day and night. I must confess that I lead a miserable life. For almost two years I have ceased to attend any social functions, just because I find it impossible to say to people: I am deaf. If I had any other profession I might be able to cope with my infirmity; but in my profession it is a terrible handicap. And if my enemies, of whom I have a fair number, were to hear about it, what would they say? — In order to give you some idea of this strange deafness, let me tell you that in the theater I have to place myself close to the orchestra in order to understand what the actor is saying, and that at a distance I cannot hear the high notes of instruments or voices. As for the spoken voice it is surprising that some people have never noticed my deafness; but since I have always been liable to fits of absent-mindedness, they attribute my hardness of hearing to that. Sometimes too I can scarcely hear a person who speaks softly; I can hear sounds, it is true, but cannot make out the words. But if anyone shouts, I can't bear it. Heaven alone knows what is to become of me. *Vering tells me that my hearing will certainly improve, although my deafness may not be completely cured.* — Already I have often cursed my Creator and my existence. *Plutarch* has shown me *the path of resignation*. If it is at all possible, I will bid defiance to my fate, although I feel that as long as I live there will be moments when I shall be God's most unhappy creature — I beg you not to say anything about my condition to any one, not even to *Lorchen;* I am only telling you this as a secret; but I should like you to correspond with *Vering* about it. If my trouble persists, I will visit you next spring. You will rent a house for me in some beautiful part of the country and then for six months I will lead the life of a peasant. Perhaps that will make a difference. Resignation, what a wretched resource! Yet it is all that is left to me. ... (A-51).

At the end of the letter, he sends affectionate greetings to Eleonore and to Hélène von Breuning. "Tell her 'that I still have now and then a raptus.' "

The two physicians mentioned here were both eminent men, though medicine had not advanced to the point of producing many specialists in otology. We have met Dr. Johann Peter Frank, director of the General Hospital of Vienna, in connection with the concert of 1801. Obviously he believed in the theory developed in the 18th century of treatment by *Tonus,* toning up the system. Dr. Gerhard von Vering held no less a position than that of the Emperor's staff surgeon. His daughter, Julia, who was then a child of ten years, became a fine pianist and married Stephan von Breuning in 1808. Before her death, only a year after the marriage, Beethoven dedicated to her his own arrangement of his Violin Concerto as a piano concerto.

It is certain that the doctors consulted by Beethoven were the best men Vienna had to offer. Yet to modern medical ears the treatment that Dr. Vering prescribed sounds like a piece of quackery. He applied a vesicatory ointment to both arms, a substance made from the seed of the daphne plant (*daphne mezereum*) that acts as a counterirritant and is capable of producing blisters. What such a treatment could possibly have to do with an intestinal disorder or with deafness is difficult to understand.*

After reading Beethoven's letter of June 29, Wegeler must have written again to ask how Beethoven was getting along and what remedies he was trying. The letter is not extant. On November 16 Beethoven replied:

> Well, it is an extremely unpleasant treatment inasmuch as for a few days (until the bark has drawn sufficiently) I am always deprived of the free use of my arms, not to mention the pain I have to suffer. True enough, I cannot deny it, the humming and buzzing is slightly less than it used to be, particularly in my left ear, where my deafness really began. But so far my hearing is certainly not a bit better; and I am inclined to think, although I do not dare to say so definitely, that it is a little weaker—The condition of my abdomen is improving, and especially when I have taken tepid baths for a few days I feel pretty well for eight or even ten days afterwards. I very rarely take a tonic for my stomach and, if so, only one dose. But following your advice I am now beginning to apply *herbs to my belly*—Vering won't hear of my taking shower baths. On the whole I am not at all satisfied with him. He takes far too little interest in and trouble with a complaint of this kind. I should never see him unless I went to his house, which is very inconvenient for me—What is your opinion of Schmidt?   (A-54).

Beethoven was dissatisfied with his physician. How often during his lifetime did he become distrustful, how often did he exchange one medical regimen for another, only to follow neither! Now he complains that Vering takes too little interest and asks for Wegeler's opinion of Johann Adam Schmidt, a physician

---

* A current medical opinion: "It was a treatment commonly called counteractive in the old days. This was much like a mustard plaster which produced a burning sensation and a blister sometimes, or the Chinese acupuncture which is simply puncturing the skin with a needle to set up an irritation. This process was not exactly quackery, but served the purpose, no doubt, to draw blood to the surface of the body and also to draw the attention away from the complaint. If the diarrhea was in any way psychosomatic, it might have worked. Surely it would not influence the deafness."—Dr. Morris Fishbein, from a letter in response to my query.

with a great reputation. He was a professor of anatomy at the Josephinum, the medical school for army doctors. Wasn't he, asks Beethoven in the same letter, a much more progressive man, more conversant with the latest discoveries? Beethoven mentions miraculous cures through the use of "galvanism." Luigi Galvani had announced this discovery in 1791, observing a current of what he called "animal electricity" in frogs' legs.* Beethoven tells Wegeler that he heard that in Berlin a deaf-and-dumb child recovered his hearing and a man who had been deaf for seven years recovered his, all through galvanism. So he casts about for some kind of treatment by electricity, after the counterirritants and the tonics.

Yet, while desperately seeking a cure and turning from a Frank to a Vering to a Schmidt and to the absent Wegeler, he does in the same letter sound a note of courage, of happiness almost:

> I am now leading a slightly more pleasant life, for I am mixing more with my fellow creatures. You would find it hard to believe what an empty, sad life I have had for the last two years. My poor hearing haunted me everywhere like a ghost; and I avoided—all human society. I seemed to be a misanthrope and yet am far from being one. This change has been brought about by a dear charming girl who loves me and whom I love. After two years I am again enjoying a few blissful moments; and for the first time I feel that—marriage might bring me happiness. Unfortunately she is not of my class—and at the moment—I certainly could not marry—I must still bustle about a good deal. Had it not been for my deafness, I should have long ago traveled half the world over; and that I must do—For to me there is no greater pleasure than to practice and exercise my art.

It was not only love which lightened his burden. There came to him at this time a marvelous courage. The will to succeed, the drive to create, the self-assurance and the pride, the conviction that he had something important to give the world, the egotism of the great artist, the clear realization that he was maturing and growing—all these were stronger than the demon hammering in his ears. He uttered the famous words, "I will seize Fate by the throat," and flung out the challenge, "It shall certainly not bend and crush me completely." Perhaps these are a young man's romantic words. They are—but they are as well the words of a man whose heart and brain were filled with valor. Beethoven was virtuous in the sense that Montaigne defined it: "The strongest, most generous, and proud-

---

* The theory was eventually proved false, the true explanation being furnished by Alessandro Volta.

est of all virtues is true courage." Of course his courage was not steadfast. There were many black times. There were the worst of times when he cursed his fate and spewed his anger out on his friends. Moments he did have, though rare, in which he entertained the thought of suicide. Bitter and resentful he often appeared. Yet nothing could debilitate that strength which carried him to the fulfillment of his genius. He was ready, then and later, to "embrace the whole world," words which echo Schiller's words he set to music. Here is the relevant passage from the November letter to Wegeler:

> Oh, if only I could be rid of it [my present affliction] I would embrace the whole world—My youth, yes, I feel it, is only just beginning, for was I not always a sickly fellow? For some time now my physical strength has been increasing more and more, and therefore my mental powers also. Every day brings me nearer to the goal which I feel but cannot describe. And it is only in that condition that your Beethoven can live. There must be no rest—I know of none but sleep, and indeed I am heartily sorry that I must now give more time to sleep than I used to do. If only I can be partially liberated from my affliction, then—I will come to you as a complete and mature man, and renew our old feelings of friendship. You will find me as happy as I am fated to be on this earth, not unhappy—no, that I could not bear—I will seize Fate by the throat; it shall certainly not bend and crush me completely—Oh, it would be so lovely to live a thousand lives—No indeed, I realize now that I am no longer suited to a quiet life—Do write to me as soon as possible.

At the *Stefanskirche* there was a priest, Peter Weiss, who had accomplished "many fortunate cures" (Schindler) of deafness. He was not merely a faith healer; he understood the physiology of the ear. Beethoven went to him at the suggestion of Zmeskall. The story is given in the so-called Fischhoff Manuscript: *

> Herr v. Zmeskall with great difficulty persuaded Beethoven to go there with him. At first he followed the advice of the physician; but as he had to go to him every day in order to have a fluid dropped into his ear, this grew unpleasant, the more since, in his impatience, he felt little or no improvement; and he remained away. The physician, questioned by Zmeskall, told him the facts, and Zmeskall

---

* This is a collection of some sixty pages comprising miscellaneous biographical material, including some personal recollections of Zmeskall. The material was left to Beethoven's nephew and after his death to Karl's widow. She gave the greater part of the collection to an unknown person who sold it for his own gain. The material was lost. Fortunately one of Karl's guardians, Jakob Hotschevar, had copied it previous to its disappearance. The copy came into the possession of Joseph Fischhoff, a professor in the Vienna Conservatory of Music. It is a valuable source, though as Thayer has pointed out, the manuscript must be regarded as secondhand information; it was edited and censored.

begged him to accommodate himself to the self-willed invalid, and consult his convenience. The priest, honestly desirous to help Beethoven, went to his lodgings, but his efforts were in vain, inasmuch as Beethoven in a few days refused him entrance, and thus neglected possible help or at least an amelioration of his condition.   (TQ).

Eighteen years later, being once again dissatisfied with another physician's treatment, he returned to the priest. But he grew impatient and skeptical again and gave it all up.

·⊰[5]⊱·

Most people imagine that suddenly a curtain fell and Beethoven could no longer hear. His companions are supposed to have shouted at him through ear trumpets—most of us have seen pictures of these naïve instruments—but it was no use; he was stone deaf. That is not a correct picture.

Beethoven's deafness was not a soundproof curtain. It was a veil of varying opacity at varying times. Sometimes, even rather late in life, he could hear well enough. He was severely—not to say totally—deaf only in the last eight to ten years. Some hearing remained as late as 1814 and possibly even as late as 1818, when he was forty-eight years old. In those later years he still attempted to lead rehearsals and conduct performances.

The state of his hearing was influenced by the general state of his health. Perhaps the weather had something to do with it. Obviously, there were differences in clarity of diction of the men and women with whom he was conversing; some voices are more easily understood than others. One suspects that his hearing was influenced also by his interest or lack of it in his interlocutor or the subject at hand. The testimony of friends and visitors is conflicting. Some said that one had to speak directly into his left ear; some said the right. Those who wished to give a pathetic portrait of the unfortunate man wrote that he could hear nothing or hardly anything. Ries recalled a time as early as 1802:

> I called his attention to a shepherd who was blowing the flute ... quite charmingly in the woods. Beethoven could not hear anything for half an hour, and though I assured him repeatedly that I too could hear nothing more (which was not the truth), he became extraordinarily silent and morose.

On the other hand, Czerny remembered about his visit in 1800 that Beethoven gave no sign of being deaf. As late as 1817 Beethoven asked Streicher whether he could adjust one of the pianos he manufactured "as loud as possible," suitable for "my weakened hearing." So he could hear something. He played the piano as late as 1814 in public—in the Trio in B-flat Major, Op. 97. The composer Louis Spohr happened to be in Beethoven's rooms at one of the rehearsals:

> It was hardly a treat, for in the first place the piano was badly out of tune, which did not bother Beethoven much, since he could not hear it; and second, because of his deafness, hardly anything was left of the virtuosity of the artist who had formerly been so greatly admired. The poor deaf man—in *forte* passages he pounded so that the strings jingled, and in *piano* he played so softly that whole phrases were unheard.

Yet in the same year Schindler reports that he successfully conducted the complicated *Battle Symphony*. Not quite so, another witness remembered. There was a second conductor standing behind him who really gave the beat.

We must make a distinction between his ability to hear words * and his ability to hear music. The first he lost sooner than the second. It is probable that he could "hear" music by feeling its vibrations. In the Beethoven House a wooden stick is preserved which Beethoven may have used by holding it between his teeth while he touched strings on the piano.

The diagnosis of the cause of his deafness remains uncertain. Many essays have been penned by medical authorities, but no agreement exists. As late as 1964 the *Zeitschrift für Laryngologie, Rhinologie, Otologie* in Stuttgart published a new analysis. Dr. A. Laskiewicz writes that his diagnosis is *"neuritis acoustica* after typhoid fever . . . smallpox, repeated headcolds and influenza." To the layman this rather sounds as if Beethoven was deaf because he was deaf.

Whether the degeneration was due to an illness in the year 1796 caused by Beethoven's coming home on a hot summer day, disrobing down to his trousers, and cooling himself in a draft at the open window (very improbable), or worsened in 1810 by Beethoven's throwing himself in a rage on the ground (unbelievable), or by a typhoid infection (not proved), or by a venereal infection (to be discussed later), the certainty remains that we have no certainty.

It was a bitter fate. Who can read without sorrow the story of the *Fidelio*

---

* The famous interview with Major General Alexander Kyd, which will be related in due time and which took place in 1810, suggests that a lively conversation took place in that year.

revival in 1822 which Schindler tells, and probably tells truthfully because, after all, he was there? The question was whether Beethoven should take over the conducting of the performance:

> We all advised against it, in fact we pleaded with him to resist his own desires and to remember the difficulties that had attended the concert in the University auditorium as long ago as 1819, and again at the Josephstadt Theater perform-ance. After several days of indecision, he finally declared his readiness to conduct the work, a deplorable decision on many counts. At his request I accompanied him to the dress rehearsal. The E-major overture went perfectly, for despite several hesitations on the part of their leader, the bold army of the orchestra moved in their customary disciplined ranks. But in the very first number, the duet between Marzelline and Jacquino, it was apparent that Beethoven could hear nothing of what was happening on the stage. He seemed to be fighting to hold back. The orchestra stayed with him but the singers pressed on, and at the point where knocking is heard at the prison door, everything fell apart. Umlauf [the other conductor] told the musicians to stop without telling the master the reason. After a few minutes' discussion with the singers, the order was given: *da capo*. The duet began again and as before the disunity was noticeable, and again at the knocking there was general confusion. Again the musicians were stopped.
> The impossibility of continuing under the direction of the creator of the work was obvious. But who was to tell him, and how? Neither the manager, Duport, nor Umlauf wanted to have to say, "It cannot be done. Go away, you unhappy man!" Beethoven, now growing apprehensive, turned from one side to another, searching the faces to see what was interrupting the rehearsal. All were silent. Then he called me to him. I stepped to his side in the orchestra and he handed me his notebook motioning for me to write down what was wrong. I wrote as fast as I could something like "Please don't go on. I'll explain at home." He jumped down on to the floor and said only, "Let's get out of here." Without stopping he hastened to his apartment in Pfarrgasse in the suburb of Laimgrube. Once there he threw himself on the sofa, covered his face with both hands, and remained so until we went to dinner.   (S).

Yet our sympathies must not lead us astray from the facts. In 1822, at that moment, it *was* complete deafness; but for many years before, he was intermit-tently deaf, or perhaps only hard-of-hearing. For a long period after he wrote the letters to Wegeler and Amenda, Beethoven still contemplated a career as executant musician. He was hopeful and he was not. He was patient one moment and wildly rebellious the next. "To be forced to become a philosopher when one is only twenty-eight years old—it is hard," he wrote. He did attain a philosophy of a sort, but the "resignation" which he mentions so often did not come to him until the last period in his life. Perhaps it is fortunate that this is so; it is fortunate that he did not enter the state of nirvana, that he did *not* free himself from passion, desire, and suffering until he had run the obstacle course of the human condition and had expressed that condition in music. When he soliloquized (in 1810), "For you, poor Beethoven, no happiness exists from without; you have to create everything for yourself, you can find friends only in an ideal world"; and similarly (in 1812), "Happiness for you no longer exists, except in yourself, in your art. You are not permitted to be a man, not for yourself, only for others," he was contradicted by his actions. He did not abdicate as a man. He was not a peaceful anchorite. He was then—and later— very much of a man in this, the un-ideal world.

He must have occasionally wearied his friends with jeremiads; contact with him must often have proved a chore. Yet the life-force within him was so strong that few abandoned him. He himself did not abandon life. The clouds did not forever hang on him, nor did he refuse to cast his nighted color off. He was often cheerful—there is general agreement on this point—and sometimes boisterously so. "Oh, it is so beautiful to live life a thousand-fold," were his words.

The theory has often been advanced that his deafness turned out to be a boon to art, that Beethoven, no longer able to play the piano or conduct orchestras, could spend more time and thought on composition; that because he was shut out from so much of the world, he was able to deepen and ennoble his work. The curse was a blessing for posterity. Let me say, with all due modesty, that I do not believe in this theory. I think he would have grown equally had he been in full possession of his ears and had his "lower body" been in perfect working order at all times. He was not only one of the great thinkers in the realm of art but he was one of those artists who arrive at greatness through inner compulsion. His outer fate was not as significant as his inner life. The blessing would have come with or without the curse. The nine symphonies would have been composed had Beethoven been surrounded by a wife and six rosy children, had he been as worldly as Goethe or as healthy as Verdi.

Lest the recital of his suffering tempt us to see him in the fellowship of saints, let us shift the mood by recalling an episode in which he appears in a fractious role:

It happened in the summer of 1800, which Beethoven spent in Unter-Döbling. There was a farmer living in a house near him who had a rather unsavory reputation, but also a daughter who was remarkably good-looking. She, too, was no model of virtue. Beethoven was attracted by her and on his walks used to stop to look at her while she worked in the farmyard. She did not return the compliment and only laughed at his admiration. Presently the father engaged in a brawl, there was a public disturbance, and the man was imprisoned. Beethoven stood up for the farmer, and though he was in no way concerned in the matter, he insisted on going to court to obtain his release. Naturally the local magistrate took a dim view of such meddling, whereupon Beethoven became angry, shouted, and used abusive language. He would have been arrested had it not been for the intervention of his powerful friends.

Beethoven was highly susceptible to the female face and figure.

Letter to the "Immortal Beloved." The first and last pages (State Library, Berlin).

CHAPTER 11

THE WOMEN
IN BEETHOVEN'S LIFE

···✷[1]✷···

Compared to what we know of other famous composers, we know very little of Beethoven's involvements with women. The paradox is extraordinary, indeed unique; in the biography of a man whose most casual everyday missives have been preserved; whose ephemeral word dropped at the dinner table was immediately caught in the hands of an eager disciple and fixed piously on a sheet of paper (thereby often unduly magnifying its importance); whose tastes in wine and song and poetry and prose have been recorded; with whose business dealings we are familiar; a man who left us, though unwillingly, the details of the sorry stratagems by which he tried to capture a child who could fill the empty spot in a paternal heart; an artist who—rarity of rarities!—occasionally afforded us a glimpse into the workshop—in all that topography of fact and impression, there is one swamp which offers no firm foothold to the steps of the explorer. How many biographers have ventured into the quagmire and yet nobody is certain as to who, when, where were the women important in Beethoven's love life, or how deeply they intertwined his existence! We do know the names of women who in one way or another are linked with Beethoven. More than names, we know much biographical detail about them. Yet in no case—not one—are we sure that the normal love relationship between a man and a woman existed. We know he loved. Was his love ever fully reciprocated, was it ever consummated?

We know much about Haydn's cantankerous wife, and the consolation he found in Luigia Polzelli at Ezterhaza and later with the comely and complaisant widow in England, Johanna Schroeter. We know a good deal about the strong sexual attraction which Constanze exercised over Mozart, the "indiscretion" he confessed to her, their jealousies, his dalliances. Through Richard Wagner's life treads a pageant of caryatids from Minna Planer to Mathilde Wesendonk to Cosima Bülow to Judith Gautier, on whose bosom he sobbed when he was a man of sixty-three. Wagner's affairs are copiously documented, not least by the ladies involved.

But Beethoven? We have contradictory tales, witnesses who merely hint, a few obscure letters by himself, a partially dated, unaddressed, and volcanic letter to the "Immortal Beloved," a suggestion of a "Distant Beloved" (*"Die Ferne Geliebte"*), mumbled memories, a scrap or two of ungracious remarks, a little scandal-mongering, shadowy references which can be, and have been, interpreted one way or another. Little more. In vain do we search for straightforwardness, simple fact, plain admission. No woman has said in so many words, "Yes, I loved Beethoven and was his." No woman has stated directly, "Beethoven loved me." Yes—one did, but she was a notorious liar.

Even during Beethoven's lifetime contradictory tales about his love life were told, to proliferate after his death. The list of his inamoratae is either long or short, depending on who is compiling the list. As to the "Immortal Beloved," there are at least seven candidates for the recipient of that enigmatic cry.

Why all the mystery? Beethoven himself is responsible for most of it; the social position of the women to whom he opened his heart may be responsible for a little of it, the trend of the times could be adduced in explaining the silence, and lastly his most important biographer cannot be declared entirely guiltless of obfuscation.

Taking the last point first, let me say that there never existed a biographer more accurate or honest than Alexander Wheelock Thayer. Making the biography of Beethoven his life's work, he amassed the facts industriously, he sifted them carefully, and he told the truth. But Thayer was a New Englander, a "proper Bostonian" (though not born in Boston proper), and he lived in Victorian times, when one did not freely discuss a man's sex life. The internal evidence of Thayer's *Life* suggests more than once that he suppressed certain facts in his possession and was purposely vague about others. This suppression has been noted by several scholars, including Ernest Newman. Let some passages from the book illustrate Thayer's attitude:

> Beethoven was no exception to the general rule, that men of genius delight in warm and lasting friendships with women of superior minds and culture—not meaning those "conquests" which, according to Wegeler, even during his first three years in Vienna, "he occasionally made, which if not impossible for many

an Adonis would still have been difficult." Let such matters, even if detail concerning them were now attainable, be forgotten.

Spending his whole life in a state of society in which the vow of celibacy was by no means a vow of chastity; in which the parentage of a cardinal's or archbishop's children was neither a secret nor a disgrace; in which the illegitimate offspring of princes and magnates were proud of their descent and formed upon it well-grounded hopes of advancement and success in life; in which the moderate gratification of the sexual was no more discountenanced than the satisfying of any other natural appetite—it is nonsense to suppose, that, under such circumstances, Beethoven could have puritanic scruples on that point. Those who have had occasion and opportunity to ascertain the facts, know that he had not, and are also aware that he did not always escape the common penalties of transgressing the laws of strict purity. But he had too much dignity of character ever to take part in scenes of low debauchery, or even when still young to descend to the familiar jesting once so common between tavern girls and the guests. Thus, as the elder Simrock related, upon the journey to Mergentheim recorded in the earlier pages of this work, it happened at some place where the company dined, that some of the young men prompted the waiting-girl to play off her charms upon Beethoven. He received her advances and familiarities with repellent coldness; and as she, encouraged by the others, still persevered, he lost his patience, and put an end to her importunities by a smart box on the ear.*

Aside from retelling a story which does little credit either to young Beethoven's chivalry or his sense of humor, Thayer does not specify who were the ones "who have had occasion and opportunity to ascertain the facts" (was it he, himself?), nor what were the "common penalties" which Beethoven did not always escape. After another paragraph, he continues:

The names of two married women might here be given, to whom at a later period Beethoven was warmly attached; names which have hitherto escaped the eyes of literary scavengers, and are therefore here suppressed. Certain of his friends used to joke him about these ladies, and it is certain that he rather enjoyed their jests even when the insinuations, that his affection was beyond the limit of the Platonic, were somewhat broad; but careful enquiry has failed to elicit any evidence that even in these cases he proved unfaithful to his principles.

If that was so, why did Thayer not give the names of the two married women? Thayer includes some reminiscences written by Dr. Alois Weissenbach,

---

* Both excerpts from the chapter "Beethoven's Friends and Fellow Musicians."

surgeon and author, who met Beethoven in 1814, enjoyed a brief acquaintance with him, and admired him enormously. In his book, *My Journey to the Vienna Congress,** Weissenbach wrote: "As to the sin of lust—he is unspotted." Thayer comments: "Remarks [by Weissenbach] follow upon Beethoven's ignorance of the value of money, of the absolute purity of his morals (which unfortunately is not true), and of the irregularity of his life." **

"Which unfortunately is not true"—there Thayer drops the hot coal! ***

There is evidence of a further suppression by Thayer which will be discussed when we consider the question of whether Beethoven did or did not suffer from a venereal disease. Suffice it to say here that Thayer's delicacy seems to have prevented him from telling us all he knew.

Why did the women keep silent? Wouldn't you think that a woman would gladly proclaim her love to the world? That she would boast of an intimacy with the famous man? That she would seek the opportunity to have her name inscribed in the diary of history? That to charm Beethoven would be considered an achievement which would far outweigh any moral censure? There is a possible explanation: Wegeler says that "so far as I know, every one of his sweethearts belonged to the higher social stations." They were all members of the nobility; not, of course, because Beethoven was a snob, but because the nobility was the circle in which he moved. One needs to think oneself back into Austrian ways and customs in the early 19th century to understand how wide was the cleft between the aristocrat and the commoner, particularly if the commoner was a man and the aristocrat a woman. That Beethoven was offered respect, friendship, admiration—even adoration as an artist—by titled ladies does not negate the fact: she would hardly confess an affair with a man not of her station, though he were a Beethoven.

Besides, there now sneaked into social life a hypocrisy which was a waste-product of Romanticism. The free, frank sexual roguishness of the 18th century gave way to pretense. The erotic impulse was hidden under high-flown poetizing. The gasconades of the French novelists were replaced by sentimental tales

---

* It was a very popular book. Beethoven read it. (1816.)
** These comments are omitted from the current (Forbes) edition of the Thayer book; they are included in the three-volume edition edited by Krehbiel, Chapter XV, Vol. II.
*** Ernest Newman wrote in *The Unconscious Beethoven:* "The words 'which unfortunately is not true,' coming from Thayer, are significant. Thayer was the last man in the world to wish to dwell upon the failings of Beethoven; when he permits himself a reference to them it is with no malicious desire to reduce the great composer to the ordinary level of mankind, but purely and simply from a conviction that the biographer's duty is to speak the truth and nothing but the truth. Speaking the whole truth is a different matter."

by German authors who conjured up virtues which were not there. The trend eventually led in England to Victorian cant and in Germany to the ideal of the blond maiden with the golden tresses whose place was in the home and whose motto, according to Wilhelm II, was *"Kaiser, Kinder, Kirche, und Küche."* (Emperor, Children, Church, and Kitchen.) Promiscuity may have been just as widespread, but it pullulated under cover. In the years of Beethoven's manhood there sprang up in Germany "Associations of Virtue" (*Tugendbunde*); they shouted phrases both of patriotism and morality. The double standard was strongly upheld in the early 1800's: men could enjoy themselves away from the marital bedroom, but if a woman were to do so she needed to conceal her action, or face social ostracism. The women Beethoven knew were not women who would proclaim a passion publicly.

But it is Beethoven himself who is the chief author of the concealment. In love he is secretive, sensitively silent, equivocal when he does confess. At times one almost has the impression that he is playing games with the curiosity of his friends. Yet love was not a game to him. It was serious—serious in delight, hope, disappointment, inquietude.

"Uncertainty" is the word to describe Beethoven's search for love. That proud heart needed love, needed it very much, and sought it often. But when he did find it, he sooner or later turned away as if in fear. He could not bind himself. It was not the practical difficulties, not the social status of the woman, not his deafness, his illnesses, nor his disorderly household which wholly prevented lasting attachments or marriage plans; but an inner hesitancy, as if he were loath to give love house-room in his heart, letting it share the lodging with music. Perhaps he never found the right woman. More likely he subconsciously did not want to find her. He flamed high, but the flames died down quickly.

Even after he must have known that there was no cure for his deafness he did not renounce love. "And what love can do, that dares love attempt"—he marked the passage in *Romeo and Juliet,* which was one of his favorite plays. Certainly he was not a misogynist. He wrote Ries that he was not a *Weiberfeind,* an enemy of women. In the same letter (May 8, 1816) he writes, "Unfortunately I have no wife." He implies that he found only one woman whom he wanted to marry but "whom no doubt I shall *never possess."* But again he is being mysterious: he does not tell Ries who she is.

Sexually he was a normally constituted man with a normal man's appetite. He was attracted to women both sensually and spiritually. Women were attracted to him. No doubt he showed them the best of his nature, his nobility and the deep sweetness which they heard in his music and his improvisations. In addition to Wegeler's statement about his "several conquests," we have the statement of Dr. Andreas Bertolini, his friend and physician from 1806 to 1816, who wrote that Beethoven was generally involved in one entanglement or another "from which he did not always escape unscathed" (. . . *daneben miselte er auch gewöhnlich, wobei er nicht immer gut wegkam*. The word *"miseln,"* used by Goethe, was a fashionable expression of the times, its meaning being stronger than "flirting" and weaker than "having an affair."). "The truth as I learned to know it"—once more it is Wegeler speaking—"and also my brother-in-law Stephan von Breuning, Ferdinand Ries, and Bernhard Romberg [cellist and a colleague of Beethoven in the Bonn orchestra] is that there was never a time when Beethoven was not in love, and that in the highest degree."

Further testimony, from Ferdinand Ries: "Beethoven loved to see women, particularly pretty youthful faces; and usually when we passed a reasonably charming girl on the street, he turned around, looked at her sharply through his glasses, and laughed or grimaced if he saw that I had observed him. Once when I teased him with the conquest of a beautiful lady, he confessed that she was the one who attracted him the strongest and the longest, that is, fully seven months." *

Gerhard von Breuning once overheard a conversation between his parents: How was it, his mother asked, that Beethoven could please women, since he was neither handsome nor elegant? His father answered: And yet he always had success with women.

The testimony, however, is not unanimous. In addition to Weissenbach's, we have the positive statement of Ignaz von Seyfried in his *Beethoven Studies* (1832): "Beethoven was never married, and curiously enough he never had a love affair." In 1823 a young journalist, Johann Chrysostomus Sporschill, approached Beethoven and no doubt as a result of several conversations (Sporschill's name appears several times in the Conversation Books) he wrote an article for the *Stuttgarter Morgenblatt für gebildete Stände* ("Stuttgart Morning Paper for the Educated Classes"—what a name for a newspaper!) in which he assured his readers, "Toward women he harbors a tender respect, and his feelings for them are of virginal purity." The whole article is fulsome, indicative of the general climate. Nevertheless, could this be true? Could Beethoven

---

* F. G. Wegeler and Ferdinand Ries, *op. cit.*

have lived and died a virgin? Or could he have stilled his sexual appetite only in the most transient and casual ways? Neither extreme seems likely. One of the friends and confidants of his last years, Karl Holz, did write that Beethoven expressed himself to him by saying that he long regretted when the "miserable necessity" of his body seduced him to do something which was contrary to his better nature. But the matter is couched in such vague terms that we cannot be sure what Beethoven meant. In the Fischhoff Manuscript there is a copy of an entry in Beethoven's journal which reads: "Sensual pleasure without uniting of souls is and remains bestial; after it there remains no trace of noble sentiment, regret only." Was this written after an actual experience? Again we cannot be sure. Schuppanzigh, relates Holz, on one occasion "took Beethoven to a girl after a convivial evening. Afterward it was weeks before he could appear again at Beethoven's."

One bridles at some words that Beethoven wrote in a Conversation Book when Schindler and he were discussing Giulietta Guicciardi: "And if I had wished to give my vital powers with that life, what would have remained for the nobler, the better [life]?" One must find an excuse for Beethoven for that ungallant conversation by saying that a disappointed lover (now fifty-three years old) was reminiscing. Unattractive too are other of his moralistic words and actions. Schindler says that he broke off a friendly relationship with a distinguished composer and conductor, hardly returning his greetings, for no other reason than that the man was having an affair with another man's wife. Otto Jahn, Mozart's biographer, tells the story that Beethoven refused to play in the presence of a Madame Hofdemel, and only the urgent entreaties of the Czerny family made him change his mind. The reason for the refusal was the generally current story that the lady had had an affair with Mozart, as a result of which her husband had made an attempt on her life and then committed suicide. (Jahn stated that the story was false; Mozart was innocent.)

Illuminating, too, is the episode with Marie Bigot. She was the wife of M. Bigot de Moroges, who was Rasoumovsky's librarian. She came to Vienna in 1804 and became friendly with Haydn, Beethoven, and Salieri. She was not only an adorable-looking young woman but a superb pianist, and the old Haydn, who liked a pretty face, said to her when she played his music, "My dear child, I did not write this music — it is you who composed it." Upon the printed sheet from which she had played, he wrote, "On February 20, 1805, Joseph Haydn was happy." Beethoven too was enraptured by her playing: when she played a new sonata of his, he said, "That was not exactly my idea of how I wanted this piece played. If it is not altogether I, it is better than I." * One fine day (March 4, 1807) Beethoven invited Marie Bigot for a drive in the country, the weather being "divinely beautiful." He wrote: "As Bigot has presumably gone out already, we cannot take him with us, of course." All the same she must not refuse:

> It would be quite alien to the outlook of our so enlightened and cultured Marie
> if for the sake of mere scruples she were to rob me of my greatest pleasure —
> (A-138).

If she were not to accept, he would interpret this as "distrust of my character." Her baby Caroline, Beethoven suggested, could be wrapped up from head to foot and taken along.

Marie Bigot refused the invitation. Something must have happened that day or the next: probably the husband saw the letter, or Marie showed it to him and, his jealousy aroused, he may have pointed out to Beethoven that his attentions to his wife were somewhat too enthusiastic. The admiration of a seventy-five-year-old Haydn was a different matter from going for a drive with the thirty-seven-year-old Beethoven. The following day Beethoven wrote the husband a very excited letter in which he protests that he feels "very much hurt," the slight being dealt by "the *dearest people* I have met since I left my native town," an obvious exaggeration of the moment. Shortly after, he sends a very long letter to *both* of them in which he says that he has been "made to realize that the purest and most innocent feelings can often be misunderstood ..."

> Besides, it is one of my chief principles *never to be in any other relationship
> than that of friendship with the wife of another man. For I should not wish by
> forming any other kind of relationship to fill my heart with distrust of that
> woman who some day will perhaps share my fate* — and thus by my own action
> to destroy the loveliest and purest relationship — Possibly once or twice I did
> indulge with Bigot in some jokes which were not quite refined. But I myself
> told you that sometimes I am very naughty — I am extremely natural with all my
> friends and I hate any kind of constraint. Now I count Bigot among my friends;
> and if something about me annoys him, friendship demands that both of you
> should tell me so — and I will certainly take care not to offend him again — But
> how can our kind Marie put such an evil construction on my actions? —

---

* For her remarkable feat in playing the *Appassionata* from manuscript see page 376.

He closes:

> For *never, never* will you find me dishonorable. Since my childhood I have learned to love virtue—and everything beautiful and good—Indeed you have hurt me very deeply—But your action will only serve to strengthen our friendship more and more—I am really not very well today and it is difficult for me to see you. Since the performance of the quartets yesterday my sensitiveness and my imagination have been constantly reminding me that I have made you suffer. I went last night to the Redoute in order to amuse myself, but in vain; visions of all of you pursued me everywhere, and the whole time I was being reminded that "the Bigots are so good and are suffering perhaps through your fault."—So in a fit of depression I hurried away—Write me a few lines—
>
> Your sincere and loyal friend
> BEETHOVEN
> embraces you all—   (A-139).

It all passed over, and later the Bigots moved to Paris and lost contact with Beethoven.

What are we to make of these letters, seemingly so stiff in righteousness? Does it not sound as if the genius protests too much? That he is trying to deny —to himself as much as to the husband—the attraction he feels for the young wife? Is it natural for a thirty-seven-year-old man to insist that his feelings are "pure," that he "loves virtue"? Why was that drive with Marie minus husband so important to him, if all that was involved was an excursion of two friends?

As one tries to arrive at a general view of Beethoven's relationship with women, one sees a man "perplex'd in the extreme," easily wounded, given to enunciating precepts which he did not always follow, capable of love but never quite willing or able to give enough to it, confused in his notions of what was moral and what was not, sometimes striking out at what he called "loose women" in revenge for his own disappointments or possibly as a reaction to his own transgressions, sometimes overflowing with emotion, at other times shoring up the warmth of his soul; but never quite grown up, never quite an adult, never secure when face to face with a woman. This man, who considered and felt so much of all that is human, this man who was able to order our disordered emotions and give them shape and voice in music, this man who must have loved love because he loved people, was an awkward stammerer when he waxed serious about a woman. The uncertainty sometimes hardened into a holier-than-thou attitude, an almost fanatic intransigence, which is particularly noticeable in his hatred of the wives of his two brothers. More than sexual feelings are involved in this; yet the nursing of his contempt for them, pursued with the pertinacity of a zealot, is the visible sign of a hidden disturbance in his character. When he was twenty-six he wrote to his brother Johann, "Beware of the whole tribe of loose women!" Hardly fitting language for a young man of twenty-six to use. Occasionally Beethoven talks like a prude—perhaps because he had seen too much of what was going on in the earlier years at the Lichnowskys and the Zmeskalls. (He sometimes calls Zmeskall "Commander of *rotten fortresses*," which is probably his expression for loose women.)

He probably had sexual relations with a few women; as Thayer suggests (but does not attempt to prove), it is silly to call him "pure"—he was too human for that. But these relations, of whatever duration or intensity they were, did not satisfy him. He wanted more from a woman; yet he could not give a woman more. One suspects that women must have felt the lack, at least those women who possessed sensitive intuition.

He thought several times of getting married. Gerhard Breuning's sister Marie related that Beethoven often spoke to her mother about "domestic happiness" and that "he regretted never to have married." But to a young friend, Nanni Giannatasio del Rio, he said "he knew of no marriage in which one or the other did not regret the step after a time and that he was glad that none of the few women whose capture he might once have considered the greatest bliss became his wife: it was good that mortal wishes often remained unfulfilled."

The wavering continued over the years. When he does fall in love, he seems to be captivated as much by an idea as by the person. Was that because so much of his "real" life was spent in a world constructed by himself?

Something unreal clings to his utterances of love, something almost fictional. He was never play-acting, never fabricating. Beethoven stood high above the pretenses of ordinary men; he did not know, nor would have used, the gambits of ordinary lovers. If ever a great man was free of affectations or attitudinizing, it was Beethoven. He wrote to Josephine Brunsvik such words as:

> Oh, beloved J, it is no desire for the other sex that draws me to you, no, *it is just you, your whole self* with all your individual qualities—this has compelled my regard—this has bound all my feelings—all my emotional power to you— (A-110, written in the spring of 1805).

> Long—long—of long duration—may our love become—For it is so noble—so firmly founded upon mutual regard and friendship—   (Same letter)

Oh you, you make me hope that *your heart* will long—beat for me—*Mine* can only—cease—to beat for you—when—*it no longer beats*—*Beloved J[osephine]* (Same letter)

Beat, though in silence, poor heart—*you*—only *you*—eternally *you*—only *you* until I sink into the grave—My refreshment—my all. (A-112. It is probably a fragment of a lost letter to Josephine and exists only as a copy made by her.)

These assertions are written from a full heart. Yet, while acknowledging their veracity of feeling, we hear in them overtones of the language of Romanticism; a literary flavor drifts through the surge of words. Sincerity becomes mixed with the remembrance of what he had read in Goethe and Novalis. It is a sign of uncertainty, as if he summoned literature to help him give words to an emotion of which he was not sure, and which passed relatively quickly.

When one compares these letters to his one letter to the "Immortal Beloved," the difference becomes striking: it is the love letter by Beethoven from which emanate the deepest feelings—and it is much simpler than the others. It is one of the most "immortal" letters a non-literary man has penned. He managed to keep it totally secret. His friends did not know he had written it—until they discovered it in a secret drawer after his death. The secrecy must have been important to him.

There seems little point in compiling, like Leporello, a complete catalogue of names. Aside from Lorchen Breuning, we hear of some early infatuations such as Jeanette d'Honrath, a vivacious blonde to whom both he and Stephan von Breuning were attracted; a Baroness von Westerholt; "La Comtesse Babette," Anna Louisa Barbara Countess Keglevics, to whom Beethoven dedicated several works and to whom he gave lessons in his early Vienna years.

·=[MAGDALENE WILLMANN]=·

Possibly more important than they was the singer Magdalene Willmann. Beethoven had known her in Bonn as a member of the Bonn theater. She left Bonn about a year after Beethoven did, to sing in Venice and in other cities, and eventually she was engaged at the Court Opera in Vienna. There Beethoven met her again and was supposed to have offered her marriage. She refused him. The story is based largely on an interview which Thayer obtained with the daughter of Magdalene's brother, Max Willmann, who was still living in 1860 and who told him that she had heard her father speak of the proposal. Thayer asked why Magdalene did not accept Beethoven's offer and was told, after a moment of hesitation, "Because he was so ugly and half crazy!" It all seems doubtful, third-hand recollection after more than half a century. In the 1790's, when this was supposed to have occurred, Beethoven was neither remarkably "ugly" nor "half crazy." *

·•ᶘ GIULIETTA GUICCIARDI ᶗᵉ··

In the letter which Beethoven wrote to Wegeler in November, 1801, he mentions that his life had become ameliorated "by a dear and enchanting girl who loves me and whom I love." After two years, he says, he once more experiences some happy moments. He has even considered the possibility of marriage, though the girl's station is above his own. Who was she? It is generally agreed that she was the young Countess Giulietta Guicciardi, whom Beethoven met about 1800 and to whom he gave piano lessons. Beethoven was then thirty years old, she sixteen or seventeen. Though she was born in Trieste, she belonged on her mother's side to a Hungarian aristocratic family. That family was the Brunsviks. Giulietta's father was an Austrian Court Councilor who had been transferred from Trieste to Vienna in 1800. The evidence, as Thayer pieced it together from people who were still living in Vienna when Thayer was interviewing, indicates that Beethoven did make an offer of marriage to the Countess, "that she was not indisposed to accept it," but that her father opposed the marriage to a man "without rank, fortune, or permanent engagement." The Guicciardis were not particularly wealthy, and prudence spoke against the union. Such at least is Thayer's opinion. Another possibility is that a girl so young was not ready for such a step. There are also some indications that Giulietta was somewhat of a flirt and that she enjoyed exerting her charm on distinguished men. A miniature of her in ivory shows a mischievous little face with a sly sideways glance from dark eyes, her hair arranged in a whirlwind of curls all over her head. This is the portrait found in Beethoven's desk after his death. In a later portrait, perhaps done at the time of her marriage, the suggestion of flirtatiousness has disappeared but the beauty remains.**

When she was nineteen, Giulietta married a man hardly a year older than herself, Count Wenzel Robert Gallenberg. He was a ballet composer, and after

---

* Nevertheless, Magdalene Willmann became one biographer's (Frimmel) choice for the "Immortal Beloved." He later changed his mind.
** However, the marble bust which was fashioned of her and now stands prominently in the Beethoven House in Bonn is one of those meaningless "historic" relics.

their marriage the couple went to Naples, where he became the director of the ballet. Years later the famous impresario of the Naples theater, Domenico Barbaja,* was called to Vienna as director of the opera house and brought the Gallenbergs with him. Thus it happened that in 1823 Schindler called on Gallenberg with some business question about *Fidelio*. When he returned, Beethoven asked Schindler about the outcome of the interview. The Conversation Book records:

> SCHINDLER: He [Gallenberg] didn't make much of an impression on me today.
> BEETHOVEN: Through others I have acted as his invisible benefactor.
> SCHINDLER: He ought to learn that, so that he would have greater respect for you than he seems to have.

The conversation then veered to other topics. But Beethoven returned to Gallenberg:

> BEETHOVEN: It seems, then, that you did not find him very sympathetic toward me. By the way, I don't care in the least. But I'd like to know what he said.

How human, this curiosity! A further interruption, and then Giulietta came into the conversation. They were probably talking in a restaurant; Beethoven answered Schindler's Boswellian inquiries in French (and what French!). He must have been fearful not only that someone might overhear them but that someone might be able to read what he was writing if he wrote in German. Schindler not only made some comments at the time but used the material as a source for his biography and added several words, here given in brackets. The dashes indicate separate entries:

BEETHOVEN: j'etois bien aimé d'elle et plus que jamais son epoux. il' etoit pourtant plûtot son amant que moi, mais par elle j'en apprinois de son misère et je trouvais un home de bien, qui me donnoit la some de 500 fl pour le soulager.	She loved me much more than she ever did her husband. However, he was her beloved more than I was. But it was through her that I learned of his misery, and I found a man

---

* This fabulous character presented to Vienna such stellar singers as Sontag, Grisi, Rubini, and Lablache and helped to make Rossini famous.

il' etoit toujours mon ennemi, et c'etoit justement la raison, que je fusse tout le bien que possible

of good will who gave me the sum of 500 fl. to help him out.
He was always my enemy, and the reason was that I did him all the good I could.

SCHINDLER: It was for this reason that he added, "He is an intolerable fellow." Probably because of pure gratitude. But forgive them, Lord, they know not what they do!! —
mad: la Comtesse?

était-elle riche?
elle a une belle figure, jusqu'ici!

was she rich?
She has a beautiful face, even now!

MONS. G

est ce qu'il ya long temps, qu'elle est mariée avec Mons. de Gallenberg?

Has she been married long to Mons. de Gallenberg?

BEETHOVEN: elle est neé guicciardi
ell' étoit encor l'Epouse de lui avant [son voyage] de l'Italie, —
[arrivée a Vienne] elle cherchait moi pleureant, mais je la meprisois. —

She was born Guicciardi
She was already his wife before [her voyage] to Italy —
[Returned to Vienna] she sought me out weeping, but I despised her.

SCHINDLER: Hercules at the crossways! —

BEETHOVEN: And if I had wished to give my vital powers with that life, what would have remained for the nobler, the better?

The accuracy of Schindler's interpolation (probably a later addition), *"arrivée a Vienne,"* is doubtful. More probably Giulietta sought out Beethoven before she married Gallenberg, before she went to Italy, and he rejected her.

There are some indications that Giulietta was not happy in her marriage.*

---

* Kalischer says so in *Beethoven und seine Zeitgenossen* ("Beethoven and His Contemporaries"). He quotes Nohl, Schindler's sister, and a writer Mielichhofer. The evidence is not entirely convincing.

Prince Hermann von Pückler-Muskau, a well known Don Juan and a fascinating figure, is supposed to have had an affair with Giulietta. (He was involved with Bettina Brentano as well.) A letter from him to Giulietta, written in French and addressing her by *tu,* was published by Pückler's biographer, Ludmilla Assing-Grimelli. The letter is dated 1810, gossips away, and closes, "Adieu, my beloved Julie, love me a little and be sure that in the entire world you haven't got a better friend than I."

Giulietta Guicciardi lived a long life, dying at the age of seventy-one. In 1852, when she was sixty-eight, Jahn interviewed her. In her recollections of Beethoven, she appeared reticent, cool, noncommittal. If ever she had suffered because of him, if ever she had sought him out weeping, she gave no inkling of remembering it.

Whatever the degree of her love for Beethoven, or his for her, it was sufficient to bestow on her a certain immortality, because it was to her that he dedicated the *Moonlight Sonata.* It was she, too, who became a favorite candidate for the "Immortal Beloved" (Schindler, Nohl, Kalischer).

·°◦[THE BRUNSVIK SISTERS]◦°·

The Brunsviks, related to Giulietta and on friendly terms with her family, were Hungarian nobles of fairly recent lineage. They were landowners, their woods and fields being administered from two castles in which they lived alternately, Korompa and Martonvásár. What wealth they possessed was bound to the soil: they never had a large fortune of ready money.

The parents of the children whose lives crossed Beethoven's were Count Anton Brunsvik and the Countess Anna Elizabeth. The countess had a brother, Philipp, who was a friend of Zmeskall, and it is possible that Beethoven met the Brunsviks through Zmeskall. Countess Anna was one of the subscribers to Beethoven's first published work, the Trio Opus 1. Count Anton was an enthusiastic democrat. He followed with lively interest the careers of Washington and Benjamin Franklin, and tried to instill the ideals of the American Revolution into his children, not with complete success.

There were four: Count Franz and three sisters, the oldest Therese, the middle Josephine, and the youngest Charlotte. Therese was five years younger than Beethoven and Josephine nine. Their father died at the age of forty-seven in 1793. Therese was his favorite child. She had been named after the Empress Maria Theresa, whose godchild she was. When the count died, Countess Anna must have decided that there was not much future for the young people on the isolated estates of the Hungarian plains, that the children ought to learn the ways of the world in the metropolis, and that the girls would have more of a chance to find husbands in Vienna. In 1799 they came to the metropolis.

The children were all musical. The sisters played the piano, and Franz was a first-rate cellist. Therese was perhaps the most talented. One of the first things they did in Vienna was to seek the acquaintance of the famous man. By and by Franz became a fast friend of Beethoven, intimate enough so that they addressed each other by *Du*. Seven years younger than the composer, Franz was another one of those young men who persevered in his devotion through the years, even after he returned to Hungary. Franz was quite as proud as Beethoven himself. His sisters used to call him "le Comte Ego."

Therese was gifted not only as a musician but as a painter. In addition, she dearly loved to write down her thoughts and impressions in words freighted with a full charge of female romantic fancy. It was the fashion to confess one's secret feelings to a locked diary—Rousseau had started the drive toward self-confession—and Therese did so over many years. Then, in her old age, she wrote her memoirs, titled *My Half Century*. Both are important sources of information about the Brunsvik-Beethoven relationship, but both must be read with caution. Let Therese now tell of her first encounter with Beethoven:

> During the extraordinary sojourn of 18 days in Vienna, my mother desired that her two daughters, Therese and Josephine, receive Beethoven's invaluable instructions in music. Adalbert Rosti, a schoolmate of my brother's, assured us that Beethoven would not be persuaded to accept a mere invitation; but that if Her Excellency were willing to climb the three flights of stairs of the house in St. Peter's Place, and make him a visit, he would vouch for a successful outcome of the mission. It was done. Like a schoolgirl, with Beethoven's Sonatas for Violin and Violoncello and Pianoforte under my arm, we entered. The immortal, dear Louis van Beethoven was very friendly and as polite as he could be. After a few phrases de part et d'autre, he sat me down at his pianoforte, which was out of tune, and I began at once to sing the violin and cello parts and played right well. This delighted him so much that he promised to come every day to the Hotel zum Erzherzog Carl—then zum Goldenen Greifen. It was May in the last year of the last century. He came regularly, but instead of an hour frequently stayed from twelve to four or five o'clock, and never grew weary of holding down and bending my fingers, which I had been taught to lift high and hold straight. The noble man must have been satisfied; for he never missed a single day in the 16. We felt no hunger until five o'clock. My good mother bore her hunger—the inn-people, however, were indignant, for it had not yet become the custom to eat dinner at five o'clock in the evening.

It was then that the most intimate and cordial friendship was established with Beethoven, a friendship which lasted to the end of his life. He came to Ofen [Budapest], he came to Martonvásár; he was initiated into our social republic of chosen people. A round spot was planted with high, noble lindens; each tree had the name of a member, and even in their sorrowful absence we conversed with their symbols, and were entertained and instructed by them.

From the Memoirs, as given by La Mara, pen name for Marie Lipsius, in *Beethoven's unsterbliche Geliebte.* (TQ).

Therese was chosen as the Immortal Beloved by no less an authority than Thayer. (Later also by W. A. Thomas-San Galli, La Mara, and Romain Rolland.) The evidence for such an accolade is flimsy and more speaks against than for it.* Those who believe that a great love existed point out that Therese gave Beethoven her portrait and that he kept this portrait along with the Immortal Beloved letter in the secret drawer. The dedication on the back of the portrait reads, "To the rare genius, the great artist, the good human being, from T.B."—hardly a passionate dedication. She also made him a gift of a sketch showing an eagle gazing into the sun; it may well have expressed her feelings about Beethoven. Beethoven, in his typical fashion, lost the sketch and then asked her to do him another one, "if you feel inspired by the deity of painting." "But," he added, "you must not assume that in this connection I am thinking of myself, although such a thought has already been imputed to me." (This is the only letter from Beethoven to Therese extant.)

There is a further story, believed by Romain Rolland and Edouard Herriot, among others, that Beethoven, on a certain moonlit May night in the park at Martonvásár in the year 1806, proposed marriage to Therese. Yet Therese never mentions such an incident, either in her diary or in her memoirs, nor was Beethoven in Martonvásár in May, 1806. I am convinced that the story is a ray of moonlit fiction, one of the many rays which shine upon a dead man and show him in a fictive light. Therese was a warm, gentle friend of Beethoven. She appreciated him more when she got older and lived away from Vienna, distance lending enchantment to the friendship she once possessed. But no moonlight envelops the pair. There was no romance. Therese was not a beloved, let alone the Immortal Beloved. It is unlikely that Beethoven would be in love with two of three sisters and about at the same time. Therese was not particularly

---

* Krehbiel in his edition of Thayer summarizes the various opinions. He himself remains of an open mind.

attractive. She had a prim mouth and suffered with a curvature of the spine, for which she sought relief in the fashionable watering places.

More important, the internal evidence of Therese's writings—to which Thayer did not have access—makes it improbable that she was ever seriously in love with Beethoven or he with her. Her nature, as it emerges from these pages, is not one which would be inclined to give herself to so strange a man as Beethoven, or to become her sister's rival. She was an almost fanatically religious woman, ascetically inclined, given to sermonizing and moralizing. A custom of her times? Yes, but she rather overdid it. She had a particularly handy pen for an adage. As a mature woman (in 1812, when she was thirty-seven), she made herself a naïve plan of "Good Resolutions," dividing the plan, like a school program, into days of the week and listing qualities such as "Cleanliness," "Tranquillity," "Chastity," "Justice," "Economy," "Humility," etc., with blank spaces to grade herself. In her memoirs she recollected that when she was only sixteen, she dedicated herself "most solemnly as a Priestess of Truth and decided never to get married." Further, "I have always despised the thought of marrying; to become somebody else's property (according to our civil laws) is abominable." She does confess that early in her youth a "passion consumed my heart." But this passion was almost certainly not Beethoven but a young hussar officer.

As she grew older she devoted herself to Josephine with a singlemindedness which transgresses the normal and which, even making allowance for the sentimentality of the period, appears sickly. "Just think," she writes in her diary in 1811, "that my life never knew a springtime, that I know nothing which would make life worthwhile except you, my one and only! [Josephine] Up to now I lived only in an unpleasant dream; now I shall begin to live: *for you. I have no future.*" In point of fact, her future was that of a servant and ministrant to her sister. Therese never married, never really had a life of her own, and (as we shall see) was cruelly treated by fate. The sisters often quarreled. Therese wept, disapproved of Josephine's doings and decisions; sometimes, though rarely, rebelled against her sister's domination and then only in the pages of the diary; and darkly prophesied further disaster. Events proved her right. Yet the two sisters were bound together. (Charlotte married normally and seemingly happily.) Therese wrote in the diary, "Oh Josephine! Your existence is in peril! And yet it is necessary to my life and to my happiness!"

What was this peril? It all started out so gaily when the girls came to Vienna. They were young, they were curious, they had eager minds, they were ready for experiences and such adventures as may befit cultured countesses. Of course they had to see all the show places of the city. Not the least famous of these was the Müller Gallery of Statues. The French guidebook from which I have quoted described it in glowing terms. The proprietor of the gallery had invented an astonishing "colored paste which he successfully employed to give modern statues a perfect lifelike quality," and in addition the gallery contained "reproductions in colored wax of antique statues, such as the Apollo of Belvedere and the Venus of Medici." The collection was housed in a large palace of over a hundred rooms. At the entrance the Brunsvik family were met by two liveried servants. Presently the proprietor himself appeared, an "elderly man." This was Herr Müller. He told them later that he took the mother for the widow of an officer. He thought her poor, as he noticed that her sleeve was slightly torn. He looked at Josephine and immediately was captivated by her beauty. When the party got ready to depart, one of the servants said to the mother, "Would Her Excellency care to put on her shawl?" At the appellation "Her Excellency," Müller sprang to attention. These were people of rank, then? At nine o'clock the next morning he was at the hotel, offering his services as a guide. He could not do enough for them. Would they care to be shown the Imperial private art collections which were closed to the public? Would they like to be invited to the fashionable garden parties or excursions to Baden which, in private carriages and in jolly company, got under way at five o'clock in the morning? Would they want to attend the masked balls with the Court? The young girls hardly slept; they were in a whirl. How did they have time to take lessons from Beethoven? Presently Herr Müller told the countess that he was not just plain Herr Müller, that he was no other than Count Joseph Deym, now back in Vienna after his banishment. To the provincial countess, he seemed the incarnation of Viennese elegance. After a suitable interval, he sought a private interview with her and formally asked for Josephine's hand. The countess was overjoyed: a count, owning a famous palace and, as he took care to let her know, one of her Emperor's chamberlains (*Kammerherr*) — it was a brilliant proposal and the mother urged Josephine to accept it, though she was twenty and he was forty-seven.

Therese recalled that Josephine did not want to marry Deym, "the strange old man" (she said he was fifty, which he wasn't), that she wept and protested, but that her mother insisted. Therese's testimony is not unprejudiced: she hated Deym. She relates that Deym was an intellectual zero, that when he saw Josephine with a book in her hand he took the book away, and worst of all that he disapproved of Josephine's love for music. "Deym detested music." Perhaps there is some truth in this; on the other hand, we know that Deym had been at least an acquaintance of Mozart, and that Beethoven was a welcome guest in his palace.

Josephine became Countess Deym June 29, 1799, about a month after the Brunsviks came to Vienna. This "o'erhasty marriage" did not turn out well. Deym had counted on a considerable dowry from the Hungarian landowners, but had received only 2000 gulden "for the trousseau"; Josephine, who loved luxury, spent more than 4000. Not very long after, it appeared that the count was deep in financial troubles, had been virtually bankrupt even before the marriage, but had managed to hide the fact. Legal wrangles threatened. The Countess Anna Elizabeth, who had returned home to Hungary, hurried post-haste back to Vienna, was present at the birth of Josephine's first child (May 5, 1800), realized that she had married her daughter to "half a beggar," stormed and threatened and now pressed for a separation. Yet Deym, even Therese admits, loved Josephine with his whole heart, and Josephine refused to leave him. She said, "I have sworn to share fortune and misfortune with him." She remained with him, now as a young mother more beautiful than ever—*"belle comme une ange et mise à peindre"* (beautiful as an angel and fit to be painted) was the Viennese verdict—and in the following two years she had two more children by him.

Beethoven proved to be an admiring friend to the young Countess and, Therese says, was "a faithful visitor." He gave her lessons gratis. At Josephine's home several of his new works, sonatas and quartets as yet unpublished, were performed, and Beethoven brought along his helpers, such as the indispensable Schuppanzigh.

Late in 1803, Josephine, brother Franz, and Deym set out on a journey to Prague. The new baby, a girl named Victoire, was taken along. They were going to spend the winter in Prague. The two little boys, Fritz and Carl, aged three and a half and two and a half, were in Budapest (Ofen) with their grandmother and Therese. Presently Deym came from Prague to Budapest to fetch the two boys: he wanted his family together. He arrived in Budapest more dead than alive, with a horrible cough. Nevertheless he insisted, after a few days, on departing with the two children and a nurse to return to Josephine in Prague. There he had to take to his bed. Josephine nursed him day and night. He knew he was dying. He appointed his young wife the guardian of his children and of whatever capital he had left (which turned out to be chiefly the Palace and the statues); he also wrote a testament in which he spoke glowingly about her sacrificial love; and on January 27, 1804, he died of galloping consumption.

Josephine, pregnant once again, and her three children returned to Vienna to take up residence in the Müller Palace. There the fourth child was born. Josephine, dressed in black, called on the Emperor and weepingly asked for help. The Emperor said, "Your children are my children. I shall not abandon them." Then he forgot about the matter. She now had to assume the management of the art gallery and she let out rooms to strangers visiting the city. There were eighty such furnished rooms in the Palace. The young Countess was plunged into a cauldron of household and business duties for which she had neither training nor inclination. When the winter was over, Josephine was exhausted and took up residence (summer, 1804) in Hietzing, then a verdant suburb of Vienna. She had asked Charlotte to stay with her. Therese was still in Hungary. (She joined Josephine later, after Charlotte got married, and took up most of the burden.) During this summer Beethoven renewed his acquaintance with Josephine. He visited the sisters and they him.

One can watch Beethoven's interest in the beautiful young widow ripen slowly into love. Charlotte, too, watched it. In June, Charlotte wrote to Therese, "We have visited Beethoven, who looked very well and promised to come to see us. This summer he is not going to travel; possibly he will live in Hütteldorf, so that we will be very near one another." After September, returning to the city, to Deym's house and to further uncertainties, Josephine suffered a nervous breakdown, "laughing and crying alternately." "Her nights were especially terrible," writes Charlotte. But by November she was far enough cured to organize several musical evenings with Beethoven. On November 10, Charlotte reports to Therese (in French) that Beethoven had played twice at the house and in addition to taking part in his quartets, he was "gracious enough immediately to play a sonata and variations when he was asked to do so." "Pepi" (Josephine) had invited him to dinner. Ten days later Charlotte writes (again in French):

"Beethoven is charming. He comes almost every second day and gives Pepi lessons; he always inquires after you. He is composing an opera and played us some selections from it. Charming." On December 19: "Our little musicales have finally begun again. Last Wednesday was the first. Pepi played the piano excellently. I do not yet find the courage to let myself be heard. *Beethoven vient très souvent, il donne des leçons à Pepi; c'est un peu dangereux, je t'avoue."* * It was "dangerous," to Charlotte's way of thinking. To Franz, her brother, she writes two days later: "Beethoven is with us almost daily, giving instruction to Pipschen—*vous m'entendez mon coeur."* **

He composes a song for "Pepi" which Charlotte sends on to Therese, urging her not to show the song to anybody. The song is called *"An die Hoffnung"* (*To Hope*). In the score of the song, Charlotte underscores several words as a message to Therese. On January 20, 1805, Therese, much troubled, writes to Charlotte: "But do tell me, Pepi and Beethoven, what is to become of it? She ought to watch out! I believe that the words you have underscored in the piano score refer to her. Her heart must have the strength to say no; it is a sad duty if not the saddest of all!"

The crescendo of their relationship which Charlotte reports can be noticed as well in Beethoven's letters. The parallel is striking.

In the autumn of 1804, Beethoven writes that yesterday when he saw Josephine he did not know "that I should be able to satisfy your longing for *something new."* Now, today, here was that something new, and he earnestly begs her not to show it to anyone. It was the charming Pianoforte Sonata in E-flat Major, Op. 31, No. 3, which had recently been published in Zurich. Beethoven is afraid that "it might fall into the hands of a Viennese publisher" who might pirate it, so the sonata was destined for her eyes only. And when was he going to see Josephine again?

In the next note he says that yesterday he did not pay proper attention to what J[osephine] was telling him. *"Did you not say* that I was to dine with you? —If you *really said it,* then I will come." He signs: "Your Beethoven who worships you."

The next letter, in December, speaks of a planned musical evening at her home in which Schuppanzigh and Zmeskall are to take part. Then Beethoven asks Josephine for the kind of favor that one friend asks of another. Would she allow his brother Carl to call on her? It seems that Carl would like some kind of a recommendation from her:

> I don't know what it is all about. But I merely add that if you can perhaps help my *brother* in some way, then I too recommend him to you. Although *wicked people* have spread a rumour that he does not treat me honourably, yet I can assure you that all that is not true, but that he has always looked after my

---

* "Beethoven comes frequently, he gives Pepi lessons; it is a bit dangerous, I admit."
** "You understand me, my dear."

interests with sincere integrity. He used to have *something uncouth* in his behaviour and that is what put *people* against him. But he has completely lost *all that* as the result of some *journeys* he has undertaken on behalf of his office ... So dear, kind J[osephine], let me know when he may call on you—

Your—your—your
BEETHOVEN (A-103).

The attraction of the composer to the countess, at first tentatively expressed by wanting to see her, wanting to come for dinner, calling her dear and kind, telling her that "Beethoven ... worships you," bursts the bonds of caution soon after. When spring came, love came, and Beethoven expressed it in a letter which is unmistakably rhapsodic. The direct cause of the letter was this: The manuscript of the song "To Hope," with a dedication to Josephine, must have been in his room; Lichnowsky saw it. He guessed the secret of the relationship. This is disturbing news to Josephine, and Beethoven tries to calm her:

[VIENNA, Spring, 1805]

As I said, the affair with L[ichnowsky], my beloved J[osephine], is not as bad as was made out to you—Quite by chance L[ichnowsky] had seen *the song "An die Hoffnung" lying about at my place, although I had not noticed this. And he too said nothing about it.* But he gathered from this that I must surely have some affection for you. And then when *Zmeskall went to him about the affair in which you and Tante Gu * were involved,* he asked him if he knew whether I went to see you *fairly often.*** Zmeskall said neither yes nor no. After all, there was nothing he could say, for I had dodged his vigilance as much as possible—Lichnowsky said that he thought he had noticed by chance (the song) that I must surely have some affection for you. But he did not say anything to Z[meskall] about the song; and that he solemnly assured me,—and Z[meskall] was to have a word with Tante Gui—and suggest that she should speak to you so that you might encourage me more earnestly *to finish my opera,* because he believed that this might do a lot of good. For he knew for certain what a great regard I cherished for you—that is the whole factum—S[meskall]—magnified it—and Tante Gui—likewise—Meanwhile—you may now be calm about it all, seeing that apart from those *two persons* no one else is *involved.*

L[ichnowsky] himself said that so far as he was concerned he had far too great a feeling of delicacy to *mention* a single word, *even if he had assumed with certainty the existence of a more intimate association between us*—On the contrary, there was nothing which he desired more than the formation of such an association between you and me, if it were possible. For what had been reported to him *about your character,* such a

---

* The Countess Susanna Guicciardi, born Brunsvik, mother of Giulietta. She was the sister of Josephine's father.
** These two words are heavily underscored.

friendship could not but be advantageous to me—basta così—Well, it is true that I have not been as diligent as I ought to have been—but a *private grief*—robbed me for a long time—of my usual intense energy. And for some time after the feeling of love for you, my adored J[osephine], began to stir within me, this grief increased even more—As soon as we are together again with no one to disturb us, you shall hear all about my real sorrows and the struggle with myself between death and life, a struggle in which I was engaged for some time—For a long period a certain event made me despair of ever achieving any happiness *during my life on this earth*—but now things are no longer so bad. I have won *your heart*. Oh, I certainly know *what value* I ought to attach to this. My activity will again increase and—here I give you a solemn promise that in a short time I shall stand *before you* more worthy *of myself and of you*—Oh, if only you would attach some value to this, I mean, to founding *my happiness* by means of your love—to increasing it—Oh, beloved J[osephine], it is no desire for the other sex that draws me to you, no, *it is just you, your whole self* with all your individual qualities—this has compelled my regard—this has bound all my feelings—all my emotional power to you—When I came to you—it was with the firm resolve not to let a single spark of love be kindled in me. But you have conquered me—The question is, whether *you wanted to do so?* or whether *you did not want to do so?*—No doubt J[osephine] could answer that question for me sometime—Dear God, there are so many more things I should love to tell you—how much I think of you—what I feel for you but how weak and poor are those words—at any rate, my words—

Long—long—of long duration—may our love become—For it is so noble—so firmly founded upon mutual regard and friendship—Even the great similarity between us in so many respects, in our thoughts and feelings—Oh you, you make me hope *your heart* will long—beat for me—*Mine* can only—cease—to beat for you—when—*it no longer beats* —*Beloved* J[osephine], I send you all good wishes—*But I also* hope—that *through me* you will gain a little happiness—otherwise I should certainly be—*selfish*.   (A-110).

The letter contains its share of mysteries. What was the "private grief" which had robbed him of his usual intense energy? What was the struggle between death and life within him? Was it due to deafness or another cause?

Whatever his griefs, he felt joy as well. The joy emanates equally from the next letter, which exists only in a copy made by Josephine:

[VIENNA, Spring, 1805]

... from her—

the only beloved—why is there no language which can express what is far above all mere regard—far above everything—that we can ever describe—Oh, who can name *you*—and not feel that however much he could speak about *you*—that would never attain—to *you* only in music—Alas, am I not too proud when I believe that music is more at my command than words—*You, you*, my all, my happiness—alas, no—even in *my music* I cannot do so, although in this respect thou, Nature, hast not stinted me with thy gifts. Yet there is too little for *you*. Beat, though in silence, poor heart—that is all you can do, nothing more—for *you*—always for *you*—only *you*—eternally *you*—only *you* until I sink into the grave—My refreshment—my all. Oh, Creator, watch over her—bless her days rather let all calamities fall upon me—

Only *you*—May you be strengthened, blessed and comforted—in the wretched yet frequently happy existence of us mortals—

Even if you had not fettered me again to life, yet you would have meant everything to me—   (A-112).

The next, a short note, written probably around this time, is significant for one phrase, though the letter deals with so mundane a matter as six bottles of eau de cologne which Beethoven sent Josephine. The phrase is, "I love you as dearly as you do not love me." A hint of this already appears in Letter 110.

From then on it was Beethoven himself who became less ardent. The thermometer drops, the ecstasy passes. Was it brief because he could not love in fullest measure, as I have suggested? Was it brief because Josephine would not be his in fullest measure, could not give herself wholly to him? Both may be causes. We cannot be sure; we can only sense the downward curve, though in the next missive he still calls her "angel of my heart," and in one shortly after he speaks of her as the person dearest to him in this world. But the letters glow with a feebler light.

No answers to Beethoven's letters from Josephine have survived. No doubt Beethoven destroyed them. Fragments of proposed letters have been found. Josephine did not trust herself to write on the impulse of the moment; she composed her letters in the rough. The fragments make it appear that Josephine's love for him was not as unquestioning as Beethoven's was at its brief height. A certain circumspect coolness emanates from her words:

Closer acquaintance with you, dear *Beethoven*, during these winter months left impressions in my soul which neither time nor circumstances can wipe out— Are you happy or grieving?—You yourself can decide this—It is *you* who can lessen or heighten your feelings—through self-control or yielding.

To Beethoven's wish that they become lovers she replied:

My soul, which felt enthusiasm for you even before I knew you personally— was nourished by your affection. A feeling which lies deep in my soul and which is ineffable made me love you; even before I knew you your music made me enthusiastic for you—the goodness of your character, your affection augmented it.—The distinction you bestowed on me, the pleasure of your company, could have been the greatest adornment of my life if you could love me in a less sensual way—Because I cannot satisfy this sensual love—you are angry with me —I would have to tear holy bonds if I acceded to your desire—Believe me—that it is I who suffer most through the observance of my duty—and that certainly noble motives guide my actions.

Holy bonds? Her duty? How so—her husband was dead, she was a free woman, she could become his love? She could marry him, had she desired to do so. Beethoven must have stormed at her, for she replied in hurt tones:

Knowing that I feel affection for you, that I value your friendship, how could you wound me, me who trustfully let you gaze deeper into my soul than our short acquaintance would properly permit, you who have come to know how little cause for gladness [I] possess—and *you* can grieve me through lack of trust in the steadfastness of my character!—Your heart does not protest, when you accuse me of certain things.

You do not know how you hurt my heart—You treat me quite wrongly—

Often you do not know what you are doing—how deeply I feel—

If my life is dear to you—then treat me with more consideration—and above all *do not doubt me*—I cannot express how deeply wounding it is to be equated with low creatures, even if only in thought and slight suspicion, conscious as I am of my sacrifice to virtue and duty—

Believe me, d. g. B. [dear, good Beethoven] *that I suffer much more, much more* than you—*much more!*

This suspicion which you impart to me so frequently, that is it which pains me beyond all expression. Let it be far from me—I despise the low, the very low, artifices of our sex. They are beneath me—

And I do not think I need them. Only the belief in your inner value made me love you. If you are not as noble as I deem you to be, then I could not have the least value in your eyes—for only in the supposition that you know how to judge good human beings can I have some value in your eyes.

I love you and value your moral character—You have demonstrated much that is dear and kind to me and my children, that I will never forget and as long as I live I will always take an interest in your fate, and contribute to your happiness what I can—But you must not take it amiss if I—

View of Vienna from the Belvedere, by Bellotto, detail showing the famous gardens leading from the upper to the lower Belvedere (Historical Museum, Vienna).

Germany's greatest poet, Johann Wolfgang von Goethe, in garb of Privy Councilor to the Duke of Weimar. Kügelgen's painting dates from about the time Beethoven met Goethe (Culver Pictures).

Therese's diary furnishes a possible explanation for Josephine's refusal to yield: it was mother-love, the concern for her four children which prevented her. It was natural that Josephine should not consider Beethoven the ideal husband for a woman surrounded by a quartet of very young children whose future life had to be secured. It was equally natural that Josephine, the spoiled darling of an aristocratic house, could not in her soul bridge that gap which divided commoner from nobleman by that little magic word "von." It was understandable that she had not strength enough to ignore the prejudices of Charlotte and Therese, mother, brother, aunts, friends. "The highest circles here are filled with unbelievable pride. They think of nothing except their ancestors" —thus wrote the Duchess Hedvig Södermanland in her diary when she visited Vienna in 1798–1799. It held equally true for the nobility of slightly less than highest circles, such as the Brunsviks.

Nevertheless, if Josephine did not want to marry Beethoven (assuming that he asked her), there was little reason why they should not have become lovers —except the cogent reason that she was not sexually sufficiently attracted by him.

For two years after the springtime of their love there is silence—at least nothing written is extant. Beethoven's next letter, written in the spring of 1807, is much cooler. He asks Josephine to ask her brother to send back as quickly as possible some scores which Beethoven had given him. Beethoven has searched everywhere and cannot find them. He promises to return them immediately after he has had them copied. He still calls her "Beloved and only J," yet he who two years before could not see enough of Josephine, twice excuses himself for his inability to see her, "owing to many affairs."

They then must have decided to break the relationship, not to see each other, not even to write to each other. This appears from a letter written on September 20, 1807, from Heiligenstadt. The letter indicates an upwelling of his former feeling for her:

Dear, Beloved and Only J[osephine]!
Again even a few lines, only a few lines from you—have given me great pleasure—How often have I wrestled with myself, beloved J[osephine], in order not to commit a breach of the prohibition which I have imposed upon myself—But it is all in vain. A thousand voices are constantly whispering to me that you are my only friend, my only beloved—I am no longer able to obey the rule which I imposed upon myself. Oh, dear J[osephine], let us wander unconstrainedly along that path where we have often been so happy—Tomor-

row or the day after I shall see you. May Heaven grant me one undisturbed hour to spend with you, so as to have just once that talk we have not had for a long time, when my heart and my soul may again be united with yours—Until now my health has continued to be very poor, but it is slowly improving—When your sister Therese was in Vienna, I was still unwell; and this condition persisted for almost that whole month—My sensitiveness prevented me from feeling well anywhere, not even in the company of my best friends—At the beginning of September I went to *Heiligenstadt,* but that trip did me no good and I had to return to town. Then I went down to *Eisenstadt* to stay with Prince *Esterházy* and there my Mass was performed—I returned from Eisenstadt a few days ago. I had hardly been back in Vienna for a day when I called on you *twice* but I was nót so fortunate—as to see you—that hurt me deeply—and I assumed that your *feelings* had *perhaps* undergone some change—But I still hope— Down at E[isenstadt] too and wherever I happened to be, your image pursued me the whole time—That is a full account of my life since we parted.—My health is daily improving, and so I hope—to be able to live more for my friends —Do not forget—do not condemn

your ever faithfully devoted
BTHVN

I am just coming into town today—and I could almost deliver this letter myself —if I did not suspect—that I might for the third time fail to see you.   (A-151).

So Beethoven tried twice to see her but did not find her in. Was it bad luck or did Josephine not want to see him? The latter seems more probable. Perhaps the following fragment by Josephine is in answer to Beethoven's letter:

I did not mean to insult you! dear *B.* but since you took it as such and I am well aware of the conventional code [*Convenienz*], to transgress which I deem of little importance, it is my turn to beg your pardon—so I beg your pardon all the more since I cannot understand very well how there could be room for touchiness where true mutual esteem exists. A malady which usually could be suspected only in weaker souls.

Some time later in the autumn Beethoven writes:

[In the country, autumn, 1807]

Dear, Dear J[osephine],
Today I can send you only a few lines—If you fancy that I am enjoying an excessive amount of entertainment, you are mistaken. My head is beginning to feel better and so—I am living in greater solitude—the more so as here I can

find hardly any company congenial to me—You are not well—How sorry I am not to be able to see you—But it is better for your peace of mind and mine not to see you—You have not offended me—I was sensitive, I admit, but for a very different reason from the one you are inclined to adduce—Today I cannot write to you more fully about this. But come what may, our opinion of one another most certainly rests on such favourable foundations that trifles can never separate us—and yet trifles can certainly produce reflections—which, Heaven be thanked, do not occur too late—nothing against you, dear J[osephine], all—all in your favour—and yet it must be so—All good wishes, beloved J[osephine] —more of this in a few days.   (A-153).

It is better "for your peace of mind and mine" not to see each other. This is followed by a letter which gives substance to Beethoven's suspicion that Josephine no longer *wanted* to see him:

[VIENNA, autumn, 1807]

Dear J[osephine],
Since I must almost fear that you no longer *allow yourself to be found* by me—and since I do not care to put up with the refusals of your servant any longer—well then, I cannot come to you any more—unless you let me know what you think about this—Is it really *a fact*—that you do not want to see me any more—if so—do be *frank*—I certainly deserve that you should be frank with me—When I kept away from you, I thought I must do so, because I had an idea that you desired it—although when doing so I suffered a good deal—yet I controlled my feelings—but it occurred to me again later on that—I was mistaken in you—the letter I sent you a short time ago contains everything else. —Do let me know, dear J[osephine]—what you think. Nothing shall bind you —In the circumstances I can and certainly dare not say anything more to you.—
All good wishes, dear, dear J[osephine]—
Please send me back the book in which I enclosed my lines to you—I was asked for it today.   (A-154).

We have one further fragment of a letter by Josephine:

For a long time I have desired to receive news about your wellbeing, and I would have informed myself about it long ago if modesty had not held me back. —Now tell me, how are you, what are you doing? How is your health, your mood, your way of life?—The deep interest which I take in all that concerns you and which I will take as long as I live, gives me the desire to have news about everything. Or does my *friend Beethoven,* surely I may call him that, believe that I have changed?—Such a doubt would imply to me nothing else but that you yourself are no longer the same.

Beethoven's response to this letter is distant in tone, indeed almost icy, though an echo of his former feeling sounds in the signature:

[VIENNA, autumn, 1807]

Please deliver this sonata to your brother, my dear Josephine—I thank you for wishing still to appear as if I were not altogether banished from your memory, even though this came about perhaps more at the instigation of others—You want me to tell you how I am. A more difficult question could not be put to me —and I prefer to leave it unanswered, rather than—to answer it *too truthfully* —All good wishes, dear J[osephine].

As always, your Beethoven
who is eternally devoted to you. (A-156).

Here speaks a man whose pride has been wounded. It was the last letter. It was the end of the relationship.

Incomplete as it is, we owe our knowledge of the Josephine-Beethoven affair to a remarkable discovery, indeed the most remarkable find of Beethoven material of the last fifty years. The thirteen letters which Beethoven wrote to Josephine were discovered in 1949 and were acquired by Dr. H. C. Bodmer, a Swiss industrialist who over many years amassed the great "Bodmer Collection" of Beethoven documents. He willed this collection to the Beethoven House in Bonn. The director of the Beethoven House, Dr. Joseph Schmidt-Görg, immediately began to decipher these letters—no easy task!—to furnish them with elucidating comments, to arrange them in chronological order, and to set them within the frame of known material, such as the memoirs of Therese and other papers of the Brunsvik family, which had previously been examined by Marie Lipsius and others. It took Dr. Schmidt-Görg the better part of seven years to accomplish what proved to be a model of scholarship. In 1957 the letters were published in a superb facsimile edition.

Long before the letters came to light, Beethoven scholars divined that some kind of relationship existed between Josephine and Beethoven.

Three years before the publication of the thirteen letters, Siegmund Kaznelson published an amazing book, *Beethovens Ferne und Unsterbliche Geliebte* ("Beethoven's Distant and Immortal Beloved"). This book set out to prove not only that Josephine was the Immortal Beloved but that Josephine's last child, a daughter by the name of Minona, was Beethoven's illegitimate child. The book piled the Pelion of deduction on the Ossa of conjecture. Mr. Kaznelson studied every scrap of the Brunsvik papers, he searched contemporary records, police

reports, passport descriptions, registers, letters of intimate and casual acquaintances, diaries, hints, reminiscences of diverse people, and so on. Gathering each
tiny straw, he wove the whole into an elaborate basket. The trouble is that the
basket fell apart once the thirteen letters were published. The "sensational
revelations" proved untenable, the premise being false. Josephine could not
have been the Immortal Beloved, for the letter containing that appelation is
now placed by most scholars, including Kaznelson, in the year 1812. The
Josephine-Beethoven relationship ended in 1807, and there is not an iota of
evidence that it was ever taken up again.

But what of Josephine? What happened to her? How often in after years she
must have thought of that spring of 1805, when the world around her looked
ominous, when she read of Napoleon's being crowned King of Italy in the
Duomo in Milan, when she saw Vienna preparing for further wars, but when
she lived in the privilege of Beethoven's company, when she was with him so
often, when she may well have heard an early performance of a new symphony
called the *Eroica* and when Beethoven played for her portions of an opera he
was composing!

The year after the break with Beethoven, Josephine persuaded her mother to
let Therese join her. The two sisters took Josephine's two boys to Germany,
while the two little girls remained in Vienna, well cared for. The purpose of the
trip was to find a suitable educational institution into which to place the boys.
Being dissatisfied with the strict discipline of a German school which had been
recommended to them, they journeyed farther to visit the most famous educator
of his time, Johann Heinrich Pestalozzi,* whose school was in Yverdon, Switzerland. Even though Josephine was much impressed by this educational wiz-
ard, she could not bear to separate herself from the two boys and leave them at
the school. One of Pestalozzi's friends whom they met at the school was an
Estonian baron, Baron Christoph von Stackelberg. He was a tremendously
learned and intellectual young man, who discussed with Therese and Josephine
the writings of Montaigne, Kant, Benjamin Franklin, Fénélon, and others—
Therese wrote that she "became acquainted with men great and noble"—and he
seemed the ideal man to undertake the instruction of the boys. After six weeks
at Yverdon, the sisters decided to embark on a still longer journey; Stackelberg
offered to accompany them as a tutor. Josephine gladly accepted. But Stackelberg had no money; he was always expecting some, but it never came. So the

---

* Pestalozzi was a follower of Rousseau, being inspired in his educational ideas by *Émile*.

sisters paid all expenses. As Vienna was occupied by Napoleon, they could not easily return there, and so after wandering at a leisurely pace through Italy, they settled in a village called Gran. Josephine longed to see her daughters again; now that the excitement of traveling was over she wanted all her children around her. Stackelberg was instrumental in bringing the little girls from Vienna. He then declared that he could no longer endure remaining in Josephine's company merely as a tutor. He loved Josephine. He couldn't live without her. He wanted to marry her. Josephine accepted him—Therese says "out of love for her children"—and they were married in Gran on February 13, 1810. Their first child, Laura, was born there. They all returned to Vienna and to the Müller Palace once peace had been declared.

Stackelberg did not have the faintest notion of how to deal with the management of the art gallery and the apartments to be let. All he wanted to do was to read. The proprietors of all the book stores in Vienna were his friends, and Therese describes how masses of books appeared every day at their house, the bills for them mounting up to extraordinary sums.

Therese took over the management of the Palace. Neither Josephine nor Stackelberg was happy in Vienna. Perhaps the city and the Deym house were too full of memories for Josephine, and probably Stackelberg wanted to get away from the disapproving Therese. So Josephine and her husband made a down payment on a grandiose country property belonging to a Countess Trautmannsdorff, whose husband had recently died. A complicated contract was entered into and signed by Stackelberg alone. Josephine, Stackelberg, and the four Deym children moved there, as well as the baby born the year before. After a year Stackelberg was unable to meet the payment that was due. In spite of oral promises the former owner insisted on taking back the property, currency in the meantime having been devalued. Stackelberg sued: he lost the case, became morose, melancholy, unable to act in any way. (Josephine didn't help: about the time that the payment was due she bought a "sleeping-equipage" with four fine Polish horses for 10,000 gulden—about $12,000 in the new currency!) Josephine and he quarreled. She refused to give him any money. He left her, and for many months his whereabouts were unknown.

So this marriage too turned out unhappily. While they were still living together, Josephine bore Stackelberg three children, Laura, Theophile, and Minona. He reappeared toward the end of 1814 and demanded that Josephine give up these three children and that they go with him to Russia, where he had inherited property from an older brother. Josephine pleaded, "Let me have the children. I have borne them in pain." But Stackelberg took them with him.

Two years later Josephine and Therese heard that Stackelberg had used up all the money that had been left him, that he had absconded, leaving debts behind, and that they were to send for the children. This they did. Yet at the last minute a younger brother appeared and prevented the departure of the children. Finally, in 1819, Stackelberg himself turned up once more in Vienna with the children, but soon departed, to take them to his mother. Josephine, by this time sick and exhausted, let him go without protest and let the children go as well.

In 1816 Therese had taken over the management of the Deym house. She describes how at five o'clock in the morning she began her working day, doing the marketing, regulating the accounts, supervising the making up of the rooms, listening to complaints, hiring and watching chambermaids and porters, and trying desperately to make the enterprise go. It was she, mostly, who looked after the Deym children, it was she who cared for Josephine; until Josephine, economically pressed, in spirit bewildered and lost, unable to cope with life, no longer surrounded by luxury or smiling servants, her nerves torn to pieces, died in 1821, only forty-two years old.

Therese lived on, and in her old age she found consolation by working with homeless children and by organizing schools for orphans. She became quite prominent in this work. A lithograph shows her as an old woman with a sunken mouth, but eyes still dreamy, teaching the Bible to a young child. She died at the age of eighty-six.

How much did Therese know about Josephine's and Beethoven's relation? Quite a lot, if perhaps not everything. In her diaries we find these entries:

> July 12, 1817 [or 1818?]. I wonder if Jo[sephine] does not suffer punishment because of Luigi's hurt! His wife—what could she not have made out of this hero!
>
> February 4, 1846. Speech is silver, but silence, silence at the right time, is pure gold. This beautiful proverb was set to music by Beethoven.* Beethoven! It is like a dream that he was the friend, the confidant of our house—a magnificent spirit! Why didn't my sister J take him as her husband when she was the widow Deym? She would have been happier with him than with S[tackelberg]. Mother-love decided her to renounce her own happiness.
>
> March 17, 1848. He [a certain Herr Dörfler from Vienna] spoke of Beethoven and admired his power of isolation, which would not let anything trivial

---

* Correct. Beethoven composed it as a canon in 1815.

touch him. O! How I remember that classic epoch of my life, when Josephine, my sister, expressed exactly the same quality through her life, which ended early, just like his, he who was spiritually so closely akin to her. Perhaps he [Dörfler] knew him only a half hour, and I, fortunate one, possessed Beethoven's intimate spiritual acquaintance for so many years! The friend of Josephine's house and heart! They were born for each other, and both of them would still be alive had they been united.*

Schindler's biography of Beethoven appeared in 1840. In it was the letter to the Immortal Beloved, and Schindler thought that she was Giulietta Guicciardi, Therese's own cousin. Therese notes:

> November 12, 1840. Three letters of Beethoven's, purported to be to Giulietta. Could they be a fraud?

(The letter was originally supposed to be three letters, as it is in three parts.) Then she read Schindler's book:

> December 22, 1846. For two days I occupied myself with the biography of Beethoven by Schindler, in 1845, second edition. Many interesting and instructive facts for musicians and pianists, in the higher sense particularly, but about the man as well. How unhappy, with all those great spiritual gifts! At the same time, Josephine was unhappy! Le mieux est l'ennemi du bien ** —together both of them might have been happy. (Perhaps) He lacked a woman, that is certain, just because he did not know how to act—But how happy he could have become! His friends should have guided him toward a good woman.

> January 15, 1847. They [the letters] must be to Josephine, whom he loved passionately.

Therese was mistaken; a natural mistake, both because Schindler had dated the letter 1806 when Beethoven *did* love Josephine, and because Therese now, after so many years, dearly wished that her sister could have been the "Immortal Beloved." (See the discussion later in this chapter.)

·❧[MARIA ERDÖDY]❧·

Of all the women Beethoven knew, the most enigmatic, the least decipherable is Countess Erdödy. She seems like a trick picture which changes as the

---

* One scholar who chose Therese as the Immortal Beloved wrote that she hid her true feelings for Beethoven behind such words! How improbable can theories become?
** "The better is the enemy of the good." Voltaire.

observer passes by. Had she been a creature of fiction, Thomas Mann might have invented her. Because she was a figure of history, one cannot invent but must try to find facts. Little in Beethoven's biography is a more frustrating task. No letters by the countess exist, and for once there is not even a diary to give us a hint. Documents touching her life are incomplete and contradictory. A scandal beclouds her, though guilt has never been proved. Neither has innocence. Was she a woman whose nobility of birth was matched by her nobility of spirit, as Schindler put it? Was she an amicable and good woman, as Reichardt described her? Was she a depraved creature, as some of the police reports imply? Was she a criminal? And if she did commit a crime, what was it? What is the meaning of the statement by Alfred Kalischer, the German editor of Beethoven's letters: "It is not at all clear what Countess Erdödy's crime was—so serious that she, the descendant of one of the most renowned families in the Austro-Hungarian realm, was banished forever from this country"? If she was a criminal, how was it possible that Beethoven counted her among his best friends for years, that he called her his "father-confessor"; and that he never said a word against her, even when damning information reached him? Was it only friendship which united these two? She too has not failed to be elected a candidate for the Immortal Beloved. Like Josephine, she has had a thick book written about her containing the latest of the hypotheses, compiled of insubstantial clues. The book is entitled *Beethoven's Beloved;* it was written by Dana Steichen, the wife of the famous photographer.*

The Countess Anna Maria von Erdödy was the daughter of Count Niczky von Niczk. Her father was something like an "overlord" of a fief (*comitat*) in Hungary. Maria was born in 1779, and when she was seventeen she was married—whether by her own volition or by family contract one does not know—to the Hungarian Count Peter Erdödy. The Erdödys were among the most important families of the Hungarian aristocracy; we find the name strewn throughout the history of the Austrian monarchy in the late 18th and early 19th century (sometimes the name is spelled Erdöd). For example, a Count Carl Erdödy accompanied the Czar back to Russia after the battle of Austerlitz in 1805. A Count Joseph Erdödy (uncle of Maria) entertained Their Imperial Majesties at his hunting lodge "Erdöhaz." **

---

* Mrs. Steichen died before she could put the finishing touches to her manuscript. The book was published in 1959, two years after her death.
** *Wiener Zeitung,* October 19, 1808.

Anna Maria and Peter Erdödy had three children—two girls, Marie (Mimi) and Friederike (Fritzi), and a son, August (Gusti). The marriage proved unhappy and the countess lived separated from her husband, divorce being impossible among Catholics. After the separation from her husband she experienced some financial difficulties; soon enough, however, the husband proved generous to her—or to the children—and enabled the countess to live very well. She owned an estate a few miles north of Vienna in a place called Jedlersee. That was her summer residence. Winters she spent in Vienna. Being an Erdödy, she was received into the most exclusive Vienna society, not only the Hungarian part of it. Both Zmeskall and Lichnowsky knew her. Her household consisted of the children and a tutor named Joseph Xaver Brauchle whom she employed about 1803. Brauchle was jokingly referred to as the *Magister*—Beethoven called him that—a sobriquet which would be equivalent to "The Professor" in our parlance. Then there was the steward of the household, named Sperl. "Sperl" in German means sparrow, and of course Beethoven did not let the opportunity pass to pun on the name. She also employed a cellist, Joseph Linke,* a slightly deformed, shy young man. Linke's name, too, gave Beethoven a chance for punning about left (*links*) and the right one (*der Rechte*). The elder daughter, Mimi, had a personal maid. In addition, the mother employed for the children what was then called a *Gesellschafterin,* a companion. Her name was Nina and she came from Croatia. All these members of the household were eventually to play roles in the drama.

The countess herself, judging by the portrait of her which is extant, possessed the type of looks which we associate with the Age of Romanticism. Goethe might have fallen in love with her had he known her. If the painter portrayed her truly, she must have been conscious of her charm, because confidence emanates from this face, these inviting eyes, this proud posture, this long neck around which dark locks cascade, this discreet but revealing décolleté. But the painting tells only a part of the story: ever since the birth of her first child, Maria was a semi-invalid. Her circulation had become impaired, her feet were swollen. Reichardt wrote (in 1808) that her illness was incurable, that "in ten years she spent but two or three months out of bed, and yet had given birth to three healthy, darling children who hang on her like burrs," and that "she

---

* When the Rasoumovsky Quartet was formed in 1808 with Schuppanzigh as the leader, the selection of the other members was entrusted to him and he chose Linke as the cellist. Obviously he was a good one.

dragged herself with her swollen feet from one forte-piano to another, yet was always merry, amicable and good — it made me melancholy during a dinner, otherwise really quite gay . . ." An afflicted creature she was. It is possible that because of her own suffering she was drawn to Beethoven as he, being himself afflicted, was drawn to her.

What was the nature of their relationship? Schindler says that she caught him "on the rebound," that he sought solace with the countess after the break with Giulietta Guicciardi. He visited her in Jedlersee; they played music together. It happened long before Schindler knew Beethoven; he heard the story from Cherubini many years later in Paris. He weakens the credibility of his report by telling an absurd tale of Beethoven disappearing somewhere within the confines of Maria's estate. The countess thought he had returned to Vienna. Three days later Brauchle discovered him in a distant part of the gardens. Beethoven was supposed to have tried to starve himself to death. Well, the story does not sound right. In the first place, Cherubini did not come to Vienna until 1805, so it is extremely unlikely that he would have known such an intimate detail of Beethoven's life as the broken Guicciardi love affair of four years before. In the second place, Brauchle was not in the countess's service, says Thayer, "until after the year 1803," and Schindler dates the incident earlier than that. In the third place, while Beethoven did fleetingly, in his blackest moments, entertain the thought of suicide, it is pretty ridiculous to suppose that he would consider starving himself to death at the home of a friend.

In the fall of 1808 Beethoven moved to an address which he gave as "1074 Krugerstrasse, at Countess Erdödy's." Other people occupied the apartment house in the Krugerstrasse, including Prince Lichnowsky, who had a *pied-à-terre* there. But Beethoven did move in with Countess Erdödy, occupying rooms in her apartment. This fact has strongly suggested an intimate relationship between them. Dana Steichen adds it to her other tenuous "proofs" of the identity of the Immortal Beloved. While he was living at the countess's, Beethoven composed the two Trios in D and E flat, Op. 70, and played them for the countess at Christmastime of 1808. Reichardt, who was present, wrote that he was quite carried away by the trios; they contained "such a heavenly songlike movement as I have never heard from him before. Indeed, it is the most lovely and most graceful [music] which I have ever heard; — it uplifts and melts my soul every time I remember it . . . The dear, sickly, and yet so charmingly joyful Countess and one of her friends, also a Hungarian lady, felt such inward, enthusiastic pleasure at every beautiful and bold idea, every successful, fine turn of phrase, that I took almost as much delight in seeing them as in Beethoven's masterly work and execution. Fortunate artist who can assure himself of such listeners!" The marvel of these two trios—one of which (in E flat major) is a happy work, though the other (in D major) has so mysterious a slow movement that the work has been nicknamed the "Ghost Trio"—is due to Beethoven's being in love. So is his great productivity around that time, say those who believe that the countess and he were lovers.

But one must be wary of drawing a direct line between heart and brain. Cause and effect of creativity are not so simply diagrammed. Wagner did not compose *Tristan* because he was in love with Mathilde Wesendonk; perhaps the reverse is nearer the mark—he fell in love with Mathilde because *Tristan* was germinating in his mind. Beethoven's creativity at that period—the period begins when his connection with Maria Erdödy was not as yet a close one—may have had little to do with love and its "inspiration." Who will ever know when and where and how Beethoven got his inspirations? A woman may have awakened slumbering thoughts. Then again, she may not have.

Another interpretation of the Erdödy relationship is possible, one which seems more probable to me. Beethoven, who, as I have said, was secretiveness itself about his loves, here made not the slightest attempt to hide his intimacy with the countess. He openly announced her address as his.* Just at that time a most important proposal came his way, one which will be discussed later. Suffice it to say here that he had received an offer from the new King of Westphalia to become official composer to the Court. When his friends heard about it they feared that they would lose Beethoven—for themselves and for Vienna. A plan was put forth to subscribe to a fund which would guarantee Beethoven an annual income on condition that he would remain in Vienna. The Countess Erdödy took an active part in formulating this plan. Not only did Beethoven approve of her role in the plan but he approved of her becoming the negotiator in drawing his friends together and finalizing the proposal. Again not the slightest secret was made of the relationship; Beethoven wrote to Gleichenstein in February, 1809: "The Countess Erdödy thinks that you ought to draw up with her a plan, on the basis of which, if she is approached, as she certainly believes she will be, she will be able to negotiate—" (A-198). A month later,

---

* For example: he wrote to Count Oppersdorf (November 1, 1808) that he was living at Countess Erdödy's apartment, underneath that of Prince Lichnowsky, "in case you wish to honor me sometime by visiting me . . ." In the advertisement for his benefit concert (*Wiener Zeitung*, December 17, 1808), the address where tickets may be bought is given as 1074 Krugerstrasse.

March 14, 1809, Beethoven wrote again to Gleichenstein, telling him that the contract had been satisfactorily settled, that remaining in Vienna had now become honorable for him, and that "Now you can help me to look for a wife. Indeed you might find some beautiful girl at F[reiburg] where you are at present, and one who would perhaps now and then grant a sigh to my harmonies . . . But she must be beautiful, for it is impossible for me to love anything that is not beautiful—or else I should have to love myself" (A-202). Even if he was half joking, he doesn't sound like a man who is deeply in love. True, just about that time he quarreled with the countess. Yet to suppose that in one month Beethoven changed from a lover to a man who merrily asks a friend to find him a wife is to impute a mercurial temperament to him which he did not possess. In short, it is more reasonable to suppose that he and the countess were friends, good friends, two human beings, kindred in several characteristics and interests, but not lovers.

The cause of the quarrel was so absurd as to be hard to believe. It was about a servant. It seems that the countess gave Beethoven's servant some extra money, without telling Beethoven about it, to make it attractive for the servant to stay in the employ of his difficult master. Beethoven found out about it, took umbrage at what was obviously an act of unselfish generosity, moved out of the countess's apartment, and asked Zmeskall to settle the matter of the servant. He wrote to him: "I am leaving it entirely to you to settle the question with my servant. But the Countess *Erdödy* must not exert even the slightest influence on him. According to her *statement* she has made him a present of 25 gulden and given him five gulden a month simply *in order that he shall stay with me*—I am now *compelled* to believe in this generosity—but I refuse to allow it to be practiced any longer—" (A-208). He had been living at the countess's home some five months, but now posthaste he fled, not even taking the trouble to find suitable rooms but taking quarters in a house of ill repute (*Walfischgasse* 1087). He was under no illusion as to where he was, for he wrote to Gleichenstein in April, giving him his new address: "It's a b[rothel], you will know it." He didn't stay there long. He repented and wrote the countess the kind of letter we have come to expect from him when he put on sackcloth and ashes:

[VIENNA, March, 1809]

My Dear Countess,

I have acted wrongly, it is true—Forgive me. If I offended you, it was certainly not due to deliberate wickedness on my part—Only since yesterday evening have I really understood how things are; and I am very sorry that I behaved as I did—Read your note calmly, and then judge for yourself whether I have deserved it and whether you have not paid me back sixfold for all I have done, seeing that I offended you without wishing to do so. Do return my note today and do write just one word to say that you are fond of me again. If you don't do this I shall suffer infinite pain. I shall be unable to do anything if this state of affairs is to continue—I am awaiting your forgiveness.   (A-207.)

Did she become fond of him again? There are no letters for six years, but of course this does not mean that none was written. He now wanted to change the dedication of the two Trios and wrote Breitkopf and Härtel on May 26, 1809, asking that the name of Archduke Rudolph be substituted for that of Countess Erdödy. It was too late. The original dedication remained.

Baron Louis-Philippe Trémont, whose impressions of Beethoven we will record later, said that the countess was to Beethoven what Madame Houdetot was to Rousseau. That is a very fine compliment to the countess. Madame Houdetot (Comtesse Elisabeth-Sophie de Bellegarde) was an altogether attractive and brilliant woman, quite unconcerned with what the neighbors thought: when she wanted to see Rousseau, she dressed in man's clothing and rode over to seek him out in his retreat. She served Rousseau as the model for his Julie in *La Nouvelle Héloïse.* But Rousseau and she were never lovers, and perhaps that is what Trémont meant to imply of Beethoven and Erdödy.

The correspondence resumed in 1815.* In February of that year Beethoven wrote to the countess a warm and friendly letter. He himself spoke of "friendship":

VIENNA, February 29, 1815 [must be March 1]

I have read your letter with great pleasure my beloved Countess, and also what you say about the renewal of your friendship for me. It has long been my wish to see you and your beloved children once again. For although I have suffered a great deal, yet I have not lost my former love for children, the beauties of nature and friendship—The trio and everything else that has not been published are most certainly at your service, my dear Countess—As soon as the trio has been copied you shall have it. It was not without sympathy and interest that I frequently enquired after your state of health. But now I will call on you sometime in person and I shall have the pleasure of being able to participate in everything that concerns you—

The prospect of the coming spring will, I trust, have an excellent influence on

---

* There is an entry in Beethoven's journal (Fischhoff manuscript) of 1814: "34 bottles from Countess Erdödy." Could it have been a peace offering of wine she sent him?

your health as well, and perhaps surround you with the happiest of life's realities —May all that is good be your portion, dear and beloved Countess. I send my greetings to your dear children whom I embrace in spirit—I hope to see you soon—

Your true friend
LUDWIG VAN BEETHOVEN (A-531).

In July when the countess was, as usual, living at Jedlersee, she sent him through Sperl a whimsical invitation in verse to come and visit her, to which Beethoven replied whimsically:

[DÖBLING, *shortly after July 20, 1815*]

My dear and beloved Countess!

You are again bestowing gifts upon me and so soon too; and that is not right. For you thereby rob me entirely of the merit of having rendered you a small service—

It is uncertain whether I can go to you tomorrow, however much I should like to do so. But certainly I shall visit you in a few days' time, even if it has to be in the afternoon. My situation at the moment is very difficult. I shall tell you more about this when I see you. Greet and press to your heart in my name all your children who are so dear to me—Give the Magister a gentle box on the ear, and the chief steward a solemn nod. To the violoncello the task has been allotted of betaking himself to the left [*linke*] * bank of the Danube and continuing to play until everything on the right bank has been drawn across to the other side. In this way your population will soon increase. Let me add that I shall confidently take the road across the Danube as I did before. *Courage,* provided it *be justified,* enables one to triumph everywhere—

I kiss your hands many times. Remember with pleasure your friend

BEETHOVEN

So don't send a carriage. I would rather *dare!* than take a *carriage!* **
The music I have promised will be sent from town.   (A-549).

Surely these are anything but love letters.

In the fall of that year the countess and her household moved to an estate she owned in Croatia. Beethoven wrote her a letter in which he expressed his

---

* His pun on the name of Joseph Linke, the Erdödys' cellist.
** Another pun: "carriage" is *Wagen;* to "dare," *wagen.*

anxiety about the difficulties and the pain she might have experienced during the long journey. He tried to console her:

> We finite beings, who are the embodiment of an infinite spirit, are born to suffer both pain and joy; and one might almost say that the best of us obtain *joy through suffering*—

The year after, we find the countess in Padua. Beethoven let her have news of himself:

VIENNA, May 13, 1816

My dear and beloved Friend!

Perhaps you believe, and quite rightly, that I have completely *forgotten all about you.* But indeed that is only what appears to be the case. My brother's death [Carl] caused me great sorrow; and then it necessitated *great efforts* to save my nephew, who is very dear to me, from the influence of his depraved mother. I succeeded in doing this. But so far I have not yet been able to make a *better arrangement* for him than to place him at a boarding school, which means that he is separated from me; and what is a boarding school compared with the immediate sympathetic care of a father for his child? For I now regard myself as his father; and I keep on wondering how I can have this treasure, who is very precious to me, nearer to me, so as to be able to influence him more directly and to his greater advantage—But how difficult is that for me!—Moreover, for the last six weeks I have been in very poor health, so much so that frequently I have thought of my death. I do not dread it. Yet I should be dying too soon so far as my poor Karl is concerned—I gather from your last few lines to me that you, my dear friend, are still suffering a great deal. Man cannot avoid suffering; and *in this respect his strength must stand the test,* that is to say, he must *endure without complaining and feel his worthlessness* and *then again* achieve *his perfection,* that perfection which the Almighty will then bestow upon him— Well, Linke will by this time be with you. May he *afford you pleasure by means of his gut strings*—Brauchle, no doubt, will not refrain from *using everything* and, as usual, you will make use of him day and night [pun on the verb *brauchen,* to use]—As for that bird Sperl, I hear that you are not satisfied with him, but why I do not know. I hear, however, that you are looking for another steward. I beg you not to be hasty and to acquaint me with your *views and intentions* in this matter. Perhaps I can give you *some helpful information;* but perhaps you are not quite fair to *Sperl in his cage?*—I embrace your children and I am expressing this in a trio. No doubt your children are progressing every day towards perfection—Let me know quite soon, very soon, how you are faring on that little *foggy spot of the earth* where you are now. Certainly, even if I do not always mention or express this to you at once, I take the greatest interest in *your joys* and *sorrows.* How long do you intend to stay at Padua and where are you going to live in future? — There is going to be an alteration in the dedication of the *violoncello sonatas,* which, however, will not alter either *you* or *me* —

Dear precious Countess, in haste I remain your friend

BEETHOVEN   (A-633).

Before mailing this letter he receives shocking news. He meets Linke in Vienna and hears that the countess's son has died. From the fullness of his heart he writes to her, enclosing both letters in the same envelope.

VIENNA, May 15, 1816

Dear and beloved Friend!

I had already written the enclosed letter when I met Linke today and heard about your grievous blow, the sudden loss of your dear son — What comfort can I give you? Nothing hurts more than the rapid and unforeseen departure of those who are near and dear to us. Thus I too cannot forget the death of my poor brother. The only consolation is — that one can believe that those who have suddenly departed suffer less — But I feel the deepest sympathy for you in your irreparable loss — Perhaps I have not yet told you that I too have not been feeling at all well for a considerable time. That is another reason for my long silence. Then, in addition, there are the cares connected with my Karl whom I often intended to attach to your dear son — I am overcome with grief on your account and also on my own, for I loved your son — Heaven watches over you and will not want to increase the great sorrows with which you are already afflicted, particularly as your state of health may possibly become still more enfeebled. But bear in mind that your son might have had to go into battle and like millions of others there meet his death. And remember that you still are the *mother* of two dear and promising children — I trust that I shall soon have news of you. I weep with you here. And now let me ask you not to lend an ear to all the gossip about why I was not writing to you. And pay no attention to Linke who is devoted to you, I admit, but who is *very fond of gossiping* — Besides I firmly believe, dear Countess, that you and I need no go-between.

In haste, with kind regards, your friend

BEETHOVEN   (A-634).

Now we must navigate in strange waters. We have to trace the fate of Maria Erdödy from the available facts. Most of these facts have been obtained from the original police records now housed in the Vienna House of Documents — Court and Government Archives, Vienna I, Waldnerstrasse 6. Unfortunately, these documents are incomplete. At one time they were kept in the Palace of

Justice. When that building was stormed in the uprising of 1927, a fire broke out; some of the documents were saved, but many burned altogether and others were singed so that they are now difficult to decipher.

Maria Erdödy, along with several Hungarian aristocrats, had come to the attention of the police in 1811 (Document 1262Z2). It was at the time that Austria was bankrupt and currency was devalued. Metternich was in charge, and Austrian censorship, always severe, had been tightened to a degree which made even slight criticism of government policy dangerous. Moreover, the dissatisfied and unruly Hungarians were giving trouble to Metternich. Maria Erdödy was called for a hearing before the Police Commission. She, along with her Hungarian friends, was accused of criticizing the Finance Law of 1811 and its "maladroit application in Hungary" (Document 1917).* Letters of incriminating content were produced; the writer of these letters reports discontent in Agram, desertion by soldiers, and so on. Countess Erdödy sent friendly greetings to the recipient of these letters. The evidence, however, seems to have been insufficient to warrant police action and the countess was dismissed.

Shortly afterward, in 1812, Count Peter Erdödy published in the *Wiener Zeitung* an official notice to the effect that "he was entrusting the management of his fortune to his wife." What the purpose of that notice was is difficult to say. It is possible that Peter Erdödy intended to take an active part in Hungarian affairs and wished to protect his wife, estranged though she was, and his children in case he got into trouble. It is also possible that the countess forced him to do this either because she was already *persona non grata* with the police or because Erdödy's family was starting a family war.

In 1815 and 1817 Countess Erdödy visited her estate in Croatia, where Beethoven planned to visit her. In 1816 she was in Padua, as I stated. She and her household returned to Vienna sometime in 1819.

Early in the spring of 1820 her daughter Mimi attempted suicide. Her mother thereupon sent her to a cloister in St. Pölten where the nuns were to take care of her.

In addition, there were rumors that the countess's son had not died a natural death in Padua, that Brauchle had beaten him to death. Some rumors even claimed that the mother had a hand in the son's death.

---

* Griesinger reported to Dresden: "The Hungarians, writing petitions a mile long couched in bad Latin, are protesting that they cannot accede to the demands of their King. They want the Finance Law repealed and gold and silver currency re-introduced as soon as possible. What is going to be the consequence of such protest?"

The police then stepped in. An Inspector Sicard was appointed to investigate the Erdödy household. In April or early May the countess was summoned to the "Supreme Bureau" (*Oberdirektion*) of the Vienna Police.

The inspector's report sketches the people employed by the countess, mentioning Nina from Croatia, a "Secretary" Brauchle, and a chambermaid "who took the young girl's part" (Sperl is not mentioned). Sicard states that Mimi had been maltreated by "employees of the mother and as a result had become extremely frightened and shy." She seemed, to be sure, well nourished, but poorly dressed. From Sicard's report of April 14, 1820:

> Indeed it seems advisable that the young Contessa ... be freed from the clutches of the Secretary and the so-called Fraulein Nina ... [The mother] has tongue-lashed the daughter with such words that in a kind of despair she went into her room and decided to poison herself with opium.

To add to Countess Erdödy's troubles, the police now brought to light the fact that she had previously been involved in an investigation in Hungary, one instigated by her sister-in-law, Countess Sigismund Erdödy. The sister-in-law had accused her of being a spendthrift and willfully wasting Erdödy property.

Brauchle was called for questioning and was then taken into custody.

Countess Erdödy pleaded not guilty, both for herself and Brauchle. In answer to the accusation by her sister-in-law, she stated that there was no truth in it, that it was prompted by the hatred which her sister-in-law felt for her, and was one of the many intrigues which Countess Sigismund had thought up against her. Both she and her husband were powerless against these intrigues and considered them as a tribulation from God. In a petition to the Prefect of the Police * on June 29, 1820, she begs that "in all fairness and kindness the judgment be set aside that Brauchle may not be released from prison before her daughter had left her house." (But she *had* left her house.) She points out that

> such a judgment constitutes a dreadful offense against my own and my daughter's honor; everybody would, quite naturally, jump to the conclusion that an affair was going on between Brauchle and my daughter, and that the High Police Bureau ... had—partly to protect the ailing mother—assumed the task of ending the affair by force ... Was it not hard to rob a human being of her holiest possession, her honor, just because she found herself in a state of human

---

* His name was Count Sedlnitzky. He was one of Metternich's important functionaries.

confusion, intending no evil? As to the question of the maintenance of my daughter in a style commensurate with her station, I assure you that you need not be concerned with it, nor trouble a mother's heart with such impugnation. Some time ago when both my husband and my father refused me any financial support I was capable of making things with my hands [*Handarbeit*], sell them to a shop here, and bring up my children decently. It is many years since I or my children have received the slightest financial support from the shaken fortune of my husband ... I have been able not only to bring my father's possessions, once robbed of livestock and furnishings by the provisions of his testament, into a flourishing state but was successful even in paying off most of the debts which my father left, using that part of the Erdödy fortune which is my rightful due by marriage.

The document is marked *"expedirt* 29 July 820." That may mean "expedited" or "settled" and probably means that the countess was found not guilty. Brauchle was released. Maria obviously acquiesced to the decree issued by the *"K.K. Polizey Ober Direktion"* which read in part: "It is the duty of the POD carefully to watch that the above-mentioned Countess will leave her daughter, who is at the moment residing in the house of the English sisters in St. Pölten, in this abode or in any other decent place of residence until the danger to her life, her health and her good morals has passed and a renewal of the stormy scenes which have taken place in her mother's house and which have given rise to the present ... official action is no longer to be feared."

Later, however (Document 9053/1823), the mother submits a new petition: she wants her daughter back. She writes that her daughter had been "incited by the rest of the family" and had now had a change of heart. She encloses letters from her daughter showing that the separation is making the daughter suffer, that she weeps a lot, that she worries about her mother's health. Indeed, her mother's health is nothing short of "catastrophic." The countess is unable to leave her room for weeks. She is suffering with ulcers, vomits frequently, and cannot even retain opium. Mimi complains that her mother hardly writes to her because she lacks the strength to write, and Mimi has to receive news about her mother from a mutual friend (female). (This friend is characterized by Inspector Sicard as a "dangerous person who will bear watching.") In Mimi's many letters, submitted by the countess, there occurs but one mention of Beethoven (letter of August 21, 1820): "One more request I have, my good mother. My music master honestly desires that I do not forget the pieces by Buthoven [*sic*] which I have learned. But we have no music here by Buthov ..."

To her new petition Maria Erdödy appends testimonials from friends repudiating the accusation that she neglected or maltreated her children. One of these reads in part:

> I testify that from their birth on she never let her three children from her side and she treated them with unique tenderness and self-sacrifice. She nursed them herself like a wetnurse in spite of the fact that for twenty years * she has suffered a serious illness which is painful, strange and rare. She has guided their education herself, though the children had decent and able governesses, etc.
>
> Vienna, 8 November 1820
> (signed) THERESIA FREYFRAU V. SCHLUTITZKY,
> nee COUNTESS STRASOTVO

On January 25, 1821, another petition was sent by the countess to the Prefect of Police. She says that after being accused by her sister-in-law a Court inquiry was begun in Hungary in which the Court not only exonerated her but testified to her extremely good economic management. She feels that her troubles are due to a plan hatched by her sister-in-law Countess Sigismund: that plan calls for her daughter to marry her sister-in-law's son so that Countess Sigismund would get her hands on the fortune which Maria possesses and help Count Sigismund, who "has squandered everything . . ." No answers to these petitions have been found.

But in 1822 there is further trouble (Document 7498). The Police are informed (from Hungary) that on hearing the news that a Count Joseph Erdödy had died, the manager of the estate of Countess Erdödy-Niczky had gathered 300 peasants and had invaded the castle where Joseph Erdödy lived. This happened during the night of July 26–27. The manager proclaimed that since the countess had been half owner of this estate she was now the rightful inheritor of the whole castle. The report states: "Since Joseph Erdödy was still alive, he promptly made arrangements to have his niece thrown out of the castle." But was she really there? Did she really invade the castle with the 300 peasants? Did she incite the manager to this action? The matter is by no means certain.

This fresh report could hardly have made a good impression on the Vienna Police. When Countess Maria and her household returned to Vienna the year after, she attempted to smuggle in an actor who was employed by her as her

---

* Maria was now forty-one years old. The "twenty years" seems a truthful statement.

"reader." He had not been furnished with a proper passport. Not a serious offense—but the police immediately proceeded against her. Inspector Sicard reported on October 28, 1823: "The Countess Erdödy, known to us from the investigation of J820 [sic], has arrived here from Agram with her notorious secretary Brauchle and an actor from the Agram Theater by the name of Walther." He wished instructions on "what measures should be taken against the Countess and her two lovers?" *

In reply the countess takes upon herself the entire blame for smuggling in young Walther. She asks for clemency, because he is the sole support of his old parents. She also asks that in view of the wretched state of her health she be not deprived of the "pleasure of being able to hear the trained voice of Walther who reads to her."

Here end the documents. There are no indications of the disposition of Countess Erdödy's case. We do know that the countess moved to Munich the following year. Thayer was led to understand that she was banished from Austria, but that is not proved. She lived out her life in Munich. In 1830 Brauchle and his wife joined her there. She died in 1837 in her fifty-seventh year.

Her brush with the police in 1820 could not have been kept a secret and must have been known at least to the "inner circle" of Vienna. In a Conversation Book of that year the following is written by an unknown hand:

> Curious things have been happening for some time. Brauchle was [is?] locked up by the police. Comtes Mimi is in the cloister St. Pölten since several days.
>
> On account of the young Gusti, that he [obviously Brauchle] maltreated him so and he is accused of having killed him.
>
> Sperl and the servants, including the chambermaid, were very often interrogated, indeed Sperl was always present at the interrogation of Brauchle—in the Manggasse 274, ground floor—but also at one time [?] at the old Wieden.
>
> The police is informed about everything conceivable, including her way of life, though he is free for a few hours he is always under surveillance.
>
> It would be best to appoint an administrator for her estates; that will happen, she now resides in the Landstrasse.
>
> The old man [Joseph Erdödy?] is still living and so is his family.

---

* Sicard's reports sound inimical enough to make one suspect he had a personal grudge against the countess.

The little Gustav in Italy, City of Padua. Now the police have written there.

He renewed the contract for a year and he is much fatter than he used to be [Linke?]. He plays cards the whole day long, but also violin. They say he plays much worse than he used to when he was here.

What did Beethoven say to all that?

The whole case is such a maze that even the careful Thayer got tangled in it. Thayer thought that "Fritzi" was a boy and it was he who died (in Croatia, not in Padua). Gunther Haupt, in his article *"Gräfin Erdödy und J. X. Brauchle,"* * points out that the death could not have taken place in Croatia and that the countess had only one son. In a letter to the countess, Beethoven sends his greetings to "the daughters." They were Mimi and Fritzi. Nothing is known about the fate of Fritzi.

Where is the truth? Was the Countess Erdödy a criminal? Or was she the victim of political anti-Hungarian prosecution? Was she involved in her son's death? Is it conceivable that Brauchle beat the young count to death and that the mother protected him? Why did Mimi attempt suicide? Did the police inspector know what he was talking about when he called Brauchle and Walther the countess's lovers or was he making an irresponsible statement? What *was* the character of this countess?

May I be permitted a guess? I am inclined to a kindlier view of Maria Erdödy than the one taken by such men as Kalischer, Romain Rolland, and Thayer. I do not believe she was a criminal. I believe:

1. Beethoven and the countess were united in warm friendship occasionally cooled by Beethoven's suspicious temper. He loved her as a trusted companion, as a well-wisher, as a woman in whom he could confide. He admired her as a woman who understood and appreciated and played his music. He liked her practical sense, the leadership she showed in getting his contract for a lifetime subsidy. He liked her because she was an attractive woman. But there was no burning passion, no sexual relation.

2. The countess had an unstable personality. There is no doubt that she suffered much bodily pain for many years, and it is probable that she took opium to alleviate that pain. Like most addicts, her actions often became irresponsible, occasionally violent.

3. She talked too much, and that was dangerous in a city where Metternich

---

* In *Der Bär,* Leipzig, 1927.

was listening. She was politically suspect as a Hungarian patriot. When the police moved to investigate her, they did so with gusto. They might have been lenient had she been an adherent of the official government policy.

4. Unless new evidence to the contrary can be brought forth, I prefer to believe her: she *did* love her children. Gusti probably died a natural death in Padua. No doubt there were "stormy scenes," but it is difficult to conceive that she committed a crime against her children.

5. She liked money, was a good manager, spent freely. She may have made some of her friends envious, in addition to her sister-in-law. Beethoven benefited by her hospitality.

6. She did not tell the entire truth to the police. At least she exaggerated or underplayed, whatever she thought helped her cause. Her testimony reads like doubtful mumbo-jumbo, hardly the deposition of an entirely innocent person, but this may be due to its being transmitted in a garbled version. She may have been hiding not only political activities but also her addiction to opium.

7. If Brauchle was the countess's lover, Beethoven did not know about it. The letters that Beethoven wrote Brauchle, though they are few in number, contain not the slightest hint that he was privy to such a secret.

8. Beethoven derived happiness from knowing her—and she from knowing him. In spite of the servant quarrel, it was a beneficent friendship.

Having said that, I repeat that it is all more or less a guess. Maria Erdödy, one of the women most important in Beethoven's life, remains shrouded in mystery. But I do not for a moment believe that Countess Erdödy was the Immortal Beloved. Aside from other indications, the stylistic difference between the letters that Beethoven wrote her and the letter to the Immortal Beloved is too great to be reconciled.

·❧[BETTINA BRENTANO]❧·

By way of contrast to the sad story of the Brunsvik sisters and the lurid Erdödy story, let us turn to a lighter episode, that of Bettina Brentano.

Bettina was the daughter of an Italian merchant and of Maximiliane La-roche, a fascinating woman with whom Goethe had been very much in love. As a child Bettina had sat in openmouthed admiration before Goethe's mother, and when Frau Goethe spoke she wrote down every word. The old lady was fond of her and used to talk to her at length about her famous son. Bettina was brought up in a convent, where she soon astonished her teachers not only with the brilliance of her mind but with her excessive vanity. Very early she saw herself in the role of the Muse of Genius, an intellectual Helen of Troy or a Heloise who would serve more than one Abelard. To prepare herself for such a role she acquired a wide knowledge of all she thought "beautiful and spiritual": she avidly read classic and modern literature, could quote the new Romantic poetry by the yard, spoke several languages, dabbled in painting, composed and listened to music while striking a soulful pose. She did all this with "style," enjoying every experience; the one thing that made her life in the convent unhappy was the absence of a mirror.

When she was twenty-four, that is in 1809, she appeared before the sixty-year-old Goethe—a girl with the black eyes of her mother and a sensuous bosom. Telling him stories of her childhood memories, of the hours spent with his mother, she not only succeeded in being received in Goethe's house but very soon in being placed on his lap. She knew all about Goethe's life, his love affairs; and she had, to do her justice, exact knowledge not only of Goethe's poetic writing but of his scientific essays. Goethe's wife Christiane, now the august and corpulent Mme. Privy Councilor, looked with understandable misgiving on this young lady who, beautifully dressed and sparkling with life, stopped at nothing to conquer the Olympian. Bettina had said to her friend the poet Tieck, "You know, Tieck, I have got to have a child by Goethe—why, it will be a demigod!"

In the book which she later wrote, she relates that Goethe visited her one night at her inn, climbing three flights of stairs to her room, clasping her in his arms on the sofa and covering her with his dark cloak. Whether that is true is a moot question. True it is that later she and Christiane literally came to blows, and that Goethe soon found her a bit too impetuous for comfort.

She was always fabricating glittering adventures that happened to her, all implying that one great man or another lost his head or his heart to her. But it was not all invention: Bettina *did* have charm, she did have the insatiable desire for admiration which constitutes half the requisite for being admired, she was impudently attractive. The poet Karl August Varnhagen described her: "If I didn't resist, Bettina would turn me entirely into her slave; it is incredible how she captures and spins her web around people ... She makes you feel that you have nothing more important to do than to please her ... She always wants something from the man who is with her, she wants to admire him and use him and tease him, or be admired, used, teased by him." * She was small and dainty

---

* From his Diary, written when Bettina was well advanced in years.

and she emphasized the childlike quality of her looks. Like a child she spun her yarns with eyes wide open. Whether we call her an embellisher of truth or just a plain liar depends on the charity of our view. To his wife Varnhagen wrote, "Bettina, the charming, sensitive and brilliant Bettina is brazen and shameless in lying." But she did not lie all the time; she sometimes told the truth about Goethe and Beethoven and the others. The trouble is we cannot know when she did and when she did not.

Three years after Goethe's death in 1832, Bettina published a book titled *Goethe's Correspondence with a Child.* The letters there published probably contain phrases of truth, but they are set within a field of flowery inventions, Bettina's own. She even quoted some love poems which Goethe was supposed to have written her, but which we now know were meant for somebody else.

One day in the spring of 1810, Beethoven, sitting at the piano with a song just composed before him, suddenly felt a pair of hands being placed upon his shoulders. Angrily he glanced at the intruder, but at once his face broke into a smile as he saw a girl standing there who put her mouth to his ear and said, "My name is Bettina Brentano." Beethoven knew who she was. He said to her, "I have just composed a beautiful song for you. Do you want to hear it?" He sang it in a hoarse, rasping voice. It was the beautiful song of Mignon to Goethe's words, *"Kennst du das Land?"* ("Do you know the land?"). Beethoven asked, "How do you like it?" She nodded, overcome with emotion. "Yes, it is beautiful," he said, "marvelously beautiful. I will sing it again." He sang it again, looked at her, and seeing her eyes glow, delighted in her approval. He then sang another song to words by Goethe, "Do not dry the tears of eternal love." Such is the description of their first meeting as she wrote it in a letter to a friend and as she told it years later to Thayer.*

Beethoven spent the entire day with her, in great good humor. She invited him to a dinner party at her brother Franz's. Bettina told Beethoven to change his shabby coat. "Oh," he replied, "I have several good coats," and he opened the closet to show them to her. He put on one of the good coats, went down to the street with her, stopped, excused himself, went upstairs again and returned dressed in his old coat. She wouldn't have it that way, so laughingly he ascended once more to dress himself properly.

---

* Thayer, while he was well aware of her tendency to invent romantic stories, believed her in this instance. Other scholars did not, and doubted the story of her meeting with Beethoven and his immediate capitulation to her.

Beethoven fell under Bettina's spell. She possessed, no doubt, the intuitive skill of drawing him out and of supplying gaiety. She made him talk. She knew how to listen. She was genuinely stirred by his music. She recognized the extraordinary power, the introspective intensity, the honesty of this man who preferred dressing in an old coat. She wanted to effect an acquaintance between him and her other hero, Goethe. "Yes," said Beethoven, "speak to Goethe about me." She wrote to Goethe (but the long letter which she published as having been written on May 28, 1810, is not only a montage of several letters, but contains some material she never wrote), and Goethe replied, in part:

June 6, 1810

Give Beethoven my heartiest greetings and tell him that I would willingly make sacrifices to have his acquaintance, when an exchange of thoughts and feelings would surely be beautifully profitable; mayhap you may be able to persuade him to make a journey to Karlsbad whither I go nearly every year and would have the greatest leisure to listen to him and learn from him. To think of teaching him would be an insolence even in one with greater insight than mine, since he has the guiding light of his genius which frequently illumines his mind like a stroke of lightning while we sit in darkness and scarcely suspect the direction from which the daylight will break upon us.

It would give me great joy if Beethoven were to make me a present of the two songs of mine which he has composed, but neatly and plainly written. I am very eager to hear them. It is one of my greatest enjoyments, for which I am very grateful, to have the old moods of such a poem (as Beethoven very correctly says) newly aroused in me ...

Bettina sent the two songs—and enclosed two of her *own* composition!

Two years later Goethe and Beethoven did meet in Teplitz, the fashionable watering place. We will quote Goethe's impressions later.

In the meantime Bettina had married. Her husband was the poet Achim von Arnim, who, with Bettina's brother Clemens Brentano, collected and published an anthology of folk poems, *Des Knaben Wunderhorn.* ("The Youth's Magic Horn." Gustav Mahler set some of the songs to music.) Arnim was a remarkably handsome man, and the marriage turned out very happily for both of them. After the wedding, Beethoven sent Bettina a congratulatory sonnet (a very lame piece), which does not indicate that his heart was broken.

After Beethoven's death Bettina published three letters which she claimed Beethoven had written her, in 1810 (the year they became acquainted), 1811 (the year she got married), and 1812. At first these documents were taken seriously, but soon doubts of their genuineness began to arise, because of both factual inconsistencies and stylistic incongruities; Beethoven delivered himself in two of the three letters of unexpected animadversion.* Schindler called on her in 1843 and asked for the originals of the letters, but "the lady wrapped herself in silence." Otto Jahn called on her, and she became (according to Varnhagen) "visibly embarrassed." No one has seen the manuscripts of the two doubtful letters.

Yet one letter, that of February 10, 1811, is genuine. Beethoven writes her (in part):

> I carried your first letter about with me during the whole summer; and indeed it often made me feel supremely happy. Even though I do not write to you very often and although you see nothing of me, yet in thought I write a thousand letters to you a thousand times—Even if I had not read your remarks about it in your letters, I could imagine how you were getting on in Berlin ** with those dregs of international society; nothing but talk and chatter about art, without doing anything!!!!! ... You are getting married, dear Bettine, or perhaps you are already married; and I have not even been able to see you again before the event. Well, may all the happiness and blessings which marriage bestows upon a wedded couple be yours and your husband's in full measure—What shall I tell you about myself? "Pity my fate," I cry with Johanna.*** If I am spared for a few more years, I shall render thanks for this, as for all other weal and woe, to the All-embracing Divinity.... —If you write to Goethe about me, choose all the words which will tell him of my warmest regard and admiration. I am just about to write to him myself on the subject of *Egmont* which I have set to music, and, what is more, purely out of love for his poems which make me feel happy. But who can sufficiently thank a great poet, a nation's most precious jewel?—Well, no more of this, dear, kind B[ettine]. I did not get home until four o'clock this morning from a bacchanalia, where I really had to laugh a great deal, with the result that today I have had to cry as heartily. Exuberant jollity often drives me back most violently into myself— (A-296).

Once again, this does not read like the letter of a heartbroken lover.

One of the other two letters, supposedly by Beethoven, relates an incident which has become a famous anecdote.

---

* There is no general agreement. Some (like André Maurois) think that Beethoven may have made such observations to Bettina in person, and then Bettina dressed them up. I think they were Bettina's free inventions.
** Bettina and Arnim had moved to Berlin.
*** A quotation from Schiller's *The Maid of Orléans*.

Goethe and Beethoven were taking a walk in Teplitz and they saw from a distance the entire Imperial Family approaching them. Goethe immediately stood aside. It was useless for Beethoven to protest; Goethe would not move another step. Beethoven pulled his hat over his head, buttoned his coat, and, with his arms crossed, strode through the crowd. Princes and flunkies made way to let him pass. The Archduke Rudolph took off his hat. The Empress was the first to greet him. Goethe, however, stood at the side with his hat off, making low bows. Afterward Beethoven remonstrated with Goethe for his servile behavior. This was supposed to have occurred in August, 1812.

Probably this is all fiction. The entire Imperial Family were not in Teplitz in August, 1812, nor was Beethoven himself, and Archduke Rudolph wasn't in Teplitz at all that year. Nor is it reasonable to suppose that Beethoven, rough though he could be, would behave in such a boorish manner. He admired and stood in awe of Goethe—as late as 1823 he wrote Goethe, "I have lived since my youth in your immortal and ever youthful works"—and it is improbable that he would "give him what-for" (*"Dann hab' ich ihm noch den Kopf gewaschen"*), as Bettina has him say. Beethoven did write—to the publishers Breitkopf and Härtel—that Goethe seemed to him to be a little overfond of the atmosphere of the Court, but that is different from face-to-face censure.

Bettina told the story not only in the spurious letter but in a description she sent to her friend Prince Pückler-Muskau. In that report she has Beethoven running to her and Arnim and relating the whole incident. Then why did he find it necessary to describe the same episode in a letter?

Equally suspect is an anecdote told by the novelist August Frankl. According to him, wherever Goethe and Beethoven went, the people on the Promenade respectfully made way for them and saluted. Goethe, annoyed by these constant attentions, said, "What a nuisance! I can never avoid this sort of thing!" Smilingly Beethoven answered, "Do not let it bother Your Excellency; the homage is probably meant for me."

In her old age Bettina maintained with great assurance that Beethoven was desperately in love with her and wanted to marry her. She spoke of "My Beethoven." Varnhagen, who judged Bettina dispassionately, noted in his diary almost half a century after the events (entry of February 15, 1856):

Bettina speaks of Beethoven and says he was in love with her and wanted to marry her! However, she was used to the contemplation of the handsome face of Arnim and she did not consider the matter; but if she had become his wife, she would never have regretted it. He composed the song "Heart, My Heart, What Will Happen?" for her. Nothing but fantasy and dreams! (*Schaum und Traum*). Beethoven never thought of marriage when he knew Bettina, and he had published the song in 1808, before he knew of Bettina's existence!

·◦[THERESE MALFATTI]◦·

Of other women with whom Beethoven was supposed to be in love, we can say less because we know even less. In the years in which Bettina appears, two others play a role. One was Therese von Malfatti. Her uncle, Dr. Johann Malfatti, was one of the most celebrated physicians of his time, founder of the Vienna Society of Physicians, and author of a treatise titled, "A Plan for Pathogenesis." * This book was published in 1809 and gained him world-wide fame. Dr. Malfatti became Beethoven's physician after Professor Schmidt died in 1808.

Malfatti's brother, a wealthy real-estate owner, had two daughters. One was Therese, the other Anna (Nanette). In 1811, Nanette married Baron Ignaz Gleichenstein, who had recently become one of Beethoven's best friends. They addressed each other by *Du*. Gleichenstein, an exceptionally sanguine and charming man, eight years younger than Beethoven, did innumerable favors for Beethoven. He sketched out details of business arrangements, advised Beethoven in dealings with publishers, drew up contracts, and, in short, used his practical sense to protect his friend. Their correspondence reflects an easy camaraderie and real affection. Beethoven calls him "Dissolute Baron" and writes, "You don't know music, but you are a friend of everything that is beautiful and good."

Probably through Gleichenstein, Beethoven met both branches of the Malfatti family, including Therese, who in 1810 was seventeen or eighteen years old. Once again we learn that Beethoven is captivated by physical beauty: both sisters were beautiful, "the two most beautiful girls in Vienna," judged the actress Antonie Adamberger. Therese was described as a real brunette, brown locks, dark complexion, dark eyes, clever, of fiery temperament, but flighty and "entirely turned toward the easy side of life." It was with this teen-age girl that the forty-year-old man now seems to have fallen in love. Dr. Malfatti, the uncle, must have looked at the affair with mixed emotions. He said of Beethoven: "He is an odd fellow—and in addition perhaps the greatest of all geniuses."

---

* The science of tracing the origin and development of disease.

Now (1810) Beethoven seems seriously to contemplate marriage. Suddenly he is concerned with his wardrobe and his personal appearance. He borrows a mirror from Zmeskall because his own is broken and asks Zmeskall to buy him another one. He sends Gleichenstein a considerable sum to buy him fine-quality Bengal cotton shirts and "at least half a dozen neckcloths." He goes to one of the best tailors in Vienna (Joseph Lind) and orders some suits. He writes to his old friend Wegeler in Bonn—to whom he hasn't written for a long, long time—and asks him to obtain his certificate of baptism and to make sure to obtain the right one, because there was a brother also named Ludwig born before him. It is probable that Therese was the object of these marriage plans. He writes to Therese:

[VIENNA, May, 1810]

...I am leading a very lonely and quiet life. Although here and there certain lights would like to awaken me, yet since you all left Vienna, I feel within me a void which cannot be filled and which even my art, which is usually so faithful to me, has not yet been able to make me forget— (A-258).

He also tells her that he hopes to go to the country very soon, that he is looking forward to it "with childish excitement":

How delighted I shall be to ramble for a while through bushes, woods, under trees, through grass and around rocks. No one can love the country as much as I do. For surely woods, trees and rocks produce the echo which man desires to hear—(Same letter)

He promises her that he will send her a few more of his compositions, not too difficult for her to understand. Has she read Goethe's *Wilhelm Meister* and Shakespeare in Schlegel's translation? One has leisure to read in the country. Perhaps she would like him to send her these works. She should cultivate her music, she has such a splendid gift for it. He calls her volatile and tells her that she treats lightheartedly the affairs of life.

I wonder what difference you will have found in the treatment of a theme which was invented one evening and the way in which I have recently written it down for you. Work it out for yourself, but please do not take punch *to help you.* (Same letter)

He concludes:

> Forget my mad behaviour—Rest assured that nobody can wish you a gayer and happier life than I and that I desire it even if you take no interest whatever in your most devoted servant and friend—

It isn't much of a love letter. It has a bantering tone, an older man to a young girl. Once more we have no clear picture, not any inkling of how Therese felt about Beethoven. It is possible that he asked Gleichenstein to be his messenger of love. He wrote to him:

[VIENNA, spring, 1810]

> Here is the s[onata] which I promised Therese.—As I cannot see her today, do give it to her—My best regards to them all. I am so happy when I am with them. I feel somehow that the wounds which wicked people have inflicted on my soul could be cured by the Malfattis. Thank you, kind G[leichenstein], for introducing me to that house—   (A-253).

Something must have happened, some rebuff, perhaps a refusal by Therese, perhaps a harsh word from the father. "Kind" Gleichenstein must have had to carry a sad message to Beethoven. What was it? Beethoven wrote him this touching letter:

[VIENNA, spring, 1810]

> Your news has again plunged me from the heights of the most sublime ecstasy down into the depths—And why did you add the remark that you would let me know when there would be music again? Am I then nothing more than a music-maker * for yourself or the others? —At any rate, your remark can be interpreted thus. Therefore only in my own heart can I again find something to lean upon; and so for me there is to be no support outside. No, friendship and emotions of that kind only spell wounds for me—Well, so be it. For you, poor B[eethoven], no happiness can come from outside. You must create everything for yourself in your own heart; and only in the world of ideals can you find friends—I beseech you to set my mind at rest by letting me know whether I was to blame yesterday. Or if you cannot do that, tell me the truth. I am as glad to hear it as I am to speak it—There is still time; truths can still be of use to me—All good wishes—Do not let your special friend Dorner [a physician] hear anything about all this.   (A-254).

---

* *"Musikus,"* writes Beethoven, a somewhat derogatory word.

Some time during the summer Beethoven wrote him again. He seemed perplexed and troubled and he begged Gleichenstein not to conceal the whole truth from him in an effort to spare his feelings:

[VIENNA, summer, 1810]

You are either sailing on a calm and peaceful sea or are already in a safe haven * — You do not feel the anguish of a friend who is struggling against a tempest — or perhaps you are not allowed to feel it — What will be thought of me in the star of Venus Urania, and how shall I be judged without being seen — My pride is humbled; and even if you had not invited me I would travel there with you — Let me see you at my rooms tomorrow morning. I shall expect you for breakfast at about nine o'clock — Dorner can come with you some other time — If you would only be more candid; surely you are concealing something from me, and you want to spare me; and you are causing me greater pain by leaving me in this uncertainty than if you were to disclose a certainty, however disagreeable it may be — All good wishes. If you cannot come, let me know this in advance — Think and act for me — I dare not entrust to paper anything more of what I am thinking and feeling — (A-265).

What is Gleichenstein concealing? Is it the fact that Therese does not reciprocate Beethoven's feeling? Or has it nothing to do with Therese — could it be the news of a disease from which Beethoven is suffering and which Dr. Malfatti has diagnosed? Is that why Gleichenstein wants to bring Dr. Dorner along? Sheer guesswork, all of it!

In 1816 Therese married Baron Johann Wilhelm von Drosdick. It is possible that Therese's refusal hurt Beethoven deeply, though this hurt, too, passed. He did not altogether lose track of her. In the Fischhoff Manuscript we find several entries between 1812 and 1818 which may refer to her. "As to T, let it be nothing else but God's decision; do not go there where one could commit a wrong out of weakness; only to Him, to Him alone, the all-knowing God, let this be entrusted!" . . . "Toward T be as kind as possible. Her loyalty deserves never to be forgotten — even if it can have no results advantageous to yourself." And, when he was forty-seven years old, he wrote on a scrap of paper, "Only love — yes, love alone could give you a happier life — Oh God! Let me find her — let me at last find her — one who can strengthen me in virtue — One who can be allowed to be mine — Baaden [sic] 27th of July, as M. passed by, and it seemed as if she glanced at me."

---

* Meaning that Gleichenstein was, or was about to be, married.

Who was M? Was it Malfatti? No conclusion can be drawn, because in Beethoven's handwriting the M is so unclear that it might just as well be some other sign, some cipher secret to himself.

How sad this affair, too, appears! The magnificent genius at the height of his fecundity, sure of himself in every way except the way of a man with a woman, now attracted to a "volatile" girl of whom he almost seems afraid, and whom he tries to educate, or at least interest, in those regions in which he is at home: music, Goethe, Shakespeare. For her he tries to make himself into what he is not, a man of the world. True, it lasted but a spring and summer and he must have derived some joy from the relationship: "Thank you, kind Gleichenstein, for introducing me to that house." But then, for what reason we are not sure, his pride "is humbled." He sinks back into isolation. He did not find the love which could have given him "a happier life"—because he was clumsy and because he could not spare enough light to light the way.

·◦](AMALIE SEBALD)◦··

Amalie Sebald was a singer whom Beethoven met in Teplitz in 1811. She was a friend of Christoph August Tiedge, a poet of considerable reputation whose major work, *Urania,* was known to Beethoven. The song "To Hope" is taken from that poem. Writing to Tiedge from Teplitz in 1811, Beethoven sends "Amalie a passionate kiss when no one sees us." Surely this, written to a third person, is meant jocularly. In an album owned by her, Beethoven wrote:

> Ludwig van Beethoven
>> Den Sie, wenn Sie auch wollten,
>> Doch nicht vergessen sollten.
> ["Whom, even if you would
> Forget, you never should."—Translation by Thayer.]

The short letters which Beethoven wrote her indicate a light, by no means an emotionally involved relationship. In one of them he humorously repudiates the charge with which she must have teased him that he was a "tyrant." At his insistence she sends him a bill for some food which she has bought for him, as he was ill and unable to leave his bed. Beethoven writes: "Tyrants do not pay, but the bill must be receipted, and you can do that best if you come in person, *n.b.,* with the bill, to your humbled tyrant." In still another note he says that he still cannot leave his bed, but if she thought it proper to come to him alone, it would give him great pleasure. "But if you think it improper, you know how I respect everybody's liberty."

In the most personal of the notes, Beethoven writes: *

> ...What on earth are you dreaming of when you say that you cannot be anything to me? When we meet again, dear A[malie], we must discuss this point. It was my constant wish that my presence would fill you with calm and peace and that you would confide in me—I hope to be better tomorrow; and during the remainder of your stay we shall still have a few hours left for our mutual uplifting and cheering surrounded by the beauties of nature—Good night, dear A[malie], very many thanks for the proofs of your feelings for your friend—   (A-390).

Amalie Sebald passed from his life, as did the others.

·•[RAHEL LEVIN]•·

Siegmund Kaznelson spins a romance from a few recollections he found in Varnhagen's Memoirs. The poet Varnhagen was part of the lively summer-resort society of Teplitz and Karlsbad which Beethoven usually avoided, though he was sent to these famous spas by his doctor. "Taking the waters" was the prescribed regimen for diverse ailments: most people expected to counteract in two or three weeks a year's overindulgence in food and drink; if the cure didn't do much good, it couldn't do much harm. In 1812 a particularly illustrious group of celebrities from the royal, diplomatic, and intellectual world foregathered in Teplitz. Varnhagen was there and he spent some time with Beethoven, who generally kept very much to himself. Varnhagen called him a solitary rambler. On one of his lonely walks in the castle park Beethoven saw the girl Varnhagen was to marry, Rahel Levin, "and her facial expression, which reminded him of somebody close to his heart, gave him pleasure." Rahel was an ethereal, idealistic girl, herself a poet, to whose fascination and sensitivity Varnhagen paid an eloquent tribute.** Beethoven refused to play for the important people vacationing in Teplitz, but willingly played for Rahel. From this, and a few other microscopic indications (such as a temporary estrangement between Rahel and Varnhagen), Kaznelson concludes that she was Beethoven's

---

* These letters were written in September, 1812, when they were both in Teplitz.
** In his *Rahel, a Book of Reminiscences* (1833). When Rahel did marry Varnhagen and move to Berlin, her home became one of the centers of German intellectual and artistic society, and many of the famous men of her times were her admirers, including Grillparzer.

"Distant Beloved," the woman for whom the song cycle *An die Ferne Geliebte* (Op. 98) was composed. It is all very dubious.

·❦[MARIE PACHLER-KOSCHAK]❦·

Marie Pachler-Koschak is often called Beethoven's autumnal love. She was a woman of extraordinary beauty, culture, and musical talent. She visited Beethoven in August or September, 1817, when she was only twenty-three years old, he forty-six. She was well known as a pianist, though the year before she had renounced the concert stage to marry a successful advocate, Dr. Carl Pachler, in Graz. In Graz she was called "heaven's daughter," so beautiful was she. She wanted to meet Beethoven personally; her brother-in-law brought her to him. She had never before been in Vienna, Beethoven never in Graz, so they had never met. But Beethoven must have known of her fine musicianship. Nothing is known of their relationship except that ten years later she wrote that in 1817 they saw a great deal of each other, and that in a penciled scrawl Beethoven sent her he praised her extravagantly:

> I am delighted that you are sparing us another day. We will make a great deal more music. Surely you will play for me the sonatas in F major and C minor, won't you? I have not yet found anyone who performs my compositions as well as you do; and I am not excluding the great pianists, who often have merely mechanical ability or affectation.
>
> You are the true fosterer of my spiritual children—   (A-815).

·❦[DOROTHEA VON ERTMANN]❦·

We have left Dorothea von Ertmann to the last because, whatever may have been her relation with Beethoven, whether it was deep friendship or something more which united them, she was one of his first admirers and she remained steadfast in that capacity through the years. Hers is one of the longest-lasting roles in Beethoven's biography, extending over more than twenty years.

In 1798, at the age of seventeen, she had married an Austrian army officer, Baron Stephan von Ertmann. In 1803 she began taking lessons from Beethoven, and was considered one of the foremost women pianists of her time.

Let Johann Reichardt, a professional musician competent to judge, who heard her frequently, give his impressions of her as an artist:

> A lofty noble manner and a beautiful face full of deep feeling increases my expectation still further at the first sight of the noble lady; and then as she

288

performed a great Beethoven sonata I was surprised as almost never before. I have never seen such power and innermost tenderness combined even in the greatest virtuosi; from the tip of each finger her soul poured forth, and from her hands, both equally skillful and sure, what power and authority were brought to bear over the whole instrument! Everything that is great and beautiful in art was turned into song with ease and expression!   (TQ).

She and her husband lived in or near Vienna till 1824 (not 1818 as Schindler says), when he was transferred to Milan. Felix Mendelssohn visited them there in 1831. He wrote to his family on July 14, 1831:

I asked by chance on my arrival at Milan the name of the Commandant, and the *laquais de place* named General Ertmann. I instantly thought of Beethoven's Sonata in A major, and its dedication; and as I had heard all that was good of Madame Ertmann, from those who knew her; that she was so kind, and had bestowed such loving care on Beethoven, and played herself so beautifully, I, next morning, at a suitable hour for a visit, put on a black coat, desired that the Government-house should be pointed out to me, and occupied myself on the way thither by composing some pretty speeches for the General's lady, and went on boldly.

I cannot however deny that I felt rather dismayed when I was told that the General lived in the first story, facing the street; and when I was fairly in the splendid vaulted hall, I was seized with a sudden panic, and would fain have turned back: but I could not help thinking that it was vastly provincial on my part to take fright at a vaulted hall, so I went straight up to a group of soldiers standing near and asked an old man in a short nankeen jacket, if General Ertmann lived there, intending then to send in my name to the lady. Unluckily the man replied, "I am General Ertmann: what is your pleasure?" This was unpleasant, as I was forced to have recourse to the speech I had prepared. The General, however, did not seem particularly edified by my statement, and wished to know whom he had the honour of addressing. This also was far from agreeable, but fortunately he was acquainted with my name, and became very polite: his wife, he said, was not at home, but I should find her at two o'clock, or any hour after that which might suit me.

I was glad that all had gone off so well, and in the meantime went to the Brera, where I passed the time in studying the "Sposalizio" of Raphael, and at two o'clock I presented myself to Freifrau Dorothea von Ertmann. She received me with much courtesy, and was most obliging, playing me Beethoven's Sonata in C sharp minor, and the one in D minor. The old General, who now appeared in his handsome grey uniform, covered with orders, was quite enchanted, and had tears of delight in his eyes, because it was so long since he had heard his wife play; he said there was not a person in Milan who cared to hear what I had heard. She mentioned the trio in B major, but said she could not remember it. I played it, and sang the other parts: this enchanted the old couple, and so their acquaintance was soon made.

Since then their kindness to me is so great that it quite overwhelms me. The old

General shows me all the remarkable objects in Milan; in the afternoon his lady takes me in her carriage to drive on the Corso, and at night we have music till one o'clock in the morning. Yesterday at an early hour they drove with me in the environs; at noon I dined with them, and in the evening there was a party. They are the most agreeable and cultivated couple you can imagine, are both as much in love with each other, as if they were a newly wedded pair,—and yet they have been married for four-and-thirty years. Yesterday he spoke of his profession, of military life, of personal courage, and similar subjects, with a degree of lucidity, and liberality of feeling, that I scarcely ever met with, except in my father. The General has been now an officer for six-and-forty years, and you should really see him galloping beside his wife's carriage in the park! ...

She plays Beethoven's works admirably, though it is so long since she studied them; she sometimes rather exaggerates the expression, dwelling too long on one passage, and then hurrying the next; but there are many parts that she plays splendidly, and I think I have learned something from her. When sometimes she can bring no more tone out of the instrument, and begins to sing in a voice that emanates from the very depths of her soul, she reminds me of you, dear Fanny, [his sister] though you are infinitely her superior. When I was approaching the end of the adagio in the B major trio, she exclaimed, "The amount of expression here is beyond any one's playing"; and it is quite true of this passage. The following day, when I went there again to play her the symphony in C minor, she insisted on my taking off my coat, as the day was so hot. In the intervals of our music she related the most interesting anecdotes of Beethoven, and that when she was playing to him in the evening, he not unfrequently used the snuffers as a tooth-pick! She told me that when she lost her last child, Beethoven at first shrank from coming to her house; but at length he invited her to visit him, and when she arrived, she found him seated at the piano, and simply saying, "Let us speak to each other by music," he played on for more than an hour, and, as she expressed it, "he said much to me, and at last gave me consolation."

FELIX.

Dorothea outlived Beethoven by twenty-two years. In her old age, after her husband had died, she took into her home a niece, who later wrote a book * of reminiscences. Her description confirms Mendelssohn's story:

My life with Aunt Ertmann had a special charm. For hours I sat next to her and listened both to her magnificent playing and to her reminiscences about Beethoven.

"In the beginning," she told me, "there was much talk against the great master and his [musical] goal. I was curious to become acquainted with his newest

---

* The book was published in two separate versions: (1) *Aus meinem Leben,* von Mathilde Marchesi Marquise de la Rajata de Castrone. Düsseldorf, Felix Bagel, publisher, no date. (2) *Erinnerungen aus meinem Leben,* von Mathilde de Castrone Marchesi geb. Graumann. Wien, Carl Gerold's Sohn, publisher, 1877.

sonatas. So one day I went to the music store of Herr Haslinger, had several of them shown to me, and at once began to play them on a piano which was placed there. In my absorption, I never noticed a young man who stood modestly in the corner and who by and by approached me silently. What was my astonishment when of a sudden he took my hand and thanked me in the warmest terms for the excellent rendition of his sonatas!

"It was Beethoven.

"We became friends from this moment on. Never will I forget"—my aunt continued—"what warm and close affection Beethoven showed to me and to my family. Therefore I could not understand at all that after the death of my uniquely loved child he did not visit me. After several weeks he finally appeared. He greeted me silently, sat down at the piano, and improvised for a long time. Who could describe such music? I felt as if I were listening to choirs of angels celebrating the entrance of my poor child into the world of light. When he had finished, he pressed my hand sadly and went away as silently as he had come.

"During a long series of years"—my aunt continued her narrative—"Beethoven was a daily guest in our house. Often he would complain that he had no appetite at all; then he would suddenly remember that he had already partaken of an excellent meal. Other times he forgot, though plagued by bitter hunger, that in his peregrinations of many hours he had partaken of no nourishment whatever. He was very irritable, very jumpy, very sensitive and therefore often unjust to and suspicious of his best friends. But who could have been angry with the unfortunate man and his ever-increasing deafness? One had to remember his physical and moral suffering and forgive everything. Thus did we live for many years in unclouded friendship."

Every day my aunt made me play Beethoven sonatas. If now and then I held my hands too high, she pushed them down with her arm, saying, "That is how my great master wished them."

"Unclouded friendship"—true, for once we have no evidence of quarrels, no hitting out by Beethoven, no recriminations. This may suggest a placid relationship, untroubled by love's emotion—or it may suggest a perfect understanding between the two. We have a letter from Beethoven to her (February 23, 1817) in which he calls her "My dear and beloved Dorothea Caecilia" * and sends her a copy of the Sonata Op. 101, which he had dedicated to her.

·⊰[FANNY GIANNATASIO'S RECOLLECTIONS]⊱·

When Beethoven, in 1816, looked about for a school in which he could harbor his nephew (see pages 499 on), he decided on an institution directed by

---

* Caecilia is the patron saint of music.

Kajetan Giannatasio del Rio. Kajetan had three daughters, of whom two were living at home and helping with the administration of the school. Fanny was twenty-six years old and Anna (Nanni) was twenty-four. Beethoven was, for a time at least, on the friendliest terms with the whole family and grateful to them. The two girls admired him, Fanny to the point of hero worship. Fanny, a small girl with gray-green eyes and a warm and loving temperament, but not particularly handsome (she never married), understood the turbulence which then obsessed Beethoven, though she could help him only by a quiet sweetness. She loved him in her own way, knowing the hopelessness of her love, as Beethoven was not attracted to her. Fanny helped with the household, and when Beethoven saw her walk around with the bunch of keys at her waist, he called her the "Lady Abbess." Fanny did not like that at all.

Nanni was engaged to be married when Beethoven met her, and three years later she did marry a Dr. Leopold Schmerling, on which occasion Beethoven composed a charming wedding song for her.

Fanny kept a diary. She also wrote her memoirs (1857), which agree substantially with the diary. Let Fanny tell the story of a visit they all made to Beethoven at Baden in September, 1816:

> While his nephew was still with us, Beethoven once invited my father and us two to visit him at Baden with Karl where he was spending the summer months. Although our host had been informed of our coming we soon noticed that no arrangement had been made for our lodging. B. went with us in the evening to a tavern where we were surprised to note that he dickered with the waiter about every roll, but this was because owing to his bad hearing he had frequently been cheated by serving-people. For even then one had to be very close to his ear to make him understand and I recall that I was often greatly embarrassed when I had to pierce through the grayish hairs which concealed his ear. He himself often said: "I must have my hair cut!" Looking at him cursorily one thought that his hair was coarse and bristly, but it was very fine and when he put his hand through it, it remained standing in all directions which often looked comical.

Since no arrangements for putting the girls up overnight had been made, they were hastily quartered in the room in which Beethoven worked. There a notebook "in particular received our attention"; in plain language this means that the girls picked it up and read it surreptitiously. Fanny continues:

> When we came to his lodgings in the afternoon a walk was proposed; but our host would not go along, excusing himself saying he had a great deal to do; but

he promised to follow and join us, and did so. But when we came back in the evening there was not a sign of accommodations for our lodging to be seen. B. muttered excuses and accusations against the persons who had been charged with the arrangements and helped us to settle ourselves; O how interesting it was! to move a light sofa with his help. A rather large room in which his pianoforte stood, was cleaned for us girls to use as a bedroom. But sleep remained long absent from us in this musical sanctuary. Yes, and I must confess to my shame that our curiosity and desire to know things led us to examine a large round table which stood in the room. A note-book in particular received our attention. But there was such a confusion of domestic matters, and much of it which to us was illegible that we were amazed; but, behold, one passage I still remember—there it stood: "My heart runs over at the sight of lovely nature— although she is not here!"—that gave us a great deal to think about.

In the morning a very prosaic noise roused us out of our poetical mood! B. also appeared soon with a scratched face, and complained that he had had a quarrel with his servant who was leaving, "Look," he said, "how he has maltreated me!" He complained also that these persons, although they knew that he could not hear, did nothing to make themselves understood. We then took a walk through the beautiful Helenenthal [a valley in the Vienna woods], we girls ahead, then B. and our father.

On this walk the girls tried their best to overhear the conversation between their father and Beethoven:

My father thought that B. could rescue himself from his unfortunate domestic conditions only by marriage, did he know anybody, etc. Now our long foreboding was confirmed: he was unhappy in love! Five years ago he had made the acquaintance of a person, a union with whom he would have considered the greatest happiness of his life. It was not to be thought of, almost an impossibility, a chimera—"nevertheless it is now as on the first day." This harmony, he added, he had not yet discovered! It had never reached a confession, but he could not get it out of his mind!   (TQ).

He never told his love. And he never told them who it was with whom he would have gladly united himself.

When we group the female protagonists into one chapter, we may perhaps leave the impression that women played more important roles in the life of Beethoven than actually they did. The cast of characters is considerable: fifteen are mentioned here (not counting the Immortal Beloved), and more there may have been. Until he was close to fifty he seems to have been "generally involved in one entanglement or the other." These "entanglements"—they came and they went, they gave joy and they wounded, but hardly one of them seems to have been an ineluctable part of his being. When Beethoven was in love, the intensity of that love was of short duration, as with Giulietta Guicciardi, Josephine Brunsvik, Therese Malfatti, and Amalie Sebald. The exception was his confession to his friend Giannatasio that there was somebody he had loved for five years. The eight women most important in his life were:

Name	Approximate Duration of Active Relationship	Beethoven's Age
Giulietta Guicciardi	1801	31
Josephine Brunsvik	1804 to 1806	34 to 36
Therese Brunsvik	1804 to 1806	34 to 36
Maria Erdödy	1807 to 1817	37 to 47
Bettina Brentano	1810 to 1812	40 to 42
Therese Malfatti	1810	40
Amalie Sebald	1811 to 1812	41 to 42
Dorothea Ertmann	1803 to about 1820(?)	33 to 50

Can we distill a general impression of these women?

First, all—except possibly one—were beautiful. It is certain that Beethoven could not warm up to a homely woman whatever her other qualities. He was very impressionable to physical beauty. Second, several of the women were much younger than he. They were young girls when he was a mature man. Third, they were women of high social standing. There was no baker's daughter in his life. If, like Horace, he was ever attracted to a servant girl, we do not know about it. Fourth, they were women of comprehensive education and good minds, able to talk to him about books, politics, and philosophical ideas (Therese Malfatti may have been an exception). And fifth, they were women interested in music, most of them being themselves accomplished musicians.

When we have said that, we must, rondo-like, return to the theme stated at the beginning of the chapter. The subject is shrouded in half-light, and it was Beethoven himself who dimmed the light. We may cite Fanny's memoirs once again: "My sister who had observed a gold ring on his finger asked him jocularly whether he had any other loves than the 'Distant Beloved.' He did not seem to have vouchsafed her any information."

·◄[2]►·

THE "IMMORTAL BELOVED"

"He did not seem to have vouchsafed her any information." That brings us to the document known as the "Letter to the Immortal Beloved," though, as Emily Anderson has pointed out, Beethoven's words *Unsterbliche Geliebte*" mean "eternally beloved."

As I have indicated, the existence of this letter constitutes a great mystery in Beethoven's biography; it has been the basis of speculation, controversy, and scholarly acrimony. The day after Beethoven's death, three of his friends (they were Stephan von Breuning, Anton Schindler, and Karl Holz, and it was Holz who pulled out the nail) and his brother, Johann, were looking for some bank shares which they knew Beethoven had possessed and which he had willed to his nephew, Karl. They could not find them in the morning, but returned in the afternoon to renew their search. Finally, they saw a drawer from which a nail protruded. They drew out the nail, the drawer fell, and in it they found not only the bank shares but other mementos, among them the letter. Well known though it is, let us read the letter before we briefly review the attempts of various scholars to clear up its mystery:

> [*Autograph in the Deutsche Staatsbibliothek, Berlin*]
> *July 6 and 7,*
> *July 6th, in the morning*

My angel, my all, my very self.—Only a few words today, and, what is more, written in pencil (and with your pencil)—I shan't be certain of my rooms here until tomorrow; what an unnecessary waste of time is all this—Why this profound sorrow, when necessity speaks—can our love endure without sacrifices, without our demanding everything from one another; can you alter the fact that you are not wholly mine, that I am not wholly yours?—Dear God, look at Nature in all her beauty and set your heart at rest about what must be—Love demands all, and rightly so, and thus it is *for me with you, for you with me*—But you forget so easily that I must live *for me and for you*; if we were completely united, you would feel this painful necessity just as little as I do—My journey was dreadful and I did not arrive here until yesterday at four o'clock in the morning. As there were few horses the mail coach chose another route, but what a dreadful road it was; at the last stage but one I was warned not to travel by night; attempts were made to frighten me about a forest, but all this only spurred me on to proceed—and it was wrong of me to do so. The coach broke down, of course, owing to the dreadful road which had not been made up and was nothing but a country track. If I hadn't had those two postilions I should have been left stranded on the way—On the other ordinary road Esterházy with eight horses met with the same fate as I did with four—Yet I felt to a certain extent the pleasure I always feel when I have overcome some difficulty success-fully—Well, let me turn quickly from outer to inner experiences. No doubt we shall meet soon; and today also time fails me to tell you of the thoughts which during these last few days I have been revolving about my life—If our hearts were always closely united, I would certainly entertain no such thoughts. My heart overflows with a longing to tell you so many things—Oh—there are moments when I find that speech is quite inadequate—Be cheerful—and be for ever my faithful, my only sweetheart, my all, as I am yours. The gods must send us everything else, whatever must and shall be our fate—

Your faithful
LUDWIG

MONDAY EVENING, JULY 6TH

You are suffering, you, my most precious one—I have noticed this very moment that letters have to be handed in very early, on Monday—or on Thursday—the only days when the mail coach goes from here to K.—You are suffering—Oh, where I am, you are with me—I will see to it that you and I, that I can live with you. What a life!!!! as it is now!!!! without you—pursued by the kindness of people here and there, a kindness that I think—that I wish to deserve just as little as I deserve it—man's homage to man—that pains me—and when I consider myself in the setting of the universe, what am I and what is that man—whom one calls the greatest of men—and yet—on the other hand therein lies the divine element in man—I weep when I think that probably you will not receive the first news of me until Saturday—However much you love me—my love for you is even greater—but never conceal yourself from me—good night—Since I am taking the baths I must get off to sleep—Dear God—so near! so far! Is not our love truly founded in heaven—and, what is more, as strongly cemented as the firmament of Heaven?—

GOOD MORNING, ON JULY 7TH

Even when I am in bed my thoughts rush to you, my eternally beloved, now and then joyfully, then again sadly, waiting to know whether Fate will hear our prayer—To face life I must live altogether with you or never see you. Yes, I am resolved to be a wanderer abroad until I can fly to your arms and say that I have found my true home with you and enfolded in your arms can let my soul be wafted to the realm of blessed spirits—alas, unfortunately it must be so—You will become composed, the more so as you know that I am faithful to you; no other woman can ever possess my heart—never—never—Oh God, why must one be separated from her who is so dear. Yet my life in V[ienna] at present is a miserable life—Your love has made me both the happiest and the unhappiest of mortals—At my age I now need stability and regularity in my life—can this coexist with our relationship?—Angel, I have just heard that the post goes every day—and therefore I must close, so that you may receive the letter immediately—Be calm; for only by calmly considering our lives can we achieve our purpose to live together—Be calm—love me—Today—yesterday—what tearful longing for you—for you—you—my life—my all

296

—all good wishes to you—Oh, do continue to love me—never misjudge your lover's most faithful heart.

ever yours
ever mine   L. (A-373).
ever ours

Ever since this letter was discovered, ever since the astonished friends perused these ten pages in which the penciled handwriting mounts from what for Beethoven is reasonable legibility to the final pages in which the words seem to tear themselves apart, ever since Schindler took possession of it for use in his contemplated biography, ever since then a line of learned men have attempted to pierce the dark, to name the unnamed woman, to point—sometimes tentatively but more often triumphantly—to this or that candidate. For more than a century a detachment of desk detectives has searched the letter for internal clues and rummaged among contemporary records for external clues, to construct from them the "great theory" and to conclude with the "great discovery." A whole shelf can be filled with books and monographs written about the Immortal Beloved.

Not idle curiosity alone nor the fascination which a riddle always offers has spurred the scholars on. The solution, if it could be found, would in truth be an important addition to our knowledge. This letter disrobes Beethoven's feeling for a woman. Stripped of caution, bare of reserve, the words which were slung unto these pages well up at us with elemental force. Who was this woman who could unloose such feelings? Who was this woman whose love made him "both the happiest and the unhappiest of mortals"? Were we to know who *she* was we could very likely know him better. It is understandable that the letter has created almost as much speculation as the identity of "the onlie begetter" of Shakespeare's sonnets, or the disappearance of Leonardo's *Leda.*

In the previous pages I have indicated who some of the candidates were, beginning with Schindler's assertion that the Immortal Beloved was Giulietta Guicciardi. Suffice it here to list the choices and the scholars who chose them. It is all in vain—there is something wrong with every theory, and none of the choices has proved satisfactory. One by one they have been discarded as further data have come to light.

	Chosen by
Giulietta Guicciardi	Anton Schindler
	L. Nohl
	Alfred Kalischer

Therese Brunsvik	A. W. Thayer, La Mara, W. A. Thomas-San Galli, Romain Rolland, K. Smolle
Amalie Sebald	W. A. Thomas-San Galli
Magdalene Willmann	Theodor v. Frimmel
Bettina Brentano	Hugo Riemann (with reservations)
Josephine Brunsvik	S. Kaznelson
Maria Erdödy	Dana Steichen

The principal questions concerning the letter, all interconnected, are:

1. To whom was it addressed? Who was the Immortal Beloved?

2. Was it sent? If it was, how did it get back into Beethoven's possession? Was it returned by the woman?

3. If it was not sent, if Beethoven wrote it in an excess of emotion and then decided not to send it, why did he keep it in the secret drawer? Was he motivated by the same sort of self-confessing impulse that made him write and then preserve the "Heiligenstadt Testament"? (See next chapter.)

4. Where was the letter written?

5. In what year was the letter written?

6. On what day was the letter written? The letter is marked July 6 (and 7). Is the dating to be trusted? Beethoven often misdated letters and even contracts.

7. Where was the letter to go if it was sent? Beethoven says that he is posting the letter to a place of which he gives only the initial "K," but which is obviously large enough to get the benefit of regular mail-coach service. Where is "K"?

Question 1 I would like to answer with a theory of my own, one which I advance tentatively and which may or may not prove to be valid.

Questions 2 and 3 cannot be answered.

Questions 4, 5, 6, and 7 can be answered, with fair certainty.

The date of the letter. Scholarship is now almost unanimously agreed that the year is 1812. Among the reasons which led to this conclusion are:

a. Beethoven mentions that he had a dreadful journey; that he did not arrive till four o'clock in the morning. He came by mail coach; since there was a shortage of available horses the mail coach chose another (less steep) route; but it was a dreadful road; at the penultimate stage he had been warned not to travel by night and to beware of the bad road through the forest. He had insisted on proceeding—"it was wrong of me"—and the coach had broken down.

The relief coachman (postilion), obviously an expert driver, had rescued him. "Esterházy," traveling "the other ordinary road" with eight horses, instead of Beethoven's four, had met with a similar fate.

It is established that two roads led from Prague to Teplitz, one skirting the mountains and leading through the forest (the one taken by Beethoven), the other steeper one through the mountains (the one taken by Esterházy). With four horses the first road would be preferable; but it was a bad road.

It is proved (by Kaznelson) that an Esterházy, Prince Paul Anton Esterházy, traveled from Prague to Teplitz at that time *in 1812*. He was Austrian Envoy to the Saxon Court at Dresden. He wrote a report in Prague dated June 30 and sent a letter to Metternich from Teplitz dated July 8, 1812, telling him that he was proceeding to Dresden. Esterházy's whereabouts are proved and the dates fit —for the year 1812.

b. The weather fits. While no exact weather reports for Teplitz are extant, the general reports for northern Austria indicate particularly bad *rainy weather* at the beginning of July, 1812. Max Unger, in tracing the weather, refers to Goethe's diary. Goethe was in Karlsbad, not in Teplitz, but Karlsbad lies in the same mountainous region, and it is not unreasonable to assume that the same weather conditions prevailed.

Goethe, who was very influenced by weather and who often begins an entry in his diary by describing the day, notes:

> July 3: Early cloudy, then heavy rain.
> July 4: Early rain. Afternoon covered sky.
> July 5: Dark day and cold.

c. The business of "Monday, July 6" fits. July 6 fell on a Monday in 1812, as well as in 1795, 1801, 1807 and 1818. Each of these dates has been examined, and none will serve as well as 1812. For example: In 1795 Beethoven, not yet twenty-five years old, was too young to use such an expression as "At my age I now need stability." In 1801 he was in love with the seventeen-year-old Giulietta Guicciardi, and it is generally agreed that the letter could not possibly have been addressed to her. Besides, while Beethoven's movements in July, 1801, are not known day by day, the evidence we do have shows that he was in

Hetzendorf near Vienna, not traveling.* Similarly, in 1807 he was in Baden and he was still somewhat in love with Josephine (see the letter to her of September 20, 1807). In 1818 he did not leave his nephew.

d. Accepting "Monday, July 6" as correct dating by Beethoven is reasonable. While Beethoven did misdate letters, it is inconceivable that he would make a mistake *three* times in one letter. There is no reason to doubt the correctness of his dating.

e. Joseph Schmidt-Görg made an analysis of the watermarks of the paper of some 800 Beethoven letters. He found that the paper of the letter to the Immortal Beloved has the same watermark as a letter to Breitkopf and Härtel (July 17, *1812*) and one to Varnhagen (July 14, *1812*).

In short, we may take it as virtually certain that the letter was written on Monday, July 6, and Tuesday, July 7, in the year 1812.

Where was the letter written? If we assume that the date is correct, then the letter *must have been written in Teplitz.* He arrived there on July 5—again this checks with the letter—and this fact is confirmed by a letter he wrote to Breitkopf and Härtel on July 17: "This is just to tell you that I have been here since July 5. . . ." He was not registered until July 6 in the register of arriving guests (*Kurgäste-Protokoll*). But that is not important because first, such registry, as opposed to the compulsory police registry, was voluntary (as a matter of fact, one had to pay a small fee for it) and there was no rush about it; and second, July 5 was a Sunday, and the protocol office may have been closed. And third, he was not sure where he was going to stay. ("I shan't be certain of my rooms here until tomorrow.")

Where was the letter sent, if it was sent? To "K."

In the second part of the letter (Monday evening, July 6) Beethoven writes, "I have noticed this very moment that letters have to be handed in very early, on Monday—or on Thursday—the only days when the mail coach goes from here to K."

He regrets that she will not be hearing from him till Saturday. This being

---

* Nevertheless, I have recently received an elaborate monograph by Vladimir Karbusicky, written on the occasion of a symposium of the "Beethoven Society of Czechoslovakia" held in Piestany, July 10–13, 1968. The monograph is titled *Beethoven's Letter to the Immortal Beloved and His Musical Work.* It suggests 1801 as a possible date and Hungary as the place where it all happened. But the arguments adduced are mostly of a musical nature; that is, that the music he composed in 1801 fits stylistically better the tone of the letter than the music he composed in 1812. It goes without saying that such parallels are biographically invalid. All the same, it is interesting that the question of the identity of the Immortal Beloved is still being pursued, even in Czechoslovakia.

Monday *evening*—too late for the Monday morning mail—he thinks the letter will go off Thursday morning and arrive Saturday. Therefore "K" must be near enough to Teplitz for mail to arrive, be sorted and delivered within forty-eight hours.

Unger has found a "Postal Notice" for Teplitz, though it deals with the year 1815, not 1812. He assumes, reasonably, that no major changes were instituted in the postal service between 1812 and 1815. The notice says:

DEPARTING MAILS:

Monday, AM 8 o'clock, the government Post (*Reichspost*) via Saaz, Karlsbad and Eger . . . Thursday AM 8 o'clock same as Monday morning.

(The notice contains information about mail to other cities and countries, but the excerpt above is the pertinent quotation. It lists no service to Karlsbad on Tuesday or Wednesday.)

It is possible that Beethoven got his information—which subsequently proved wrong—from a similar Postal Notice displayed at the Teplitz post office. (The post office was located in the same street as Beethoven's inn, "The Oak.")

In the third part of the letter (Tuesday morning) Beethoven writes: "Angel, I have just heard that the post goes every day—and therefore I must close, so that you may receive the letter immediately—"

He found out he had been mistaken about the postal service. Well, interestingly enough, the same Postal Notice from which we have quoted contains on the bottom an amendment:

NOTE

From May 15 to September 15 the Post from all I. R. Austrian States arrives daily in the morning, and departs daily 11 o'clock forenoon.

Again, one should remember that this notice dates from 1815. All the same, the facts are suggestive: because of increased tourism the postal service was augmented to run daily, and this may already have been the case in 1812. Beethoven may have at first overlooked this improvement of the postal service, and then learned better, probably early on Tuesday morning. He writes, "I must close," to get the letter ready for the 11 o'clock departure.

All this is conjecture—reasonable conjecture—but all the clues point to Karlsbad.

The fact that the mail coach went every day is further confirmed by some random jottings in Goethe's diary from which it appears that Goethe traveled from Karlsbad to Teplitz on a Monday (July 13, 1812); his wife, from Teplitz to Karlsbad on a Sunday (July 19), and that he returned from Teplitz to Karlsbad on a Tuesday (August 11).

Finally, scholars have pointed out that Beethoven referred to Karlsbad as "K" in several letters. He was in the habit of abbreviating names—"V" for Vienna, for example—in the letter to the Immortal Beloved.

To summarize, Unger writes: "There is no doubt that Karlsbad is the pertinent place." *

The Immortal Beloved, then, was in Karlsbad. Before pursuing this clue, let us first retrace Beethoven's movements, and second, see if the letter itself furnishes any helpful internal evidence.

Date	Beethoven's Whereabouts	Evidence	Fact or Conjecture
June 28 or June 29	Leaves Vienna for Prague	On the 28th he writes a letter to Baumeister, secretary of Archduke Rudolph. However, the date is added to the autograph by another hand; it could be wrong. The latest he could have left Vienna was the 29th to arrive in Prague on July 1. Travel time, Vienna-Prague: 3 to 4 days.	Fact
July 2	In Prague **	Varnhagen (poet, friend of Beethoven) writes from Prague to Rahel (his fiancée), July 2: "I write you, immediately after Beethoven and Willisen have arrived."	Fact
July 3	In Prague. Calls on Prince Kinsky.	Beethoven told Princess Kinsky of this visit. Letter of December 30, 1812	Fact

* Max Unger, *Auf Spuren von Beethovens "Unsterblicher Geliebten,"* 1911.
** I have been able to find further corroboration of Beethoven's stay in Prague through a publication called "Supplement to the Imperial-Royal Official Newspaper of the Prague Higher Post Office"

Date	Beethoven's Whereabouts	Evidence	Fact or Conjecture
July 3, 4	In Prague. Meets the Immortal Beloved. Departs for Teplitz, late July 4.	Letter to the Immortal Beloved suggests recent meeting (see below). If so, Prague would have been the most likely place. He would not have had time to go from Prague to Karlsbad, meet her there, then go on to Teplitz.	Conjecture
		He traveled directly from Prague to Teplitz, same as Esterházy.	Fact
		He was "incommunicado" on his last evening in Prague. At least, he wrote apologetically to Varnhagen (from Teplitz, July 14):	
		"I was sorry, dear V[arnhagen], not to be able to spend my last evening in Prague with you, and I myself found this all wrong. But a circumstance which I could not foresee prevented me from doing so—Therefore you must forgive me for my omission—I will tell you more about this when we meet—" (A-374).	Much has been made of this statement. Yet there could be a dozen reasons why Beethoven could not or did not want to see Varnhagen. Conjecture.
July 5	Arrives in Teplitz	(Distance, Prague to Teplitz, about 75 miles.) Two letters by him.	Fact
July 6 July 7	Writes letter to the Immortal Beloved	The letter itself.	Fact
July 7	Addresses letter to Karlsbad	"K" indubitably Karlsbad, as demonstrated by Unger.	Virtual fact

(*Beilage zur kaiserlich-königlichen privilegierten Prager Oberpostamts-Zeitung*). This little sheet, published apparently three times a week, gives a summary of local news. One column of it lists arrivals and departures of persons of rank and consequence. Number 80 of the Supplement (published July 3, 1812) lists among the arrivals on July first "Herr v. Beethoven, composer, from Vienna, staying at the 'Black Horse' [*Schwarzen Ross*]." Number 81 of the Supplement (published July 6) lists among the departures on July 4: "Herr Beethoven, composer, to Töplitz."

These newspaper items, which to the best of my knowledge have not been published before, fit the timetable: Beethoven arrived on the first and departed on the fourth, giving him time enough not only to see Kinsky but to see the Immortal Beloved.

What psychological, or shall we say what *human,* evidence can we distill from the letter without reading meanings into it which are too speculative?

1. Beethoven's relationship with the Immortal Beloved is not one where passion sprang up suddenly. It is not a temporary infatuation by which he is seized. A man is talking to a woman whom he has known and loved for a long time, a woman who shares his joys and despairs. In turn he knows her "profound sorrow." The letter breathes familiarity and an intimacy which is almost conjugal. He wants to be "completely united" with her—"ever yours, ever mine, ever ours"—and wants her "for ever" as "my faithful, my only sweetheart, my all, as I am yours."

He does not appear as the impulsive lover: "At my age [he is forty-one] I now need stability and regularity in my life."

They are resolved "to live together."

2. An obstacle to a permanent and full union exists. Is this compatible with his wish for "stability"? What is the obstacle? The first and obvious guess is that she is a married woman. The next guess is that he is ill and must be cured before he can say, "I am yours." Right now she is not wholly his, he not wholly hers.

I believe that the first guess is more probable than the second, judging from the tone of the entire letter.

3. The obstacle is not insuperable, Beethoven thinks. He has not given up hope. The important sentence is: "Yes, I am resolved to be a wanderer abroad until I can fly to your arms and say that I have found my true home with you and enfolded in your arms can let my soul be wafted to the realm of blessed spirits." Romantic though the words are, the intention is clear: he proposes to go away and not to see her until he can "live altogether with you." He *was* planning to go to England after the war.

4. The letter is by a man who has consummated his relationship with a woman. This cannot be proved; it can only be felt. I believe that the atmosphere the letter breathes is that of fulfilled love. He addresses her as *"Du."* A man did not do so unless he knew the woman intimately. *"Du"* among adults not members of the same family was usually used only by lovers. The letter is the *only* instance we know of in which Beethoven uses the familiar form to a woman. Even his love notes to Josephine Brunsvik use *"Sie."*

5. The lovers had met recently. (Unger does not quite agree—but most other scholars do.) The beginning of the letter, "Only a few words today," implies this, as well as the vividness of recollection. He has her pencil; would Beethoven still have it if they had not met for some time?

In summary: The Immortal Beloved was probably a married woman whom Beethoven had known intimately for a considerable time. If so, she most probably lived in Vienna. It is unthinkable that she was only a "summer acquaintance."

Whether or not these deductions are correct, of one fact we can be almost certain: *she was in Karlsbad in the first days of July, 1812.*

Unless she was a woman who resided permanently in Karlsbad—a highly unlikely supposition considering how seldom and how little Beethoven was in Karlsbad—she must have arrived in Karlsbad.

Does this give us any help?

Unger examined the Karlsbad *Kurliste* of 1812—the voluntary registry which cost 30 kreuzer—and found "only a few ladies whom Beethoven knew or knew well." He lists:

Elisabeth von der Recke	Arrival June 7
Princess Moritz Liechtenstein with husband	Arrival June 25
Baroness Dorothea Ertmann	Arrival June 25
Antonie Brentano, with husband and child	Arrival July 5

Unger says: "None of these women can up to now be considered the 'Immortal Beloved.' " But he gives no reason for this statement.

However, Unger does not seem to have examined the Police Register of Karlsbad. Possibly it had been mislaid or lost. Kaznelson did examine it—but says nothing about 1812. He cites entries in 1811 for Josephine Brunsvik's husband Stackelberg. The Police Register (*Anzeigs-Protokoll*) was a mandatory list. Regulations made it *compulsory* for all strangers arriving in Karlsbad to register with the police. One did not fool with Metternich's police rules.*

What does the Police Register teach us? First, a negative fact: *none of the women mentioned as possibilities for the Immortal Beloved is listed here.* That

---

* After a prolonged search we *were* able to find this Police Register. We searched (1) the Karl Marx Museum; (2) the Resort Office; (3) the City Museum; (4) the City Archive. The list was found in the City Archive. (Thanks are due to the help offered by Mr. Karel Nejdl, a citizen of Karlsbad, retired bank employee, who for many years has studied the history of the city.) The records are much the worse for dust and mildew, and some of them have become virtually undecipherable. This Police Register—that portion of it which runs from May 30, 1812, to August first—has been microfilmed, and the film is now in my possession. It comprises seventy-two sheets, containing over 900 entries. Anybody interested in the subject of the Immortal Beloved is welcome to consult the film. I also have photographs of the *Kurliste* from May 1 to July 31, 1812. Photographs of the front pages of the *Prager Oberpostamts-Zeitung,* June 22 to July 13, 1812, are likewise available.

is discouraging—but may help to explain why all the previously proposed theories have broken down. Second, all arrivals mentioned by Unger *are* registered. Unger was right. They seem to be the only possibilities. Can any of them be considered seriously as a candidate?

Elisabeth von der Recke was a poet. Long separated from her husband, Baron Magnus von der Recke, she lived with the poet Christoph August Tiedge, a very intimate friend of Beethoven. She is listed as arriving with "Herr Tiedge and servants." She was a steady visitor to the Bohemian resorts and was acquainted with Varnhagen, Rahel Levin, Bettina Brentano, etc. She was fourteen years older than Beethoven—therefore fifty-five in 1812. A virtually impossible candidate. She arrived June sixth. Her "voluntary" registration in the *Kurliste* is dated a day later than her police registration.

Princess Moritz Liechtenstein. She was the daughter of Prince Nikolaus Esterházy and his wife, the Princess Hermenegild Esterházy. Her name was Marie Leopoldine (1788–1846), and she married Prince Moritz von Liechtenstein on April 13, 1806. The marriage did not prove a happy one. Her husband neglected her, though she was "Vienna's most beautiful woman" (Lulu von Thürheim). Her brother-in-law adored her, yet she never "swerved a hair's breadth from the path of marital virtue." Metternich, in letters to his mistress, the Countess Lieven, praised her gentleness and naturalness. Beethoven's connection with her was of the slightest, if any. He certainly harbored no kindly feelings toward her father. An intimate relationship between Beethoven and her is totally improbable. She arrived June 25 *with* her husband and daughter.

Antonie von Brentano. A very good and fine friend of Beethoven. She was ten years younger than he and happily married to Franz Brentano, half-brother of Bettina. Beethoven received financial help from Franz, and Antonie advised him about nephew Karl's education. The evidence of their relationship is clear and excludes even a remote chance of anything but friendship. We have a number of letters to the Brentanos from Beethoven. In none of them is there the slightest sign of a romantic involvement with Antonie. The Brentanos, Franz and Antonie, arrived in Karlsbad July sixth "with child": this was Maximiliane (Maxe), then ten years old, to whom Beethoven dedicated in

1821 his Piano Sonata Op. 109. Antonie is highly improbable in the role of the Immortal Beloved.

That leaves Dorothea von Ertmann, who *is* a possibility. She arrived in Karlsbad on June 25: both the *Kurliste* and the Police Register agree as to the date. She arrived *alone.* Her entry in the Police Register reads:

Number	Month and Date of Arrival	Family and First Name	Occupation	Place of Birth and Country of Origin	Residence
412	June 25	Dorothea Baroness von Ertmann	Wife of I.R. Major	Frankfurt am Main	Vienna

Purpose of Visit and Means of Travel	Proposed Address and Duration of Stay	Details of Passport or Document	Day of Departure	Destination and Means of Travel
Cure. Post-Chaise	"The Knight" 4 Weeks	I.R. Austrian War Bureau. Vienna, June 11, 1812. Also, Prague June 23, 1812	[left blank]	[left blank]

She had what we might now call a "visa" for Prague, obtained two days before she reached Karlsbad. She may have been in Prague or she may have provided herself with this visa because she *intended to go to Prague.* She gave no information as to the day of her departure or destination, but quite a few visitors omitted such information.

At any rate, it is certain that she was in Karlsbad, and it is at least possible that she had made arrangements for a visit to Prague.

I find these facts telling. Yet I do not want to assert positively that Dorothea v. Ertmann *was* the Immortal Beloved. To make such an assertion we need grounds more relative than a listing which fits as to time and place. We need to know more than we do know. And I am wary of increasing the lengthy list of candidates by one more name. Still, the facts are significant, and I think the matter worth further investigation. This will be difficult—little is known about the Ertmanns—unless a diary or family papers come to light.

In several respects Dorothea v. Ertmann makes an ideal choice. It is not scientific to say so, but let us say it anyway: there could hardly be among the women Beethoven knew a more fitting "Beloved." She was pretty (see miniature, p. 451); the right age—ten years younger than he was, and he did prefer younger women—she was musically gifted and understood his music; she did admire and love the artist and the man; the relationship between them stretched over many years; she seems to have been very charming and sensitive; she was a baroness but not of so exalted a social station as to make a connection with Beethoven out of the question (she was not a member of the *Hochadel,* the high nobility).

The Conversation Books confirm that, to the very last, Beethoven remained interested in Dorothea—and Dorothea in him:

She and the general were planning to visit Vienna in 1826, the year before Beethoven died. Beethoven must have known about this visit. Perhaps she wrote to him. Entry, between May 22 and June 4, 1826: "The [*die,* feminine form] Ertmann is expected any day." Obviously, this is an answer to Beethoven's question as to when Dorothea was arriving.

Entry, second half of June, 1826:

> BEETHOVEN: What did Ertmann say? [*die*].
> KARL (?): She plays your work better than the men.

Entry, first half of July, 1826:

> HOLZ (?): My Lord [Schuppanzigh] says Ertmann [*die*] wants to have a quintet; she is even willing to pay for it.

Entry, July 13 to 27, 1826:

> SCHUPPANZIGH: Have you already seen [*die*] Ertmann? She wants very much to hear your new quartets.

Entry, end of August, 1826:

> SCHUPPANZIGH: Her father is one of the richest men in Frankfurt. Frank [not identified], a stingy fellow, would not have married her sister, if she hadn't had a dowry.

After it was decided that Karl, Beethoven's nephew, was to pursue a military career, somebody must have suggested that General Ertmann could help him obtain a post. (Perhaps it was Beethoven's own suggestion. Eventually Stephan Breuning helped Karl.)

Entry, beginning of September, 1826:

> HOLZ: Ertmann leaves on September 15. Because she expressed the wish to hear some of your new quartets, we could arrange this here on one of the next evenings. Then you can easily consult him about Karl.

> HOLZ: Yesterday I spoke with Ertmann in the city. You need not trouble yourself to go to him. Tomorrow morning after the review of the troops on the *Schmelz* [a field used for maneuvers] he will have the honor to call on you.

We do not know whether this meeting ever took place or whether Dorothea saw Beethoven before her departure. Yet the entries do point to a continuing relationship.

What are the indications against the theory that Dorothea was the Immortal Beloved? First, Mendelssohn reported in a letter (written nineteen years after Dorothea came to Karlsbad and came *without* her husband) that the Ertmanns were an exceptionally happy and loving couple. In Mendelssohn's letter she does not sound as if she ever entertained the idea of leaving her husband. But who can tell what was in her mind when she was a young woman of thirty-one?

Second, the letter from Beethoven to her, written in 1817, to which I have referred (page 291), is very affectionate and friendly, but *nothing more.* However, it was a kind of "official" letter, sending her the engraved copy of the Sonata Op. 101. Let it serve, writes Beethoven, as "a proof of my devotion both to your artistic aspirations and to your person."

Third, there is the assertion by Beethoven that he would never enter into any other relationship than that of friendship with the wife of another man. (Letter to the Bigots—see page 226.) He expressed himself similarly on one or two other occasions. Beethoven meant what he said. He was too direct, too elemental, too unworldly a personality to be able to equivocate. Yet we do have instances of his acting in ways inconsistent wtih the mantle of morality with which he covered himself. He did this without seeing the contradiction.

A man who is inundated by so high and so forceful a wave as the letter indicates can no longer stand safely on the beach, thinking of "correct" principles. To assume that Beethoven could not fall in love with a married woman because he said he would not is to impute a righteousness to him which is unnatural. Shall we not accord this man—strong in several aspects of his will, yet vulnerable in the region of the heart—the privilege of lack-logic? Shall we use granite to sculpt his statue? "No law is made for love," wrote Dryden. Not even a self-postulated law.

One other detail is to be noted: Suppose Dorothea Ertmann was the Immortal Beloved. We know she arrived at Karlsbad on June 25. Suppose she went from there to Prague (about seventy miles away) to meet Beethoven. Suppose that she returned to Karlsbad, while Beethoven went on to Teplitz. Did she have to re-register with the police on re-entering Karlsbad? No, according to the information I received. If you were registered and left town for a short while, an oral declaration sufficed on re-entry—particularly if you did not relinquish your rooms.*

Finally, there are questions 2 and 3—what are the answers? I have none, not even a glimmer. Whether the letter was sent and returned to Beethoven, or whether Beethoven never sent it, or why he kept it, remain insoluble puzzles.

Let us once more lay the clues on the table:

1. All the probabilities are that the letter was written in 1812.

2. All the probabilities are that the "K" to which it was sent was Karlsbad.

3. If (1) and (2) are true, then all names hitherto proposed for the Immortal Beloved must be eliminated.

4. Of the names listed in the Police Register of Karlsbad, the one which is most worthy of consideration is that of Dorothea Ertmann.

5. In more ways than one, Dorothea Ertmann seems a logical choice: age, beauty, interests, social station, and duration of relationship with Beethoven. She may well be worth further research.

We who love Beethoven will never cease being tantalized by the mystery. Who was this woman who created in him so great a turbulence that he who was not particularly healthy at the moment—who had behind him a grueling and bone-breaking journey of many hours, during which he suffered not only the

---

* I have this information from Mr. Walter Goldinger of Vienna, an expert on Austrian police regulations. Foreigners had to re-register; Austrian citizens did not. Dorothea Ertmann was an Austrian citizen.

inclement weather but the accident to the coach—forthwith sat down and wrote a long letter of such longing, of so strong a mixture of hope and sadness that his other letters pale beside it? That letter—it sprang from the depth of his tormented soul; it remains one of love's most moving documents and will remain so whether or not we ever discover the whole truth about it.*

·◦[3]◦·

DID BEETHOVEN HAVE SYPHILIS?

The first public voicing of this possibility appeared in the original edition of the famous *Grove's Dictionary of Music and Musicians,* which still serves as one of the standard encyclopedias of musical knowledge. The first edition was published in 1878, and Sir George Grove himself wrote the article on Beethoven (as well as on Mendelssohn and Schubert).** Discussing the postmortem examination of Beethoven's auditory system, Grove stated that "The whole of these appearances are most probably the result of syphilitic affections at an early period of his life." The statement is accompanied by this footnote: "This diagnosis, which I owe to the kindness of my friend Dr. Lauder Brunton, is confirmed by the existence of two prescriptions, of which, since the passage in the text was written, I have been told by Mr. Thayer, who heard of them from Dr. Bartolini [*sic*]." Grove was a man of highest probity. He was also a careful scholar, though he did misspell Dr. Bertolini's name. Since Grove wrote this, there can be no doubt that Thayer *did* tell him of these prescriptions; yet they have not been found. Nor is Grove explicit enough to present a tight case.

Thayer knew Dr. Andreas Bertolini, Beethoven's physician from about 1806 till about 1816, and discussed Beethoven's illnesses with him. A caprice of

---

* For a contrary iconoclastic view read Bernard Shaw: "I have been in love, like Beethoven, and have written idiotic love letters, many of which, I regret to say, have *not* been returned; so that instead of turning up among my papers after my death, they will probably be published by inconsiderate admirers during my lifetime, to my utter confusion. My one comfort is, that whatever they may contain—and no man is more oblivious of their contents than I am—they cannot be more fatuous than Beethoven's. I have a modest confidence that at the worst I shall not fall below the standard of punctuation set by that great man. . . ." From *Music in London,* Vol. 3.

** He earned his place in musical history not only through the *Dictionary* but by the discovery of Schubert's *Rosamunde* music. He and the composer Arthur Sullivan journeyed to Vienna and began a search among dusty and forgotten manuscripts which had been lying unheeded for almost half a century. When after several disappointments they finally found the score, the two respectable and middle-aged Englishmen were so excited that then and there they played leapfrog (C. L. Graves' *Life of Sir George Grove.* London, MacMillan and Company Ltd., 1903).

Beethoven terminated the relationship; but, wrote Thayer, Bertolini, though pained and regretful, "retained his respect and veneration for his former friend to the last. In 1831 [four years after the composer's death] he gave a singular proof of his delicate regard for Beethoven's reputation; supposing himself to be at the point of death from cholera, and being too feeble to examine his large collection of the composer's letters and notes to him, he ordered them all to be burned, because a few were not of a nature to be risked in careless hands."

The impression left here is that Bertolini died in 1831 of cholera. This was not so. He recovered and lived on into his nineties.

Why did Bertolini burn Beethoven's letters and notes? If they concerned Beethoven's known ailments, his deafness or his intestinal disorders, there surely was no need to burn them. Such information could not possibly have injured Beethoven's "reputation." Was Bertolini really trying to destroy medical data which he thought would have been deleterious to the fame of his erstwhile friend, then four years dead? If so, what could they have been but data concerning a venereal infection?

The problem has long occupied physicians and Beethoven scholars. As early as 1907 the famous physician William Osler thought that the symptoms of Beethoven's putative typhoid infection pointed rather to a venereal infection. Three years later the otologist Dr. Leo Jacobsohn published an article * in which he argued the strong possibility of syphilis, though he did not conclude that it was the cause of the deafness.

Theodor von Frimmel, the Beethoven scholar and also a physician, wrote in 1912 that, though he did not completely reject the opinion of Dr. Weissenbach, Beethoven's friend, that Beethoven's deafness was due to a "terrible typhus," it was "practically impossible" that there was not present a contributory cause in the form of a "previous infection." Frimmel continues in words which, for a medical man, seem needlessly veiled: "One suspects a severe case of common exanthema [skin eruption] . . . and something else about which I may not entirely keep silent since many years ago I received, thanks to the kindness of A. W. Thayer, definite written facts about this other illness of Beethoven." Obviously, a venereal infection is meant. He concludes, "Beethoven's deafness was a symptom. The disease itself had another name."

Ten years after that an otologist fully as reputable as Jacobsohn, Dr. Waldemar Schweisheimer, published an opposite view. He believed that Beethoven's

---

* *Ludwig van Beethovens Gehörleiden, Deutsche Medizinische Wochenschrift,* No. 34, 1910.

deafness was most probably due to typhus. "One always has to consider typhus with inhabitants of Vienna. The disease was endemic there. Schubert died from it, as well as Schubert's mother." He felt that the postmortem examination testified *against* the presence of venereal infection. "The cirrhosis of the liver cannot be traced to luetic origin, but was the result of a chronic stomach-intestinal illness, perhaps initiated by typhoid." *

André de Hevesy ** wrote that Beethoven in 1819 made a note that he must get a book titled *L'art de connaître et de guérir toutes les contagions vénériennes* (*The Art of Recognizing and Curing All Venereal Infections*) by L. V. Legunan. Beethoven was then forty-eight years old. Could he have wanted the book for the future education of his nephew?

A whole clinic of physicians has published diagnoses. Walther Forster *** lists no fewer than forty-three names of medical men who have written on the subject. Nor is there an end to it: in the last decade more articles have appeared in medical journals all over the world—in the U.S.A., Italy, Germany, Brazil, France, Sweden. Despite the scant evidence, the subject cannot be laid to rest.

One wonders at the seeming suppression and disappearance of evidence. Ernest Newman † believes that "Thayer had in his possession evidence which he could not bring himself to make public" and bases that belief on the statement by Sir George Grove. Jacobsohn, in another article,†† quoted Frimmel, who had sent him a partial copy of a letter by Thayer dated October 29, 1880. Thayer wrote that Beethoven's "venereal disease" was "well-known to many persons." The original of this letter has disappeared, to the best of my knowledge. Jacobsohn continues: "Of a further proof I can only give some general information. In a private collection there is a note in Beethoven's handwriting, one which has never been made public, which points with great probability to a venereal disease of the Master. I cannot give more details since the possessor of the document does not wish its publication." That note has not been found, nor has a prescription for a salve of tincture of mercury (a standard treatment then) supposed to have been at one time in the possession of a Berlin

---

* *Beethovens Leiden* [*Beethoven's Malady*], 1922.
** *Beethoven: Vie Intime*, 1926.
*** *Beethovens Krankheiten und ihre Beurteilung* [Beethoven's Maladies and their Diagnosis], 1955.
† *The Unconscious Beethoven*, 1927.
†† *Beethovens Gehörleiden und letzte Krankheit* [*Beethoven's Hearing Defect and Last Illness*], *Deutsche Medizinische Wochenschrift*, No. 53, 1927.

collector.* It is virtually impossible that any of these documents will now come to light, after the destruction of the last war.

Obviously, the time has long passed when one took seriously the opinion that the creator of the Ninth Symphony and the last quartets could have been morally infallible. On the contrary, it has now become fashionable—perhaps overly fashionable—to seek a connection between disease and the nature of genius. Readers of biography know of the venereal infections of Boswell and Tolstoy and Schubert and de Maupassant and Nietzsche. On more or less firm evidence, syphilis has been attributed to a large number of famous men, from Benvenuto Cellini to Manet.

It goes without saying that to the music itself it makes not the slightest difference whether Beethoven's troubles were due to spirochetes or a hangnail. Yet the search for a definitive diagnosis is prompted by better motives than prurience or the wish to cut the composer down to size. If he did suffer an infection, that fact may help us to offer fresh and more cogent interpretations of anomalies which up to now have been attributed to his deafness or, for want of a more tangible cause, to the eccentricity of his character.

The hatred of his sisters-in-law, his fear of immoral women, his never getting married, his frequent change of doctors, his frantic attempts to exercise strict control over his nephew lest he fall into "temptations" which were widely available in Vienna—these might be better understood if we knew that he knew that he had a disease which was then often incurable. Yet if he did have it and knew he had it, his physicians at one time must have held out the hope of his being cured; for he thought of getting married. Read from that point of view, several of the notations in his journals could be reinterpreted. For example, the one in 1814:

> Decision of the doctors about my life. If no salvation is possible I must use. . . . ??? It only remains to end it quicker what was formerly impossible. Consultation with . . . .

This does not sound as if he were writing about deafness, but about a disease which he fears to be mortal. It is difficult to explain the entry on other grounds. Beethoven is not known to have been seriously ill in 1814. In 1816 he writes about "a malady which he cannot change and which brings him gradually nearer to death." Deafness could hardly be described in such words.

---

* It was later supposed to have been bought for the Bodmer Collection. The Beethoven House states that it has no such document.

Did that curious letter he wrote to Gleichenstein (A-265) — "if you would only be more candid; surely you are concealing something from me" — express his pain over the Therese Malfatti affair or was he referring to another disclosure? Why does he mention a Dr. Dorner in the letter? (See page 285.)

In the early 19th century, long before Paul Ehrlich, it was difficult to diagnose venereal diseases, and little distinction was made between the various forms of infection. A terrible stigma was attached to such diseases. They had to be treated in secrecy, though advanced cases were put into a special hospital in Vienna; * in the 18th century some heartless men — and women — in search of a cheap thrill visited that hospital to laugh at the sufferings of the patients.

If it was difficult then to diagnose living patients, it is impossible to diagnose a dead man after more than a century and after facts have been obfuscated, whether carelessly or willfully. It is probable that Thayer did suppress certain data; yet, to give him the benefit of the doubt, he may have done so because he himself was not convinced of their validity.

There is another argument against the syphilis theory: is it probable that Beethoven could have hidden such a secret from all his friends or from all the Viennese gossipmongers? If they knew, nobody said anything. That is not likely; usually such "scandal" slips out. Is it probable that none of the many doctors he consulted ever dropped a word, even after he died? We have no such word, save the story of Dr. Bertolini's burned records.**

At any rate, after perusing the many medical papers, the layman must sum up the matter by noting that for every ten authorities who said that he had it, there are ten who said that he did not. We have to counter an Ernest Newman statement, "The fact of Beethoven's malady seems then to be beyond dispute," by asserting that there *is* a dispute. There is no certainty, and we must leave it at that.

---

* The *St. Marx Hospital for Syphilis*. Joseph II ordered the rooms opened to visitors, probably to show people the results of the disease.

** Donald MacArdle, the distinguished Beethoven scholar who died in 1964, planned to issue a Beethoven encyclopedia. He was at work on this when he died. The manuscript, which has not been published, is in the Library of Congress. Under the entry which refers to Dr. Bertolini, MacArdle discusses a statement by Jahn quoted by Kerst in his biography (vol. 2, p. 193) similar to the statement I have quoted, to the effect that Beethoven did not always escape unscathed from his adventures in love. MacArdle writes: "This statement by a physician who felt it prudent to destroy all his professional records dealing with B would seem to be of the greatest significance in arriving at a conclusion on the much-debated question as to whether B was luetic, but it seems to have been overlooked by writers on the subject." As is apparent, it has not been entirely overlooked.

CHAPTER 12

THE PREMATURE TESTAMENT
AND THE EROICA

If you needed help to discover the worthwhile goings-on in Vienna's musical and theatrical life, you could obtain it by buying a little volume titled "Historic Pocketbook with Special Regard to Austria." The edition covering the year 1802 * states that Vienna lagged behind other European cities, particularly the smaller German cities, in the "art of song." Little in the way of fine new songs or good new operas was being created by Austrian composers. "When one did hear singing in Vienna, it was more likely to be a bravura Italian aria by Paer or Salieri." However, conditions were very different in the field of instrumental music. There Vienna was preeminent:

> Father Haydn gave us as his seventy-seventh work three new Quartets. They are of a simple, unforced greatness, as good as his *Creation* or the heavenly *Seven Last Words* ... Beethoven has written his First Symphony in C Major. It is a masterpiece which does equal honor to his power of invention and his musical skill. It is as beautiful and excellent in design as in execution; a clear and radiant order reigns, and the work is marked by such a stream of the most pleasant melodies, as well as such a rich but never fatiguing instrumentation, that this symphony can be rightly considered the equal of any by Mozart or Haydn. A Violin Quintet and a Septet (Opus 20) with Horn and Clarinet are finely invented and adroitly executed. Unprejudiced listeners to Beethoven's music are less satisfied with his new works for the piano, in which one perceives a conscious effort to be unconventional and original, all too often at the expense of beauty. This characteristic, bordering on the abstruse, is to be found especially in Opus 23 and in certain movements of Opus 26 and 27, though these works do offer in recompense several brilliant and significant delights.

---

* Published in Vienna 1806 by the enterprising publishing house Anton Doll.

Archduke Rudolph of Austria, Beethoven's noted pupil and protector (Historical Museum, Vienna).

What were these new works which seemed so unconventional as to border on the abstruse? They were the Violin Sonata No. 4 in A Minor, Op. 23, which did perplex Beethoven's contemporaries because it sacrifices prettiness in favor of boldness; the Piano Sonata No. 12 in A-flat Major, Op. 26, decidedly a sonata which begins with a shock, an opening movement not in sonata form but a theme-and-variation, and proceeds to a slow movement which bears the title, "Funeral March on the Death of a Hero." According to the above-mentioned composer Paer, it was he who took Beethoven to hear his opera *Achilles,* and Beethoven enjoyed himself no end. The opera contained a Funeral March, and Beethoven exclaimed, *"Il faut que je compose cela."* *

Opus 27 consists of two piano sonatas, both called by Beethoven *"Sonata quasi una fantasia"* ("Sonata in the manner of a fantasy"). The first of these is in E-flat Major; the second, in C-sharp Minor, is the *Moonlight Sonata.* It was not called "Moonlight" by Beethoven nor was it known by that name until well after Beethoven's death. The poet-critic Ludwig Rellstab named it so in 1832, saying that the opening movement made him think of moonlight rippling on the waves of Lake Lucerne. What would Beethoven have thought of the sentimental and quite inappropriate title?

Yes, these works must have fallen strangely on the ears of some of the auditors. Yet they were listened to, eagerly, curiously, receptively. They had many partisans. They became "conversation pieces." And, as the "Historic Pocketbook" indicates, Beethoven in his thirties rivaled Haydn in his seventies as Vienna's most celebrated composer.

In 1800 Beethoven worked on a ballet called *The Creatures of Prometheus.* In doing so, he not only undertook to solve an artistic problem which interested him, the problem of music which could serve bodily expression, but took advantage of a lucrative opportunity. Salvatore Vigano, the ballet master whose idea *Prometheus* was, was a particular favorite not only of the Empress but of all Vienna. So was his beautiful wife, who invented flattering maternity dresses "a la Vigano." The opportunity to collaborate with the ballet master of the Court Theater, a man who enjoyed a high artistic reputation, was one which Beethoven seems to have appreciated, and he was decently recompensed for his work. The ballet was given on March 28, 1801, and had a good but not an unqualified success, fourteen performances being recorded that year and nine the following year. Prometheus, who stole the fire from the gods, was

---

* "I must compose that."

a figure who must have made a particular appeal to Beethoven's imagination. He was familiar with Goethe's great symbolic poem on the theme of man's defiance of the gods.

Also around 1800 Beethoven began the composition of his Third Piano Concerto, though almost three years elapsed before he brought that magical work to completion. No doubt about it, in the first two years of the century he was vigorously busy. Whether in love or not, miserable in his fate or temporarily hopeful, plans and inventions and ideas were germinating in his mind, sequences, melodies, modulations were coursing in his blood, his musical thinking encompassed both the tempest and the zephyr, and what he finally let stand on paper after countless erasures, reshapings, impatient scratching out, compression, and correction is music that is equally persuasive when it mutinies against pain as when it murmurs in tender serenity. He continued the piano sonatas, the violin sonatas (the *Kreutzer Sonata* was begun sometime in 1802), the chamber music, songs, "bagatelles," variations, and he essayed an oratorio, *Christ on the Mount of Olives,* which, to be sure, is hardly one of his more successful works. But for those spells of deafness he might have been at peace, or as much at peace as Beethoven could be.

··≎[2]≎··

Even the world was for the moment at peace, that is, in 1801. Early that year, on February 9, peace had been concluded between Austria and France (at Lunéville); * in July Napoleon had arrived at an understanding with the Papacy, signing a Concordat which permitted French ecclesiastics to be appointed by France's government and merely confirmed by the Pope. This was a signal diplomatic victory for Napoleon. In return for this, the Pope was allowed to keep his papal states, with three exceptions. Further peace moves were initiated in October between Britain and France. Egypt was to be restored to Turkey, and Napoleon agreed to evacuate Naples. The agreement was formalized by the Peace of Amiens, March 27, 1802.

In that year a lady suggested to the publisher Hoffmeister that Beethoven compose a sonata celebrating the "Revolution." Hoffmeister passed the suggestion on to him; he rejected it with humorous scorn:

---

* Austria had no choice. She was temporarily beaten. The Peace of Lunéville marked the virtual disintegration of the Holy Roman Empire.

THE PREMATURE TESTAMENT AND THE EROICA

VIENNA, April 8, 1802

Has the devil got hold of you all, gentlemen?—that you suggest that *I should
compose such a sonata*—Well, perhaps at the time of the revolutionary fever—
such a thing might have been possible, but now, when everything is trying to
slip back into the old rut, now that Buonaparte has concluded his Concordat
with the Pope—to write a sonata of that kind?—If it were even a Missa pro
Sancta Maria a tre voci, or a Vesper or something of that kind—In that case I
would instantly take up my paint brush—and with fat pound notes dash off a
Credo in unum. But, good Heavens, such a sonata—in these newly developing
Christian times—Ho ho—there you must leave me out—you won't get anything
from me—Well, here is my reply in the fastest tempo—The lady can have a
sonata from me, and, moreover, from an *aesthetic* point of view I will in general
adopt her plan—but without adopting—her keys—The price would be about 50
ducats—for that sum she may keep the sonata for her own enjoyment for one
year, and neither I *nor she* will be entitled to publish it—After the expiry of
that year—the sonata will be exclusively my property—that is to say—I can and
will publish it—and in any case—if she thinks it will do her any honor—she
can ask me to dedicate the sonata to her—Now may God protect you, gentlemen
— (A-57).

Fifty ducats was his price. For fifty ducats in 1802 you could buy a whole
piano! In the same year, Beethoven's compositions were published by no fewer
than seven different publishers.

Two men who were to become important to him entered his life sometime in
the early years of the century. One was Ferdinand Johann Nepomuk Joseph
Kinsky, Prince of Wchinitz und Tettau. Born in Vienna, he owned estates in
Bohemia. His palace on the Freyung was a superb edifice designed by Lukas von
Hildebrandt; it had served under Maria Theresa as the headquarters of her
proud Swiss Guard. Now it served for many an hour of music, as Kinsky and his
new wife (they were married in 1801) were particularly captivated by all that
Beethoven brought.*

The other was Rudolph Johann Joseph Rainer Habsburg—Archduke Rudolph—youngest son of Leopold II, brother of reigning Emperor Franz. Born
in Florence, he was brought to Vienna in 1790 when he was but two years old.
Since the age of fifteen he was surrounded by his own court attendants headed

---

* The Palace still stands, though when last seen by the author it was in a state of disrepair. One of
its features was a huge painting on the ceiling of the Room of State, painted by Carlo Carlone, the
Venetian painter who worked in the style of Tiepolo.

by two counts and a tutor. He lived in luxury; he took that for granted and it did not debilitate him.

To be the brother of a reigning Emperor was a fate both enviable and frustrating, enviable because, standing at the top of the social pyramid, he had the opportunity to observe and influence the intellectual and artistic events of his time; frustrating because as the younger son of a royal house he found it difficult to define his mission in life. It was no longer possible to plot a brother's murder and to usurp the crown, as it had been possible in the bad old medieval days. Nor was it possible to take an active part in a political career; the reigning monarch did not wish a younger brother to interfere in government. One could lead troops. Or one could lead souls, by joining the Church. Or one could be idle. But if there was any feeling of uselessness in Rudolph's mind, or if he resented having to stand at the side of Franz's baldachin, he gave no inkling of it. He had a purpose in life.

Even as a youngster his health had not been good. Possibly as a recompense for this weakness, he had become genuinely devout, a man of piety and true goodness of heart. He did begin his career in the military, but very soon switched to theological studies, eventually becoming the coadjutor of the Prince-Archbishop of Olmütz, the archbishop's seat in Moravia. After the death of the archbishop, Rudolph assumed the office. In this his career paralleled that of his uncle, Maximilian Franz. Rudolph's portrait in later life, clothed in the bishop's robes, shows him with a soft face, almost feminine in contour, eyes that seem to look away from the world, hands folded in a peaceful gesture, the hair combed stiffly and straight back like a hood protecting the vulnerable head. His whole life must have been lived under a shadow: he was a Habsburg and he knew that he was threatened by the disease endemic to the Habsburgs, epilepsy. He did not escape it.

He was a modest man. His private correspondence shows that when Rudolph wrote to the Emperor he always addressed him as "Your Majesty" and in the polite form.* When he was away from Vienna, he asked his tutor, Baumeister, to procure for him this or that work by Beethoven. He wanted to be kept up to date. His great passion was music. He wanted not only to play; he wanted to compose. He really worked at it, though as a composer he remained a talented dilettante. He took an active part in Vienna's musical affairs. When the

---

* Brother Ferdinand, Archduke of Tuscany, and brother Carl, who became the hero of Aspern, addressed Emperor Franz as "Du."

Society of the Friends of Music was founded, Rudolph was appointed its first "Protector." He willed to the Society a valuable luxury edition of Handel's oratorios and a special edition of Beethoven's works, copied in a fair hand, along with several original Beethoven manuscripts. Aside from music,* he was much interested in the art of engraving. Several of his drawings and engravings have been preserved.

Such was the man who proved to be a friend to Beethoven to the end of the composer's life. Beethoven dedicated more compositions to Rudolph than to any of his other patrons. The friendship began with a pupil-teacher relationship. When Beethoven met him, and how, is not certain. Rudolph was a friend of Lichnowsky; they were on good enough terms for him to visit Lichnowsky on his estate; it is possible that it was Lichnowsky who effected the introduction. As to the year, it may have been 1803, at which time Rudolph was a boy of fifteen.** The archduke had already taken some lessons before Beethoven became his tutor and had made enough progress to display his skill in the palaces of Lobkowitz, Kinsky, and others. Well, the Lobkowitzes and the Kinskys hardly had any choice but to listen to and praise the performance of a Habsburg archduke.

Rudolph's talent is better attested by the fact that Beethoven did teach him and respected him. The music that Beethoven was to write for Rudolph's use, such as the *Triple Concerto* and the *Archduke Trio,* was not music that could be ventured by a clumsy pianist.

It is consistent with Beethoven's character that he rather made a point of treating Rudolph as if he were just another pupil. He underscored with a thick stroke his democratic principles; Rudolph took this lightly, as he could afford to do. Perhaps Beethoven acted that way to hide the fact that he *was* impressed. He exaggerated the prerogatives of an instructor, though we must view skeptically the several stories of his almost impudent behavior, stories which have formed part of the legend—such as that he would rap Rudolph over the knuckles when he did not play well—and the tale that Ries tells that once, when Beethoven was kept waiting by the archduke, he angrily forced his way into Rudolph's private chamber and flatly declared that much though he respected the archduke himself, he could not possibly be expected to observe Court etiquette and

---

* One of his compositions was a set of forty Variations on a theme of Beethoven. He modestly called the composition "an assignment" and dedicated it to Beethoven. It was published by Steiner in Vienna, 1819.
** Other authorities give 1805 as the year, but the earlier date seems more probable.

submit himself to being "ceremonialized." The archduke laughed and told his staff that Beethoven was to be admitted at once when he called.

The evidence of Beethoven's letters and notes to Rudolph contradicts these stories. We have a quantity of such missives.* They indicate that Beethoven never was really at ease with Rudolph. He held Rudolph in affection, but a ceremonial curtain hung between them which prevented too close an approach. One feels the difference between Beethoven's outspoken and undiplomatic relationship to a Lichnowsky or a Lobkowitz and the more circumspect attitude he assumed toward the archduke. Beethoven did not really enjoy the archduke's company because he did not like to breathe the air of a Court. Time and again he postpones visiting Rudolph, puts off giving him lessons, while asserting that he hopes to "grow and thrive in your grace and favor." The following letter is typical:

> Your Imperial Highness!   [VIENNA, late March, 1811]
>
> For over a fortnight now I have again been afflicted with a headache which is plaguing me. I have kept on hoping that the pain would subside, but in vain. Now that the weather is improving, however, my doctor has promised me an early recovery. As I regarded every day as the last one of my ailment, I did not send you word about it, partly too because I fancied that, since Your Imperial Highness had not sent for me for so long, you did not require my services— During the festivities in honor of the Princess of Baden and when Your Imperial Highness was hampered by your sore finger I began to work rather hard; and one of the fruits of this diligence is a new pianoforte trio. Since I was very much taken up with my own affairs I did not think that Your Imperial Highness would be annoyed with me, as I am now almost inclined to believe that you are—Meanwhile I hope soon to be able to appear in person before your tribunal.
>
> Your Imperial Highness's
> faithful and most devoted servant
> LUDWIG VAN BEETHOVEN   (A-300).

So it goes on: "I am better and in a few days I shall again have the honor of waiting upon you and of making up for lost time—I am always desperately worried if I cannot be zealous in your service and if I cannot be with Your Imperial Highness as often as I should like." . . . "I am not yet in the best of health" . . . "You must have almost thought my illness was feigned but I

---

* They are written with a more careful penmanship than are Beethoven's other letters.

assure you that it was not" ... "I have again had to remain in my room," etc., etc. No doubt all true, but at the same time psychological excuses for not doing what he did not want to do. Conversely, a letter from Rudolph to Beethoven written when the archduke was called to Olmütz, March 25, 1820, illustrates the respect with which the royal pupil treated the tutor:

Dear Beethoven: Since my task lies here, I had to leave Vienna in a hurry. Otherwise I would never have been able to separate myself from so much that is dear to me. So that you may see that even at a distance I think of all that, I write you these few lines. I am sorry not to have seen you before my departure. Persuaded as I am of your intentions, I hope that you will compose industriously for me. If only I were capable of producing something that would be worthy of you! Since I have so many proofs of your tolerance, I will send you something as soon as I have finished it—till now I haven't had a moment of free time—for your correction and my instruction. I only hope that my wish be granted that your health and your spirit be at peace ...

Since music will always remain my most welcome relaxation, I have already been to a few amateur concerts ... They know here of my justifiable predilection for your compositions and therefore they treated me to a performance of your symphony in A Major [the Seventh], one which was for Olmütz surprisingly good. There were passages which I heard performed worse in Vienna, especially the first *allegro* which I love so much. I was quite enraptured.

I will be very happy soon to receive good news from you. Once Holy Week has passed, which is a somewhat difficult time for me, I will try to translate my thoughts into notes and to send you a new proof of how—even at a distance—I am your devoted

RUDOLPH, M. P.

Rudolph died four years after Beethoven, at the early age of forty-three.

·>[3]<·

The growing number of his compositions and the bruiting about of the esteem in which he was held in high places may have turned a light of notoriety on Beethoven too bright for his own comfort. He didn't want the knock on the door, the idle visitor. Was that the reason he moved about? Or was it merely his bodily irresolution, the alternating moods, which made it hard for him to sit still? He was a nomad within city walls. He no longer lived on the Graben; in the spring of 1801 he was occupying a lodging on top of one of the Bastions (the *Wasserkunstbastei*) with which he could well have been pleased, as it gave him a beautiful view of the Glacis, with plenty of light and sun. Yet in the fall of 1802 we find him again in a new quarter, in the Petersplatz, in a location practically where he started from, right in the center of the city. As Thayer asks, what whim could have induced him to go there, "with the bells of St. Peter's on one side and those of St. Stephen's sounding down upon him on the other, and he so suffering with his ears?" Then early in 1803 he moved again to the quarters offered him by Schikaneder in the new Theater-an-der-Wien.*

In the summer, as usual, he went to the country, and in 1802 he went to Heiligenstadt, a particularly quiet and restful retreat, choosing it perhaps on the advice of his doctor, Professor Schmidt. It did not turn out to be the best of medical counsels. Though Beethoven lived in charming surroundings, among flowery fields and gentle woods in a house high on top of a hill, he was much alone. As the summer wore on, he knew that his hearing was not improving. He could hear no better than before the familiar noises of the country, the singing of the shepherd, the bleating of the sheep, the threshing of the grain. Taking stock of a condition which he had up to recently tried to hide from all but his most intimate friends, he was overcome by a realization of its hopelessness. Lonely, solitary, his mind tangled with new problems he wanted to solve, with no Zmeskall handy to cheer him up, no Schuppanzigh with whom to play music, deprived of the society of the Vienna Palaces, possibly recovering from one of his disappointments in love—in short, brooding in the country's isolation, he fell into a despondency in which he must have seen himself as an outcast, marked for death and forced to settle his accounts with the world.

In such a mood, at such a moment, he wrote the Heiligenstadt Testament, one of the most heartbreaking documents to be found in the long literature of lamentations.** Here it is, as translated by Emily Anderson:

THE HEILIGENSTADT TESTAMENT

HEILIGENSTADT, *October* 6, 1802

FOR MY BROTHERS CARL AND — — — — BEETHOVEN

O my fellow men, who consider me, or describe me as, unfriendly, peevish or even misanthropic, how greatly do you wrong me. For you do not know the secret reason why

---

* With all those moves it is no wonder that so few letters addressed to Beethoven have been preserved.

** The Heiligenstadt Testament came into possession of Stephan von Breuning, who died on June 4, 1827, shortly after Beethoven. His widow turned the document over to Schindler. Schindler showed it to Rochlitz, who published it. Then the autograph passed through many owners. At one time Franz Liszt owned it, and later Jenny Lind. Otto Goldschmidt, Jenny Lind's husband, offered it to the Library of Hamburg, where it now is.

I appear to you to be so Ever since my childhood my heart and soul have been imbued with the tender feeling of goodwill; and I have always been ready to perform even great actions. But just think, for the last six years I have been afflicted with an incurable complaint which has been made worse by incompetent doctors. From year to year my hopes of being cured have gradually been shattered and finally I have been forced to accept the prospect of a *permanent infirmity* (the curing of which may perhaps take years or may even prove to be impossible). Though endowed with a passionate and lively temperament and even fond of the distractions offered by society I was soon obliged to seclude myself and live in solitude. If at times I decided just to ignore my infirmity, alas! how cruelly was I then driven back by the intensified sad experience of my poor hearing. Yet I could not bring myself to say to people: "Speak up, shout, for I am deaf." Alas! how could I possibly refer to the impairing *of a sense* which in me should be more perfectly developed than in other people, a sense which at one time I possessed in the greatest perfection, even to a degree of perfection such as assuredly few in my profession possess or have ever possessed—Oh, I cannot do it; so forgive me, if you ever see me withdrawing from your company which I used to enjoy. Moreover my misfortune pains me doubly, inasmuch as it leads to my being misjudged. For me there can be no relaxation in human society, no refined conversations, no mutual confidences. I must live quite alone and may creep into society only as often as sheer necessity demands; I must live like an outcast. If I appear in company I am overcome by a burning anxiety, a fear that I am running the risk of letting people notice my condition—And that has been my experience during the last six months which I have spent in the country. My sensible doctor by suggesting that I should spare my hearing as much as possible has more or less encouraged my present natural inclination, though indeed when carried away now and then by my instinctive desire for human society, I have let myself be tempted to seek it. But how humiliated I have felt if somebody standing beside me heard the sound of a flute in the distance and *I heard nothing,* or if somebody heard *a shepherd sing* and again I heard nothing—Such experiences almost made me despair, and I was on the point of putting an end to my life—The only thing that held me back was *my art.* For indeed it seemed to me impossible to leave this world before I had produced all the works that I felt the urge to compose; and thus I have dragged on this miserable existence—a truly miserable existence, seeing that I have such a sensitive body that any fairly sudden change can plunge me from the best spirits into the worst of humours—*Patience*—that is the virtue, I am told, which I must now choose for my guide; and I now possess it—I hope that I shall persist in my resolve to endure to the end, until it pleases the inexorable Parcae to cut the thread; perhaps my condition will improve, perhaps not; at any rate I am now resigned—At the early age of 28 I was obliged to become a philosopher, though this was not easy; for indeed this is more difficult for an artist than for anyone else—Almighty God, who look down into my innermost soul, you see into my heart and you know that it is filled with love for humanity and a desire to do good. Oh my fellow men, when some day you read this statement, remember that you have done me wrong; and let some unfortunate man derive comfort from the thought that he has found another equally unfortunate who, notwithstanding all the obstacles imposed by nature, yet did everything in his power to be raised to the rank of noble artists and human beings. — And you, my brothers Carl and [Johann], when I am dead, request on my behalf Professor Schmidt, if he is still living, to describe my disease, and attach this written document to his record, so that after my death at any rate the world and I may be reconciled as far as possible — At the same time I herewith nominate you both heirs to my small property (if I may so describe it) — Divide it honestly, live in harmony and help one another. You know that you have long ago been forgiven for the harm you did me. I again thank you, my brother Carl, in particular, for the affection you have shown me of late years. My wish is that you should have a better and more carefree existence than I have had. Urge your children to be *virtuous,* for virtue alone can make a man happy. Money cannot do this. I speak from experience. It was virtue that sustained me in my misery. It was thanks to virtue and also to my art that I did not put an end to my life by suicide — Farewell and love one another — I thank all my friends, and especially *Prince Lichnowsky* and *Professor Schmidt.* I would like Prince L[ichnowsky]'s instruments to be preserved by one of you, provided this does not lead to a quarrel between you. But as soon as they can serve a more useful purpose, just sell them; and how glad I shall be if in my grave I can still be of some use to you both — Well, that is all — Joyfully I go to meet Death — should it come before I have had an opportunity of developing all my artistic gifts, then in spite of my hard fate it would still come too soon, and no doubt I would like it to postpone its coming — Yet even so I should be content, for would it not free me from a condition of continual suffering? Come then, Death, *whenever* you like, and with courage I will go to meet you — Farewell; and when I am dead, do not wholly forget me. I deserve to be remembered by you, since during my lifetime I have often thought of you and tried to make you happy — Be happy —

LUDWIG VAN BEETHOVEN

For my brothers Carl and — — — —
To be read and executed after my death —
HEILIGENSTADT, October 10, 1802 — Thus I take leave of you — and, what is more, rather sadly — yes, the hope I cherished — the hope I brought with me here of being cured to a certain extent at any rate — that hope I must now abandon completely. As the autumn leaves fall and wither, likewise — that hope has faded for me. I am leaving here — almost in the same condition as I arrived — Even that high courage — which has often inspired me on fine summer days — has vanished — Oh Providence — do but grant me one day *of pure joy* — For so long now the inner echo of real joy has been unknown to me — Oh when — oh when, Almighty God — shall I be able to hear and feel this echo again in the temple of Nature and in contact with humanity — Never? — No! — Oh, that would be too hard.

A few comments: First, we must not judge it as a document representing Beethoven in his totality or for a protracted period of time. It represents Beethoven at a particular moment and in a particular mood, that of "hitting bottom." As such it touches us deeply—but we must not think of Beethoven as a Niobe, "all tears." Not for long!

Second, it is not a real will, the paper of an old man saying farewell to the world. Beethoven was not quite thirty-two and, aside from the deafness which varied in severity and was to continue to vary for years to come, he was physically robust. Nor does he think he is at death's door. Even as he is writing the Testament he is shaping plans for music of the future. He does say, "Joyfully I go to meet death," but adds immediately, as if in fear that Death would take him seriously, "Should it come before I have had an opportunity of developing all my artistic gifts, then in spite of my hard fate it would still come too soon." He does not expect to die.

Third, the Testament has little practical application, since Beethoven leaves his estate to his two brothers, who would have been the heirs had he died intestate, but does not particularize or give an inventory. The only part of his property he thinks worth mentioning are the musical instruments which he had received as a gift from Prince Lichnowsky, but even those he leaves vaguely to "one of you" and hopes that this will not "lead to a quarrel between you." What about his manuscripts, his jewelry, whatever money he had, his books, his personal belongings? Even Beethoven could not have thought that this was putting his affairs in order.

What was the purpose of the Testament? I believe it was, first, a Rousseau-like self-confession and, second, an effort to cleanse his mind of the horrible depression and by this catharsis to be able to go on with life, go on for another twenty-five years, go on to the great achievement still before him.

He knows that his brothers and the friends around him, such as Lichnowsky, must have thought him "unfriendly, peevish, or even misanthropic." He acknowledges the charge, but he explains it by the confession that he is ashamed of his deafness, that he cannot bring himself to admit it, that he has been living in "burning anxiety" lest people notice the true state of his hearing, and that he has been suffering from this affliction for six years—which we know to be an exaggeration by at least two years.

But unfriendliness, peevishness, misanthropy were not his true characteristics. He describes himself—rightly—as "imbued with the tender feeling of good-will"; in his soul there dwelt both "the love for humanity and a desire to do good." It is true. Love for humanity and goodness are in him, though often strangely miscarried. The tenderness which we hear in the music emerges from his words. The greatness of heart is mirrored in the lines.

It is music, obviously, that gives him the desire to live. Yet music is not the only thing he wants out of life. He speaks of his fondness for the "distractions offered by society," he would like to seek "relaxation in human society," he enjoys "refined conversations." He knows that he is "endowed with a passionate and lively temperament."

He has had to become a philosopher in his twenty-eighth year. He was to become more of a philosopher after he had tucked away the Heiligenstadt Testament. (Probably he never looked at it again.) If by a "philosopher" he means a man who reasons with himself, one who accepts his fate "philosophically," then he has used the Testament to help him become one. The act of writing down his thoughts has defined for him the resolve to "endure to the end," whether his condition will improve or not. "Patience" is the word. The Testament is a soliloquy, a "To be or not to be" which was of greater curative value than any of Dr. Schmidt's prescriptions.

There are several other noteworthy points about the document. First, when he speaks of not being able to hear a flute in the distance or the shepherd singing, we are reminded of Ries's statement quoted on page 212. It must actually have happened as Ries relates it. Second, the document is very neatly written and shows few erasures, suggesting that Beethoven sketched it out in the rough and then made a clean copy. How different it is from his actual last testament, a few words which the dying man scribbled on a piece of paper! Third, though it is addressed to both brothers, he consistently omits Johann's name in the superscription, in the text, and in the postscript. One scholar has suggested that he did so because he did not know whether to call his brother Johann or Nikolaus Johann! This seems absurd. It is more likely that he had just had a quarrel with Johann and that Carl was the current favorite, to whom he gives special thanks for the "affection you have shown me of late years." * He does let fly a little arrow aimed at both of them: he forgives them "for the harm you did me." And he cannot refrain from adding a bit of Beethovian moralizing.

Finally, without detracting a jot from the poignancy of the document, one must point out that the style bears similarities to the Romantic literature of the period. Again, a few phrases, particularly in the postscript, are echoes of

---

* Ries, however, says that Beethoven had had a terrible argument with Carl that summer, which ended in blows. If that is true, then perhaps the affectionate words in the Testament serve as an apology.

Werther. Here too, as in the letters to Josephine, Beethoven was subconsciously quoting.

Before we leave the Heiligenstadt Testament, we must again ask, What was this matter with Johann and why did he single out Carl for approbation? Carl at that time was helping him with his business dealings. We have a letter from Carl written about six weeks after Beethoven returned from Heiligenstadt, November 23, 1802, to the publisher Johann André in Offenbach in which Carl signs himself "Imperial Royal Treasury Official" * and in which he treats André's inquiries in a high-handed manner. He gives the prices at which "we" are willing to sell a symphony and a piano concerto. André can also have three piano sonatas but not all at once, just "one every five or six weeks, because my brother does not trouble himself with such trifles any longer and composes only oratorios, operas, etc." (Not true, of course.) One can just hear Carl saying pompously to Ludwig: "Let me deal with those publishers. I know how to do it."

Johann, on the other hand, was doing very well. Still employed as a pharmacist, he was managing to save money from which he soon bought an apothecary shop in Linz. Later, about 1809, he was to furnish the Austrian army with pharmaceutical supplies and to become a wealthy man. Beethoven may have felt that Johann paid too much attention to his own life and not enough attention to him. At any rate, possession was Johann's chief desire in life. He became a bit of a parvenu. Gerhard von Breuning recalled that Johann used to drive in the Prater in an old-fashioned phaeton, with two or four horses, lolling carelessly in the seat with two servants on the box. When Johann signed a letter to his brother, "Real Estate Owner," Ludwig replied, "Brain Owner." Or so the story goes.

The relationship with both of his brothers was a troubled one: Carl's place in the sun did not last long. Soon enough, Beethoven began to distrust him. From time to time he had harsh things to say about both Carl and Johann. But the repeated breaches were always healed, and even when they committed some act which offended Beethoven he forgave them, saying, "What shall I do? They are my brothers."

They were ordinary enough men, but they were not the villains which they were pictured to be in early Beethoven biographies. Both Schindler and Ries described them so. Ries accused them of trying to keep Beethoven's intimate

---

* He was, in point of fact, an unimportant clerk.

330

friends away from him in an effort to gain ascendancy over the famous composer. Schindler, who knew Johann only slightly and Carl probably not at all, was jealous of practically everybody who approached Beethoven. Listen to him rant in his biography:

> These brothers possessed such hypocrisy, such cunning and malice, that they were able by evil and persistent methods to negate the kindly ministrations of Beethoven's friends and often estrange them, though not always without bitter conflict.
>
> Surely Nature played a curiously malevolent trick when she gave Beethoven, who was highly moral and singularly gifted but also in certain respects weak, a pair of brothers capable of nothing above the mentality of a shopkeeper. (S).

There is no basis for portraying Carl or Johann as if either had been Edmund Gloucester. Thayer's estimate is near the mark: what is really known about them "though it sufficiently confutes much of the calumnious nonsense which has been printed about them, is not fitted to convey any very exalted idea of their characters."

·∘⟦ 4 ⟧∘·

Before the year was out (1802), Beethoven had completed the Second Symphony. He seems to have brought it home right from the meadows of Heiligenstadt, so full is it of summer air and summer flowers. The joyous symphony adds one more caution to any attempt at connecting an artist's work with his mental state at the time of creating it. Often the work is the purgative of its creator's melancholy.

Yet not only as a composer, as a man too, Beethoven was in anything but a negative mood. He was ever ready to do battle when he thought his interests had been slighted, but never more so than after his return from Heiligenstadt, when he became embroiled in a quarrel with the Viennese publishers Artaria and Mollo. The man who sighed in Heiligenstadt spouted in the city. The change came virtually overnight. The facts of the case are intricate. Beethoven had composed a string Quintet, Op. 29, and had sold it to the Leipzig publishers Breitkopf and Härtel. Artaria and Company wished to have the Quintet for publication in Vienna, and consequently borrowed a copy of the manuscript from Count Moritz von Fries, to whom the Quintet was dedicated, telling him —according to Beethoven—that the Quintet was already published and on sale in Vienna, but that they wanted a better copy for the purpose of correcting their edition, which was faulty.

Count Fries gave them his copy, and in short order the work was published in a version competitive with that of Breitkopf and Härtel. When Beethoven saw it, he flew into a rage, saying that it constituted a breach of agreement between himself and Breitkopf and Härtel, publishers who were friends of his and whose good will was important to him. He dashed off a long letter to Breitkopf and Härtel, dated November 13, 1802, in which he called Artaria and Company "arch-villains," "scoundrels," pointing out that both Mollo and Artaria, though two different publishers, were really only one firm—that is, "one whole family of scoundrels"—proposed to take legal action against them, and said that he approved of any steps, "even of a personal character," that could be taken. At first he thought that to straighten out the matter he should offer "these low fellows" two new works of his own on condition that they would suppress their whole edition of the Quintet. But then he thought better of it, on the advice of a cool-headed friend. "Do you want to reward these rascals?" his friend had said to him. He called the whole affair "the greatest swindle in the world," and mentioned too that his brother Carl had been acting as an agent between himself and Artaria and in doing so, in the general confusion of running to and fro, Carl had lost a faithful dog of whom he was particularly fond.

Not content with intramural attempts to straighten things out, Beethoven rushed into the open and published in the *Wiener Zeitung* of January 22, 1803, the following notice:

> TO MUSIC LOVERS. In informing the public that the original Quintet in C Major, long ago advertised by me, has been published by Breitkopf and Härtel in Leipzig, I declare that I have no part in the edition published at the same time by Herren Artaria and Mollo in Vienna. I am the more constrained to make this declaration because this edition is highly faulty, incorrect, and quite useless to players, whereas Herren Breitkopf and Härtel, the rightful owners of this Quintet, have done all in their power to produce the work as beautifully as possible.
>
> LUDWIG VAN BEETHOVEN

Obviously Artaria and Company, a respectable publishing house, could not let so direct an accusation pass uncontested. They filed a petition on February 14, 1803, in the High Police Court, demanding a retraction by Beethoven. Artaria deposed that Count Fries had bought the Quintet and was within his rights to hand over a copy to Artaria for publication. Soon after doing so the count had requested that publication be delayed until the Breitkopf and Härtel edition had been on sale in Vienna for fourteen days. This was done. They accompanied their deposition by a written statement from Count Fries, who confirmed these points. They also stated that Mollo had nothing whatever to do with the edition. As to the faults which Beethoven claimed, Beethoven himself had corrected two copies of the edition and consequently, if there were any mistakes, it was Beethoven who was responsible for them.

Beethoven replied that Count Fries had told him personally that Artaria had obtained the Quintet by "trickery"; later he had to admit that he did correct two copies; out of anger he had not done a thorough job. In the meantime, he called for all available copies and asked his pupil Ries to "correct" them by smearing them with ink as coarsely as possible, to make them unsalable. Ries did this.

The court appointed an impartial musician to study Artaria's edition. He found that all of Beethoven's corrections had been observed by the publishers. He also found that it was true that Mollo had nothing to do with the edition.

On September 26, 1803, the court ruled against Beethoven. They ordered him to retract his notice of January 22, submitting such a retraction to the court prior to its publication. Should he fail to comply with this decision, he would give cause to the plaintiffs "to secure their rights through process of law." A report dated December 4, 1803, shows that Beethoven was summoned to court and was clearly told that he must publish his disavowal. And yet he did not. He would not. Indeed, he never came forth with a retraction, in spite of a further judgment by the court on March 8, 1805. All he would concede by way of apology was to insert the following on March 31, 1804:

ANNOUNCEMENT TO THE PUBLIC

After having inserted a statement in the *Wiener Zeitung* of January 22, 1803, in which I publicly declared that the edition of my Quintet published by Mollo did not appear under my supervision, was faulty in the extreme and useless to players, the undersigned hereby revokes the statement to the extent of saying that Herren Mollo and Co. have no interest in this edition, feeling that I owe such a declaration to do justice to Herren Mollo and Co. before a public entitled to respect.

LUDWIG VAN BEETHOVEN

Artaria and Company never exercised their rights to proceed against Beethoven. Perhaps their skirts were not entirely clean. Or they may have decided that it was imprudent to offend Beethoven further. The matter dragged along for almost three years until the lawyers for both parties signed an agreement (September 9, 1805) concerning future editions of that particular work. Beethoven got over his anger, Artaria over theirs. The firm continued to publish some of Beethoven's works.

It is plain that compositions by Beethoven were properties the publishers sought because they were salable. Beethoven said, "I ask and they pay." It was not an empty boast: publishers were vying for his latest output. Muzio Clementi, who was not only a good composer but a progressive businessman, and who with a partner was engaged in the music-publishing business in London, made an arrangement with Breitkopf and Härtel by which he bought for England all the compositions Beethoven might cede to that firm. He agreed to pay Breitkopf and Härtel half of whatever fee they paid Beethoven. Not a bad affair for Clementi, considering that the British market for musical scores was extensive.

··э[5]c··

With a wave of his gay Tyrolean hat and an actor's bow, Schikaneder now entered Beethoven's life. The Theater-an-der-Wien, Schikaneder's ambitious undertaking, had finally been completed and opened on June 13, 1801. Immediately a lively competition ensued between Schikaneder's new theater and the Burgtheater, which was under the direction of Baron Peter von Braun. In addition Braun managed the Kärntnertor Theater; both were the official Court Theaters. Schikaneder had the best of it for a time. A contemporary writer, Johann Gottfried Seume,* wrote that one could hardly scold the Viennese for occasionally preferring Schikaneder's livelier performances to those at the Court Theaters. His people sang better, acted better, and were better costumed, "the boots of their heroes not being quite as down-at-the-heel." Schikaneder scored a great success with *Lodoiska,* a new opera by the important French (French by adoption) composer Luigi Cherubini. To meet the competition Braun, himself an alert theater man, now obtained the score of another opera by Cherubini, *Les Deux Journées,* retitled in German *The Days of Peril, or The Water Carrier.* What Braun did not know was that Schikaneder was secretly rehearsing the same work, having sent Kapellmeister Seyfried all the way to Munich to obtain a score. One day in advance of the scheduled performance at the Burgtheater,

---

* *Ein Spaziergang nach Syrakus,* 1801.

Schikaneder announced on the billboards of the Theater-an-der-Wien an opera called *Count Armand, or The Two Unforgettable Days;* it was none other than *Les Deux Journées.* The opera proved so popular that it filled both houses, and years later Beethoven remembered the great impression that Cherubini's music had made on him. Baron Braun, understandably, fumed over Schikaneder's pulling so fat a rabbit out of the hat and in retaliation he himself journeyed to Paris and entered into a contract with Cherubini.

Schikaneder looked around for another magic trick. His assistant was Sebastian Meyer, second husband of Mozart's sister-in-law Mme. Hofer, who had sung the Queen of the Night in the original performance of *The Magic Flute.* Meyer was a bass, though a better actor than a singer, and a man of cultivated musical taste. It is probable that it was he who advised Schikaneder to turn to Beethoven for a new attraction with which to best the rival theater.

Beethoven had given no evidence of being able to compose an opera or of knowing his way around the opera house. Nevertheless his name was sufficiently renowned to make Schikaneder's move a reasonable gamble. Three offers were made to Beethoven. First, he was to write an opera for Schikaneder; second, he was to take charge of the orchestra at the Theater-an-der-Wien; and third, he could conduct there whenever he wanted to. There was a further inducement: Schikaneder offered Beethoven free lodging in the building of the Theater-an-der-Wien. Beethoven moved there early in the spring of 1803 and took his brother Carl with him.

As it turned out, Beethoven was far too deeply occupied with ideas and sketches for his Third Symphony to pay much attention to the opera Schikaneder wanted. But the immediate result of Beethoven's engagement was a famous concert, given for his own benefit, in which the program consisted entirely of his own compositions. The concert was first announced in the *Wiener Zeitung,* March 23,* 1803:

NOTICE

On the 4th of April Herr Ludwig van Beethoven will produce a new Oratorio set to music by him
Christus am Oelberge
in the I. R. Privil. Theater-an-der-Wien. The other pieces to be performed will be announced on the large billboard.

---

* Not the 26th, as given in Thayer.

It was for this concert that Beethoven composed the oratorio *Christ on the Mount of Olives,* but it is not certain whether he wrote it in a short time or whether he had been thinking of the work for a long time. Later, when Beethoven became dissatisfied with the oratorio, he said that he had not taken enough time with it.*

The concert was postponed one day and took place on April 5.

Ries tells us that he called on Beethoven early in the morning of the concert, about five o'clock. He found Beethoven in bed, writing on separate sheets of paper. To his question of what he was working on, he answered, "Trombones." The trombone players played from these original sheets.

The rehearsal started at eight o'clock in the morning. It was a terrible rehearsal. At half past two everybody was exhausted and more or less dispirited. Prince Lichnowsky, who attended the rehearsal from the very beginning, now sent out for bread and butter, cold meat, and wine for all the musicians. He asked all to help themselves, and, after everybody had eaten heartily, tempers were restored. Lichnowsky requested that the oratorio be rehearsed once more from the beginning, so that it might go well in the evening. So they began to rehearse once more from the beginning. They must have finished not long before the actual commencement of the concert, at six o'clock. Ries remembered that the concert was so long that a few of the pieces were not performed. The program included the First and Second Symphonies; the Third Piano Concerto, and the oratorio. As no copy of the printed program has been found, we do not know what else might have been played. Even assuming that nothing else was given—customarily short selections or songs were interspersed between the longer works—the concert would have presented two and a half hours of music!

Seyfried was at the concert to turn the pages while Beethoven played the Third Piano Concerto. His report:

> In the playing of the concerto movements he asked me to turn the pages for him; but—heaven help me!—that was easier said than done. I saw almost nothing but empty leaves; at the most on one page or the other a few Egyptian hieroglyphs wholly unintelligible to me scribbled down to serve as clues for him; for he played nearly all of the solo part from memory, since, as was so often the case, he had not had time to put it all down on paper. He gave me a

---

* Thayer believed that Schindler was wrong when he wrote that sketches for the work were made "as early as 1801."

secret glance whenever he was at the end of one of the invisible passages and my scarcely concealable anxiety not to miss the decisive moment amused him greatly and he laughed heartily at the jovial supper which we ate afterwards. (TQ).

Beethoven had increased the admission prices to as much as twelve ducats for a loge (the usual price was four florins). He must have had a good audience, for his take from the concert was 1800 florins (over $10,000).

The reviews were mixed. The *Zeitung für die Elegante Welt,* No. 46, April 16, 1803, reported:

> Herr van Beethoven even augmented the price of the seats for his Cantata and announced several days in advance and with much pomp that all of the pieces to be played would be of his composition.... They consisted of two symphonies, of which the first is essentially of more value than the second, because it is developed with an unforced lightness, while in the second the striving for the new and astonishing is more apparent. However, it goes without saying that in both works there was no lack of surprising and brilliant beauties. Less successful was the Concerto in C Minor which followed, which Hr. v. B ... did not perform to the complete satisfaction of the public.

Beethoven conducted the entire concert, barring the concerto, which he might have guided while seated at the piano. What was he like as a conductor? The same Ignaz von Seyfried, who turned the pages, left us an account:

> Our master could not be presented as a model in respect of conducting, and the orchestra always had to have a care in order not to be led astray by its mentor; for he had ears only for his composition and was ceaselessly occupied by manifold gesticulations to indicate the desired expression. He often made a down beat for an accent in the wrong place. He used to suggest a *diminuendo* by crouching down more and more, and at a *pianissimo* he would almost creep under the desk. When the volume of sound grew he rose up also as if out of a stage-trap, and with the entrance of the power of the band he would stand upon the tips of his toes almost as big as a giant, and waving his arms, seemed about to soar upwards to the skies. Everything about him was active, not a bit of his organism idle, and the man was comparable to a *perpetuum mobile.* He did not belong to those capricious composers whom no orchestra in the world can satisfy. At times, indeed, he was altogether too considerate and did not even repeat passages which went badly at the rehearsal: "It will go better next time," he would say. He was very particular about expression, the delicate nuances, the equable distribution of light and shade as well as an effective *tempo rubato,* and

337

without betraying vexation, would discuss them with the individual players. When he then observed that the players would enter into his intentions and play together with increasing ardor, inspired by the magical power of his creations, his face would be transfigured with joy, all his features beamed pleasure and satisfaction, a pleased smile would play around his lips and a thundering "Bravi tutti!" reward the successful achievement. It was the first and loftiest triumphal moment for the genius, compared with which, as he confessed, the tempestuous applause of a receptive audience was as nothing. When playing at first sight, there were frequent pauses for the purpose of correcting the parts and then the thread would be broken; but he was patient even then; but when things went to pieces, particularly in the scherzos of his symphonies at a sudden and unexpected change of rhythm, he would shout with laughter and say he had expected nothing else, but was reckoning on it from the beginning; he was almost childishly glad that he had been successful in "unhorsing such excellent riders." (TQ).

To return to the concert, we may find a partial explanation for its lack of critical success through a source which has hitherto been unused. To describe this source, a short digression is needed.

·◦≡[6]≡◦·

The man's name was Joseph Carl Rosenbaum. He was the son of an employee of the Esterházy family, was born in Eisenstadt, and came to Vienna in 1797. He fell in love with the singer Therese Gassmann, who was quite famous, the Queen of the Night being one of her favorite roles. Rosenbaum's employer, Prince Nikolaus Esterházy, disapproved of the relationship, as did Therese's mother, who envisaged for her daughter a marriage more advantageous than one with a simple young man, not of the nobility. She intrigued against him and eventually he lost his post with Esterházy. Yet nothing swerved him from his love, nor Therese from her love for him, and they were married in 1800. He went into business and turned out to be so capable a businessman that he became wealthy; when he died in 1829, he owned several houses and left Therese and the five children of their marriage a considerable fortune. From 1797 to 1829 he hardly ever left Vienna; from the moment he got to Vienna until he died he kept a diary, writing down every day what seemed interesting to him: gossip, the weather, incidents of war, social affairs. Through Therese he got to know many of the artists of Vienna and several of the composers, among them Haydn, though seemingly he never met Beethoven. He was a kind of ingenuous Mr. Pepys, neither diplomat nor scientist nor artist but a shrewd and good-hearted observer of the scene. He was passionate for the theater, and almost every day he was to be found there or at the opera. His diaries shed a homey light on the everyday life of the period.* We shall have occasion to quote Mr. Rosenbaum more than once.**

What we glean from him of the 1803 concert is that Baron von Braun decided to revenge himself on Schikaneder by scheduling on the day of Beethoven's concert a performance of Haydn's *Creation,* for which he engaged the best available musicians and singers in Vienna.*** It was a spiteful move on Braun's part. Rosenbaum's pertinent entries read:

> Tuesday, April 5, 1803. I went to Fuchs [not identified], where we spoke of today's performance of the Cantata by Bethowen [*sic*], which was certainly a very faulty performance, since Braun in the Burgtheater gave the *Creation* with both orchestras as a benefit for indigent theater employees.
>
> Wednesday, April 6. Near the Lusthaus [in the Prater] I spoke with Willmann [Max, a brother of the singer Magdalena Willmann whom supposedly Beethoven wanted to marry] about Bethowen's Accademie, which he praised. But from everybody else I heard the opposite. Eberl [Anton Eberl, Viennese composer and friend of Mozart] told me that Bethowen in his Accademie yesterday did not in any way live up to the legitimate expectations of the public and that nothing was worthy of a great master.

One concludes that the performance was anything but adequate, since the good musicians of "both orchestras" were occupied with Haydn. Beethoven had experienced his first failure.

---

* The diaries slumbered for years in the manuscript collection of the Austrian National Library, but have now been examined, edited, and furnished with commentary by H. C. Robbins Landon and Else Radant. They became interested in Rosenbaum through their work on Haydn and then continued the research for this book.

** Rosenbaum achieved a peculiar kind of notoriety because two nights after Haydn's funeral he and one or two of his trusted friends went to the cemetery, bribed the caretaker, dug up the grave, and removed Haydn's head. He wanted it both as a souvenir and as an object to study, he being a student of phrenology. Though the smell made him very ill, he bore the head home in triumph and hid it in his house. The theft was discovered eleven years later when Prince Nikolaus Esterházy, grandson of Haydn's employer, had the body exhumed with the object of burying Haydn in Eisenstadt near the Esterházy Palace. The prince offered Rosenbaum a good deal of money if he would admit to the possession of the skull and give it up. Rosenbaum agreed. Whereupon the prince refused to pay the money and threatened Rosenbaum with police action. Rosenbaum sent the prince a skull, saying it was Haydn's skull. It was not. But on his death Rosenbaum bequeathed the real skull to the Vienna Society of The Friends of Music. It was not until a few years ago that Haydn's body and his head were finally reunited at Eisenstadt.

*** The date is confirmed by a history of the Theater-an-der-Wien, *150 Jahre Theater an der Wien,* by Anton Bauer.

A little more than a month after this concert, a violin virtuoso, George Augustus Polgreen Bridgetower, came to Vienna, preceded by high fame, to give a concert in the Augarten Hall. Beethoven met him at the Lichnowskys' and proposed to him that at his concert he play a new sonata. It was not ready, but Beethoven would get it ready in time. Yes, surely he would get it ready in time. Bridgetower agreed enthusiastically, knowing that the premiere of a new work by Beethoven could but add luster to his own appearance.

Bridgetower aroused much curiosity in the musical circles of Vienna. They knew that, though he was only twenty-four years old, he had long been in the service of the Prince of Wales. They were intrigued by him because he was a mulatto, the son of an African father and a mother who was either German or Polish, and because he had what was to them a strange name, which they hardly ever managed to spell correctly—"Bridgethauer" was one version, "Bride Tower" another, and "Brishdower" Beethoven's spelling. Schindler in his biography called him an American ship captain. Bridgetower never was in America and most probably never stood on the bridge of a ship.

The Sonata in A Major was of course not ready till the very last moment. The faithful Ries was summoned at half past four in the morning on the day of the concert to copy the violin part of the first allegro. The piano part was merely sketched in. Bridgetower played from Beethoven's manuscript, there being no time to copy it, except the final allegro, which was neatly written, since it originally belonged to a previous sonata (Op. 30). Beethoven played the piano. The sonata was a great success and Bridgetower left in his copy of the sonata a note in which he speaks lovingly of Beethoven's beautiful and "chaste" playing. Before Bridgetower departed from Vienna, he and Beethoven quarreled—about a woman, it is said—and Beethoven then dedicated the work, Sonata, Op. 47, to Rodolphe Kreutzer.

Kreutzer never played the *Kreutzer Sonata*.

Further distinctions were accorded to Beethoven. In the summer he received as a gift an Erard piano from the famous Parisian manufacturer. An inquiry came from Edinburgh, from a George Thomson, a Scottish gentleman who was secretary to the Board of Trustees for the Encouragement of Arts and Manufactures in Scotland, asking whether Beethoven would be willing to compose six sonatas for him. Scotland had but recently passed through the heady experience of the Enlightenment. Now, suddenly, the country broke away from dour religion and fog-bound isolation and began to pay attention to the arts. It had produced in a short space of time some remarkable talents: in economics Adam

Smith, in poetry Robert Burns, in science James Watt, in literature Boswell, whose *Life of Johnson* had appeared twelve years previously (1791). To be sure, nothing came of Thomson's plan because Beethoven demanded 300 ducats for the six sonatas, and Thomson, being a Scotsman, wished to give only half that sum. But it was to lead to other projects later.

From the Rhineland came Willibord Joseph Mähler, who was born in Ehrenbreitstein, near Bonn, and, as a fellow countryman and an attractive personality, was welcomed by Beethoven. He was a man of varied artistic endowments; he wrote quite good poetry, he sang well, and he was a portrait painter. He now asked to be allowed to paint Beethoven's portrait. Stephan von Breuning took him to Beethoven's lodgings in the Theater-an-der-Wien, where they found Beethoven busily at work on the *Eroica*. Thayer, interviewing Mähler, who lived until 1860, reports him as relating that they asked Beethoven to play, and Beethoven, after some urging, gave his visitors, instead of an extempore performance, the Finale of the new symphony. At its close, and without a pause, he continued to improvise for two hours, "during all which time there was not a measure which was faulty, or which did not sound original." Mähler added that one characteristic impressed him particularly: "that Beethoven played with his hands so very still; wonderful as his execution was, there was no tossing of them to and fro, up and down; they seemed to glide right and left over the keys, the fingers alone doing the work."

Mähler did paint Beethoven's portrait around that time; ten years later he did a second portrait. The first is a prettified, romantic falsification, freeing Beethoven's face of all its imperfections. Only the eyes, dark and deep-set, are expressive. In his left hand he holds the lyre, his right hand is raised in a conductor's gesture, quieting the orchestra. The figure is set against the usual dramatically illuminated sky; in the background stands Apollo's temple.*

·∘⊰ 7 ⊱∘·

After a while Beethoven abandoned the work on the opera he was to produce for Schikaneder, finding the subject, *Vestas Feuer* (The Vestal Fire), uncongenial. The new symphony absorbed him. He said to his old friend Krumpholz that "I am by no means satisfied with my work up to now and I intend to make a fresh start from now on."

---

* The portrait is in the Historical Museum of Vienna. Thayer possessed a copy of it, which is now in the New York Public Library, Lincoln Center.

He went to Oberdöbling that summer, taking quarters in a vintner's house.* There were gardens and vineyards all around, the Danube Canal flowed nearby, and almost under his very windows Beethoven could see the gorge which separates Döbling from Heiligenstadt. It was here that he grappled with the "heroic" concepts which must have lain in his mind for a long time and toward which Bernadotte may have given him the original impulse.

Napoleon was present in his consciousness. Beethoven could hardly have escaped being aware of him. The recess in the war had not lasted long. The paper written at Amiens was at first riddled by occasional rifle shots; before long the whole document had to be thrown into the wastepaper basket. Napoleon had not quieted his determination to conquer all of Europe or softened the intensity of his craving to subjugate his two arch-enemies, Austria and England. Night and day he prepared. He got at Austria first by nibbling again at the appetizing lands in Italy, annexing Piedmont six months after the Treaty of Amiens and the rich Duchies of Parma and Piacenza the month after. England, until then in a mood to compromise, knew that it was impossible to compromise, impossible to set a limit to Napoleon's ambitions. The British were well aware that Napoleon was still planning an invasion of England, postponing it again and again since the French fleet was no match for Britain's naval superiority. They knew too that Napoleon was scanning the horizon of the world through his spyglass and wondering how to establish a colonial empire which might hamper the British. He sent an expedition to Haiti under Leclerc which, however, failed. He negotiated the Louisiana Purchase with the young United States on April 30, 1803. England retaliated first by refusing to part with Malta, second by placing an embargo on all French and Dutch ships in British ports, and finally by renewing hostilities on May 18, 1803.

Pitt forged a new liaison against Napoleon and drew Russia, Sweden, and Austria into it; Austria, still bleeding from her previous wounds, joined the alliance with great reluctance.

All these preparations for ever more bloody tugs at the rope of power happened at or about the time that Beethoven was working on his Third Symphony. He still believed that Napoleon would liberate Europe from the kind of bigotry, police control, and Habsburg-worship with which he was familiar.

---

* The house is now known as the Eroica House, though it has been somewhat altered since the time Beethoven occupied it. The address is Vienna XIX, Döblinger Hauptstrasse 92.

THE PREMATURE TESTAMENT AND THE EROICA

We know for certain that it was his intention to dedicate the *Eroica* to Napoleon. The original manuscript of the symphony has disappeared, but early in the spring of 1804 a fair copy had been made to be forwarded to Paris through the French Embassy. At that time Napoleon was still First Consul. Ries says that he saw a copy of the score lying on Beethoven's table with the word "Buonaparte" at the extreme top of the title page. Ries was the first to bring him the intelligence that Napoleon had proclaimed himself Emperor. Napoleon's assumption of royalty took place on May 18, 1804, and the solemn proclamation was issued on the twentieth. Therefore, at the latest, the *Eroica* must have been completed in early May of 1804.

There exists a copy of the score—one which Beethoven used and which is full of erasures and corrections—which confirms the original dedication, although the title page does not answer to Ries's description. On this page there are two technical remarks in Beethoven's hand. The title was written by a copyist. It reads:

> Sinfonia grande
> intitolata [?] Bonaparte
> 804 im August
> del Sigr.
> Louis van Beethoven

The words "intitolata Bonaparte" are erased, the "Bonaparte" so violently that a hole is left. Under Beethoven's name there appears written in pencil by him in large letters: GESCHRIEBEN AUF BONAPART. The writing of these words seems to have been erased and is barely legible. The "804 im August" is written in a different ink and may have been inserted afterward, by somebody else.*

Both Ries and Count Moritz Lichnowsky testified to the terrible scene which ensued when Beethoven heard of Napoleon's elevation. He flew into a rage and cried out: "Is he then, too, nothing more than an ordinary human being? Now he, too, will trample on all the rights of man and indulge only his ambition. He will exalt himself above all others, become a tyrant!" Beethoven went to the table, took hold of the title page by the top, tore it in two and threw it on the floor. The first page was rewritten, and only then did the symphony receive the title, "Sinfonia eroica." **

---

* This manuscript is in the library of The Friends of Music in Vienna.
** Ries, *Notizen*.

THE PREMATURE TESTAMENT AND THE EROICA

When the *Eroica* was published, it bore the subtitle, *"per festeggiare il sovvenire di un grand Uomo"* ("to celebrate the memory of a great man").

Hearing the *Eroica* for the first time must have been an experience similar to that of hearing the news of the splitting of the atom. To some it was maddeningly incomprehensible. To others it was frightening. To others it was altogether thrilling. Those who knew music well must have perceived that here was the discovery of a new galaxy of music in which constellations moved in bold new patterns and dizzying motion, yet following discernible laws and bending to a purpose.

There had been grand and mighty works of symphonic music before. This symphony was not just grander and mightier: Beethoven had taken familiar building material and had constructed a universe of a symphony into which he fitted the noblest and strongest qualities of man, those qualities which he called heroic. For such an ambition he needed to deal in new terms and in proportions, depth and height, which dwarfed preceding symphonic compositions. Whoever heard of starting with two such hammer blows? Whoever needed not one or two but three transitions to arrive at the second theme, which when it does arrive is so intimate and pleading? Whoever designed a first movement on such a scale and then added to it as a coda another section of majestic importance? Everything about this first movement is astonishing and nothing is superfluous. Coleridge called the second movement "a funeral procession in deep purple." Whoever heard of interrupting such a procession by an unmannerly cry to heaven, one which brings us consolation by the very intensity of its grief? What did those first audiences, used to the Theme and Variation form, make of the last movement, where Beethoven took a theme from *Prometheus* and formed it into a turbulent life-story, the variations ranging from the ominous to a vision of pure, untroubled beauty?

The *Eroica* unites elements of the Enlightenment—man helping himself through strength and reason—with elements of the Romantic Movement—the work of art as an expression of the artist's heart and soul—and achieves a perfect synthesis.

How much has been written about this work! It has been parsed by technicians, assayed for philosophic content, and furnished with programmatic commentary. If that commentary tries to explain the music literally, it gets itself tied in knots; it puzzles as to why the hero dies in the middle of the symphony and must then describe the Scherzo as Berlioz did: "Funeral games around the grave of the warrior." * If the commentary is spiritual, it can become as turgid as Richard Wagner's words about the Finale: "Man entire, harmoniously at one with self, in those emotions where the memory of sorrow becomes itself the shaping force of noble deeds."

Explanations in words do not help, nor are they needed. What Nietzsche wrote about Beethoven's music in general is specifically true of the *Eroica:* "Beethoven's music is music about music." One is reminded of Toscanini, who said of the first movement: "To some it is Napoleon, to some it is Alexander, to me it is *allegro con brio.*"

What it is, and as such acknowledged by fame, is one of humanity's stablest and strongest artistic treasures.

That it was not immediately recognized as such is not surprising. First it was tried out privately at Prince Lobkowitz's Palace—probably in December, 1804. Nothing is known about the reception of this performance.**

Ries tells a little anecdote, quoted by Thayer:

> In the first Allegro occurs a mischievous whim (*böse Laune*) of Beethoven's for the first horn; in the second part, several measures before the theme recurs in its entirety, Beethoven has the horn suggest it at a place where the two violins are still holding a second chord. To one unfamiliar with the score this must always sound as if the horn player had made a miscount and entered at the wrong place. At the first rehearsal of the symphony, which was horrible, but at which the horn player made his entry correctly, I stood beside Beethoven, and, thinking that a blunder had been made I said:
>
> "Can't the damned hornist count?—it sounds infamously false!" I think I came pretty close to receiving a box on the ear. Beethoven did not forgive the slip for a long time." *** (TQ).

---

* A sample of early "literary" interpretations is a program note printed by the Philharmonic Society of New York, which performed the *Eroica* at the second concert of the Society's existence, on February 18, 1843: "This great work was commenced when Napoleon was first Consul, and was intended to portray the workings of that extraordinary man's mind. In the first movement, the simple subject, keeping its uninterrupted way through harmonies that at times seem in almost chaotic confusion, is a grand idea of Napoleon's determination of character. The second movement is descriptive of the funeral honors paid to one of his favorite generals, and is entitled 'Funeral March on the Death of a Hero.' The winding up of this movement represents the faltering steps of the last gazers into the grave, and the listener hears the tears fall on the coffin ere the funeral volley is fired, and repeated faintly by an echo. The third movement (Minuet and Trio) describes the homeward march of the soldiery, and the Finale is a combination of French Revolutionary airs put together in a manner that no one save a Beethoven could have imagined."

** An article did appear in the *Wiener Musik-Zeitung* stating that the symphony did not please. But this was written in 1843 (almost forty years after), and it is not even certain that the writer of the article was present at the private performance at Lobkowitz's.

*** Ries frequently seems to have put his foot in it!

The fact that Lobkowitz soon scheduled another private performance—and that on the occasion of doing honor to a particularly important guest—would suggest that he, at least, recognized the importance of the work. This performance took place at Lobkowitz's country seat, and the honored guest was Prince Louis Ferdinand of Prussia. It was supposed to have pleased the prince so much that he requested an immediate repetition of the entire symphony.

During the same winter a semiprivate performance was given at the home of the bankers Würth and Fellner, and a report of it appeared in the *Allgemeine Musikalische Zeitung* * on February 13, 1805. The report calls the symphony a "daring and wild fantasia." The critic is perplexed: the work

> lacks nothing in the way of startling and beautiful passages, in which the energetic and talented composer must be recognized; but often it loses itself in lawlessness . . . The reviewer belongs to Herr van Beethoven's sincerest admirers, but in this composition he must confess that he finds too much that is glaring and bizarre, which hinders greatly one's grasp of the whole, and a sense of unity is almost completely lost.

The first public performance took place at the Theater-an-der-Wien on April 7, 1805, at a concert conducted by the concertmaster and conductor of the theater, Franz Clement; ** but Beethoven conducted his symphony himself. Czerny told Jahn that on this occasion somebody in the gallery cried out, "I'll give another kreuzer if the thing will but stop!" I doubt the story; Viennese audiences did not shout out at concert performances, nor is it likely that Czerny was sitting in the gallery where he could have overheard such a remark. It sounds too pat to be true.

The symphony was reviewed by a correspondent of the periodical *Der Freymüthige* (*The Liberal*). The writer says that the audience could have been divided into three factions; first, Beethoven's friends, who "assert that it is just this symphony which is his masterpiece . . . and that if it does not please now, it is because the public is not cultured enough, artistically, to grasp all these lofty beauties; after a few thousand years have passed it will not fail of its effect"; another faction denies that the work has value "and professes to see in it an untamed striving for singularity, which has failed, however, to achieve in any of

---

* It was the leading publication dealing with musical matters; Breitkopf and Härtel had an interest in it.
** We shall meet him again in connection with the Violin Concerto.

its parts beauty or true sublimity and power." The third faction takes a middle-of-the-road position, admitting that the symphony contains many beauties but conceding "that the inordinate length of this longest, and perhaps most difficult of all symphonies, wearies even the cognoscenti, and is unendurable to the mere music-lover." The report concludes: "The public and Herr van Beethoven, who conducted, were not satisfied with each other on this evening; the public thought the symphony too heavy, too long, and himself too discourteous, because he did not nod his head in recognition of the applause which came from a portion of the audience. On the contrary, Beethoven found that the applause was not strong enough." (TQ).

If Beethoven read these reports, he was undeterred by them. To the complaint of "inordinate length" he was supposed to have replied, "If I write a symphony an hour long it will be short enough." He made no changes in the score but did suggest that the symphony be played near the beginning of a concert, before the audience was fatigued. The popularity and understanding of the work grew at a sure pace. It was published (orchestral parts) in Vienna in 1806 with a dedication to Lobkowitz. In 1809 Cianchettini and Sperati, in London, published an orchestral score in which the subtitle was changed to a maudlin "Heroic symphony composed to commemorate the death of a hero." Death is only one part of a work which deals with life.

Having quoted some myopic critical opinions about the *Eroica,* I find it necessary to redress the balance and to try to eradicate the impression promulgated by the romantic school of biography, that Beethoven's music for the most part met with an uncomprehending reception, and that he had to struggle against the stubborn asininity of the pundits. Beethoven himself is guilty of spreading this impression. He railed against the critics, often unjustly. One begins to wonder if he read his reviews. The truth is that the critics were deeply impressed by Beethoven's genius. The truth is that he found much and quick recognition among them in spite of the newness of the music, in spite of what must have sometimes sounded to them like willful eccentricity. The musicologist Henry Pleasants has pointed this out after having made a special study of fifty volumes (1798–1848) of the *Allgemeine Musikalische Zeitung,* the journal from which I have quoted above. Its chief critic, Johann Friedrich Rochlitz, published as early as 1807 — that is, two years after its premiere — a perceptive review of the *Eroica* which occupied fifteen columns! As early as 1804 a correspondent in the same journal wrote of the Second Symphony:

To no community of musicians and music-lovers can a second symphony by Beethoven be a matter of indifference. It is a remarkable, colossal work, hardly equaled by any other in depth, strength and artistic mastery, and unexampled in the demands it makes upon a large orchestra. Even the best orchestra will have to play it again and again before the admirable totality of original and exotically associated ideas can be united, rounded off and presented as they appeared in the composer's imagination. The listener, too, even the most sophisticated, will require repeated hearings before he can be in a position to appreciate the details in relation to the whole, and the whole in detail, and to savor it with properly objective enthusiasm.

The Vienna correspondent reporting on the first performance of the Ninth Symphony wrote of its slow movement that "Art and truth have celebrated their greatest victory, and one might say with every good reason: *Non plus ultra!*"

These examples could be prolonged, though of course there was a fair amount of dissension. On balance one must arrive at the conclusion that critical appreciation *was* vouchsafed to Beethoven.

Fourteen years after the *Eroica* lay behind him Beethoven happened to be dining with the poet Christoph Kuffner. Beethoven liked to converse with Kuffner; he was witty, "extremely instructive," was especially well versed in the writings of Voltaire and Rousseau and wrote some interesting studies of them. Kuffner, noticing that Beethoven, having just enjoyed a good fish dinner, was in an expansive mood, asked which of the symphonies was his favorite. (He had composed eight up to then.) Beethoven answered, "The *Eroica.*"

CHAPTER 13

FIDELIO—VIENNA OCCUPIED

··›❈[I]❈‹··

"The Theater is an insane asylum and the Opera the department for the incurables." If that saying, attributed to Rossini, is true today, it was true then. While preparations for the big war were hurrying apace in much of Europe, the little footlight war was sharpening in Vienna. Here Schikaneder. There Braun.

Braun had the audacity to put on his stage that surefire box-office success, *The Magic Flute,** which Schikaneder considered his exclusive property. Braun had even omitted Schikaneder's name from the playbill. It was a puerile bit of discourtesy. Schikaneder hit back by putting on *his* stage a *Magic Flute* which was a parody of Braun's performance at the Court Theater. In Braun's staging, the quick change of Papagena from an old woman to a luscious young thing seldom succeeded; Schikaneder now staged the scene by sending a couple of tailors on the stage who slowly and deliberately changed Papagena's costume in full view of the audience. It was an inside joke, but the audience, which knew *The Magic Flute* by heart, appreciated it.

Bartolomeo Zitterbarth, the financier, had purchased the leasing rights of the Theater-an-der-Wien from Schikaneder, but he had retained Schikaneder as director. Now Zitterbarth, in financial difficulty, sold his rights to Braun, and consequently Braun became director of all three major Vienna theaters. Promptly Braun dismissed Schikaneder and appointed in his stead a man who had served as Secretary of the Court Theaters, Joseph von Sonnleithner.

Sonnleithner, now thirty-eight, had a fine career behind him: Emperor Franz had commissioned him to travel widely, to collect portraits and books for the

---

* The Queen of the Night at that performance in 1801 was Therese Gassmann, now the wife of Rosenbaum.

French arrival in Vienna in 1805. Napoleon is on horseback at center (Austrian National Library).

Imperial library. Beethoven was a frequent guest in his house. One of his first ideas in attaining his new position was to suggest to Beethoven the subject for an opera, after Beethoven had turned down Schikaneder's libretto.

Because the Theater-an-der-Wien had come under new management, existing agreements were no longer valid. Beethoven was under no further obligation to furnish an opera. All the same, Braun and Sonnleithner wanted one by him, and he himself was sufficiently intrigued by the challenge to want to compose an opera, whether it was Schikaneder or Braun who was to stage it. Beethoven respected Sonnleithner and mistrusted Braun. At least so it would appear from a letter he wrote to Sonnleithner in March, 1804—Beethoven's trusts and mistrusts had a way of changing suddenly—a letter in which he complained that Braun had shown himself "persistently unfriendly." He wasn't going to ask him for any favors: *"I shall never crawl. My world is the universe."*

As matters turned out, Beethoven did not need to deal with Braun. For Braun took the extraordinary step of recalling his rival and enemy, the irritating but seemingly indispensable Schikaneder. He was back at the Theater-an-der-Wien in the autumn of 1804. What a triumph that must have been for the showman! The competitors got together, that happens in business, politics and the theater. Schikaneder appealed to Beethoven to compose the opera, suggested by Sonnleithner. Beethoven agreed.

In the meantime Beethoven did have to move out of the Theater-an-der-Wien. It was then that he moved with Breuning into a large building known as "The Red House," which was located near where the *Votivkirche* now stands. After the quarrel with Breuning, he moved first to the country, changing his address three times in the summer of 1804—Baden, Döbling, Hetzendorf.* Then in October he moved to the fourth floor of an imposing house belonging to Baron Johann Pasqualati. The house was on the Mölkerbastei, placed quite high, its view extending all the way to the mountains in the distance.** Pasqualati became very fond of Beethoven, often advising him on financial matters; and though Beethoven moved out several times, Pasqualati would say, "I won't rent these rooms; Beethoven will come back" (Ries). Beethoven even moved back briefly to the Theater-an-der-Wien; nevertheless the Pasqualati house became as permanent an abode as he ever had, till his last years.

---

* In Hetzendorf the next year he did much of the final work on the score of *Fidelio*.
** The house still stands, and Beethoven's rooms have been turned into a museum, though the contents are few and the rooms are ill kept. Nevertheless, seeing this house, climbing those stairs, and walking through these rooms will give one a good idea of how Beethoven lived.

The libretto which Sonnleithner proposed was merely an adaptation of a plot which had been set to music three times before. The text was by J. N. Bouilly, a French playwright who had served Cherubini with the libretto of *Les Deux Journées*. The first use of Bouilly's text was by a French composer, Pierre Gaveaux, and was entitled *Leonore ou l'Amour conjugal.* Later it was taken up by Ferdinando Paer,* rewritten in Italian, and performed in Dresden on October 3, 1804, in the very year in which Beethoven was working on his version. A third version, by one Simon Mayr, was given in Padua the following spring.

What attracted Beethoven to this thrice-told tale? We may conjecture that there were two motives which fired his imagination. The first was revolt against political subjugation. Bouilly stated that he based his play on an actual incident which occurred in France during the Reign of Terror, but to avoid censorship he had transferred the action to the Spain of the 16th century. The play belonged to the type of drama then widely known as Rescue Drama. Bouilly wanted to show that it was possible for a man, unjustly accused by a powerful tyrant, to be vindicated. *Les Deux Journées,* too, was a Rescue Drama.

To the man who at just about that time erased Napoleon's name, the figure of the noble prisoner Florestan, who dared to oppose the oppressor and who now lay in chains in the deepest and coldest recess of the dungeon, must have made a poignant appeal. To Beethoven that prisoner appeared as a symbol of courage, a courage that knew no compromise with the libertarian drive. Florestan steps out of the book of the Enlightenment. In his rescue lies an assertion in which Beethoven believed.

The libretto, which reads almost as if it were a propaganda piece for the French Revolution, came to him at a time when Beethoven thought deeply about man's struggle against fate, whether such fate brought repression from without—or deafness from within. *Fidelio* stands between the Third and the Fifth Symphonies, and we are not astonished to find Beethoven jotting down ideas for the Fifth Symphony in his Sketch Books, among musical ideas for the Dungeon Scene. The positiveness, the will to win, the triumph which the Finale of *Fidelio* represents are apparent in the last movements of the Third and the Fifth, while the hymn to Leonore at the very end foreshadows the Ninth.

The second motive which prompted Beethoven to accept what in truth was a naïve play must have been a desire to express in music a condition he had never experienced and which—as he may have known already—he was never to

---

* Paer had become Kapellmeister in Dresden in 1803.

experience. That condition was conjugal love, with the loyalty, the order, the understanding, the calm, the complement of one through the other, the wordless language between man and wife, the private humor and the private puzzles which marriage can attain. How could Beethoven ever have known such a relationship, even had he not been ailing? Here he was able to compensate for his lack by creating so beautiful a wife as only imagination can create. "Nature meant woman to be her masterpiece," Lessing wrote. Beethoven, who read Lessing's *Emilia Galotti,* expressed his ideal in music.

The whole libretto is replete with idealism, too much so, and sets a high moral tone. Its morality appealed to Beethoven. He confessed that he would not have been able to set either *Don Giovanni* or *Così fan tutte* to music, both subjects being too immoral for his taste. Was this stricture, too, a compensation? Was it merely a defense he set up to refuse operatic project after operatic project while continuing to tell all his friends that he was looking for a suitable libretto? How many did he contemplate! *Macbeth, Attila, Ulysses' Return, Romulus, The Founding of Pennsylvania, Bacchus, Brutus, Bradamante, Undine, Faust, Alexander the Great, Romeo and Juliet,* and the play which Grillparzer prepared for him, *Melusine*—these were some of the ideas he considered. The truth, as everybody has recognized, is that Beethoven was essentially an instrumental composer and did not feel comfortable behind the footlights.

Though Sonnleithner had an official position, he had to submit the text to the I. R. Censorship Bureau, just as any other author. He was adroit in preserving the illusion that the story happened far away and long ago. That was advisable in a play where such lines occur as, "Boldly I dared to tell the truth and chains are my reward" (Florestan), or "No. No longer need you kneel like slaves" (Fernando); or such dialogue as:

LEONORE: He must be a great criminal.
ROCCO: Or he must have great enemies. It is approximately the same thing.

The severity of the Austrian censorship is shown by the printed rules which were handed to the traveler at the border. The visitor was informed:

All books are subject to the I. R. Censorship. They will be taken in custody and examined by the I. R. Central-Book-Revision-Bureau, Vienna, Old Fleischmarkt No. 752. Books that are permitted will immediately be restored to their owner. Those which are prohibited remain in the Bureau either until the traveler begins

354

his return journey or until the I. R. Police and Censorship-Court-Bureau has ruled that they may be imported. Books in Hebrew or prayer and religious books printed abroad are banned under all circumstances.

Sonnleithner had trouble with the I. R. Censorship. That is apparent from his petition:

> Court Secretary Josef Sonnleithner begs that the ban of this September 30th on the opera Fidelio be lifted since this opera from the French original of Boully [sic] (entitled Leonore, ou l'amour conjugal) *has been most especially revised because the Empress had found the original very beautiful and affirmed* that no opera subject had ever given her so much pleasure; secondly: this opera which was revised by Kapellmeister Paër in Italian has been given already in Prague and Dresden; thirdly: *Beethoven* has spent over a year and a half with the composition, also since the ban was completely unanticipated, rehearsals have already been held and other arrangements have been made in order to give this opera on the name-day of the Empress (October 15); fourthly: the plot takes place in the 16th century, thus there could be no underlying relationship; finally in the fifth place: there exists such a big lack of opera libretti, this one presents the quietest description of womanly virtue and the evil minded governor is executing only a private revenge like Pedrarias in Balboa.   (TQ).

The petition is dated October 2, 1805. The libretto was approved on October 5 (remarkably fast action for a government office) after a few changes. But the music was not ready and the premiere was postponed for five weeks.

We have called Sonnleithner's libretto naïve. It is certainly no literary masterpiece. Yet it has dramatic virtues. He does succeed in making the central character, Leonore, warm and real and sympathetic. She belongs among the few treasurable women who inhabit the opera stage. Then, too, the librettist made it possible for Beethoven to compose the heartbreaking scene in which the prisoners see the sunlight for a few brief moments. The chorus "Oh God! What a moment" in the second act, in which all participate (*Sostenuto assai*), is a sublime Beethovian inspiration, but of a purely musical, not of a dramatic, nature. The Dungeon Scene is great drama, very suitable for musical expression, proceeding in a continuous crescendo of excitement from Florestan's dark soliloquy to the final shouts of joy of husband and wife united. Are there many stage effects more thrilling than the two trumpet calls which herald liberation?

If the *Fidelio* book has strength, it also has weaknesses. Nobody except Leonore is a believable human being; everybody is a representative. Pizarro is the arch-villain, a Desperate Desmond of melodrama. Florestan is the man who "did his duty." Rocco represents middle-class mediocrity, and he seems to be particularly obtuse about the state of affairs in his prison. Fernando is a *deus ex machina*. As to Jacquino and Marzelline, these are stock characters, young-girl-in-love-with-the-wrong-man, inept-fellow-in-love-with-the-wrong-girl, result: comic complications—all delivered ready-made from the *Singspiel*. The uneven quality of the dramatic material may be blamed for the fact that *Fidelio* contains some of Beethoven's greatest and some of his worst music. If you love Beethoven you love it all. If you love Beethoven, the very naïveté to be found here is endearing. It is easy enough to scoff at the heaping helping of morality. It is easy enough to say that nobody as noble as Leonore could exist. It takes no great perspicacity to observe the awkward corners, the improbable disguise, the convenient arrival of the minister, and so forth. These defects do not matter, if we respond to the beauty of the music. There is an art which functions with disregard of probability and can dispense with an obligation toward verisimilitude because it gives you more than probability and verisimilitude: it gives you deep truth. Though Beethoven could not rise above the conventional in the conventional *Singspiel* scenes, in those scenes which concern Leonore herself and the moral issue involved he became as great as he is in his instrumental music.

Beethoven took no end of trouble with the music; the Sketch Books are a veritable labyrinth of themes, false starts, improvements, more improvements. They testify to Beethoven's struggle in subjugating the operatic medium to what he wished to express. He made eighteen starts on the tenor soliloquy in Act II. There are ten versions of the final chorus, and many studies for the Leonore-Florestan duet.

·◦〖 2 〗◦·

Under what conditions did the rehearsals for *Fidelio* proceed and what was the situation at the first performance of the opera?

The large historical events are familiar to most of us. We will, I think, get a sharper impression by observing the daily life of Vienna, as Napoleon was approaching and as war threatened its citizens and the singers who were rehearsing the opera. Let us follow Rosenbaum's diary and the *Wiener Zeitung:*

As early as July, 1805, when Napoleon was still far away, the necessity of supplying the Austrian army caused food shortages in Vienna. Riots began.

The following are extracts from Rosenbaum's diary:

Sunday, July 7th. We came to the bakery "At the Peacock." The whole shop and all the rooms were robbed clean ... The mob had broken the fence, the iron gate, the house door and the inner door ... The riot was started by a baker's wife refusing to sell to a young apprentice a groschen worth of bread while she still had some. The tumult began at five o'clock and lasted the whole night through ... The Court is in Baden. The news won't be exactly pleasant to them.

Monday, July 8th. A bunch of demonstrators came along, boys carrying whole bags full of bread. Others carried clubs and bedslats. As soon as we arrived the grenadiers began to shoot ... Some rowdies took a baker's stick with a rag of linen and used it as a flag. Another an old drum. They proceeded furiously to pelt the soldiers with a hail of stones. A cavalryman split the head of the flag carrier, another slashed the armpit of the drummer, a grenadier plunged his bayonet into his body. Then the grenadiers had to seek refuge in the Cadet-School. They closed the door, the mob threw stones and threatened to force the doors. The grenadiers fired on the people from the windows. More than a hundred were injured or killed.

Tuesday the 9th. Soldiers are quartered in all the suburbs. War preparations. Hordes of demonstrators [*Arrestanten*] are rounded up. The order is that at nine o'clock all houses in the suburbs are to be locked and all inns cleared out.

In the autumn Napoleon's army reached the Danube, traveling swiftly by a series of forced marches. The marches were "a triumph of careful planning and staff work," writes David Chandler.* At Ulm, Napoleon confronted the Austrian-Russian army under General Mack. The battle lasted the better part of thirteen days and ended in a complete defeat of General Mack, on October 20, 1805. The *Grande Armée,* which was to scourge Europe for almost a decade to come, had proved itself. Napoleon was jubilant. A drop of wormwood in his cup of joy was the news that, exactly at the time of the Battle of Ulm, Lord Nelson had defeated the Franco-Spanish fleet at Trafalgar. Napoleon's greatest foe was still ruler of the sea, though Nelson was mortally wounded. But at least Napoleon's road to Vienna was open, and further humiliation for Austria was almost inevitable. In a few days the Viennese knew that they were likely to be invaded.

From Rosenbaum's diary:

Monday, November 4th. Every moment one sees baggage and travel-carriages passing. In the afternoon I went with TH[erese] to the Danube. We saw the possessions of the

---

* In his fascinating book, *The Campaigns of Napoleon,* 1966.

Court [being shipped off] ... The Court is sending everything away, even bedwarmers and shoetrees. It looks as if they have no intention of ever coming back to Vienna.

Wednesday the 6th. After lunch Eppinger [a doctor?] came with the devastating news that the Russians have retreated as far as St. Pölten. Vienna is in great danger of being swept over by marauding Chasseurs ...

On the Josephsplatz 100 horses were standing, ready to be hitched to transport carriages ... [The carriages] are loaded with kegs of gold, the Treasury, Medallion and Natural History Collections, Silver, Linen, etc. Many people gathered who resented this removal of all movable objects ...

Friday the 8th. TH along with the rest of the company is summoned by Braun to the Redoutensaal for half past nine. Braun appeared before ten o'clock. He said approximately this: his situation was extremely awkward; by the command of His Majesty he has to remain, but it is possible that he as Court Banker and landowner would be taken in custody as hostage by the enemy, who is expected to arrive in a few days. He is prepared to share fortune and misfortune with all his people; performances were to continue; only in case of a bombardment would he have passes for all.

Saturday the 9th. Proclamation by Count Rudolph Wrbna: * His Majesty has set apart a ship located near the Franz Bridge. Because of the dire danger everybody is allowed to stow his gold, silver and jewels on this ship, against a receipt. His Majesty guarantees the safety of these goods, barring acts of God ... After five o'clock a group of deputies started on their way to meet the enemy in order to begin negotiations with them about the fate of Vienna.

Sunday the 10th. All three Tabor Bridges will be burned. Ships loaded with firewood are placed under their vaults ... Wrbna summoned the entire magistrate to City Hall and announced: His Majesty has determined not to permit a single shot to be fired on the city and therefore has sent a deputation to the enemy to negotiate the question of how Vienna can be spared. His Majesty expects, however, that all citizens of Vienna will avoid excesses and behave in a quiet and friendly manner.

Monday the 11th. For the first time bank notes of 12- and 24-kreuzer denomination were put into circulation ... Offenheimer stopped payments three days ago and has disappeared. Neupauer and Wertheimer have closed their establishments [these were bankers].

Tuesday the 12th. Murat is quartered in Hütteldorf in the villa of Princess Franz Liechtenstein. He informed her that Emperor Napoleon is expected this evening for supper and asked for more porcelain dishes.

Wednesday the 13th. At half past eleven a mass of people pressed through the portals of the *Burg*. Everybody screamed "The French are coming." The cavalry was in the vanguard. Some of them had beards like Jews. In their midst rode Prince Murat, surrounded by generals, a tall, strong, handsome man ... The infantry looked very sloppy, not uniformed alike. One wore a hat, another a cap, a shako, one a silk scarf, another

---

* Count Wrbna was city governor during the 60 days of the occupation, later director of the Court Theaters.

mousseline cloth, boots, shoes, slippers, linens, Manchester trousers; everything topsy turvy. The troops look quite wild. Nothing is known of our army. They have retreated far from Spitz. The French are the masters of the whole region.

Rosenbaum's description is confirmed by that of a Salzburg soldier:

You now see many of them [the French soldiers] dressed in peasant's blouses, sheepskin cloaks or wild-animal skins; some are laden down in the most singular fashion, carrying long strips of lard, hams, or chunks of meat dangling from their belts. Others march all hung about with loaves of bread and bottles of wine. Their penury, however . . . does not prevent them from lighting their pipes with Viennese banknotes.*

So the French marched in during the final week of *Fidelio* rehearsals. Rosenbaum's diary continues:

Thursday the 14th. The French behave most considerately, even gallantly. All the streets were and still are full of people. That must make a curious impression on them because in other cities which they occupied everybody hid from them and here they are received amicably. If only they would amicably go away again from Vienna! . . . On the *Mehlmarkt* people are killing one another for one eighth of a kilo of flour; in the other markets almost nothing is to be had. Nobody is delivering anything.

The considerate and gallant bearing of the army did not last long; it never does:

Friday the 15th. Nothing is to be found in the market. Yesterday a pound of butter cost two, even three florins. Nobody dares to bring anything here because they [the French] take everything; even the horses are unharnessed . . . On the Laimgrube at noon a French soldier who had torn shoes grabbed an apprentice and wanted to take his boots by force. When he struggled, the soldier hit him in the mouth with his sword and cleaved his mouth. Then our people came running to help the boy, disarmed the Frenchman, and took him to the next guard-station . . . Women are hardly to be seen in the theaters, except the whores.
Saturday the 16th. Last night a French infantryman at the windmill in Lamm demanded food, drink and lodging. All this was given him in plenty. Then he wanted a girl for temporary amusement. Since such a one was not readily to hand, he grabbed the innkeeper's wife, and when she slipped away he shot after her with a pistol. He was arrested at once . . .
His I. R. Majesty Napoleon has traversed the city to join his army on the other side of the Danube where the Russian troops are gathering in considerable strength . . . Every-

---

* Quoted by David Chandler, *op. cit.*

body tacitly rejoices over the victory of the Russians.* The French fear them, as they give no pardon. In the last skirmish they captured a Major, speared him through the ass on a bayonet, and carried him to their bivouac. They are very cruel.

Sunday the 17th. Every day the Magistrate has to deliver 50,000 measures of bread, meat, wine, grain and hay. Everybody is scared of famine. The burden of the billeting is unbelievable ... In an Extra Edition I read that Tirol has been conquered, Archduke Johann has fled into the mountains, and Prince Carl in Italy has retreated. Terrible loss!

It was under these circumstances, with singers and musicians continuing to do their work because an Imperial edict had so decreed it, with people dragging themselves through hungry days and noisy nights, with none knowing what a drunken soldier might do to him, with everybody wishing to hide at home, that the preparations at the Theater-an-der-Wien proceeded.

Beethoven himself was nervous. Several incidents show his state of mind. He had not as yet forgiven Ries for the joke Ries played in connection with the Waldstein Sonata. Beethoven punished him now. Ries recounts:

> One day when a small company including Beethoven and me breakfasted with Prince [Lichnowsky] after the concert in the Augarten (8 o'clock in the forenoon), it was proposed that we drive to Beethoven's house and hear his opera *Leonore,* which had not yet been performed. Arrived there Beethoven demanded that I go away, and inasmuch as the most urgent appeals of all present were fruitless, I did so with tears in my eyes. The entire company noticed it, and Prince Lichnowsky, following me, asked me to wait in an anteroom, because, having been the cause of the trouble, he wanted to have it settled. But the feeling of hurt to my honor would not permit this. I heard afterward that Prince Lichnowsky had sharply rebuked Beethoven for his conduct, since only love for his works had been to blame for the incident and consequently for his anger. But the only result of these representations was that Beethoven refused to play any more for the company.   (TQ).

This instance of Beethoven's ungraciousness is immediately balanced by an act of kindness. Since Bonn was now under French government, and Ries was a citizen of Bonn, he was liable for conscription. His name was drawn and he had to return home forthwith, as any disobedience would have exposed his father and family to grave risks. Beethoven gave Ries a letter to Princess Josephine von Liechtenstein:

---

* There was no Russian victory. It was a rumor that proved false.

[September, 1805]

Forgive me, most illustrious Princess! if the bearer of this letter gives you perhaps an unpleasant surprise—*Poor Ries,* who is a pupil of mine, must shoulder his musket in this unfortunate war and—as he is a foreigner, must also leave Vienna in a few days—He has nothing, absolutely nothing—and he has to undertake a long journey—*In these circumstances* he has no opportunity whatever of giving a concert—So he must have recourse to *charity*—I recommend him to you—I know that you will forgive me for taking this step—It is only in extreme necessity that a noble-minded man can resort to such measures—Convinced of this I am sending the poor fellow to you so that you may perhaps alleviate to some extent his difficult circumstances—He is compelled to appeal for help *to all* who know him.

With the deepest homage
L. van Beethoven (A-121).

It was three years before Beethoven and Ries were to see each other again.

The painter Mähler is the authority for another incident, one which has become famous:

Mähler remembered that at one of the general rehearsals the third bassoon was absent; at which Beethoven fretted and fumed. Lobkowitz, who was present, made light of the matter: two of the bassoons were present, said he, and the absence of the third could make no great difference. This so enraged the composer, that, as he passed the Lobkowitz Palace, on his way home, he could not restrain the impulse to turn aside and shout in at the great door of the palace: "Lobkowitzian ass!" (T).

Schindler tells the story of Sebastian Meyer, who sang Pizarro, and who had a very high opinion of his own musicality: he boasted that he could sing anything and never be thrown off the track, no matter how complicated the accompaniment of the orchestra. To take him down a peg, Beethoven wrote a passage in Pizarro's aria in which the voice moves over a series of scales played by the strings, the singer hearing at each note the interval of a minor second. The players in the orchestra, in on the joke, maliciously emphasized this minor second, and Meyer got confused, flew into a rage, and shouted at Beethoven, "My brother-in-law [Mozart] would never have written such damned nonsense!"

The Leonore of the first performance was Anna Milder, now only twenty years old, of whom Haydn had said when she was even younger, "My dear child! You have a voice like a house." She had not really mastered the part, although later she was to become a very fine Leonore.

The first version of *Fidelio* (contrary to a general impression, it was never called *Leonore,* thought that was the title Beethoven preferred) * was in three acts, rather too long for the material at hand, and the final scene remained in the dungeon. Thus the action seemed more static than in later versions.

·⊰[3]⊱·

The opera was given at the Theater-an-der-Wien on November 20, 1805, exactly a week after the French marched into Vienna. On the day of the occupation, the editor of the *Wiener Zeitung* was dismissed from his post, and a new editor, a minion of the French, filled the paper with pro-French propaganda. On the day of the *Fidelio* premiere General Hulin, appointed "Commanding General of Vienna," issued orders from his headquarters, established in the Palace of Prince Lobkowitz. One may imagine Beethoven's feeling when he heard that Lobkowitz had had to cede his Palace to the invader. A proclamation of the same day announced: "It has been regrettably observed that a few citizens were spreading rumors and inciting tempers ... which had caused several incidents insulting to the Imperial French troops."

Many of Beethoven's friends and patrons had by that time left the city. In the audience, what there was of it, there were many French officers, no doubt in search of light entertainment to while away a boring evening in a strange city. It was hardly to be expected that they could make much of the German text. The Viennese women, to whom Leonore could have made a special appeal, were of course absent from the theater, all "except the whores." Such is the general tenor of contemporary accounts. We do have a specific one from Rosenbaum, an entry in his diary:

> November 20th. At the Wien today for the first time, Beethowen's grand opera Fidelio or Conjugal Love in 3 a. freely from the French by Joseph Sonleither [*sic*] ... In the evening I went to the W. th to hear Louis Beth opera ... The opera contained beautiful, artful, heavy music, a boring, uninteresting book. It had no success. And it was empty.

---

* The textbook, published 1805, of the first version by Sonnleithner, was titled "Fidelio." This libretto says "opera in two acts," while the first version was performed in three acts. In the revision made by Stephan von Breuning for 1806 the textbook gives the title as "Leonore or the Triumph of Conjugal Love." For the actual performances the title "Fidelio" was adhered to. The original version (1805) was called "Fidelio or Conjugal Love," the third and final version (1814) simply "Fidelio."

The first performance of *Fidelio* was a fiasco. Whatever scant critical reviews it received were negative. At the end of the second performance leaflets containing laudatory verses were showered down from the gallery. This gesture was due to Stephan von Breuning, who had written the verses and arranged for the surprise to please Beethoven. But it did not help. One more performance was given, and then the opera was dropped.

The day after the third performance the *Wiener Zeitung* wrote (November 23): "The French army ... will remain here until peace is made, the early conclusion of which depends solely on the Austrian Emperor." Conditions had if anything got worse. Rosenbaum wrote in his diary that the French robbed the church treasure of Mariazell (one of the holy places near Vienna), that they used other churches as slaughterhouses, and that the wounded "filled all hospitals, even those of the Jews, as well as all cloisters." Rosenbaum, as well as the other Viennese, felt that a huge battle was in preparation. Archduke Carl, who had the command in Italy, was trying to break through to the north and to unite his troops with Kutusov's Russian army stationed in Moravia. Before Carl could get there, Napoleon struck at Austerlitz. The battle began on December first, and when it ended, some 27,000 Austrians and Russians lay dead on the field. The Austrians panicked. The Russian troops pillaged and robbed—or so at least Franz reported to his Empress—and many deserted. Emperor Franz sought an armistice. Napoleon, who had been on the battlefield for eight days and nights, said, *"Soldats! Je suis content de vous,"* * and returned to Vienna.

There he sat in Schönbrunn, issuing edicts and preparing the terms for peace with Austria. He was within a half-hour carriage ride of Beethoven's lodging. But Napoleon did not know of Beethoven's existence nor did he care greatly about music, certainly not Viennese music. A private concert in his honor was given in Schönbrunn on December 14; he sat stiffly on a specially erected throne, while Cherubini, who happened to be in Vienna, performed excerpts from Zingarelli's opera, *Romeo e Giulietta,* and other selections. Two paces behind Napoleon stood Murat. Three hundred ministers, adjutants, and officers stood around "in Oriental despotic silence." Napoleon's "mien was dour, almost defiant." ** When the concert was over, Napoleon turned on his heels and left the room without applauding or saying a word.

The *Wiener Zeitung* published, on December 18, the new taxes made

---

* "Soldiers! I am pleased with you."
** Rosenbaum's diary—but he wasn't invited. A friend described the concert to him.

necessary by the French occupation. They amounted to a "forced loan" equivalent to a full year's taxes. And all citizens whose annual rent amounted to more than a hundred gulden were taxed a surcharge of half a year's rent. "In case of non-payment, the moneys will be collected by force through the French Army Commission, with the addition of a suitable fine."

Napoleon exacted thirteen million gulden of war reparations, and appropriated many works of art, including 400 paintings from the Belvedere. They were shipped to Paris. In 1815, after the defeat of Napoleon, these pictures were found in Paris, and all but thirty-six were returned to Vienna.

How extraordinary it is that under such conditions anybody in Vienna should have paid attention to an opera which had just failed! Yet such was the case. Stephan von Breuning, though he was much occupied as a member of the War Council, offered to do what he could to tighten and improve the libretto. Some time early in December Prince Lichnowsky called a meeting to discuss ways and means of saving *Fidelio*. It was suggested that the entire opera be run through with the assembled cast and with Beethoven and a few friends present, so that all could agree on what parts were weak and what needed rewriting. One of the men present was a young tenor, Josef August Röckel,* who had been discovered in Salzburg by Braun. Braun hoped for good things from him. He had a fine voice and was intelligent, and was just the man to take the place of Demmer, who had sung Florestan at the first performance and whose voice was becoming a little white. Röckel was invited to come to the meeting and to sing through the part. He was frightened but he was game. He has left us a vivid and moving description of all that happened at the meeting: **

We were led into a music-room with silken draperies, fitted out with chandeliers lavishly supplied with candles. On its walls rich, splendidly colorful oil paintings by the greatest masters, in broad, glittering golden frames bespoke the lofty artistic instincts as well as the wealth of the princely family owning them. We seemed to have been expected; for Mayer had told the truth: tea was over, and all was in readiness for the musical performance to begin. The Princess, an elderly lady of winning amiability and indescribable gentleness, yet as a result of great physical suffering (both her breasts had been removed in former years) pale and fragile, already was sitting at the piano. Opposite her, carelessly reclining in an arm-chair, the fat Pandora-score of his unfortunate opera across his knees, sat Beethoven. At his right we recognized the author of the

---

* His son, August Röckel, became Wagner's friend and assistant.
** Quoted from O. G. Sonneck, *op. cit.*

tragedy "Coriolan," Court Secretary Heinrich von Collin, who was chatting with Court Counsellor Breuning of Bonn, the most intimate friend of the composer's youth. My colleagues from the opera, men and women, their parts in hand, had gathered in a half-circle not far from the piano. As before, Milder was Fidelio; Mlle. Müller sang Marzelline; Weinmüller, Rocco; Caché the doorkeeper Jacquino; and Steinkopf the Minister of State. After I had been presented to the Prince and Princess, and Beethoven had acknowledged our respectful greetings, he placed his score on the music-desk for the Princess and—the performance began.

The two initial acts, in which I played no part, were sung from the first to the last note. Eyes sought the clock, and Beethoven was importuned to drop some of the long-drawn sections of secondary importance. Yet he defended every measure, and did so with such nobility and artistic dignity that I was ready to kneel at his feet. But when he came to the chief point at issue itself, the notable cuts in the exposition which would make it possible to fuse the two acts into one, he was beside himself, shouted uninterruptedly "Not a note!" and tried to run off with his score. But the Princess laid her hands, folded as though in prayer, on the sacred score entrusted to her, looked up with indescribable mildness at the angry genius and behold—his rage melted at her glance, and he once more resignedly resumed his place. The noble lady gave the order to continue, and played the prelude to the great aria: *In des Lebens Frühlingstagen*. So I asked Beethoven to hand me the part of Florestan. My unfortunate predecessor, however, in spite of repeated requests had not been induced to yield it up, and hence I was told to sing from the score, from which the Princess was accompanying at the piano. I knew that this great aria meant as much to Beethoven as the entire opera, and handled it from that point of view. Again and again he insisted on hearing it—the exertion well-nigh overtaxed my powers —but I sang it, for I was overjoyed to see that my presentation made it possible for the great Master to reconcile himself to his misunderstood work.

Midnight had passed before the performance—drawn out by reason of many repetitions—at last came to an end. "And the revision, the curtailments?" the Princess asked the Master with a pleading look.

"Do not insist on them," Beethoven answered sombrely, "not a single note must be missing."

"Beethoven," she cried with a deep sigh, "must your great work then continue to be misunderstood and condemned?"

"It is sufficiently rewarded with your approval, your Ladyship," said the Master and his hand trembled slightly as it glided over her own.

Then suddenly it seemed as though a stronger, more potent spirit entered into this delicate woman. Half-kneeling and seizing his knees she cried to him as though inspired: "Beethoven! No—your greatest work, you yourself shall not cease to exist in this way! God who has implanted those tones of purest beauty in your soul forbids it, your mother's spirit, which at this moment pleads and warns you with my voice, forbids it! Beethoven, it must be! Give in! Do so in memory of your mother! Do so for me, who am only your best friend!"

The great man, with his head suggestive of Olympian sublimity, stood for many moments before the worshipper of his Muse, then brushed his long, falling curls from his face, as though an enchanting dream were passing through his soul, and, his glance turned heavenward full of emotion, cried amid sobs: "I will—yes, all—I will do all, for you—for my your—for my mother's sake!" And so saying he reverently raised the Princess and offered the Prince his hand as though to confirm a vow. Deeply moved we surrounded the little group, for even then we all felt the importance of this supreme moment.

From that time onward not another word was said regarding the opera. All were exhausted, and I am free to confess that I exchanged a look of relief not hard to interpret with Mayer when servants flung open the folding-doors of the dining-room, and the company at last sat down to supper at plenteously covered tables. It was probably not altogether due to chance that I was placed opposite Beethoven who, in spirit no doubt still with his opera, ate noticeably little; while I, tormented by the most ravenous hunger, devoured the first course with a speed bordering on the ludicrous. He smiled as he pointed to my empty plate: "You have swallowed your food like a wolf—what have you eaten?" "I was so famished," I replied, "that to tell the truth, I never noticed what it was I ate."

"That is why, before we sat down, you sang the part of Florestan, the man starving in the dungeon, in so masterly and so natural a manner. Neither your voice nor your head deserves credit, but your stomach alone. Well, always see to it that you starve bravely before the performance and then we will be sure of success."

All those at the table laughed, and probably took more pleasure in the thought that Beethoven had at last plucked up heart to joke at all, rather than at his joke itself.

When we left the Prince's palace Beethoven spoke to me again: "I have the fewest changes to make in your part; so come to my house in the course of the next few days to get it; I will write it out for you myself."

A few days later I presented myself in the anteroom, where an elderly servant did not know what to do with me, since his master was bathing at the moment. This I knew because I heard the splashing of the water which the noble eccentric poured out over himself in veritable cascades while giving vent to bellowing groans, which in his case, it seemed, were outbursts of content. On the old servant's unfriendly countenance I read the words: "Announce or dismiss?" in grumpy, wrinkled letters, but suddenly he asked: "Whom have I the honor——?"

I gave my name: "Joseph Röckel."

"Well, that's all right," said the old Viennese, "I was told to let you in."

He went and immediately afterward opened the door. I entered the place consecrate to supreme genius. It was almost frugally simple and a sense of order appeared never to have visited it. In one corner was an open piano, loaded with music in the wildest confusion. Here, on a chair, reposed a fragment of the *Eroica.* The individual parts of the opera with which he was busy lay, some on other chairs, others on and under the table which stood in the middle of the room. And, amid chamber music compositions, piano trios and symphonic sketches, was placed the mighty bathing apparatus in which the Master was laving his powerful chest with the cold flood. He received me without any fuss, and I had an opportunity of admiring his muscular system and his sturdy bodily construction. To judge by the latter the composer might look forward to growing as old as Methuselah, and it must have taken a most powerful inimical influence to bring this strong column to so untimely a fall.

Beethoven greeted me affably, gave me a contented smile, and while he was dressing told me what pains he had taken to write out my voice part from the illegible score with his own hand, so that I might receive it as soon as possible and in an absolutely correct form.

The new, second version of *Fidelio* was to be put on the stage the following spring.

In the meantime, preparations for the peace conference were progressing: on December 21 the congress of diplomats, including Talleyrand, journeyed to Pressburg. There the treaty was signed on December 26. As expected, the terms were cruel. Austria was compelled to cede all of its possessions in Italy and in Dalmatia, to swell Napoleon's new Kingdom of Italy; the Tirol and Voralberg were awarded to Bavaria as a French ally; Swabia was given to the Duke of Württemberg. William Pitt's Coalition was dissolved. The shattering of his hope proved too great a burden for the ailing Prime Minister; he died within a few weeks, in January, 1806.

Napoleon left Vienna on December 28. On that day a solemn *Te Deum* for peace was sung in St. Stephen's Church. On January 11, the *Wiener Zeitung* announced that its former editor had been reinstated. On the 12th the French troops left. Before Napoleon's departure from Vienna, he issued a proclamation which was a masterpiece of propaganda. It read in part:

PROCLAMATION

Citizens of Vienna: I have signed the peace with the Emperor of Austria. Since I am now ready to depart for my capital, I wish to express to you the esteem in which I hold you, as well as my satisfaction for your behavior during the time in which you were subject to my laws . . .

Citizens of Vienna, I know that all of you find that war abhorrent which the ministers who have sold themselves to England have instigated on the Continent. The head of your State knows of the machinations of these corrupt ministers . . .

Citizens of Vienna, I did not often show myself among you, not, I assure you, out of disdain or vain pride; no, only because I did not wish to detract from the respect which you tender to your Emperor, with whom I was willing to conclude a prompt peace. In parting from you, take back as a gift, one which proves my esteem for you, your Supply Depot. It is untouched,* though by the laws of war it had become my property . . .

Schönbrunn, the 6th Nivose, Year 14
NAPOLÉON

It is clear that Napoleon was ready to turn his attention once more to "Perfidious Albion." Vienna belonged again to the Viennese. Gradually Beethoven's friends returned. He set about the task of revising *Fidelio*. But the changes which were wrung from him with so much trouble were not significant. He eliminated a couple of the lighter numbers and Rocco's mediocre "Gold" aria, and he recast the music into two acts. He did compose a new overture, one which was destined to become the most famous part of the famous opera. The overture used with the first version of the opera is now known as *Leonore No. 2*. For the 1806 performances, he expanded the overture, giving it greater symphonic weight and scope, and forming it into a dramatic synthesis which is almost too mighty for the confines of an opera house: that is the magnificent *Leonore No. 3*.**

The first or second version of *Fidelio* is hardly ever given today. Yet the original version, while being in certain respects weaker dramatically, contains musical ideas which, if not superior to those in the final version, are as potent.***

As usual, Beethoven could not bring himself to let go the notepaper, to send to the theater the changes he had promised to deliver. Braun pressed him in January, he pressed him in February; March came along and the new overture still was not delivered. Braun then took matters in his own hands: he told Beethoven that he had definitely fixed the date of Saturday, March 29, for the performance. It was to be given then or not at all. This worked. Even so, the

---

* Not true.

** The so-called *Leonore No. 1* was not discovered until after Beethoven's death and was long thought to have been written for a special performance of the opera in Prague. (Both Nottebohm and Thayer held this theory.) More recent scholarship inclines to the view that No. 1, after all, is an early work, discarded by Beethoven in favor of No. 2. This later view has been supported by a careful examination of internal evidence by Josef Braunstein (1927). As to the *Fidelio* Overture which is now used to begin the performance (*Leonore No. 3* being usually played after the Dungeon Scene), this was a serviceable short piece which Beethoven composed for the 1814 performances. Yet he was never satisfied with any of these overtures, and there is some evidence that he was planning a fifth.

*** The 1805 version was given on August 5, 1967, by the Boston Symphony under the direction of Erich Leinsdorf in a performance in Tanglewood. It was an unforgettable experience. One critic, Michael Steinberg of the *Boston Globe,* called it "a work of surging vitality with a life all its own."

orchestra had a chance to rehearse the difficult overture only once. Seyfried conducted.

·◦§ 4 §◦·

Now the opera pleased much more. Indeed, it was on its way toward becoming popular when Beethoven had a falling out with Braun. To tell this story, we again quote Röckel:

While I accidentally chanced to be waiting in the anteroom to the Baron's business office, I heard a violent altercation which the financier was carrying on with the enraged composer in the adjoining room. Beethoven was suspicious, and thought that his percentage of the net proceeds was greater than the amount which the Court Banker, who was at the same time director of the *Theater an der Wien,* had paid him. The latter remarked that Beethoven was the first composer with whom the management, in view of his extraordinary merits, had been willing to share profits, and explained the paucity of the box-office returns by the fact that the boxes and front row seats all had been taken, but that the seats in which the thickly crowded mass of the people would have yielded a return as when Mozart's operas were given, were empty. And he emphasized that hitherto Beethoven's music had been accepted only by the more cultured classes, while Mozart with his operas invariably had roused enthusiasm in the multitude, the people as a whole. Beethoven hurried up and down the room in agitation, shouting loudly: "I do not write for the multitude—I write for the cultured!"

"But the cultured alone do not fill our theatre," replied the Baron with the greatest calmness, "we need the multitude to bring in money, and since in your music you have refused to make any concessions to it, you yourself are to blame for your diminished percentage of return. If we had given Mozart the same interest in the receipts of his operas he would have grown rich."

This disadvantageous comparison with his famous predecessor seemed to wound Beethoven's tenderest susceptibilities. Without replying to it with a single word, he leaped up and shouted in the greatest rage: "Give me back my score!"

The Baron hesitated and stared as though struck by lightning at the enraged composer's glowing face, while the latter, in an accent of the most strenuous passion repeated: "I want my score—my score, at once!"

The Baron pulled the bell-rope; a servant entered.

"Bring the score of yesterday's opera for this gentleman," said the Baron with an air; and the servant hastened to return with it. "I am sorry," the aristocrat continued, "But I believe that on calmer reflection—." Yet Beethoven no longer heard what he was saying. He had torn the gigantic volume of the score from the servant's hand and, without even seeing me in his eagerness, ran through the anteroom and down the stairs.

When the Baron received me a few minutes later this composed gentleman was unable to conceal a slight apprehension; he appeared to realize the value of the treasure with which he had parted. Out of sorts, he remarked to me: "Beethoven was excited and over-hasty; you have some influence with him; try everything—promise him anything in my name, so that we can save his work for our stage."

I excused myself and hastened to follow the angry Master to his Tusculum. All was in vain, however, he would not allow himself to be soothed.

Röckel's account has been cited by biographers as one more example of Beethoven's habit of suspecting people without cause. No doubt his anger was largely unjustified. No doubt he behaved unreasonably. Yet the question has not been asked whether Braun was entirely to be trusted. Had Beethoven no justification whatever for his action? It is curious that nobody has asked this question, because evidence exists which places Braun's character in a dubious light. He was so universally distrusted that a group of Viennese theater lovers (anonymous) wrote a petition in verse and presented it to the Emperor, begging him not to entrust Braun with the management of the Court Theaters.* Johann Reichardt, that confidential chronicler of Viennese affairs, stated that pejorative stories were circulated about Braun accusing him of manipulating funds belonging to the Court Theaters for his own use, to acquire "vast manorial estates." I do not know the truth of the matter; I merely suggest that we must not judge Beethoven invariably in the wrong, just because he was frequently in the wrong.

At any rate, this was the end of *Fidelio* for the time being. Eight years were to elapse before the opera was to be heard again and then under very different circumstances.

---

* Heinrich Kralik, *The Vienna Opera.*

First pages of the "Appassionata Sonata." Manuscript shows spots of a downpour that penetrated the trunk of a post-chaise in which Beethoven was traveling back to Vienna after a quarrel with Lichnowsky. See page 376 (Bibliothèque Nationale, Paris).

CHAPTER 14

CREATIVITY

··ɔ[I]ɕ··

ike all Gaul, Beethoven's output is usually divided into three periods. That division could apply to most artists. If there are seven ages of man, they shrink to three in the creator: apprentice work; maturity; the work of the final years.

But the work of Beethoven which we prize most highly belongs to two periods: the middle one, which is long, and the final one, which is sparse and short and was terminated by death at a time when he felt "he had only begun to know how to compose."

The works which are especially beloved, those compositions to which most people respond, the parts of him which most music lovers think of as "Beethoven," belong to the middle period.

It is these toweringly famous creations which we must now place within his biography. An astonishing number of them was composed in a relatively short time. From 1804, when he began the composition of the *Waldstein Sonata,* to 1810, by which time he had finished the music to Goethe's *Egmont,* the list is a succession of successes. We have before us a period of seven fat years in which he created:

Opus No.	Title of the Composition	Year (Approx.)
53	*Waldstein Sonata*	1804
54	F Major Piano Sonata	1804
55	*Eroica Symphony*	1804
72	*Fidelio*	1805
57	*Appassionata Sonata*	1806
61	Violin Concerto	1806
58	Piano Concerto No. 4	1806

What a record of achievement this represents! What a miracle of creativity! We must be careful not to explain this creativity by overt causes, such as Beethoven's being in love, or his compositions' being in demand, or a marked improvement in his health. Can a better reason be suggested?

Through the *Eroica* and *Fidelio* he had arrived at a promontory from which he had a wide and unobstructed view. He had, so to speak, found the place where he could build his own world, a world of lofty mountains, quiet glades, deep waters, in which he could express himself in a variety of ways. This brave new world, built by himself, needed to be explored in many excursions. It was a world of deeper shadows and brighter lights, now inducing contemplation, now quickening a bold step. It was a comprehensive landscape, but never barren.

The artist-explorer in him pressed on to variegated adventures. Yet they have a characteristic in common: his assertion of the arrival at joy through suffering. He was to write of this thought to Countess Erdödy. He writes it in his music: struggle alternates with peace, strife leads to tenderness, determination is not inimical to reverie. Again and again we find the interaction of the dreamlike state with a state of high wakefulness. Only when both are present can man fulfill himself.

Beethoven merged, if only subconsciously, the two concepts of the Enlightenment and the Romantic movement; both the clear resoluteness of the one and the dark introspection of the other are present in his music. Through this merger, this chemistry of genius, he created music which reaches the understanding of the plain man and the musically knowledgeable one. Both of us feel he has very much to say that we cannot say ourselves, because, in a sense, the best sense, we are a product of enlightenment and a romantic impulse. Both of us feel that he is our personal representative.

He was the most personal of great artists. Berenson, discussing Piero della

Francesca and Velazquez, speaks of "the impersonal art": we never know what Piero or Velazquez is thinking, much though we may be moved by their works. With Beethoven—as with Rembrandt or Michelangelo or Dostoievsky—we get the sense of personal involvement. We seem to see him storm or smile, suffer or exult. Not outward circumstances, but the maturing of his experience, ambition, strength, and beliefs is responsible for this paragon of output during the seven years.

There is one outward circumstance, however, that we can cite. From the departure of the French troops at the end of 1805 to the renewed hostilities in the spring of 1809, the war rolled away from Vienna. In 1806, Napoleon had other foes to conquer. And conquer them he did, beating Naples, beating Holland, beating Prussia (at the Battle of Jena on October 14, occupying Berlin on October 27), beating the Dukedom of Warsaw (occupying Warsaw on December 15). Wherever he went he left "branch managers" behind; Bonapartes sat down on various thrones, Louis in Holland, Joseph in Naples, and the following year Jerome in Westphalia.

The Holy Roman Empire came to a formal end: with so many of the principalities now vassals of France, there was no longer any sense to it. On August 6 Franz II laid down the crown of the Holy Roman Empire and became Franz I, Emperor of Austria. The vestments and the jewels heavy with the history of ten centuries were locked away in the Treasury of the *Hofburg*. They became and have remained a tourist attraction.

Though the Viennese—some of them—were ashamed of defeat, though some mourned a son or brother lost at Austerlitz, though most were a good deal poorer, they could again buy bread, listen to music, go to the theater, and imitate the new French fashions. Let us chronicle the events of Beethoven's life during the next few years:

First, a marriage. His brother's. On May 25, 1806, brother Carl married Johanna Reiss, daughter of an upholsterer. Some three months after the marriage—on September 4—a son was born to them and named Karl. In this marriage and in this son lay the cause of the future destructive tragedy in Beethoven's life.

In the summer of that year Beethoven for some reason did not move to the country.* But in September he was in Silesia, visiting with Prince Lichnowsky

* Some believe that he visited the Brunsviks in Hungary, but evidence is lacking. We have only two dated letters, one in May, one in July, both from Vienna.

the castle belonging to Count Franz von Oppersdorff, who was an admirer of Beethoven and to whom the Fourth Symphony is dedicated. Then he went to Lichnowsky's country estate, in Grätz, near the city of Troppau in Silesia. Among the guests at Prince Lichnowsky's was a group of French officers. One evening they urged Beethoven to play. He refused. They insisted. Somebody, probably the prince himself, threatened him with house arrest if he didn't play, a threat obviously meant as a joke. Beethoven took it seriously, packed his belongings, said nothing to anybody, and walked out at night. He walked to the nearest city, Troppau, and hurried "on the wings of the wind by extra post to Vienna" (from an account given to Thayer by the daughter of Moritz Lichnowsky). The incident is confirmed by Seyfried and by a Dr. Weiser, who was house physician to the Lichnowskys. Dr. Weiser remembered that Beethoven wrote Lichnowsky a letter saying:

> Prince, what you are you are by accident of birth; what I am I am through myself. There have been and will still be thousands of princes; there is only one Beethoven.

This letter has not been found; it may never have been written.

When he arrived at home, he took a bust of Prince Lichnowsky which stood on his cabinet and dashed it to the floor, breaking it into a hundred pieces.

There must have been more to this outburst than his usual reluctance to perform. It is possible that he was feeling particularly bitter against Napoleon. The failure of *Fidelio* and his recent experience with the French occupation could have instilled in him a resentment against the French. His friend Krumpholz met him on the street around that time, and when Beethoven, always interested in what was going on in the world, asked him, "What's the news?" Krumpholz told him about Napoleon's victory at Jena. Beethoven said, "It is a pity that I do not understand the art of war as well as I do the art of music. I would conquer him!"

Returning from Troppau, Beethoven had the manuscript of the *Appassionata Sonata* * in his trunk. On the way back, the post-chaise was overtaken by a torrential rain which penetrated the trunk. Arrived in Vienna, he went immediately to see his friends the Bigots and laughingly showed them the manuscript which had become spotted by the rain. Marie Bigot looked carefully at the

---

* It was not called that by Beethoven; the title was appended later by a publisher.

beginning and immediately sat down at the piano and began playing it. Beethoven had not expected this. He was astonished that Marie could make anything out of the manuscript with its many erasures and alterations, in addition to the rain spots. But Marie played the whole difficult sonata at sight. When she finished it, she begged Beethoven to give her the manuscript. He brought it to her later.

He heard again from Thomson in Scotland, who had approached Haydn as well. Beethoven now wrote him—on November 1, 1806—expressing his willingness to furnish various compositions. He said he would take care to make the compositions easy and pleasing, insofar as he was able to, and insofar as this was consistent with the *"élévation"* and *"orginialité"* of his style.* He proposed chamber music and sonatas, but all that came of it was his setting of various Scottish, Irish, and other folk songs (composed between 1810 and 1816) and some Themes and Variations for the piano (composed between 1818 and 1820).

Possibly as a relief from the mightier works, he composed in this *annus mirabilis* of 1806 a light piece, the 32 Variations for Piano in C Minor. Some time after, he found Streicher's daughter practicing the Variations and asked who composed the work. "You did," she answered. "Such nonsense by me? Beethoven, what an ass you were!"

For a concert which Franz Clement, first violinist and conductor at the Theater-an-der-Wien, was to give, Beethoven that year composed his Violin Concerto. It was his unique essay in this form, and Beethoven was a pianist, not a violinist; yet in that one try he created the Mount Everest of violin concertos. It is an equal partnership of symphony and solo instrument, encompassing grandeur and mystery and sweetness and humor. It remains today the wonder of the form, the challenge to every artist.

Clement played it on December 23, 1806, to fair approval. The concert must have been a strange one. In addition to selections by other composers, Clement played a sonata of his own "on one string with the violin turned upside down," inserting this trick after the first movement of the Beethoven Concerto! The concerto did not really begin to be appreciated until after Beethoven's death: on May 27, 1844, Joseph Joachim, then a child prodigy of thirteen, played it in London, with Felix Mendelssohn conducting. Then it received its rightful due.

The manuscript bore the punning dedication: *"Concerto par Clemenza pour*

---

* The letter was written in French by somebody else for Beethoven.

Clement," but when it was published Beethoven dedicated it to Stephan von Breuning.

If the Violin Concerto had to wait years before it was understood, the *Rasoumovsky Quartets* met at first not only with puzzlement but with some irritation. Czerny told Jahn that at the first play-through of the Quartet in F the players laughed and thought that Beethoven was playing a joke on them. An Italian musician, Felix Radicati, related that when he looked over the Quartets he asked Beethoven whether in all seriousness he considered these works to be music, to which Beethoven replied calmly, "Oh, they are not for you but for a later age."

Yet these three masterpieces are not difficult; they abound with gaiety as well as sentiment. Nor did they frighten the man for whom they were composed: Rasoumovsky was aware of Beethoven's mastery of the quartet style, and had asked Beethoven to give him lessons in music theory with emphasis on quartet composition. Beethoven refused. But in the first and the second of the three quartets Beethoven used Russian themes—a gracious compliment to the count. Unfortunately, Rasoumovsky lost his wife in the year the Quartets were completed—she died on December 23, 1806, only forty-three years old—and for some time there could be no music in the house of mourning. Eventually the Quartets were heard in Rasoumovsky's new palace—with increasing frequency and to increasing approbation.

In the Fourth Piano Concerto (no doubt composed for Beethoven's own use in a concert in which he was planning to present his new works), there occurs the famous dialogue between the piano and the orchestra (in the second movement) which Liszt likened to Orpheus taming the beasts of the under-world. Though this is a fanciful description, it seems apt to me: there *is* a kinship to Gluck's scene in which Orpheus quiets the furies. The movement is ineffably moving, one of the great inventions in all of music.

There was no slackening in creativity in the year following, 1807. During that year he finished—or almost finished—both the Fourth Symphony and the Fifth. Is it not astonishing that he could compose these disparate two not only at the same time, but going from one to the other alternately without ever losing his footing? It is as if Shakespeare had worked on one act of *As You Like It*, turned the page, and wrote a scene of *Macbeth*. Of the Fourth, Robert Schumann said that it was "a slender Greek maiden between two Norse giants," but it seems more like a Viennese Countess than a Greek maiden.

In the Fifth, all sorts of extra-musical meanings have been found. Schindler's reporting of Beethoven's reply when he was asked the meaning of the opening is hard to believe. Did Beethoven really say anything as fatuous as "Thus Fate knocks at the door"? But whatever Beethoven did or did not intend to say, there is one trait that this symphony has beyond every other, "and that is the quality of epic valor" (Lawrence Gilman). Because of this quality, because its drama combines largeness with clarity, the Fifth has procured a special admiration from listeners whose relationship to music is somewhat less than encompassing. E. M. Forster called it "the most sublime noise that has ever penetrated into the ear of man." To achieve it not only did Beethoven agonize over three years in preliminary sketches, but even the final manuscript shows such feverish crossings-out, so many alterations, so much striving for the still better and more pungent, that in one passage of the first movement he has no more room for the final version and must write it as a footnote at the bottom of the page.

Though some critics accused him, now more than ever, of being "original at all costs" and "striving for newness at the expense of beauty," * his reputation was increasing even abroad. In the spring of 1807 he signed the contract with Muzio Clementi for England. He wrote to Franz Brunsvik about it, and in the same letter apprised him of another bit of cheerful news—Schuppanzigh was married:

May 11, 1807

Whenever *we* (that is to say, several amici) drink your wine, we drink your health—All good wishes. Hurry—hurry—hurry and send me the quartets ** — if you don't you may cause me the greatest embarrassment—Schuppanzigh has got married—*to somebody very like him,*** I am told—what will their family be like????—Kiss your sister Therese and tell her that I fear that I shall have to

---

* For example: *Zeitung für Theater, Musik und Poesie,* issue of January 8, 1807, wrote after the first performance of the Violin Concerto: "The educated part of the audience marveled how Clement could have lowered himself to indulge in the sort of tricks and stunts which might amuse the plebs, since he is capable of expressing beauty and nobility in good music. We do not disagree with that opinion. A division of opinion exists about Beethoven's concerto; some acknowledge much beauty in it, others feel that its continuity seems frequently to be torn apart and that needless repetition of a few commonplace passages prove ... fatiguing. It is said that Beethoven could employ his admittedly great talents better to give us works like his first symphonies in C and D, as well as several others of his earlier compositions, which place him in the rank of foremost composers. One fears that if Beethoven will pursue his present path, he and the public will come to no good end. He could arrive at the point where those who are not expert in the rules and intricacies of the art will find no pleasure in his music ... etc., etc."
** The *Rasoumovsky Quartets,* the manuscripts of which Beethoven must have sent to the Brunsviks.
*** Schuppanzigh's wife was as fat as he.

become a great man without a monument of hers contributing to my greatness *—Send me tomorrow, send me immediately the quartets—quar—tets—t—e—t—s.

Your friend
BEETHOVEN (A-143).

The great *Coriolan Overture* belongs to this period; it was composed for a tragedy by the popular Viennese playwright Heinrich von Collin. Collin's play was then famous, though it is now so little known that it is generally assumed that Beethoven's overture is one for Shakespeare's play.

Some time in the early spring of 1807, Beethoven received an invitation from Prince Nikolaus Esterházy, Haydn's employer, to compose a Mass. To honor his wife, the prince wanted the Mass to be performed in September for her name day. As usual, it took Beethoven a long time to answer. When he did, like a schoolboy he enclosed a letter from his physician testifying that he had been ill. But he did promise to deliver the Mass by the end of August. He worked on the Mass along with the Fifth Symphony in Heiligenstadt. Early in September Beethoven journeyed to Eisenstadt to conduct the performance, which took place on September 13, 1807.

Schindler writes that it was the custom at the prince's palace for friends and guests to meet in the chambers of the prince after a performance for the purpose of discussing the works they had just heard. When Beethoven entered the room the prince turned to him, saying, "But, my dear Beethoven, what is this that you have done again?" At the same time Beethoven saw the prince's Kapellmeister, J. N. Hummel, laugh. One can hardly blame Beethoven, raw from the labors of composition and the conducting of the work, for feeling insulted. He left Eisenstadt the same day. Schindler says that Hummel had not laughed at Beethoven at all but at the curious way in which the prince had criticized the Mass. There might have been another reason, cited by Elliot Forbes, which contributed to Beethoven's annoyance. Beethoven was not housed in the castle but in the rooms of a Court secretary, in quarters which were not fit to be lived in and, indeed, had been refused by a tenor two years earlier. How humiliating for the man who was used to being received in the Lichnowsky and Lobkowitz palaces! How irritating to the man who was inclined to be a hypochondriac. It left such an impression on him that he told Schindler about it some fourteen

---

* Therese never painted a portrait of Beethoven.

years later. He neither gave the prince the manuscript of the Mass nor did he dedicate the work to him.

·◦[2]◦·

The withdrawal of *Fidelio* caused by the quarrel with Braun must have been regretted by Beethoven in his calmer moods. But there was little he could do about it just then, for Braun himself was in trouble. In attempting to run three theaters, Braun could not work out an individual program policy for each one. The mixture of German and Italian operas, plays, cheap comedies, and ballets which he presented palled on the public, and box-office receipts decreased. He tried to stave off this indifference by arranging for ever more extravagant productions. The result was the threat of financial disaster. He had gone through a difficult time during the French occupation, his theaters were now out of fashion, and at the end of 1806 he had no choice but to resign. Schikaneder could be of no further help: he had been called to Budapest to consider running the theater there. On the way he became insane and was brought back to Vienna hopelessly ill.

A group of nobles calling themselves the Society of the Cavaliers agreed to take over the Theater-an-der-Wien as well as both Court Theaters. The group included Prince Joseph von Schwarzenberg, Prince Joseph Franz Lobkowitz (Beethoven's patron), Prince Nikolaus Esterházy (Haydn's employer), Count Ferdinand Palffy von Erdöd, Count Hieronimus zu Lodron, Count Stefan Zichy, Franz Nikolaus Count Esterházy, and Franz Count Esterházy. This management of the theaters by amateur aristocrats was a throwback to the 18th century. It no longer worked in the 19th century. Nevertheless, the committee started out with high hopes. Beethoven, too, hoped that he might play a role in Vienna's operatic life.

The leading member of the Society of the Cavaliers was Prince Lobkowitz, whose special responsibility was the presentation of opera performances. Not all the members of the society were favorably inclined toward Beethoven, but certainly Lobkowitz was. Beethoven grasped what he thought was an opportunity and addressed a detailed petition to the directors. No doubt he had help in drafting this petition—perhaps from Gleichenstein or from Lobkowitz—for it is logically and convincingly written. Beethoven stated that while he had enjoyed some success in Vienna, while his works had won him a reputation in foreign lands, he was yet obliged to struggle with various practical difficulties, which had prevented him from living wholly for his art. He intimated that if these difficulties could not be solved he would "leave the city so dear to him." Perhaps the new directors would be willing to employ him in an official position at the opera house. Such a position would assure him of a "comfortable livelihood" and would guarantee his further stay in Vienna. He would be willing to contract for at least one grand opera a year. In addition, he would deliver each year a small operetta or a *divertissement,* small choruses or occasional pieces, as needed. (Can one imagine Beethoven composing an operetta?) Finally, he asked, should his petition be granted, that he be given the theater one day per year for a concert for his own benefit.

Nothing happened. The directors may have known that Beethoven was not the man to be held to the punctual delivery of a work a year, be it opera or *divertissement.* Or there may have been inimical voices raised among the committee, such as Palffy's or Nikolaus Esterházy's, who just then had had an unpleasant brush with the composer. Or the Society of the Cavaliers may at that stage have been quite uncertain of what they wanted to do and therefore did not wish to enter into a binding arrangement. At any rate, no reply is extant to Beethoven's petition. It is ironic that we might have had one or two more operas by Beethoven had the Society of the Cavaliers been endowed with farsight.

··∘[3]∘··

In March, 1808, Beethoven was suffering from an infected finger. It gave him stinging pain, but he bore it patiently. It finally had to be lanced. Yet his "poor finger" did not prevent him from paying tribute to his former teacher, Haydn, whom he honored as a musician, though the two men, so very different in character and viewpoint, had never become close friends. Haydn was now seventy-six years old. He had largely retired from the world and looked older than his years; he who had been so adventurous and filled with life had now become frail and shadowy. To honor Haydn's approaching birthday a committee of ladies of high society arranged for a special festival performance of *The Creation* in the auditorium of the university on March 27, 1808. The entire artistic and aristocratic world of Vienna assembled.*

So as not to excite Haydn needlessly before the performance, the plan was kept secret until the last moment. Then the Princess Esterházy sent her carriage to call for him. When he arrived at the university he was greeted by the rector and a number of musicians, Beethoven among them.

---

* The painter Balthasar Wiegand painted the gathering, showing more than 200 portraits of "celebrities." The painting was then affixed to the cover of a chest and given to Haydn as a gift.

He was carried into the hall on a litter. He was as pale as a shroud. Frightened by the noise, the ovation, and the flourishes of the trumpets which greeted his entrance, he shrank into himself. Presently the audience quieted down and Haydn was placed in the first row, directly in front of the orchestra. The performance began. Salieri conducted; Kreutzer played the piano. When, at the famous passage "Let there be light," the audience burst into applause, Haydn pointed upward with an unsteady hand.

At the end of the first part, when those standing near him rushed forward to congratulate him, they found that Haydn had fainted, though he recovered at once. "Don't you see that he is cold?" exclaimed the French ambassador. At that, the women standing near took off their shawls and furs and piled them at Haydn's feet. The second part was about to begin when Haydn's physician sternly insisted that Haydn could bear no more: he had to return home. The litter bearers raised him up, but they found it difficult to make a path through the crowd. Beethoven thrust his way toward Haydn, everybody respectfully giving Beethoven precedence. He knelt beside him and covered Haydn's hand with kisses.

So exuberant a celebration was possible while Vienna was drawing an easy breath between wars. Interest in matters of the mind and spirit was at its height. As if to make up for lost time or as a premonition of conflict to come, people flocked to lectures and poetry readings. The famous August Wilhelm Schlegel, poet, philosopher, translator of Shakespeare, came to Vienna to hold a series of lectures at the university.

Said a contemporary observer: "Princes, Counts and Lords, Ministers, Generals, scholars, artists, and ladies of top rank were present ... A silence, attention and interest reigned which honored both the speaker and the listeners. The princesses and the other ladies of the nobility usually appeared at twelve o'clock, modestly dressed, without pretension or coquetry ... The good Schlegel was absolutely nonplused. Such a thing had never happened to him" (Lorenz Leopold Haschka, a Viennese writer).

It seemed a propitious time for Beethoven to give that benefit concert which he had long planned. The large theaters were available for concerts only at Easter or Christmas, being otherwise engaged for theatrical performances. Since the Easter season had passed, he had to wait until Christmas time for the Theater-an-der-Wien. He had created enough new music to fill *two* programs, not one. One symphony, the Fourth, was virtually new to the public; two unheard symphonies, the Fifth and the Sixth, were ready when they needed to be.

Into the Sixth he poured that delight in the outdoors, the exhilaration of the open sky, the smile of the sun, the incessant gossip of the brook, the feel of grass against the walker's foot, which were part of his life ever since he had roamed in the woods at Bonn. But he goes beyond the sensual pleasures which Nature bestows. He treats as well of Nature's role in regenerating the spirit. He assigns to Nature not only the power to "awaken pleasant feelings" but also the power to help man lift his eyes and begin to understand eternal and stable beauty and goodness. A shepherd's piping becomes a hymn, without changing the melody. He sees the shepherd as the representative of a good life; he advocates man's return to "naturalness." He expresses in music the beliefs he had arrived at in Döbling, Heiligenstadt, or Baden and converts into sound what his eyes had seen. Yet he also echoes what he has learned from the men of his time: from Klopstock's bucolic verses; from Sturm, the ingenuous pastor of Hamburg; from Goethe, who found peace *"im Walde,"* and from Rousseau, who wrote:

> Send your children out to renew themselves; send them to regain in the open field the strength lost in the foul air of our crowded cities *(Émile).*

As I indicated, it seemed a good time to bring this music to the public; yet Beethoven experienced ill luck with his big concert project, partly because the Society of the Cavaliers had made more or less of a mess of the direction of the Court Theaters and nobody was making decisions. Presently one by one they turned away until only Count Palffy and Prince Lobkowitz remained active, and even they turned the actual direction over to one Joseph von Hartl.*

As early as February, 1808, Beethoven wrote to Heinrich von Collin, author of *Coriolan,* asking him to help obtain the Theater-an-der-Wien. As usual when things were not going well, Beethoven growled angrily and was sure that there was foul work afoot. "I have already become accustomed to the basest and vilest treatment in Vienna," he wrote to Collin. He told him that he had three documents in his possession promising him "a day in the theater last year . . .

---

* Lobkowitz's efforts on behalf of the Court Opera caused him to make expenditures from his own pocket, expenditures so substantial that at one time he found himself in financial difficulties.

Hartl, good administrator and practical theater man though he was, could not pull the heavy cart of the three theaters out of the financial mire. By 1813 the Society was dissolved and the administration of the theaters was taken over by a government bureau which appropriated annual subventions to the "official" theaters. Today the Austrian State Opera, the Burgtheater, and their subsidiary theaters are government-supported.

which has never been allotted to me ... I repeat, a day which they *owe me,* for, *if I choose to do so, I can by virtue of my right* compel the T[heatrical] D[irectors] to give me that day. And indeed I have discussed this point with *a lawyer* ..." (A-164).

He stormed and fumed and threatened to leave Vienna, yet continued to try to get the day for his concert fixed and concurrently to attempt to find an operatic project with Collin which might be accepted by Hartl for the Vienna Opera. Finally he succeeded. The day of the concert was to be December 22. He was to have the Theater-an-der-Wien.

In granting this date Lobkowitz seems to have been of no help. Why not? Probably because he had troubles of his own and did not want to push Beethoven's cause too hard with the other members of the committee. It was all handled badly, in typical committee fashion, and it was Beethoven himself who obtained what he desired. He gave his services freely to several charity concerts; he was generous in aiding public causes, and gladly undertook the labors of conducting and playing when he thought he could do good. In recognition of this he was given the theater. His benefit concert, the "Akademie," was advertised five days before the event in the *Wiener Zeitung:*

MUSICAL AKADEMIE

On Thursday, December 22, Ludwig van Beethoven will have the honor to give a musical *Akademie* in the I. R. Priv. Theater-an-der-Wien. All the pieces are of his composition, entirely new, and not yet heard in public.

First Part: 1, A Symphony, entitled: "A Recollection of Country Life," in F major (No. 5).*

2, Aria.

3, Hymn with Latin text, composed in the church style with chorus and solos.

4, Pianoforte Concerto played by himself.

Second Part: 1, Grand Symphony in C minor (No. 6).*

2, Sanctus with Latin text composed in the church style with chorus and solos.

3, Fantasia for Pianoforte alone.

4, Fantasia for the Pianoforte which ends with the gradual entrance of the entire orchestra and the introduction of choruses as a finale.

Boxes and reserved seats are to be had in the Krugerstrasse No. 1074, first story. Beginning at half past six o'clock.

---

* Note that the *Pastoral Symphony,* No. 6, is here listed as No. 5; the Fifth Symphony is No. 6.

There was trouble right from the start. The recollections of those of his friends who were there are conflicting. They do agree that the event so long in planning, from which the composer had hoped so much, and in which he presented two of his greatest symphonies, that event which one might have thought would overwhelm the Viennese audience and overcome them with wonder, turned out to be pretty much of a disaster. At a previous concert—the charity concert of November 15—Beethoven had already run into trouble with the orchestra. His behavior was hardly diplomatic; possibly too his beat was not the simplest to follow. The orchestra had insisted that he should not conduct. At the rehearsal, then, he had to remain in an anteroom, impatiently pacing up and down. Later the quarrel was smoothed over and Beethoven conducted the performance, but it was not a friendly orchestra he now faced and which was expected to grapple with the new music.

A singer had to be found to sing the selection for No. 2 of the first part, the aria *Ah! Perfido!* Milder, who had sung Leonore, consented at once. Beethoven was eager to get her and wrote to Röckel that he was willing to come himself "to kiss the hem of her garment." He then quarreled with Milder; she refused to appear. Röckel looked around for someone else, and finally engaged the sister of Schuppanzigh's new wife, a Fräulein Josephine Killitschgy,* who was young and inexperienced. When Beethoven led her on the stage she had such an attack of nerves that she trembled all over and butchered the aria.

The most embarrassing incident of the concert occurred during the final number, the Fantasia for Orchestra, Piano, and Chorus. Beethoven had composed this specially for the occasion, feeling that the concert ought to end with a rousing finale, as a contrast to the preceding number, which presented Beethoven alone at the piano. Let Seyfried tell the story:

> When the master brought out his orchestral Fantasia with choruses, he arranged with me at the somewhat hurried rehearsal, with wet voice-parts as usual, that the second variation should be played without the repeat. In the evening, however, absorbed in his creation, he forgot all about the instructions which he had given, repeated the first part while the orchestra accompanied the second, which sounded not altogether edifying. A trifle too late, the Concertmaster, Unrath, noticed the mistake, looked in surprise at his lost companions, stopped playing and called out drily: "Again!" A little displeased, the violinist Anton

---

* Later she became a famous singer and sang Leonore at the first performance in Berlin.

Wranitzky asked "With repeats?" "Yes," came the answer, and now the thing went straight as a string.

With some variations, Seyfried's story is confirmed by other friends and musicians who were there, including Czerny and a young man of fourteen who had just come to Vienna to pursue his studies with Salieri and the old Albrechtsberger. This was Ignaz Moscheles, who was to become one of Beethoven's warm-hearted champions and write eloquent reminiscences about him.* Of the incident Moscheles wrote:

> I remember having been present at the performance in question, seated in a corner of the gallery, in the Theater-an-der-Wien. During the last movement of the Fantasia I perceived that, like a run-away carriage going down-hill, an overturn was inevitable. Almost immediately after . . . I saw Beethoven give the signal for stopping. His voice was not heard; but he had probably given directions where to begin again, and after a moment's respectful silence on the part of the audience, the orchestra recommenced and the performance proceeded without further mistakes or stoppage.

Seyfried comments further:

> At first he could not understand that he had in a manner humiliated the musicians. He thought it was a duty to correct an error that had been made and that the audience was entitled to hear everything properly played, for its money. But he readily and heartily begged the pardon of the orchestra for the humiliation to which he had subjected it, and was honest enough to spread the story himself and assume all responsibility for his own absence of mind.

Still another incident was recorded by Spohr in his autobiography. This, though it is a famous Beethovian anecdote, is a secondhand one, as Spohr was not present at the concert. The story goes that Beethoven, in his violent conducting motions, first swept the candles off the piano and then inadvertently knocked down a choirboy whose task it was to hold one of the candles. The audience is supposed to have been convulsed with laughter. The story is almost certainly apocryphal.

But even if the concert had proceeded without incident; even if it had been

---

* Moscheles edited the Beethoven sonatas and in doing so spoke of his personal connections with Beethoven. This aroused Schindler's jealousy to such an extent that he stated that Moscheles never had any relationship whatsoever with Beethoven. Later he corrected himself.

performed to the hilt by a great orchestra and experienced singers, it could not but have wearied the best disposed of audiences. How could they have been expected to understand and absorb both the Fifth and the Sixth Symphonies, the Fourth Piano Concerto—which was probably what Beethoven played—not to mention an aria, a hymn, and other miscellaneous pieces? Four hours of music, new sounds demanding new strength of response and comprehension, played in an unheated theater three days before Christmas. Reichardt described it:

> I accepted the kind offer of Prince Lobkowitz to let me sit in his box with hearty thanks. There we continued, in the bitterest cold, too, from half past six to half past ten, and experienced the truth that one can easily have too much of a good thing—and still more of a loud. Nevertheless, I could no more leave the box before the end than could the exceedingly good-natured and delicate Prince, for the box was in the first balcony near the stage, so that the orchestra with Beethoven in the middle conducting it was below us and near at hand; thus many a failure in the performance vexed our patience in the highest degree. Poor Beethoven, who from this, his own concert, was having the first and only scant profit that he could find in a whole year, had found in the rehearsals and performance a lot of opposition and almost no support. Singers and orchestra were composed of heterogeneous elements, and it had been found impossible to get a single full rehearsal for all the pieces to be performed....

Such then was the result of a year of effort. The labor which it entailed, the scant enthusiasm which this oversupply of glories aroused in auditors anxious to get home and warm their hands and feet, the quarrel with the orchestra, and the nerve-racking incident at the final moment could hardly have added to Beethoven's satisfaction with the Viennese public or Vienna's artistic conditions. As to the financial results, we have only Reichardt's words for it that they were scanty.

·⊰[4]⊱·

About two months before the concert, a card was handed in to Beethoven by a servant, announcing an official visitor. He was Count Truchsess-Waldburg, High Chamberlain to His Majesty the King of Westphalia. The King of Westphalia was Napoleon's brother, Jerome Bonaparte, a young man, indolent, superficial, weak—at least to Napoleon's way of thinking—and of doubtful masculinity. Napoleon, in his moves of nepotism, fobbed him off on one of the least important of the little kingdoms, the city of Cassel and surrounding territory. The new King thought it advisable to show that he too was capable of doing something for "culture"; he dispatched his chamberlain to offer Beethoven the position of First Kapellmeister. Cassel was smaller than Bonn and had never distinguished itself for artistic excellence. The offer entailed the lightest of duties, no other than to conduct at the King's infrequent concerts, and to work in any way that Beethoven liked with an orchestra which was to be put at his disposal.

It was obvious that the offer was made merely to attract a celebrated name to the King's Court. Ordinarily Beethoven might have scoffed at it. However, it came at a time when he felt unappreciated in Vienna; as the weeks passed and the troubles with his *Akademie* multiplied and as there was no answer forthcoming to his petition addressed to the director of the theaters, Beethoven began to consider it seriously. One feels that he considered it almost as a vengeful move against a public which had let him down. Hovering between a calm confidence in his own powers and an almost autocratic fury that these powers were not sufficiently acknowledged, that the other musicians, envious creatures, were trying to stifle him, he wrote, and no doubt spoke, bitter phrases: "I have so little reason to expect anything favorable from them [the directors of the Opera] that the thought that I shall certainly leave Vienna and become a wanderer haunts me persistently." Or the long letter which he wrote to Breitkopf and Härtel on January 7, 1809, in which he states:

> At last owing to intrigues and cabals and meannesses of all kinds I am compelled to leave my German fatherland which is still in its way unique. For I have accepted an offer from His Royal Majesty of Westphalia to settle there as Kapellmeister at a yearly salary of 600 gold ducats—I have just sent off by today's post my assurance that I will go, and am only awaiting my certificate of appointment; whereupon I shall make my preparations for the journey, which will take me through *Leipzig*—

In the same letter, he says about his last concert:

> The promoters of the concert for the widows, out of hatred for me, Herr Salieri being my most active opponent, played me a horrible trick. They threatened to expel any musician belonging to their company who would play for my benefit—In spite of the fact that various mistakes were made, which I could not prevent, the public nevertheless applauded the whole performance with enthusiasm—Yet scribblers in Vienna will certainly not fail to send again to the *Musikalische Zeitung* some wretched stuff directed against me—The musicians, in particular, were enraged that, when from sheer carelessness a

mistake had been made in the simplest and most straightforward passage in the world, I suddenly made them stop playing and called out in a loud voice: *"Once more."* — Such a thing had never happened to them before. The public, however, expressed its pleasure at this— (A-192).

Whether Salieri really intrigued against Beethoven, as he was accused of having done against Mozart, is something we cannot know but we greatly doubt. Nor was his diatribe against the *Allgemeine Musikalische Zeitung* quite just. At any rate, Beethoven was angry, and the Cassel offer helped to assuage him. He told all his friends about it. The sizable remuneration, too, might have tempted him, 600 ducats being the equivalent of at least $15,000 today, and that for doing virtually nothing. But he did not really want to go. He did not really want to leave Vienna. To the letter to Breitkopf and Härtel quoted above, he appended a curious postscript:

> Please do not make public anything definite about my appointment in Westphalia until I let you know that I have received my certificate—Accept my good wishes and write to me soon—We shall discuss the question of new works at Leipzig—Of course, a few hints about my leaving Vienna might be inserted in the *Musikalische Zeitung*—and with the addition of a few digs, seeing that people here would never do anything worth mentioning for me—

This postscript is written inside the envelope of the letter. Was he trying to stir up publicity about his leaving Vienna so that he would be urged to stay? On the envelope itself somebody, perhaps a member of the firm of Breitkopf and Härtel who knew Beethoven's mentality, wrote, "Oh, how very interesting!"

He did not have to go: When the news that Beethoven was thinking of signing the Cassel contract spread among his patrons, some of them realized that his departure not only would represent a historic disgrace to Vienna but also would be an ill-advised step for Beethoven himself. He *had* to be retained in Vienna. The way to accomplish this was to assure him of a regular income. An offer competitive to King Jerome's had to be made. It was the Countess Erdödy who organized the contra-Cassel expedition, and it was Gleichenstein, Beethoven's good friend with the legal mind and the precise pen, who drew up the necessary details. There was no doubt a good deal of running about, of conferring, of writing notes, of palace oratory, of consideration of one scheme or another. How Beethoven must have enjoyed it all! In a short time a plan was formulated, a document was drawn up, and subsequently a formal agreement was signed by three of Beethoven's patrons, Archduke Rudolph, Prince Lob-kowitz, and Prince Kinsky. The document is one of the most remarkable testimonials to a composer in the history of music.

In brief, after complimenting the offer from the King of Westphalia, it postulates the necessity that a composer must be allowed to be left undisturbed for "the invention of works of magnitude." For this a financial provision must be made, as well as for the composer's old age.

The document states that Beethoven prefers life in Vienna, having received many proofs of esteem here. He feels such patriotism for his second fatherland that he counts himself an Austrian artist. Therefore persons of high and highest rank have asked him to state under what conditions he would remain in Vienna. These were the conditions he proposed:

1. Beethoven should receive the assurance of an annual salary for life, to which a number of persons of rank might contribute. This salary can be no less than 4000 florins a year, considering the present high cost of living.

2. Beethoven should have freedom to undertake artistic tours, so as to add to his fame and to acquire additional income.

3. It is Beethoven's greatest desire to obtain an official position in His Majesty's service. The title of Imperial Royal Kapellmeister would make him very happy; if it could be obtained for him, he would all the more willingly stay in Vienna. Should at any time his wish come true and he receive a salary from His Majesty, Beethoven would forgo his claim on whatever part of the 4000 florins the imperial salary amounted to. And if the imperial salary were a full 4000 florins, he would forgo the entire subvention.

4. Beethoven desires an assurance from the Court Theater directors or their successors that on Palm Sunday of each year he shall have the use of the Theater-an-der-Wien for a concert for his own benefit. In return for this assurance, Beethoven will obligate himself to arrange and conduct a charity concert every year, or should he be unable to do so, contribute a new composi-tion for such a concert.

The demands were met. The 4000 florins were made up by the following contributions: Archduke Rudolph, 1500; Kinsky, 1800; Lobkowitz, 700.

The agreement was signed by the three men on March 1, 1809. The arch-duke handed Beethoven the document. There was one additional provision, as generous as the whole agreement: should Beethoven be prevented from practic-ing his art by sickness or accident or old age, the three participants guaranteed him the salary for life nonetheless. The only pledges Beethoven had to give were to remain in Vienna or in a city in the Austrian monarchy, and to undertake only short artistic or business trips, for which the participants had to be consulted in advance and give their consent.

Several points of the agreement deserve to be commented upon:

1. The 4000 florins represented about $2400, or less than a sixth of the Cassel offer. Yet it was enough to make Beethoven stay.

2. Neither Lichnowsky nor Rasoumovsky contributed, and these two were as close to Beethoven as the three others. Rasoumovsky may not have wanted to contribute because he was Russian and did not consider Vienna his permanent domicile. But the absence of Lichnowsky is inexplicable. Smashed bust or not, their relations were as cordial as ever, and after all he was Beethoven's first and staunchest patron. Nor had he suffered any financial reverses.

3. Archduke Rudolph and Kinsky were the chief contributors, Lobkowitz the least. That may have been because so many demands were being made on his purse that he was beginning to feel pinched for ready money. Yet the disparity is curious.

4. Kinsky, the generous one, probably did not know Beethoven personally and did what he did merely for the sake of art. At least, Kinsky is not mentioned in Beethoven's letters or notes. He seems to have met him only seven years later.

5. Surely none of the three thought that Beethoven could handle the duties of an Imperial Kapellmeister, the sort of duties which a Salieri performed. But perhaps Rudolph felt he might obtain the title as an honorary measure by using influence on his brother. If so, he was due to be disappointed, for Beethoven never received official recognition from the Emperor.

6. The three were in no position to guarantee Beethoven a performance in the Theater-an-der-Wien for a benefit concert. In the official agreement this clause was omitted.

It was a high-minded gesture these three men made, even when one recognizes that the amounts involved were far less than the moneys they spent on their stables. It was a delicately conceived salute to music. It was a generous tribute to Beethoven, whether or not the princes knew that they were carving for themselves a memorial as enduring as marble. That it did not in the end work out altogether satisfactorily was not their fault.

The document was signed. Beethoven was elated. He could now devote himself to his next "invention of works of magnitude," the *Emperor Concerto*. That is, he could have done so had not war interfered once more.

Vienna bombarded, the night of May 11, 1809 (Austrian National Library).

CHAPTER 15

SECOND OCCUPATION
OF VIENNA

It was merely a question of time before Napoleon would again move toward that inchoate foe of his, so vast in territory, so rich in coal and minerals, so arrogant in its ruling house, the Austrian monarchy. Emperor Franz knew it. So did his advisers. Without Austria utterly prostrate, France could not exercise that complete hegemony of the European continent which was Napoleon's goal. Franz and his war cabinet, among whom a new diplomat, Metternich, became important, saw the threat. From any or all of the four cardinal points the foe could strike: from the west through conquered Prussia, from the north through conquered Poland and a Russia with whose Czar Napoleon had made an uneasy alliance in 1808, from the south through conquered Italy. In the east there were always the Turks. One had to prepare for war. War was inevitable. Exhausted as she was, Austria came to this conclusion. In June, 1808, the Austrian State Guard, the *Landwehr,* was created, which was to fight the *Grande Armée.* In addition, Austria sought help from Britain, who agreed to send an expedition and money. After sparring for a little time, Emperor Franz declared war on February 8, 1809, perhaps more out of fear than conviction.

Some of the Austrian leaders, including Lobkowitz, who stood high in the council of war, were sure that they could at least prevent Napoleon from succeeding in another occupation, and the more optimistic felt that with England's help and with the possibility of seducing Russia to its side, Austria had a chance to win. At first it seemed so. Austrian troops marched against Poland and occupied Warsaw on April 22. But once again experience had not taught them to evaluate the Corsican general properly. Once again, like a tragic play repeated with the same cast, Napoleon became the quick victor. He reached the outskirts of Vienna as early as May, 1809.

But now, unlike four years previously, the decision was taken to defend the city. Day and night the bastions were strengthened by stones dug from the pavements. The portals were rammed closed by wooden fortifications. The cannons were in place. Artillery soldiers stood on the walls carrying burning torches, ready to hurl them into the camps of the enemy. While the Viennese took their usual walks on the Glacis and gaped, the suburbs were ordered closed, the barest kind of communication being kept up by using ladders to scale the walls, and the people of the inner city became captives in their own city.

Dipping once more into Rosenbaum's diary, one reads with a mixture of pity and irritation the preparations for the defense of the city, undertaken in typical Viennese fashion at the last moment and superficially. How amateurish they seem, how inadequate! Characteristically Viennese is his statement that all arms which could be found were pressed into service, including the guns, lances, halberds and sabers from the property rooms of the Court Theaters. (Entry of May 6.) Napoleon's army did not need theater properties as arms. They had come prepared with heavy and efficient bombs.

A few days before the bombardment started, on May 4, the Empress had left Vienna with the entire Imperial Family. Archduke Rudolph accompanied her, and Beethoven commemorated his departure with the famous first movement of the Sonata Op. 81a, which we know as *Les Adieux*. The manuscript bears this inscription in Beethoven's hand: "The Farewell [*Das Lebewohl,* which Beethoven preferred to the French title as being more personal], Vienna, May 4, 1809, on the departure of His Imperial Highness the revered Archduke Rudolph." The slow movement of the sonata, composed during Rudolph's absence from Vienna, he titled *Die Abwesenheit* (The Absence). The joyful last movement, *Das Wiedersehen* (The Return), he composed in 1810, and marked the manuscript "The Arrival of His Imperial Highness the revered Archduke Rudolph, January 30, 1810."

The night of May 11 was hellish. Rosenbaum wrote:

> At a quarter past nine the French began their bombardment and fired incessantly until midnight; then a little less until three o'clock. Not until dawn did they cease. Our batteries shot off a few shots; they were ineffective. Terrible it was to see all the fires. The poor city suffered so because nobody was really prepared, nobody had foreseen such a misfortune. Everything was covered with

glass splinters; you could not walk ... People tried to find refuge in our cellar. I had nothing but my light robe on, I was freezing. With a thousand words of encouragement, I tried to quiet the moaning mob. From time to time I went up to the street, to the *Graben,* to see how far the pernicious fires had spread and how our house could be saved. I gathered all my people together to carry water, and our house was saved.

This is another contemporary description of that fearful night:

> In the morning, everybody in the suburbs was as still as a mouse ... In the city, the people tried to pass the hours and lighten their fears by swapping jokes. When night fell, it became quieter and quieter. The noise of the far-off shelling subsided. We sat down to supper with a will. As the plates for the first course were being served, we heard detonations. We looked out of the window and we saw, sailing through a starless night sky, black objects which trailed fiery tails behind them. Suddenly such a body descended from the air, danced in great hops on the granite pavement, and—whoever had stood at the window was now lying on the ground. A sixty-pound bomb had exploded. As the autumn wind shakes the tree, so did the air pressure shake the whole street. The windows shattered. We heard the chimes from the Stephansdom, ten o'clock ... A few shadowy figures groped along the houses to escape the bombardment ...*

Beethoven's quarters in the Walfischgasse were directly in line of the shell-fire. According to Ries, he took refuge in the cellar of the house of his brother Carl, "where he covered his head with pillows" to save his ears from the loud noise of the bursting shells. This statement is contradicted by recent findings of Josef Bergauer,** which indicate that Beethoven took refuge in the house of Ignaz Franz Castelli, a very successful Viennese poet whom Beethoven liked. His house was in the Ballgasse No. 4. It is my opinion that this is the more likely version; first, because Beethoven had just quarreled with Carl—writing to Johann on March 29 that he wished "our other worthy brother" would acquire some feeling instead of his "heartlessness"—and second, because the Ballgasse was nearer to Beethoven's lodgings.

The next day Vienna capitulated. The garrison of 16,000 troops, the few hundred students, and the *Landwehr* proved no match for the French army. At half past two in the afternoon the white flag was run up.

---

* Friedrich Anton von Schönholz, *Traditionen zur Charakteristik Oesterreichs.*
** *Tracing the Paths of Famous Men of Vienna,* 1949.

The French soldiers who now marched in were no longer ill dressed, as they had been four years before. They were "magnificently equipped through the wealth pressed from half of Europe, well nourished at the cost of the ruined Austrian peasant." While they disposed themselves in elegant camps around the city and bathed luxuriously, food and drink "disappeared from Viennese mouths to be plunged into the seemingly inexhaustible abyss of a hundred thousand Gallic stomachs"—Schönholz. Business and commerce came to a standstill. Communication with the rest of the country was cut off. The Prater, the Augarten, and Schönbrunn were closed. Beethoven, who at that season of the year was accustomed to seeking the peace of the woods, was confined in a city in which the prices of whatever food could still be bought doubled, tripled, quadrupled day by day, while the value of money, now almost all paper, sank. So terrible was this progression that the occupying French government itself took fright and finally opened the captured granaries. It was then discovered that the flour had mildewed to such an extent that as one chewed the bread baked from it one had to sneeze. The Stephansplatz became the center of the black market. Every French soldier came there to buy and sell plundered objects. The Viennese now called the Stephansplatz "The Exchange." Only the vendors of the little hot Vienna sausages were able to do business: they had somehow managed to hide their supplies and appeared on the streets a few hours after the occupation.

Once again the *Wiener Zeitung* became a French organ and displayed Napoleon's eagle on its front page. On May 20 the newspaper stated:

> The consequence of the short opposition with which the demand for capitulation on the eleventh had been met would have been unpleasant had it taken place with any other conquering army. But Emperor Napoleon acts like a father to everyone, even to the peoples against whose armies and leaders he is forced to make war.

Caught in the siege and the occupation was a young man who was to become Austria's national poet, Franz Grillparzer. He had met Beethoven the year before in Döbling and was to become one of Beethoven's staunchest friends. Years later (in 1861) Thayer interviewed him. Thayer wrote:

> Mme Grillparzer, mother of the poet, was a lady of great taste and culture, and was fond of music. She used to stand outside her door in order to enjoy Beethoven's playing, as she did not then know of his aversion to listeners. One

day Beethoven, springing from his piano to the door to see if anyone were listening, unfortunately discovered her there. Despite her messages to him through his servant that her door into the common passageway would remain locked, and that her family would use another, Beethoven played no more.

Now virtually all of Beethoven's friends had left the city. There was hardly anybody to whom he could turn for comfort. Kinsky and his family, Prince Lobkowitz, the Lichnowskys, and Waldstein had all left, some to the war, some to their estates. The Countess Erdödy took refuge probably in Croatia. Breuning did remain. Bigot and Marie had gone off to Paris, and Beethoven was never to see them again. Even Zmeskall had fled to safety. Fortunately the first payment of his new annuity had been delivered, and he could use this and the money which was coming in from the publishers to buy food.

Napoleon levied enormous tributes on the city, nearly ten million florins. Again taxes were raised on all possessions and on rents. A note in Beethoven's handwriting on the margin of a musical manuscript reads: "From ten to one thousand florins a quarter—all resident or parties to rent-contracts without distinction." Rosenbaum noted the same in his diary on July 28: a quarter of rentals (ranging up to 1000 Fls.) had to be paid as a "forced loan" within forty-eight hours. Higher rents were taxed half the amount (up to 4000 Fls.), and above 4000 the tax rose to two-thirds. For many householders this was tantamount to bankruptcy. Respectable families began to beg openly in the streets, grouped around a little table on which a plate was placed. Only those who had things to sell did well. Among them was Johann van Beethoven. With the impartiality of the merchant, he supplied the French as well as the Austrian troops with medicines. Napoleon had placed an embargo on English tin, and by luck Johann's pharmaceutical supplies were stored in tin containers. He transferred them to earthenware and sold off the tin, laying a foundation for his future wealth.

There was little "fraternization" this time. Even the "leftish" aristocrats who had flirted with the ideas of the French Revolution now turned Habsburgian. Their women, by and large, no longer found the French attractive. Napoleon knew this, and in connection with the negotiations for the exchange of the captured French general Durosnel, he said, "If anything happens to Durosnel, I will have all the Austrian prisoners massacred. No, they are innocent. I will have my drum corps rape all the Viennese ladies."

Yet suddenly the city, dull with the weight of defeat, gray with fear, its lively gait slowed to a conspirator's creep, was illumined by a bright ray. The news, penetrating only as rumors, seemed incredible. Whitsuntide had come; it was a bright spring Sunday when the Viennese heard the noise of cannon far away, then heard it in increasing frequency and force. There was a battle going on somewhere. From the roofs of the houses the people strained to see from where the noise was coming. It was the battle of Aspern. It raged for two days (May 21 and 22). Archduke Carl had massed the Austrian forces in that field on the banks of the Danube and attacked the main part of the French bivouacking army with the kind of feint and thrust he had learned from his enemy. Archduke Carl was perhaps the only thoroughly capable Austrian general; he emerged victorious at Aspern. (As was characteristic of Austrian politics, he was dismissed from his post in July through intrigues.) For the first time, then, the invincible *Armée* had suffered a defeat. But Napoleon rallied the armies, devised a new plan, and in a series of terrible battles at Znaim, and decisively at Wagram (July 5 and 6), reconquered what he had lost, and held Vienna in a tighter grip than ever.

Rosenbaum recalls the misery of the new defeat:

> July 6. At two in the night the battle began anew. I cannot sleep nor eat. Our misfortune is certain ... We pressed through to the Rennweg [one of Vienna's principal streets] through the mass of the wounded and came to the Linien Wall. There we found everything unfortunately confirmed ... Our retreat is precipitous. [I counted] twenty-one officers—among them they had only four-teen uninjured feet ... Devastating is the sight of so much misery ... At the B Th [Burgtheater] today there were at the beginning [of the performance] three people, later seven. The receipts were eleven florins ... I passed an almost sleepless night.

A week later an armistice was declared and its conditions posted for all the Viennese to read. On August 4 Metternich became Chief Minister of Austria. Both he and Archduke Carl had warned that "Austria's military preparedness had been completely inadequate." Napoleon now was at his zenith—and Vienna got ready to celebrate, willingly or not, his birthday on August 13. It is instructive to contrast Rosenbaum's entry with the official report of the birthday celebration in the *Wiener Zeitung*. Rosenbaum: "August 18. My thoughts during the illumination on the 13th: Long live the Emperor! My little lamp too is burning because that is the law. FORCE! Viennese, do not light your lamps! You can see your misery without light!" *Wiener Zeitung*, August 16: "The

Napoleon festivities took place in brilliant and glad fashion . . . People sang in the streets. There was not the slightest disorder. Not since the time of Joseph has there been a festival so universally celebrated. Never before has there been seen such a great crowd, happy and decently behaved."

All this time Beethoven was continuing to work on what was to be the last of his piano concertos, the *Emperor*. This proud, bold, ringing work has nothing to do with defeat or victory; it is rather an expression of the spirit which permeates the *Eroica,* an assertion of that belief in humanity which was so strong in Beethoven that even hiding in a cellar could not diminish it. *"Emperor"* is not his title for the work, nor was he concerned with the Emperor who now ruled in Vienna.

Perhaps by way of contrast Beethoven in the same period completed as well the charming Quartet No. 10, E-flat Major, Op. 74, the *Harp Quartet,* so called because of the dreamy arpeggios which occur in the first movement.

On July 26, 1809, he wrote to Breitkopf and Härtel, saying that he had suffered misery in a concentrated form:

> Normally I should now be having a change of scene and air—The levies are beginning this very day—What a destructive, disorderly life I see and hear around me, nothing but drums, cannons, and human misery in every form . . . (A-220).

He asked his publishers for some money, as well as for some music, and scores of other composers: Mozart's *Requiem,* Haydn's Masses, Johann Sebastian Bach, Emanuel Bach, and so on. Not long after, he wrote again asking for editions of Goethe's and Schiller's complete works. "These two poets are my favorites, as are also Ossian and Homer, though unfortunately I can read the latter only *in translations.*" And on September 19: "Curse this war!" he exclaimed—and also asked for the works of Wieland. Previously he had thanked the publishers for sending him "the really beautifully translated tragedies of Euripides."

Thus in the stringently restrictive days of the French occupation Beethoven occupied himself with literature—when he was not busy with his music or in copying off some extracts from theoretical works for use in the instruction of Archduke Rudolph. Unable to take the long walks he wanted,* with hardly

---

* Thayer believed that late in the summer Beethoven did manage to get away from the city for visits to Baden and Hungary. Neither of these visits can be documented.

anybody in the mood to make music, no doubt disgusted with the mendacious twaddle that the *Wiener Zeitung* served to its readers, he spent time with his favorite authors. Indeed, it was now easier for him to get whatever books he wanted. Napoleon, still appearing as the champion of a free press, counter-manded the Austrian censorship regulations. On July 19 the *Wiener Zeitung* announced: "All persons who have forbidden books on deposit at the former Censorship Bureau may now claim these; the Bureau is commanded to restore them." On the 26th: "Because of the new decree, all those books are now for sale in Vienna and all those plays may be performed which are for sale or are performed in German states." For the first time *Don Carlos* was performed in Vienna, on August 23. Court Director Hartl planned two further important new productions, one of Schiller's *Wilhelm Tell*—certainly an indication that censorship was relaxed altogether, for the play is a call to freedom, the Swiss shaking off the yoke of the oppressors, the oppressors being the Austrians!— and one of Goethe's *Egmont.* According to Czerny, Beethoven was anxious to write the incidental music for the production of *Tell.* But Gyrowetz was en-trusted with the music for *Tell,* while Beethoven was asked to write the music for *Egmont,* a play "supposed to be less adaptable to music . . . It turned out, however, that he could make masterly music for this drama also, and he applied the full power of his genius to it." Egmont, like Tell, is a champion of liberty; opposing the tyrant Duke of Alva he meets death on the scaffold, but his spirit lives on in the people. Beethoven wrote ten numbers for *Egmont* (including the famous Overture) and finished the composition in 1810.

It was fortunate that Haydn did not survive to experience this summer of discontent. He died on May 31, 1809, in his seventy-eighth year. He was buried on June 1. Rosenbaum was one of the many who were invited to the funeral. He described Haydn as "lying in a large room, clothed in black, looking very lifelike. At his feet lay the seven honor medallions, from Paris, Russia, Sweden, etc., and his honorary citizenship of Vienna." Rosenbaum's wife sang at the requiem. We do not know whether Beethoven attended the funeral.

Negotiations for peace began some time in July, 1809, but peace did not come about until October 14, so difficult proved the negotiations which would allow Austria some kind of existence, if only that of an invalid. One of Napoleon's demands was the razing of Vienna's fortifications. Two days after the treaty was signed the French engineers began to drill shafts in the wall, fill them with gunpowder, and detonate it. Did Beethoven again flee from the noise? We do not know, but on November 2 he wrote to Breitkopf and Härtel:

We are enjoying a little peace after violent destruction, after suffering every hardship that one could conceivably endure—I worked for a few weeks in succession, but it seemed to me more *for death* than for *immortality* ... (A-228).

He asked: "What do you say to this *dead peace?*"

The destruction of the fortification around the city seemed a tragedy then. It eventually made it possible for Vienna to plan its beautiful Ringstrasse in 1865. Emperor Franz returned to Vienna at the end of November. He practically crept back, alone, in a simple equipage. Before him many members of the aristocracy, including some of Beethoven's patrons, had returned to the city.

While the French soldiers were still occupying Vienna, Beethoven had a visitor who has left us a famous account of the occasion. His name was Louis-Philippe-Joseph Girod de Vienney. He was in the diplomatic service. A year after the Vienna occupation he was created a baron of the French Empire, Baron de Trémont. Though he was but thirty, he had acquired a wide knowledge of music and knew Beethoven's music well. A man of means, hospitable and generous, he entertained at his home in Paris many famous musicians, both French and foreign. His "Musical Reunions" were celebrated affairs. Did any of these musical experiences equal the satisfaction he obtained when through his own persistence and tact he became friendly with Beethoven? Baron Trémont published a diary of five volumes, which is preserved in the National Library in Paris. The passages pertinent to Beethoven were first published by Michael Brevet in the *Guide Musicale* in 1892. I give some of the passages here as they were reprinted in Sonneck's *Beethoven: Impressions of Contemporaries.*

Although my departure was hurried, I made up my mind that in case the army should take Vienna I must not neglect the opportunity to see Beethoven. I asked Cherubini to give me a letter to him. "I will give you one to Haydn," he replied, "and that excellent man will make you welcome; but I will not write to Beethoven; I should have to reproach myself that he refused to receive some one recommended by me; he is an unlicked bear!"

Thereupon I addressed myself to Reicha. [Composer and friend of Beethoven; living in Paris since 1808.] "I imagine," said he, "that my letter will be of no use to you. Since the establishment of the Empire in France, Beethoven has detested the Emperor and the French to such a degree that Rode, the finest violinist in Europe, while passing through Vienna on his way to Russia, remained a week in that city without succeeding in obtaining admission to him. He is morose, ironical, misanthropic; to give you an idea of how careless he is of convention it will suffice to tell you that the Empress sent him a request to visit her one morning; he responded that he would be occupied all that day, but would try to come the day after."

This information convinced me that any efforts to approach Beethoven would be vain. I had no reputation, nor any qualification which might impress him; a repulse seemed all the more certain because I entered Vienna after its second bombardment by the French army, and besides, was a member of Napoleon's Council.

However, I intended to try.

I wended my way to the inapproachable composer's home, and at the door it struck me that I had chosen the day ill, for, having to make an official visit thereafter, I was wearing the every-day habiliments of the Council of State. To make matters worse, his lodging was next the city wall, and as Napoleon had ordered its destruction, blasts had just been set off under his windows.

The neighbors showed me where he lived: "He is at home (they said), but he has no servant at present, for he is always getting a new one, and it is doubtful whether he will open."

I rang three times, and was about to go away, when a very ugly man of ill-humored mien opened the door and asked what I wanted.

"Have I the honor of addressing M. de Beethoven?"—"Yes, Sir! But I must tell you," he said to me in German, "that I am on very bad terms with French!"—"My acquaintance with German is no better, Sir, but my message is limited to bringing you a letter from M. Reicha in Paris."—He looked me over, took the letter, and let me in. His lodging, I believe, consisted of only two rooms, the first one having an alcove containing the bed, but small and dark, for which reason he made his toilet in the second room, or salon. Picture to yourself the dirtiest, most disorderly place imaginable—blotches of moisture covered the ceiling; an oldish grand piano, on which the dust disputed the place with various pieces of engraved and manuscript music; under the piano (I do not exaggerate) an unemptied *pot de nuit;* beside it, a small walnut table accustomed to the frequent overturning of the secretary placed upon it; a quantity of pens encrusted with ink, compared wherewith the proverbial tavern-pens would shine; then more music. The chairs, mostly cane-seated, were covered with plates bearing the remains of last night's supper, and with wearing apparel, etc. Balzac or Dickens would continue this description for two pages, and then would they fill as many more with a description of the dress of the illustrious composer; but, being neither Balzac nor Dickens, I shall merely say, I was in Beethoven's abode.

I spoke German only as a traveller on the highways, but understood it somewhat better. His skill in French was no greater. I expected that, after reading my letter, he would dismiss me, and that our acquaintance would end then and there. I had seen the bear in his cage; that was more than I had dared hope for. So I was greatly surprised when he again inspected me, laid the letter unopened on the table, and offered me a chair; still more surprised, when he started a conversation. He wanted to know what uniform I wore, my age, my office, the aim of my journey; if I were a musician, if I intended to stay in Vienna. I answered, that Reicha's letter would explain all that much better than I could.

"No, no, tell me," he insisted, "only speak slowly, because I am very hard of hearing, and I shall understand you."

I made incredible conversational efforts, which he seconded with good will; it was a most singular medley of bad German on my part and bad French on his. But we managed to understand each other; the visit lasted nearly three-quarters of an hour, and he made me promise to come again. I took my leave, feeling prouder than Napoleon when he entered Vienna. I had made the conquest of Beethoven!

Do not ask how I did it. What could I answer? The reason can be sought only in the *bizarrerie* of his character. I was young, conciliatory and polite, and a stranger to him; I contrasted with him; for some unaccountable reason he took a fancy to me, and, as these sudden likings are seldom passive, he arranged several meetings with me during my stay in Vienna, and would improvise an hour or two for me alone. When he happened to have a servant he told her not to open when the bell rang, or (if the would-be visitor heard the piano) to say that he was composing and could not receive company.

Some musicians with whom I became acquainted were slow to believe it. "Will you believe me," I told them, "if I show you a letter he has written me in French?" — "In French? that's impossible! he hardly knows any, and he doesn't even write German legibly. He is incapable of such an effort!" — I showed them my proof. "Well, he must be madly in love with you," they said; "what an inexplicable man!"

This letter — so precious an object to me — I have had framed....

I maintain that unless one has heard him improvise well and quite at ease, one can but imperfectly appreciate the vast scope of his genius. Swayed wholly by the impulse of the moment, he sometimes said to me, after striking a few chords: "Nothing comes into my head; let's put it off till — —." Then we would talk philosophy, religion, politics, and especially of Shakespeare, his idol, and always in a language that would have provoked the laughter of any hearers.

Beethoven was not a man of *esprit,* if we mean by that term one who makes keen and witty remarks. He was by nature too taciturn to be an animated conversationalist. His thoughts were thrown out by fits and starts, but they were lofty and generous, though often rather illogical. Between him and Jean-Jacques Rousseau there was a bond of erroneous opinion springing from the creation, by their common misanthropic disposition, of a fanciful world bearing no positive relation to human nature and social conditions. But Beethoven was well-read. The isolation of celibacy, his deafness, and his sojournings in the country, had led him to make a study of the Greek and Latin authors and, enthusiastically, of Shakespeare. Taking this in conjunction with the kind of singular, though genuine, interest which results from wrong notions set forth and maintained in all good faith, his conversation was, if not specially magnetic, at least original and curious. And, as he was well affected towards me, by a whimsey of his atrabilious character he preferred that I should sometimes contradict him rather than agree with him on every point.

When he felt inclined to improvisation on the day appointed, he was sublime. His tempestuous inspiration poured forth lovely melodies, and harmonies unsought because, mastered by musical emotion, he gave no thought to the search after effects that might have occurred to him with pen in hand; they were produced spontaneously without divagation.

As a pianist, his playing was incorrect and his mode of fingering often faulty, whence it came that the quality of tone was neglected. But who could think of the pianist? He was absorbed in his thoughts, and his hands had to express them as best they might.

I asked him if he would not like to become acquainted with France. "I greatly desired to do so," he replied, "before she gave herself a master. Now, my desire has passed. For all that, I should like to hear Mozart's symphonies—(he mentioned neither his own nor those of Haydn)—in Paris; I am told that they are played better at the Conservatoire than anywhere else. Besides, I am too poor to take a journey out of pure curiosity and probably requiring great speed."—"Come with me, I will take you along."—"What an idea! I could not think of allowing you to go to such expense on my account."—"Don't worry about that, there's no expense; all my charges for the post are defrayed, and I am alone in my carriage. If you would be satisfied with a single small room, I have one at your disposal. Only say yes. It's well worth your while to spend a fortnight in Paris; your sole expense will be for the return journey, and less than fifty florins will bring you home again."—"You tempt me; I shall think it over."

Several times I pressed him to make a decision. His hesitation was always a result of his morose humor. "I shall be overrun by visitors!"—"You will not receive them."—"O-verwhelmed by invitations!"—"Which you will not accept."—"They will insist that I play, that I compose!"—"You will answer that you have no time."—"Your Parisians will say that I am a bear."—"What does that matter to you? It is evident that you do not know them. Paris is the home of liberty, of freedom from social conventions. Distinguished men are accepted there exactly as they please to show themselves, and should one such, especially a stranger, be a trifle eccentric, that contributes to his success."

Finally, he gave me his hand one day and said that he would come with me. I was delighted—again from vanity, no doubt. To take Beethoven to Paris, to have him in my own lodgings, to introduce him to the musical world, what a triumph was there!—but, to punish me for my pleasurable anticipations, the realization was not to follow them.

The armistice of Znaim caused us to occupy Moravia, whither I was sent as intendant. I remained there four months; the Treaty of Vienna having given this province to Austria, I returned to Vienna, where I found Beethoven still of the same mind; I was expecting to receive the order for my return to Paris, when I received one to betake myself immediately to Croatia as intendant. After spending a year there, I received my appointment to the prefecture of l'Aveyron, together with an order to wind up an affair at Agram with which I had also been charged, and then to travel in all haste to Paris to render an account of my mission before proceeding to my new destination. So I could neither pass through Vienna nor revisit Beethoven.

His mind was much occupied with the greatness of Napoleon, and he often spoke to me about it. Through all his resentment I could see that he admired his rise from such obscure beginnings; his democratic ideas were flattered by it. One day he remarked, "If I go to Paris, shall I be obliged to salute your emperor?" I assured him that he would not, unless commanded for an audience, "And do you think he would command me?" — "I do not doubt that he would, if he appreciated your importance; but you have seen in Cherubini's case that he does not know much about music." — This question made me think that, despite his opinions, he would have felt flattered by any mark of distinction from Napoleon. Thus does human pride bow down before that which flatters it. . . .

The baron wrote an excellent, and apparently a just, account.

The fateful year of 1809 ended with Metternich's great *coup.* He acted as a marriage broker to form a political alliance. Time was what he and Austria needed, and time was what he gained by the union of Napoleon to Emperor Franz's daughter. So improbable a result could not have been achieved without Napoleon's own fantastic dynastic ambitions. Being King was not enough. Commanding Europe from the southern tip of Portugal to the Baltic Sea was not enough. He needed to continue his glorification by handing to a son the crown he had set upon his own head. Josephine was unable to bear him children. At first Napoleon thought that the fault was his. However, when his mistress, the beautiful Eleonore de la Plaigne, bore him a son, his doubts were resolved. He divorced Josephine and now looked around for a new wife, who of course had to be chosen from an imperial family: only two royal houses really measured up, those of Austria and Russia. The Czar remained cool to the idea, but Metternich persuaded Franz that one of Franz's daughters, the young Marie Louise, would serve the purpose admirably. A union between Austria and Napoleon was most desirable, if for no other reason than to give Austria time to lick its wounds. On March 11, 1810, Marie Louise was married to Napoleon by proxy. Metternich, as he wrote to Prince Schwarzenberg, had no illusions that this marriage could fundamentally change "Napoleon's system of subjugation." But it gained a respite for Austria.

Like Marie Antoinette forty years before, Marie Louise journeyed to Paris, accompanied by 300 attendants traveling in eighty-three equipages. At the border, Napoleon's wedding gifts were presented to her, including 500,000 francs in gold. As soon as she arrived, Napoleon consummated the marriage, ignoring the travel fatigue that Marie Louise felt. Though he had married her for the sake of procreating children — "I am marrying a belly," he had expressed it — he fell in love with her. He was forty, balding, and corpulent; she was eighteen, pretty, and heartless.

For the next three and a half years Beethoven lived in an atmosphere of an armed and suspicious truce. Napoleon, the new bridegroom, despised his father-in-law. The father-in-law and his coldly calculating minister bided their time.

In such an atmosphere the fullness of music which Beethoven's three patrons expected and for which they had given him a lifelong mandate did not come forth as copiously as that of previous years would have led one to anticipate. What he composed was created only in intermittent issue, with considerable pauses between the wondrous creations. Kinsky did not live to hear any of them. Lobkowitz heard only three. Archduke Rudolph, being younger and living longer, had a better opportunity to assure himself, as he looked back on Beethoven's achievement, that the money had not been "wasted"; but even he must have wondered why his teacher did not put notes on paper at the rate he used to.

That is not to say that the period from 1811 to 1820 or 1821 was barren: one could hardly characterize a period in which the Seventh and Eighth Symphonies, the Trio Op. 97, and others were composed as fruitless. It is to say that this period does not compare to that astonishing play of the fountain which spurted forth with the *Eroica* and lasted till *Egmont*.

Why the decrease?

Two reasons are possible: first, that Beethoven was seeking to express new thoughts; as the thoughts of the older man became more profound, the voicing of them became more difficult. That would be true particularly of his instrumental (piano, violin) and chamber music. Second, that the troubles with his nephew which began in 1816 sapped his energies.

Even before that, however, there came years when the winds blew harshly and the climate was inclement. His music was not time-bound, but *he* was. He could escape temporary detonations, but not the general exhaustion of Vienna, not the devaluation of the money, not the more difficult "economics of music" (his expression), not the frowns of his worried patrons, not, as he wrote in December, 1809, the "melancholy reminders of this German country which has so declined *partly through its own fault, I admit.*"

Conditions improved again, eventually. Vienna rose; Beethoven rose; yet some fatigue of war remained. It had a greater effect on Beethoven than his biographers have accounted for.

CHAPTER 16

BEETHOVEN
AS A MATURE MAN

As Beethoven grew older the mystic component in him grew stronger, the worldly grew weaker. By necessity he had long ago renounced the dazzle and delight of virtuosity with which in his young days he forced even professional musicians to be "all ears when he plays." Yet even had there been no necessity, had ears and hands retained their services, his genius would have led him to mine among the regions where the wellsprings of human thought are to be discovered—or thrown him up among the stars.

As an artist his career could be compared to Michelangelo's as he proceeded from the young "David," a work of bold virtuosity, to the final and unfinished "Pietà." As a man, now in his forties, he raised his sight upward more and more frequently; when he lowered it, he became more and more impatient, cantankerous, obstreperous, unreasonable. Several contemporaries remarked on his *"Blick nach oben,"* his glance upward. When he did see what was going on around him, he often saw it wrong.

We have observed that as a young man his imagination was so nimble that his first task was one of rigorous selection. In the Sketchbooks, themes and fragments are set down sufficient for several times nine symphonies. Even when he alighted on an idea which he determined as useful, its first form was often casual and sometimes spineless. Evolution, concentration, and clarification were the quintessential ingredients of Beethoven's working process. That process was a slow, painful, and truculent one. The pages of his Sketchbooks and even many pages of his finished manuscripts look like battlefields in which inferior thoughts and ideas fight thoughts and ideas of superior worth. Through disorder he arrived at order. His major compositions are buildings in which an infinity of detail combines to give us a total experience: no superfluous ornament sticks

...rawing for a lost painting by A. Klöber. Beethoven was then forty-eight (Beethoven House, Bonn).

out, no rosette is pasted on. "Seen" from afar or from close up, the work is equally of a piece, a Parthenon in sound, the product of a great thinker who was at the same time a great planner. As he grew older the flood of ideas did not abate. In organizing them he placed requirements on himself which became ever more compelling. The architect built with greater boldness and yet with no less attention to each stone.

It is often said that Beethoven was not a great melodist. This is one of those facile half-truths which are not true at all. When he needs melody, particularly in his lyrical slow movements, he commands it. When he commands it, it possesses the lovely, inward quality which only that artist can conjure whose brain and heart work together in perfect agreement. Neither runs away with the other. When he has finally set his plan, constructing it from the melodic elements supplied by the heart and the dramatic elements supplied by the brain, once he has arrived at the musical scheme which satisfactorily carries his meaning, there is no uncertainty, no turning back. "I am not in the habit of rewriting my compositions," he told Thomson.

As a mature man he cogitates over lofty riddles. He searches the sky and the book. He does not become more "religious" in the churchgoing sense, but turns to mystic and religious thought of diverse cultures. He interests himself in the current Oriental researches, Hindu and Persian literature, the essays of Herder, Hebrew writings, Schiller's essay on the nature of wisdom, "The Mission of Moses," and so on. He copies passages (the provenance of some of which has not been traced) of mystic import. Three sentences he keeps framed under glass on his desk: *

I am that which is.
I am all what is, what was, what will be; no mortal man has lifted my veil.

---

* Schindler wrote that these three sentences are inscriptions in the temple of the goddess Neith at Sais and that Beethoven found them in the writings of Napoleon's great Egyptologist Champollion, the decipherer of the Rosetta stone. It is almost certain that Beethoven could not have read Champollion, since his findings did not become known to laymen till after Beethoven's death.

In his analysis of James Joyce's *Ulysses,* Stuart Gilbert discusses the Smaragdine Table of Hermes Trismegistus. He calls it "one of the most ancient and authoritative records of occultism." The first words of this Table are:

"It is truest and most certain of all things.
"That which is above is as that which is below, and that which is below is as that
    which is above, to accomplish the one thing of all most wonderful."

These words seem to echo the meaning of the three sentences which so impressed Beethoven. The axiom, known in diagrammatic form as Solomon's Seal, postulates that everything existing, from the tiniest atom to the largest and most complex structure, contains within itself all the elements of the entire universe.

He is only and solely of himself, and to this only one all things owe their existence.

These sentences mean little to us. They are murky mysticism. Perhaps they are an expression of the deistic creed, a God in "all things." They must have carried a particular meaning to Beethoven.

With his exploration of various philosophies—the quotations he writes down range from Goethe to Kalidasa's Indian epic work *Sakuntala*—he combines keen interest in the political world around him and in the latest scientific inventions. Jakob Degen, a Swiss living in Vienna, has invented a crude flying machine in 1808. In 1816 he even attempts the construction of a model helicopter. Beethoven is fascinated. He wants to know all about it.

He believes that some form of supreme intelligence exists to order and regulate the physical laws of the world. Because all Nature must obey fixed laws, it follows that Nature herself is a product of supreme wisdom. It is not possible that the universe was created by a haphazard combination of atoms, a chance coming-together. More frequently than in his younger days he calls on the creator of the universe, the "Almighty."

He believes that the structure of animals and plants becomes increasingly complex the farther they live from the sun. Similarly he believes that the spiritual and material characteristics of life on the planets, ranging from Mercury to Uranus and "perhaps even farther should there be such planets," become perfected in proportion to their distance from the sun. He makes a note showing that he is interested in "troglodyte cave-dwellers."

While his mind was constantly expanding, constantly learning something new, constantly being stimulated by books, newspaper reports and examination of musical scores, his character was, so to speak, contracting. The factors which etched into his character were principally two: his increasing deafness and the uncertainty of his income. From the first sprang his tendency to isolate himself. There were moments when this sociable man became *menschenscheu* (to use the expressive German word), "shy of humanity." Never a misanthrope, sometimes he was a man who pulled down the shutters and sat in the dark. Then he seemed purposely to neglect his appearance and forget his manners.

The variability of his earnings and the economic depression through which he lived, the inability to know what money was worth the day after he earned it, the instability of the fortunes of his patrons, all these caused in him a mixture of extravagance and penuriousness. He could be generous when he had money,

413

and haggle at the top of his voice over pennies when he felt poor. He often made himself out poorer than he actually was. A side effect of the alternation between very good earnings—and they *were* very good at certain times, such as in 1814—and the dry spells was an envy of other musicians' successes. The envy grew as he became older. No one could criticize him for looking askance at the ubiquitous popularity which Rossini enjoyed: that was too much to bear. But Beethoven was not very kind to Meyerbeer, a beginner.

His nature was so variable, his behavior so changeable, that it is dangerous to describe him: the minute we adduce proof of one characteristic we find proof of the opposite. There was no logic to Beethoven's makeup. For example, his appearance. Though he preferred an old shabby coat to a new one (according to Bettina), he wrote to Zmeskall on October 28, 1810:

> Please let me have the recipe for boot polish. A well polished head needs also a well polished boot—No doubt the thing can be done without the help of your servant, with whom once and for all I don't want to have anything to do, never mind why—
>
> In haste, your
> BEETHOVEN (A-282).

He wore a blue frock coat with brass buttons, the flaps of which were open to the wind. But they were well anchored, for in the pockets he carried his Conversation Book (after 1819), a Sketchbook, and a heavy thick pencil, like a carpenter's pencil. He liked such a pencil because it didn't break easily. His spectacles hung from a chain.* Sometimes he would wind a large kerchief around his neck.

A young engraver, Blasius Höfel by name, who worked on an engraving of a portrait made of Beethoven, told Thayer that

> The effect upon him of his pecuniary embarrassments, his various disappoint-ments, and of a mind ill at ease, was very plainly to be seen in his personal habits and appearance. He was at that time much accustomed to dine at an inn where Höfel often saw him in a distant corner, at a table, which though large was avoided by the other guests owing to the very uninviting habits into which he had fallen; the particulars may be omitted. Not infrequently he departed without paying his bill, or with the remark that his brother would settle it; which Carl Caspar did. He had grown so negligent of his person as to appear

---

* He did not use them much in his last ten years.

there sometimes positively "schmutzig" (dirty). Now, however, under the kind care of the Streichers, cheered and inspirited by the glory and emolument of the past eight months, he became his better self again; and—though now and to the end, so careless and indifferent to mere externals as occasionally to offend the sensitiveness of very nice and fastidious people—he again, as before quoted from Czerny, "paid attention to his appearance." (TQ).

Yet at the time he had grown so negligent of his person he was once more busily engaged in looking for a servant. Those endless servant troubles he had! They drag their dirty shoes over the carpet of his life. The couple he employs in 1809, the Herzogs, are "wicked people." Out they go. The servant in 1811 is "a vagabond." He finds another couple in 1813 (Schindler says a tailor, who carries on his trade in the anteroom, and his wife) who stay with him almost three years. In 1816 he has other servants. He dislikes them. The following year he takes a housekeeper (Nanni) and a kitchen-maid (Baberl). They are "stupid." A new cook appears, Peppi. She cooks well. But she is "treacherous" and conspires against him. Out she goes, along with a new housekeeper "the old woman" (Frau D.). They are all "in league against him." His servant makes his way "into other people's rooms with counterfeit keys." He wants one without "murderous tendencies." He has reason to suspect another couple of committing a theft.

There are long calculations as to how much he should pay, including food allowances, charges for livery, "boot money." Beethoven shared this picayune quirk with Kant, who personally locked up the cutlery after meals, and quarreled with his domestics, though in all other respects the philosopher was good nature itself. Nanette Streicher tries to help Beethoven in domestic matters; he gets her to check over the household accounts. He asks questions about how to treat servants:

> What ought one to give 2 servants to eat at dinner and supper both as to quantity and quality?
> How often ought one to give them roast meat?
> Ought they to have it at dinner and supper too?
> That which is intended for the servants, do they have it in common with the victuals of the master, or do they prepare their own separately, i.e., do they have different food from the master?
> How many pounds of meat are to be reckoned for 3 persons?
> What allowance per day do the housekeeper and maid receive?
> How about the washing?

Do the housekeeper and maid get more?
How much wine and beer?
Does one give it to them and when?
Breakfast?

But it is no use. He cannot keep servants, or will not.

Were all his servants malefactors? Hardly. Some probably took advantage of the impractical employer. But others could not stomach his fear of being taken advantage of, the constant suspicions. He was peculiarly stingy with them at times, giving them insufficient money to run the house. When he had to occupy himself with the little annoyances of everyday life, he could display a very unpretty temper.

But his heart could be compassionate. Xaver Schnyder von Wartensee, a Swiss musician, recalled:

> At this moment two Austrian peasants entered the room and showed Beethoven a document. It was a kind of begging letter. The peasants had lost their house in a fire and had received permission from the authorities to collect alms. Beethoven cursed and ranted, growled that something of the sort turned up every minute of the day, went to his writing-desk and took out a great deal of money which, still grumbling, he gave to the peasants, who left the room amidst the most fervent expressions of gratitude and countless bows.

His personal belongings, the few which were not lost, show that they were of good quality. He did not stint on his walking stick, his spectacles, his watches, his pipes—he liked to smoke a peaceful pipe.

He liked to display ornaments on his desk; these were mostly gifts. He bought two little metal figures representing Cossacks and used these statuettes as paperweights. He used a metal handbell. He treasured a figurine of Lucius Brutus, the leader of the Romans against the Tarquins.

When an article did not measure up to his expectations, he could take time to complain:

> Your purchase of a hat has been a failure, for yesterday already, as I came out here very early in the morning, it developed *a tear*. Seeing that this hat cost too much for us to be so horribly swindled, you must see that those people take it back and give you another one. In the meantime you may tell that to those vile *tradespeople;* and I will return it to you—It is really too bad— (A-144).

Beethoven wrote this to Gleichenstein on June 13, 1807, from Baden, while he was wrestling with the problems of the Fifth Symphony!

A good description of him appears in a letter which a young musician—later a teacher—Wilhelm Rust, wrote to his sister in 1808:

> He is as original and singular as a man as are his compositions; usually serious, at times merry but always satirical and bitter. On the other hand he is also very childlike and certainly very sincere. He is a great lover of truth and in this goes too far very often; for he never flatters and therefore makes many enemies. A good fellow played for him and when he was finished Beethoven said to him: "You will have to play a long time before you will realize that you can do nothing."

He could be charming to children. Here is a letter of his, written from Teplitz, to a little girl of whom nothing is known except that she was about eight to ten years old and that she had sent Beethoven a wallet:

> To Emilie M. at H.
>
> TEPLITZ, July 17, 1812
>
> My dear, kind Emilie, my dear Friend!
>
> My reply to your letter to me is late in arriving. My excuse must be a great amount of business and persistent illness. The fact that I am here for the recovery of my health proves the truth of my excuse. Do not rob Handel, Haydn and Mozart of their laurel wreaths. They are entitled to theirs, but I am not yet entitled to one.
>
> Your wallet will be treasured among other tokens of a regard which several people have expressed for me, but which I am still far from deserving.
>
> Persevere, do not only practice your art, but endeavor also to fathom its inner meaning; it deserves this effort. For only art and science can raise men to the level of gods. If, my dear Emilie, you should ever desire to have anything, do not hesitate to write to me. The true artist has no pride. He sees unfortunately that art has no limits; he has a vague awareness of how far he is from reaching his goal; and while others may perhaps be admiring him, he laments the fact that he has not yet reached the point whither his better genius only lights the way for him like a distant sun. I should probably prefer to visit you and your family than to visit many a rich person who betrays a poverty of mind. If I should ever go to H., then I will call on you and your family. I know of no other human excellences than those which entitle one to be numbered among one's better fellow creatures. Where I find people of that tpye, there is my home.
>
> If you want to write to me, dear Emilie, just address your letter to Teplitz where I am staying on for four weeks. Or you may write to Vienna. It really

doesn't matter. Look upon me as your friend and the friend of your family. (A-376).

Wherever we examine Beethoven's personality we find a protean aspect strange and confusing to behold. The thinker behaved often like a naïve jokester. The man who kept complaining about his infirmities could exult in the strength of an athlete. As he tramped through streets and fields with his quick, firm steps he left many a younger companion footsore. As young people loved him, so did he love young people. In 1819 he composed a wedding song for Nanni Giannatasio, then hid during its performance, popped up in glee and barricaded himself behind some chairs to escape the effusive thanks. He liked the poet Castelli, partly because he regaled him with *bons mots* and jokes, the rougher the better. Every time Beethoven met him he asked, "What new stupidities have you got to tell me?" When the music publisher Schlesinger visited Vienna, he gave a splendid dinner to which Beethoven and Castelli were invited. After dinner Beethoven was pressed to play the piano. He refused. Finally he said, "In the name of all the devils, all right, I'll play. But Castelli, who hasn't the faintest idea of music or the piano, must suggest a theme." Castelli went to the piano and picked out four notes at random. Beethoven laughed and said, "Very well." Then he improvised "for an hour by the clock, using the four notes, so that the whole company was transported." *

We have learned how he quarreled with Stephan von Breuning, though the friendship endured to the end of Beethoven's life. When Breuning lost his wife after but a year of marriage, Beethoven wrote to Gleichenstein:

[VIENNA, April, 1809]

Dear, kind Gleichenstein!

I find it impossible to resist my impulse to tell you of my fears about Breuning's hysterical and feverish condition and at the same time to beg you so far as possible to attach yourself to him more closely or, rather, to contrive to draw him more closely to yourself. *My circumstances* allow me far too little time to discharge the supreme duties of friendship. So I beg you, I adjure you in the name of the good and noble feelings you certainly possess, to shoulder the burden of this anxiety which is really torturing me. It would be a very good thing if you could persuade him to accompany you here and there and (however much he may try to spur *you* on to work harder) to restrain him a little from his excessive and, as I 'think, not always absolutely necessary exertions—You

---

* Castelli's *Memoirs*, written *circa* 1860, published by Georg Müller, Munich, 1913.

would hardly believe in what an excited condition I once found him—You will have heard of his outburst of annoyance yesterday—nothing but the result of his dreadful irritability which, unless he checks and controls it, will certainly ruin him—

Hence, my dear Gleichenstein, I am entrusting to your care one of my best and staunchest friends, the more so as your business affairs have already established a kind of connection which you will strengthen still further by frequently making him realize your anxiety for his welfare; and this you can do the more easily because he is really attached to you—But your noble heart, which I know so well, certainly needs no injunctions—Act, therefore, in my interest and in that of your good friend Breuning.

I embrace you with all my heart.   (A-216).

This same man can sound like a jealous actor. Johann Wenzel Tomaschek, music teacher and composer (Goethe preferred his setting of *Mignon's Song* to Beethoven's) wrote copiously about Beethoven in his autobiography.* He reports two conversations about Meyerbeer, who had certainly done Beethoven no harm:

T.—I am told that there is a young foreign artist here who is said to be an extraordinary pianoforte player.

B.—Yes, I, too, have heard of him, but have not heard him. My God! let him stay here only a quarter of a year and we shall hear what the Viennese think of his playing. I know how everything new pleases here.

T.—You have probably never met him?

B.—I got acquainted with him at the performance of my Battle, on which occasion a number of local composers played some instrument. The big drum fell to the lot of that young man. Ha! ha! ha!—I was not at all satisfied with him; he struck the drum badly and was always behindhand, so that I had to give him a good dressing-down. Ha! Ha! Ha!—That may have angered him. There is nothing in him; he hasn't the courage to hit a blow at the right time.

Before the next conversation Meyerbeer's opera *The Two Caliphs* had been given:

T.—Were you at [Meyerbeer's] opera?

B.—No; it is said to have turned out very badly. I thought of you; you hit it when you said you expected little from his compositions. I talked with the opera singers, and that night after the production of the opera at the wine-house where they generally gather, I

---

* Published in the yearbook *Libussa,* Prague, 1847–1849.

said to them frankly: You have distinguished yourselves again! —what piece of folly have you been guilty of again? You ought to be ashamed of yourselves not to know better, nor to be able to judge better, to have made such a noise about this opera! I should like to talk to you about it, but you do not understand me.

T.—I was at the opera; it began with hallelujah and ended with requiem.

B.—Ha, ha, ha, ha, ha! It's the same with his playing. I am often asked if I have heard him—I say no; but from the opinions of my acquaintances who are capable of judging such things I could tell that he has agility indeed, but otherwise is a very superficial person.

T.—I heard that before he went away he played at Herr——'s and pleased much less.

B.—Ha, ha, ha, ha! What did I tell you?—I understand that. Let him settle down here for half a year and then let us hear what will be said of his playing. All this signifies nothing. It has always been known that the greatest pianoforte players were also the greatest composers; but how did they play? Not like the pianists of today, who prance up and down the keyboard with passages which they have practiced—*putsch, putsch, putsch;* —what does that mean? Nothing! When true pianoforte virtuosi played, it was always something homogeneous, an entity; if written down it would appear as a well thought-out work. That is pianoforte playing; the other thing is nothing!   (TQ).

Meyerbeer was a Jew. So were Moscheles, the Schlesingers, and some of the bankers he knew. Beethoven had some curious ideas about Jews: they were not to be trusted and they "cooked badly." Yet his prejudice was mild and inconsequential; he admired Rahel Levin and was fond of Moscheles. Whether about Jews or food, Beethoven gave forth his opinions with an air of finality, and by this time few dared to contradict him. One of his favorite expressions was *"Dixi"* ("I spoke"), and though he meant it half as a joke, he meant it.

His imperious nature peeped out in his humor. The music publisher Sigmund Anton Steiner, who became connected with Beethoven around 1814, he called his "Lieutenant General." Steiner's young associate Tobias Haslinger was "the Adjutant." Diabelli, then employed by the firm, was "Diabolus" and "Provost-Marshal." There was much talk about "court martials" when the firm made mistakes. Beethoven was of course the "Generalissimo" or "Chief General."

As a mature man he had lost none of his love for nature. If anything, his love intensified after the *Pastoral Symphony.* The British pianist Charles Neate spent a part of the summer of 1815 with Beethoven in Baden. The forty-five-year-old composer took a long walk every morning and toward evening. Neate said he never met a man who enjoyed nature so intensely: "Nature was like food to him, he seemed really to live in it." In the summer, when walking in the woods, he used to shed his outer clothing, stripping down to his underpants (Gerhard Breuning was told so by his father).

He said he hated Vienna and its frivolity. Yet he was pleased when a magisterial deputation conferred on him the citizenship of Vienna in December, 1815. He wrote to his old friend Amenda that if Amenda sent him a letter he needed to put no fuller address than "my name."

He felt hurt—justifiably so—that the Imperial Family of Vienna accorded him no official recognition. He loathed Emperor Franz. Dr. Karl von Bursy, a friend of Amenda, reported this conversation in 1816:

> BURSY: Why do you remain in Vienna when every foreign ruler would have to make a place for you near his throne?
> BEETHOVEN: Conditions hold me here, but here things are shabby and niggardly. It could not be worse, from top to bottom everyone is a scoundrel. There is nobody one can trust. What is not down in black and white is not observed by any man, not even by the one with whom you have made an agreement.

Four years after this conversation, Beethoven was still talking politics and was chafing under the absolutism of the Metternich regime. We can surmise this from entries in the Conversation Books by his friends. They deplored conditions in Austria. No doubt they turned the conversation to this subject because they knew that Beethoven was interested, and they gave vent to their feelings because they had before them a man who sympathized. Examples (all from the early part of 1820):

> Entry by Karl Bernard, journalist: Now the Assembly is working on a law which prescribes how high the birds are permitted to fly and how fast the rabbits may run.
> Entry by Franz Oliva, bank employee: The police go into all the bookstores to investigate; even books which have been published in this country are now being prohibited ... Obscurantism is gaining the upper hand in a terrible manner ...
> Karl Peters, teacher, describes Europe under absolutism as "an old torn garment which can no longer be patched up."

He accused others of not living up to agreements. Yet we will have to observe his dubious dealings with the London Philharmonic Society and his doubtful probity with publishers. To be sure, not all the publishers with whom he did business were models of rectitude. Far from it! Still, the publishers could not be blamed for stepping warily. Ordinary honesty he took for granted. He lost his pocketbook containing the receipts of a benefit concert. A passer-by handed it back to him; Beethoven's thanks were casual. He took it as a matter of course.

He was willing, when he felt like it, to compose on commission. But so was every composer of his time—and surely before his time. He was willing, though rarely, to reduce his price: when some Variations offered to a British publisher at £30 proved too dear, he abated the price to £20 "for the sake of our friendship." But if he did *not* feel like it, nothing could induce him to compose in a style uncongenial to him. Major General Alexander Kyd found that out. He had served in India, his health had broken down, and he had come to Vienna to put himself under treatment by the famous Dr. Malfatti. Through him he became acquainted with Dr. Bertolini. Kyd was an ardent musical enthusiast and besought Bertolini to introduce him to Beethoven. Kyd reported his meeting to Jahn and Thayer. He and Bertolini found Beethoven

> shaving and looking shockingly, his ruddy face browned by the Baden sun variegated by razor cuts, bits of paper, and soap. As Kyd seated himself, crash! went the chair. In the course of the interview, the General, showing the common belief of Beethoven's poverty, proposed to him through the Doctor, to compose a symphony for which he would pay him 200 ducats (£100), and secure its performance by the London Philharmonic Society, not doubting that the profits of the work to the composer would thus amount to £1000. He offered also to take him himself to London. To Beethoven's leaving Vienna just now there really seems to have been no serious impediment, other than his nephew; and the boy was certainly in the best of hands so long as he remained with Giannatasio. However, he did not accept the proposition, nor even the order for the Symphony, because Kyd desired to have it rather like the earlier, than the later ones—that is, somewhat shorter, simpler, and more easy of comprehension than these last. (T).

Simrock, the Bonn publisher, confirmed this story to Thayer:

> When I visited Beethoven in Vienna on September 29, 1816, he told me that he had had a visit on the day before from an Englishman who on behalf of the London Philharmonic Society had asked him to compose a symphony for that institution in the style of the first and second symphonies, regardless of cost. ... As an artist he felt himself deeply offended at such an offer and indignantly refused it and thus closed the interview with the intermediary. In his excitement he expressed himself very angrily and with deep displeasure towards a nation which by such an offer had manifested so low an opinion of an artist and art,

which he looked upon as a great insult. When we were passing Haslinger's publishing house in the Graben in the afternoon he stopped suddenly and pointing to a large, powerfully built man who had just entered, cried out: "There's the man whom I threw down stairs yesterday!" (TQ).

Because of his fame he was subjected to pressure not only from those who wanted advice or those who genuinely admired him, but from curiosity-seekers and bores, including once or twice a father who insisted on showing him compositions of his "child genius." The tenor Ludwig Cramolini published this incident: *

One day Beethoven was visited by a certain Count Montecuccoli, who was very musical and is said to have played the oboe with virtuosity. Beethoven was very ill-tempered and did not wish to receive Montecuccoli at all. The Count, however, persisted in his intention and went into the garden where Beethoven was sitting in loud conversation with the maid. Montecuccoli spoke at great length about some composition of Beethoven's, saying that the passage in question could not be played by any oboist as it stood. Beethoven would have to alter it. Beethoven replied sharply: "You, Count, are probably incapable of playing it, but a competent oboist could certainly do so; I therefore advise you to take some lessons—I haven't time to listen to you any longer." Montecuccoli called Beethoven a boor, but in such a way that he could not hear it, and walked away. My mother, who had overheard the whole conversation in a nearby bower, went up to Beethoven and said: "You should be ashamed of yourself, Herr von Beethoven, to receive such a fine gentleman and let him see you in a torn shirt collar and torn cuffs and to treat people so roughly." Beethoven asked her: "Was I really rough with that troublesome ass? I'm delighted to know it. In that case, perhaps, he'll leave me alone in future. But as far as my torn linen is concerned, I beg you to do me the favour of having half a dozen shirts made for me. I'm always forgetting about it, and so is my sister-in-law."

My mother obeyed his wish and whenever he wore one of the new shirts he would say to her: "Well, Frau von Cramolini, I suppose that now you're satisfied with my appearance?"

As we did for the young Beethoven, so may we afford glimpses into the mind of the mature Beethoven by giving a few of his observations, remarks, and thoughts which he wrote down in the years of his maturity: **

---

* How reliable the story is one cannot say; Cramolini was very young when he met Beethoven and the reminiscences were not published till long after Cramolini's death.

** These written soliloquies are for the most part taken from the Fischhoff manuscript.

BEETHOVEN AS A MATURE MAN

1812

You may not live as a man, not for yourself, only for others; for you no happiness exists any longer except that which is created within you, in your art. O God! Give me strength to conquer myself! Nothing may bind me to life—In this way with A.[?] * everything will come to naught.

1813

O terrible circumstances which do not suppress my feeling for domesticity but its fulfillment. O God, God look down on the unfortunate B., let it not last long this way.

In the evening examine everything!

... which he has composed that day.

Occupation is the best thing for not thinking of my malady.

How do you pronounce *Eleison* in Greek? e-le-ison is correct.

Buy everything in advance to prevent the cheating of ... Ask ... about the lights, wrote to ... about—

The copyist suppressed the names. No doubt he is referring to a servant.

1814

Brushes for shoes, if a visitor comes

Decision of the doctors about my life. If no salvation is possible I must use ... ??? It only remains to end it quicker what was formerly impossible. Consultation with ...

Again names are omitted by the copyist. Does this hint that Beethoven wants to poison himself if he can't be cured? (*See the discussion of syphilis in Chapter* 11.)

---

* Not certain the letter is an *A*.

Rosamunde by Alfieri, an edition of Gozzi—Pertossi, which Theres Malfatti got from me, ask for them back.

Books he lent her.

Much is to be done on earth, do it soon!

Don't continue my present every-day life! Art demands even that sacrifice. Find rest through diversion, so that I may work more potently in art.

Do not show contempt for people who deserve it. One never knows when one needs them.

1815

Everything which might be called "life" should be devoted to the sublime and be a sanctuary for art! Let me live, even if it be with artificial aids; if they could but be found!

"Artificial aids" (*Hilfsmittel*) may mean medicines.

If it is possible to develop hearing aids, then travel! That you owe yourself, humanity and him, the Almighty; only thus can you develop everything which still must be enclosed within you. A small Court, a small orchestra—music written by me for it, performed to honor the Almighty—the eternal, the infinite!

By a small Court he may have meant Olmütz, where Rudolph was.

Portraits of Handel, Bach, Gluck, Mozart, Haydn in my room—they can help to teach me endurance.

Always study from half past five till breakfast!

1816

A peasant lodging, then you escape your misery.

O look down, brother! Yes, I wept for you and still weep for you. O, why were you not more honest with me! You would be living still and you would not

Refers to brother Carl. The missing word(s) may have been a term of

425

have perished so miserably had you ... separated and been close to me.

opprobrium about the sister-in-law.

About my library: the large books must be put upright and so that they can be easily got at.

The history of the world numbers 5816.

Meaning the number of years of recorded history.

He who is burdened by a malady which he cannot change and which brings him gradually nearer to death must consider that he could have perished even quicker through murder or other causes. O fortunate he who only....

The note breaks off.

Malheuresement les génies médiocres sont condamnés à imiter les défauts des grands maîtres sans en apprécier les beautés: de là le mal que Michel-Ange fait à la peinture, Shakespeare à l'art dramatique et que Beethoven fait de nos jours à la musique.

Perhaps copied from some contemporary French publication.
"Unfortunately, mediocre talents are condemned to imitate the faults of the great masters without achieving their virtues [beauties]: hence the harm Michelangelo does to painting, Shakespeare to drama, and nowadays Beethoven to music."

For living and existence a house in the suburbs; the country doesn't suit Karl.

There exist works of architecture, the pagodas, quarried from the stone-mountains of India, which one judges to be nine thousand years old.

He has become interested in Indian culture. He copies not only quotations from Indian literature, but the Indian scale of tones, and bits of Indian philosophy.

BEETHOVEN AS A MATURE MAN

1817

God, help! You see me abandoned by all humanity, because I do not want to commit any wrong. Hear my plea: in the future let me live with Karl alone. Now that possibility is nowhere apparent. O harsh fate, O cruel judgment! No, no, my unfortunate condition will never end!

He did not want to commit a wrong: yet as he wrote this he became involved in a wrong from which none of his friends could rescue him. He felt himself "abandoned," tapping like a Kafka creature on closed doors; yet as he wrote down these sighs and sobs he was gathering strength for that incomparable resurgence of power which resulted in the *Hammerklavier Sonata* (Op. 106), and he was beginning to do some serious sketching for that symphonic sermon on the mount, the Ninth.

As intense as was his passion for composing was his fury over a dish of ill-cooked macaroni. As intense as was his joy was his suffering. He was as exposed to triumph as to defeat. The price of universal joy and the price of a breakfast roll were both questions with which he concerned himself.

"You make upon me the impression of a man with several heads, several hearts and several souls," Haydn once said to Beethoven.

A view of Teplitz, in Bohemia, as it looked at the time Beethoven met Goethe there (Culver Pictures).

CHAPTER 17

DEVALUATION, DISCOURAGEMENT, GOETHE, MÄLZEL

··›❘ I ❘‹··

or a year after the second occupation of Vienna, Beethoven's regenerative resiliency, so often effective in lifting him from the slough of ailment and despondency, failed him. For Beethoven, 1810 was a feeble year, but the causes may have been personal as well as the aftermath of war. Did he suffer "the pangs of despised love" over the Therese Malfatti refusal? Did he bear badly "the whips and scorns of time"?

"We no longer have even decent bread fit to eat," he wrote to Breitkopf and Härtel. Even his fame gave him little satisfaction for the moment. He wrote to Zmeskall:

July 9, 1810

My master [Archduke Rudolph] wants me to be with him and my art makes the same demand. I am partly at Schönbrunn, partly here. Every day there are fresh inquiries from foreigners, new acquaintances, new circumstances connected with my art as well. Sometimes I feel that I shall soon go mad in consequence of my unmerited fame; fortune is seeking me out and for that very reason I almost dread some fresh calamity. (A-263).

As life became more expensive in Vienna, it became more important to see to it that his works be published. He kept after Breitkopf and Härtel with long harangues. They were at the moment his favorite publishers, as they deserved to be, for they were the most conscientious. Even so, many mistakes crept into the publications, partly through careless proofreading, partly through impatient negligence on Beethoven's part. He was always complaining: "Mistakes, mistakes, mistakes! You yourself are one great big mistake." Publication of his works was proceeding at too slow a pace. He was being inadequately compensated, considering that one had to pay these days "30 gulden for a pair of boots, 160 and even 170 gulden for a coat, and so forth. The deuce take the economics of music." * Aside from the *Egmont* music and the final touches for the *Emperor Concerto,* the only substantial production of 1810 is the String Quartet No. 11 in F Minor, Op. 95. It is called the *Quartetto Serioso,* because up to its jubilant end it is composed in a prevailingly somber mood. Beethoven here wrote in so new a style, chromatic and languorous, that the music foreshadows *Tristan.* This quartet was to be the last essay in the form for fourteen long years.

In 1811 Beethoven wanted the score of *Egmont* sent at once to Goethe, and he chided Breitkopf and Härtel for not complying with his request quickly enough. He could not understand how a German publisher could be so discourteous to the foremost of German poets. He wrote to Goethe, entrusting the letter to the hands of a new-found friend, Franz Oliva, who was an employee of the banking firm of Offenheimer and Herz, with whom Beethoven had some dealings. Oliva was going on a business trip to Germany. He did see Goethe on May 2 in Weimar. Later Oliva was in Teplitz when Beethoven was there, and they were a good deal in each other's company. Then a rift occurred, a violent one: Beethoven quarreled with Oliva and called him a lout (*Lumpenkerl*). The following year he renewed his friendship with him, as if nothing had happened. Once again we may observe the power of Beethoven's personality over young people. Oliva, the *Lumpenkerl,* continued to serve and help Beethoven. This is the letter that Beethoven wrote to Goethe:

VIENNA, April 12, 1811

Your Excellency!

The pressing opportunity afforded me by a friend of mine and a great admirer of yours (as I am also), who is leaving Vienna very soon, allows me only a moment in which to thank you for the long time I have known you (for that I have done since my childhood) — That is so little for so much — Bettine Brentano has assured me that you would receive me kindly, or, I should say, as a friend. But how could I think of such a welcome, seeing that I can approach you only with the greatest reverence and with an inexpressibly profound feeling of admiration for your glorious creations! — You will shortly receive from Leipzig through Breitkopf & Härtel my music for Egmont, that glorious Egmont on which I have again reflected through you, and which I have felt and reproduced in music as intensely as I felt when I read it — I should very much like to have

---

* Letter to Breitkopf and Härtel, about August, 1810.

your opinion on my music for Egmont. Even your censure will be useful to me and my art and will be welcomed as gladly as the greatest praise.—

Your Excellency's profound admirer

LUDWIG VAN BEETHOVEN (A-303).

Goethe's answer to this letter:

KARLSBAD, June 25, 1811

Your friendly letter, very esteemed Sir, was received through Herr von Oliva much to my pleasure. For the kindly feelings which it expresses towards me I am heartily grateful and I can assure you that I honestly reciprocate them, for I have never heard any of your works performed by expert artists or amateurs without wishing that I might sometime have the opportunity to admire you at the pianoforte and find delight in your extraordinary talents. Good Bettina Brentano surely deserves the friendly sympathy which you have extended to her. She speaks rapturously and most affectionately of you and counts the hours spent with you among the happiest of her life.

I shall probably find the music which you have designed for Egmont when I return home and am thankful in advance—for I have heard it praised by several, and plan to perform it in connection with the play mentioned on our stage this winter, when I hope thereby to give myself as well as your numerous admirers in our neighborhood a great treat. But I hope most of all correctly to have understood Herr von Oliva, who has made us hope that in the journey which you are contemplating you will visit Weimar. I hope it will be at a time when the court as well as the entire musical public will be gathered together. I am sure that you would find worthy acceptance of your service and aims. But in this nobody can be more interested than I, who with the wish that all may go well with you, commend myself to your kind thought and thank you most sincerely for all the goodness which you have created in us. (TQ).

They were not to meet until the following year.

After a fallow year Beethoven's strength surged back. Once again he turned to composition and, his hearing being temporarily improved, he went to concerts, theaters, and to social gatherings. His relationship with Archduke Rudolph became closer. The archduke took the liveliest interest in all Beethoven did and wanted him to come and teach more frequently than it suited the teacher. Beethoven found set duties irksome. Yet for the royal pupil he produced the incomparable B-flat Trio, Op. 97, for which he had sketched out some ideas in the previous year and which he now completed in three weeks. This was the *Archduke Trio,* a lordly work, obviously meant to be played by lordly virtuosi. Rudolph took hold of the manuscript at once; he clutched at every line

Beethoven wrote, and he wanted all of Beethoven's manuscripts to form a complete collection for his personal library.

·⊲[2]⊳·

Emperor Franz was trying to do something to placate the Hungarians. In 1808, before the outbreak of the war, he had approved a plan of building at Budapest a sumptuous new theater which would also contain ballrooms, a gambling casino, a restaurant, and a coffee house. Because of the war, the completion of this enterprise had been delayed. It was now sufficiently finished to consider the arrangements for opening the theater with a performance worthy of its splendor. A new play and new music were to be commissioned; for the music, Beethoven was the logical choice. For the play, Collin was applied to, but he was ill (he died shortly thereafter) and could not accept the task, which was then entrusted to the prolific and popular playwright Kotzebue.* He produced in practically no time three short plays entitled *Hungary's First Benefactor, Bela's Flight,* and *The Ruins of Athens.* The fact that Emperor Franz had twice taken flight from his capital, chased away by Napoleon, made it understandable that the directors in charge decided that *Bela's Flight* was hardly a suitable subject. They substituted another piece, but Kotzebue's two other plays were accepted and were submitted to Beethoven at the end of July. Beethoven composed several numbers for both plays (the first one was retitled *King Stephan or Hungary's First Benefactor*), of which only the overture to *The Ruins of Athens* is still occasionally played. These pieces were not compositions of which Beethoven could or should have been proud.

His various activities, including the tedious work of the corrections of the mistakes in the scores, strained not only Beethoven's patience but also his health. He was suffering severe headaches. Dr. Malfatti ordered him to go to Teplitz. Beethoven hesitated. He did not want to go alone, not only because as a deaf man he found it difficult to brave unfamiliar surroundings, but also because the paradox of his personality demanded both solitude and human contact. He wanted to be alone with his thoughts and yet wanted to have somebody with him—some good and comfortable friend such as Zmeskall or Franz Brunsvik—on whom he could lean. He did entreat Franz Brunsvik to go with him. He wrote him in Budapest:

---

* Kotzebue was assassinated in 1819 by a radical German student.

DEVALUATION, DISCOURAGEMENT, GOETHE, MÄLZEL

VIENNA, July 4, 1811

My friend, I simply cannot accept your refusal. I have let Oliva go off alone and, what is more, on your account. I must have somebody with me in whom I can confide, if this everyday life is not to become a burden to me. I shall expect you by the 12th of this month at latest, or perhaps I may even wait until the 15th. But there must be no refusal. It is a supreme command. The carrying out of such a command cannot be deferred without severe retribution and punishment, no, indeed, it must be obeyed unconditionally—And now all good wishes, dear faithful friend, we pray God to watch over you with His gracious care. The above order was issued this morning immediately after I rose from the coffee table.

BEETHOVEN

We are expecting with six times the speed of lightning no other answer to our supreme command but yes! yes! yes! quickly—or else my rage will reach and strike you at Ofen.   (A-318).

But Franz could not or would not go; and accordingly it was arranged for Oliva to be Beethoven's companion. Since Franz did not oblige Beethoven, he immediately drew Beethoven's anger: Beethoven called him "that wretched Hungarian count."

Beethoven stayed at Teplitz for quite a long time, returning to Vienna sometime in September, after making a detour to visit Lichnowsky. In Teplitz he made the acquaintance of Joseph von Varena, a government official residing in Graz, who was one of the founders of the Graz Musical Society. Varena told him about the plight of the Ursuline nuns and their 350 charity pupils in Graz. They needed money to continue their work of helping poor children. Almost everybody was becoming poor in Austria. Later in the year, Varena appealed to Beethoven and asked him to let him have a few of Beethoven's new works for some charity concerts he was trying to promote: he would be delighted to pay Beethoven for whatever works the composer thought fit to let him have. Beethoven responded by sending a number of his works and by refusing categorically to accept any payment. The only payment he wanted was "the feeling of inward happiness" which he would derive from his action of aiding "poor suffering humanity." Varena had the great satisfaction of telling Beethoven that the nuns had gained a very handsome sum by his generosity.

Beethoven came back to Vienna seemingly much improved in health. His will to work returned and soon mounted high, to concentrate on two symphonies, again two of them together, the Seventh and the Eighth. It is characteristic

433

of him that once his mind turned to composition, once he set himself to work, he experienced an onrush of ideas which touched not only the particular work under consideration but other projects, projects unrelated. The Sketchbook of 1811 * is an amazing document: we find a whole storehouse of seeds of which he himself could not as yet know which grain would grow and which would not. In addition to the Seventh and Eighth Symphonies, the Sketchbook contains notations for piano pieces never executed, as if he planned to follow the *Emperor Concerto* with further great concertos, overtures never put on paper, an *Adagio* in E-flat, a *Polonaise for Pianoforte* alone. Immediately following this, we read a memorandum: *"Freude schöner Götter Funken Tochter.* Work out the overture." Later, *"Freude schöner Götter Funken Tochter aus Elysium.* Detached fragments like princes are beggars, etc., not the whole." Again on the same page, "Detached fragments from Schiller's *Freude* brought together in a whole." These are indications that the idea of the Ninth Symphony was slowly emerging although it was to take still another twelve years until the symphony was put on paper.

Beethoven kept trying to obtain an opera libretto. Many were submitted; all were rejected. He knew well enough that it would aid his fame and finances to produce another opera. It was difficult to earn a great deal of money from symphonies. And neither Lobkowitz nor Lichnowsky nor Rasoumovsky commissioned Beethoven to write a symphony. Count Oppersdorff did, and paid Beethoven 350 florins in advance, because the count employed an orchestra in his castle in Silesia. The count was promised the Fifth Symphony several years earlier, but Beethoven calmly sold this to Breitkopf and Härtel, being in need of some further ready money, and promised the count the Fourth instead. As it turned out, the count got neither, though Beethoven did dedicate the Fourth to Oppersdorff. It speaks well for the count that if he took offense at being fobbed off by Beethoven, he never said so publicly.

To return to the subject of opera, even Lichnowsky, whose chief love was chamber music, thought that Beethoven ought to write an opera, and he urged the subject of Alfred the Great on him. Then along came an idea Beethoven said he liked. It was a French subject, *The Ruins of Babylon.* Beethoven was delighted when Georg Friedrich Treitschke expressed interest in collaboration. He was a poet and theatrical producer and now functioned as the deputy

---

* The so-called "Petter Sketchbook," the last 130 pages of which Unger dates from the middle of 1811 to sometime in 1812. Thayer dated it 1809, but the later date is now generally agreed upon.

director of the Theater-an-der-Wien. (We shall meet him again on the occasion of the revision of *Fidelio.*) Then Beethoven heard that a performance of this play with incidental music (melodrama) was being discussed for the benefit of an actor Scholz. Immediately Beethoven voiced a loud protest: the subject had been taken away from him; this was unjust; it was difficult to find a good libretto, the preceding year he had turned down no fewer than twelve of them, even paying for some of them out of his own pocket; at any rate the proposed plan of producing *Babylon* as a melodrama was not a sound one: as such it would fill the theater five or six times at most. "But as an opera it will be a work of permanent value and certainly it will produce for your theater incomparably more favourable results in a commercial way" (A-312). What was more, said Beethoven, he had told the archduke about *The Ruins of Babylon,* as well as other people with "intellectual interests." What was he going to do? Was he going to be embarrassed? The directors of the opera house decided that the subject should be earmarked for Beethoven's use. He could have *Babylon.* That was the end of it. He never wrote a note of the opera.

·≡[3]≡·

Now a serious misfortune befell him, as it did all of his countrymen from the highest to the lowest, the lowest of course suffering proportionately more. He could not have foreseen it, any more than many astute businessmen foresaw it. Austria went bankrupt. The condition was not called bankruptcy; the true facts were swept under a carpet of complicated decrees. The government, which had to try to meet Napoleon's levy of fifty million francs (equivalent to some hundred million dollars in today's purchasing power), which now had to buy food from other states and at high prices, whose industry and commerce had suffered grievously, could no longer meet its obligations. The money had to be devalued. On February 20, 1811, the Austrian government issued what was called the *Finanz-Patent,* effective March 15, 1811.

Let us not enter into the complicated calculations of this decree. The net effect was that the old banknotes were declared invalid, new paper money was issued—it was called *Wiener Währung*—and that this new money had the value of one fifth of the old money. This severe contraction of the citizen's capital was bad enough, but worse was to follow: even the new currency, the "W.W." florin, slid further downward, as the people and the banks had lost faith in the stability of government-issued obligations. Men who had possessions in land, in houses, in silver, in works of art, in jewels, were not harmed by the decree; quite the contrary. But imagine the fate of the teachers, the doctors, the musicians, the actors and the small officials. Anger reigned in the inner city, misery in the suburbs. Therese Brunsvik wrote in her memoirs: "The man who went to bed in March 1811 with the comfortable feeling of being a capitalist, having provided for his wife and children, got up in the morning as a beggar. The incredible happened during the night: The Austro-Hungarian currency lost four out of five parts of its value and the fifth part was devalued soon after, in an effort to pay for war's cost and prevent government bankruptcy." The decree was followed by a wave of suicides, then by a wave of lawsuits—futile for the most part—brought by people claiming that old contracts ought to be honored by old currency or its equivalent.

Beethoven had no possessions. He was dependent on income and on the subvention which had been granted to him, the 4000 florins. These now shrank to approximately 1617 florins * in the new paper money. A further shock was in store for Beethoven: Lobkowitz was in financial difficulties. The devaluation hit him hard. His affairs were in a muddle and a "curator" (financial manager) was appointed to sequestrate his estate so that no part of it could be sold. In September, 1811, Lobkowitz stopped payment on his portion of Beethoven's annuity. Payments were to remain suspended for nearly four years. Even knowing the difficulties experienced by Lobkowitz, one still is puzzled why he could not scrape up the paltry sum represented by his part of the annuity. In the absence of documents one conjectures that Lobkowitz had no say in the matter. The "curator" determined what moneys were to be paid. The annuity may have been regarded as a voluntary, not a "legal" obligation. Beethoven did not or would not understand this and had recourse to the law. Unnecessarily, as events proved.

Before the cessation of the Lobkowitz payments Beethoven appealed to his three patrons: he said that though according to the letter of the law he had no choice but to accept the annuity in devalued currency, the spirit of the contract demanded, in justice and fairness, that he be paid a sum equivalent to what he had been receiving. The three men admitted that Beethoven had a point. Archduke Rudolph at once gave orders to bring his portion of the annuity to the corrected amount.

Kinsky did not. The following year Oliva asked Varnhagen on behalf of

---

* The shrinkage was not applied to this and similar contracts on a straight one-fifth reduction, but according to a scale based on the value of the florin in silver at the time the contract was signed.

Beethoven to deliver a letter to Prince Kinsky seeking to convince the prince that he ought to do no less than Rudolph had done. Varnhagen was able to report after a personal interview that Kinsky saw the fairness of Beethoven's claim and promised to send his paymaster the necessary instructions. Unfortunately, his instructions were not carried out. Some time after, Kinsky was riding in a forest near Prague. The saddle of his horse broke. He was thrown from the horse, his skull was cracked, and he survived but ten hours. Later Beethoven appealed to his widow. When he wrote to the princess, he told her that he himself had called on her late husband (July, 1812), who had confirmed his previous promise and even paid him sixty ducats on account. Both Varnhagen and Oliva could testify to the veracity of this, since both of them had spoken with Kinsky. No answer from the princess. He sent a second letter, repeating the request, and urged that he be paid, since he was in need, being the sole support of a brother and his family * and stressing again the righteousness of his claims. In the end—that is, after the matter had dragged on for three years, after Beethoven had used up quantities of writing paper, after he had stormed that his patrons would honor neither oral nor written agreements, after he had called Lobkowitz a "princely rogue," after he protested that it was all too much for him to bear, that he was no Hercules who could help Atlas to carry the world, still less carry it for him—after all the recriminations, a compromise with the Kinsky estate was reached. He was to receive part of the annuity due him plus the sum in arrears—altogether 2479 gulden, W.W., less than $3000 in today's equivalent. The settlement was effected by Johann Nepomuk Kanka, a lawyer in Prague, a fine, cultivated, considerate man, one of the few to whom Beethoven would listen. Near the end of the affair—the decision is dated January 18, 1815—Beethoven wrote Kanka a piteous letter from which we quote a few passages:

[VIENNA, Autumn, 1814]

You yourself know that a man's spirit, the active creative spirit, must not be tied down to the wretched necessities of life. And this business robs me of many other things conducive to a happy existence. I have been compelled, and still am compelled, to set bounds to my inclination, nay more, to the duty which I had imposed on myself, i.e., to work by means of my art for human beings in distress.

---

* Carl had fallen ill, but Beethoven was hardly his sole support.

> Think of me and remember that you are acting for an unselfish artist in his dealings with a niggardly family. How ready people are to rob the poor artist of what they owe him in other ways ... To whatever heights I feel uplifted when in happy moments I find myself raised to my artistic atmosphere, yet the spirits of this earth pull me down again; and among those spirits are to be found these two lawsuits. (A-502).

While one may not altogether sympathize with Beethoven's being so very sorry for himself, the question arises why the widowed Princess Kinsky did not settle the claim at once and have done with it. The money couldn't have meant much to her. Kinsky, unlike Lobkowitz, had not been in a financial bind. A possible explanation may be found in the fact that husband and wife had not been on good terms. Perhaps the widow wanted to have nothing to do with her husband's promise, till Counselor Kanka persuaded her differently.

And Lobkowitz? Beethoven sued in 1813 (the documents are still extant), claiming that Lobkowitz had promised him, orally and in writing, to augment the stipend to the equivalent before devaluation. Lobkowitz denied this. The court found for Lobkowitz. Yet as soon as Lobkowitz's affairs were straightened out and the sequestration removed, he *voluntarily* added the difference. He wrote to Archduke Rudolph from Prague, on December 29, 1814:

> Although I have reason to be anything but satisfied with the behavior of Beethoven toward me, I am nevertheless rejoiced, as a passionate lover of music, that his assuredly great works are beginning to be appreciated. I heard "Fidelio" here and barring the book, I was extraordinarily pleased with the music, except the two finales, which I do not like very much. I think the music extremely effective and worthy of the man who composed it. (TQ).

But the former cordial relationship was never resumed by Lobkowitz. He kept Beethoven at a distance. Beethoven tried to make amends by dedicating the song cycle *An die Ferne Geliebte* to him. That was in the spring of 1816. In the winter of the same year Lobkowitz died.

From 1815, then, to his death, Beethoven received from the three men or their estates an annual income of 3400 florins (a little over $4000). Very little —but enough to keep him from starvation. But there was no question of starvation.

No doubt Beethoven's expenses at the time increased, no doubt the devaluation made it more difficult to get along. No doubt his frequent changes of lodging cost him a lot of money. Yet, adding the annuity (even though devalued) to the money he received from England (Clementi), Scotland (Thomson), Leipzig (Breitkopf and Härtel), and the Viennese publishers indicates that there was no cause for the almost frantic alarm he felt. Why this pugnacious insistence on his "rights"? Why this hunt for florins by a man who surely was not money-grubbing?

Accusation. Injustice to friends. Distortion of truth. How can they be explained? Only one theory will serve. Beethoven wanted to divest himself of everything that had to do with mundane matters, to immerse himself wholly in what to him was the only reality, music. He felt that if he had an adequate income he need no longer negotiate with publishers, appeal to patrons, or subtract the smallest thought from the sum of thought devoted to the single purpose of creating music. Concentration, consuming, burning concentration on his task—for that the artist sacrifices friends, gratitude, and ordinary notions of decent behavior. In Beethoven's mind there was no doubt that this money was his rightful due. Devaluation or depression was the government's concern, not his. He wanted his money; he did not care whom he offended in order to get it. Perhaps it was not solely a question of more or less money. He felt that the representatives of "the spirits of this earth" ought to make it possible for him to achieve his task. His music was to help "human beings in distress." When he called himself an "unselfish artist" he surely was not pretending. Never! He called on the world to enable him to *be* unselfish according to his lights.

When he did not quite succeed he fell into a stance of poverty. He wrote, so to speak, "I am poor" in large letters on the walls of his room. He seemed to *want* to be poor, to shame the world. Was he that poor in this difficult period, 1810 to 1814? Nanette Streicher, wife of the piano maker Andreas Streicher, a practical, good-hearted woman, who had both feet on the ground, related to Schindler that in 1813 she found Beethoven in a most deplorable condition: he did not have a single good coat, not even a whole shirt. Frau Streicher took over with the help of her husband, saw to it that his wardrobe was refurbished, provided him with necessities and comforts, and read him a lecture urging him to put money aside against the future. Beethoven obeyed meekly. Even assuming that Schindler exaggerated Frau Streicher's report to give it the dramatic effect of which he was so fond, it remains difficult to understand that Beethoven's condition could have been that miserable. Thayer says that Thomson paid him "90 ducats more in February 1813, and within the last years Breitkopf and Härtel had certainly paid him several thousand florins. . . ." Surely enough to buy him a "whole shirt." Yet Beethoven himself told the composer Ludwig Spohr that he had but one pair of shoes and was forced to stay home while they were at the cobbler's being repaired. Is it really possible that Vienna's leading composer, friend of counts and princes, had only one pair of shoes to his name? No—impossible. It was far more probable that he was so immersed in the creation of the Seventh and Eighth Symphonies, so challenged by the as yet vague idea of a Ninth, that he covered his eyes with his hand and did not see how many pairs of shoes he had, or what was happening to his clothes, or who was providing the food and what the food might be. The attitude of utter poverty was a gesture of defiance against a world which would not protect him sufficiently. The bills lay there in the same heap as the manuscripts. Between the musical notes there are notes of what things cost. Yet he was not as poor as he described himself to be. Even during the financially depressed years of 1811 and 1812 he had money enough to travel to and maintain himself in Teplitz; the journey and the stay at this fashionable resort were anything but inexpensive.

With all that, Beethoven preserved some of his humor, some of his generosity, some of his charm as a host. Friedrich Starke, horn player of the Vienna Opera and an industrious composer, gave Ludwig Nohl the account of a morning's visit:

A musical breakfast in the year 1812

. . . Starke was often invited to a meal and after it often had the soul-satisfying experience of hearing Beethoven improvise. The most remarkable and pleasant time was an invitation to a breakfast which for Starke was a real spiritual breakfast. . . . After breakfast *which consisted of very good coffee (and which Beethoven made himself in a glass machine)*, Starke requested a breakfast for his heart and mind, and Beethoven improvised in three different styles. . . .

·≈[4]≈·

This was the year of the Letter to the Immortal Beloved (1812). Even aside from that letter the year was an important one in Beethoven's life. It was a pivotal year in the life of Europe. Perhaps it could have been a turning point in the history of mankind, had the Czar and Metternich and Talleyrand been possessed of wider vision.

As long ago as December 28, 1811, Metternich had reported to his sovereign, "The moment has arrived, long envisaged by Napoleon, which makes the last battle unavoidable, the battle of the old order against his plans of topsy-turvy-dom." That battle, Metternich saw, was to be fought against Russia. What he didn't see was the outcome: Metternich thought Napoleon would conquer Russia.

Now, in the spring of 1812, Napoleon had convoked at Dresden the heads of his tributary nations. They had come as they had been bidden, including Emperor Franz and his Empress, Napoleon's unwilling parents-in-law. It was the first time in history that a Habsburg Emperor had to cede precedence in entering a meeting. Napoleon entered first. He told the assembled nations that he would strictly hold them to their commitment to furnish men for the *Grande Armée.** Everybody bowed. Napoleon left Dresden on May 28 and headed eastward. Franz left to seek the cure at Teplitz. No doubt he needed it.

By the end of June Napoleon had crossed the Niemen with an army of nearly half a million. He was on his way. His immediate plan was to proceed against and capture Moscow. "Within a month I'll have the Russians at my feet," he wrote to Caulaincourt, his Russian ambassador.

Napoleon's supply line was now stretched across a vast expanse of conquered territories. The dukes and princes and kings of these countries, insulted, injured, and disgraced, were only waiting for the right opportunity to hack that line. Quite a few of them came to Teplitz, ostensibly to take the waters, actually to consult with Emperor Franz and one another. From June to September one could speak of a "Congress of Teplitz," though nobody knew what in the world to propose.

All these sovereigns in Teplitz, the King of Saxony, the Prince of Courland, the Grand Duke of Würzburg, the Grand Duke of Weimar, and others knew the seriousness of the situation. If Napoleon were to conquer the Czar, then indeed all opposition in continental Europe would cease. It would mean the end of the Habsburgs, the end of individual states with even a pretense of auton-omy, the end of everything that was not French, or rather, not Napoleonic. The Napoleon of 1812 saw himself as Charlemagne and Alexander the Great rolled into one. In Dresden in a performance at the Court Theater a figure represent-ing the sun appeared: it bore the legend "Less great and less fair than He." **

Along with royalty came the politically important nobility such as Baron von

---

* It was eventually constituted of 190,000 Frenchmen, 110,000 Germans from the Rhineland, 30,000 Austrians, 20,000 Prussians, 12,000 Swiss. Other nations brought the total to over 400,000.
** I owe this fact to a recent book, Alan Palmer: *Napoleon in Russia—The 1812 Campaign.* The book is a superb study.

Humboldt, the Prussian ambassador, and Prince Lichnowsky. Kinsky had been with Emperor Franz in Dresden and now was with him at Teplitz.* The Grand Ducal Privy Councilor of Weimar, Johann Wolfgang von Goethe, arrived on July 15. Later the same month Arnim and his wife Bettina arrived; in August, Clemens Brentano and Varnhagen.

Amidst this crowd of champagne and small-beer royalty, diplomats resplendent on the outside and feeling nervous inside, statesmen of grave mien pregnant with confidential memoranda, writers, journalists, ministers and spies, women of various degrees of charm and intellect, in addition to the usual vacationing group arriving for no other purpose than the search for health—there was Beethoven, sent once more by his physician. The one person he wanted to meet was Goethe. As to the others, they meant nothing to him. He wrote to Varnhagen (who was still in Prague): "There is not much to tell you about T[eplitz], for there are few people here and no distinguished ones among the small number. Hence I am living—alone—alone! alone! alone!" The letter is dated July 14, about a week after the Immortal Beloved letter, and may be a sign of Beethoven's emotional fatigue after the upheaval. Or it may be a sign that Beethoven *wanted* to be alone. At any rate, it is an astonishing statement.

He did meet Goethe. A meeting between the two greatest artists of the early 19th century—what did it produce? Bettina Brentano and others have embellished it with imagined blossoms, but we must not exaggerate. Beethoven impressed Goethe; the artist's instinct sensed the exceptional qualities of the artist before him. Yet Goethe was far from really understanding Beethoven. Music itself meant little to the poet; his attitude toward it was that of an intelligent but passive dilettante. "Weakish sentimental melodies depress me; I need strong fresh sounds," he said. It is a dilettante's remark. There is no evidence that Goethe ever heard any of Beethoven's symphonies in full ** or even understood the *Egmont* music. Goethe might also have gone to the meeting with somewhat of a psychological prejudice: Bettina had raved so

---

* I found a little-known though characteristic, anecdote about Kinsky in Dresden. His wife, who was exceptionally beautiful, tall and striking-looking (Beethoven thought so!) caught Napoleon's eye. Napoleon asked Kinsky: "Where does your wife come from?"
Kinsky: "She comes from the Reich, Sire."
Napoleon: "What Reich?"
Kinsky: "She was born in Koblenz, Sire."
Napoleon: "You had better say she is a Frenchwoman."
(Source: *Memoirs* of Baroness Marie du Montet.)
** In 1830 the young Mendelssohn played the first movement of the Fifth Symphony for Goethe on the piano. Goethe found it exciting but erratic, "as if the house were caving in."

much about Beethoven and had been so busy in wanting to form the relationship that Goethe might instinctively have set up some resistance, all the more because there had occurred an open quarrel the year before between Bettina and Goethe's wife, and Goethe had taken his wife's part. At the time, Goethe was friendly with the musician Karl Friedrich Zelter and he accepted Zelter as an authority on musical questions. Zelter was a traditionalist and at first had very little use for Beethoven's music. He thought it was heavy and self-important and trivial in ideas, "like Hercules using his club to kill flies." Bettina was furious and called Zelter "a Philistine with large bones and a long waistcoat." *

In spite of these handicaps, Goethe did recognize some of Beethoven's quality. A few days after their meeting he summed up his impressions of Beethoven in a letter to his wife: "Never before have I seen an artist with more power of concentration, more energy, more inwardness." That is perceptive. But Goethe still could not understand—the man-of-the-world Goethe could not understand—why Beethoven seemed so truculent, why so roughly surfaced that if you touched him a splinter got stuck in your skin.

Beethoven, conversely, had come to the meeting with a predisposing fascination with the great poet and a wide knowledge of his writings. He was prepared to worship the man whose genius he had worshiped from afar. Yet he too did not understand all of Goethe. Goethe must have represented to him much of what he himself was not and could never be. The poet was never more fascinating, never more captivating, than then, at the age of sixty-three. He was impeccably dressed, his walk vigorous, his carriage erect, his full hair iron-gray; when he entered a room all conversation stopped. Everybody thought (to quote a contemporary) that an elegant god had made his appearance; now as much as when he was younger he was irresistible to women. The Privy Councilor of Weimar, who found it possible to combine the creation of some of the greatest poetry ever penned in any language with a practical participation in the political world—that of course was why Goethe was in Teplitz, in the retinue of the Grand Duke—was too smooth, too balanced, a human being for Beethoven to understand fully and respond to completely. The ease which emanated from Goethe's personality must have struck Beethoven curiously. Though it is not

---

* But Zelter was not the hidebound Tory that Bettina made him out to be. He was a fine musician, and later he changed his mind about Beethoven and became a friend and an admirer. Zelter was the teacher of Mendelssohn, in whom he instilled a great love for Beethoven.

true, as it has been said of Goethe, that he wrote with ease, though he too struggled, Goethe felt that it was possible for the artist to stand in the stream of life, that he need not isolate himself, but be part of "worldliness." Indeed, the artist should dip his hand into the fullness of human life: wherever he got hold of it he would find it interesting (*Faust*). That was not Beethoven's way of working. In spite of his genuine interest in many subjects, Beethoven needed isolation. Goethe needed sociability, in its best sense. Thus, with all the hero worship that Beethoven felt for Goethe, he could say about him, as he did in a letter to Breitkopf and Härtel on August 9, 1812: "Goethe delights far too much in the court atmosphere. Far more than is becoming to a poet."

They saw each other fairly frequently. They walked together. Beethoven played for Goethe, and Goethe responded with a show of feeling which Beethoven reputedly recognized as not being entirely sincere. (Goethe noted, "He played delightfully.")

Goethe wrote to Zelter about a month later—September 2, 1812:

> I made Beethoven's acquaintance in Teplitz. His talent amazed me; unfortunately he is an utterly untamed personality, who is not altogether in the wrong in holding the world to be detestable but surely does not make it any the more enjoyable for himself or others by his attitude. He is easily excused, on the other hand, and much to be pitied, as his hearing is leaving him, which perhaps mars the musical part of his nature less than the social. He is of a laconic nature and will become doubly so because of this lack. (TQ).

It is an analysis which seems to have been written more by Goethe the Privy Councilor than Goethe the poet.

Though Beethoven wrote to Goethe once or twice after the meeting, preserving from a distance the admiration for the poet as a poet, the two men were never to meet again. Beethoven left Teplitz on July 27. He did not return to Vienna, but on the advice of his physician went first to Karlsbad and then to Franzensbrunn, both watering places of high reputation. He then returned to Teplitz about the middle of September, his health not being any better, and remained there until the end of the month.

··◖ 5 ◗··

At the beginning of October we find Beethoven unexpectedly in Linz. He had come to visit his brother Johann, at his house known as the Water Apothecary, because of its proximity to the Danube. But it was not for the

Beethoven, circa 1804, at about thirty-four, a highly idealized portrait by W. J. Mähler—detail from the first of four that this artist painted. A copy of it, which belonged to Thayer, now hangs in the New York Public Library, Lincoln Center (Bettmann Archive).

Ignaz Schuppanzigh, "Milord Falstaff." Violinist who first played much of Beethoven's chamber music (Society of Friends of Music, Vienna).

Prince Ferdinand Kinsky. One of the three subscribers to Beethoven's annuity. Killed by a fall from his horse, 1812 (Austrian Nat. Library).

Karl Amenda. He was an intimate friend of Beethoven, although he remained in Vienna for only a short time (Beethoven House, Bonn).

Dr. Franz Gerhard Wegeler. Coauthor with Ferdinand Ries of "Notizen." The engraving dates from 1821, when Wegeler was fifty-six years old.

Jean Baptiste Bernadotte. French ambassador to Vienna. King of Norway and Sweden. Beethoven met Kreutzer through him (Bettmann Archive).

Ferdinand Ries. Pianist, composer. He moved to London, promoted Beethoven music there (Beethoven House, Bonn).

Josephine Brunsvik, to whom Beethoven wrote thirteen love letters which were only recently discovered. Twice married; her life ended in deep tragedy.

Therese Brunsvik. From a portrait that she gave and inscribed to Beethoven (Beethoven House, Bonn).

Marie Bigot. Marvelous pianist. Played the "Appassionata Sonata" from manuscript. (From a contemporary drawing).

Therese Malfatti, niece of the famous Dr. Johann Malfatti. Beethoven may have proposed marriage to her.

Bettina Brentano. Vivacious, romantic, un-reliable. Charmed Goethe and Beethoven (Goethe Museum, Frankfurt).

Countess Giulietta Guicciardi. Beethoven dedicated the "Moonlight Sonata" to her (Beethoven House, Bonn).

Countess Anna Maria Erdödy and her husband, Count Peter. From a lost oil painting, reproduced in "Atlantis" (Austrian National Library).

449

Right: Dorothea von Ertmann, whom Beethoven called his "Dorothea Caecilia." One of the greatest interpreters of his piano music. She may be the Immortal Beloved (From a contemporary oil painting). Below: Police Register of Karlsbad, June, 1812, which shows Dorothea Ertmann's entry. For complete details and translation, see page 307.

The Heiligenstadt Testament, page 1. Note omission of brother Johann's name in the superscription. Insert: Johann's portrait.

beautiful view that Beethoven came; the visit was not a friendly one. Thayer found out in Linz from "perfectly competent authority" that the principal object of Beethoven's visit was to interfere in Johann's domestic affairs. Soon after Johann had been able to buy the house in Linz, he leased part of it to a physician from Vienna whose wife's sister came to live with them. Her name was Therese Obermeyer (or Obermayer). She was described as attractive of figure, though one could not call her an out-and-out beauty. She had an illegitimate child, a little girl Amalie. Johann made Therese his housekeeper, fell in love with her, and soon she became his mistress. The relationship seems to have been perfectly calm and acceptable, not only to Therese herself but to her sister and her brother-in-law. Therese was happy. Johann was happy. The only one who strenuously objected was Beethoven. It was, to be sure, none of his business. Johann was then a man of thirty-five, doing well, certainly old enough to know what he was doing. But Beethoven seems to have made the journey to Linz—and he probably went there directly from Teplitz, without going home to Vienna—with the express purpose of breaking up the relationship and persuading his brother that his living with a woman outside of wedlock was "immoral," that a woman who entered into such a relationship was worthless, and that Therese was no better than a slut. As Thayer, for once losing his judicial calm, writes, the action seems "hardly credible," even making allowances for "all his [Beethoven's] eccentricities of character . . ."

Johann very sensibly refused to knuckle under to such brotherly tyranny and probably told Beethoven to mind his business or go back to Vienna. Seeing that he could not prevail with Johann, the infuriated Beethoven now "resorted to any and every means to accomplish his purpose." He ran around Linz, knocking on the doors of this and that authority. He who usually avoided dealings with the clergy called on the Bishop of Linz. That gentleman, a sensible minister, gave him no encouragement. He then called on local city authorities. Finally he obtained an order authorizing the police to remove the girl to Vienna on a certain day if she should still be found in Linz. Such an order would be well nigh impossible under modern law, but under the Austrian constitution of the early 19th century, it was possible to proceed against a person accused of moral misbehavior. (We have described similar police action against Countess Erdödy in Chapter 11.)

The news must have hit with the noise of a Napoleonic bomb fallen from a clear sky. One can imagine the delighted gossip, the scurrying to and fro, the factions forming, the stares at *Jause* time, the *Klatsch* in the coffee houses. The girl was disgraced, Johann was shamed, not only before the girl herself but before the townspeople. Johann confronted Beethoven, and a violent quarrel ensued. What could Johann do? How could he set matters right? How could he make it up to Therese? There was but one way, and Johann took it. He married her on November 8, 1812. Beethoven packed his bag and left for Vienna, offended, bested, checkmated. What he had gone to Linz to do he not only failed to do, but he had made matters infinitely worse by pushing Johann into a marriage which, but for his own meddling, might never have taken place. The marriage did not turn out to be a happy one, and in future years Johann always blamed Ludwig for it.

From a psychological point of view it is significant that both of Beethoven's brothers chose women whose reputations were hardly spotless. Therese was supposed to have had a number of lovers, and Johann knew about them. That is what Ludwig said; Johann did not deny it. Therese's morals concern us only insofar as they may point to a tendency in the relation of the Beethovens toward the female sex. Was there a streak in them which preferred "unchaste" women (to use the language of their time)? And was that streak so violently suppressed in Ludwig's character as to turn him into the interfering, officious, sermonizing prig which he sometimes appeared to be? Beethoven's hatred of Carl's wife was partly motivated by his love for his nephew. Beethoven's hatred of Therese was motivated by no consideration of self. Was it motivated by reminiscences in his own experiences, dark, dank reminders? Or was it simply envy of a brother who had found love while he himself could not?

The wonder grows when we know that at the time that Beethoven behaved so atrociously, at the very time that he must have caused Therese to weep, Johann to fume, and the authorities to consider him a meddler of whom they would gladly have rid themselves had he been anybody less than the famous Beethoven—at this very time he finished composing the Eighth Symphony, that quintessence of purity, lightness, grace, charm, humor, and, if one can speak of moral value in music, of goodness.

··❊[6]❊··

In Vienna a new personality entered Beethoven's life. This man, half Edison and half Barnum, was Johann Nepomuk Mälzel. He was well known as an inventor of ingenious mechanical contrivances (with or without musical accompaniment) and knew how to profit by his talent, making the most of them in an age which delighted in clocks run by steam and contraptions which could rise in the air. In Vienna Mälzel proudly sported the title of "Court Mechanician." What he did not invent he bought and introduced as his own—for example, a Mechanical Chess Player constructed by a certain Kempelen. When Napoleon was in Schönbrunn in 1809 he was supposed to have played a game with this early form of computer. It was a fake; a man was concealed in the instrument.

Beethoven, who could just about manage to do simple addition, was fascinated by mechanical contrivances, the more complicated the better.* He used to visit Mälzel's workshop, sit there and be impressed. Mälzel (or his brother) made four ear trumpets for him, one of which worked well enough for Beethoven to use it for several years.

Composers had long looked for a device which would indicate the tempo of a musical composition more accurately than the elastic descriptions of "Presto" or "Adagio." Not only Beethoven but the other composers of Vienna—Salieri, Hummel, Weigl—were excited over a development which Mälzel called "The Musical Chronometer." It consisted essentially of a small lever, set in motion by a cogwheel, which operated a little hammer which in turn struck a small wooden anvil. This was the forerunner of Mälzel's Metronome, in which hammer and anvil were replaced by a swinging pendulum, the tick of which indicated the desired rhythmic speed; but he did not perfect the later instrument until 1817.

Beethoven liked Mälzel very much, and on one companionable evening he composed a canon to the words *"Ta ta ta lieber lieber Mälzel."* The *"ta ta ta"* suggested the beat of the chronometer, and Beethoven may have used the theme for the *Allegretto* of the Eighth Symphony.**

Another of Mälzel's inventions which fascinated Beethoven was the Panharmonicon, an instrument which mechanically could imitate several instruments of the orchestra, such as the trumpet, clarinet, viola, and cello. It caused a sensation in Vienna, as did his Mechanical Trumpeter (not a fake) which blew an Austrian military march.

Mälzel sensed that Beethoven could constitute a source of profit to him. If Beethoven were to compose something for the Panharmonicon—that would be a real *coup* for a special exhibition Mälzel was planning in the major European capitals, including London. Mälzel talked to Beethoven about these plans,

---

* He inquired about a jeweler who said he had perfected a fillable and transportable pen. He was very interested in the new ships driven by steam.
** Schindler says so. Later scholarship doubts this, since the Eighth Symphony was in all likelihood substantially sketched out before the spring of 1812, when the canon was written.

stressing the profits that lay in England ready for the plucking. They had to wait till the instrument he was now constructing was finished, and perhaps it would be prudent to await the outcome of Napoleon's Russian campaign, but at the proper time would Beethoven consider journeying to England with Mälzel for a "Grand Tour"?

Before Beethoven could make up his mind, Carl's health deteriorated and Beethoven did not want to leave him. Mälzel himself decided to postpone the tour—because the startling change in Europe's fortune had given him a new idea.

Napoleon had reached Moscow—September 15, 1812—and occupied it. He had conquered, though with greater difficulty than he had anticipated, at Smolensk and again at Borodino. He had conquered, or thought he had conquered, the last of the great European capitals. Moscow was deserted on that September day. The French soldiers made their way through empty streets. The adjutant who was in the Kremlin preparing the rooms for Napoleon's formal entry idly glanced out of the window at the dead city. It was after midnight; some distance away he saw flames.

It took the French High Command three days to realize that the flames were the result of a detailed plan conceived by Moscow's governor Rostopchin; incredible though it appeared, the Russians had chosen to burn their own Holy City. Soon Napoleon had to flee the burning city. The supplies which he had counted on capturing in Moscow were now heaps of ashes. The victory proved an illusion. Retreat was necessary, and winter was coming on.

On October 19 the retreat began. It was the beginning of Napoleon's end. Of the 400,000 soldiers, only 60,000 returned home. "The Russian campaign has ended in disaster," wrote Napoleon honestly.* He left the army and, traveling day and night, secretly made his way back to Paris. Since he had departed for Russia, additional troubles had reared their heads and he had to confront them without delay: Wellington and the British had invaded Madrid, Talleyrand was plotting against him, and another conspiracy—the Malet plan—had been discovered.

By this time it became clear to Metternich that Napoleon had suffered more than a defeat. It was time to prepare a decisive thrust. In the greatest possible secrecy Austria began to rearm, while Metternich kept assuring French Ambassador Narbonne in Vienna that he could count on Austria's good will. Excite-

---

* Bulletin 29, December 3, 1812.

ment among the Viennese rose. Mälzel knew how to profit by it. He exhibited an elaborate mechanical spectacle, complete with lights, artificial snow, wind machine, and somber music (*not* by Beethoven), entitled *The Conflagration of Moscow.* It did fine business. But better was to follow.

It took more than forty lashes of the Russian winter to subdue Napoleon altogether. He raised a new army and won new victories. Then, on June 21, 1813, he was routed by Wellington at Vitoria. That news made more of an impression in Vienna than the Russian defeat, perhaps because it was the British who won the victory and the British were popular with the Viennese. Again Mälzel saw the opportunity: would Beethoven consider a composition for the Panharmonicon to celebrate Wellington's victory? It was just the thing to arouse enthusiasm not only in Vienna but in England. Let Beethoven use themes that a British audience would at once recognize—*Rule Britannia, God Save the King,* and *Marlboro s'en va-t-en guerre*—what could be more surefire? For once Beethoven accepted these opportunistic suggestions. He wrote in his diary, "I must show the English a little what a blessing they have in *God Save the King.*"

There is no question but that most of the ideas for this farrago of a composition were Mälzel's. Obviously it was he too who instructed Beethoven how to write for so novel an instrument as the Panharmonicon. It is important that we keep this in mind, in view of Beethoven's later treatment of Mälzel. Several contemporary witnesses could be cited as to Mälzel's share in the undertaking. Suffice it to quote Moscheles, a truthful man:

> I witnessed the origin and progress of this work, and remember that not only did Mälzel decidedly induce Beethoven to write it, but even laid before him the whole design of it; himself wrote all the drum-marches and the trumpet-flour-ishes of the French and English armies; gave the composer some hints, how he should introduce "Malbrook" in a dismal strain; how he should depict the horrors of the battle and arrange "God save the King" with effects representing the hurrahs of a multitude. Even the unhappy idea of converting the melody of "God save the King" into a subject of a fugue in quick movement, emanates from Mälzel. All this I saw in sketches and score, brought by Beethoven to Mälzel's workshop, then the only suitable place of reception he was provided with.*

---

* From the Moscheles edition of the Schindler biography.

The composition was ready probably early in October, to be transferred by Mälzel to one of his cylinders.

Now Mälzel had another idea, a still better one. For the journey to England he needed to raise considerable funds. His own were pretty well used up, and Beethoven's finances were in a low state. The way to raise money, he suggested to Beethoven, was to give two or three grand gala concerts. It was five years since Beethoven had had a concert for his own benefit, and his efforts to arrange for one in the spring had proved discouraging. Nevertheless, Mälzel felt that the time was propitious for another effort. Cultivated music lovers would like to hear a new symphony by Beethoven, and he, Mälzel, knew that at least one such was ready, the Seventh. But, said Mälzel, for the broad mass of auditors a surprise, a sensation, was needed. How would it be if Beethoven took his battle piece written for the Panharmonicon and now orchestrated it *for the full orchestra?* In doing so, he would be freed from the limitations of the mechanical instrument, could give unlimited rein to his imagination, could make a better composition of it. Mälzel was willing to return the score created for the Panharmonicon to Beethoven, remain in Vienna, and make the new piece Beethoven was to write the central attraction of several concerts; first, one for the benefit of wounded Austrian soldiers, and then two or three for the benefit of Mälzel and Beethoven combined. Beethoven pondered the plan. He wanted his Seventh heard. He needed money. He said yes.

While Beethoven was sitting at his desk, Mälzel was busy with the preparations for the concert. Mälzel's personal popularity, the interest in Beethoven's new works, and the excellent charitable purpose for which the first concert was destined, all enabled him to obtain the consent of the leading musicians of Vienna to play in the orchestra. He saw to it that this "all-celebrity" orchestra became widely publicized. Schuppanzigh led the violins while Spohr took second place in the violin section. Salieri cued the fanfares and salvos. A young pianist by the name of Giacomo Meyerbeer, in Vienna for study purposes, played the drum on one side of the stage while Hummel played the other. Moscheles stood beside him with the cymbals. There were many other local celebrities in the orchestra. Beethoven conducted, and Spohr remembered that he cut a pathetic figure, crouching down at the soft passages, jumping into the air at the loud passages. At the rehearsals Beethoven was patient. The musicians, after initially protesting that the music (no doubt they referred to the Seventh) was very, very difficult, rejoiced that they could give Beethoven what he wanted.

Beethoven had asked Archduke Rudolph to use his influence to obtain the large hall of the university. There the charity concert took place on December 8. The program consisted of the following:

1. An "entirely new symphony" by Beethoven. (This was the Seventh.)
2. Two marches, one by Dussek, the other by Pleyel, played by Mälzel's Mechanical Trumpeter with orchestral accompaniment.
3. *Wellington's Victory.*

The success of the performance was startling. The people applauded frantically. The audience was in ecstasy. The *allegretto* of the Seventh Symphony had to be repeated. The critical reviews raved about both the symphony and *Wellington's Victory*. Immediately a repetition of the entire concert was demanded. It was given four days later on a Sunday, December 12, at noon, at the same high prices, ten and five florins. The charity benefited to the tune of 4000 florins.

Beethoven, whose worth up to now had been often appreciated by the intelligent music lover, now became a "popular composer," in the sense that he appealed to the people who liked something of a show with their music. The banal, noisy, and naïve piece of music which Beethoven had been persuaded to produce had the beneficial effect of shedding the light of interest and curiosity on his other music, specifically the great Seventh. It all happened very much as Mälzel had predicted. There were, to be sure, extra-musical reasons which aided the success. Vienna was in a patriotic furor. Austria had declared war on Napoleon on August 12, playing the part of the hunter who, in friendly company, now moves in for the kill. On October 16 the great "Battle of the Nations" had been fought at Leipzig. Everywhere throughout Europe the subjugated people were rising against the Corsican. In Vienna it was now safe to throw mud on his picture while making believe that the Viennese had something to do with Wellington's victory. They merely wrote the music; that is, one man did. That man's Seventh Symphony rode to victory on the back of *Wellington's Victory.*

·⊰[7]⊱·

It was the first ray of bright light, the first note of optimism, which Beethoven had experienced in a year in which his health had deteriorated and he had been feeling bitter against the world. He wrote to a lawyer in Prague, Dr. Joseph Reger:

> In everything I undertake in Vienna I am surrounded by innumerable enemies. I
> am on the verge of despair—My brother [probably Carl], whom I have loaded
> with benefits, and owing partly to whose deliberate action I myself am finan-
> cially embarrassed, is—my greatest enemy! (A-441).

This letter is dated December 18, 1813; it was written only six days after the
second successful concert. Beethoven's anger had not left his soul. Grief was still
too densely packed within him. For too many months had he lived in his own
confinement for even the loud acclamation of the two concerts to break the
wall. Soon he was to turn again to the saner, sweeter, and gentler side of his
nature. But not yet. Not yet.

Before him now was the opportunity to earn money through the benefit
concert in which Mälzel was to have a share and for which Mälzel had labored
so ingeniously. What happened was that Beethoven proceeded, *ignoring
Mälzel's rightful due.*

On December 31, 1813,* the *Wiener Zeitung* carried the following notice:

MUSICAL ACADEMY

The desire of a large number of honorable music-lovers to hear again my
grand instrumental composition on "Wellington's Victory at Vittoria," makes it
my pleasant duty to inform the valued public that on Sunday, the 2nd of
January, I shall have the honor to perform the aforementioned composition with
added vocal pieces and choruses and aided by the most admirable musicians of
Vienna in the I. R. large Redoutensaal for my benefit.

Tickets of admission are to be had daily in the Kohlmarkt in the house of
Baron v. Haggmüller, to the right of the court on the ground floor, in the
bureau of Baron v. Pasquallati; [*sic*] Parterre 2 fl. Gallery 3 fl., W.W.

LUDWIG VAN BEETHOVEN

Not a word about Mälzel.

Beethoven had obtained, again largely through the good offices of Archduke
Rudolph, the use of the large Redoutensaal. Who Baron v. Haggmüller **.
was we have not been able to ascertain. It is worth noting that the tickets were
more popularly priced (about $2.50 and $3.75) than those for the first two
concerts. For this concert Beethoven discarded Mälzel's Mechanical Trumpeter
and substituted some selections from his *Ruins of Athens* music, including an

---

* The same notice appeared on January 2, 1814, the day of the concert.
** Thayer spells it "Haggenmüller."

aria for the bass, sung by Weinmüller. During the aria, the bust of Emperor Franz was made to appear from behind a curtain. This childish theatrical touch was Beethoven's own idea. He thought it very important for the dramatic effect, as is apparent from a note, half humorous, half nervous, written to Zmeskall on New Year's Day:

Dear and Beloved Friend!

All would be well if the curtain were there, but without it the aria will be a failure. Only at noon today did I hear this from S[chuppanzigh] and I am much distressed — There must be some curtain, even though it be a bed-curtain or merely some kind of screen, which can be removed in a trice, a veil or something of the sort. There must be something. As it is, the aria is more or less dramatic, for it was composed for the theater and thus cannot be effective in a concert hall; and without a curtain or something of the kind its whole significance will be lost! — lost! — lost! — The devil take the whole business! The Court will probably be present.

Baron Schweiger has begged me insistently to go to the Hofburg; the Archduke Karl has received me in person and promised to come — The Empress has not said yes, but neither has she said no —

Curtain!!! Or the aria and I will be hanged tomorrow.

All good wishes. At the New Year I press you to my heart as warmly as I did during the Old Year — With or without a curtain?

Your
BETHVN. (A-456).

Most of the musicians who had taken part in the previous concerts played on January 2. Beethoven attempted to conduct but nearly caused a shipwreck. Whereupon at the critical moment Kapellmeister Umlauf took charge and surreptitiously indicated to the orchestra that they were to follow his beat. According to the reminiscences of Franz Wild, a singer who was present,

For a long time Beethoven noticed nothing of the change; when he finally observed it, a smile came to his lips which, if ever a one which kind fate permitted me to see could be called so, deserved to be called "heavenly." (TQ).

Again the concert was a huge success. The *Battle Symphony* — with its imitations of martial sounds, its fanfares and drum rolls — made a particularly stirring impression, the large Redoutensaal offering an opportunity to deploy the opposing forces of the orchestra and give the illusion that they were approaching each other.* (Surely an early example of a stereo effect.)

On January 9, the *Wiener Zeitung* published a review of the concert which they called "a veritable feast":

> The applause was general and mounted to the highest ecstasy. Many parts had to be repeated. The spectators unanimously voiced their desire to hear these compositions frequently and to be able to praise and admire the products of the spiritual invention of this our native artist.

On January 24, Beethoven published in the *Wiener Zeitung* a note of thanks:

NOTE OF THANKS

> I had the good fortune on the occasion of a performance of my compositions at the concert given by me on January 2, to have the support and help of a large number of the most admirable and celebrated artists of the city, and to see my works brilliantly made known by the hands of such virtuosi. Though these artists may have felt themselves rewarded by their own zeal for art and the pleasure which they gave the public through their talents, it is yet my duty publicly to express to them my warmest thanks for their mark of friendship for me and ready support.
>
> LUDWIG VAN BEETHOVEN   (TQ).

Not a word about Mälzel. About a month later, another concert was announced, again in the Redoutensaal, a Sunday "Akademie" on February 27 for which Beethoven promised a new symphony and a new vocal trio. The new trio was an old trio, composed by 1802 but now completed in final form. It was sung by Beethoven's first Leonore, Milder, now married and appearing under the name of Milder-Hauptmann.** The two male parts were taken by the famous tenor Giuseppe Siboni and the bass Weinmüller. But the new symphony *was* new: it was the Eighth.

---

* From a letter by Georg Griesinger: "I am reminded of J. Haydn who was severely lectured when in 'The Creation' he imitated the quacking of the frogs, the murmur of the wind, the rain, etc. He said to me then: 'Don't people realize that I know very well what is permissible in music and what is not?' .... I heard Beethoven say something similar in connection with his Battle Symphony. When great talents sin once in a while against good taste, that doesn't prove that they haven't got taste." (To Böttiger in Dresden, October 10, 1818.)

** Hauptmann was a wealthy jeweler. The marriage proved unhappy and was subsequently dissolved, and Milder continued her stage career. In 1815 she made a great success in Berlin as Leonore. Beethoven admired her very much. While she was married he called himself her *real* "Hauptmann" (Headman), a military term.

All this music constituted a long program, beginning with the Seventh Symphony, followed by the trio, then the Eighth, and finally the now indispensable *Wellington's Victory*. The *Allgemeine Musikalische Zeitung* reviewed the concert, and the critic, whoever he was, made some intelligent remarks about the Eighth Symphony:

> The greatest interest of the listeners seemed centered on this, the *newest* product of B's muse, and expectation was tense, but this was not sufficiently gratified after the *single* hearing, and the applause which it received was not accompanied by that enthusiasm which distinguishes a work which gives universal delight; in short—as the Italians say—did not create a furore. This reviewer is of the opinion that the reason does not lie by any means in weaker or less artistic workmanship (for here as in all of B's works of this class there breathes that peculiar spirit by which his originality always asserts itself); but partly in the faulty judgment which permitted this symphony to follow that in A major, partly in the surfeit of beauty and excellence which must necessarily be followed by a reaction. If this symphony should be performed *alone* hereafter, we have no doubt of its success. (TQ).

Though the Seventh was again appreciated and though *Vittoria* drove the audience to wild applause—the *Battle* section had to be repeated—Beethoven was disappointed that the Eighth did not please better than it did. He said, comparing it to the Seventh, that the reason was that "the Eighth was much better" (Czerny). We need not take this too seriously. Czerny also remembered that Beethoven was fond of telling the story how, after this concert, when he was walking in the Kahlenberg, he bought some cherries from two peasant girls, and when he asked the price, one of them replied, "There is no charge. We saw you in the Redoutensaal and heard your beautiful music."

Schindler reported (secondhand—he wasn't there) that the audience numbered 5000. That is probably exaggerated. Thayer estimates the audience to have been about 3000. Even so, that was a very large audience, and the profits to Beethoven must have been substantial.

··⊰[8]⊱··

Mälzel must have watched all this success with a mixture of fury and envy. He was still in Vienna, probably still hoping to make some kind of arrangement with Beethoven, either for Beethoven to accompany him to London or at least to give him a share of the concert receipts. Beethoven had borrowed fifty ducats from Mälzel. These he repaid. He and Beethoven met several times at the office of one of Beethoven's legal counselors, Dr. Carl von Adlersburg. At these meetings Mälzel proposed several plans to obtain the right of first performance of the *Battle Symphony* for England, none of which proved acceptable to Beethoven. Nothing came of the meetings. Mälzel, having seen that Beethoven was intractable, did not show up for the last one. Instead, he obtained, by dubious means (probably by bribing certain musicians who had taken part in the performances), single parts of the *Battle Symphony* score, from which he was able to reconstruct a full score. With that score he departed for Munich and there produced the work in two concerts, on March 16 and 17, 1814. When Beethoven heard about it, his rage became fierce, his counterattack voiced in his usual cry: "I crave the law." He would hear no advice; he was going to sue his former friend to stop him from producing or publishing the *Battle* in England. Aside from all questions of right or wrong, it was absurdly silly to instigate a lawsuit against a man who was on his way to the other end of Europe and to a country where Austrian courts had no jurisdiction. Beethoven ran to the law at the slightest provocation; his life story is dotted with the names of lawyers.

The second step Beethoven took was to have a copy of the symphony made and to send it to the Prince Regent of England. The maneuver was prompted by the hope that the prince would interest himself in the composition, considering what a tribute to the British it represented, and would have it performed under his protectorate or at least prevent Mälzel from announcing it as his property. As it turned out, that move was as futile as the lawsuit, since the elaborate copy, expensively done, was filed away in the library of the prince, who never paid it the slightest attention. For several years Beethoven tried to obtain recognition for the *Battle* from the British Royal House and he asked a number of influential people to promote the cause. He was finally willing to settle just for the reimbursement of the cost of copying. In vain: he was met by stony silence.

The question remains: why did Beethoven act as he did against Mälzel? We can only guess that Mälzel became too forward in his claim of proprietorship in the piece, or his share in its composition. Beethoven had objected to the wording of some of the original posters, giving Mälzel too much credit.

Thayer made an analysis of the documents of the case. There are three principal ones:

1. A Deposition by Beethoven to his lawyer.
2. An "Appeal to the musicians of London."

3. A certificate testifying to the conferences that had taken place between Mälzel and Beethoven in the lawyer's office. It is signed by Adlersburg and Pasqualati.

Beethoven's Deposition (No. 1) is full of gross misstatements, inexcusable even in a document pleading one's own case to one's own lawyer. He berates Mälzel as a "coarse fellow, entirely without education or culture," which is not true. He says that the sending of the score to the Prince Regent was an opportunity offered to him, which is not true. He says that he composed the *Victory Symphony* for the Panharmonicon to encourage Mälzel to construct hearing machines for him. This is substantially untrue. The machines proved useless. "Now, assuming that I really felt under some obligation for the hearing machines, it is canceled by the fact that he made at least 500 florins . . . out of the *Battle* stolen from me or compiled in a mutilated manner."

No. 2. The "Appeal" declares that Mälzel is not the rightful owner, that the performance of the work therefore is a fraud on the public; in any case, what the London public is likely to hear is a "spurious or mutilated [version of the] work."

Mälzel's reply to his own lawyer is lost. As Thayer says: "He had no young disciple planning with zeal to preserve it and give it, with his version of the story, to posterity." Thayer concludes:

> Candor and justice compel the painful admission that Beethoven's course with Mälzel is a blot—one of the few—upon his character, which no amount of misrepresentation of the facts can wholly efface; whoever can convince himself that the composer's conduct was legally and technically just and right, must still feel that it was neither noble nor generous.

Mälzel returned to Vienna in 1817, bringing with him his now perfected metronome. What was he doing in Vienna? It was highly important to him, or rather to the manufacturers who were backing him, to obtain testimonials from leading composers. He saw Salieri, Weigl—and he saw Beethoven, risking a renewal of the quarrel. Nothing of the kind happened. Their difference was amicably adjusted, each of them paying half of the legal expenses which had been incurred. Beethoven made a thoughtful study of the metronome and in connection with this wrote a valuable analysis of the true meaning of tempo. In spite of his belief that tempo must be felt, he acknowledged the need for an objective measuring rod to substitute for those absurd descriptive terms such as *allegro, andante,* and so on. Mälzel's metronome "affords us the best opportunity of doing so." He also joined with Salieri in a public announcement praising the instrument.* In short, the whole ugly and expensive quarrel was buried "full fathom five." Beethoven again was on good terms with the man whom he had damned.

It is of tangential interest that Mälzel eventually made his way to the United States. Thayer interviewed there some of the men who had known him; they spoke of him as "a gentleman and a man of culture." He died suddenly in 1838, on board ship while on a voyage between the West Indies and Philadelphia. He was supposed to have left a fortune of half a million dollars.**

·◦[9]◦·

Such, then, reads the conscientious chronicle of four years of Beethoven's life. With moments of exception, they were not happy years either for him or the world in which he lived. As to the world—no one will ever know whether another potential Beethoven was lost at Wagram or another potential Voltaire froze to death on the banks of the Berezina. As to Beethoven—in a letter, in the summer of 1813, to Franz Brunsvik in which he calls himself a "suffering individual" (*elendes Individuum*) he writes: "Our striving is infinite, but vulgarity makes everything finite!" It was his own involvement with the finite —the three lawsuits (Lobkowitz, Kinsky, Mälzel), the family quarrels, the money problems, the printers' errors in the scores—which interfered with his infinite striving.

The world renewed itself: it had to. Within those four years Frédéric Chopin, Robert Schumann, Camillo Cavour, Alfred de Musset, William Makepeace Thackeray, Franz Liszt, Charles Dickens, Robert Browning, Richard Wagner, and Giuseppe Verdi were born. So, to be sure, was Alfred Krupp.

Beethoven renewed himself. He emerged from the lugubrious light. For him there were no easy rewards. He could not live at peace. Yet he summoned the power to struggle through—to the creation of his greatest work. The strongest geniuses are not merely born; they are renewed.

---

* In the *Wiener Allgemeine Musikalische Zeitung,* February 14, 1818.
** See Paul Nettl, *Beethoven Handbook,* 1956. Article on Mälzel.

CHAPTER 18

FIDELIO AND
THE CONGRESS OF VIENNA

·:[I]:·

At last there was a little balm in Gilead. Blow after blow fell on Napoleon, but he would not and could not accept defeat. "I am in blood stepp'd in so far"—he could say with Macbeth—"that . . . returning were as tedious as go o'er." Metternich tried to negotiate with him, because much as he desired the downfall of Napoleon he did not relish the ascension of the Czar, and he was quite willing to arrive at a compromise. It was no use. On June 26, 1813, in a historic interview which lasted eight and three-quarter hours, Napoleon said to him, "I'll know how to die—but I will not cede a hand's breadth of earth." In December the Austrians—under Karl Schwarzenberg—the British, and the Prussians invaded France. On March 30, 1814, they were in Paris. On April 1 Talleyrand called a meeting of the French Senate. Only 64 of the 140 senators showed up: they voted for the dethronement of Napoleon and the reinstatement of the Bourbons. Napoleon tried to commit suicide. He was unsuccessful. He took leave of his guard and embarked for Elba.

Dressed in a new white uniform (tailored in Paris) and riding a white horse, that somewhat less than doughty hero, Emperor Franz, returned to Vienna.

That spring was joyful to the Viennese, who had had to swallow defeats in evil-tasting and sour-smelling doses. Almost as soon as the news turned good, musical and theatrical life assumed new vigor. For a festive performance at the Court Opera, Georg Friedrich Treitschke—now highly placed in the management of the Court Theaters—wrote a one-act *Singspiel* entitled "Good News." Beethoven obligingly furnished a concluding patriotic chorus for it. For a charity concert—held on April 11, the day after the news of the occupation of Paris reached Vienna—Beethoven consented to appear; he presented the *Archduke Trio*. Moscheles noted in his diary:

Return of Emperor Franz I to Vienna, 1814. Painting is by J. P. Krafft (Austrian National Library).

> In the case of how many compositions is the word "new" misapplied! But never
> in Beethoven's, and least of all in this, which again is full of originality. His
> playing, aside from its intellectual element, satisfied me less, being wanting in
> clarity and precision; but I observed many traces of the *grand* style of playing
> which I had long recognized in his compositions.

In Vienna, Beethoven stood as the figure of the Austrian national composer.
He who years before had composed a symphony which was to honor Napoleon
had now written the work which celebrated Napoleon's defeat. The cynic may
say that it was his one major worthless work which propelled him toward
greater fame. Yet it is impossible to judge this music of the moment, this proud
patriotic noise, except within the context of the new fervor, freed from fear.

At any rate, *Wellington's Victory* was performed again and again, and
Beethoven's popularity gave three men an idea. They bethought themselves of
Fidelio, that stillborn work which nobody had heard for eight years. It was
there, available, an opera by the great Beethoven. Why not bring it out again?
Why not experiment to see if this work could now arouse interest? Conditions
were different; surely the story would now have great appeal. For "Pizarro"
read "Napoleon." So argued three *Inspizienten* * of the Imperial Royal Court
Opera. They were Saal, Vogel, and Weinmüller. They were entitled to a benefit
performance, and they felt that the name of Beethoven was sufficient to assure
them of a full house. Would he agree to let *Fidelio* be revived? The scenery was
still intact—Napoleon had hardly cared to carry that away—and the work
could be remounted without too much expense. They had all three heard the
original performance of the opera and felt that it could become successful; at
the least it could offer them three good parts as singers. What they wanted most
of all was the magic name of Beethoven.

Beethoven consented, under one condition. He felt that the opera needed
considerable revision and tightening, particularly the libretto, and that the one
man who could accomplish this was Georg Friedrich Treitschke. Would
Treitschke be willing? He would, indeed. Treitschke was delighted and, having
obtained permission from the original librettist, Sonnleithner, set to work. So
did Beethoven: in March he wrote Treitschke, "I feel more firmly resolved to
rebuild the desolate ruins of an old castle."

Treitschke felt that the opera ought to concentrate as much as possible on the

---

* A title denoting regular employees of the opera house. They worked both as singers and as stage
directors.

heroine; he therefore suggested eliminating at least two of the numbers in which she was not involved. For example, there was a little trio for Rocco, Marzelline, and Jacquino; out it went. Treitschke describes how Beethoven, the score in front of him, literally tore the pages out of it.

His principal changes were two: the first at the beginning of the second act, with Florestan alone in the prison. Florestan had to be introduced, and he needed an aria. Yet, said Treitschke, it could not be a bravura aria, because a man dying of starvation could hardly give forth a lot of florid music.* They tried one idea, they tried another. Nothing seemed right. Then one night Treitschke wrote the words "which describe the last blazing up of life before its extinguishment." Treitschke tells what happened:

> What I am now relating will live forever in my memory. Beethoven came to me about seven o'clock in the evening. After we had discussed other things, he asked how matters stood with the aria? It was just finished, I handed it to him. He read, ran up and down the room, muttered, growled, as was his habit instead of singing—and tore open the pianoforte. My wife had often vainly begged him to play; today he placed the text in front of him and began to improvise marvelously—music which no magic could hold fast. Out of it he seemed to conjure the motive of the aria. The hours went by, but Beethoven improvised on. Supper, which he had purposed to eat with us, was served, but—he would not permit himself to be disturbed. It was late when he embraced me, and declining the meal, he hurried home. The next day the admirable composition was finished.** (TQ).

The second change was this: In the original version the final scene took place in the dungeon. Treitschke suggested that a change of locale would be advantageous: after the gloomy dark the scene of liberation would be more effective played in full daylight. There were other changes, so that Beethoven could say with justice that he was virtually recomposing the opera. It was difficult for him, and of course he took more time with it than he had expected he would need. He wrote to Treitschke in April:

> Now, of course, everything has to be done at once; and I could compose something new far more quickly than patch up the old with something new, as I am now doing. For my custom when I am composing even instrumental music

---

* He was applying common sense to opera, an art which does very well without it.
** From his reminiscences published in *Orpheus, Musikalisches Taschenbuch für das Jahr 1841.*

is always to keep the whole in view—But in this case the whole of my work is—to a certain extent—scattered in all directions; and I have to think out the entire work again—To produce the opera in a fortnight is certainly out of the question. I am still convinced that it will take us four weeks. Meanwhile the first act will be finished in a few days—But there is still much to be done to the second act and I have to compose a new overture as well; but this is the easiest task of all, I admit, because I can write an entirely new one—Before my concert I had just made a few sketches here and there, both in the first and in the second acts; and only a few days ago I was able to begin to work them out—The score of the opera has been copied as wretchedly as anything I have ever seen; I have to check every single note (it was probably stolen). In short, I assure you, dear T[reitschke], that this opera will win for me a martyr's crown. Had you not taken so much trouble with it and revised everything so satisfactorily, for which I shall ever be grateful to you, I would hardly bring myself to do my share—But by your work you have salvaged a few good bits of a ship that was wrecked and stranded— (A-479).

Finally there was the question of Rocco's "Gold" aria, which Beethoven had with great difficulty been persuaded to eliminate in the 1806 version. He was never really convinced that he ought to give it up. In the contemplated new performance, Weinmüller, one of the three propounders of the plan, was to sing Rocco.* He had to be given an aria, so the "Gold" aria was reinstated. However, Treitschke changed the words.** It is interesting to compare the original words with Treitschke's version: The original was also written under the restriction of censorship. But the later version was produced in Metternich's era in an atmosphere of even stricter "conform-or-else," *** and Metternich's censors were sharp-eyed. So Treitschke wrote a bowdlerized version.

1805 version (*Allegro*)	1814 version (*Allegro*)
... *Fortuna* favors the rich. They do what they want, and hide their shameful actions behind a heap of gold.	... May good fortune smile on you kindly and favorably and bless your endeavors, your sweethearts in your arms, gold in your sack. May you live thus many a year!

---

* Saal sang Don Fernando, Vogel, Pizarro.
** This may not have been ready till a later performance, that of July 18, 1814.
*** "I don't need scholars but obedient subjects," Emperor Franz said to the professors of Graz University.

In the end—but before the performance took place—Beethoven was dissatisfied with nearly all of the opera. He hated the business of patching up here and there, a labor less congenial than "being able to indulge in free meditation or inspiration." He planned to write a new short overture for the performance. The final rehearsal was scheduled for May 22, yet the promised new overture was, in Treitschke's words, "still in the pen of the creator." On the twentieth or twenty-first, Beethoven was dining out with Dr. Bertolini. After dinner he took a menu, drew lines on its blank side, and began to write. "Come, let's go," said Bertolini, impatient with the long silence. "No," Beethoven replied, "wait a moment. I have an idea for my overture." Bertolini left, and Beethoven remained and finished his sketching. Treitschke writes:

> The orchestra was called to rehearsal on the morning of the performance. B. did not come. After waiting a long time we drove to his lodgings to bring him, but —he lay in bed, sleeping soundly, beside him stood a goblet with wine and a biscuit in it, the sheets of the overture were scattered on the bed and floor. A burnt-out candle showed that he had worked far into the night. The impossibility of completing the overture was plain; for this occasion his overture to *Prometheus* was taken and the announcement that because of obstacles which had presented themselves the new overture would have to be dispensed with today, enabled the numerous audience to guess the sufficient reason.

The overture which was played was not that to *Prometheus* but probably that of *The Ruins of Athens*. Many years later Beethoven happened to remember the incident and remarked, "The people applauded but I was ashamed. It did not belong to the rest."

The first performance of the new version of *Fidelio* took place on May 23. The production had been carefully rehearsed. Beethoven conducted, but once again the real conductor, Umlauf, gave the cues behind his back and "guided everything to success with eye and hand."

That success was very great indeed. Enthusiasm ran high. At the close of the first act Beethoven received an ovation. Leonore's great aria, in the new version, was rapturously applauded; Milder, grown older and more experienced, sang it superbly. When the liberating trumpet call was heard, the audience gasped. When, up in the sunlight, Don Fernando bade the people rise and kneel no longer, there were few in that audience who were not weeping openly. After the fall of the curtain his friends rushed backstage to embrace Beethoven. One friend, alas, was missing, the one at whose house the stormy discussion about the opera had taken place in 1805: Prince Lichnowsky, his patient and understanding protector, had died on April 15.

The opera was repeated on May 26; the new overture—now known as the *Fidelio*—was then played and "was received with tempestuous applause."

Referring again to our friend Rosenbaum's diary: He notes performances on May 23, May 26; June 2, 4, 7, 21; July 18, 22; and August 24. The June 21 performance seems to be the first time Rosenbaum heard the opera; he reports, "Full house." Of the August 24 performance he writes that Milder began her duet with Radichi (Florestan) four times, and two days later he writes to his wife, who is in Baden, that Milder had to leave the stage without being able to finish the duet. (That seems improbable. Was Rosenbaum trying to console his wife because she did *not* get a chance to sing in *Fidelio?*)

The list of performances goes on: September 4, 16, 20, 26; October 4, 9—the Congress of Vienna had now begun—18, 28; November 3, 27; and December 27.

The performance on July 18 was for Beethoven's benefit. According to the *Wiener Zeitung,* the house was full, the applause extraordinary, the enthusiasm for the composer, "who has now become a favorite of the public," showing itself in many curtain calls. All free tickets had been canceled; therefore the performance must have netted Beethoven a good sum.

What, to the audiences of more than a century and a half, is the gain? How valuable is the work which cost Beethoven so much grief and which in the end he loved so dearly? *Fidelio* is not a drawing card. It has never proved a decided box-office success; it is no "Fifth Symphony." Nor is it a failure. It never drops from the repertoire altogether because too many people want to hear it, because many have always and can today respond to its beauty, and because the role of Leonore is as challenging to a great actress as is the role of Isolde or Norma. Yet there are many who consider *Fidelio* a work to be handled with respect and reverence, but which, to put it bluntly, they find a bore. They'd exchange the whole opera for one overture, the *Leonore No. 3.*

What are the obstacles which lie in the way of the understanding of what is, in my opinion, one of the supreme works for the lyric stage?

Let us first note that *Fidelio* does not "play itself." It is by no means easy to perform. Either it comes off—or it can be quite tedious. The demand for exceptionally fine interpreters is severer here than in most operas—severer than in Verdi, Puccini, and even Wagner—and these must include a conductor who understands *both* opera and Beethoven, and a Leonore who can sing, act, and *speak* the lines. That is quite a bill of particulars. Consider: She must be able to sing her great aria, the vocal demands of which are cruel and even a little impractical—that much must be conceded. She must be able to handle lines which are something less than deathless dialogue but which must be spoken with conviction. She must combine in herself both the power of dominating the dramatic climaxes and the womanly sweetness which is the essence of Leonore's character. Let her lack either, and Leonore becomes either a virago or a ninny. Lastly, the opera demands that she give the illusion of being able to carry off her male disguise.* Let her be of mammalian amplitude, and, on her first appearance as a boy in the service of Rocco, the irreverent are bound to snicker. Wagner tells us in his autobiography of the searing impression Schroeder-Devrient, the first of the famous Leonores, made on him.** Berlioz, too, was inspired by her. Schroeder-Devrient not only was an exceptional artist, but at the time Wagner first heard her she was a young girl in her twenties. Alas, young sopranos usually cannot sing the part; older sopranos cannot look it.

A further difficulty lies in the sequence of music alternating with spoken text, a combination usual enough in Beethoven's time but now a form to which we have become unused. We accept it in musical comedy. It bothers us in serious opera. Unlike *Carmen, Fidelio* is not given with recitatives which somebody has added later. No doctoring is possible. The alternation of song and dialogue creates some extraordinary effects. But it is irritating if one does not understand German. Even if one does, one has to get used to it. Yet the work transcends its difficulties and defects because it is endowed with the compassion and the idealism which it is the special task of great art to present to us.

·◦[2]◦·

So *Fidelio,* which had been a failure during Napoleon's first invasion, now became *the* fashionable opera for those in Congress assembled. Metternich announced the Congress when he returned to Vienna on July 18, 1814. He was

---

* "Most Leonores look like the Soviet women competitors in the Olympic games."—Vincent Sheehan.
** "When I review my entire life," wrote Wagner in *Mein Leben,* "I can discover hardly another occurrence which affected me so profoundly. Whoever remembers this remarkable woman at that stage of her career will testify to the almost demoniacal warmth radiated by the human-ecstatic achievement of this incomparable artist. After the performance I dashed to the home of a friend of mine to write her a letter in which I solemnly stated that, as of that day, my life had acquired its meaning, and that if she were ever to hear my name mentioned as of consequence in the world of art, she should remember that on this evening she had made me what I herewith vowed to become. I dropped the letter at her hotel and rushed off into the night." This was in 1829. Beethoven heard her in 1822, but she was too young then to have penetrated the part, though he too was impressed.

received in triumph; the official reception was managed by Count Palffy and took place in front of the Palace of the Government Archives. An orchestra played Beethoven's overture to *The Creatures of Prometheus*.

The avowed purpose of the Congress of Vienna, to which the representatives of all European nations had been invited whether they had taken part in the war on one side or the other, was the establishment of an equilibrium which would avoid future power arrogation and future disastrous wars. The ideal was a fine one. That it was not reached; that indeed at one time the peace meeting threatened to disintegrate into another armed war between nations; that neither Metternich for Austria, nor Talleyrand for France, nor Hardenberg for Prussia, nor Viscount Castlereagh for England, nor decidedly the victorious Czar Alexander could for a moment forget national interests in favor of humanity; that many of the best efforts were turned awry by greed and trickery—all of that we have come to accept as an unfortunate truism. Italy and Germany remained fractured countries, Metternich got his wish of preserving the monarchy as if the French Revolution had never happened, the Czar sucked up a large part of Poland, and Britannia remained the ruler of the waves.

Yet the Congress did manage to lay down safeguards in such a way that a major European war was avoided till 1870. The analysis of the successes and failures of the Congress * does not lie within the province of a Beethoven biography. We must content ourselves with relating how the Congress affected Beethoven's life.

Beginning in the summer of 1814, there gradually assembled in Vienna a crowd of luminaries and their satraps which eventually numbered two emperors, two empresses, four kings, one queen, two hereditary princes, three grand duchesses, and three princes of royal blood, all with their staffs and entourages. In addition there were present 247 members of reigning houses. These were accompanied by military leaders, diplomats, experts in various fields, bankers, industrial leaders, cartographers, journalists, authors—plus wives, mistresses, expensive prostitutes, and various dubious characters. Not to mention the cooks, the valets, the equerries, the private barbers, the ladies' maids, the coachmen, the interpreters. All in all, over 10,000 persons streamed into Vienna.

The Congress has been described as a dancing affair, "Congress Dances." That is a Dumas-esque version of history. There *was* a lot of dancing. The Czar,

---

* It has been written with fine lucidity by Harold Nicolson: *The Congress of Vienna.* Metternich too has recently become the subject of a biography by the French writer Henry Vallotton.

it was said, danced forty nights through. The younger diplomats, bored to extinction by Metternich's stuffy receptions or the endless banquets, continued their evenings in the Apollo or the Redoutensaal ballrooms. A thousand chandeliers and tens of thousands of candles illuminated the city. The Viennese lost sleep watching the strange and beautiful foreign women. The Russian Princess Bagration was voted the most beautiful, perhaps because she displayed her charms generously: she was known as "the beautiful naked angel." Lady Castlereagh was considered the most ridiculous, particularly when she used her husband's Order of the Knight of the Garter to hold her hair in place. "The English ladies think that it is beneath their dignity to dress according to the fashion of the country they are visiting. . . . Their clothes, or rather their coverings, are so tight that their whole bodies are sharply outlined. Their décolletages reach down to their navel. Lord Castlereagh dances every evening for two hours with his wife or her sister, if he can't find another partner. He says he needs the exercise to recover from his daily mental exertions. If the ladies are busy, he takes a chair and dances with it" (Baroness Du Montet). Talleyrand said, "The Czar of Russia loves, the King of Denmark drinks, the King of Württemberg eats, the King of Prussia thinks, the King of Bavaria talks, and the Emperor of Austria pays." There was lots to be paid for, not only the quartering of all these illustrious guests but also the masquerades, the sledding parties, the fireworks, the balloon ascensions, the theatrical performances in Schönbrunn, the hunting expeditions, the tombolas and ridottos. It cost the Court 500,000 gulden a day to feed the guests. Special carriages were furnished to all royal guests; 1400 horses stood in the stables of the *Hofburg*.

The "Festivals Committee" appointed by the Emperor was driven to the edge of a nervous breakdown not only by the task of inventing new amusements but by the ubiquitous problems of precedence. Somebody, some minor king, was always being insulted and launching a protest.

Gone was the Vienna that Beethoven had known, where a Lichnowsky or a Rasoumovsky would invite a few people and let them be auditors to a performance of chamber music. There was little time for chamber music now; dinner for thirty people was not very practical, since there were sixty more that needed to be invited. A great deal of entertaining was done in the so-called *assemblées* —giant receptions, forerunners of our cocktail parties—during which ices and champagne were served, and during which the same people saw one another day after day in different palaces and exchanged the same inanities. (The next day the servants called at the houses of the various guests to collect a tip.) One dared not talk openly, for spies were everywhere. The Vienna police were said to open about 15,000 letters a year and skillfully to seal them again. Emperor Franz, supposedly a model of probity, avidly read at breakfast the confidential reports of the most scandalous incidents of the preceding night.

Yet this was only one side of the Congress. The famous epigram *"Le congrès danse, mais il ne marche pas"* ("Congress dances, but does not move") was no truer than most epigrams. A prodigious amount of serious labor was accomplished, and men toiled far into the night with selfless devotion. In addition to territorial and defense issues, such matters as freedom of shipping on the rivers, the abolishment of slave trade, the neutrality of Switzerland, and the establishment of copyright laws were discussed.

Many of those who worked for or were observers of the Congress were men and women of intellectual interests, and they asked for entertainment less frivolous than a masquerade. How else could *Fidelio* have become popular, how else could concerts of Beethoven's music have become events of importance both artistically and representationally? * It is strange that we do not know whether Beethoven, the representative of musical Vienna, and Metternich, the representative of political Vienna, ever met. Metternich must have known who Beethoven was, but he never mentions him. It is a safe guess that had they known each other they would have disliked each other cordially.

One of the men who left us a record of the Congress that speaks of events other than the morning receptions at Talleyrand's (while two barbers arranged his coiffure and a valet poured vinegar over his lame foot) was a Carl Bertuch from Weimar. He had arrived with a letter of recommendation from Goethe and was working as assistant to Cotta, the Augsburg book publisher. He kept a diary the pages of which "provide an admirable antidote" (Nicolson) to the snobbish recitals of the Congress' doings:

> October 25. 7 o'clock with Cotta to the Arnsteiners [powerful bankers, the firm being Arnstein and Eskeles. Beethoven later dealt with them. Baron Nathan von Arnstein and his wife Fanny entertained lavishly]. About 70 to 80 people. Overture to *Fidelio* played by Mosele [Moscheles]. Trio with Mad. Geymüller. Italian Duet, very well sung by Fräulein Werdenstein and an Italian. Quartet, in which Kraft played the cello excellently [Anton Kraft, who was the cellist in Beethoven's Triple Concerto] ...

---

* Another important artistic event was a performance of Handel's oratorio *Samson*, October 10, 1814. Then there were special performances of new compositions such as Spohr's cantata, *Germany Liberated* (text by Karoline Pichler), serious plays given in both Court Theaters, etc.

October 28. In the evening *Fidelio* by Beethoven. Profound marvelous music. Milder sang the role of Fidelio very well.

December 27. Evening. I saw *Fidelio* for the second time. An opera full of originality. Beautiful quartet in Act I, in the second act duet with the husband. Chorus of prisoners excellent. The entire treatment very skillful.

During the summer Beethoven worked on some occasional pieces to be presented during the Congress. One of these was a cantata for chorus and orchestra, *Ihr weisen Gründer,* the other an overture in C, designed as a tribute to Emperor Franz and to be called the *Name-day Festival Overture (Namens-feier Overture,* Op. 115, not performed till December, 1815).

Surprisingly, after a five-year interval, he composed a piano sonata, No. 27 in E minor, Op. 90. He dedicated it to Moritz Lichnowsky, Karl's younger brother, and on September 21, 1814, announced the dedication in a charming note to him, saying, *"I have never forgotten how much I owe you in general."* While it is not one of Beethoven's great sonatas, it is a romantic, intimate work. Schindler wrote that it was a love story, appropriate for Moritz Lichnowsky, who had just become engaged to an opera singer.

Another work came about through Alois Weissenbach who, long an admirer of Beethoven, now heard a performance of *Fidelio* and was "carried to heaven." The professor of surgery who was a poet (or vice versa) brought to Beethoven the text of a timely poem, *Der glorreiche Augenblick (The Glorious Moment).* Beethoven liked the poem as he did its author. Weissenbach, a Tyrolean, neat and elegant, was as deaf as Beethoven. The two conversed amiably by shouting at each other.

The Glorious Moment (an inglorious poem) was one of the compositions Beethoven wished to present at a "Gala Concert" which was to be one of the high points of the year's festivities. It was announced first for November 20 in the large Redoutensaal, then postponed three times—to the 22nd, the 27th and finally the 29th—the last postponement having a curious reason, if we may believe a report of the secret police: * "The English are so religious that they do not wish to go to a concert on a Sunday. Therefore the musical Academy of H. v. Beethoven was postponed from Sunday to a work day" (Tuesday, November 29). The police report states that factions existed *pro* and *contra* Beethoven. "As against Rasoumovsky, Apponyi,** Kraft, who deify Beethoven, there exists

---

* Published in *The Secret Police at the Vienna Congress* by August Fournier, Vienna, 1913.
** Count Anton Georg, an early patron.

a much greater majority of connoisseurs who do not wish to hear any compositions whatever by Herrn Beethoven." Beethoven was not precisely popular with the secret police.

The puritanical scruples of the English having been accommodated, the Grand Gala Concert took place before an audience as illustrious as any that had assembled in Vienna. It gathered shortly before noon. Among those present: Czar Alexander of Russia, the Empress of Russia, the Empress of Austria (?), both the Grand Duchesses of Russia, the King of Prussia, Frederick William III (who, however, stayed only for the first part), the Prince of Sicily; in addition, virtually every musician of note, as well as the intellectual leaders of Vienna. The program:

> First: A new large Symphony (the Seventh)
> Second: A new Cantata, "The Glorious Moment," by Dr. Alois Weissenbach
> Third: A large, full-voiced Instrumental Composition describing Wellington's Victory at the Battle of Vitoria
> First Part: Battle   Second Part: Victory-Symphony
> Prices of admission: downstairs 3 gulden, upstairs 5 gulden [*approximately $5 and $8*].

Bertuch wrote in his diary:

> [About the Seventh] a new symphony which recommends itself as much by its wealth of ideas as by its clarity; it represents a new wonderful enrichment of music. [Of the cantata] text quite mediocre, conveying nothing much more than the idea that there were many sovereigns assembled in Vienna; music excellent. [Of *Wellington's Victory*] a bold musical character picture ... The second part was given under Beethoven's direction. Beethoven's conducting is unique. The real world is too narrow for him, he strives for something beyond. He rises and bends physically, now small, now huge. The house was very full.

After it was over, the audience, white gloves and aristocratic restraint notwithstanding, broke into tumultuous applause. They had kept very quiet up to then. What did Beethoven look like, among all those uniforms and gold braid and silk scarves, dressed simply, a "short and stout" figure, waving his hands?

The *Wiener Zeitung* rushed into print the day after and reported that Beethoven "gave all music lovers an ecstatic pleasure." Beethoven does not seem to have been satisfied with the money he made from the concert. Two years later Dr. Karl von Bursy reported Beethoven as saying:

After many intrigues he gave a concert in the *Redoutensaal*. The King of Prussia paid him an extra entrance fee of ten ducats; very paltry! Only the Emperor of Russia paid the decent sum of 200 ducats for his ticket. He was very pleased that the General Director of the Imperial Theatres, Count Palffy, had received a good wigging on this occasion. He bears him a special grudge. Beethoven seems very interested in money and I must confess that this makes him more human, that is, lessens the distance between him and others.*...

The interview took place at the end of May, 1816, when Beethoven was worried about his nephew. Perhaps it should be taken with a grain of salt.

The concert was repeated in the same hall on December 2, but then the house was only half full. Probably some other event interfered. It was given for the third time on Christmas evening as a benefit for St. Marx Hospital. Bertuch was present again and noted, "The hall was very full, the receipts considerable." Even Rosenbaum, who was bored out of his wits by the Seventh Symphony and who thought Weissenbach's poem "beautiful," reported that there was a "crushing crowd."

Tragedy struck Rasoumovsky a few days after. At the Congress he had played the role of host to the Russian contingent with particular brilliance. Schindler says that it was he who presented Beethoven to the assembled monarchs, the ceremony taking place in the rooms of Archduke Rudolph. The Empress of Russia was particularly complimentary to Beethoven. At Dr. Bertolini's suggestion, Beethoven composed a Polonaise (Op. 89) to be dedicated to her. The Empress granted Beethoven a private audience (perhaps at Rasoumovsky's instigation), accepted the dedication, and handed him a gift of 50 ducats. She then asked whether the Czar had ever acknowledged the receipt of the Violin Sonatas, Op. 30, which Beethoven had dedicated to him. Upon learning that he had not, Beethoven was given 100 ducats additionally.

Because Rasoumovsky had distinguished himself both in the dealings with Napoleon and now during the Congress, the Czar made him a prince. "Prince Rasoumovsky," he was at the height of his glory. On the evening of December 30 he invited 700 guests for a gala affair. Spacious though his Palace was, it was insufficiently large to hold such an assembly, and Rasoumovsky had ordered the construction of a temporary addition made of wood on the side next to the garden. The feast proceeded with great *élan*. Between five and six in the morning a fire was discovered, and before it could be brought under control the

---

* Quoted from Michael Hamburger, *Beethoven: Letters, Journals and Conversations*, 1951.

conflagration had destroyed a great part of the Palace, with all the furniture, the tapestries, the innumerable works of art. The precious library went up in flames; so did the adjoining apartments. So did the famous Canova room, the ceiling of which fell in and buried the sculptures. Emperor Franz left his bed and hurried to the site of the fire, trying to help, while Czar Alexander did not bother to show up (or could not be found). Later Alexander offered financial assistance to Rasoumovsky, which proved insufficient. At any rate, what assistance could make good the loss of twenty years of loving and enthusiastic acquisition?

Rasoumovsky never recovered either financially or spiritually. In 1818 the Baroness du Montet found him "aged and melancholy." He who had been so sure of himself, with his charm, his brilliance, his love for music, his fascination for women, now fell into a decline of all his senses and his bodily strength. For a while he did continue his interest in music; the Rasoumovsky Quartet was not pensioned off until 1816. Yet nothing in life meant very much to him from now on. He lived on to the age of eighty-four, existed rather than lived. In effect, Beethoven had lost another of his patrons.

··◦[3]◦··

He gained an all-around useful factotum. One day Schuppanzigh, during an orchestra rehearsal, asked a musician at the next music stand, a youth of eighteen years, to take a note to Beethoven proposing a rehearsal and requiring no other answer than yes or no. The young man joyfully undertook the commission, since he had admired Beethoven's works for several years without ever having dared to approach him. The next morning, "with a beating heart," he climbed the four flights of the Pasqualati house and found himself in the presence of Beethoven, who read the missive, said "yes," asked a question or two, and then dismissed the messenger. At the door the young man surreptitiously tarried for a few moments to observe his idol, who paid no attention to him and immediately resumed his writing.

This young man was Anton Schindler. He followed up the brief encounter with better courage soon after, and gradually their acquaintance ripened. In 1817 Schindler got a job as a clerk in a law office, and in 1819 he took his law examinations. However, his predilection was for music, not for law. About 1820 he began what was to turn out to be his real mission in life, service to Beethoven. He wrote letters, he helped negotiate with publishers, he advised Beethoven in household affairs, he ran errands both important and menial. When Beethoven needed money, he found ways of obtaining it for him; and he did all this without pay and, in the beginning, at least, prompted by the purest of motives: admiration. Gradually he came to realize that he had a not unimportant role for posterity to carve for himself, that of being curator of Beethoven memorabilia. He determined that when the time came it would be he who would be best fitted to write Beethoven's biography.

Beethoven never paid Schindler any salary, though once he said that he really ought to. Most of the time he was very fond of Schindler—one could not help becoming fond of such devotion, such docile patience, such tireless willingness. Beethoven called Schindler by those playful maledictions which he was wont to bestow on those for whom he felt affection. He called him *Lumpenkerl* ("Lout"), *Hauptlumpenkerl* ("Chief Lout"), and *Samothracian Lumpenkerl*, meaning that like the Samothracians of ancient Greece he was privy to secret rites. For many months the two lived together. Yet there were periods when Beethoven could not abide Schindler. We know that practically everybody, at one time or another, grated on Beethoven's nerves. But Schindler—because of his being around all the time, because of a certain open-mouthed eagerness which he displayed, and his avidity to worm all biographical data out of Beethoven—he could stand least of all. The usual pattern repeated itself: Schindler was a "villain." The harshness of the invectives became cutting indeed: Beethoven told him he could not recompense his services by embracing him in true friendship. How could he share his thoughts with him? Schindler was so commonplace that it was impossible for him to understand what was not commonplace. He wrote to Grillparzer that if Grillparzer would be willing to come to see him, he ought to come alone without that "obstreperous appendix." And to Ries he called Schindler an "arch-scoundrel to whom he handed his walking papers." *

Yet all this passed, and when Beethoven returned to Vienna in December, 1826, a sick man, Schindler was there again after a breach of two years to care for him, attend and help.

After Beethoven's death, Schindler left Vienna to become music director in Münster, then Aachen. All this while he was writing the biography, the first edition of which was published in 1840. It represented thirteen years of labor.

No doubt Schindler was an unreliable scholar, and Thayer had to spend much time mopping up the errors. No doubt his bias against the brothers, his

---

* But at the moment he was using Schindler as a whipping boy. Beethoven had promised Ries to dedicate the *Diabelli Variations* to Ries's wife. He did not—and blamed the "mix-up" on Schindler.

faulty memory, and his careless way with dates made him less than an ideal reporter. All the same, his work is valuable, for one important reason: he was there. Whenever he speaks of scenes to which he was an eyewitness, he speaks convincingly. In later years he stalked about as a sort of official representative of Beethoven, a keeper of the keys; he became arrogant and antagonized many people. In 1841 Schindler was in Paris and there made the acquaintance of the poet Heinrich Heine, who, to be sure, was no model of modesty either. Heine, who had little feeling for Beethoven's later music, was offended by Schindler. He said that when Schindler presented himself he proffered a visiting card on which was printed *"l'ami de Beethoven."* Heine described Schindler as "a long black beanpole with a horrible white necktie and the expression of a funeral director. . . . 'How could the great artist bear such an unpleasant, intellectually poverty-stricken friend?' asked the Frenchmen who were listening to his monotonous chatter. . . . They didn't remember that Beethoven was deaf." * In the reminiscences of Moscheles, edited by his wife, the visiting card with *"l'ami de Beethoven"* is mentioned as well.

·◦[4]◦·

That Beethoven lost a Rasoumovsky, a Kinsky, and a Lobkowitz and gained instead a Schindler is somewhat illustrative of the change which the world—his world—was undergoing. At first almost imperceptible, it was nonetheless true that a new order was developing. By and by those rich, cultured, music-loving members of the older aristocracy either died out—or lost their wealth. A new bourgeoisie arose, at first more interested in amassing money and social position than in supporting music. The change was gradual, and Beethoven continued to receive some support to the end of his days. But the princes employed fewer musicians, and the cultivation of music in the palace became weaker. Some of the palaces were sold to the newly rich—and ceased being palaces.

The Industrial Revolution, which had its strongest development in England, eventually reached even the Austria of Metternich, in some ways the most backward of the great European countries, with a statesman who was still plumping for "legitimate monarchies, however 'illegitimate' the conditions." ** The industrial development did not favor a status quo.

As yet—that is, in 1815—the emperors and kings continued the game of

---

* In *Lutezia,* Chapter 33.
** Golo Mann, *The History of Germany Since 1789,* 1968.

fitting nations to frontiers, not frontiers to nations. The Congress was still sitting, negotiating, wrangling, dealing—yes, and dancing, too. Vienna was more brightly illuminated than ever. On January 25, 1815, a grand festival was given in the *Hofburg* to celebrate the birthday of the Russian Empress. Part of that celebration was a concert; unexpectedly, possibly because the Empress had shown him much favor, Beethoven appeared at the concert and played the piano once again in public to an audience quite as brilliant as that which had attended the Gala of the year before. (About a week before this, his lawsuit against Kinsky had been settled.)

A little more than a month after the festival, Metternich attended a session of the Congress which protracted itself until three o'clock in the morning (night of March 6–7). He had just undressed and lain down to rest when a courier was announced with a message which brooked no delay. The message was that Napoleon had escaped from Elba.

On March 20, Napoleon entered Paris, and the "hundred days" began. Austria, Britain, Prussia, and Russia forgot their differences (in January, Austria and Britain had formed a secret alliance against Prussia and Russia) and went to war once more. The war lasted until the decisive Battle of Waterloo on June 18, under the leadership of the Duke of Wellington and von Blücher. Here at last was journey's end for Napoleon: he was shipped off to final banishment on St. Helena.

The long wars, with their violent swings, their instabilities of currency and conditions, their death and destruction, debilitated not only the financial structure of the old order but its moral fiber. Baroness du Montet wrote as early as 1818: "The high Viennese aristocracy is the most dissolute group one can imagine, at least as far as its male members are concerned . . . so riddled with debt, so corrupt and frivolous, that if the *Fideikommisse* * were ever to be dissolved, the bearers of the noblest names of Austria would fall into the bitterest poverty within a decade." Specifically she related about the same Waldstein who early recognized Beethoven's genius:

> Count Ferdinand Waldstein has sunk terribly into debt, particularly after he had served as Finance Minister to the Elector of Cologne. He is Knight of the Teutonic Order and was entitled to substantial benefices. Yet he became diplomat without portfolio, financier without credit. He had vowed celibacy, but he

---

* The government bureau whose task it was to preserve the inheritance for the eldest son of the family.

had himself absolved from the vow and married in 1812. Through foolish speculations, he ruined both himself and the clever and charming Countess Isabella Rzewuska [his wife]. Count Waldstein possesses a superior intellect but was unable to maintain a decent reputation.

Countess Lulu Thürheim wrote that Waldstein died in such poverty (in 1823) that the doctors' bills could not be met, and a friend had to pay for the funeral.

Of Count Fries, Baroness du Montet wrote that his wife had possessed a necklace and a diadem of enormous pearls. "Those pearls were a part of the purchase price paid by King Murat's widow to Count Fries for a country estate. . . . *All that is now gone.* . . . His beautiful and virtuous wife died a few years before him. The state of his finances could have remained unknown to her, but was the Count able to hide his transgressions from her? A French actress, a little dark-skinned and ugly baggage, a Mlle. Lombard, was his evil demon. . . ." Fries lost everything, his business, his prosperous banking house, and his town *palais.* The Saxon minister, Griesinger, wrote to Dresden on December 13, 1826: "The Fries *palais* was bought by the banker Sina for 388,000 Fl., W.W. The whole amount goes to the creditors, not a penny to the children." A petition to the police is extant in which the mother-in-law of Count Fries asks for a scholarship to enable one of the younger sons of the count to continue his schooling. Her petition was granted (Police Act 3629, 1826). In 1826 the partner of the banking house, Fries and Co., a Mr. Parish, committed suicide by drowning himself in the Danube. Fries and Co. went bankrupt.

Financial decline, with new wealth going to new people, was the frequent lot of these hapless patricians; some sought forgetfulness in a desperate licentiousness. These declines touched Beethoven only tangentially: he hardly lived in the world any longer. There were still some august names around to whom compositions could be dedicated. Yet what he pondered had little relation to patrons—aside from the faithful Archduke Rudolph—and less relation to the developing pressures and changes. His music now was not "new" or "old," "conservative" or "revolutionary." It stood above such definition; it stood high above a world at unrest.

Unrest—that condition which was the aftermath of the Napoleonic wars—has been described by Harold Nicolson: *

> Meanwhile the spirit of unrest, which was the spirit of the first half of the nineteenth century, was seething in every country. It was not the lees of the old

---

* *Op. cit.*

wine of 1789; it was the ferment of a new and no less inebriating vintage. It was not the rise of the internal and external proletariat; it was the rise of the internal and external bourgeoisie, the revolt of the young intellectuals. Throughout Germany the boys and girls who in 1813 had formed the resistance movement against Napoleon, and who regarded themselves as the heroes of the War of Liberation, observed with dismay the old crust forming again in the several States and Principalities. They were enraged by the spectacle of the same old men creeping back into the same old positions;—denying to Germany the promises which they had made in the hour of danger;—denying to youth those opportunities which, in the gay dawn of Liberation, had seemed so glamorous.

In one specific aspect this revolt of youth, this contempt for "the same old men," this wriggling against "the old crust"—a phenomenon as periodic as the tide, but always more violent after the sufferings of war—may have impinged on Beethoven. He had a nephew who rebelled against him. There were many reasons for Karl's rebellion; but one of them, though not the major one, may be ascribed to the generally seething spirit of unrest. Karl was thirteen years old in 1819 when the dramatist Kotzebue was assassinated. Metternich used that as the occasion to call together the representatives of nine German states and to force through the "Karlsbad Decrees," dissolving student societies, further tightening censorship of the press, and appointing "watchdogs" to supervise the teaching in the universities. He did succeed in suppressing the movement toward freedom for twenty-nine years. In the end the movement won; Metternich lost.

Karl once called Beethoven "the old fool."

CHAPTER 19

THE TRAGEDY
OF POSSESSIVE LOVE

·≈[I]≈·

The tale of the nephew exists in two very different versions. In one, Beethoven appears as the King Lear of the heath who learns how sharper than the serpent's tooth it is to have a thankless child. In the other, Beethoven appears as the Lear of Scene I, the arrogant King who in his clutching neuroticism and foolish tyranny very nearly wrecks the lives of both a mother and a child.

Tyrant or martyr—which was Beethoven? Loving mother or salacious schemer—which was Johanna? Normal mediocre boy or callous little sneak—which was Karl?

It is no surprise that Schindler heaps most of the guilt on Johanna and Karl; he sees "reason upon reason for the master's unmitigated hatred" and he accepts Beethoven's characterization of Johanna as "wicked and vicious." Thayer, while calling Beethoven's attempt to take charge of his nephew "ill-advised and full of evil consequences" and while characterizing the methods used by Beethoven to separate the boy from his mother as "very questionable—if not utterly unpardonable," still concludes: "There can be no doubt that the woman whom Beethoven called 'The Queen of Night' was wicked and vicious." No such black-and-white view is held by Ernest Newman.* He writes:

> The popular notion of this affair is that the one person wronged, and cruelly wronged, was Beethoven. That he suffered grievously through it, and that he conceived himself to be acting throughout from motives of the utmost purity, cannot be questioned. But men who are sure that their motives are, in the abstract, of the utmost purity, can sometimes attain that certitude by way of

---

* *Op. cit.*

488

Nephew Karl, probably in the uniform of a cadet. Unsigned portrait (Austrian National Library).

quite false premises, and in the attempt to realize their virtuous purpose can unconsciously do a great deal of harm.

There has been too easy-going an assumption that in everything that happened in this affair Beethoven was right and the others wrong—that he was in every way more fitted to be the guardian of Carl * than the latter's mother was, and that Carl himself was a fundamentally bad boy who did nothing but plague his good uncle. The case did not present itself so simply to contemporary judges of it, nor does it so present itself to cool students of the evidence today.

That is a reasonable statement. It is far from the extreme claims in which Editha and Richard Sterba indulge.** The two psychoanalysts charge—of course in psychoanalytical terms, which means that to understand all is to forgive all—Beethoven with "inhuman cruelty" and attribute the immense conflict in his life to "the *polarity between the male and female principle,* which he vainly sought to reconcile in his behavior." As to Johanna and Karl:

> It must be emphasized that there is no evidence that Johanna was a bad mother, that she neglected or mistreated her son; she was concerned for her child, and she suffered under the inhuman cruelty with which Beethoven kept him from her for many years. In addition, the surviving descriptions of the boy during the time succeeding his father's death indicate that he was well behaved and exhibited no pathological traits; this supports the assumption that Johanna was not a bad mother.

This is sophism, nothing else. Few impartial readers of the documents would arrive at such a conclusion.

The two doctors did. They pronounced a diagnosis by which Johanna was furnished with a cleaner character than the most elastic interpretation of the facts would warrant, and Karl was given more than passing marks for deportment, while Beethoven became a case needing daily consultation, a patient ready for the psychiatric ward, a menace to his poor relatives, if not actually dangerous to life and limb.

A few years after publication of the Sterbas' book, along came another one, entitled *Beethoven contra Beethoven: The History of a Famous Lawsuit,* by L. G. Bachmann.*** This book, though written in semifictional style—"The door was impatiently thrown open and there stood" . . . "The fog was clutching at

---

* Newman spells the nephew's name with a *C.*
** *Op. cit.*
*** Published by Schöningh in Munich in 1963.

the houses" . . . that sort of thing—examines the documents anew and comes to the conclusion that Beethoven was a latter-day Job, shamefully and mercilessly put upon, cheated and betrayed. The book is a broad-stroked whitewash of the noble "Master."

Divergent though the *interpretations* of the facts have been, the facts themselves lead to the same conclusion: that his love for and involvement with his nephew loaded a tragic burden on Beethoven's shoulders, a burden so heavy that his steps faltered and his body bent. Whosesoever fault it was, the occupation with the nephew was a direct cause of the lessening of his productivity. Karl's guardianship and the lawsuit took a terrible toll, which must be subtracted from Beethoven's creative energy.

Therefore the tale of the nephew is a sad tale, whatever interpretation we adopt. Wasted love, wasted anger, wasted time—such is its refrain. In retelling it, I shall attempt to steer a course based on the available charts—the letters and documents, private and official—avoiding the cliffs of both specious psychoanalytical analysis and of fictive romancing.

·◦[2]◦·

Beethoven's brother Caspar Carl was a simple man. He held a small position, but he held it to the satisfaction of his employer, the Imperial Royal Bank and Chief Treasury. He was a cashier there; cashiers are usually trustworthy men. In 1813 Carl needed some money, and Beethoven arranged a loan for him through the publisher Sigmund Anton Steiner. Part of the arrangement was a clause specifying that should Carl be unable to repay the loan to Steiner, the publisher would obtain certain limited rights to a new piano sonata by the composer. Beethoven, in effect, became the guarantor of the loan.* Carl, however, was by no means penniless. His wife had brought him a dowry and he did not squander it. He owned a house with a garden, a wagon, a horse, a goat, a couple of peacocks, and so on.

Whatever Carl may have thought of his wife's morals, he seems to have lived with her contentedly. When he was barely forty-two years old, he contracted "Vienna's disease," tuberculosis. His condition rapidly worsened; in October, 1815, he applied for a leave of absence. This the bank refused. The official document bearing this refusal is preserved. Beethoven scribbled on it:

---

* The accommodation proved a good move by Steiner: Beethoven began dealing with his firm rather than with Breitkopf and Härtel, and subsequently Steiner published a number of Beethoven's works.

This miserable product of financial officialdom was the cause of my brother's death. For he was really so ill that he could not discharge the duties of his office without hastening his death—A nice memorial provided by those vulgar superior officials.

Beethoven exaggerated: he knew that Carl was not just thrown out, but retired on a small pension. Beethoven tried to help him and wrote to his friend, Antonie Brentano. She was the daughter of Melchior von Birkenstock, a famous art collector, and was married to Franz Brentano, a businessman in Frankfurt. Probably she had inherited her father's love of collecting *objets d'art;* hence the letter:

[November, 1815]

There is another matter which I must tell you about. It's about a pipe-bowl! A pipe-bowl?—Among the individuals (the number of which is infinite) who are now suffering, there is also my brother, who on account of his poor health has had to retire on a pension. His position at the moment is very difficult. I am doing all I can to help him, but it is not enough.—He possesses a pipe-bowl which he believes he could dispose of most advantageously at Frankfurt. In his weak state of health it is difficult to refuse him anything. So on that account I am taking the liberty of asking you to let him send you this pipe-bowl. So many people are constantly calling at your house that perhaps you could manage to sell it—My brother thinks that you might possibly get ten louis d'or for it—I leave that to you to decide—He needs a lot of money, he has to keep a carriage and horse in order to be able to live, for his life is very precious to him, though indeed I would gladly relinquish mine!! (A-570).

A pipe bowl worth something like $150—if it *was* worth that much—suggests that Carl treated himself well.

Carl's disease took its galloping course. He died on November 15. His end came so suddenly that Beethoven voiced the suspicion—in all seriousness—that his brother had been poisoned, obviously by Johanna. He would not rest until Dr. Bertolini performed a postmortem examination: the physician stated that there were no grounds for such an accusation.

Two days before Carl died, he made his last will and testament. It is this document which is the blueprint of the Beethoven tragedy. The salient point of the testament is the following:

Point 5. I appoint my brother Ludwig van Beethoven guardian. Inasmuch as this, my deeply beloved brother, has often aided me with true brotherly love in the most magnanimous and noblest manner, I ask, in full confidence and trust in his noble heart, that he shall bestow the love and friendship which he often showed me, upon my son Karl, and do all that is possible to promote the intellectual training and further welfare of my son. I know that he will not deny me this, my request.

That is how it read: "guardian." But that this could not have been Carl's original intention—not quite—is proved by the autograph, where the first sentence originally read: "Along with my wife I appoint my brother Ludwig van Beethoven co-guardian." The words "along with my wife" and the "co-" were then crossed out, obviously at Carl's request and with his knowledge, since the testament is a valid one signed by him. Beethoven forced his brother to change the text: at least, there is preserved at the Beethoven House in Bonn * a fragment in Beethoven's writing which reads:

I knew nothing about the fact that a testament had been made; however, I came upon it by chance. If what I had seen was really to be the *original text,* then passages had to be stricken out. This I had my brother bring about since I did not wish to be bound up in this with such a bad woman in a matter of such importance as the education of the child.

The probabilities are that, when the testament was drawn up, Carl thought that a co-guardianship of Beethoven and Johanna was possible. Beethoven refused this. Carl then amended the document. Having done so, he thought further about the problem; his heart was troubled, his mind ill at ease. The same day he had a codicil to the will prepared, which read:

CODICIL TO MY WILL

Having learned that my brother, Hr. Ludwig van Beethoven, desires after my death to take wholly to himself my son Karl, and wholly to withdraw him from the supervision and training of his mother, and inasmuch as the best of harmony does not exist between my brother and my wife, I have found it necessary to add to my will that I by no means desire that my son be taken away from his mother, but that he shall always and so long as his future career permits remain with his mother, to which end the guardianship of him is to be exercised by her as well as my brother. Only by unity can the object which I had in view in

---

* The whole question was studied by the Beethoven scholar Dr. Dagmar Weise, who worked at the Beethoven House.

appointing my brother guardian of my son, be attained, wherefore, for the welfare of my child, I recommend *compliance* to my wife and more *moderation* to my brother. God permit them to be harmonious for the sake of my child's welfare. This is the last wish of the dying husband and brother.

VIENNA, November 14, 1815
CARL VAN BEETHOVEN
M.P. (TQ).

A deep worry speaks from this codicil of "the dying husband and brother." He fears Beethoven's future course. He fears strife. He doubts that wife and brother will be "harmonious." Yet the fact that he was not content to entrust his son entirely to his wife and leave his brother out of it altogether does not prove that he felt that Johanna was unfit to bring up a child. A widow needs a man's help and advice. A co-guardian would be desirable, with *any* mother. Beethoven, however, insisted on all or nothing at all. So Carl capitulates, giving Beethoven full responsibility "in full confidence and trust in his noble heart"; and a few lines below desires that his son should not be taken away from his mother and that the guardianship be exercised jointly. In short, Carl says one thing in Point 5 and almost the opposite in the codicil. This contradiction was to provide the cutting edge of contention.

Nowhere in the testament does Carl say that the accusations which Beethoven had voiced against Johanna were unjust, although we can be quite sure that Beethoven spoke them loud and clear, just as he wrote to Ries only seven days after Carl's death: "My poor unfortunate brother has just died. He had a bad wife." All he does is to recommend "compliance" to his wife, as he recommends "more moderation" to his brother. Carl must have known that Johanna was an obstinate creature, and that the one thing his brother was incapable of was moderation. He thought that the impossible could come about because he wanted it to come about.

The object of these cares was a little boy of nine, handsome and prepossessing. Beethoven, who loved children, saw himself becoming a father to the fatherless boy. In subsequent years he often called himself "father." We cannot doubt the sincerity of his conviction: he believed that Carl meant him to have the boy, and he believed that Johanna, a woman morally depraved, was unworthy of the name of mother. He believed this because he wanted to believe it. He wanted to believe it because his whole being longed for somebody he could love. His heart groped for the object on which he could concentrate his capacity for tenderness.

He had to have Karl all to himself. Anticipating that the mother would object, Beethoven did what for him was the natural thing to do: losing no time, he applied to the law. Hardly had the flowers on Carl's grave faded and only six days after the testament had been filed (filing date, November 28, 1815), he submitted a petition to the Imperial Royal *Landrechte* of Lower Austria. The *Landrechte* was the court for the nobility and the clergy. Why did this court accept jurisdiction of the case? Could they have thought that "van" Beethoven was a nobleman? We do not know. His petition stated that he wished to undertake the plenary guardianship of his nephew without delay; his brother's last charge was sacred to him, having "committed the welfare of his son to me several times by word of mouth." The next day the court ordered the petitioner and Dr. Johann Michael Schönauer, executor of the testament, to appear on December 2. This was deferred to December 13, when Beethoven declared that he wanted sole guardianship because he could put forward cogent reasons why Johanna should be entirely excluded from the guardianship. On December 15 the court ordered him to produce such reasons within three days, failing which the testament would be carried out as originally written, including the provision of the codicil.

Beethoven now needed, in a hurry, documentary proof of Johanna's maternal unsuitability. Knowing that the woman had been criminally accused in 1811, he applied to the *Magistrat* of the City of Vienna, the court which dealt with political, civic, and criminal cases of commoners, and asked the *Magistrat* to supply him with a legally attested copy of the charges brought against Johanna. The *Magistrat* answered that they had no legal right to furnish him with such a copy, but would communicate the necessary facts to the *Landrechte.* This was done on December 21.

Right here we have a puzzle. We have made a diligent search of the pertinent Vienna archives but have been unable to locate the document accusing Johanna, supposedly of embezzlement. Dr. J. Schmidt-Görg, director of the Beethoven House in Bonn, feels that the charge concerned "probably infidelity against her husband" rather than embezzlement. Emily Anderson, on the other hand, does state that Johanna was accused of embezzlement. At any rate, no document of the 1811 charge has been found.

After the *Magistrat* informed the *Landrechte,* the superior court had in its possession the facts necessary for a ruling. In the meantime Beethoven presented to the *Landrechte* on December 20, 1815, another document, setting forth his reasons for wishing to be the sole guardian. The first sentence reads:

However reluctant the undersigned may be to reopen a wound, a deep wound that was inflicted on his family and especially on his unfortunate deceased brother and has but slowly healed, yet he feels that by reason of the legal regulation A and of the analogy of Paragraph 20 of the Civil Code it is his duty to draw the attention of the High Court to the fact that if the latter considers it compatible with the necessary care for the welfare of the nine to ten year old Karl van Beethoven to obtain official information about the earlier associations of his mother before entrusting her with the guardianship, the report B of the Worshipful *Magistrat* of Vienna will give the necessary particulars; and that honourable men holding distinguished appointments would be ready to give the most incontestable evidence about her behaviour before and after her marriage to my brother and until the time of his death, even if I refused to say anything about matters which I myself can prove up to the hilt. (A-Appendix C, Document 3).

This nonstop sentence is legal language; immediately the language becomes acerbic, and we hear Beethoven spewing out accusations: Johanna is not equipped with the necessary moral and intellectual qualities; the codicil to the will, while undoubtedly genuine, was added without Beethoven's knowledge and behind his back when he was absent for an hour and a half; it can be "proved" that the codicil was written only because the dying man was urged to do so by his wife "and was not in a condition to take an entirely free decision"; after the codicil was written, his brother had second thoughts and sent his nurse to Dr. Schönauer, demanding that the codicil be invalidated. The woman did not find the lawyer at home, and when Beethoven himself called on him at his brother's urging, Dr. Schönauer again could not be found. While all this was going on, Carl expired.

We can imagine Beethoven and a lawyer working on the petition together, with Beethoven, summoning the tremendous force of his will, telling the lawyer exactly what to say.

The decision of the court was announced on January 9, 1816. It was entirely in Beethoven's favor. He was to become sole guardian and he was to appear on the 19th to take vows for the performance of his duties. He did appear before the assembled council and vowed "with a solemn handgrasp." He now had the legal right to take Karl away from his mother.

What were the grounds for such a decision? We may rule out the possibility that the court was influenced by any undue pressure from Beethoven or that it was overly impressed by Beethoven's fame even though, a month before, Beethoven had been awarded honorary citizenship of Vienna. Assuming then that the court acted logically, we must assume that grounds sufficiently severe against Johanna's character were put forward to make them doubt that she would be a fit mother. If that were not so, the court's decision would represent a singular instance of irresponsibility. As Dr. Schmidt-Görg has said: "It was not a question of a groundless accusation by Beethoven." *

There are indices to substantiate this statement. While the story that Johanna entertained lovers in one room of the house while Carl lay dying in another is unproved, it is fairly well proved that after Carl's death Johanna took up a liaison with a man by the name of Hofbauer, a well-to-do merchant. She became pregnant, most probably by him; an illegitimate half-sister was born to Karl. (What a curious twist of fate it was that both of Beethoven's sisters-in-law had illegitimate children!) She never married Hofbauer.

Gerhard von Breuning, a kindly soul, had nothing good to say about Johanna. He calls her "giddy" and "bottomlessly wanton, vulgar in her feelings and actions." To be sure, Breuning was in the vanguard of the Beethoven worshipers, and he was a child of five or six when the lawsuit was being pursued. He simply repeated what his father had told him. Father Breuning was a man of undoubted honesty and a man of good will. He would hardly have blackened Johanna's character by careless calumnies.

Beethoven called her a strumpet and wrote to Karl's schoolmaster, del Rio, in February, 1816, that she was at the Artists' Ball until 3 A.M. "exposing not only her mental but also her *bodily nakedness*—it was whispered that she—was willing to hire herself—for 20 gulden! Oh horrible!" (A-611). Unexpectedly we find her name cropping up in Rosenbaum's diary, in 1810, when she had been married to Carl four years and was twenty-six years old: "Sunday, 4th of February, 1810. Ten o'clock to the Redoute ... We remained until 4 A.M. Several pretty masks ... *Die* Bethhowen ... So I had a fairly good time."

Even discounting Beethoven's exaggerations, we still have enough evidence against Johanna to reach the conclusion that she was hardly the ideal mother, that she preferred dancing at 4 A.M. to walking hand in hand with her son.

Yet she was Karl's mother. However "giddy," however flighty her feelings, they were maternal. If anything, motherhood must have limited her freedom in her contacts with men or in enjoying herself at masked balls. Her motives when she struggled for her son, when she raised heaven and earth to try to retain him, when she paid lawyers and ran to plead before the court, must have at least in

---

* Letter to the author, April 9, 1968.

part been prompted by feelings of tenderness, of affection, by the instinct which makes the cat lick the kitten. She must have realized, too, that Beethoven was not the ideal man to care for the boy, his household not the kind of home in which a child could grow up normally. Other motives, less selfless, may have entered into her actions. There was hatred. The more Beethoven fought her, the more adamant he showed himself, the more often she heard his opprobrious terms—"Queen of the Night," "loose woman," "beastly mother"—the more her hatred must have grown. In spite of that hatred, she must have known how important the name of her brother-in-law was; she did not want to relinquish all connection with that name. Karl was the only progeny, as Johann was childless. Finally, she may have had money in mind. She did get a pension from her husband's estate. If she were to be cast aside altogether and not allowed to contribute to the expenses of maintaining and educating her son, the pension might be contested.

To sum up the two adversaries, we had best be content with a judgment equidistant between the two extremes. Johanna, who had been living in peace with a weak but reasonably decent man, could not have been the arch-villainess which even the conservative Thayer portrayed her to be. On the other hand, Beethoven was not an utter madman when he felt that she was unworthy of bringing up a child who was a blood relative of a genius. Had there been an ounce of talent in Karl, as Beethoven was sure there was, it was not she who could have brought it out.

True, Johanna schemed and planned and plotted against her brother-in-law. Yet Beethoven's characterization of her as "Born for intrigue, well-schooled in deceit, master of hypocrisy" (in a Conversation Book, March, 1820) is little short of calumny.

That Beethoven, driven by possessive love, dug himself into a position in which his actions became fearsome, that he became a man who was passion's slave, that his later moves were those of a being unbalanced, that he did not have the faintest idea how to treat a growing boy, that he destroyed whatever affection the child may have had for him at the beginning—all that still does not warrant the charge of "inhuman cruelty." Heartsick, misguided, intransigent, suffering man—we must watch his descent into hell with pity.

·⊰[3]⊱·

Beethoven now had obtained from the court what he wanted, the exclusive guardianship of the precious ward. What was he going to do with him? He looked around for a boarding school; the best was none too good. He decided on the school of Cajetan Giannatasio del Rio, whose establishment enjoyed a first-class reputation. Beethoven had been introduced to del Rio by Josef Karl Bernard, a distinguished journalist who was shortly to become editor of the *Wiener Zeitung*. Bernard and Beethoven were good friends; Beethoven respected his worldly judgment and excellent common sense. Beethoven began frequently to visit the del Rio family. We have seen that both daughters became fond of him, and Fanny more than fond.

On February 1, 1816, Beethoven wrote del Rio that it gave him much pleasure to inform him that at last "I am bringing you tomorrow the precious pledge that has been entrusted to me." He immediately added:

> And now I beg you once more in no circumstances to allow his mother to influence him. How or when she is to see him, all this I will arrange with you tomorrow in greater detail.—But you yourself must have some sort of watch kept on your servant, for *she has already bribed my servant*, though for another purpose!—I shall give you fuller particulars about this when we meet, though indeed I would much prefer to say nothing about it—But in the interest of your future citizen of the world I must give you this information, much as I regret having to do so.— (A-603).

Underneath Beethoven's signature, nine-year-old Karl wrote in a childish scrawl: "I am greatly looking forward to going to you, and I remain your Karl van Beethoven." Did the boy read the whole letter? What kind of impression must it have left on him to have his mother thus described?

The mother was not so easily excluded. She visited Karl the day after he entered the school, and repeated her visit on each of the following three days. She interfered with the discipline, bringing Karl sweets and other delicacies which he was not supposed to have and taking him for visits to her house. On the fifth day del Rio asked her to stay away. On the tenth day he wrote to Beethoven asking for a court order forbidding her to interfere. Beethoven consulted a lawyer and told del Rio that under no pretext whatever could Johanna fetch Karl from the boarding school without express permission from him, and indeed she was never to visit him at school. He, Beethoven, would apply to the *Landrechte* to get a court order.

Beethoven did apply to the *Landrechte* on February 15, 1816, and got a favorable ruling five days afterward.

He wrote to del Rio in triumph: the ruling was exactly what he desired.

After further imprecations against the Queen of the Night, he ends the letter by doing exactly what he objects to when Johanna does it: that is, taking Karl out of school for an outing:

[February 21, 1816]

> If it *suits you,* I will fetch my *little fellow at about one o'clock today for lunch,* so that he too may see something of the *carnival,* which no doubt is being celebrated at your boarding school and especially by *his schoolmates* (as he tells me) — With all my heart I embrace you as that man to whom I shall gladly be indebted for all the good and great deeds which my Karl is likely to perform — (A-612).

He had lofty ambitions for Karl. He thought he might make a musician out of the boy, or an artist, and he arranged to have him take piano lessons. Again only the best was good enough: it was the famous Czerny who became Karl's teacher. No doubt Czerny undertook the lessons to do Beethoven a favor. Beethoven wanted Karl to study Latin and Greek.* Later he wanted him to learn English and go to England to represent his uncle.

With his increasing expenses, Beethoven had a difficult time making ends meet, or said that he did. He wrote to Ferdinand Ries in London that he needed money. The letter is dated May 8, 1816, or about three months after Karl entered del Rio's school. Beethoven writes that in spite of its cost, "it is not a good school." The words are significant; they are followed by: "Hence I shall have to start a proper household where I can have him to live with me." That was what he really wanted — full possession of the boy. Home with him.

On July 28, 1816, he announced to del Rio his decision to take Karl out of school:

> Dear Friend!
> Several circumstances induce me to have Karl to live with me. So, as I have this in view, allow me to send you the amount for the coming quarter, at the end of which Karl will leave your boarding school — Do not attribute this move to any unfavorable criticism of yourself or your respected boarding school, but ascribe it to many other urgent factors connected with the welfare of Karl. It is an experiment; and as soon as I have begun it I will ask you to assist me with your advice, in fact, to allow Karl to visit your boarding school occasionally. We shall

---

* "Karl can answer a riddle propounded to him in Greek," the doting Beethoven told a visitor.

always be grateful to you; and indeed we shall never forget your attention and the excellent care of your worthy wife, such care as can only be compared to that of the very best of mothers — ...

I would send you at least four times the amount I am now sending you, if only my situation would allow it. Meanwhile if my circumstances improve in the future, I will seize every opportunity of honouring and recalling in some definite way the remembrance of your having laid the foundations of the physical and moral well-being of my Karl — (A-644).

But Karl remained at the school for the present, since he had to undergo an operation for hernia. One can imagine Beethoven worrying over this. Shortly before the operation, performed on September 18, 1816, he sent him a note:

My dear K[arl],

According to Herr v. *Smetana's* prescription it is necessary for you to bathe a few times more before the operation. Today the weather is favorable and just now it is still the right time. I shall wait for you at the Stubentor — Of course you must first ask H[err] v[on] G[iannatasio] for permission — Put on a pair of underpants or take them with you, so that you may put them on immediately after you have bathed, should the weather again become cool — *Has the tailor not yet called?* When he does, he is to measure you for linen underpants as well, for you need these. If Frau von G[iannatasio] knows where he lives, my servant too could ask him to go to you —

Well, all good wishes — I am — even on your account

your trouser button

L. V. BEETHOVEN (A-657).

The Dr. Smetana mentioned in the letter was one of Vienna's best surgeons, and the operation was entirely successful. But Beethoven was not easily reassured, writing about a month later:

To my nephew Karl! So far as I can see, there is still a certain amount of poison in your system. Hence I do entreat you to note down your mental and bodily requirements. The weather is becoming colder. Do you need another blanket or possibly your eiderdown? — Since I requested him to do so, Herr von Smetana will have been to see you. The trussmaker has called once already, but to no purpose. He has promised me to call again, to bring you another truss and to take away the old one to have it washed. He has already been paid for everything —

All good wishes. May God enlighten your heart and soul

Your uncle and friend

BEETHOVEN (A-667).

Probably no father or guardian of any of the boys in del Rio's school gave del Rio as much trouble. In November Beethoven requests that Karl stay at the school. To be nearer to the boy, he toys with the idea of moving into a house in del Rio's garden—undoubtedly the last thing del Rio wanted. He asks del Rio's advice as to how much he ought to pay Smetana, and beseeches del Rio to be patient until he can manage to reimburse him for the expenses "entailed by Karl's illness."

A few days later, Beethoven wants Karl with him to visit the father's grave, as it is the anniversary of Carl's death. He reports to del Rio:

[November 14, 1816]

While we were still at your house I dropped some hints about his tendency to be lazy. We walked along together more seriously than usual. Timidly he pressed my hand but found no response. At table he ate practically nothing and said that he felt very sad; but I failed to find out from him the cause of his sadness. Finally, during our walk he explained *that he was feeling very sad because he had not been able to work as hard as usual.* I then did my share and was even more friendly than before. This certainly shows his feeling of delicacy; and it is precisely traits of this kind that lead me to entertain hopes of his developing a fine character— (A-672).

So it went, Beethoven devoting the substance of his thought to the boy, alternately scolding him and pouring his love over him, severe one moment, indulgent the next, preaching to him and derogating Johanna; questioning servants like a police examiner to find out whether she had been around; pressing Karl to tell him the truth and merely teaching him to lie. Karl soon learned that to curry favor with his uncle he needed only to drop a disparaging word or two about his mother. Yet he wanted his mother, a woman who did not preach, did not expect him to accomplish feats of learning, merely petted him and brought him sweets.

Johanna, apparently in financial difficulty, wanted to sell the house which she had inherited. The son, according to the father's will, was joint owner; since he was a minor, his interest had to be represented by the guardian. Beethoven's consent to the sale of the house had to be obtained. He gave this consent, no doubt after prolonged discussions, and he further agreed to the transfer of the other property held in the names of mother and son to the mother alone, provided that Johanna would (a) acknowledge legally her obligation of making a yearly contribution of at least half her pension for the education and maintenance of her son, and (b) that she would make a contribution of 2000 gulden outright to her son "for his better education and support." The contract was signed on May 10, 1817, by both Beethoven and Johanna.

·•›[4]‹•·

Thus, instead of being occupied with music, Beethoven was burdened with cares which he did not understand and with which he could not cope: property rights, servants, school, house furnishings, Karl's lessons. The more he became involved the more morose he became. Fanny del Rio wrote that he was "in one of his man-hating moods." Nothing was right: he doubted, since he wanted to doubt, del Rio's competence: Karl's boots were too tight; del Rio ought not to let the boy wear such boots and ruin his feet; Karl was not allowed sufficient time at the school for his musical studies, and so on. Entries in Fanny's diary reflect her distress over the situation. She is sad: he really ought not to treat people who love and respect him with "biting sarcasm." Why is he angry? They have not deserved such treatment. Presently she forgives him and blames Karl, who lied, saying that he had been forbidden to practice the piano.

Oppressed in spirit, Beethoven's health declined. On June 19, 1817, he wrote to Countess Erdödy, who was then in Munich, that he had once again changed doctors "because my own doctor, a wily Italian, had powerful secondary motives where I was concerned and lacked both honesty and intelligence." (A-783). The "wily Italian" must have been the famous Dr. Johann Malfatti (whom people from far and wide came to consult and who was good enough to treat Metternich's son Viktor when he fell seriously ill in 1831). In the same letter Beethoven wrote:

> Well, from April 15th until May 4th I had to take six powders daily and six bowls of tea. That treatment lasted until May 4th. After that I had to take another kind of powder, also six times daily; and I had to rub myself three times a day with a volatile ointment. Then I had to come here [Heiligenstadt] where I am taking baths. Since yesterday I have been taking another medicine, namely, a tincture, of which I have to swallow 12 spoonfuls daily.

At the beginning of 1818 Beethoven finally took the step of removing Karl from del Rio's school and taking him into his own home. He was now full of gratitude toward del Rio, but his decision remained firm. Though del Rio offered to continue Karl's education for a reduced fee, Beethoven insisted that "the arrangement must stand."

Now he had the boy at home and he tried to make a real home for him. He consulted Nanette Streicher. The patience of that friend was endless; one marvels at her sweetness. She acted like a loving elder sister (she was one year older than Beethoven). Her husband, Johann Andreas Streicher, well known in the history of German literature because of his close friendship with Schiller, acquiesced to his wife's spending many hours in her attempts to straighten out Beethoven's household. The numerous letters from Beethoven to Nanette Streicher make both prosaic and pathetic reading. What an unholy pother there is about two pairs of lost stockings, and could she please notify the laundress to let him have the wash by Sunday, and he needs a supply of feather dusters, and is it really necessary for him to buy a silver sugar bowl, and would she help him out with twenty-five gulden for just a few days? He covers pages and pages (a letter written from Mödling on June 18, 1818), with lamentations about the two servants, Peppi and "the old woman," Frau D, the "gray-haired traitress." They are in league with Johanna. Johanna has given them presents of coffee and sugar. Johanna has bribed them in spite of the great generosity that Beethoven has shown them. They have reported to her conversations which they overheard between himself and his nephew. They sneered when they saw Karl embracing Beethoven. Having received an "anonymous letter" telling him that Johanna is waiting in the wings to make trouble, Beethoven pounces on Karl, and after he gives Karl a solemn promise that everything will be forgiven if only he will confess the truth, but that lies will plunge him into an even deeper abyss, Karl does admit that with the help of the servants he has had contact with his mother. The whole affair has made Beethoven ill.

Where was Karl going to continue his schooling? Beethoven justified himself for his decision by saying to Frau Streicher that while del Rio's school was called an "educational" establishment, it should be called a "spoiling" place, a pun on the German words *Erziehung* (education) and *Verziehung* (spoiling a child). He first engaged a tutor, of whom nothing is known except that he stayed out one night, which made Beethoven furious. For a brief time he considered, and may actually have employed, a Frenchwoman as a governess. Then, at Mödling, Karl was placed in a class taught by one Johann Baptist Fröhlich, a priest. It wasn't long before Beethoven suspected the priest of holding converse with Johanna. He wasn't going to do anything about it at the moment, he wrote to Frau Streicher, unless another incident were to occur:

MÖDLING, June 18, 1818

when I shall give His Reverence such a merciless drubbing with countless spiritual flails and amulets and with my exclusive guardianship and the privileges connected therewith that the whole parsonage will quake with it— (A-904).

Presently the priest dismissed the pupil with the dangerous uncle, and Karl was placed in the hands of a private tutor to be prepared for admission to a public *Gymnasium.** To enter the *Gymnasium* one had to pass an examination. For this purpose Beethoven brought Karl to Vienna about the middle of August.

·≈[5]≈·

Johanna now decided to act. No doubt she thought she had amassed enough evidence against her brother-in-law's handling of the boy at least to diminish his authority and perhaps to enable her to wrest Karl away altogether. To this end she consulted a relative of hers, Jakob Hotschevar, a *Hofkonzipist*—a clerk in the government service possessing some legal training. He drew up a petition to the *Landrechte,* claiming that (1) Beethoven was unable to be a proper guardian because he was deaf and could not communicate with the child; (2) Beethoven was in ill health; (3) Karl's education had been badly and planlessly handled; (4) a child should be reared by his mother.

The hearings began in September, 1818, and were dismissed by the court on the 18th. Three days later Johanna applied to the court again, this time for permission to place her boy in the Imperial Royal Seminary, a school where he could have board, lodging, and education. She and Beethoven were summoned to appear in court on the 23rd. Beethoven was to bring with him the report of Karl's *Gymnasium* entrance examinations.

Beethoven prepared a full answer to Johanna's charges, one showing every sign of having been written by a competent person, probably Bernard.

As to Charge 1, Beethoven answers, with perhaps pardonable exaggeration:

> In regard to the first point, everybody who is closely acquainted with me knows only too well that all verbal communications between me and my nephew and other people as well are carried on with the greatest ease and are by no means impeded by my indifferent hearing.

---

* The lower *Gymnasium* is approximately equivalent to junior high in the United States.

As to Charge 2: "My health has never been better." That too was stretching the truth.

He enclosed the school report that the court wanted. It was a satisfactory one. As to Johanna's plan to place the boy in the seminary, it was a bad plan because

> ... in a seminary the special limitations imposed on *this* mother would not be generally known and she could easily contrive to get hold of the child and take him home with her.   (A-Appendix C, Document 7).

On October 3, 1818, Johanna's petition was rejected by the court. For the time being Beethoven was again the victor.

That fall, Karl entered the public *Gymnasium*. In addition he continued to receive instruction in piano, French, and drawing. All was going well. Beethoven was calmer. He was working on the *Hammerklavier Sonata*. He saw a few friends, including the del Rios. Fanny wrote in her diary in November:

> Yesterday Beethoven was with us once again. We have secured a housekeeper for him. He was here three hours and since his hearing was especially bad this day, we wrote everything down. One cannot be in his company without being impressed with his admirable character, his deep sense of what is good and noble. If Karl would but recompense him for the many sacrifices which he makes for his sake! My hopes are intermingled with serious doubts. He will probably make a journey to London this spring. It might be advantageous to him financially in many ways.   (TQ).

Suddenly Beethoven's peace was sharply ended. Once more a crisis came. Fanny recalled later:

> One day B. came in great excitement and sought counsel and help from my father, saying that Karl had run away! I recall that on this occasion amid our expressions of sympathy he cried out tearfully: "He is ashamed of me!"   (TQ).

In her diary on December 5 Fanny recorded the event, which had apparently happened on December 3:

> Never in my life shall I forget the moment when he came and told us that Karl was gone, had run away to his mother, and showed us his letter as an evidence of his vileness. To see this man suffering so, to see him *weeping*—it was

touching! Father took up the matter with great zeal, and with all my sorrow I feel a pleasurable sensation in the consciousness that now we are *much* to Beethoven, yes, at this moment his only refuge. Now he surely perceives his error if he has wronged us in his opinions. Ah! he never can appreciate how highly we esteem him, how much I should be capable of doing for his happiness! How the uniqueness of his character shows itself once again. The naughty child is again with him with the help of the police—the Ravenmother! Oh! how dreadful it is that this man is compelled to suffer so on account of such outcasts. He must go away from here, or she; that will be the outcome. For the present B. will give him into our care; it will be an act of great kindness on my father's part if he receives him, as he will have to look upon him as one under arrest ... It did me good when he went away to note that his thoughts were more diverted. He told me that he had been so wrought up by the matter that it took him some time to gather his thoughts. During the night his heart had beat audibly. Alas! and there remains nothing for me to say except that all that we can do is so little! I would give half my life for the man! He always thinks of himself last. He lamented that he did not know what would become of his housekeeping when Karl was gone.   (TQ).

Fanny had the facts correct. Beethoven went to Johanna in the morning to bring the boy back. Johanna promised to release him in the evening. Beethoven did not accept her word. He turned to the police. When he did get the boy back —we can imagine Karl's state of confusion and bewilderment—Beethoven asked del Rio to accept him once again at his school, at least temporarily. What a remarkable testimonial to del Rio's friendship that he was willing!

·◄[6]►·

Karl's flight, his seeking refuge with his mother, gave Johanna a new weapon. She used it immediately. On December 7 she applied again to the court and again requested that her son be sent to the seminary.

Three days later she followed this with further documents, including a letter she had received from del Rio. The letter purported to show that she had been denied her natural desire to visit her son. She could visit him only once a month, "like a thief." She then gave some financial details, intending to prove that she was well able to take care of her son.

Hotschevar supported her petition. He admitted that Johanna Beethoven had once been judged guilty of moral delinquency. This offense of long ago should not, however, excuse (1) the illegal refusal to a mother of contact with her child; (2) the exposure of her son to an uncle and guardian whose treat-

507

ment of the boy carried with it the "danger of suffering physical and moral ruin." The Beethovens, Hotschevar wrote, were all eccentric, and the brothers could more fitly be called enemies than friends. Carl had been well disposed toward his brother only when he was in need of money from him. The codicil to the will made it clear that Carl's real intention was against Ludwig's becoming the sole guardian. He, Hotschevar, had personally observed, after the boy had run away from the uncle, that his hands and feet were frostbitten, that he was not warmly enough dressed, and that his underclothes and baths had been neglected.

A statement by the priest Fröhlich was appended. Frölich deposed that Beethoven had encouraged his nephew to speak ill of his mother, lauding him when he applied evil epithets to her. Karl had confessed to the priest that he knew he was doing wrong, yet he defamed his mother to court favor with his uncle. In the priest's opinion, Karl's training was contrary to all moral principles and showed itself in indifference to religious instruction. He had been unruly in church and in the streets of the village as well, so that the priest had received complaints, and finally he had been constrained to dismiss the boy to protect his other twelve pupils.

At once, with extraordinary promptness, the court summoned Johanna, Beethoven, and Karl to a hearing. It took place on December 11, 1818. Beethoven brought Bernard with him, no doubt to write out the questions which the court would ask and to counsel him as to the proper answers.

Thayer quotes from the minutes of the meeting, and we use extracts from his quotations.

Examination of Karl:

Why had he left his uncle?
Because his mother had told him she would send him to a public school and he did not think he would make progress under private instruction.
How did his uncle treat him?
Well.
Where had he been of late?
He had been in hiding at his mother's.
Where would he rather live—at his mother's or his uncle's?
He would like to live at his uncle's if he but had a companion, as his uncle was hard of hearing and he could not talk with him.
Had he been prompted by his mother to leave his uncle?
No.

When did he leave him?

Eight days ago.

How could he say that he could not succeed under private instruction when he had made such good progress?

This had been the case since he had studied in public [school]; before that he had received 2nd class in mathematics and had not made it up.

Had his mother commanded him to return to his uncle?

She had wanted to take him back to him herself, but he had resisted because he feared maltreatment.

Had his uncle maltreated him?

He had punished him often, but only when he deserved it; he had been maltreated only once, and that after his return, when his uncle threatened to throttle him.

Who had given him instruction in religion?

The same teacher who taught him other subjects, formerly the priest at Mödling, who was not kindly disposed towards him because he did not behave himself in the street and babbled in school.

Had he indulged in disrespectful remarks about his mother?

Yes; and in the presence of his uncle, whom he thought he would please in that way and who had agreed with him.

Was he often alone?

When his uncle was not at home he was left wholly alone.

Had his uncle admonished him to pray?

Yes; he prayed with him every morning and evening.

Examination of Johanna Beethoven:

How did her son come to her from the house of his guardian?

He had come to her in the evening for fear of punishment and because he did not like to live with his uncle.

Had she advised him to return to his uncle?

Yes, but her son did not want to do so because he feared maltreatment.

It looked as if she had concealed her son?

She had written to her brother-in-law that she would send her son back to him, but she had not seen him for a long time and was therefore glad to have him with her for a while, and for this reason she had not sent him back at once.

Had she been forbidden to see her son?

Her wish to do so had been frustrated by telling her of different places where she might see him, but when she went to the places he was not there.

Had her son been taken from her by the police?

She had herself taken him to the police at 4 o'clock.

How did she learn of the plan to send her son out of the country?

Giannatasio had disclosed the project to the police.

Did she consider that her son had been well treated at his uncle's?

She thought it unsuitable for the reasons given in her former application. She wished to say in particular that v. Beethoven had only one servant and that one could not rely on servants; he was deaf and could not converse with his ward; there was nobody to look after the wants of her son satisfactorily; his cleanliness was neglected and supervision of his clothing and washing; persons who had brought him clean linen had been turned back by his guardian.

Was her husband of noble birth?

So the brothers had said; the documentary proof of nobility was said to be in the possession of the oldest brother, the composer. At the legal hearing on the death of her husband, proofs of nobility had been demanded; she herself had no document bearing on the subject.

Examination of Ludwig van Beethoven:

How did his nephew Karl leave him?

He did not know exactly; his nephew had made himself culpable; he had charged him with it and the same day in the evening he had received a note of farewell. He could not tell the cause of his departure; his mother may have asked him to come to her the day before, but it might have been fear of punishment.

What had his nephew done?

He had a housekeeper who had been recommended to him by Giannatasio; two of her letters to Frl. Giannatasio and one of the latter's had fallen into his hands; in them it was stated that his nephew had called the servants abusive names, had withheld money and spent it on sweetmeats.

In whose care was his nephew?

He had provided him with a *Correpetitor* for pianoforte playing, French, and drawing who came to the house; these studies occupied all the leisure time of his nephew so completely that he needed no care; moreover, he could not trust any of his servants with the oversight of his nephew, as they had been bribed by the boy's mother; he had placed him in the hands of a priest for the development of his musical talent, but the mother had got into an agreement with him also.

Had his nephew not spoken disrespectfully of his mother in his presence?

No; besides, he had admonished him to speak nothing but the truth; he had asked his nephew if he was fond of his mother and he answered in the negative.

How did he get the boy back?

With the help of the police. He had gone to the mother in the forenoon to demand him of her, but she would promise nothing except that she would deliver him back in the evening; he had feared that she intended to take him to Linz, where his brother lived, or to Hungary; for that reason he had gone to the police; as soon as he got him back he placed him in the care of Giannatasio.

Were he and his brother of the nobility and did he have documents to prove it?

"Van" was a Dutch predicate which was not exclusively applied to the nobility; he had neither a diploma nor any other proof of his nobility.

Beethoven's answer that he had no proof of his nobility is all that the minutes of the court show; but a tradition exists that Beethoven, when he was asked whether he was of noble birth, pointed to his head and to his heart and answered, "My patent of nobility lies here." No doubt a very fine answer, if he made it. No doubt justly said. But we can hardly blame the Imperial Royal *Landrechte* of Lower Austria for being unimpressed. The *Landrechte* decided then and there that the proceedings were being held before the wrong tribunal.* They transferred the case to the proper authority, the Vienna *Magistrat*. Perhaps they were glad to wash their hands of the messy business. It was a terrible blow to Beethoven. Now the whole question remained in a state of uncertainty. Now all the testifying had to be done again, another decision had to be awaited. Beethoven no doubt felt that he would get a less sympathetic audience with the judges of the lower court.

The *Magistrat* held a hearing on January 11, 1819, after which Beethoven drafted a twelve-page answer to Johanna's and Hotschevar's accusations. How he stormed! Here is a small excerpt:

> I could be careless and, finally wearying of the whole business, let myself fall a prey to those many intrigues and defamatory statements. But this I will not do. I will prove that he who performs *good and noble* actions, *can also suffer* for their sake and that he *must never lose sight of the noble aim which he has set himself.* I have *sworn* to act *in the best interest of my nephew as long as I live.* Even if I had not acted in this spirit, yet from *my character* and *my opinions in general* one could *only expect what is most advantageous for my nephew in every respect.* Am I to discuss as well the intrigues *against me* of a worthy Court Secretary, named Hotschevar, or talk about a *parson at Mödling* who, despised by his congregation, has the reputation of *indulging in illicit intercourse,* has his pupils put on a bench to be flogged like soldiers, and can never forgive me for watching *him* and positively refusing to have my nephew bestially treated with thrashings? Am I to do this? No.
>
> (A-Appendix C, Document 9, Feb. 1, 1819).

·∘[7]∘·

Karl went back to his mother, at least for the next few weeks. Fanny del Rio writes in her diary that she heard that Beethoven was grieving, did not see anybody, and took his meals alone.

---

* As I stated before, the question remains how the matter got before the *Landrechte* in the first place.

Though Beethoven's guardianship was now in a state of suspense pending the decision of the *Magistrat,* he still had the right to concern himself with Karl's education. He placed his nephew in an institute conducted by Johann Kudlich. He thought highly of Kudlich: his teaching methods were considered by all the experts as being the best, he said. That judgment lasted but a little while. As usual, Beethoven changed his mind, writing Bernard on June 16, 1819, that Kudlich "is either a *rascal* or a *weak fellow!!!!!*"

In March Beethoven had considered resigning the guardianship. He announced this desire perhaps to forestall his being removed by the court. Unable to come to any decision, he went around asking advice of his friends. Bernard had suggested Kudlich as a co-guardian. Beethoven was more inclined toward one Matthias von Tuscher, a magisterial councilor. In the meantime he took the boy out of Kudlich's school and proposed that he be sent back to del Rio. This was too much for the long-suffering educator. He refused to take him back.

Tuscher, though probably reluctantly, accepted the co-guardianship. The court approved this and asked Tuscher to make recommendations for the boy's further fate. Tuscher was of the opinion that the best thing for Karl was to have him sent away—we conjecture "sent away" from *both* Beethoven and Johanna —and he fell in with an idea proposed by Beethoven and Bernard that he be sent to the school of a Professor Johann Michael Sailer at Landshut in Bavaria. A passport was needed for this, and Beethoven applied to the city authorities for a passport for Karl. The passport bureau asked the *Magistrat* if there were any objections. There were: the *Magistrat* ruled that the boy was not to be sent off to a foreign country.

The Landshut plan had to be abandoned, the summer was coming on, Beethoven wanted to go again to Mödling to escape the city, del Rio had refused to accept Karl—what could be done? He was sent to still another school, that of Joseph Blöchlinger, an educator who had studied with Pestalozzi. There for the moment the boy, shuttled from school to school, from authority to authority, could find a little peace.

Beethoven, however, was not satisfied. No lower court was going to tell him what to do. No matter what the *Magistrat* decreed, he considered himself Karl's real guardian and that was all there was to it. He poured his troubles into his friends' ears. He laid his hand pleadingly on anybody who might help him, or merely sympathize with him. He even took the extreme step of appealing to Archduke Rudolph. He had heard, he wrote Rudolph in May, 1819, that

Johanna was seeking the aid of Archduke Ludwig, a younger brother of Rudolph. He begged and implored Rudolph, in language that was humble and un-Beethovian, to intercede for him. How hard he must have swallowed to write such a letter! Rudolph, however, was unable or unwilling to interfere.

Karl seems to have done fairly well in the new school. At least, somebody wrote in the Conversation Book in December, 1819, that he had seen Karl, who looked well and handsome and had become orderly in his studies.

After some months Tuscher, probably wearying of Beethoven's continuous adjurations, resigned as co-guardian. Beethoven immediately broke off friendship with him and announced to the *Magistrat* that he was resuming the sole guardianship, though the action was obviously illegal. He laid down the law to Blöchlinger, as to who was to have access to Karl and who was not, that Karl was never to leave the house without written permission from Beethoven himself, and more such infrangible rules given dictatorially. Yet behind all these dicta one feels the terror of the man fearing that he might lose what was now dearest to him. In one breath he repudiates and curses the boy—the "young miscreant" . . . "as long as I live I shall never see him again, for he is a monster"—and in the next breath he loves him again: "Once more I repeat he is *innocent of everything.*" Perhaps the most pathetic letter is the one he wrote to Bernard in July, 1819:

> I heard from Oliva that Karl *asked* Blöchl[inger] *for permission* to write *me* a letter in Latin for my name-day—Hence I am of the opinion that you should make it clear to K[arl] in the presence of Herr B[löchlinger] that I do not wish to receive *any letter* from him. He ought to have done that long ago and apologized to me for the wicked pranks which he was induced to perpetrate partly by his mother and partly by his own inclination. His stubbornness, his ingratitude and his callousness have so got the better of him that when Ol[iva] was there he never once even *asked for me.* Moreover when I took him for the first time to Blöchl[inger] and held his hand, he drew it from mine as soon as we approached the house,* and he did the same thing again on a later occasion when I was there with Ol[iva]—Away with him, my patience is at an end, I have cast him out of my heart. I have shed many tears on his account, that worthless boy. Only if he *on his own initiative* finds the way back to me and only after I first have proofs that he has reformed his bad heart will I see whether I shall acknowledge him once more. My love for him is gone. *He needed my love.* I do not need his. And since he has been in that plague-ridden

---

* A natural gesture on the part of a boy in the presence of his schoolfellows.

atmosphere and has *now gone there again,* I don't want to hear anything more about him, save that I am paying and otherwise providing for him— ...

He continues like that until toward the end of the letter his *real* feeling breaks through:

> You understand, of course, that this is not what I *really* think (I still love him as I used to, but without weakness or undue partiality, nay more, I may say in truth that I often weep for him). (A-956).

The *Magistrat* finally decided to put an end to the intramural fighting. They made their decision. Stating that the ward had been "subjected to the whims of Beethoven and had been tossed back and forth like a ball from one educational institution to another," they decreed, on September 17, 1819, that Tuscher's request for relief from his guardianship be granted, but that the guardianship should *not* be re-entrusted to Beethoven but to the mother, with a capable, honest man at her side as co-guardian. A municipal official, Leopold Nussböck, was appointed by the court.

·◦[8]◦·

The blow had fallen. Beethoven had lost. What he had feared had come to pass: the lower court had found against him. Yet he was not going to give up. Indeed not! Driven into a corner by his own intransigence—for all along the quarrel might have been arbitrated had Beethoven been willing to sit down with Johanna and work out some sort of co-guardianship—he now sought what *new* legal moves he could undertake. His newly active adviser was Johann Baptist Bach. He was one of Vienna's shining legal lights, three times dean of the Faculty of Law of the University of Vienna. Dr. Bach's willingness to take the case indicates that he felt that there was still a chance to get the judgment reversed.

In putting the details of the case before Dr. Bach, Beethoven stated that he was financially able to take care of Karl for the rest of his life. He mentioned a sum of 4000 florins in silver (approximately $24,000). It was money he had acquired during the Congress of Vienna, and he earmarked it as capital for his nephew. He had deposited it with Steiner, and in July, 1819, he had bought with it eight shares of bank stock, acting on the financial advice of Baron von Eskeles, of the firm of Arnstein and Eskeles. It turned out to be a good investment.

An appeal to the *Magistrat* was peremptorily dismissed: there were no new facts that warranted the court's changing its ruling.

Now Dr. Bach suggested an appeal to a higher tribunal, the Appellate Court. Among other arguments brought forward it was stated that Nussböck neither had enough time nor was pedagogically experienced enough to fulfill his function: Beethoven gave as his choice for a co-guardian the name of Karl Peters. He was a tutor of the Lobkowitz children. Beethoven liked him * because he was a kindly, talkative, pleasant man who could perhaps exert a beneficial influence on Karl.

The Appellate Court ordered the *Magistrat* to file full particulars of all previous proceedings for review. The *Magistrat,* prompted by the wish to justify its ruling, not only did what was asked but wrote an explanatory brief which reads more like the summation of an accusing district attorney than the document of a judiciary body. All through the case the *Magistrat* seems to have been influenced by a certain bias against Beethoven, possibly because Beethoven showed them that he scorned them, considering them "a lower court," fit to judge clerks and workmen but not able to comprehend the actions of a Beethoven.

Beethoven in his turn wrote a memorandum to the Appellate Court, an unbridled statement speckled with underscoring, Latin quotations, lamentations, and accusations which went so far as to charge Johanna with having given the boy alcoholic drinks and making him ill for three weeks. Only the draft of the memorandum has survived: it is the longest piece of writing in Beethoven's hand, covering more than twenty printed pages in Emily Anderson's book. Whether it was ever presented to the court we do not know; it is possible that Dr. Bach advised his client against submitting so raw a document.

The Appellate Court examined the case from A to Z. They asked for more and more information, taking their time before coming to a decision. In the meantime, both adversaries were doing spadework of their own. Beethoven wrote letters to a judge who was a member of the Appellate Court and personally visited two other members of the court for "private talks." Such a practice would of course be unthinkable under British or American law—or Austrian law of today.

Karl was in school and was behaving quite well for the time being. He

---

* Beethoven wrote a humorous little canon dedicated to him.

apologized to Beethoven (what he said to his mother we do not know). He wrote in the Conversation Book:

> She promised me so many things that I could not resist her; I am sorry that I was so weak at the time and beg your forgiveness; but I will certainly not again permit myself to be led astray—I did not know what results might follow when I told the Magistrates what I did. But if there is another examination I will retract everything that *I said* at the time which was *untrue!* (TQ).

After three months the Appellate Court issued its decision—on April 8, 1820. They set aside the decision of the *Magistrat* and found in Beethoven's favor. Johanna and Nussböck were dismissed as guardians, and Karl was put under the joint guardianship of Beethoven and Karl Peters.

Beethoven had won.

Though Johanna appealed to the highest authority in the land, the Emperor, she had to abide by the decree.

·•:[9]:•··

Karl remained at Blöchlinger Institute. Blöchlinger, who must have smarted severely under the insulting letters which Beethoven had written him previously, now was all on Beethoven's side. He expressed himself in the Conversation Book concerning Johanna:

> ...It has seemed to me of late that the Beethoven woman was expecting. I would be very glad to know for sure, one would have new evidence for saying to Karl that his mother was immoral, moreover he will have observed it when he was with her. I would like to know it for certain. Karl must get a clear understanding as regards his mother, as you have said yourself; for if he depends on her, he is lost, and to alienate him from her, he must have proof that she is immoral. The other day I also told him that she had been in a house of correction and let him judge whether what his mother had done till now was good for him. (TQ).

What a thing for an educator to impart to a young boy! Blöchlinger seems to have been as fit for his profession as Beethoven was for a diplomatic career.

What were the results? Karl once more ran away—to his mother. He had to be brought back forcibly to the school.

During the next few years an uneasy truce prevailed. At the beginning of 1824 Johanna fell ill. Beethoven immediately rallied to her aid. Now that she was in need, this woman whom he hated, "she must be helped at once" (he wrote to Bernard), and he was going to persuade his "pigheaded brother also to contribute something." He offered to relieve her of her obligation to contribute half her pension to Karl. Yet he did not want *to have anything to do with her personally.*

In the summer of 1825, when Beethoven was at Baden, the relationship between Karl and Beethoven worsened. He was no longer a child, he was a young man of nineteen and fighting for an independence which he could not wring from his uncle. It was clear to everybody except Beethoven that Karl did not possess sufficient talent for "either a musician or an artist," but Beethoven still hoped to make a scholar of him, and Karl had enrolled at the University of Vienna, pursuing studies in languages. Beethoven wanted to form Karl in his image. Yet Karl's mind was not inclined toward the intellectual, the spiritual, or the artistic. His was a practical bent. When Beethoven entrusted him with certain business transactions, Karl did well.

He asked his uncle to let him enter the army. One understands his longing for discipline, for order, for a career in which he would not have to make decisions. Failing this, he wanted to become a businessman; after long reluctance he was successful in persuading Beethoven to let him enter a business school. He wrote in the Conversation Book in April, 1825:

> You know that I will not oppose you if you *wish* me to continue to study; but I really feel that I will progress much better there [in the business school] since in times past I have lost interest. Nevertheless, I will never forget my Greek but continue with it consistently and industriously, the more since I am far enough along in it so that reading it is no longer a strain for me but rather a pleasure. (TQ).

Karl entered the Polytechnic Institute in 1825, and Beethoven arranged to have its vice-director, a Dr. Franz Reisser, appointed co-guardian in place of Peters. Karl took lodgings with the family of one Matthias Schlemmer. The young man remained in the city while Beethoven moved to the country. Karl had a good deal of work to make up, having entered the school late in the term. A tutor was engaged to help him.

Beethoven watched Karl from afar and set his friends, the Bernards and the Holzes * and the Schindlers, to spy on him. Some of Beethoven's letters read like

---

* Karl Holz became one of Beethoven's best friends in the last years.

Polonius' instructions to Reynaldo secretly "to make inquiry of his behavior." But Karl was not a Laertes, not a very noble youth.

On Sundays and holidays Karl was expected to visit his uncle in Baden. He did not want to go. He preferred going to the theater. He loved to play billiards. No doubt he wanted girls. What fun was there to journey to Baden to hold converse with a deaf man for whom one had to write out every word? Lame indeed are the entries in the Conversation Books in which Karl makes excuses for not coming. Bitter and harsh are Beethoven's reproaches.

Beethoven wrote to Matthias Schlemmer:

> ... one might be led to suspect that perhaps he really is enjoying himself in the evening or even at night in some company which is certainly not so desirable—I request you to pay attention to this and not to let Karl leave your house at night under any pretext whatever,* unless you have received something in writing from me through Karl— (A-1380).

To Karl:

> I was glad when I could help my poor parents. What a difference compared with you, in the matter of your behaviour to me.   (A-1400).

To Karl:

> Write me a few words—send them to me tomorrow. Here is another florin. Don't forget to bathe—Keep well. Take care of yourself so that you do not *fall ill*—and only spend your money in *the right way*—Be my dear son.   (A-1406).

> Last Sunday you again borrowed 1 gulden, 15 kreuzer from the housekeeper, that vulgar old skivvy—I had long ago forbidden you to do this—Everywhere it is the same story. I would have managed for two years with the one frock-coat. Admittedly I have the bad habit of putting on a worn out coat at home. But that gentleman Karl, faugh, the shame of it, and why should he do it? Well, because Herr L. v. B[eethove]n's money-bag is there solely for that purpose—You need not come this Sunday either, for owing to your behaviour there can never be true harmony and concord between us—And why this hypocrisy? ...

---

* This—I repeat—about a young man nineteen years old!

However, don't be anxious, I shall always provide *for you*, as I am doing now continually. But you provoke me to make *such scenes*—for instance, when I again found that sum of 1 gulden, 15 kreuzer on the housekeeper's bill.

Do not write on such thin sheets in future, for the housekeeper can read them by holding them against the light.   (A-1430).*

When Karl rebelled and stayed away for some time, the proud Beethoven wrote like a feverish supplicant:

[Autumn, 1825]

My Beloved Son!

Stop, no further—Only come to my arms, you won't hear a single hard word. For God's sake, do not abandon yourself to misery. You will be welcomed here as affectionately as ever. We will lovingly discuss what has to be considered and what must be done for the future. On my word of honour you will hear no reproaches, since in any case they would no longer do any good. All that you may expect from me is the most loving care and help—But do come—come to the faithful heart of

your father
BEETHOVEN

Volti sub[ito]

Come home as soon as you receive this note.

　Si vous ne viendres pas
vous me tûerès surement
　lisés la lettre et restés
a la maison chez vous, venes
　de m'embrasser votre pere
vous vraiment adonné soyes
assurés, que tout cela resterà
　entre nous.

For God's sake, do come home again today. If not, who knows what danger may confront you? Hurry, hurry.   (A-1445).

The words in French are written on the outside of the letter; they are in French so that the servants could not read them. "If you don't come, you will surely kill me. Read this letter and stay home. Then come to embrace me, your devoted father. Be assured that all this will remain between us."

It did not help when friends such as Holz told Beethoven that Karl was not a bad fellow. Holz's report (in part) written in the Conversation Book:

---

* All of these letters are from 1825.

> I have lured him into going to a beer house with me because I [wanted] to see if
> he drinks much; but that does not appear to be the case. Now I will invite [him]
> at some point to play billiards; then I will see immediately if he has already been
> practising a long time— (TQ).

The struggle continued: Karl tried to put distance between himself and his glowering guardian, while Beethoven strained to hold him, enlisting in the effort even his brother Johann.

Karl had a friend, Niemetz, of whom Beethoven disapproved because he suspected him of leading Karl into temptation. But Karl showed strength and, in spite of his uncle, held on to the friend. There is a discussion about this in a Conversation Book, dated by Schindler "Fall 1824 in Baden." Curiously, Beethoven's part in the conversation is given as well as Karl's:

> BEETHOVEN: I am very ill pleased with your choice of this friend. Poverty
> certainly deserves sympathy, but not invariably. I would not want to be unfair to
> him but to me he is a burdensome guest, lacking completely in decency and
> manners, which belong in some degree to all well brought up youths and men.
> —Besides I suspect that his interests are more with the housekeeper than with
> me—Besides I love quiet; also the space here is too limited for several people
> since I am constantly busy, and he cannot engage my interest at all.—You still
> have a very weak character.
> KARL: Concerning my choice, I believe that a close acquaintance of four years'
> duration is really sufficient to get to know a man from *all angles,* especially a boy
> who cannot possibly remain disguised for such a long time—Thus there cannot
> be a question of lack of conviction, but merely of the reasons which led me to it,
> and they are in a word: the very great similarity of character and tastes. If he has
> been unable to please you, you are free to send him away, but he has not deserved
> what you have said about him. (TQ).

There is much more in the same tenor, all testifying to the struggle between nephew and uncle.

A note to Niemetz from Karl has been found:

> I had to write you in such a great hurry from fear and worry of being discovered
> by the old fool.

··❧[10]❧··

The "old fool" was not to be spared further sorrow. In the last days of July, 1826, Beethoven was told that Karl had disappeared. Schlemmer had learned that Karl had dropped some hints about wanting to end his life. He told Holz, who told Beethoven, and then both of them went to see Schlemmer. Schlemmer's entries in the Conversation Book:

> The story in brief, since you have heard it already from Mr. Holz: I learned today that your nephew intended to shoot himself before next Sunday at the latest. As to the cause I learned only this much that it was on account of his debts, but not completely, only in part was he admitting that they were the consequences of former sins.

> I looked to see if there were signs of preparation; I found in his chest a loaded pistol all right, together with bullets and powder. I tell you this so that you may act in this case as his father. The pistol is in my keeping.

> Be lenient with him or he will despair.   (TQ).

Holz searched for Karl at the institute. He was not there. Then the men searched among Karl's belongings for clues. They found two more pistols. Karl had left his weapons behind. Beethoven, instead of being reassured, now thought, "He will drown himself." What happened next is uncertain, because pages of the Conversation Book are missing. Perhaps Schindler removed them in later years or, as Thayer conjectures, "they may have been torn out by Beethoven himself when, some weeks later, Holz advised him to look through his books against their possible demand for examination by the police magistrate; they might contain references to affairs which he did not want to bring into public discussion."

Even without the missing pages, the progression of events can be pieced together. Karl, having escaped his watchers, did not dare to return to his lodging: he went to a pawnshop to pledge his watch. Instead of using the pistols which he had prepared, he bought two new ones. He went to Baden and spent the night writing letters, one to his uncle. The next morning the distraught youth climbed up to the old ruin of Rauhenstein and there discharged both pistols toward his left temple. One bullet missed altogether, and the second inflicted a flesh wound; it grazed but did not penetrate the skull.* He fell to the

---

* For the theory that Karl only pretended to commit suicide and purposely inflicted only a superficial wound no corroboration exists.

ground and lost consciousness. After some hours a teamster with horses and wagon came along, heard a moan, investigated, saw the prostrate figure, and lifted him onto his wagon. Karl stammered that he wanted to be taken back to the city. Where to? To his *mother's* house.

There Beethoven sought him out. There both Johanna and he bent over him. To Beethoven's questioning he wrote, "Do not plague me with reproaches and lamentations; it is past. Later all matters may be adjusted." (TQ).

Then Beethoven asked, "When did it all happen?" Johanna answered:

> He has just come. The teamster carried him down from a rock in Baden and has just driven out to you ... I beg of you to tell the surgeon not to make a report or they will take him away from here at once, and we fear the worst. (TQ).

Beethoven dashed off a note to Smetana, the surgeon who had operated on Karl for hernia:

> [VIENNA, July 30, 1826]
>
> Most Honoured Herr von Smetana,
> A great misfortune has happened, a misfortune which *Karl* has accidentally brought upon himself. I hope that it is still possible to save him, but my hope depends particularly on you, provided you can come soon. Karl has a *bullet* in his head. How this has happened you will learn in due course.—But come quickly, for God's sake, quickly.
>
> Yours respectfully,
> BEETHOVEN
>
> As help had to be provided quickly, he had to be taken to his mother's where he now is. I enclose her address. (A-1495).

Holz took the letter, but before he left the house with it a surgeon named Dögl had arrived. Holz returned with a message from Smetana saying that Dögl was a perfectly competent physician, and medical ethics being what they were, he could not come unless Dögl called him in consultation.

The "accident" had to be reported to the police. Holz undertook this onerous task. He returned to say that the police would investigate and that Karl would have to be placed under police surveillance. He also told Beethoven that after Beethoven had left, Karl said, "If only he would not show himself again!" and "If only he would stop his reproaches!" He threatened to tear the bandages from his wound if another word were spoken about his uncle.

After a few days Karl was removed from his mother's house by the police and placed in the General Hospital. He was getting along well and was soon out of danger. Because attempted suicide was considered an offense against the Church, Karl was put in charge of a priest. Beethoven, through Holz and other friends, tried time and again to have Karl answer the exacerbating question: Why did he do it? What was it that drove him to it? Karl lay in the hospital bed and would not answer. Perhaps he himself could not clearly articulate the reason. Holz described him as "weary of life" and "weary of imprisonment." To the examining police magistrate Karl said that his uncle had "tormented him too much," but added, "I became worse because my uncle wanted me to be better." All kinds of reasons have been put forward: debts, the possibility that he stole some books from Beethoven to sell,* mental aberration, the heat, fear of not passing the examinations at the institute, and so on. Whatever the immediate cause, the true cause lay in Karl's inability to endure a position in which he stood in the center while two adults clawed at him tooth and nail.

Being young, Karl eventually recovered. The act shattered not Karl but Beethoven. It was he who was wounded, not by a grazing blow, but by an injury which reached the core of his being. It was a wound from which he never recovered. Gerhard Breuning described Beethoven after the attempted suicide:

> The pain which he received from this event was indescribable; he was cast down as a father who has lost his much-loved son. My mother met him on the Glacis completely undone. "Do you know what happened? My Karl has shot himself!" "And—is he dead?" "No, it was a glancing shot, he is still living, there's hope that he can be saved;—but the disgrace that he has brought upon me; and I loved him so."

After Karl recovered, the question of his future again became pertinent. It was necessary to decide this immediately, for the criminal aspect of the case was still threatening. Holz became firm:

> Here you see ingratitude as clear as the sun; why do you want further to restrain him? Once with the military, he will be under the strictest discipline, and if you want to do anything more for him you need only make him a small allowance monthly. A soldier at once.   (Conversation Book).

Holz also urged Beethoven to give up the guardianship. A replacement would then become the court's responsibility, and Beethoven would be free to

---

* Holz indicates this in an entry in the Conversation Book.

decide what he wanted to do for his nephew, if indeed he wanted to do anything more. Breuning, Dr. Bach, and Schindler joined Holz. Beethoven would not heed them.

The court investigated and, according to the report that Holz supplied to Beethoven, said that they would respect any decision Beethoven would arrive at. When Karl left the hospital, Beethoven took him immediately to his home; he was not to stay with his mother, not even for a day.

Finally, not knowing what else to do, Beethoven gave his consent to Karl's embarking on a military career. Stephan von Breuning now came to his aid. Through his connections in the War Department, he got in touch with a Baron Joseph von Stutterheim and got his agreement to enroll Karl in his regiment. In gratitude, Beethoven dedicated no less a work than the String Quartet in C-sharp Minor, Op. 131, to Stutterheim. In addition, it is probable that Beethoven gave the money to purchase a commission for Karl. Breuning agreed to accept the co-guardianship, as Reisser had resigned. Now Beethoven instructed the new co-guardian, his intimate friend, Breuning:

[September, 1826]

> In Karl's case three points should be borne in mind, I think. First, he must not be treated like a convict, for such a treatment would not produce the result we desire, but precisely the opposite—secondly, if he is to be promoted to the higher ranks, he must not live too frugally and shabbily—thirdly, he would find it hard to face too great a restriction in eating and drinking—But I do not wish to forestall you.   (A-1523).

The indulgent treatment—it was still there.

While waiting for the formalities to be completed, uncle and nephew took refuge on brother Johann's estate in Gneixendorf. The story of that visit and the fateful return journey to Vienna will have to be told in its chronological place.

Let us here merely trace Karl's further fate.

His army career was undistinguished but satisfactory. After five years he resigned from the army and became a farm manager. He had inherited Beethoven's estate. In 1848 his other uncle, Johann, died. Since Johann's wife Therese had long been dead and since there were no children, Karl became Johann's heir as well. There was enough money to enable him to live the last decade of his life in comfort. He died in 1858, at the age of only fifty-two.

Karl had married and had five children, one son and four daughters. The son, Ludwig, born in 1839, had a checkered career. Ludwig Nohl, the Beethoven scholar, gave Ludwig an introduction to Richard Wagner, who in turn recommended Beethoven's grandnephew to King Ludwig of Bavaria. He used these introductions, taking advantage of the gullibility of the King, to commit systematic frauds, such as trading in fictitious Beethoven memorabilia. He called himself Baron van Beethoven and pretended to be the grandson of the famous composer. In 1872 he was condemned by a Bavarian court to four years' imprisonment, while his wife was locked up for six months.

Another version, based on researches by Paul Nettl,* states that while Ludwig was found guilty, he never served his sentence. He was tried *in absentia,* having escaped to the United States the year before. He lived for a time in Rochester, New York, and then moved to various cities in the United States and Canada. There was a streak of bad blood in him; yet he possessed some sort of talent as well. He inaugurated a messenger service, based on the European system, which was successful. Moving to New York, he changed his name to Louis von Hoven, evidently to obliterate his traces. For a New York fair in 1874 he developed a project of renting wheel chairs. This venture too was successful. Ludwig died in New York in moderate wealth.

Ludwig had a son Karl, born in 1870. He died in 1917 in an army hospital in Vienna. He was the last to bear the name of Beethoven.

Of Johanna's life we have almost no information. She was supposed to have ended her days in Baden as a woman of doubtful reputation. It was said of her daughter that she too led an indecorous life.

The lives of great men have taught us that they can embrace the world in noble unselfishness, that they can spend blood and spill tears for the benefit of mankind, and yet wound and offend those nearest to them, treating wife and children and friends like the tyrants they are the first to despise. Rousseau and Tolstoy are examples in point. That Beethoven, who set to music the words, "This embrace to the whole world," was a tyrant to the boy is indisputable. His tyranny was caused by love, long unfulfilled, and now concentrated, like rays caught in a magnifying glass, on a mediocre little soul who was singed by such heat. The opposite of his devotion was his icy rebuff of the mother. One was as extreme as the other. He had plenty of excuse to hate Johanna; but that does not mitigate his behaving like a thin-lipped bigoted fanatic. From fire and ice he forged his own poniard, which he plunged into his own heart.

---

* *Beethoven's Grandnephew in America.* In *Music and Letters,* Vol. 38, No. 3, July, 1954.

Ludgate Hill, St. Paul's Cathedral in the background. William Marlow's painting shows London as it looked in Beethoven's time (Courtesy of the Governor and Company of the Bank of England).

CHAPTER 20

TO ENGLAND—BUT WHEN?

·∘][I][∘·

To a man living in Vienna in the early 19th century, London was as romantically distant as Paris was to a Cleveland schoolteacher of the 1890's. To a citizen of Austria, St. Petersburg or Naples seemed a good deal more accessible than England; at least he did not need to submit to the perilous channel crossing.

England was a country regarded by thoughtful Europeans, artists, scientists, musicians, and statesmen as a citadel of hope. Ever since it had given refuge to many of the *philosophes* of the 18th century, since the workings of the Parliament had come to be better understood, since with the rise of the Romantic Movement Shakespeare had begun to be valued, since Pope had written:

> Nature and Nature's laws lay hid in night:
> God said, Let Newton be! and all was light;

since a street in London called Pall Mall had been lit by gas (1809), since a steam wagon called a locomotive was put into service (1814), since the new painters, the Gainsboroughs and Reynoldses, had pictured the splendor of British uniforms, the Continent looked with admiration at the foggy island. With admiration—and with puzzlement. The English were an incomprehensible people, calculating, parochial, imperturbable, with their peculiar ideas of how to spend a Sunday, their haughty women, their indigestible beef, their passion for the sea, and their skill at preserving through all the ups and downs of war the power of the pound sterling.

A voyage to London was not an easy undertaking: it required thought and preparation. A great many more Englishmen came to Vienna than did Viennese to London. The trip needed time. Castlereagh, traveling to the Vienna Congress by private carriage, in a style in which money was no object, left London on August 16, 1814, made a short stay in Brussels and Antwerp, reached Paris on the 24th, left Paris on the 27th, and arrived in Vienna on September 13. He was almost a month en route.

Still, the journey to London was worth a great deal—as Haydn had learned. For a musician it was rewarding both artistically and financially. Several of Beethoven's friends sooner or later worked in London, happily and profitably. He had known Johann Peter Salomon and Ferdinand Ries since his Bonn days. Salomon, violinist, conductor, concert impresario, friend of Haydn, who had suggested the idea of *The Creation* to him, well-wisher of musicians, and a generous spirit, had earned a great reputation for his manifold activities. Salomon had lived in London off and on since he was thirty-six years old and now, in 1815, he was nearing seventy and was regarded as the grand old man of London's music. Around him there were grouped such men as the young pianist Charles Neate, who was the first to play the *Emperor Concerto* in England; Muzio Clementi, but one year younger than Salomon, pianist, composer for the piano, and music publisher who had met Beethoven in 1807; and Johann Baptist Cramer, Clementi's pupil, whom Beethoven had known and liked in the early years in Vienna. Moscheles, the famous virtuoso, settled in London in 1821. Spohr, Weber, and Cherubini appeared there during Beethoven's lifetime.

The musical life of London was vigorous. Long ago Handel had stamped on it the force of his personality. Rival opera companies and their rival stars had turned opera into a sport. There were good halls and theaters available; when they burned down, as they inevitably did, the Londoners were not slow to rebuild them. The old Covent Garden was destroyed by fire in 1808, the Drury Lane in 1809; the first was rebuilt in 1809, the second in 1812. Opera houses employed orchestras which performed at concerts as well. Concerts, while seeking the patronage of this duke or that duchess, were more generally regarded as public events than the Court concerts of Vienna. A measure of democracy had entered artistic life, though the division between peer and tradesman was still wide.

In 1813 a group of musicians formed the Philharmonic Society. It was to be "essentially an instrumental institution," * its purpose to promote symphonic

---

* Adam Carse, *The Orchestra From Beethoven to Berlioz,* 1948.

music as a change of diet from the vocal offerings with celebrated singers. Salomon, Clementi, and the conductor George Smart—recently knighted for his services to music—were among the founders of the society, which was to exercise an important influence on the history of orchestral music in England.

The Philharmonic was a cooperative affair. Only members could play (except certain trumpet and other wind players who were hired as the need arose), and only excellent musicians could become members. Salomon led the first concert, on March 8, 1813. They all played for the love of it, earning no emolument of any kind. That is, at the beginning. The concerts became popular, the expenses were small, the receipts large, and after about three years all members of the orchestra began to be paid. In addition, funds were used to commission new works.

The leaders of the concerts were chosen from among the playing members, but visiting celebrities were not excluded (Cherubini in 1815, Spohr in 1820). Most of these leaders, whether personally acquainted with Beethoven or not, were Beethoven enthusiasts. The programs of the first ten years show these performances of symphonies:

> Haydn 49
> Mozart 37
> Beethoven (I to VII) . . . 32
> Spohr 3
> Other composers 28*

In their first season the society performed three Beethoven symphonies and the Septet; the *Eroica* the next season.

It was natural, then, that Beethoven should be favorably disposed toward these proselytizing friends, who spoke a language of which he understood but a few words. Even apart from music, Beethoven entertained an idealized view of England, a view to which distance lent enchantment. The parliamentary system, and what he conceived to be true democracy, delighted him. He used to scan the newspapers avidly for news from the island and would read the debates in Parliament. Schindler says: "As one would expect, he sided with the Opposition, and was a great admirer of Lord Brougham,** Hume, and other orators in

---

* Figures compiled by Carse.
** Lord Henry Brougham was an eloquent opponent of the slave trade.

that party's cause." Looking at the country from afar, he did not see its imperfections, nor did he understand that the British royal family cared no more about musical development than his Emperor Franz. He could not judge that George IV was a King desirous of something less than nourishing his country's intellectual life; extravagant and dissolute, his enthusiasms confined themselves to horses and girls. What Beethoven could observe was the devotion of the men who were infusing seriousness into the musical life of England; he contrasted this with the "frivolity of the Viennese taste," forgetting that there never is such a thing as general taste, that taste is a multilayer cake of unequally thick layers, and that there was frivolity to be found in London as in Vienna, though perhaps the Anglo-Saxon temperament favored a more serious approach to art. Beethoven said: "In London everybody knows something and knows it well; but the man of Vienna can only talk of eating and drinking, and sings and pounds away at music of little significance." *

When *Wellington's Victory* became a success in Vienna, Beethoven logically assumed that it would be an even greater success in England. We have noted that he sent the score to the Prince Regent, asking whether he might dedicate the composition to him. He expected that a composition so obviously pro-British would be enthusiastically received and that the prince would express himself in a tangible way. There is extant the draft of a long letter written in 1815 which speaks of Beethoven's disappointment. The letter seems to have been so important to him that he had a French version prepared as well. It is not certain for whom the letter was intended: it might have been Prince Paul Esterházy, who in October, 1815, was appointed Austrian envoy to London, or it might have been Viscount Castlereagh, whose acquaintance he probably made during the Congress. Beethoven wrote:

> All the papers were full of the praises and the extraordinary applause which this work [*Wellington*] had won in England. Yet no one thought of me, its composer; nor did I receive the least mark of gratitude or acknowledgment of indebtedness; nay more, not even a syllable came to me from London in reply! (A-546).

It is true that the *Battle Symphony* was performed that year at the Drury Lane Theater with great success. The conductor was Sir George Smart, who had

---

* From a conversation with Johann Stumpff.

introduced the *Mount of Olives* oratorio to the London public the year before.

While the Prince Regent did nothing, Smart, Salomon, and Ries put forth their best efforts. They persuaded Robert Birchall, one of England's good music publishers, to buy four works: the piano arrangement of *Wellington's Victory* and of the Seventh Symphony, the *Archduke Trio,* and the Sonata for Piano and Violin Op. 96. For the right of publishing these in the British Isles, Birchall paid sixty-five pounds sterling (about $1500 in today's purchasing power).

As in Vienna so in London were the young musicians champions of Beethoven's music. Ferdinand Ries was fourteen years younger than Beethoven. Charles Neate was exactly the same age as Ries. In 1815—that is, after the end of the Napoleonic Wars—Neate undertook the voyage from London to Vienna with the express purpose of seeing Beethoven and the hope of taking lessons in composition from him. Beethoven declined to take him as a pupil, but gave him much good advice. Neate spoke German, and the two used to go strolling in Baden discussing music, with Neate shouting into Beethoven's left ear and both of them gesticulating wildly and laughing. Neate remained in Vienna for eight months. When he left, Beethoven dedicated two canons to him: *Rede, rede* and *Lerne Schweigen*—"Speak, speak" and "Learn Silence." Beethoven wrote, "My dear English Countryman, Do not forget your sincere friend Beethoven, whether you are silent or not."

Neate told Beethoven that his sonatas and chamber music were often played in England and that his Septet was much admired. "I wish it were burned," said Beethoven, much to Neate's embarrassment. But the exciting message that Neate could impart to Beethoven was a commission from the Philharmonic Society—obtained no doubt through the recommendation of the pillars of that society, Salomon and Smart—for three overtures. He was to compose those and was to be paid seventy-five guineas, with the understanding that the Philharmonic Society would obtain exclusive rights for their publication; Beethoven was to retain the right to perform them wherever and whenever he wanted.* Beethoven was delighted.

When Neate left to return to England, Beethoven entrusted to him several of his important works, such as *Fidelio,* the Violin Concerto, and the Seventh Symphony, asking Neate to try to sell them to British publishers.

All the auguries were favorable. Beethoven had but to deliver his part of the bargain, and his London admirers would have sent other commissions his way.

---

* There was a bit more to the contract; I am simplifying it.

Ears were open at Covent Garden, and minds were receptive at Drury Lane for the fullness of Beethoven's harmony.

What demon was it that seduced him to an action as unfair to his well-wishers as it was detrimental to his own best interests? Instead of composing three new overtures—for which he had been paid a good fee in advance, seventy-five guineas being the equivalent of about $2000—Beethoven sent the Philharmonic Society three already existing overtures, *The Ruins of Athens,* the *King Stephan,* and the *Name-day.* None of these, to be sure, had as yet been published. But they were not new, not specially composed. Moreover, they were casual works written for specific occasions and hardly of top-drawer quality.

The Philharmonic Society had given the first London performance of the Fifth Symphony and the public had acclaimed it.* The musicians themselves who had played the work were thrilled by its bold beauty. Now they had the eagerly awaited, supposedly fresh products from Beethoven's pen in front of them—and they turned out to be old compositions, the existence of which some of the members of the society had known. As Thayer puts it:

> Imagine the disappointment of these men, fresh from the performance of the C minor Symphony, when they played through the overtures to *Die Ruinen von Athen* and *König Stephan,* which, however interesting to a Hungarian audience as introductions to a patriotic prologue and epilogue in the theatre, possess none of those great qualities expected from Beethoven and demanded in a concert overture! Nor was the "Namensfeier" thought worthy of its author. (T).

Beethoven's action was tantamount to an insult to the Philharmonic Society, and it would have been quite understandable had the men broken off any future relations with the composer. That they did not do so speaks as much for their tolerance as it does for the importance of Beethoven's music in England. But their chagrin was great. It was just as well that Salomon was no longer alive to witness the delusion. In August he had had a bad fall from his horse, breaking his shoulder. He did not recover, though he lingered on until November 28, 1815, dying at the age of seventy. Long before his death Salomon had rehearsed parts of the Fifth Symphony with the Philharmonic Society. He could make nothing of it and called the music "rubbish." He tried again some time after; at the end of the first movement Salomon laid down his violin, walked to the front

---

* The date was April 15, 1816. In the program there are detailed instructions to coachmen where to park the horses and in which direction their heads should be pointing.

of the orchestra and said, "Gentlemen, some years ago I called this symphony rubbish; I wish to retract what I then said. I now consider it one of the great compositions I know." Salomon is buried in Westminster Abbey next to Handel. He deserves such a resting place.

⋯⊰[2]⊱⋯

Beethoven could not have been under any illusion that he was fulfilling his obligation, that the overtures, being new to England, were new in point of fact. If he thought that the British gentlemen would not know any better, he grossly underestimated both their knowledge of current musical events and their taste. He tried to justify himself later by writing to Sir George Smart that while he admitted that the three overtures "do not belong to my best and greatest works, they being all occasional pieces composed for the theater," they had been successful wherever performed, and that *it was Neate* who had chosen them, although he had in his possession other more essential works. So now the whole imbroglio was Neate's fault, and Beethoven peremptorily withdrew the other works which Neate had in his possession and asked Smart to dispose of them.

VIENNA, October, 1816

> At least I am thoroughly persuaded that the two Englishmen, who have treated me very ill—very meanly—are very rare exceptions of the general character of your great nation. These two are the Prince Regent and Mr. Neate—enough of them! (A-664).

The biographer searching for an explanation of Beethoven's behavior can only admit that he draws a blank. There is no explanation. Only a rather feeble excuse can be docketed: it may be that his brother's death lamed Beethoven's inventive power temporarily and the appeal to the *Landrechte* preempted his attention.* Yet, if so, there would have been no reason why Beethoven could not have asked for more time.

His dealings with Birchall were equally nonsensical. Having received the compositions agreed upon, Birchall immediately deposited the stipulated sum to Beethoven's credit. He forwarded a declaration form for Beethoven's signature; it was a receipt for the sixty-five pounds and a legal statement assigning interest,

---

* There is some indication that Beethoven decided to send the old overtures *before* Carl's death, which of course would make this statement invalid.

"present and future, vested or contingent, or otherwise within the United Kingdom of Great Britain and Ireland."

Instead of signing this perfectly normal document, Beethoven asked for an additional five pounds for expenses he had incurred in copying and postage. Not getting an immediate answer, he kept insisting that he was entitled to the additional payment. He jeopardized his whole relationship for this trifling sum. Birchall did deposit the five pounds, though Beethoven somehow or other did not learn of this until much later. The months passed by and Beethoven's signature did not arrive. (He never did sign.) All this became known in London. Neate remembered the letter he got from one of the publishers which read, "For God's sake don't buy anything of Beethoven!" When he spoke to Birchall, asking him to purchase the overtures, the publisher replied, "I would not print them if you would give me them gratis."

Then Beethoven read in what he called the "Morning Cronigle" about a performance of one of his symphonies and he judged it to be the Seventh. He immediately jumped to the conclusion that Neate had sold the symphony without telling him about it, or in other words that his friend had acted in an underhanded manner.

The news about the symphony, combined with the failure of Neate to sell any of the compositions, a failure which certainly was not Neate's fault and the true reason for which he could hardly communicate to Beethoven, as well as continued silence on Neate's part, made Beethoven feel that again he had been betrayed. He vented his anger against Neate in letters both to Ries and Sir George Smart. Smart, an upright and honorable man, felt that the only way to clarify the issue was to show Neate the letter. This he did. Neate was bitterly hurt. On October 29, 1816, he wrote Beethoven a long, dignified, and beautiful letter in which, instead of becoming furious, he took a conciliatory tone:

> Nothing has ever given me more pain than your letter to Sir George Smart. I confess that I deserve your censure, that I am greatly in fault; but must say also that I think you have judged too hastily and too harshly of my conduct.   (TQ).

How painful it was to stand accused by the man whom in all the world he most admired and esteemed and for whose welfare he had done his level best! Neate pleaded guilty only to the charge of silence. The cause of it was his terrible state of mind. He had fallen in love with an English girl whose family had objected to her marrying a musician. It looked as if he would have to make the choice between giving up the woman he loved or renouncing his profession, a dreadful dilemma. Fortunately he was able to persuade the girl's parents to let him continue to be a musician. Now he was married. All was well. "I remain in my profession, and with no abatement of my love of Beethoven!"

During the period which he had just passed he had to remain inactive, nor could he have served as director of the Philharmonic Society. Now he was reelected for the next season. The symphony, continued Neate, which was mentioned in the *Morning Chronicle* was most certainly not the Seventh; it was probably the Fifth. Neate did not hide the difficulty he experienced in selling Beethoven's works, though he put the matter in tactful terms:

> I have offered your Sonatas to several publishers, but they thought them too difficult, and said they would not be saleable, and consequently made offers such as I could not accept, but when I shall have played them to a few professors, their reputation will naturally be increased by their merits, and I hope to have better offers.

Finally, as to the compositions which Beethoven had entrusted to him, he was willing to give up every one of them if Beethoven really desired it. Yet Beethoven must believe in his goodwill, a friendship for which he has "... even offered my purse, which you generously always declined."

Beethoven, as usual, was sorry and he replied to Neate in a charming letter. (The letter is written in English by another hand.) He congratulates Neate on reaching the "port of love" safely. All happiness to him and let past ills be forgotten.

Beethoven, having duly received the five pounds, did apologize to Birchall finally, in a letter on October 1, 1816. But Birchall, being made of grosser clay, told Beethoven that he could not enter into any fresh arrangement with him until the composer had signed the declaration. Beethoven now misunderstood this and thought Birchall wanted a receipt for the five pounds. He wrote, "I give you my word of honor that I have signed and delivered the receipt. ..." The business relationship might have continued had not Birchall died suddenly. His successor did not think it worth the trouble to take up the connection again.

·≈[3]≈·

Though it was maddening to deal with this genius, who answered letters only spasmodically, who attempted to sell leftover music and haggled over five pounds, it was nevertheless well-nigh mandatory to overlook his quirks—so popular had his music become with English audiences. This was true not of London alone. A report of a music festival held in Liverpool as early as the fall of 1813 says:

> ...the evening concerts were so crowded, as to render it necessary to break the windows of the Music Hall to afford relief. We already begin to trace the effects of the establishment of the Philharmonic Society, which held its first meeting on the 8th of March preceding, on this occasion, when the instrumental compositions of Beethoven and Cherubini ... formed one of the chief attractions.*

Almost two years had passed since the episode of the three overtures. Anger had softened. Perhaps the Philharmonic Society thought it the better part of valor to ignore the past. Accordingly—and surprisingly—Beethoven received in June, 1817, an invitation to visit London. The invitation was given in an official and gracious letter written by Ries. It reached Beethoven after he had recovered from an illness and while he was becoming more and more immersed in his troubles with Johanna.

June 9th, 1817

My dearest Beethoven,

For a very long time I have been forgotten by you, although I can think of no other cause than your too great occupation, and, as I was compelled to hear from others, your serious illness. Truly, dear Beethoven, the gratitude which I owe you and always must owe you—and I believe I may honestly say I have never forgotten it—although enemies have often represented me to you as ungrateful and envious—is unalterable, as I have always ardently desired to prove to you in more than words. This ardent desire has now (I hope) been fulfilled, and I hope to find again in my old teacher, my old and affectionate friend. The Philharmonic Society, of which our friend Neate is now also a director, and at whose concerts your compositions are preferred to all others, wishes to give you an evidence of its great respect for you and its appreciation of the many beautiful moments which your great works have so often provided for us; and I feel it a most flattering compliment to have been empowered with Neate to write to you on the

---

* This quotation is taken from an elaborate Folio which contains a history of concert events in England in the early 19th century. The book, published by five publishers simultaneously, bore this title: "An Account of the Grand Musical Festival, held in September, 1823, in the Cathedral Church of York; for the benefit of the York County Hospital, and the General Infirmaries at Leeds, Hull, and Sheffield: to which is prefixed A sketch of the Rise and Progress of Musical Festivals in Great Britain; with biographical and historical notes.

"By John Crosse, F. S. A., F.R.S.L., M.G.S., honorary member of the antiquarian society of Newcastle-upon-Tyne, and of the Yorkshire Literary and Philosophical Society, &c. and a member of the Committee of Management."

subject. In short, my dear Beethoven, we should like to have you with us in London next winter. Friends will receive you with open arms; and to give you at least one proof of this I have been commissioned on behalf of the Philharmonic Society to offer you 300 guineas on the following conditions:

1st. You are to be here in London next winter.

2nd. You are to write two grand symphonies for the Philharmonic Society, which are to be its property.

3rd. You must bind yourself not to deliver any composition for grand orchestra for any concert in London, nor direct any concert before or during our eight concerts, which begin towards the end of February and end in the first half of the month of June (without the consent of the Philharmonic Society), which certainly will not be difficult.

Do not understand by this that we want to tie your hands. ... We are all cordially disposed in your favor and I believe that every opportunity to be helpful to you in your plans would sooner give us pleasure than any desire to restrict you in the least.

4th. You are not to appear in the orchestra at any concert until our first two concerts are over, unless you want to give a concert yourself, and you can give as many of your own concerts as you please.

5th. You are to be here before the 8th of January, 1818, free from all obligations to the Society except to give us the preference in the future in case we meet the same conditions offered you by others.

6th. In case you accept the engagement and need money for the journey you may have 100 guineas in advance. This is the offer which I am authorized to make to you by the Society.

All negotiations with publishers are left to you as well as those with Sir G. Smart, who has offered you 100 guineas for an oratorio in one act, and who has specially commissioned me to remind you of an answer, as he would like to have the work for next winter. The intendant of the grand opera, G. Ayrton, is a particular friend of ours. He does not want to commit himself, but he promised us to commission an opera from you.

Your own concert, or as many concerts as you choose to give, may bring in a handsome sum to you as well as other engagements in the country. Neate and I rejoice like children at the prospect of seeing you here and I need not say that I will do all in my power to make your sojourn profitable and pleasant. I know England, too, and do not doubt your success for a moment. Moreover, we need somebody here who will put life into things and keep the gentlemen of the orchestra in order.

Yesterday evening our last concert took place and your beautiful Symphony in A-sharp [B-flat No. 4] was given with extraordinary applause. It frightens one to think of symphony writers when one sees and hears such a work. Write me very soon an explicit answer and bid me hope to see you yourself here before long.

I remain always
Your thankful sincere friend

FERD. RIES.   (TQ)

That Beethoven was excited and pleased by the offer is apparent not only by his reply to Ries but from the fact that he replied promptly, on July 9. But being Beethoven, he could not simply say yes. He answered that were it not for his "unfortunate infirmity" he would accept the proposal unconditionally. As it was, he had to overcome "many more obstacles than any other artist" and therefore he asked for additional money for traveling expenses for himself and a traveling companion. It was essential that he have one. He promised:

1. I shall be in London during the first half of January, 1818, at latest.
2. The two grand symphonies which are entirely new, will then be ready and they will become and remain the sole property of the Society. (A-786).

He accepted the other proposals made in Ries's letter.

The letter was written for Beethoven by somebody else, and Beethoven appended a note in his own handwriting:

> Dear Ries:
> I embrace you with all my heart. I have purposely asked somebody else to write the above letter, so that you may read it all with greater ease and then expound it to the Society. I am convinced of your good intentions with regard to myself; and I hope that the P[hilharmonic] S[ociety] will accept my proposal. The Society may rest assured that I will exert myself to the utmost to perform as worthily as possible the honourable task entrusted to me by such a select company of artists—How powerful is the Society's orchestra, how many violins and so forth; and are there *one or two of each wind-instrument?* Is the hall large and resonant?
>
> Your sincere admirer and friend
> L. V. BEETHOVEN   (A-787).

Beethoven wanted an advance of 150 guineas: the whole difference between his demand and the Philharmonic's offer was a matter of fifty guineas (though that was not an inconsiderable sum), and the Society would undoubtedly have accommodated him. Had he gone, how much might he have benefited, how much the world might have benefited through a tenth symphony, how less odious his last year of life might have become!

It was not to be. Something within him held him back. He could not go through with the journey. He remained anchored to his own uncertainty. And by the time November rolled around, he was setting up household with his nephew and he would not dream of abandoning the boy. Nor had he by that time done any further work on either of the symphonies. Whatever time he could spare for music he devoted to the *Hammerklavier Sonata*.

··❦[4]❦··

The disappointment in England over Beethoven's nonappearance must have been considerable and must have underscored the impression that Beethoven's promises were written in vanishing ink. Yet the English friends tried again. From time to time emissaries from England arrived. One of these was Cipriani Potter, who later became the director of the Royal Academy of Music. He heard that Beethoven had repelled all efforts by strangers to approach him. Potter had been in Vienna for two weeks when one day he was asked why he had not called on Beethoven. He said he was afraid of a rebuff; that was nonsense, he was told. Accordingly, Potter did call on Beethoven, and Beethoven turned out to be kindness itself, taking the liveliest interest in Potter's work. He asked to see one of Potter's compositions. Potter showed him an overture, and Beethoven leafed through it so hurriedly that Potter thought he had only glanced at it to be polite, without in the least examining the music. Potter was dumbfounded when Beethoven pointed to a certain note in the bassoon and said that it was not practical, and then made other telling observations about the piece.

The following year a Mr. Smith visited Beethoven, bearing a letter from Thomson, the Scottish publisher. Somebody wrote in the Conversation Book in 1819:

> These Englishmen speak of nothing else than your coming to England;—they give assurance that if you were to come for a single winter, from September until sometime in May, to England, Scotland and Ireland, you could earn so much that you could live the rest of your life on the interest.   (TQ).

Thus it went, Beethoven making himself believe that he *would* go—the day after tomorrow. When in 1822 he was in the very thick of the composition of the Ninth Symphony, he wrote to Ries to inquire whether the Philharmonic Society would buy a symphony from him and at what price. Ries raised the question at a meeting of the directors of the Society on November 10, 1822, and they resolved to offer Beethoven fifty pounds. Beethoven answered almost immediately: he accepted, though he thought the honorarium rather small. He wrote, in a letter of December 20, 1822:

My dear Ries!

Even though the fee to be paid by the English cannot be compared with the fees paid by other nations, yet I would compose even without a fee for the leading artists of Europe, were I not still that poor Beethoven. If only I were in London, how many works would I compose for the Philharmonic Society! For, thank God, Beethoven can compose—but, I admit, that is all he is able to do in this world. If God will only restore my health, ... then I shall be able to comply with all the offers from all the countries of Europe, nay, even of North America; and in that case I might yet make a success of my life.   (A-1110).

"Beethoven can compose"—and the world knew it. He did receive requests for his music from as far away as North America. The Handel and Haydn Society of Boston asked him for an oratorio.*

Two more years passed. Again an invitation came—in 1824. This time he was surely to embark on the voyage. Then he procrastinated. Then, on December 20, 1824, another letter from Neate arrived, so blandishing that it seemed difficult to resist. Neate said that Beethoven's genius was better appreciated in England than in any other country, that if he came he would earn enough money to make the inconveniences of the journey worthwhile, that the Philharmonic Society was willing to offer him 300 guineas for conducting at least one of his works at each of the society's concerts in the coming season and for composing a new symphony and a concerto which were to have their world premiere in London but would remain Beethoven's property. In addition, Beethoven could give a benefit concert of his own from which he would derive at least 500 pounds. If he would bring along his new quartets, they would yield him a further 100 pounds or more. In short, Beethoven could through this one visit earn such a sum as to make the remainder of his life carefree.

The Ninth had arrived in England, continued Neate, and the first rehearsal of it was set for January 17, 1825.** He hoped that Beethoven would be present to direct it at its premiere and he further hoped that a rumor he heard that a copy of this symphony had been sent to Paris was false.

Beethoven replied on January 15th and again on the 27th. He said that he found the conditions offered by the Philharmonic Society satisfactory but he

---

* In 1825 he had a visitor from Quebec, a music teacher and organist by the name of T. F. Molt. He asked Beethoven for a souvenir to take back to the New World, "a distance of 3,000 hours." Beethoven, no doubt touched by this visit from so distant a part of the globe, complied and wrote a little canon to the words *Freu Dich des Lebens* ("Enjoy Life"). The manuscript is now in the Lawrence Lande Collection of McGill University in Montreal.
** The fifty pounds had been duly paid in April, 1824.

proposed that in addition to the 300 guineas he be allotted 100 guineas for traveling expenses. He needed to buy a carriage and he needed to pay the expense of his companion. As for the question of the Ninth Symphony and Paris, there was no truth at all to the rumor.

The 300 guineas, representing something like $6000 in today's purchasing power, was a generous offer. Only an organization which by dint of artistic excellence and good management had amassed a sizable fund could have made the gesture. One can imagine the impression that Neate's transmittal of Beethoven's demand must have made on the directors. Neate had to report to Beethoven that the Philharmonic Society did not see its way clear to make any change in the offer.

Beethoven's friends urged him to accept and to undertake the journey. Johann said that it would benefit him physically as well as financially. Karl reminded him that he was certainly not too old: Haydn had gone to London when he was fifty. Schuppanzigh exhorted Beethoven to "pick up enough courage." To no avail. On March 19 Beethoven wrote Neate that he would come some other time, perhaps in the autumn. On March 21 the Ninth Symphony was given for the first time in London to great wonder and acclaim, but without the composer present. Sir George Smart conducted.

Smart made a trip through Germany in company with the actor Charles Kemble in the summer of the same year. He came to Vienna and called on Beethoven in September. The Conversation Book indicates that Smart was still trying to persuade Beethoven:

> [KARL]: He asked why you had not come before now; he said the three hundred pounds of the Philhar. Society were not to be looked upon as the principal thing. For that you needed only to appear 2 or 3 times in the orchestra and make money with your own concerts.
>
> ———————
>
> He said that in a short time you could make at least 1000 pounds and carry it away with you.
>
> ———————
>
> You can do better business with the publishers there than here.
>
> ———————
>
> And you'll find 1000 friends, Smarth (*sic*) says, who will do everything to help you.

... We'll wait till the year is over before going to England.   (TQ).

The year was over and Smart was still in Vienna. From the Conversation Book of January 3–8, 1826, it appears that Beethoven gave a festive dinner for him. It may have been a farewell dinner, and it was a good one. Schuppanzigh and Holz were present. From the Conversation Book:

> "A double portion for Mylord (Schuppanzigh)."
> "Mylord wants to steal your cook—everything is so delicious."
> [SCHUPPANZIGH]: "Such topers you invited today! As for me, I was moderate."
> [HOLZ]: "Smart knows how to drink."

From that time on, there was no further mention of a voyage.

·⊰[5]⊱·

When Beethoven lay on his deathbed, suffering not only bodily pain but anxiety over the morrow, since there was no further money coming in and under no circumstances would he touch the patrimony which he had set aside for Karl, he wrote to Stumpff in London:

VIENNA, February 8, 1827

> ... I well remember that several years ago the Philharmonic Society wanted to give a concert for my benefit. It would be fortunate for me if they would now decide to do so. Perhaps I might still be rescued from the poverty with which I am now faced. I am writing to Mr. S[mart] about this. And if you, dear friend, can contribute something to this object, do please come to an agreement with Mr. S[mart]. A letter about this is being written to Moscheles as well. And if all my friends combine I do believe that it will be possible to do something for me in this matter.... (A-1550).

Stumpff immediately reported Beethoven's condition to Smart and Moscheles (Ries had left London in 1824 for Godesberg, where he became music director), and they placed the facts before the directors of the Philharmonic Society. In a meeting of the directors held on February 28, 1827, the following resolution was taken:

> It was moved by Mr. Neate, and seconded by Mr. Latour: "That this Society do lend the sum of One Hundred Pounds to its own members to be sent through

the hands of Mr. Moscheles to some confidential friend of Beethoven, to be applied to his comforts and necessities during his illness."
Carried unanimously.

Stumpff and Moscheles wrote the news to Beethoven, Moscheles adding that the Philharmonic Society would be willing to aid him further whenever Beethoven should have need of help. The gift arrived, and the money was transmitted through the banking house of Eskeles.

One of the last letters which Beethoven sent—he no longer wrote himself but dictated to Schindler—was to Moscheles.

> VIENNA, March 18, 1827
>
> My Dear, Kind Moscheles!
>
> I cannot put into words the emotion with which I read your letter of March 1st. The Philharmonic Society's generosity in almost anticipating my appeal has touched my innermost soul.—I request you, therefore, dear Moscheles, to be the spokesman through whom I send to the Philharmonic Society my warmest and most heartfelt thanks for their particular sympathy and support . . .
>
> In regard to the concert which the Philharmonic Society has decided to give for my benefit, I do beg the Society not to give up this noble plan but to deduct from the proceeds of this concert the 1000 gulden A.C. which they have already advanced to me. And if the Society will be so kind as to let me have the remainder, I will undertake to return to the Society my warmest thanks by engaging to compose for it either a new symphony, sketches for which are already in my desk, or a new overture, or something else which the Society might like to have.
>
> May Heaven but restore my health very soon and I shall prove to those magnanimous Englishmen how greatly I appreciate their sympathy for me in my sad fate.
>
> But *your* noble behaviour I shall never forget; and I will shortly proceed to express my thanks particularly to Sir Smart and Herr Stumpff.   (A-1566).

There was to be no new symphony, though it was true that some sketches for it were lying in his desk. There was to be no new overture nor anything else "which the Society might like to have." The letter to Moscheles, flowing with the gratitude of the moribund man, was sent about a week before Beethoven died. He never reached England: it is comforting to know that England reached him. It is comforting as it is an example of man's humanity to man.

Beethoven gesticulating with a cane. Drawing is by J. P. Lyser (Society of Friends of Music, Vienna).

CHAPTER 21

THE MISSA, THE NINTH, AND VISITORS

·❈[I]❈·

he attempt to narrate Beethoven's struggle for and with his nephew as a consecutive presentation necessitated an impropriety against biographical procedure: the story had to be carried to its climax and therefore almost to the end of Beethoven's life. Similarly, it seemed preferable to present his relations with England in one chapter, rather than divide them into chronologically placed chunks. We by-passed events and we must now retrace our steps and speak of that penultimate period in which Beethoven completed his last symphony and his major religious work. The period extends from about the winter of 1818 to the spring of 1824. We might call this period Beethoven's philosophical period: in the Ninth he points the way toward a philosophy of daily and communal life, while in the *Missa Solemnis* he seeks to probe "the undiscover'd country" and occupies himself with the question which each man asks in solitude. One work deals with man's conduct, the other with the reaches of his soul. Yet no sharp philosophical distinction need be drawn between the two works: in the Ninth we hear of a creator who dwells above the stars, and in the *Missa* we hear almost realistic echoes of the wars through which Beethoven had suffered. And, of course, both works are emotional expressions in music, not philosophic treatises.

That both of these compositions are the products of many years of musical and general cognizance is certain. That both of them represent an antidote against the bitterness he felt and the grief he had experienced is more than probable. The works stand in complete contradiction to the behavior of Beethoven the man during that period; that alone could indicate their medicinal origin.

After Beethoven had somewhat recovered from the first shock of Karl's running away and the decision of the *Landrechte* to push the case to a lower court, he turned again toward music. He had too much to give to be permanently stunned into silence. While in the year 1818 he lay almost completely fallow, the year following saw him immersed in thoughts of the Mass, which he felt was to become one of his proudest achievements; and it saw him broaching with ever greater intensity the problems of the symphony. In the next year, in 1820, he turned once again to piano sonatas, completing his last three sonatas by 1822. Schindler relates that when Beethoven heard there was a rumor going around that he had written himself out and that his invention now sufficed only for trivia, he seemed amused and said, "Wait a while; you will soon learn differently."

The origin of the *Missa Solemnis* is this: Archduke Rudolph, having first become a Cardinal, was elevated to the archbishopric of Olmütz. In June, 1819, Rudolph was officially informed of this honor; the date of his elevation was set for March 20, 1820. Beethoven heard about this and wrote to Rudolph, congratulating him and saying:

[June, 1819]

The day on which a High Mass composed by me will be performed during the ceremonies solemnized for Your Imperial Highness will be the most glorious day of my life; and God will enlighten me so that my poor talents may contribute to the glorification of that solemn day — (A-948).

Beethoven, then, intended to compose a Mass for the ceremony, which was to take place nine months from the date of this letter; he had done some preliminary sketching as early as the beginning of 1819, when rumors of Rudolph's promotion must have reached him.

There is no reason to doubt his original intention of completing the work in time for Rudolph's installation. But we are familiar with the process by which a composition which he had intended for a certain date grew as he thought about it and how, as he labored on it, it swelled so gigantically in his hands that it was difficult for him to carry it; how he revised — though the final manuscript of the Mass is written on excellent quality paper, Beethoven erased one spot of it so many times that he rubbed a hole in it — and how therefore what was to be ready in six or nine months took years for completion. Of none of his works is this truer than of the *Missa Solemnis,* which he just could not let go and from which he finally had to tear himself away with an almost physical effort. It was not to be ready till 1823.

Schindler has left us a picture of Beethoven at work on the *Missa* which might have been painted by Goya in his black period:

> Toward the end of August (1819) I arrived at the master's rooms in Mödling accompanied by the musician Johann Horzalka, who is still alive in Vienna. It was four o'clock in the afternoon. As soon as we entered we were told that both Beethoven's maids had left that morning and that there had occurred after midnight an uproar that had disturbed everyone in the house because, having waited so long, both maids had gone to sleep and the meal they had prepared was inedible. From behind the closed door of one of the parlours we could hear the master working on the fugue of the Credo, singing, yelling, stamping his feet. When we had heard enough of this almost frightening performance and were about to depart, the door opened and Beethoven stood before us, his features distorted to the point of inspiring terror. He looked as though he had just engaged in a life and death struggle with the whole army of contrapuntists, his everlasting enemies. His first words were confused, as if he felt embarrassed at having been overheard. Soon he began to speak of the day's events and said, with noticeable self-control, "What a mess! Everyone has run away and I haven't had anything to eat since yesterday noon." I tried to calm him and helped him to make his toilet. My companion hurried to the bathhouse restaurant to order something for the famished master. While he ate, he complained to us about the state of his household.   (S).

(As usual, Schindler got things a little wrong, though the essence of the episode is undoubtedly true: Horzalka claimed to know nothing of the incident, and it is fairly certain that Beethoven was not working on the fugue of the *Credo* but possibly on the *Gloria*.)

Long before the *Missa* was finished, Beethoven had begun to negotiate for the publication of the work. These negotiations represent one of the least creditable moves of Beethoven's life. Indeed, not to mince words, he behaved shockingly. The purpose of his maneuvers was obviously to obtain the best possible price and the most advantageous conditions for a work which he felt—or said he felt—was the most significant he had ever produced. Nothing was wrong with such a purpose. But what he did was to promise the Mass to one publisher after another, to give his word that this one and only this one was to obtain the coveted composition, only to break his word, playing off one offer against another, exacting new conditions, inventing new excuses; and all the while asseverating that he really could not help himself, that circumstances forced him to do what he did and that he loved "honesty and sincerity."

He offered the Mass to seven publishers. The first of these was his old friend from Bonn, Nikolaus Simrock. He bought publication rights for 100 louis d'or (about $1000 in today's equivalent). There was a misunderstanding: Simrock thought of the louis d'or as equivalent to the friedrichs d'or, which was about twenty percent less. Simrock said that he was not in a position to give more. He was then informed that Beethoven was satisfied. In November, 1820 (negotiations had started in March) Beethoven wrote him:

> Since I understand nothing whatever about business affairs, I was waiting for my friend who, however, has not yet arrived in Vienna. Meanwhile I had to learn from other people that I shall be losing at least 100 gulden A.C. With my usual frankness I must confess to you that previously I could have had a fee of 200 gold ducats in Vienna. Yet we gave the preference to your offer, because according to the particulars quoted to us 100 louis d'or were supposed to be worth more. It is too late now to cancel the arrangement, since the firm which was to get the grand Mass has commissioned another big work from me, and since I too should not like to appear as if I had had to refuse an offer which I had already accepted—all of which you will find quite natural. As soon as the German text has been completely written out in the Mass, I will send it to you through Herr v[on] Brentano at Frankfurt, to whom you can then remit the 100 pistoles, as you have stated, instead of louis d'or. The translation is costing me at least 50 gulden V.C. I trust that you will add this amount at any rate to my fee—and so requiescat in pace—I would rather write 10,000 notes than one letter of the alphabet, particularly when it is a question of taking money *in this way* and not *in that way*. I trust that you in turn will treat me all the more favourably in the publication of my collected works which, as you know, I have very much at heart. (A-1037).

Double talk! Simrock never did get the score, even though, being dunned several times, Beethoven kept reassuring Simrock through Franz Brentano, who acted as the intermediary, that he would abide by his agreement.

Then he wrote to the publisher Schlesinger in Berlin.* It was the same procedure. The price was satisfactorily settled with Schlesinger when Beethoven turned around and offered the Mass to Peters of Leipzig:

---

* This was Adolf Martin Schlesinger, who had established his music-publishing firm in 1810. His eldest son, Moritz, established his own firm in Paris in 1821. Both of them, the one in Paris, the other in Berlin, published Beethoven's final Piano Sonata, Op. 111, and both of them wondered whether they had got their money's worth, since the Sonata was written in two movements, lacking the usual *Finale*.

Above: Title page of "Wellington's Victory" (Beethoven House, Bonn). Left: Ignaz Moscheles, composer, pianist (Otto Haus). Right: Franz Grillparzer, Austrian poet, friend of Beethoven.

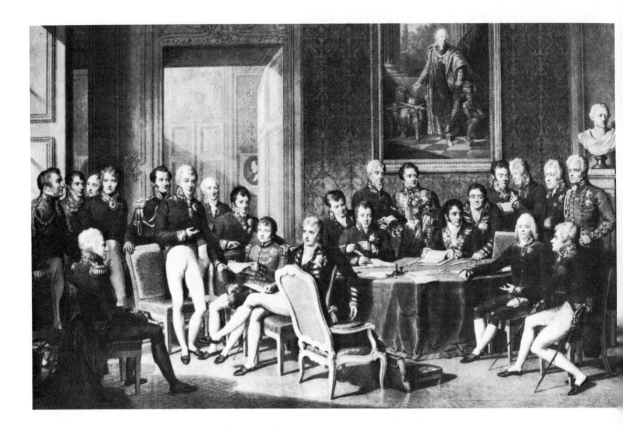

"The Vienna Congress." Painting by Isabey. Talleyrand is at the extreme right, seated. Metternich stands in front of a chair and points at the Duke of Wellington, seated nonchalantly. Below: Caricature of the various powers greedily cutting up Europe (Austrian National Library).

Karl Holz, a violinist and intimate friend of Beethoven in the composer's last years. Miniature on ivory. (Historical Museum, Vienna).

Sir George Smart, the fine British conductor who visited Beethoven and espoused his cause. Painting by W. Bradley (National Portrait Gallery, London).

Anton Schindler, Beethoven's sometimes irritating but always devoted friend and aide as well as his first biographer (Beethoven House, Bonn).

Beethoven's frantic note to Dr. Smetana after Karl's attempted suicide: come "quickly for God's sake quickly," he implored (Beethoven House, Bonn).

Große
musikalische Akademie

von

Herrn L. van Beethoven,

welche

morgen am 7. May 1824,

im k. k. Hoftheater nächst dem Kärnthnerthore,

abgehalten wird.

Die dabey vorkommenden Musikstücke sind die neuesten Werke des Herrn Ludwig van Beethoven.

Erstens. Große Ouverture.

Zweytens. Drey große Hymnen, mit Solo- und Chor-Stimmen.

Drittens. Große Symphonie, mit im Finale eintretenden Solo- und Chor-Stimmen, auf Schillers Lied, an die Freude.

Die Solo-Stimmen werden die Dlles. Sontag und Unger, und die Herren Haizinger und Seipelt vortragen. Herr Schuppanzigh hat die Direction des Orchesters, Herr Kapellmeister Umlauf die Leitung des Ganzen, und der Musik-Verein die Verstärkung des Chors und Orchesters aus Gefälligkeit übernommen.

Herr Ludwig van Beethoven selbst, wird an der Leitung des Ganzen Antheil nehmen.

Die Eintrittspreise sind wie gewöhnlich.

Die Logen und gesperrten Sitze sind am Tage der Vorstellung an der Theaterkasse, in der Kärnthnerstraße Nro. 1038, im Eckhause beym Kärnthnerthore, im ersten Stocke, zu den gewöhnlichen Amtsstunden zu haben.

Freybillete sind ungültig.

Der Anfang ist um 7 Uhr Abends.

*From the Conversation Books we know that the two charming young singers—
Henrietta Sontag, left, Caroline Unger, right—helped to overcome Beethoven's
reluctance to give the premiere of his Ninth Symphony in Vienna. The announcement of this historic concert, which was given on May 7, 1824, shows that "Herr
Schuppanzigh would direct the orchestra, Herr Kapellmeister Umlauf is to supervise
the total forces," and that "Herr Ludwig van Beethoven himself will take part in
the direction of everything" (Sontag's portrait from the Opera Library, Paris; Unger's
from the Austrian National Library).*

The funeral procession on the afternoon of March 29, 1827. From a contemporary watercolor. The honorary escort precedes and follows the coffin; carriages and riders are in line to form a cortège; spectators hurry to the scene to catch a last glimpse while a part of the populace stands behind a fence (left). The crowd was estimated as numbering between 15,000 and 20,000 (Beethoven House, Bonn).

Beethoven's signature on the last of his testaments, written by him in a faltering script three days before he died. Karl was the sole heir.

THE MISSA, THE NINTH, AND VISITORS

June 26, 1822

In no circumstances will Schlesinger ever get *anything more from me,* because he too has played me a Jewish trick. In any case he is not one of the publishers who might have got the Mass. At the moment, however, the competition to secure my works is very keen; and for this I am grateful to the Almighty.... I am keeping all our dealings secret, a thing which *in any case I much prefer to do;* and please treat my present connexion with you as a secret. I shall not forget to inform you when the time has come to talk. (A-1083).

The time elapsed between the letter to Schlesinger and that to Peters is less than two months—all this, while he kept Simrock on the string, writing to him:

Sept. 13, 1822

In regard to the Mass, you know that on this subject I did write to you some time ago that a larger fee had been offered to me. Indeed it is not my practice to be greedy just for the sake of obtaining one or two more gulden. My poor health, however, and very many other untoward circumstances compel me to pay attention to such things. The lowest fee which at least four publishers have offered me so far for the Mass is 1000 gulden A.C. at the rate of 20, or fixing the gulden at three Austrian pieces of 20 A.C. However sorry I feel at our having to part company particularly about this composition, yet I know that your integrity would not let me lose over this work which is perhaps the greatest I have ever written. You know that I am no braggart and that I don't like to hand on the letters of other people or even quote extracts from them; but if I chose to do so, I could give you proofs of my statement about this from near and far. Well, I must trust that this question relating to the Mass will be settled as soon as possible, for on its account I have already had to deal with intrigues of all kinds. I should be glad if you would reply as soon as possible and say whether you are prepared to pay me that fee. If you are satisfied, then you need only send the balance to Brentano, whereupon I will immediately send you a carefully corrected copy of the score of the Mass, from which you can engrave it without more ado. I trust that my dear Simrock, whom I consider at any rate to be the wealthiest of all publishers, will not let his old friend slip away for the sake of a few hundred gulden. (A-1098).

Later he tried to satisfy Simrock by promising him other works: he would get *a* Mass. "I have written another Mass and am still hesitating which one I should give to you." (Letter of March 10, 1823.) That was simply not true. Beethoven did plan to compose another Mass, but the work which he here described as already composed was never written. It may have been composed in his mind, never on paper.

Peters was similarly treated and he was similarly told that two Masses were in existence. Then Beethoven tried to assuage Peters' feelings by promising him that he was going to get another great work, and he resented Peters' huffy refusal of a slight work, the *Bagatelles,* Op. 119, saying that Peters had no artistic judgment. Beethoven had accepted an advance from Peters.*

It is wearying to follow all of Beethoven's twists and turns with the publishers. Suffice it to note that before a decision was taken he had collected bids from Diabelli, Steiner and Haslinger, Artaria, Schlesinger, Simrock, and Peters. Each of them was assured that the coveted prize was his. Each of them was due to be disappointed. Beethoven finally awarded the Mass to Schott and Sons in Mainz, though not till July, 1824, and not till after much letter writing back and forth.

The firm of Schott and Sons had been founded by Bernhard Schott in the year 1773, in the city of Mainz. Bernhard had died in 1817, and his two sons, Andreas and Johann Josef, carried on the business and developed it along progressive lines. In addition to publishing music, they now owned a review devoted to music, *Cäcilia.* The two sons liked to do business in the grand style; they were willing to take chances and did not haggle. Beethoven liked their methods.** They paid Beethoven—for the *Missa,* the Ninth Symphony, and one of the last Quartets, Op. 127—1600 silver florins, or roughly about $10,000 in today's purchasing power. (They also bought some smaller works, as well as the Quartet 131.) The price, though large in contemporary terms, was small enough for what the Schotts received, small enough a recompense for Beethoven's work of almost five years. Still, that has nothing to do with Beethoven's bargaining behavior.

Is there an explanation for this behavior? The one usually put forward is Beethoven's pressing need of money, his being in debt,*** his haunting fear that upon his death he would leave Karl insufficiently provided for. There may be another explanation: he may have played the game of "who-will-get-the-Mass?" for a psychological reason. Even while he wanted to sell it he wanted to hold on to it. He wanted to hold on to it as long as there was still one phrase or one bar left which could be improved, one thought for which he could find expression apter still. Not only would money have come in faster had he been

---

* This is apparent from a letter to Peters dated September 13, 1822. On that one day Beethoven wrote business letters to Simrock, Franz Brentano, and Peters.
** Later in the 19th century the firm grew to even greater prominence and became the publishers of Richard Wagner's works.
*** He was quite heavily in debt in 1822, owing, among others, 3000 florins to the publisher Steiner and 1000 florins to Artaria. (T).

able to write *finis* to the *Missa* sooner, but during those years he had many opportunities to earn money by composing smaller works. He could do neither one nor the other. The cleft between his ordinary morality—that is, the manner in which he dealt with "mere" businessmen—"hell hounds" he called them— and his artistic morality was as wide as the difference "twixt amorous and villainous." For a parallel example one must look forward to Wagner, who sold the publishing rights to *Das Rheingold* to Wesendonk—and soon sold it again to Schott. At least Beethoven tried to pay his debts; Wagner never bothered.

At the end of 1822, Beethoven conceived another plan. Instead of merely publishing the Mass, he wanted to sell prepublication manuscript copies of it to whatever patrons he could interest, particularly the sovereigns of Europe. He enlisted Schindler and Johann to help him with the project. Schindler wrote what were in effect circular letters and Beethoven signed them. Appeals to subscribe were sent to the Courts of Baden, Württemberg, Bavaria, Saxony, Weimar, Mecklenburg, Hesse-Darmstadt, Berlin, Copenhagen, Hesse-Cassel, Nassau, Tuscany, and Paris. The letters offered what was called "the most excellent product" of Beethoven's mind in a manuscript copy for the "not excessive" fee of fifty ducats ($1250). Beethoven himself was active in the solicitation, writing to Cherubini in Paris and asking him to put in a good word for him; to his acquaintance of long years ago, Bernadotte, now King Charles XIV of Norway and Sweden; and to Goethe. Neither from Goethe * nor from Bernadotte did Beethoven receive an answer.

In the end there were ten subscribers, the first being the King of Prussia, who inquired of Beethoven through the Embassy whether he would prefer a royal order to the fifty ducats. Without hesitation Beethoven replied, fifty ducats. The King of France, Louis XVIII, proved more generous: he not only subscribed to the Mass but within the year sent Beethoven a valuable medal made of heavy gold. (Beethoven was very proud of the medal.) The subscribers were: the Czar of Russia, the Kings of France, Prussia, Saxony, and Denmark, the Grand Dukes of Tuscany and Hesse-Darmstadt, the Russian Prince Nikolas Galitzin, and another Russian friend of Beethoven, Prince Anton Radziwill. In addition, a subscription came in from a singing society in Frankfurt, the Cäcilia Society. At the request of the publisher Artaria and against Beethoven's better judgment, an appeal had been sent to Prince Paul Esterházy. Beethoven was right: Esterházy did not subscribe. Archduke Rudolph obviously could not be asked.

---

* Goethe was very ill at the time.

But it is significant that no member of the Austrian government showed any interest. No letter was sent to the English Court, which had ignored *Wellington's Victory.* From the 500 ducats Beethoven collected, the expenses of copying had to be deducted; Beethoven gained probably no more than $2000 from the project.

One of the subscribers, Prince Galitzin, was shortly to play an important role in Beethoven's life. Beethoven asked Galitzin to use his influence to persuade the Russian Court to buy a copy of the *Missa,* and Galitzin was delighted to report to Beethoven that he had been successful. He himself became a subscriber as well. Even more important, Galitzin was eventually responsible, or largely responsible, for the first performance of the *Missa Solemnis,* which took place in St. Petersburg in April, 1824. The work was not given in Vienna in its entirety during Beethoven's lifetime.

·∞[2]∞·

The question may be asked why Beethoven, with his lack of orthodoxy and his disinterest in ritual, should have turned to the solemn Catholic service as material from which to construct a *magnum opus.* Ernest Newman has suggested an answer: *

> Beethoven, at the climax of a spiritual crisis that had racked him for years, had found the best subject imaginable for the expression of himself as a musician in the admirable drama which the genius of the Church in ages past had evolved in the ritual of the Mass. Neither an opera nor an oratorio would have suited him one quarter as well, for there he would have been bound hand and foot to the commonplaces and divagations and paddings of his librettists. The words and the solemn ceremony and implications of the Mass having provided him with his emotional starting-point, his imagination was then able to play in perfect freedom upon them in terms of his special art. Thus four preliminary words — "Kyrie eleison Christe eleison" — gave him all he needed to paint in music a vast panorama of human hopes and fears; four words — "Gloria in excelsis Deo" — to sing exuberantly the praises of the Creator of the cosmos; two words — "Miserere nobis" — to enable him to reach to the very heart of human pain and sorrow. A better "libretto," if we may use the word without risking misunderstanding, he could not have found.

Beethoven made painstaking preparations for his task. He studied Church music, obtained copies of the chorales used in monasteries, examined Palestri-

---

* From an essay on the *Missa Solemnis* accompanying the Toscanini recording.

na's music, and had an accurate translation made of the Latin text so that no meaning of the words would escape him.

The core of the work may lie in "A prayer for inner and outer peace," his own heading of the section *"Dona nobis pacem."* The peace he yearned for—"inner and outer"—would come about both through the raising of the vision toward the sky, as Prince Andrew's glance flew to the sky as he lay wounded on the battlefield, and the introspection which it is given to every man to practice. The solace of such introspection one feels particularly in what is perhaps the most magical part of the *Missa,* the beginning of the *Benedictus,* an orchestral prelude from the depth of which arises a solo violin. Its melody seems indeed to be a "messenger of peace" (as expressed in the Jewish prayer) or the "Rahmat Allah" (in the Arabic phrase) or "the peace of God, which passeth all understanding" (of which we read in Philippians).

There is one highly unorthodox episode in this work. In the *"Dona nobis pacem,"* just when it seems that Beethoven is heading toward a serene conclusion, there are to be heard drumbeats and distant trumpet fanfares, and the contralto breaks into an anguished cry which Beethoven marked *Ängstlich, timidamente* (fearfully, timidly). What else could this have been but a reminder of the wars that he had lived through? Was it as well a reminder of Napoleon, who died while Beethoven was working on the *Missa* (1821)?

Though the *Missa* is one of Beethoven's profoundest and noblest works, it is not one of his most beloved creations. He wrote at the head of the score, "From the heart—may it in turn go to the heart," but it has not gone to the hearts of listeners who find no difficulty in responding to the last sonatas or the Ninth. Perhaps its introvert reveries make it seem distant; perhaps its moments of labored polyphonic writing, combined with a strangeness of harmony, as well as passages which lie ungratefully for the voice, bewilder the listener. It is difficult to say.

The opposite is true of the Ninth. It has become possibly the most universally appealing major work in the literature of symphonic music. It is held in awe but it is also held in affection, and rivals the Fifth and the Third in popularity. To that popularity not only the music itself contributes, but the high moral sentiment. The fact that there is a poetic idea here, an extra-musical thought to hold onto, a main theme enunciated in words, is of help, at least to some listeners.

What attracted Beethoven to Schiller's poem—by no means one of the best of the poet's creations—was undoubtedly the consonance between its main concept and Beethoven's belief in the "arrival at joy through suffering."

"Freude" may be interpreted in a broad sense: gladness, happiness, fulfillment of life. While it would be presumptuous to ascribe any "program" to this music, it is allowable to assume that Beethoven indicates the direction toward fulfillment: struggle in the first movement, humor in the second, contemplation in the third, finally to arrive at the jubilation of the paean. Schiller's poem contains the line, "All creatures drink in joy from nature's breast." Schiller echoed Rousseau, and the words may have made a special appeal to the creator of the *Pastoral Symphony.* Yet we must be cautious: the Ninth is not a spiritual travelogue; nor is it, as I have said, a philosophical disquisition in tones. With whatever interpretation we choose to endow it, it remains a *musical* creation and as such we must feel it.

There is some evidence that Beethoven first planned the last movement as an instrument finale without the chorus. What gave him a great deal of trouble was the link between the orchestral passage and the vocal conclusion. Schindler states that one day he burst into the room crying, "I have it! I have it!"; whereupon he showed him a sketchbook bearing the words, "Let us sing the song of the immortal Schiller Freude." This was followed by a solo voice which began the hymn. Whether, as Carl Czerny asserted, Beethoven later planned to write a new finale without the vocal parts is questionable. The matter is of historical interest only; we can no longer think of the Ninth without its gloriously exciting choral end. Useless, too, is the reflection—voiced by some critics—that the Ninth would have been "better" without the choral part. To dissect is not necessarily to reflect.

·⊰[3]⊱·

Beethoven worked on the Ninth during the summer of 1823 while staying in a villa in Hetzendorf which belonged to a Baron Pronay. It was a beautiful villa, and he was content until the baron insisted on making low, obsequious bows every time he managed to meet Beethoven. Beethoven could not tolerate this "humility of man toward man" and insisted on moving out. He went to Baden.

In Baden there was one house, at which he had stayed the year before, which he wanted again. But to Schindler, on whom he had called for help, Beethoven confessed that the landlord had declared that he would not take Beethoven in again. When he arrived at the house, Beethoven asked Schindler to go and see if he could persuade the landlord to change his mind, promising in Beethoven's name a quieter behavior and neater order. At first Schindler failed. Sent once more by Beethoven's urging, and bearing "the flag of truce" with protestations of good conduct, he succeeded on the second visit.

> Yet there was another unconditional requirement; Beethoven must have shutters put on the windows overlooking the street as he had had the year before. In vain we tried to guess the reason for this strange request. When the landlord explained that the shutters were needed to spare the composer's suffering eyes from the harsh sunlight, Beethoven complied immediately. Within a few days the move was completed.
>
> But what was the reason for the shutters, and why were they a condition of Beethoven's tenancy? The reason was simple: Beethoven ... would, during his stay at the same house the year before, stand at one or another of the unpainted window-shutters and, as was his custom, make long calculations—for example, how many florins were 50, 100, or 200 ducats? Then there were some musical ideas, and in short a whole stream of consciousness written out in pencil so that these thin boards formed a kind of diary. In the summer of 1822 a family from North Germany lived across the street. They used to watch him at this occupation, and when he moved away they paid the landlord a piece of gold for one of these shutters, apparently as a kind of souvenir. Once he realized the value of his window-shutters and their inscriptions, the landlord had no trouble in selling all four pieces to other guests of the baths. When the apothecary T. in Baden told Beethoven of this strange commerce, the master is said to have exploded in Homeric laughter. (S).

Scribbling on window shutters or in his notebooks, at the time of the *Missa* and the Ninth he was resuming his old love for the instrument to which he had given a new dimension. He had never lost that love: even in the gray year of 1818 he had pondered the *Grosse Sonate für das Hammerklavier,* No. 29, Now —that is, roughly between 1820 and 1823—he composed the *Diabelli Variations* and the three last sonatas.

We mentioned that one of the publishers who made a bid for the Mass was Antonio Diabelli and that he, too, was doomed to disappointment. At least he received a handsome consolation prize: the *Diabelli Variations.* Diabelli was not only a partner in a music-publishing firm (Cappi and Diabelli), but also a composer. In 1821 he invited a number of composers to contribute variations on a waltz theme of his own invention. Beethoven, who one would have said would be the last man to be interested in such an enterprise, was intrigued.* He

---

* Among the other contributors were Schubert, Czerny, Hummel, Moscheles, Weber, and the boy Liszt, then ten years old. Archduke Rudolph contributed as well.

did some sketches, thinking that he would compose at most six or seven variations. But, again, the work grew beyond the original plan: thirty-three variations were the final result, all on an undistinguished enough tune, which Beethoven himself called "a cobbler's patch" (*Schusterfleck*). The tune served Beethoven to construct what Bülow termed the "microcosmos of Beethoven's genius," a wide world of fantasy within the framework of a piano.

Schindler says that Beethoven said that he composed the last three sonatas "in a single breath." Perhaps so. Though he may have conceived their main ideas quickly, the working out of these summit achievements of the piano literature took time: No. 30 was completed in 1820, No. 31 in 1821, and No. 32 the following year.

Sonata No. 30 in E Major, Op. 109, is enriched by the most wonderful set of variations which Beethoven composed for the piano; he used for them a beautiful theme which he marked, "Like a song with deepest feeling."

Sonata No. 31 in A-flat Major, Op. 110, seems easygoing, at least up to its final fugue. It is like an extended melody that a certain amount of strife cannot really disturb.

The final Sonata, No. 32 in C Minor, Op. 111, is in two movements only, the first a demonstration of great power; the second, in its unearthly and remote contemplativeness, is the product of a man who breaks his staff and drowns his book. After this movement nothing more was to be said. Thomas Mann, in *Dr. Faustus,* wrote imaginatively on the reason for the lack of a final movement. That lack puzzled not only the publisher but also Schindler; Beethoven gave him the impatient answer that he "had no time" to write a third movement, proving that a foolish question provokes a foolish answer.

·∘[4]∘·

The building of this domain exacted so fierce an effort from Beethoven that he seemed at times to have lost all sense of his surroundings and circumstances. He appears like a creature imprisoned within a globe of sounds.

Thayer tells us of a conversation he had with a Professor Blasius Höfel, a teacher of fine arts at Wiener Neustadt, a little town near Vienna. One evening Höfel was in a tavern with some of his colleagues, the Commissioner of Police being a member of the party. A constable appeared and said to the commissioner, "We have arrested somebody who will give us no peace. He keeps on yelling that he is Beethoven; but he surely is a tramp. He has no hat, wears an old coat, and has nothing on him by which he can be identified." The commissioner, perhaps unwilling to have his convivial evening spoiled by so trifling an incident, told the constable to keep the man under arrest until morning and he would then investigate the matter. At eleven o'clock that night the commissioner was awakened by a policeman with the information that the prisoner insisted that the musical director of Wiener Neustadt, a man by the name of Herzog, be called to identify him. Troubled now, the commissioner got up, dressed, went out, woke up Herzog, and both men went to the jail. As soon as Herzog saw the man, he exclaimed, "That is Beethoven!" Herzog took him home, gave him his best room, and the next day the mayor of the town came, falling over himself with profuse apologies.

What had happened was that Beethoven had arisen early in the morning and gone out for a walk, had lost his way, had continued to walk, immersed in thought, and finally, not knowing where he was, he was observed looking in at the windows of some houses. The inhabitants of one of the houses had been frightened by the appearance of this disheveled man and had called the policeman who had arrested him. When he was arrested, Beethoven said, "I am Beethoven." The policeman answered, "Sure! You are a tramp. Beethoven doesn't look like that." Herzog gave Beethoven some respectable clothes, and the mayor sent him back to Baden in the state coach.

Of his standing as a famous man there was no doubt. The provincial constable did not recognize him, but in Vienna itself almost everybody did. He could not walk down the street without people staring and pointing him out. The street urchins followed him, partly because he was Beethoven and partly because his appearance was so curious: this embarrassed Karl when he had to walk with his uncle.

Musicians and writers from various parts of Europe sought him out. He would not receive many visitors. He had to protect himself. Among those who did succeed in seeing him were:

·≈[SIR JOHN RUSSELL]≈·

He wrote a book, *A Tour in Germany, and Some of the Southern Provinces of the Austrian Empire, in 1820, 1821, 1822* (Published by Constable & Co. in Edinburgh, 1824). I am not sure who Russell was.* He may possibly have been the man who later, as Lord John Russell (1792–1878), became a famous

---

* Constable and Co., of whom I made inquiries, replied that the book was published prior to the liquidation of the firm in 1830. There was a period of sixty years before the firm started operating again, and during this time many of the old records were lost.

Liberal leader, serving twice as England's Prime Minister, engaging in debates with Lord Palmerston, and coining the slogan, "Italy for the Italians." In the book's first edition,* Russell described Beethoven as he appeared in 1821:

> The neglect of his person which he exhibits gives him a somewhat wild appearance. His features are strong and prominent; his eye is full of rude energy; his hair, which neither comb nor scissors seem to have visited for years, overshadows his broad brow in a quantity and confusion to which only the snakes round a Gorgon's head offer a parallel. His general behaviour does not ill accord with the unpromising exterior. Except when he is among his chosen friends, kindliness or affability are not his characteristics. Even among his oldest friends he must be humoured like a wayward child. He has always a small paper book with him, and what conversation takes place is carried on in writing. In this, too, although it is not lined, he instantly jots down any musical idea which strikes him. These notes would be utterly unintelligible even to another musician, for they have thus no comparative value; he alone has in his mind the thread by which he brings out of this labyrinth of dots and circles the richest and most astounding harmonies. The moment he is seated at the piano, he is evidently unconscious that there is anything in existence but himself and his instrument; and, considering how very deaf he is, it seems impossible that he should hear all he plays. Accordingly, when playing very *piano,* he often does not bring out a single note. He hears it himself in the "mind's ear." While his eye, and the almost imperceptible motion of his fingers, show that he is following out the strain in his own soul through all its dying gradations, the instrument is actually as dumb as the musician is deaf. It is exceedingly difficult to prevail upon him to perform, as he has a perfect horror of being exhibited; but when he does place himself at the piano, it is interesting to observe how the music of the man's soul passes over his countenance. He seems to feel the bold, the commanding, and the impetuous, more than what is soothing or gentle. The muscles of the face swell, and its veins start out; the wild eye rolls double wild; the mouth quivers; and Beethoven looks like a wizard, overpowered by the demons whom he himself has called up.

·≈[FRIEDRICH ROCHLITZ]≈·

He was the excellent critic of the *Allgemeine Musikalische Zeitung.* He was not a blind admirer, but it was exactly his intelligent approach to Beethoven's work which made Beethoven respect him. He had never met Beethoven. When he got to Vienna in 1822, he was told that Beethoven was in the country and

---

* He seems to have changed the text somewhat in later editions; Sonneck in *Beethoven: Impressions of Contemporaries,* uses a later text. I have used the original text.

had become such a recluse that a visit might prove fruitless. But Beethoven did come to Vienna at least once a week and often he was then approachable. Rochlitz decided to wait for Saturday. On that day a messenger came with an invitation from Beethoven.

In broken sentences he made some friendly and amiable remarks to me. I raised my voice as much as I could, spoke slowly, with sharp accentuation, and thus out of the fulness of my heart conveyed to him my gratitude for his works and all they meant to me and would mean to me while life endured. I signaled out some of my favorites, and dwelt upon them; told him how his symphonies were performed in model fashion in Leipzig, how all of them were played each recurring winter season, and of the loud delight with which the public received them. He stood close beside me, now gazing on my face with strained attention, now dropping his head. Then he would smile to himself, nod amiably on occasion, all without saying a word. Had he understood me? Had he failed to under-stand? At last I had to make an end, and he gave my hand a powerful grip and said curtly to N. N. [probably Haslinger]: "I still have a few necessary errands to do." Then, as he left, he said: "Shall we not see each other again?" N. N. now returned. "Did he understand what I said?" I queried. I was deeply moved and affected. N. N. shrugged his shoulders. "Not a word!" For a long time we were silent and I cannot say how affected I was. Finally I asked, "Why did you not at least repeat this or that to him, since he understands you fairly well?" "I did not wish to interrupt you and, besides, he very easily gets sensitive. And I really hoped he would understand much of what you said, but the noise in the street, your speech, to which he is unaccustomed and, perhaps, his own eagerness to understand everything, since it was perfectly clear to him that you were telling him pleasant things.... He was so unhappy." I cannot describe the sensations which filled me as I left. The man who solaced the whole world with the voice of his music, heard no other human voice, not even that of one who wished to thank him. Aye, it even became an instrument of torture for him. I had my mind made up not to see him again, and to send Mr. Härtel's proposal to him in writing.*

Some two weeks later I was about to go to dinner when I met the young composer Franz Schubert, an enthusiastic admirer of Beethoven. The latter had spoken to Schubert concerning me. "If you wish to see him in a more natural and jovial mood," said Schubert, "then go and eat your dinner this very minute at the inn where he has just gone for the same purpose." He took me with him. Most of the places were taken. Beethoven sat among several acquaintances who were strangers to me. He really seemed to be in good spirits and acknowledged my greeting, but I purposely did not cross over to him. Yet I found a seat from which I could see him and, since he spoke loud enough, also could hear nearly all that he said. It could not be called a conversation, for he spoke in monologue, usually at some length, and more as though by hapchance and at random.

Those about him contributed little, merely laughing or nodding their approval. He

---

* The proposal: Beethoven was to write music for Goethe's *Faust*.

philosophized, or one might even say politicized, after his own fashion. He spoke of England and the English, and of how both were associated in his thoughts with a splendor incomparable—which, in part, sounded tolerably fantastic. Then he told all sorts of stories of the French, from the days of the second occupation of Vienna. For them he had no kind words. His remarks all were made with the greatest unconcern and without the least reserve, and whatever he said was spiced with highly original, naïve judgments or humorous fancies. He impressed me as being a man with a rich, aggressive intellect, an unlimited, never resting imagination. I saw him as one who, had he been cast away on a desert isle when no more than a growing, capable boy, would have taken all he had lived and learned, all that had stuck to him in the way of knowledge, and there have meditated and brooded over his material until his fragments had become a whole, his imaginings turned to convictions which he would have shouted out into the world in all security and confidence.

When he had finished his meal he rose and came over to me. "And is all well with you in this old Vienna of ours?" he asked amiably. I answered in the affirmative by signs, drank to his health and asked him to pledge me. He accepted, but beckoned me to a little side-room. This suited me to a T. I took the bottle and followed him. Here we were by ourselves, save for an occasional peeper who soon made himself scarce. He offered me a little tablet upon which I was to write down whatever my signs did not make clear. He began by praising Leipzig and its music; that is to say the music chosen for performance in the churches, at concerts and in the theatre. Otherwise he knew nothing of Leipzig and had only passed through the city when a youth on his way to Vienna. "And even though nothing is printed about the performances but the dry records, still I read them with pleasure," he said. "One cannot help but notice that they are intelligent and well inclined toward all. Here, on the contrary...." Then he started in, rudely enough, nor would he let himself be stopped. He came to speak of himself: "You will hear nothing of me here." "It is summer now," I wrote. "No, nor in winter either!" he cried. "What should you hear? 'Fidelio'? They cannot give it, nor do they want to listen to it. The symphonies? They have no time for them.* My concertos? Everyone grinds out only the stuff he himself has made. The solo pieces? They went out of fashion here long ago, and here fashion is everything. At the most Schuppanzigh occasionally digs up a quartet, etc." And despite all the exaggeration in what he said a modicum of reason and truth remains. At last he had relieved himself and harked back to Leipzig. "But," said he, "you really live in Weimar, do you not?" He probably thought so because of my address. I shook my head. "Then it is not likely that you know the great Goethe?" I nodded my head vigorously. "I know him, too," said Beethoven, throwing out his chest, while an expression of the most radiant pleasure overspread his face.

Our third meeting was the merriest of all. He came here, to Baden, this time looking quite neat and clean and even elegant. Yet this did not prevent him—it was a warm day—from taking a walk in the Helenenthal. This means on the road all, even the Emperor

---

* That, of course, was not so. The symphonies were being performed. *Fidelio* was once more revived in the year of Rochlitz's visit.

and the imperial family, travel, and where everyone crowds past everyone else on the usually narrow path; and there he took off his fine black frockcoat, slung it across his shoulder from a stick, and wandered along in his shirt-sleeves. He stayed from about ten in the forenoon to six o'clock in the evening. His friends Jener and Gebauer kept him company. During the entire visit he was uncommonly gay and at times most amusing, and all that entered his mind had to come out. ("Well, it happens that I am unbuttoned to-day," he said and the remark was decidedly in order.) His talk and his actions all formed a chain of eccentricities, in part most peculiar. Yet they all radiated a truly childlike amiability, carelessness, and confidence in every one who approached him. Even his barking tirades—like that against his Viennese contemporaries, which I already have mentioned—are only explosions of his fanciful imagination and his momentary excitement. They are uttered without haughtiness, without any feeling of bitterness and hatefulness—and are simply blustered out lightly, good-humoredly, the offsprings of a mad, humorous mood. In his life he often shows—and for the sake of his own subsistence only too often and too decidedly—that to the very person who has grievously injured him, whom he has most violently denounced one moment, he will give his last dollar the next, should that person need it.

To this we must add the most cheerful recognition of merit in others, if only it be distinctive and individual. (How he speaks of Handel, Bach, Mozart!) He does not, however, where his greater works are concerned, allow others to find fault (and who would have the right to do so?) yet he never actually overvalues them; and with regard to his lesser things is more inclined, perhaps, to abandon them with a laugh than any other person. He does this the more since once he is in the vein, rough, striking witticisms, droll conceits, surprising and exciting paradoxes suggest themselves to him in a continuous flow. Hence in all seriousness I claim that he even appears to be amiable. Or if you shrink from this word, I might say that the dark, unlicked bear seems so ingenuous and confiding, growls and shakes his shaggy pelt so harmlessly and grotesquely that it is a pleasure, and one has to be kind to him, even though he were nothing but a bear in fact and had done no more than a bear's best. (1822).*

It was Rochlitz whom Beethoven chose as his official biographer. Rochlitz, however, declined the honor.

·•✠[ROSSINI]✠•·

This was the man who Beethoven claimed—and with some justice—had supplanted him in popularity.** Vienna, long enamored of mellifluous Italian melody, succumbed to a Rossini craze. Beethoven too admired the Italian art of vocal writing—to which Salieri had introduced him in the early days but which

---

* From Sonneck, *Beethoven: Impressions of Contemporaries.*
** Writing to Spohr (July 27, 1823), Beethoven said that in Vienna they were having a rich "harvest of raisins" (*Rosinen* in German).

he had never mastered completely—and he thought Italian singers much superior to the German ones. Nevertheless he felt that Rossini morning, noon, and night was rather overdoing it.

In the spring of 1822 Rossini was in Vienna, invited there by the impresario Barbaja. Rossini was on his honeymoon, having recently married Isabella Colbran, long his mistress. In his trunk he had brought along an opera especially written for Vienna, *Zelmira,* which he had tried out at the San Carlo in Naples the preceding December. *Zelmira* enjoyed a sensational success and Rossini was wined, dined, and feted, so that he hardly found time to sleep. He was full of life and spirits. He had elegant manners and an extraordinary wit. He was everything that Beethoven was not. But he was also a true musician, and a genius. He had heard some of Beethoven's music and he expressed a great desire to meet him. We have a full account of this historic meeting: Rossini described it to Wagner when Wagner called on him in Paris in 1860. Edmond Michotte, a friend of both Wagner and Rossini, was present, took detailed notes which he transcribed immediately afterward. Some of Rossini's remarks (or rather Michotte's notes of them) are quoted here as they are given in *Rossini,* a recent (1968) biography by Herbert Weinstock:

ROSSINI: The Beethoven portraits that we know render the whole of physiognomy faithfully enough. But what no burin would know how to express is the indefinable sadness spread across all his features, so that from under heavy eyebrows there shone, as if from the depths of caverns, two eyes which, though small, seemed to pierce you. The voice was soft and very slightly fogged.

When we first entered, he paid no attention to us, but for some moments remained bent over a piece of printed music, which he was finishing correcting. Then, raising his head, he said to me brusquely in Italian that was comprehensible enough: "Ah, Rossini, you are the composer of *Il Barbiere di Siviglia?* I congratulate you; it is an excellent *opera buffa;* I read it with pleasure, and it delights me. It will be played as long as Italian opera exists. Never try to do anything but *opera buffa;* wanting to succeed in another genre would be trying to force your destiny." When Carpani,* who had accompanied Rossini in order to present him to Beethoven, pointed out that Rossini had written a large number of *opere serie* and mentioned *Tancredi, Otello* and *Mosè in Egitto,* Beethoven said:

"In fact, I have looked through them. But, look, *opera seria*—that's not the Italians' nature. They don't have enough musical science to deal with real drama; and how could they acquire it in Italy? ... In *opera buffa,* nobody would have the wit to match you, you Italians. Your language and your vivacity of temperament destine you for it. Look at

---

* Giuseppe Carpani, poet and friend of Rossini.

Cimarosa: how superior the comic part of his operas is to all the rest! It's the same with Pergolesi. You Italians, you make a great thing of his religious music, I know. I agree that there is very touching feeling in his *Stabat,* but its form lacks variety . . . the effect is monotonous, whereas *La Serva padrona—*"

At this point the conversation with Wagner turned to Rossini's operas, then to Mozart, Haydn, Bach ("a miracle of God!"), and Mendelssohn. Wagner brought the talk back to Beethoven, asking about the meeting thirty-eight years before. Rossini remembered it vividly:

ROSSINI: Oh, it was short. You understand that one whole side of the conversation had to be written out. I told him of all my admiration for his genius, all my gratitude for his having allowed me an opportunity to express it to him. He replied with a profound sigh and exactly those words: "*Oh! un infelice!*" After a pause, he asked me for some details about the Italian opera houses, about famous singers, whether or not Mozart's operas were performed frequently, if I was satisfied with the Italian troup at Vienna.

Then, wishing me a good performance and success for *Zelmira,* he got up, led us to the door, and said to me again: "Above all, make a lot of *Barbers.*"

Rossini then continued to reminisce:

Going down that ramshackle staircase, I felt such a painful impression of my visit to that great man—thinking of that destitution, that privation—that I couldn't hold back my tears. "Ah!" Carpani said, "That's the way he wants it. He is a misanthrope, morose, and doesn't know how to hold on to a single friendship."

That very evening, I attended a gala dinner given by Prince Metternich. Still completely upset by that visit, by that lugubrious "*Un infelice!*" which remained in my ears, I couldn't, I assure you, protect myself from an inner feeling of confusion at seeing, by comparison, myself treated with such regard by that brilliant Viennese assemblage; that led me to say stoutly and without any discretion at all what I thought about the conduct of the court and the aristocracy toward the greatest genius of the epoch, who needed so little and was abandoned to such distress. They gave me the very reply that I had received from Carpani. I demanded to know, however, if Beethoven's deafness didn't deserve the greatest pity, if it was really charitable to bring up again the weaknesses with which they were reproaching him, to seek reasons for refusing to go to his assistance. I added that it would be so easy, by means of drawing up a very small subscription, to assure him an income large enough to place him beyond all need for the rest of his life. That proposal didn't win the support of a single person.

After dinner, the evening ended with a reception that brought to Metternich's salons the greatest names in Vienna society. There was also a concert. One of Beethoven's most recently published trios figured on the program—always he, he everywhere, as was said of

Napoleon. The new masterpiece was listened to religiously and won a splendid success. Hearing it amid all that worldly magnificence, I told myself sadly that perhaps at that moment the great man was completing—in the isolation of the hovel in which he lived —some work of high inspiration which was destined, like his earlier works, to initiate into beauties of a sublime order that same brilliant aristocracy from which he was being excluded, and which, amid all its pleasure, was not at all disquieted by the misery of the man who supplied it with those pleasures.

Not having succeeded in my attempts to create an annual income for Beethoven, I didn't lose courage immediately. I wanted to try to get together sufficient funds to buy him a place to live. I did succeed in obtaining some promises to subscribe; but even when I added my own, the final result was very mediocre. So I had to abandon that second project. Generally I got this answer: "You don't know Beethoven well. The day after he became the owner of a house, he would sell it again. He never would know how to adjust himself to a fixed abode; for he feels the need to change his quarters every six months and his servant every six weeks." Was that a way of getting rid of me?

·∘[LOUIS SCHLÖSSER]∘·

Schlösser, a young man not quite twenty-two when he arrived in Vienna, was just getting started on a musical career. He met Schubert and became friendly with him and his circle. But for a long time he was unsuccessful in meeting Beethoven. It was his dearest wish; yet being unknown to fame and timid, he did not know how to bring about such a meeting. He used to follow Beethoven on his walks, "until darkness hid him from sight." Then what he regarded as the impossible happened: the Ambassador of the Grand Duke of Hessen, who liked the young man, gave him a letter to be delivered to Beethoven. The letter was an affirmative answer to Beethoven's appeal to subscribe to a copy of the *Missa Solemnis.*

The delight with which I seized the missive mocks all effort at description; and the thought of soon seeing Beethoven thrust every other sensation into the background. I had no more than hastily thanked the good Baron than I hurried down into the street and threw myself into the first carriage which came my way, loudly shouting the address of the house—No. 60, *Wiedener* suburb—as I did so. My fancy had painted the happiest pictures of Beethoven's home, but the nearer I drew to it toward the end of my drive, moving uphill between the steep rows of housefronts in the uncomfortable *Kotgasse* and finally stopping before a low, mean-looking house with a rough stone stairway leading to its entrance, the greater my surprise and an emotion I could not suppress at the thought of hunting up the great tone poet amid such surroundings.

Opposite, in a workshop open to the street, a herculean bell-founder, like Vulcan the Smith, swung a most hefty hammer, so that the strident blows made the air tremble within a wide radius, and drove me as quickly as possible into the interior of the house

No. 60, where, without paying any attention to a man, presumably the proprietor, who stepped forward to meet me on the threshold, I at once hurried up the uncomfortable, nearly dark stairs to the first story, door at the left. At times one is overtaken by moods which do not admit of verbal expression and which instinctively, at the thought of soon confronting some extraordinary celebrity, occasion a shyness beyond control. This was my case when, since neither servant nor maid appeared, I carefully opened the outer door and —quite unsuspecting, found myself standing in a kitchen, through which one had to pass to gain the living-rooms. At any rate, I never knew of any other way, for on every subsequent occasion when I came to Beethoven and remained a long time, he himself, at parting, invariably led me through this kitchen anteroom to the stairs. After repeatedly knocking in vain at the real living-room door, I entered and found myself in a rather commodious but entirely undecorated apartment; a large, four-square oak table with various chairs, which presented a somewhat chaotic aspect, stood in the middle of the room. On it lay writing-books and lead-pencils, music-paper and pens, a chronometer, a metronome, an ear-trumpet made of yellow metal and various other things. On the wall at the left of the door was the bed, completely covered with music, scores and manuscripts. I can recall only a framed oil-painting (it was a portrait of Beethoven's grandfather for whom, as is known, he had a childlike reverence) which was the sole ornament I noticed. Two deep window-niches, covered with smooth paneling I mention only because in the first a violin and a bow hung from a nail, and in the other Beethoven himself, his back to me, stood busily writing down figures and the like on the wood, already covered with scribblings.

The deaf Master had not heard me enter, and it was only by stamping vigorously with my feet that I managed to attract his notice and he at once turned around, surprised to see a young stranger standing before him. Yet before I could address a single word to him, he commenced to excuse himself in the politest manner imaginable because he had not sent out his housekeeper, and no one had been in attendance to announce me, the while quickly drawing on his coat; and then first asking me what I wished. Standing so near this artist, crowned with glory, I could realize the impression which his distinguished personality, his characteristic head, with its surrounding mane of heavy hair and the furrowed brow of a thinker, could not help but make on every one. I could look into those profoundly serious eyes, note the amiably smiling expression of his mouth when he spoke, his words always being received with great interest.

My visit probably occurred shortly after he had eaten breakfast, for he repeatedly passed the napkin lying beside him across his snow-white teeth, a habit, incidentally, in which I noticed he often indulged. Steeped in my contemplation of him I entirely forgot the unfortunate man's total deafness, and was just about to explain my reason for being there to him when, fortunately, I recalled the uselessness of speaking at the last moment, and instead reverentially handed him the letter with its great seal. After he had carefully opened it and read its contents his features visibly brightened; he pressed my hands gratefully, and after I had given him my visiting-card, expressed his pleasure at my visit and added (I shall use his very language): "These are heartening words which I have read. Your Grand-Duke expresses himself not alone like a princely Mæcenas, but like a thorough musical connoisseur with comprehensive knowledge. It is not only his accept-ance of my work which pleases me, but the value he attaches to art in general, and the recognition he concedes my activities." He had seized his ear-trumpet, so I explained the unbounded veneration accorded his genial works, with what enthusiasm they were heard, and what an influence the perfection of his intellectual creations had exercised on the cultural level of the day. Though Beethoven was so impervious to flattery of any kind, my words which came stammering from the depths of my soul, nevertheless seemed to touch him, and this induced me to tell about my nocturnal pursuit of him after the performance of "Fidelio." "But what prevented you from coming to see me in person?" he asked. "I am sure you have been told any amount of contradictory nonsense; that I have been described as being an uncomfortable, capricious and arrogant person, whose music one might indeed enjoy, but who personally was to be avoided. I know these evil, lying tongues, but if the world considers me heartless, because I seldom meet people who understand my thoughts and feelings, and therefore content myself with a few friends, it wrongs me." *

·❧[SCHUBERT]❧·

Did Beethoven know Schubert personally? Around the time of Schlösser's visit, Diabelli announced the publication of Schubert's *Variations on a French Song for Piano, four hands,* which was "Dedicated to Ludwig van Beethoven by his worshipper and admirer Franz Schubert." The legend persists that Schubert, who did worship and admire Beethoven, submitted the *Variations* to Beethoven personally, that the two composers met, that Beethoven criticized the *Varia-tions,* though in a kindly manner, and that Schubert was so completely shaken by this criticism that he lost control of himself and fled Beethoven's house.

It is true that Beethoven knew of the *Variations* and was aware of Schubert as an artist. In the last year of his life he looked at a number of Schubert's *Lieder* and said that a divine spark lived in Schubert. Schubert seems not to have succeeded in making Beethoven's acquaintance. He went once to his lodging, taking with him a gift copy of the *Variations;* Beethoven was not at home, and Schubert left the copy with the servant. That was the end of it. The supposed meeting of Schubert and Beethoven is probably a fabrication by Schindler.**

·❧[LISZT]❧·

Beethoven's meeting with the young prodigy, then a boy of eleven, in 1823, belongs to the famous anecdotes of both Beethoven's and Liszt's biography. Like

---

* O. G. Sonneck, *op. cit.*
** Schubert told the correct story to his close friend, Joseph Hüttenbrenner.

most famous anecdotes, it is differently related by different tellers. Schindler told one story in the first and another in the third edition of the biography. Liszt's own account, given to his pupil Ilka Horowitz Barnay in 1875, may also have been polished for posterity.

The essence of the story is this: the boy Liszt, who was studying with Czerny, gave a concert in the small Redoutensaal in April, 1823. A few days earlier he was taken, in company with his father, to Beethoven's house. There is an entry in the Conversation Book, probably written by the father:

> I have often expressed the wish to Herr von Schindler to make your high acquaintance and am rejoiced to be able now to do so. As I shall give a concert on Sunday the 13th I most humbly beg you to give me your high presence.

Schindler wrote:

> Little Liszt has urgently requested me humbly to beg you for a theme on which he wishes to improvise at his concert tomorrow. [Some words crossed out] humilime dominationem Vestram, si placeat scribere unum Thema. [He humbly begs for the contribution of a theme, if you will be so kind.] He will keep it sealed until he opens it there.

> The little fellow's free improvisations cannot yet, strictly speaking, be interpreted as such. The lad is a true pianist; but as far as improvisation is concerned, the day is still far off when one can say that he improvises.

> Do come, it will certainly amuse Karl to hear how the little fellow plays.

After other entries, Schindler returns to the subject:

> Won't you make up for the rather unfriendly reception of the other day by coming tomorrow to little Liszt's concert?

According to Nohl and Liszt himself, Beethoven did attend the concert, and much moved by the boy's phenomenal playing, went onstage, lifted the boy in his arms, and kissed him. Liszt's own account of his meeting Beethoven is this:

> I was about eleven years old when my respected teacher Czerny took me to see Beethoven. Already a long time before, he had told Beethoven about me and

asked him to give me a hearing some day. However, Beethoven had such an aversion to infant prodigies that he persistently refused to see me. At last Czerny, indefatigable, persuaded him, so that, impatiently, he said, "Well, bring the rascal to me, in God's name!" It was about ten o'clock in the morning when we entered the two small rooms in the Schwarzspanierhaus, where Beethoven was living at the time,* myself very shy, Czerny kind and encouraging. Beethoven was sitting at a long, narrow table near the window, working. For a time he scrutinized us grimly, exchanged a few hurried words with Czerny and remained silent when my good teacher called me to the piano. The first thing I played was a short piece by Ries. When I had finished, Beethoven asked me whether I could play a fugue by Bach. I chose the Fugue in C minor from the Well-Tempered Clavichord. "Could you also transpose this fugue at once into another key?" Beethoven asked me. Fortunately, I could. After the final chord, I looked up. The Master's darkly glowing gaze was fixed upon me penetratingly. Yet suddenly a benevolent smile broke up his gloomy features, Beethoven came quite close, bent over me, laid his hand on my head and repeatedly stroked my hair. "Devil of a fellow!" he whispered, "such a young rascal!" I suddenly plucked up courage. "May I play something of yours now?" I asked cheekily. Beethoven nodded with a smile. I played the first movement of the C major Concerto. When I had ended, Beethoven seized both my hands, kissed me on the forehead and said gently, "Off with you! You're a happy little fellow, for you'll give happiness and joy to many other people. There is nothing better or greater than that!" This event in my life has remained my greatest pride, the palladium for my whole artistic career. I speak of it only very rarely and only to my intimate friends.**

It is almost certain that Beethoven did *not* attend Liszt's concert. This did not prevent a 19th-century artist from picturing the scene: Beethoven, having climbed onto the stage, embraces the boy. "Beethoven's kiss," if indeed it was bestowed, was more likely given in his room.***

---

* At that time he was *not* living there.

** Michael Hamburger, *op. cit.*

*** Sacheverell Sitwell in his biography of Liszt writes: "It seems unlikely that Beethoven attended the concert. He was too deaf to derive any pleasure from another person's playing. He certainly did not give Liszt the theme he had asked for upon which to improvise. But, on the authority of Liszt himself, the story is true that Beethoven climbed upon the stage at the end of the concert, lifted him in his arms, and kissed him. This personal testimony cannot be lightly contradicted, although it has been argued by his detractors that the story was merely invented as an advertisement for the young virtuoso.

"It is sufficient that Liszt knew Beethoven and that on some occasion, in public or more probably in private, perhaps in the master's own house, Beethoven should have been so impressed by his playing that he embraced him. This possibility, that the episode took place in Beethoven's own house, is certainly in accord with the version of it that used to be told by Ferdinand Hiller, a musician who was one of Liszt's early pupils."

THE MISSA, THE NINTH, AND VISITORS

·⊰[FRANZ GRILLPARZER]⊱·

Grillparzer was more than a visitor. He had known Beethoven for many years and now, in 1823, serious consideration was being given by both men to a collaboration. Grillparzer, though still in his early thirties, had become a famous playwright, having written *Sappho, The Ancestral Woman,* and *The Golden Fleece.* He was delighted at the prospect of creating an opera with Beethoven, though it is probable that he had some doubts that Beethoven could really understand his aims—or he Beethoven's. (His *Memories of Beethoven,* published in 1840, indicate this.) Patiently, and with that sense of both respect and equality which one artist can feel for another, Grillparzer suggested several ideas. He even sketched an entire libretto on the subject of the beautiful Melusine; there are quantities of entries in the Conversation Book discussing details. It all came to nothing, but Grillparzer never lost his fondness for the composer. We owe a charming anecdote to the poet:

> We took a promenade and entertained each other as well as was possible half in conversation, half in writing, while walking. I still remember with emotion that when we sat down to table Beethoven went into an adjoining room and himself brought forth five bottles. He set down one at Schindler's plate, one at his own, and three in front of me, probably to make me understand in his wild and simple way that I was master and should drink as much as I liked. When I drove back to town without Schindler, who remained in Hetzendorf, Beethoven insisted on accompanying me. He sat himself beside me in the open carriage but instead of going only to the edge of the village, he drove with me to the city, getting out at the gates and, after a cordial handshake, starting back alone on the journey of an hour and a half homeward. As he left the carriage I noticed a bit of paper lying on the seat which he had just vacated. I thought that he had forgotten it and beckoned him to come back; but he shook his head and with a loud laugh, as at the success of a ruse, he ran the faster in the opposite direction. I unrolled the paper and it contained exactly the amount of the carriage-hire which I had agreed upon with the driver. His manner of life had so estranged him from all the habits and customs of the world that it probably never occurred to him that under other circumstances he would have been guilty of a gross offence. I took the matter as it was intended and laughingly paid my coachman with the money which had been given to me. (TQ).

Beethoven said to Grillparzer: "Your work lives here," pointing to his heart. Grillparzer said of Beethoven: "He was an artist—and who shall arise to stand beside him?"

CHAPTER 22

THE LAST YEARS

··❧[I]❧··

PREMIERE OF THE NINTH

Breitkopf and Härtel wanted a new portrait of Beethoven, to be used for an elaborate edition they were planning, and they commissioned Ferdinand Waldmüller to paint it. Their decision represented a compliment to Beethoven, as Waldmüller was one of Vienna's highly esteemed painters. Though he was not a "great painter" (Austria never produced a great painter), he was a charming one, and his *genre* scenes, in which "scrubbed urchins" * play and a shepherd flirts with a milkmaid, were much in demand. Beethoven never liked to sit for a portrait. Right now, at the beginning of 1823, he was less than ever inclined to do so: he was immersed in work, and his eyes were bothering him. He put off the appointment as long as he could and when he could no longer do so he received Waldmüller less than graciously. In addition, wrote Schindler, Waldmüller made the mistake of approaching Beethoven deferentially, "a bearing that Beethoven generally found most irritating."

> No matter how much Waldmüller hurried with sketching the head and roughing out the portrait, the preoccupied master was impatient to get back to his work, and would repeatedly stand up, pace the floor irritably, and go to his writing-table in the next room.
>
> The under layer of paint had not yet been completed when Beethoven made it clear that he could tolerate the procedure no longer. When the painter had left, the master gave vent to his spleen and called Waldmüller the worst artist in the world because he had made him sit with his face towards the window. He obstinately refused to hear any argument in the man's defense. No further sittings took place and the artist completed the portrait from memory because,

---

* The phrase is John Canaday's, in *Mainstreams of Modern Art.*

578

The famous painting of the composer by Ferdinand Waldmüller, done in 1823 (Bettmann Archive).

as he replied to my suggestions to the contrary, he could not afford to give up the fee of twenty ducats that had been agreed upon. (S).

That last statement is not correct: we know that Waldmüller's fee was twelve ducats, not twenty, and it is hardly likely that the successful painter would be in great need of such a sum (about $300, if they were full-value ducats). Schindler called the finished painting worthless, and some of Beethoven's other friends were incensed by it.

Yet it is the product of a real artist who in that one sitting saw his model with the artist's eye and fixed on canvas an impression which comes nearer to conveying Beethoven as he was than do the other polite portraits of the composer.* Waldmüller, inspired by his subject to unwonted seriousness, seems to have caught the image of the man not only as he was but as he was shortly to be.

The gray hair, matted with the perspiration of thought, frames a forehead as high and smooth as a prison wall. The mouth is drawn in pain or deprecation. The jowls are becoming indeterminate in outline, a sign of advancing years. But the eyes are those of a man in full possession of his power, the glance glowing and strong. He gazes into the distance, yet there is nothing vague, imprecise, or idle in that gaze.

We have plenty of testimony about Beethoven's strength in his latter years. To Julius Benedict,** friend of Weber and Mendelssohn, who saw him in the year of the Waldmüller portrait, he appeared like King Lear or one of the old Celtic bards,

with his white hair, that streamed down over his powerful shoulders, his knitting of the brows when anything specially moved him, and his prodigious laughter, that was indescribably painful for the hearer.

Benedict was struck by the expression of his eyes: "It was a feeling of sublimity and melancholy combined."

Now he occasionally showed a gentleness of bearing and a pliancy of manner which moved some of his friends to tears. Ludwig Rellstab, essayist and historian and later a famous critic who rebuffed the young Richard Wagner, was one

---

* The sketches made of Beethoven, on the other hand, do give an excellent idea of his looks and bearing. Such sketches were made by J. D. Böhm, Johann Peter Lyser, Joseph Weidner, Martin Tejeck, and others.
** He went to England in 1827, was knighted, and conducted *Elijah* when Jenny Lind first sang in it (1848). When he met Beethoven he was only nineteen years old.

of those who made a special journey in 1825 from Berlin to Vienna with the object of seeing Beethoven. He wrote:

> I read sadness, suffering and kindness in his face; yet I repeat not a trace of the harshness, not a trace of the impetuous boldness which characterizes the impetus of his genius was even evanescently noticeable ... For the suffering, the mute, silent anguish therein expressed, was not the consequence of a momentary indisposition, since a number of weeks later, when Beethoven felt much better, I recognized it again and again—but was the outcome of the whole unique fatality of his life, which welded the loftiest awards of substantiation with the most cruel renunciatory tests....
>
> It called for great powers of self-control to sit opposite him and hold back the tear which would out.*

The calm of resignation, the belief that the fight had been fought, the conviction that "the readiness is all," were not at variance with the impression of power he conveyed. On the contrary, composure only rendered strength the stronger.

Nor did he summon tranquillity at all times. Sublimity did not sustain him every day. He did not become the wise man of the mountain. In his music only did he reach a level beyond good and evil. In his personality the lion was still rampant; the paw could pounce with punishing speed. His anger could be as heedless, his fury as fierce. A case in point (perhaps a trivial one) is his set-to with a copyist, Ferdinand Wolanek. He was newly employed after the death of Schlemmer, Beethoven's previous copyist, who had worked for him for about thirty years and who had learned how to decipher Beethoven's scrawl. Beethoven must have taken Wolanek to task for one reason or another, and Wolanek decided that he was not going to stand for Beethoven's outbursts any longer. Let him get another copyist. So he quit—and wrote Beethoven a letter the irony of which is apparent behind the politeness:

[1825]

To Herr Ludwig v. Beethoven!
Since I cannot add the finale to the score until Easter and you will no longer need it at this time, I am sending over the complete parts along with what has already been begun for your favorable disposition.
I remain gratefully obliged for the honor rendered by your employment of

---

* Quoted from Sonneck, *op. cit.*

me; as for more concerning the discordant behavior towards me, I can only regard it smilingly as a good-natured outburst to be accepted. In the ideal world of tones there are so many dissonances, shouldn't they exist also in the real world?

My one comfort is the firm conviction that with Mozart and Haydn, those celebrated artists, I would have shared a similar fate as with you in the position of copyist.

I request only not to mix with those common copyists who consider themselves happy to be able to maintain their existence by being treated as slaves.

At any rate be assured that I will never have the least bit of cause to blush in front of you on account of my behavior.

Respectfully yours FERD. WOLANEK (TQ).

Beethoven read the letter and in a rage drew zigzag lines across it from corner to corner. Then in letters two inches long he wrote over Wolanek's writing the words, "Stupid, conceited ass of a fellow." But that was not enough. There was a margin at the bottom of the sheet just large enough for Beethoven's next remark: "Am I to exchange compliments with such a scoundrel who filches my money? Instead of that, I ought to pull his ass's ears." He turned the letter over and there was a whole blank page for him to fill. He did so. In the center he wrote, "Slovenly copyist! Stupid fellow! Correct the mistakes you have made through your ignorance, arrogance, conceit and stupidity. That is more fitting than to want to teach me. For to do so is exactly as if the *sow* should want to teach Minerva."

On the right in the margin he wrote, *"I beg you to do* Mozart and Haydn *the honour* of not mentioning *their names."* Even then his anger was not spent. There was a margin left; he wrote on it: "Indeed yesterday and even before then it was decided *not to employ you any more* to copy for me." (A-1463).

He could become just as furious at his brother—his "pseudo-brother"—as he was at Wolanek. The ambivalence he felt toward Johann we can understand: most of us both love and hate our relatives. But Beethoven's love-hate was extreme. He longed for his brother's companionship, though he had so often berated him. In May, 1822, he asked Johann to come to Oberdöbling that very day with his wife and her daughter (Therese's illegitimate child, Amalie, now fifteen years old), instead of going for a drive in the Prater. He writes:

I have nothing against your wife. I only hope that she will realize how much could be gained for you too by your living with me and that all life's wretched trivialities need not cause any disturbances between us.

He adds a postscript:

> Peace, let us have peace. God grant that the most natural bond, the bond between brothers, may not again be broken in an unnatural way. In any case my life will certainly not last very much longer. I repeat that I have nothing against your wife, although her behaviour to me on a few occasions has greatly shocked me.... (A-1078).

A year later, when Johann was convalescing from an illness, Beethoven writes:

BADEN, August 19 [1823]

> I received your letters of August 10th through that miserable rascal *Schindler.* Remember that you need only send your letters straight to the post where I shall certainly receive them all. For I avoid as far as possible that low-minded, contemptible fellow—Karl can't join me until the 29th when he will write to you. But you will not be entirely neglected, whatever those two canailles, that loutish fat woman and her bastard, may do to you,* and you will receive letters from Karl and from me through him. For, however little you may deserve it so far as I am concerned, yet I shall never forget that you are my brother; and in due course a good spirit will imbue your heart and soul, a good spirit which will separate you from those two *canailles,* that former and still active whore, with whom her fellow miscreant slept no less than three times during your illness and who, moreover, has full control of your money, oh, abominable shame, is there no spark of manhood in you?!!! (A-1231).

He has nothing against Johann's wife—except that he calls her a whore!

·◦[2]◦·

As his group of friends grew smaller—some he no longer wanted to see, and a few found social intercourse with him too difficult—he gained a new friend in Karl Holz. He was the last of the young faithful who gathered around him. Holz was twenty-eight years younger than Beethoven. He was a cultured man, a good conversationalist, and a great deal stronger and more forthright in his opinions than Schindler dared to be, even when these opinions differed from Beethoven's. Holz was second violinist in the Schuppanzigh Quartet—a fine musician according to all accounts—and Beethoven treated him with greater

---

* He means of course Therese and her daughter.

respect than he ever did Schindler. His name gave Beethoven the opportunity for endless puns on *"Holz,"* the German word for wood. In ecclesiastic German the word is also a synonym for Christ's cross. Holz therefore was showered with such appellations as "Best mahogany," or "Dearest *lignum crucis,"* "Best splinter from the cross of Christ," and so on, but he didn't mind. He loved Beethoven —"the mere thought of Beethovian music makes me glad to be alive," he said —and willingly helped him by copying scores and writing letters.

Schindler, relegated to a lesser role, gave vent to his jealousy. Entry in the Conversation Book:

> SCHINDLER: The behaviour of certain people who are around you reminds me—now and as long as I have known you—of what you read about the courts of the Oriental nabobs—Sultan Beethoven!

In addition to Holz, one or two other new and several old acquaintances moved within the circle of his last years. Proust has observed that in the end we are apt to return to the impressions we first form of people and places. Beethoven returned to first impressions, to remembrance of things past, to thoughts of Bonn and to Wegeler, to whom in the last few months of his life he wrote two moving letters, recalling their youth. "I remember all the love which you have always shown me, for instance, how you had my room whitewashed and thus gave me such a pleasant surprise,—and likewise all the kindness I have received from the Breuning family." (A-1542, December 7, 1826.) He became deeply attached to Stephan Breuning, the friendship growing closer than it had been before.

Among the new acquaintances was Ignaz Dembscher, an official of the War Department, a very wealthy man, and a chamber-music enthusiast. He gave chamber-music evenings at his house. Dembscher had at one time neglected to subscribe to a series of concerts which Schuppanzigh gave. Then when Dembscher asked Beethoven to let him have the manuscript of one of his quartets in order to have it played at his house, Beethoven jokingly refused: Dembscher was to be punished for not attending Schuppanzigh's concerts. Dembscher begged Holz to intercede and to find some means of restoring him to Beethoven's favor. Holz suggested that to make amends he ought to send Schuppanzigh fifty florins, the price of a concert subscription. Dembscher laughingly asked, "Must it be?" (*"Muss es sein?"*) When Holz related the incident to Beethoven, he too laughed and at once wrote down a canon to the words, "It must be, yes, it must be. Out, out with the money!" From this joke sprang an idea which Beethoven was to use for the ultimate movement of his ultimate quartet; the movement bears the superscription, "The Difficult Resolution."

Johann Nepomuk Wolfmayer, a successful cloth merchant, was an admirer of Beethoven in the composer's last three years. He would show his admiration by occasionally having a brand-new coat made for Beethoven, bringing it to his rooms, placing it upon a chair, and spiriting away an old one. Sometimes Beethoven objected, but Wolfmayer paid no attention. Some years previously Wolfmayer had commissioned Beethoven to write a Requiem for him and had paid 1000 florins as an advance. Nothing came of it, though Holz said that Beethoven had every intention of composing the work. Instead, Beethoven dedicated his last quartet to Wolfmayer.

Beethoven's mind, in addition to its miraculous creativity, was as intellectually active as it had been twenty years before. The Conversation Books indicate the nature of his conversations with Grillparzer: they discussed the evils of censorship, Weber, the lot of Austrian artists. Grillparzer, inclined to melancholy, was buoyed up by Beethoven. Somebody, probably Holz, wrote after Grillparzer left, "you certainly made a great impression on Grillparzer, because you gave him so much courage today." With Christian Kuffner, the poet, Beethoven discussed the "new English poets," Byron and Thomas Moore (author of "Believe Me, If All Those Endearing Young Charms"), Goethe's poetry, the Voss translation of Homer. There is talk of Rousseau and Voltaire. But there is a bit of gossip, too, which Beethoven enjoyed. And sooner or later the talk swings to politics and the deplorable state of the world.

The great revolutionaries often turn toward the past after the hurly-burly is done. In the years in which Beethoven immeasurably widened the horizon of music, the years of the last quartets, he turned from the contemporary and the immediate past to the men of long ago. Bach and Handel offered him new inspiration. He expressed himself about Handel in glowing terms. An English visitor, Edward Schulz, who saw Beethoven in Baden in the summer of 1823 in company with Haslinger, wrote an account of his visit for the British magazine *Harmonicon:* *

> In the whole course of our table-talk there was nothing so interesting as what
> he said about Handel. I sat close by him and heard him assert very distinctly in

---

* The article was reprinted in John Crosse's book.

German, "Handel is the greatest composer that ever lived." I cannot describe to you with what pathos, and I am inclined to say, with what sublimity of language, he spoke of the *Messiah* of this immortal genius. Every one of us was moved when he said, "I would uncover my head, and kneel down at his tomb!" H. and I tried repeatedly to turn the conversation, but without effect. I only heard him say, "In a monarchy we know who is the first"; which might or might not apply to the subject. Mr. C. Czerny—who, by-the-by, knows every note of Beethoven by heart, though he does not play one single composition of his own without the music before him—told me, however, that B. was sometimes inexhaustible in his praise of Mozart.

The year following, he answered another visitor from London, Johann Andreas Stumpff:

Whom do you consider the greatest composer that ever lived?
"Handel," was his instantaneous reply; "to him I bow the knee," and he bent one knee to the ground.

Stumpff then asked Beethoven if he owned all of Handel's works, since he admired him so highly. Beethoven replied, "How should I, a poor devil, have got them?" At that moment Stumpff made a secret vow: Beethoven should have the works for which his heart was longing. He kept his promise, though it took two years. He sent Beethoven a fine edition of Handel in forty volumes. The gift reached Beethoven in 1826, in the middle of December, when he was lying ill. He used to lean the books against the wall, turn the pages, and now and then break into exclamations of praise and joy as he read.

Here, too, he returned to first impressions. Neefe had introduced him to Handel's music and he had heard it played at the house of the august van Swieten when he first came to Vienna.

·•❧[3]❧•·

Beethoven's steadfastness in musical taste was opposed by an increasing incertitude in living and instability in action. Again he moved from lodging to lodging to lodging—four city addresses in 1823–24 and four summer residences—ate irregularly, slept irregularly.

His vacillation, when a decision taken at noon became in his mind the mistake of the afternoon, and today's ally became tomorrow's adversary, was maddeningly apparent in the question of performing the *Missa* and the Ninth. He drove his friends to distraction. Of course he wanted the Ninth and the

Missa performed. But he had got it into his head that Vienna had gone Italian, that the public was no longer in sympathy with him, that his new works would not be understood, and that in undertaking their presentation, with the many rehearsals, much work, and huge apparatus it required, he could at best expect respectful indifference. What was the use? Why perform these works to a public which preferred whipped cream? The comparative failure of his subscription plan for the *Missa* could hardly have improved his mood. Schindler, Schuppanzigh, Lichnowsky, *et al.* could not persuade him.

Two girls, however, made an impression. He had become acquainted recently with two young singers, Caroline Unger, a contralto, and Henrietta Sontag, a soprano.* He wrote to Johann on September 8, 1822:

> Two women singers called on us today and as they absolutely insisted on being allowed to kiss my hands and as they were decidedly pretty I preferred to offer them my mouth to kiss. (A-1097).

Sontag and Unger kept at him, urging him toward a performance. (Perhaps the fact that there were roles for them to sing in both compositions contributed to their enthusiasm.) Unger wrote in the Conversation Book:

> If you give the concert, I will guarantee that the house will be full.
> You have too little confidence in yourself. Has not the homage of the whole world given you a little more pride? Who speaks of opposition? Will you not learn to believe that everybody is longing to worship you again in new works? O obstinacy! (TQ).

Spoken like a pretty girl—and well said.

It all took place at the dinner table (probably on January 25, 1824). The charm of the two girls can be sensed from the Conversation Books.

Beethoven invited them to dinner. This caused much upset in the Beethoven household, because the girls did not accept the invitation promptly enough for adequate preparations to be made. When they did accept, Beethoven decided to make himself presentable and hurried to the barber. Entry by Sontag: "When we arrived, you were at the barber; when I saw that, we turned left and waited so as

---

* In 1824 Unger was twenty-one, Sontag a mere eighteen. Unger later sang mostly in Italy. Sontag became a European star of first magnitude and toured America. A year after she sang in the Ninth, Berlin went mad over her; it was said that audiences were suffering with "Sontag-fever." (Henry Pleasants: *The Great Singers.*)

not to disturb you." The cook grumbled that she was notified too late. They would have to make do with the food that was in the house or could be sent for from a restaurant. Entry by the cook: "All the shops are closed. Chicken with a few portions of meat from the restaurant—how many people? We have salad and *Kugelhof* [*Gugelhupf*—a popular Viennese yeast cake] afterwards."

Beethoven makes excuses for the meal to Unger, who reassures him. Unger: "I did not come to eat well but to make your precious acquaintance, to which I have looked forward for so long.* Schindler told us that you have finally decided, to everybody's satisfaction, to give a concert; we are grateful to you if you deem us worthy to sing in it." Schindler reported later that the two girls drank too much wine—probably in the excitement of the occasion—with calamitous results. Sontag, who was supposed to sing that evening, had to cancel. Schindler: "Some heroines! They are not used to wine. In addition, the wine must have been bad. . . . The two pretty witches send you their compliments and beg that the next time you will serve better wine. . . ." If the wine was bad, it wasn't because Beethoven was stingy. He was probably cheated right and left by the tradespeople.

Yet, in spite of the girls, for a while Beethoven persisted in his Vienna-hating mood. He turned to Count Karl Brühl, the intendant of the Court Theater in Berlin, and asked whether a performance of the Mass or the Ninth Symphony could be given in that city. Brühl answered, "By all means." The news that Beethoven might favor a foreign city with so important a premiere spread through the musical circles of Vienna, causing regret mingled with recriminations. Something had to be done to avoid what in after years would appear as a historic blot. Such was the opinion particularly of Count Moritz Lichnowsky. The friends drew up a flowery petition, and Lichnowsky secured signatures. The petition pleads: "though Beethoven's name and creations belong to all contemporaneous humanity and every country which opens a susceptible bosom to art, it is Austria which is best entitled to claim him as her own . . ."

> We know that a new flower glows in the garland of your glorious, still unequalled symphonies. For years, ever since the thunders of the Victory at Vittoria ceased to reverberate, we have waited and hoped to see you distribute new gifts from the fulness of your riches to the circle of your friends. Do not longer disappoint the general expectations! Heighten the effect of your newest creations by the joy of becoming first acquainted with them through you! Do

---

* She had, of course, made his acquaintance previously.

not allow these, your latest offspring, some day to appear, perhaps, as foreigners in their place of birth, introduced, perhaps, by persons to whom you and your mind are strange! Appear soon among your friends, your admirers, your venerators! This is our nearest and first prayer. (TQ).

The petition is signed by familiar names, such as those of his Viennese publishers, the poets Castelli and Kuffner, Czerny, Zmeskall, Sonnleithner, Palffy. When Beethoven read the document, he was much moved. Schindler— on whom we base our knowledge of the events leading to the first performance of the Ninth, since he was not only present but an active agent—tells us that Beethoven, having read the paper, went to the window and gazed out for a long while. Then he turned to Schindler and said, "Let us go out." They went for a walk and he was silent, "an unmistakable sign that his soul was greatly moved."

The petition was published in the *Theater Zeitung*. Malicious gossip arose that Beethoven himself had inspired both the writing and the printing of it. He was "sickened" by such an imputation. He wrote in the Conversation Book:

> Now that the thing has taken this turn I can no longer find joy in it. The atrocity of attributing such an act to me sickens me with the whole business and I am scarcely able to address even a few words to men of such intellectual prominence. Not a single critic can boast of having received a letter from me. I have never— (TQ).

Here the note breaks off, as if his anger had overpowered him. Schindler tried to soothe him and wrote, "Your honor has not been compromised."

The petition achieved its object: Beethoven took new courage and decided within the month that the premiere was to be given in Vienna. Excitement ran high, and offers of help poured in. Schindler kept reassuring Beethoven not to worry, that everything would go well; the best musicians of Vienna would deem it an honor to take part. The circle of friends gathered and discussed all the details: which was the best theater, what date was suitable, which orchestra should be chosen, what the prices of admission should be, how many rehearsals would be necessary, who should sing the solos, who was to conduct. There would be only a little time left to prepare everything before the summer would put an end to the concert season. His friends kept urging Beethoven to make commitments. Beethoven would not. He still vacillated, he still doubted, and he became confused by his oversupply of advisers. Even Karl and Johann gave their opinions. Beethoven listened to everybody and trusted no one. The only point on which he made a decision was the musical direction: he wanted Umlauf to be general conductor and Schuppanzigh to be leader of the orchestra.

The first hall chosen for the concert was the Theater-an-der-Wien. Its intendant, Count Palffy, who had not always been favorably inclined toward Beethoven but who had now signed the petition, was ready to provide not only the theater but the musical forces for a reasonable price (1200 florins), an unlimited number of rehearsals, and to leave it to Beethoven to fix the price of the tickets. At once there arose a difficulty: at the Theater-an-der-Wien Seyfried was general conductor and Clement was leader of the orchestra. Count Palffy was unwilling to insult Clement, though he thought that Seyfried would not mind too much. He suggested that Beethoven write a conciliatory letter of explanation to Clement, giving him his reasons for choosing another leader.

In the meantime, Schindler had got in touch with Duport, the director of the Kärntnertor Theater. Duport, too, was anxious to obtain the premiere and was quite willing to accept Umlauf and Schuppanzigh.

Still Beethoven hesitated. Moritz Lichnowsky, Schindler, and Schuppanzigh now hatched a little plot. They planned to call on him, all three together, and after the usual amenities lead the conversation casually around to the points which it was necessary to clarify. Then they were going to write down Beethoven's decisions and ask him to sign the paper.

It happened as the three had planned—except that after they left, Beethoven saw through the ruse, thought he had been tricked, and wrote all three.

(To Ignaz Schuppanzigh)
Don't visit me any more. I am not giving a concert.

B-----VN

(To Anton Felix Schindler)
I request you not to come again until I send you word to do so. There will be no concert.

B-------N

(To Count Moritz Lichnowsky)
I despise what is false—
Don't visit me any more. There will be no concert—

B------VN
(A-1279, 1282, 1283).

The three missives seem like commands issued by a Japanese emperor. But the three friends, far from committing hara-kiri, paid no attention, called on Beethoven again, were welcomed, and continued the deliberations. In the Conversation Book there appears a humorous record of a meeting, opened by a formal ritual:

Present:

Herr. L. van Beethoven, a *musikus*.
Herr. Count v. Lichnowsky, an amateur.
Herr Schindler, a fiddler.

Not yet present today:

Herr Schuppanzigh, a fiddler representing Mylord Fallstaff. [*sic*]

Every detail was chewed and rechewed, and finally the decision was arrived at that Beethoven was to accept Palffy's offer and that he was to write to Clement explaining his wishes. Schindler told Beethoven:

Palffy certainly does not want you to take Clement, but only to take the trouble to write him a billet and tell him about the matter. He will certainly be agreeable.

But Clement was not so easily pacified. One can hardly blame him. The orchestra sided with him and roundly declared it would not play under Schuppanzigh. Palffy said that he could force the men to accept Schuppanzigh, but he could not take the responsibility for any sabotage that might result from such a move.

Negotiations with the Kärntnertor Theater were taken up again, and presently two other halls, the Redoutensaal and the Landtständischer Saal, came under consideration. Lichnowsky begged Beethoven not to consider a move toward another hall: there would be trouble with Palffy, and he himself would be embarrassed, since he had by this time promised the coveted event to him. Nevertheless, the difficulties surrounding a performance at the Theater-an-der-Wien finally forced the choice to the Kärntnertor Theater. Palffy behaved in a gentlemanly fashion: he said he would rather lose a considerable sum than the honor of presenting the concert in his house, but that he realized he was powerless against the orchestra's refusal to accept Schuppanzigh. Beethoven's insistence on Schuppanzigh was not merely a whim: being intimately acquainted with the Beethoven style, Schuppanzigh was better able to essay the difficulties of the new works.

Now came the question of when the concert was to be given. Beethoven at first preferred the noon hour. But Johann, his mind ever alert to a possible profit, told him that an evening concert was worth 1500 florins more than one in the daytime. The date first agreed upon proved impractical, since Sontag and Unger were that day performing at a gala event at the Redoutensaal. Beethoven had considered other soloists but soon settled on the two girls. Of their artistic abilities he could have obtained only a secondhand idea.

Finally May 7, 1824, was determined as the date.

Now—the prices of admission. Beethoven wanted them raised, but the Minister of Police, who regulated such matters, refused.

Beethoven had originally intended to present his overture, *The Consecration of the House* (which he had composed for the opening of the new Theater in der Josefstadt but was still virtually unknown), then the entire *Missa,* and finally the Ninth Symphony. Soon realizing that such a program would make the concert long beyond endurance, he first decided to omit the *Gloria* of the Mass, and later, after rehearsals had begun, he gave up the *Sanctus.*

Another difficulty arose here. Church music was not supposed to be performed in a theater; when the program was submitted to the authorities, it was vetoed. Beethoven made a personal appeal to the censor: he expostulated that he had gone to considerable expense for copying the music, there was no time to produce other music, and if the ban were not lifted, he had no choice but to cancel the concert, which would mean a loss not only to him but to the participating artists. He was willing to list the three pieces from the Mass as "Hymns," if that would help. The censor was adamant, and it was not until Moritz Lichnowsky made a private appeal to Count Sedlnitzky (we have met him in connection with the Erdödy case) that the performance was permitted.

In the meantime, the various forces were rehearsing separately and with singular devotion, the choral director with the chorus, Schuppanzigh with the strings, and the solo singers with Beethoven himself. Both Sontag and Unger, accustomed to the smooth road of the Italian style, found the music of the Ninth a rough obstacle course. Unger called Beethoven a "tyrant over all the vocal organs." And both girls tried good-naturedly to charm him into making changes. He would not. "Well then," Unger said to Sontag, "we must go on torturing ourselves in the name of God." The sopranos of the chorus, too, jibbed at the many high notes. Beethoven would not change a single note, with the result that at the performance they simply left out the notes they couldn't reach. Beethoven, of course, did not notice it.

We can imagine the bewilderment of the double basses when during rehearsal they were first called upon to play the exposed recitative passages (*Presto*) and melody (*Allegro assai*) of the final movement of the Ninth. Used to leading the sheltered life and marking the thump, thump of the rhythm, what did this composer now demand of them? This was worse than the passage in the Fifth Symphony. Were they now to become "soloists"?

Entries by Schindler in the Conversation Book:

> The recitatives for the double-basses are enormously difficult. . . . They cannot execute them in tempo. You can play them with 20 [musicians] but not the way you want.
> How many double-basses are to play the recitatives?
> Is it possible? *All!* In strict tempo that would cause no difficulty. But to play them in a singing style will cost great patience at the rehearsals. If the old Kraus were still living, one would not need to worry, because he was able to conduct twelve basses and they had to do what he wanted.

Beethoven then proposed to explain to the double-bass players the poetic meaning of the text in order to guide their phrasing. Schindler: "As if the words were written underneath?" Beethoven must have replied, "Exactly so." Schindler: "If necessary, I will write the words into the parts so that they can learn to 'sing.' "

After the special rehearsals, everybody came together and two full rehearsals were held. Two only—hardly enough.

The final program was:

1. The Overture *The Consecration of the House*
2. The *Kyrie, Credo,* and *Agnus Dei* from the *Missa Solemnis*
3. The Ninth Symphony.

It was announced that "Herr Ludwig van Beethoven will himself participate in the general direction." At the concert he stood at Umlauf's right and marked the tempo at the beginning of each movement. All had been instructed not to pay any attention to him but to follow Umlauf's beat.

As his friends had predicted, the prospect of the concert had created wide interest, reinforced by a few preliminary announcements. The *Allgemeine Theater Zeitung* wrote on May 1: "France and England will envy us the privilege of being able to pay tribute in person to the composer known in all the world as the greatest [living] genius. No one whose soul responds to the great and the beautiful will want to miss this evening." Curiosity must have played a part: not only was this the first opportunity in a long while to hear new works by Beethoven, but what was this business of a symphony which employed chorus and soloists? Who ever heard of a symphony ending in a song?

Whether or not the house was completely filled is not certain. Schindler said that it was; Thayer said so too. However, Rosenbaum noted in his diary:

> Friday the 7th. Warm. Kärntner Theater. van Bethoowens Concert. Sontag, Unger, Heitzinger, Seipelt sing. Umlauf conducts. He [Beethoven] takes part. Overture and three hymns with Kyrie and *Lied an die Freude*. Beautiful but boring—Not very crowded.... Many boxes empty, nobody from the Court. Considering that numerous cast—little effect.
> B[eethoven] partisans noisy, the greater part remained quiet, many left before the end.

What concert did Rosenbaum hear? Was he there or did he fake his entry in the diary? It is true that the Emperor's box remained empty, though Schindler and Beethoven had gone in person to present an invitation to the Imperial family. Emperor Franz and his Empress happened to have left Vienna a few days before; he probably would not have attended a Beethoven concert had he been in Vienna. But the elite of Vienna *were* there * —and all accounts agree that the giant of a symphony made an overwhelming impression. At one point in the *Scherzo* of the Ninth, presumably at the point where one hears the start-ling outburst of the tympani, a gasp went through the audience, and it seemed as if right then and there they would insist on a repetition of the movement. Beethoven, neatly garbed in a black frock coat,** white neckerchief, black silk stockings, and buckled shoes, was oblivious of the reaction of the audience. He stood there, his eyes riveted on the score.

Either after the *Scherzo* or more probably at the end of the symphony—the accounts differ—the audience broke into an ovation. They stood, they clapped,

---

* Zmeskall, bedridden with gout, was carried to his seat in a sedan chair.
** The pianist Thalberg, who was present, told Thayer it was a black coat. However, there is an entry by Schindler in the Conversation Book: "We will take everything with us now; also take your green coat, which you can put on when you conduct. The theater will be dark and no one will notice it. . . . Oh, great master, you do not own a black frock coat! The green one will have to do; in a few days the black one will be ready." (TQ). Did Beethoven borrow a black coat (the conventional concert garb) at the last moment?

they stamped their feet, they waved handkerchiefs. Beethoven heard nothing: he was still looking at the music. Unger plucked him by the sleeve and gently turned him around toward the audience. When he saw what was going on, he bowed, and when the audience realized that he had heard nothing of their previous expression of enthusiasm, they redoubled it. He had to bow again and again.

◦⊰[4]⊱◦

Though this enthusiasm may have represented in part a personal tribute to Beethoven, though the excitement of the moment undoubtedly fed the fever, the fact that the listeners did respond to these complex works must be counted to the credit of Viennese taste, so often scourged by Beethoven. The *Allgemeine Musik Zeitung* (No. 437) wrote of the "enthusiastic shouts raised to the master from overflowing hearts" and the *Allgemeine Theater Zeitung* (May 11, 1824) reported that the "gigantic creations" were received "with deepest appreciation" and "closest attention."

After the concert Beethoven's friends, who had worked so long and so hard to persuade him to bring the concert about, gathered to celebrate and exchange impressions. In the Conversation Book, there are entries such as these:

Never in my life did I hear such frenetic and yet cordial applause.

Once the second movement of the Symphony was completely interrupted by applause.

---

and there was a demand for a repetition.

The reception was more than imperial.

---

for the people burst out in a storm four times. At the last there were cries of Vivat!

When the parterre broke out in applauding cries the 5th time the Police Commissioner yelled Silence!

Obviously Beethoven had heard none of this, and his friends were luxuriating with him in the recollection. Entries by Schindler the next day:

> The whole audience was impressed, crushed by the greatness of your work.

> In Paris and London the concert would certainly have yielded from 12 to 15 thousand florins; here it may be as many hundreds.

> After yesterday you must now too plainly see that you are trampling upon your interests by remaining longer within these walls. In short, I have no words to express my feelings at the wrong which you are doing yourself.

> Have you recovered from yesterday's exertions? (TQ).

The gross receipts of the concert amounted to only 2220 florins W.W. (about $3000). After deducting expenses, there remained for Beethoven a sum of only 420 florins (less than $600), and even against that pitifully small sum some minor costs had to be charged. Beethoven was utterly dejected. According to Schindler, "he collapsed" when he saw the accounts.

He had invited Schindler, Umlauf, and Schuppanzigh to a festive meal at a restaurant in the Prater. Beethoven arrived, his face dark, his brow contracted. He brought Karl along. He had ordered a very fine meal, but the moment everybody sat down at the table, the explosion came. He accused Schindler of having cheated him and, in league with the management, withholding money that was due him. Umlauf and Schuppanzigh, shocked to the core, tried to reason with him: it was out of the question that cheating could have taken place, since the box-office reports had passed through the hands of two theater cashiers, and their accounts agreed. In addition, Karl had been asked by Johann to check the accounts. Beethoven persisted: he had been informed of the fraud by a "reliable source." Thayer thought that this reliable source was brother Johann, who was

> jealous of Schindler's participation in the composer's business affairs and probably took advantage of a favorable opportunity to strengthen Beethoven's chronic suspicion and growing distrust of what the composer himself looked upon as Schindler's officiousness.

Schindler and Umlauf got up and left the room. Schuppanzigh remained behind and after enduring Beethoven's outbreak for a few more moments followed the other two. The three men went to another restaurant and ate by themselves, we can imagine with how little appetite.

Yet Schindler and Schuppanzigh knew how to deal with the volcano that was Beethoven. They returned because they loved him and because they realized that these eruptions were necessary to him to relieve the smoldering pressure of his mind.* Like a phenomenon of nature, he broke out against the just and the unjust, whoever was at hand.

Before a second concert, scheduled for May 23 (a repetition of the Ninth), Schindler was back at his post. So were Schuppanzigh and Umlauf. For this concert, Duport had guaranteed Beethoven 1200 florins W.W. (about $1500). The program was a popular version of the first program, the Ninth Symphony being preceded by Rossini's aria from *Tancredi, "Di tanti palpiti!"* **

The concert took place at midday on Sunday, May 23. Since the weather was exceptionally fine, people preferred to go to the country, and the house was not half full. There was a considerable deficit, and Beethoven was most reluctant to accept the 1200 florins.

From the Conversation Book:

> KARL: A part of the public stayed away because they were indignant about the Rossini aria. I felt the same way. I was in the hall partly to overhear remarks. Everybody was incensed about this aria. It should not have been permitted to happen.

Did he write this to mollify Beethoven? It is hardly a convincing explanation.

After other performances of the Ninth, tributes flowed in from many countries. The London performance, on March 21, 1825, was acclaimed. Music lovers sent souvenirs, messages, and expressions of delight. Beethoven was elected an honorary member by the Royal Academy of Music of Sweden. He was so pleased that he wrote to the editors of two Vienna newspapers asking them to print this news.

---

* In one or two biographies Beethoven's intimates have been characterized as spineless sycophants. I cannot agree with this view. In this instance even Schindler lost some of his docility. He writes in a Conversation Book: "You create such scenes! I almost did not return. One cannot advise or help you."
** The aria was responsible for establishing Rossini's initial popularity. Wagner made a humorous reference to it in *Die Meistersinger*, Act III, in the ditty the tailors sing.

Beethoven loved to receive gifts, large or small. He was extremely proud of a Broadwood piano, a magnificent instrument which had been sent to him from England as long ago as 1818. When he was notified that Thomas Broadwood, the head of the firm, was sending him such a piano, Beethoven was profuse in his thanks. The question then arose how the piano could be delivered without putting Beethoven to the expense of paying the import duty. Beethoven enlisted the help of Moritz Lichnowsky and of Nanette Streicher; they managed it. The Austrian authorities decreed that as a gesture to Beethoven neither Broadwood nor Beethoven would have to pay duty. Beethoven would not let anybody touch the piano or tune it. It was inscribed with the autographs of well-known pianists, and he showed these to his visitors. He kept the instrument as long as he lived. (It is now in the National Museum in Budapest.) It may have been that piano with its powerful tone which helped him to conceive of piano music in larger and more symphonic terms, a conception which led to the *Hammerklavier* and the last sonatas. When, in 1824, Beethoven was making one of his several testaments, he wrote to Dr. Bach that of course Karl was to be the sole heir. But

> since one must bequeath something to relatives as well, even if one has nothing at all in common with them, my worthy *brother* is to have my French pianoforte from *Paris*— (A-1302 *).

It wasn't the Broadwood he willed to Johann but the Erard—like Shakespeare willing his second-best bed to Anne.

Because the King of Prussia had been the first subscriber to the *Missa,* Beethoven decided to dedicate the score of the Ninth to him, having obtained permission from the Prussian ambassador to do so. He instructed Haslinger to have the score bound as beautifully as befitted a King, at Beethoven's expense. In return, the King sent him as a gift a ring of reddish hue, of which the jeweler to whom it was shown said that it was worth very little and which he appraised at 300 florins W.W. (about $450). Beethoven was with difficulty prevented from sending the ring back with a sarcastic note. He sold the ring to the jeweler at the appraised value.**

---

* In 1968 the original of this letter (August 1, 1824) was sold at auction at Sotheby's for 2200 pounds ($5280).
** There is a theory that the ring the King sent was stolen and an inferior one substituted for it. This has never been proved.

·≼[5]≽·

In his last three years, Beethoven was attacked by various ills to which a man with a less robust constitution would have succumbed more quickly than he did. His intestinal disorders were due to the bad food he ate and the irregularity of his meals. He was the most impatient of patients: if the prescription read that the medicine was to be taken a spoonful every four hours, he would swallow four spoonfuls in one hour. Then he would forget about it. If a physician told him to stay in bed, he would get up as soon as he felt a little better and tramp through the fields. In 1825 he suffered serious stomach pains. Dr. Jakob Staudenheim had been his physician, but Beethoven had ignored his advice and was now apparently unsuccessful in getting him to come to the house. Beethoven sent for another doctor, Anton Braunhofer, well known in Vienna, whom he had consulted previously. Dr. Braunhofer was one of those honest, no-nonsense doctors whom the Vienna school at its best produced. He was gruff and stern, and demanded—no, ordered—that Beethoven follow his regimen. Beethoven, somewhat cowed, obeyed, with beneficial results. Braunhofer writes in the Conversation Book:

> Then I will guarantee you full recovery which means a lot to me, understandably, as your admirer and friend.

> A sickness does not disappear in a day. I shall not trouble you much longer with medicine, but you must adhere to the diet, you'll not starve on it.

> You must do some work in the daytime so that you *can sleep at night*. If you want to get entirely well and live a long time, you must live according to nature. You are very liable to inflammatory attacks and were close to a severe attack of inflammation of the bowels; the predisposition is still in your body. (TQ).

The doctor then asked for a souvenir.

> Do not forget the bit of music, just something unimportant, what matters is that it is your handwriting.

Beethoven's condition improved sufficiently for him to move to his beloved Baden in May. From Baden he sent Dr. Braunhofer a quizzical note:

May 13, 1825

Esteemed Friend!

D[OCTOR]: How are you, my patient?

PAT[IENT]: We are rather poorly—we still feel very weak and are belching and so forth. I am inclined to think that I now require a stronger medicine, but it must not be constipating—Surely I might be allowed to take white wine diluted with water, for that poisonous beer is bound to make me feel sick—my catarrhal condition is showing the following symptoms, that is to say, I spit a good deal of blood, but probably only from my windpipe. But I have frequent nose bleedings, which I often had last winter as well. And there is no doubt that my stomach has become dreadfully weak, and so has, generally speaking, my whole constitution. Judging by what I know of my own constitution, my strength will hardly be restored unaided.

D[OCTOR]: I will help you, I will alternate Brown's method with that of Stoll.*

PAT[IENT]: I should like to be able to sit at my writing desk again and feel a little stronger. Do bear this in mind—*Finis.* I will look you up as soon as I go into town. Just tell Karl at what time I can find you. But it would help me if you could inform Karl what other remedies I should use. The last medicine you prescribed I took only once and then lost it—With kindest regards and my gratitude,

Your friend
BEETHOVEN (A-1371).

He sent along a little canon to the words, "Doctor, close the dooor to Death." ** Braunhofer had his souvenir.

After his return from Baden in October, he moved to what was to be his final residence, the Schwarzspanierhaus. This large house stood near the spot where the Votivkirche stands today. The Breunings lived nearby and their little boy Gerhard, twelve years old in 1825, was taken to visit Beethoven. Gerhard, endowed with a sensitivity which Karl lacked, became a kind of benevolent sprite around the house, a lovable little busybody always underfoot, spending every moment he could spare from school and from his piano lessons with Beethoven, often merely sitting still and watching him. Beethoven called him "Ariel" and "trouser button"; they took walks together, and on Sundays the boy's father would come along. When Gerhard grew up,*** he wrote a little book, *Aus dem Schwarzspanierhause,* which in those episodes in which he was

---

* Brown was a Scottish physician, Stoll of Württemberg his antagonist.
** Joseph Kerman has pointed out that the canon is a "Mephistophelian travesty" of the "Song of Thanksgiving" of the Quartet Op. 132.
*** He became a prominent physician.

an eyewitness is vividly written and affectionately informed. It is indeed a delight to read.

Among the anecdotes Gerhard relates, there is a charming one concerning a picture of Haydn's birthplace, which Diabelli gave to Beethoven as a gift. He took great pleasure in it, showed it to Gerhard, and said, "Look what I received today. Look what a small house, and there so great a man was born. Ask your father to have a frame made for the picture. I want to hang it." Gerhard took the picture, and his father asked Gerhard's piano teacher to order a simple frame of black polished wood. The teacher, delighted to be able to do something for Beethoven, not only had the picture framed but on the white margin underneath he himself wrote, in elaborate calligraphy, "Jos. Hayden's [*sic*] birthplace in Rohrau." The Breunings, father and son, noticed the mistake in spelling but were sure Beethoven would not. They brought the picture to him. Instead of being pleased, his face reddened, his expression darkened, and in a veiled voice he asked Gerhard, "Who wrote this?" "My piano teacher." Then Beethoven broke out: "What is the name of that ass? Such an ignoramus is supposed to be a piano teacher, a musician, and does not even know how to spell the name of a master like Haydn." * Gerhard took the picture back, had it corrected, and brought it again after a few days; but Beethoven was still grumbling away.

He then insisted on paying for the frame. Stephan Breuning protested, but when Beethoven would not have it otherwise, Stephan wrote in the Conversation Book, "all right. 2 guld. and 15 kr. W.W." Beethoven then said, "Take the little box there on the commode. You'll find the money there." Gerhard writes:

> My father did so, but found no change and therefore took a five-gulden note in order to make change. Beethoven was quite weak and sleepy and had closed his eyes. When my father noticed this, he waited with the open box until Beethoven opened his eyes again to show him what he had taken and what change he put back. Then, pressed for time, he hurried away to his office. Beethoven paid no attention and answered as if he had been unpleasantly disturbed in his slumber, briefly and with a gesture of dismissal, "Quite all right." No sooner had my father left when Beethoven, now fully awake, spoke in hurt tones about the seeming distrust which my father had shown. "Why did your father show me

---

* Beethoven himself misspelled practically everybody's name—including in his youth the name of Haydn.

the banknote? Did he think that I do not trust his honesty? I thought we were old enough friends to be convinced of our probity."

⊰[6]⊱
THE LAST QUARTETS

The works which occupied him almost exclusively in the last years were the final five string quartets. These late-harvest products are unique, unique for Beethoven, unique in all music. The quartets carry music to a summit of exaltation and to the deepest depth of feeling. There is no "message" in these works, no "philosophy." They are beyond definition in words. To probe their variety of mood, sweetness, power, intensity, humor, compassion, assertion of life, a book by itself is needed, one which it would be beyond my ability to write.* Yet we may let the music speak—without a preliminary word. Each of the five quartets is an experience which makes one break out in perspiring superlatives. (I think that the slow movement of Opus 135 is the most beautiful piece of music ever written.) Each is peerless. They have a reputation for being difficult, and some listeners shy away from them. Difficult they may be, as *The Tempest* or *Faust* or *The Idiot* is difficult; but not abstract, not severe, not inaccessible, save possibly the Great Fugue (Op. 133).

All great artists travel the road upward. For some the climb is not a steep one, and the level they reach lies near the level at which they started. Others ascend continuously from youth to age, and reach so high a plateau that they leave their early works far in the valley. Raphael and Mendelssohn were accomplished artists almost from the start, and while their work shows development, it is not a startling development. (Both died young, however.) Beethoven is like Rembrandt: a world separates "The Anatomy Lesson," painted when Rembrandt was twenty-six, from the "Self Portrait" in the Frick museum, painted at the age of fifty-two. When Beethoven was twenty-six, he worked on the Piano Sonata, Op. 7, a charming piece known in his lifetime as "The Maiden in Love"; when he was fifty-two he was thinking of the first of the last quartets. It was an immense journey.

Prince Nikolaus Galitzin wanted compositions he could play in his home in St. Petersburg; he played the cello—by itself a cumbersome instrument—and he desired chamber compositions in which the cello could be an equal partici-

---

* A number of such books have been written, including a recent one by Joseph Kerman: *The Beethoven Quartets* (Knopf). It is superb critical analysis, though highly technical.

pant. He wrote to Beethoven late in 1822, asking for "one, two, or three new quartets, for which labor I will be glad to pay you what you think proper." It took Beethoven the better part of three months to answer. He wrote (in French, written by Karl and signed by him): ". . . since I perceive that you are cultivating the violoncello, I will take care to content you in this regard." He fixed the honorarium for each quartet at fifty ducats (about $1250, if they were meant to be full-value ducats); it was a high fee, but quite agreeable to the prince.

Galitzin had to wait a long time. More than a year elapsed, and no quartet had as yet been delivered. The manuscript of the Mass to which he had subscribed had arrived, and the prince, after expressing his joy, wrote:

> I am really impatient to have a new quartet of yours, nevertheless, I beg you not to mind and to be guided in this only by your inspiration and the disposition of your mind, for no one knows better than I that you cannot command genius, rather that it should be left alone, and we know moreover that in your private life you are not the kind of person to sacrifice artistic for personal interest and that music done to order is not your business at all. (TQ).

This is the letter of a patron who understands the mentality of the artist, though his subsequent action would negate this assertion. At any rate, in a letter written a few months later, Prince Galitzin had the pleasure of informing Beethoven of the success of the Mass at its premiere in St. Petersburg:

> The effect of this music on the public cannot be described and I doubt if I exaggerate when I say that for my part I have never heard anything so sublime; I don't even except the masterpieces of Mozart which with their eternal beauties have not created for me the same sensations that you have given me, Monsieur, by the *Kyrie* and *Gloria* of your Mass. (TQ).

The first of the Galitzin quartets eventually arrived (No. 12), and by the middle of 1826 all three were in the prince's hands. In the meantime Galitzin had become a kind of official representative of Beethoven in St. Petersburg. He was proud of every sheet of Beethoven music in his library and he asked Beethoven to have copies made of new works, such as the Ninth, at his expense.

The prince's role of a gallant Maecenas must be emphasized, since shortly afterward his behavior became incomprehensible to the Beethoven circle in Vienna. What happened? Galitzin, after remitting the fifty ducats for the first quartet and assuring Beethoven that should he need money he must feel free to draw on his purse, did not pay for the second and third quartets, nor for a dedicatory copy of *The Consecration of the House* overture which Beethoven had sent at the prince's request. In vain did Beethoven wait for his fee. In vain were letters dispatched reminding Galitzin of his obligation. The prince answered that he was going to pay, but the months dragged on and nothing arrived. Holz knew of a courier named Lipscher who had the route to St. Petersburg. His services were retained: he was to jog what seemed to be the prince's failing conscience. In May, 1826, Holz wrote in the Conversation Book:

> The courier Lipscher, who took the third quartet and was supposed to bring back the money, has written from Petersburg: he went to the home of the Prince, who excused himself, he had no time, he should come another day; Lipscher then went 5 or 6 times but was never received; all kinds of excuses were given. A so-called blue note for 5 fl. given to a servant helped him finally to get through to the Prince again; he was embarrassed again, fumbled through his scores and finally said that Lipscher might come to him before his departure for Vienna and receive the money. (TQ).

Lipscher did *not* succeed in collecting the money and advised Beethoven to turn to the banker Stieglitz in Vienna, who had connections with the Russian government and perhaps could exert pressure. Stieglitz reported to Beethoven: an inquiry disclosed that Prince Galitzin was not in St. Petersburg but somewhere in a remote province in Russia where he could not be reached. A letter from Galitzin arrived in November, 1826, showing that he had received all of the quartets, acknowledging his indebtedness, and promising payment soon. But though Beethoven sent a final appeal (to Stieglitz) five days before he died, the money did not arrive in his lifetime. The Beethoven acolytes accused Galitzin of cheating the composer out of his rightful due. Holz wrote in the Conversation Book of "a Russian trick," and Schindler pontificated, "If you had followed my advice you would have sent at most *one* quartet and then stopped." Thayer, while not joining in such accusations, does not make clear what the cause of Galitzin's peculiar behavior was. Nor did editor Krehbiel, who followed the further history of the Galitzin affair, elucidate the case altogether. It remained for later research to do so. A recent article by Lev Ginsburg, a Russian scholar, published in the Beethoven Annual of 1959–60 (Beethoven House, Bonn, 1962), sheds light on what really happened.

It was this: Late in 1825 Galitzin suffered one tragedy after another. One of his children died, his wife fell ill, he was involved, if only indirectly, in a revolutionary movement, and in the summer of 1826 he was faced with bankruptcy. Persia declared war on Russia, and Galitzin, possibly to escape his troubles, joined the army. He went through hard months. After Beethoven's death, Galitzin's financial condition improved; then he *was* guilty of dilatoriness in quitting the debt. He disputed with Karl as to the exact sum he owed, and it was not until 1852 (twenty-six years later!) that the sum was paid in full. In the meantime, two books had appeared (one on Beethoven, the other a history of music) in which it was stated that Galitzin had "cheated Beethoven." Galitzin's son took up the defense of his father's name.

Eventually the Beethoven estate was paid. The total sum from Galitzin's coffers amounted to 279 ducats instead of the contractual 225,* the difference representing a voluntary gift "to the memory of Beethoven" by Galitzin's son. A confusion arose in transferring this money; the money may never have reached the Beethoven heirs.

The last Quartets are:
No. 12, E-flat Major, Op. 127. Completed 1824, dedicated to Galitzin.
No. 13, B-flat Major, Op. 130. Completed 1825, except that its original Finale was a Grand Fugue which Beethoven then decided to publish as a separate work. The new finale was composed late in 1826 and is the last music Beethoven wrote. Dedicated to Galitzin.
No. 14, C-sharp Minor, Op. 131. Completed 1826. Dedicated to Baron von Stutterheim.
No. 15, A Minor, Op. 132. Completed 1825, probably before No. 13 and 14, but numbered 15 because it was published later. Dedicated to Galitzin.
No. 16, F Major, Op. 135. Completed 1826. Dedicated to Wolfmayer.

A lively competition arose over who was going to perform the first of the last quartets (No. 12) for the first time. Beethoven, as was right and just, chose Schuppanzigh—not, however, before wavering for a while. He turned over the parts to the Schuppanzigh Quartet too late for them to rehearse adequately so difficult a work. Beethoven was worried about the reception of this new music.

---

* Fifty for the Mass, 50 each for the three Quartets, 25 for the Overture.

At a meeting in his house he made the four musicians sign a humorous little document:

> Most Excellent Fellows!
>
> Each of you is receiving herewith his part. And each of you undertakes to do his duty and, what is more, pledges himself on his word of honour to acquit himself as well as possible, to distinguish himself and to vie in excellence with the others.
>
> Each of you who is participating in the said undertaking must sign this paper.
>
> BEETHOVEN
> Schindler secretarius
>
> Schuppanzigh,
>> Weiss,
>> Linke,
> the accursed cello of the great master.
>> Holz,
> the last of all, but only when signing this paper.   (A-1356).

The performance took place on March 6, 1825, as part of the Schuppanzigh concert series. No doubt all four players acquitted themselves "as well as possible," but the quartet was a failure. Beethoven held Schuppanzigh responsible; the poor Falstaff defended himself as best he could, saying that there simply had not been enough time for the players to enter into the spirit of the music. The technical difficulties were nothing; the spirit of the work was difficult to grasp. He was hurt when Beethoven, who had not been at the performance, cited *Johann's* opinion as an authority in judging the performance. Schuppanzigh was willing to try again, but acquiesced when Beethoven said that he now wanted the quartet to be performed under the leadership of Joseph Böhm. Böhm was a Hungarian violinist who, during Schuppanzigh's absence in Russia, had achieved prominence by his own series of quartet concerts. He was undoubtedly a fine artist; later he became the teacher of Joseph Joachim.

Böhm left Thayer an account of his part in the performance:

> He sent for me first thing in the morning—In his usual curt way, he said to me, "You must play my quartet"—and the thing was settled.—Neither objections nor doubts could prevail; what Beethoven wanted had to take place, so I undertook the difficult task.—It was studied industriously and rehearsed frequently under Beethoven's own eyes: I said Beethoven's *eyes* intentionally, for the unhappy man was so deaf that he could no longer hear the heavenly sound of his compositions. And yet rehearsing in his presence was not easy. With close

attention his eyes followed the bows and therefore he was able to judge the smallest fluctuations in tempo or rhythm and correct them immediately. At the close of the last movement of this quartet there occurred a *meno vivace,* which seemed to me to weaken the general effect. At the rehearsal, therefore, I advised that the original tempo be maintained, which was done, to the betterment of the effect.

Beethoven, crouched in a corner, heard nothing, but watched with strained attention. After the last stroke of the bows he said, laconically, "Let it remain so," went to the desks and crossed out the *meno vivace* in the four parts. (TQ).

The quartet was again performed and was now received with stormy applause. Steiner, who heard it, was particularly enamored of it and at once offered to buy it for sixty ducats. Beethoven, curiously enough, remained loyal to Schott, though he did not fail to point out to the Mainz publisher that he could get a higher price for the work.* (Beethoven was at liberty to sell it outside of Russia.)

Beethoven derived great satisfaction from the success of the first quartet and set to work on No. 13. It is the last of the three written for Prince Galitzin, and it seems as if Beethoven was trying to explore the largest possible variety of which the form was capable; thus it grew to six movements. Some of these movements are quite short, the second, the *Presto,* lasting no more than a hundred seconds. Of the fifth movement, the *cavatina* (song), Holz reported that it cost the composer tears when he wrote it, and whenever Beethoven recalled it he paid it "the tribute of tears." The Finale was originally the Great Fugue. At the first performance, again by Schuppanzigh's Quartet (March 21, 1826), the Fugue proved an obstacle, though the quartet as a whole was a success and the *Presto* and the *German Dance* had to be repeated. There followed a lively debate, some of Beethoven's friends arguing that the difficulty of the Fugue would disappear after several hearings, while others felt that the movement was too long and too powerful and that it overshadowed the rest of the work. Artaria discussed the matter with Beethoven on practical grounds: he suggested that Beethoven write a new Finale and that the Fugue be published as an independent piece. Beethoven consented. He himself must have been persuaded of the artistic rightness of this move.

Holz is the authority, too, for the statement that when he told Beethoven that

---

* The publisher Schlesinger told him, "If you'll compose quartets, you'll earn more money than with your other great works. He who lives with wolves has to learn to howl. The world these days is a den of wolves." (Conversation Book, September, 1825).

this quartet was the greatest of the three, Beethoven replied, "Each in its way. Art demands of us that we shall not stand still. You will find a new manner of voice treatment [part writing] and thank God there is less lack of fancy than ever before."

Some time after, Beethoven declared the C-sharp Minor Quartet (No. 14) to be his greatest. When he delivered the work to Schott, he wrote on the manuscript, "Stolen together from various odds and ends." The sense of humor of the Schott brothers must have been somewhat deficient: they took fright at this, and Beethoven had to assure them that it was all a joke and the quartet was "really *brand new.*" "You said in your letter that it should be an original quartet. I felt rather hurt; so as a joke I wrote beside the address that it was a bit of patchwork." (A-1498).

No. 15 is, as indicated above, an earlier composition. Sketches for it date from 1824, and work on it was interrupted by Beethoven's illness in 1825. When he recovered, he recast most of the work and he rewrote the slow movement, "Song for Thanksgiving in the Lydian mode * offered to the Deity by a Convalescent." It was tried out in private first, once again by the Schuppan-zigh faithful four, and then presented to the public, again with success.

There remains his ultimate complete work No. 16, composed a few months before his death. He never witnessed a performance of it. It is smaller than the others, and while some analysts with the wisdom of hindsight have found in it "an instinctive premonition of death," such an interpretation seems completely unwarranted. The man was near death; the artist was not. Transcendental though the work appears to us, it bears all the marks of abundant life. The last movement is superscribed, "The Difficult Resolution. Must it be? It must be. It must be."

What must be? What is the purpose of these words? Nobody has guessed the meaning. They may simply have been one of those Beethovenian jokes which walk on two left feet.

The explanation Beethoven gave to Moritz Schlesinger explains nothing: "Here, my dear friend, is my last quartet. It will be the last; and indeed it has given me much trouble. For I could not bring myself to compose the last movement. But as your letters were reminding me of it, in the end I decided to compose it. And that is the reason why I have written the motto: *The decision taken with difficulty—Must it be?—It must be, it must be!——*"(A-1538a).

---

* A Greek mode characterized by its softness. Milton wrote: "Lap me in soft Lydian aires."

THE LAST YEARS

Elizabeth Barrett Browning wrote, a generation after Beethoven's death:

> What is art
> But life upon the larger scale, the higher,
> When, graduating up in a spiral line
> Of still expanding and ascending gyres,
> It pushes toward the intense significance
> Of all things, hungry for the Infinite?

The gyres along which Beethoven ascended led to the musical expression of the "intense significance of all things." Perhaps we may for once indulge in the idle speculation that this final ascension could only have been possible to an artist no longer able to hear the sounds of the finite world.

But he still tried to hear. He still hoped. With pity and astonishment one reads an entry in the Conversation Book, set down as late as August, 1826, some seven months before he died:

> Linke knows of a quite newly discovered remedy for deafness. It did wonders for one of his friends.
> Green nut-rinds crushed in lukewarm milk. A few drops into the ear.

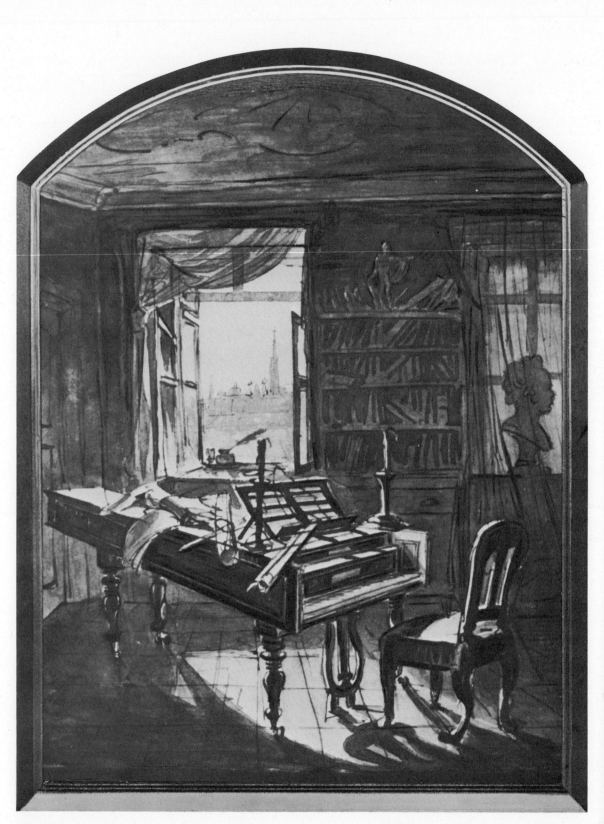

Beethoven's study in the Schwarzspanierhaus. Drawing by Hoechle, three days after Beethoven's death. Note disarray of manuscripts on piano, the much-used bookcase (Historical Museum, Vienna).

CHAPTER 23

THE LAST MONTHS

·•][1][•·

After Karl's attempted suicide, Beethoven decided that he should take Karl away from Vienna for a time so as to remove him from easy access by the police. It would be just as well if he were to be asked no further questions. Before he could join the army, time was needed to let his hair grow over the wound so that when he did become a soldier there would be no visible marks to shame him. Where could uncle and nephew find a retreat, a place where Beethoven would be left alone and Karl could quietly recuperate?

Johann had acquired an estate in Gneixendorf, in the Danube Valley, a few miles from Krems. The estate comprised nearly 400 acres, most of which were leased to tenants. Johann and Therese lived in a large and handsome house surrounded by a garden and isolated by a sheltering wall. Johann had invited Beethoven several times to visit him, and Beethoven, no doubt because he knew he would have to endure the company of his sister-in-law, had consistently refused. Beethoven wrote to Johann:

July 13, 1825

As for your desire that I should visit you, I already expressed my opinion long ago. I beg you never to mention the subject again, for in this you will find me, as always, adamant. (A-1398).

After Karl's "accident," Johann must have repeated the invitation. On August 28, 1826, Beethoven replied:

I am not coming —

Your brother??????!!!!
LUDWIG (A-1499).

A few weeks after that, Johann was in Vienna and again offered his place as a haven to Beethoven and Karl. This time Beethoven, who had declared himself "adamant," *accepted* the invitation. He wanted to get away from the scandal, the inquisitive looks, the whispered comments—he would go anywhere, away from Vienna.

Three days after Karl was discharged from the hospital, Beethoven and he started off and, passing the night at an inn on the road, reached Gneixendorf on September 29, in the afternoon.

They were a curious pair of guests, the older man ailing and sick at heart, the young man with his wound still raw, afraid of his uncle and yet secretly rejoicing that at last there seemed to be a prospect of obtaining what he wanted most, to free himself from Beethoven's Argus-eyed fretting and to live a life of his own. Late in the afternoon of their arrival, Johann showed Beethoven around his property. The walk through the fields and woods cheered him up. The next day he and Karl took a very long stroll.*

At first everything went well. Beethoven had been given a pleasant room with a view of the Danube Valley. Being in the country let him breathe more easily. He took an interest in the activities of the estate. One day Johann went to a nearby village to visit a doctor named Karrer, who was a friend of his. The doctor had been called away to a patient, but there were other guests at the home, and the doctor's wife, very pleased by the visit of the estate owner, whom she could show off to her friends, entertained Johann lavishly. She noticed a man, sitting by himself on a bench behind the stove, who took no part in the general conversation. Thinking that he was somebody's servant, she filled a little jug with wine and handed it to him, saying, "He too shall have a drink." When the doctor came home that night and heard an account of the incident, he exclaimed, "My dear wife, what have you done? The greatest composer of the century was in our house today and you treated him with such disrespect!"

Therese assigned one of her servants, a young man named Michael Krenn, to look after Beethoven. The cook, a woman, was supposed to make up his room. One day, while she did so, she saw Beethoven sitting at a table waving his arms violently, beating time with his feet, muttering and singing. This struck the woman as funny, and she burst into a loud guffaw. Beethoven saw her laughing

---

* Thayer has done such a superb job of research concerning Beethoven's visit and his subsequent return to Vienna that I can do no better than to follow him. The main facts of this chapter are taken from Thayer, though the interpretation of Beethoven's, Johann's, and Karl's motives is my own.

and chased her out of the room. Michael followed, but Beethoven drew him back, gave him a tip, told him not to be afraid, and said that from now on *he* was to make the bed and clean the room by himself. He was told to come to the room early in the morning, but usually he had to knock for a long time before Beethoven opened the door.

Beethoven got up at half past five, immediately sat down to work, and went through the business of singing, stamping, and shouting. But Michael got used to it. At half past seven Beethoven would go down for breakfast, after which he went into the fields and roamed for miles, shouting and waving his arms, stopping at times to write in a notebook. At half past twelve he would return home for dinner, after which he would rest until about three. Then he resumed his walks until shortly before sunset. Supper was at half past seven, and after eating he worked until about ten and then went to bed. Nobody was allowed to enter his room except Michael. On one or two occasions Michael found money lying on the floor, and when he carried this to its owner, Beethoven made him show him the exact spot where he had found the money. Then he gave him the coins. Sometimes Beethoven asked Michael what had been said about him at dinner or at supper, and Michael would obligingly write down the answers to his questions.

While Beethoven was walking, the peasants working in the fields used to observe his wild gestures. At first they thought he was mad and carefully kept out of his way. When they found out that he was the brother of the estate owner, they used to greet him politely. Lost in thought, he seldom noticed their greeting. One day a peasant who was driving a pair of young oxen scarcely broken to the yoke saw Beethoven's gesticulations; the peasant, being afraid for his oxen, called out, "Hold on a little." But Beethoven paid no attention. What the peasant feared would happen did happen: the oxen took fright, ran down the steep hill, and were calmed only with the utmost difficulty.

One day Therese sent Michael shopping and gave him a five-florin note. Michael lost the money. He went back to the house in consternation and told Therese. She promptly discharged him. That night, when Beethoven came to dinner, he asked where Michael was, and Therese told him what had happened. Beethoven grew terribly angry, gave her five florins—whether Therese accepted them we do not know—and demanded that Michael be recalled to his job. It was done. After that, Beethoven never had dinner or supper with the family but had the meals brought to his room, and Michael prepared breakfast for him.

Karl enjoyed himself doing nothing. He visited people in nearby villages, played billiards, sat in the wine cellars, and talked to the peasants. He did continue to practice the piano. "Karl plays very well," Therese notes in the Conversation Book.

Experience had taught Beethoven nothing; even now he often reproached Karl. There were scenes between uncle and nephew. Karl writes: "Yours is the right to command, and I must endure it all." The reproaches continued, Karl replying, "I beg you once and for all to leave me alone," or—in more outspoken words:

> But I beg of you once more not to torment me as you are doing; you might regret it, for I can endure much, but too much I cannot endure. You treated your brother in the same way today without cause. You must remember that other people are also human beings.

> Why do you make such a disturbance? Will you let me go out a bit today? I need recreation. I'll come again later.

> I only want to go to my room.

> I am not going out, I want only to be alone for a little while.

> Will you not let me go to my room? (TQ).

Beethoven, looking at Karl with the gun wound showing, must have been under continual nervous apprehension. Once, when Karl stayed away for a few hours, Beethoven's fears mounted. Where was Karl? Was he contemplating some new irresponsible deed? Therese tried to calm him:

> Do not be concerned. He will certainly come home by 1 o'clock. It seems that he has some of your rash blood. I have not found him angry. It is you that he loves, to the point of veneration. (TQ).

The visit was supposed to have been a short one. But the two stayed on. Beethoven avoided Therese and spoke little to Johann; he was totally immersed in the completion of the Quartet in F. Karl was anxious to stay until he could appear "without any visible sign left of what happened to me." I believe he may have wanted to stay also because he did not have enough strength to face life. Much as he hated the fetters with which his uncle bound him, he may yet have been afraid to break them and to walk alone. Being taken care of in Gneixendorf suited his weak nature. Schindler says that Karl slept with Therese. That may be another of Schindler's inventions,* but if it was true, it would furnish an additional reason for Karl's wanting to stay.

The weather turned colder, and still they stayed. Beethoven quarreled with Johann; he wanted Johann to make a will in favor of Karl, bypassing his wife. By that time Johann must have been more than anxious to get rid of brother and nephew, both. Near the end of November, when they had been there two months, Johann wrote his brother a letter (Thayer suggests that he wrote a letter to avoid a face-to-face argument) which reads in part:

> I cannot possibly remain silent concerning the future fate of Karl. He is abandoning all activity and, grown accustomed to this life, the *longer* he lives as at present, the more difficult it will be to bring him back to work. At his departure *Breuning* gave him a fortnight in which to recuperate, and now it is two months. —You see from Breuning's letter that it is his decided wish that Karl *shall hasten* to his calling; the longer he is here the more unfortunate will it be *for him,* for the harder it will be for him to get to work, and it may be that we shall suffer harm.
>
> It is an infinite pity that this talented young man so wastes his time; and on whom if not *us both* will the blame be laid? For he is still too young to direct his own course; by which reason it is your duty, if you do not wish to be reproached by yourself and others hereafter, to put him to work at his profession as soon as possible. Once he is occupied it will be easy to do much for him now and in the future; but under present conditions nothing can be done.

---

* Schindler indulges in particularly wild fabrications when he comes to relate the last days of Beethoven. He writes that Karl was playing billiards in a coffee house when Beethoven needed a doctor and Karl told the "marker" in the billiard room to fetch one. The marker, being himself unwell, could execute this commission only after a few days. Schindler implies that Karl did nothing about caring for his uncle. This story (told also by Gerhard Breuning) has been exposed as false. Schindler also says that during Beethoven's stay at Gneixendorf "there was an unbelievable lack of consideration for the master's physical needs as to both lodging and food." Donald W. MacArdle, the editor of the present edition of Schindler's book, *Beethoven as I Knew Him,* comments: "The painstaking inquiries conducted by Thayer in Gneixendorf in 1860, corroborated by the evidence that he educed from the Conversation Books, give so completely different a picture of the composer's life with his brother during these two months that no effort can succeed in reconciling the two accounts. Thayer's integrity and the care with which he conducted his researches and formed his judgments are beyond challenge. One can assume only that Schindler allowed his malice towards brother Johann to get the better of his obligations as a biographer."

> I see from his actions that he would like to remain with us, but if he did so it would be all over with his future, and therefore *this is impossible.* The longer we hesitate the more difficult will it be for him to go away; I therefore adjure you—make up your mind, do not permit yourself to be dissuaded by Karl. I think it ought to be *by next Monday.* (TQ).

A reasonable and forthright statement. Instead of acting upon it immediately, Beethoven let several more days elapse before he decided that he wished to return to Vienna with Karl. Having so decided, and probably having taken offense at Johann's letter, nothing would do but to leave *at once.* Johann seems to have told Beethoven that if he wanted to leave on Monday (the Monday mentioned in Johann's letter), the carriage must be got ready on Sunday. Whether Beethoven did not let Johann know that he needed the carriage, or whether the carriage was broken, or whether Therese had driven in it to Vienna is unclear. It is almost impossible to believe Schindler:

> In addition to all his other inconsiderateness, the "pseudo-brother" refused to lend them his closed carriage for their journey to nearby Krems, and they were forced to travel in an open calash.

No public conveyance was available, because none went from the tiny village to Vienna. So Karl and Beethoven set out in an open wagon—"a vehicle of the devil, a milk wagon," Beethoven described it—early in the morning of a cold December day.

Before following the two on this journey, we must ask—is it possible that Johann would let his brother depart in so perilous a conveyance, exposed to the winter winds? Even if the departure had been preceded by a quarrel, could Johann have been so heartless as to endanger Beethoven's health, which was already precarious? What were Johann's feelings toward his brother? Here we are treading on uncertain ground. Johann's motives are irreconcilable with one another. At one moment he seems genuinely eager to help his brother, is fond of him, concerned for him. Just the contrary in his next action. He did want Beethoven to live with him; that is proved by his repeated invitations, extended in spite of Beethoven's refusals.

In 1824 Johann wrote in the Conversation Book: "My wife has surrendered her marriage contract and entered into an obligation permitting me to drive her away without notice at the first new acquaintance which she makes" (TQ).

What a dreadful thing for a man to say about his wife to another man, were he ten times his brother! Beethoven must then have said to Johann, "Yes, *do* drive her away," for the next entry reads: "I cannot do that. I cannot know but that some misfortune might befall me." Karl, joining the "conversation"—he had to hear fine things not only about his mother but about his aunt—pleads:

> Your brother proposes that you spend the four months at his place. You would have four or five rooms, very beautiful, high and large. Everything is well arranged; you will find fowl, oxen, cows, hares etc. Moreover, as regards the wife, she is looked upon as a housekeeper only and will not disturb you.... You will scarcely see the woman. She looks after the housekeeping and works. (TQ).

If Therese's role had really been reduced to that of a slavey whom her husband could "drive away without notice," if she had surrendered the rights of a wife, would she not have cried out in protest then or later? Or would she not have left Johann for one of the lovers she was supposed to have had? The scraps of evidence we possess—admittedly few—show that Therese was quite content with her lot and, far from a menial, was regarded by Johann as a real wife and mistress of his household. One must suspect that Johann was tampering with the truth when he pictured his relationship with Therese as worse than it actually was.* Did he do this because he wanted to curry favor with Beethoven? Did he tell him what he wanted to hear, whether it was the truth or not? It could be that at the time Johann made the accusatory statements about Therese to Beethoven he had caught her with one of her lovers, was furious, and meant what he said, for the moment at least. Then a reconciliation could have taken place. Johann could have accepted Therese anew, because he was used to her or was attracted to her or wished to avoid the scandal of an open break.

All this is guesswork. Whatever happened, it seems strange that Johann should confide the details of his marital troubles to his brother, the same brother who years ago, when Johann was happy with Therese, had appeared in their midst to churn a calm pond.

If Johann lied about Therese's behavior, then he capitulated to his brother in

---

* Equally suspect is an entry in the Conversation Book of late 1823 because it was written by Schindler, with obvious malice: "We have reason to be satisfied with the *fratello;* only rarely does he permit his wife to go out and he says that at the first concrete proof of the suspicion he now harbors he'll have her arrested. He can't divorce her because according to our laws he would have to give her half his fortune, but more and more he is exercising his rights as head of the house."
This, on the face of it, is nonsense. A little later Karl writes: "Most of all he is happy that she is now getting old; no rooster crows after her and she has to behave herself."

a shameless way. If he told the truth, then he was imprudent indeed to invite Beethoven to share his home with Therese. Either way, the only kindly explanation one can give of Johann's action is to ascribe to him a fond wish to please Beethoven and come closer to him. One must add that this wish was mixed with a pinch of vanity and social ambition. Johann's later actions show that he basked luxuriously in the luster of Beethoven's fame. He wanted to be cock-of-the-walk of the Beethoven house. Thus it is possible—and not inconsistent with Johann's character—that he summoned submissiveness in handling Ludwig, even at the expense of his wife, who may have cuckolded him but whom he certainly did not drive away, neither then nor later. In sum, he either accepted a wife who slept around, or he lied about the matter to fall in with Ludwig's imaginings. Probably the truth is in the middle, as usual. Therese was probably neither as ruttish as Beethoven thought her to be, nor was she a model wife. In either case, there is something repellent about Ludwig's brother, at least in these later years. An ulcerous cell festered in all four Beethovens, Carl, Johann, Ludwig, and Karl—but in one it was encapsuled and allowed a man to grow who, in spite of asperity, was great of heart.

Another astonishing fact can be gleaned from the Conversation Book: Johann charged Beethoven for board and lodging. It is scarcely credible; in Johann's handwriting an entry reads: "I will charge nothing for the first fortnight; I would do more if I were not so hard pressed with taxes." Johann stands before us, then, as a man who may have held his brother in affection, but who loved him less because he loved money more.

·•⟨ 2 ⟩•·

Even if Johann did not refuse Beethoven the carriage, he let him go in the rickety vehicle. Off he went, on a journey which has been described by Dr. Andreas Wawruch, who attended Beethoven during his last illness: *

That December was raw, damp, cold and frosty. Beethoven's clothing anything but adapted to the unfriendly season of the year, and yet he was urged on by an eternal unrest and a gloomy foreboding of misfortune. He was compelled to spend a night in a village tavern where, besides wretched shelter, he found an unwarmed room without winter shutters. Towards midnight he experienced his first fever chill, a dry hacking cough accompanied by violent thirst and cutting pains in the sides. When seized with the fever he drank a few measures of

---

* From the *Medical Review of Ludwig van Beethoven's Last Period,* May 20, 1827.

ice-cold water and longed, helplessly, for the first rays of the morning light. Weak and ill, he permitted himself to be lifted into the *Leiterwagen* and arrived, at last, weak, exhausted, and without strength, in Vienna. (TQ).

Having arrived in Vienna, Beethoven went to bed: a doctor was needed at once. Braunhofer refused to come, giving as an excuse that the distance was too great. Nohl, in a study of the case, suggests that because of recent experience, Braunhofer had already diagnosed that Beethoven was in the last stages of a fatal illness, and he could not bear to be the doctor in charge of Beethoven's death. Dr. Staudenheim was sent for, promised to come, but failed to show up. It was then that Dr. Wawruch, a competent but not an eminent physician belonging to the staff of the General Hospital, was called in. Holz was the one who thought of him, having hurried to Beethoven's side immediately after receiving a message from Beethoven.

Dr. Wawruch came and introduced himself in the Conversation Book: "One who greatly reveres your name will do everything possible to give you speedy relief. Prof. Wawruch." Then he wrote out medical questions, designed to help him diagnose Beethoven's illness. What the questions were we do not know because at this point certain pages of the Conversation Book were removed, presumably by Schindler. Wawruch's diagnosis was "pneumonia." He gave Beethoven whatever treatment was at that time possible, and Beethoven's strength did the rest. He rallied and on the seventh day he could get out of bed. Dr. Wawruch was pleased. He had visited Beethoven daily from December 5 to the 14th, and one day twice. But when he came on the eighth day he was greatly alarmed. Beethoven looked very ill: he was yellow, the telltale sign of jaundice. During the preceding night he had suffered a frightful attack of vomiting. Dr. Wawruch's report (in part):

> Trembling and shivering he bent double because of the pains which raged in his liver and intestines, and his feet, thitherto moderately inflated, were tremendously swollen. From this time on dropsy developed, the segregation of urine became less, the liver showed plain indication of hard nodules, there was an increase of jaundice. Gentle entreaties from his friends quieted the threatening mental tempest, and the forgiving man forgot all the humiliation which had been put upon him. But the disease moved onward with gigantic strides. Already in the third week there came incidents of nocturnal suffocation; the enormous volume of collected water demanded speedy relief and I found myself compelled to advise tapping in order to guard against the danger of bursting. (TQ).

"Dropsy" was the name given to a condition (edema) which may have any number of causes but the effect of which is the inability of the body to eliminate fluids, causing the accumulation of fluids and swelling.*

Beethoven's friends gathered to comfort him; they braved the fearful mess and stench of the sickroom, in which the first operation was soon to be followed by further tappings. Beethoven must have refused to be transferred to a hospital: that is the only explanation why so seriously ill a man should have been operated on in his room, under unsanitary conditions which were deplorable even for those days. Karl, far from neglecting his uncle, occupied himself with the care of the patient, giving him his enemas, watching over his food. Johann came to Vienna to be in attendance. Schindler returned from "exile." Little Gerhard acted as a tireless messenger, bringing provisions from the Breuning kitchen. Holz, newly married, still came as often as he could. A ring of love surrounded the ill man.

When Dr. Wawruch made the decision that an operation was advisable, he called Dr. Staudenheim for consultation. The latter came and agreed. Dr. Johann Seibert, the principal surgeon at the hospital where Dr. Wawruch was active, was chosen to perform the operation. It took place on December 20. The operation consisted of making an incision in the belly, inserting a tube, and siphoning off the fluids. Johann, Karl, and Schindler were present. Beethoven showed grim humor. When Dr. Seibert inserted the tube and the fluid spurted out—an enormous quantity of it—he said, "Professor, you remind me of Moses striking the rock with his staff." Wawruch wrote in the Conversation Book:

> Thank God it is happily over! • If you feel ill you must tell me. • Did the incision give you any pain? ** • From today the sun will continue to ascend higher. • God save you! [This in English.] • Lukewarm almond milk. • Do you not now feel pain? • Continue to lie quietly on your side. • We shall soon measure off the water. • I hope that you will sleep more quietly tonight. • You bore yourself like a knight. (TQ).

---

* I owe this information to Dr. Max Ellenberg of New York. "Dropsy" is a term hardly used in modern medicine. The condition may be due to a malfunction of the kidney, or occur in certain forms of heart disease, or be caused by a cirrhosis of the liver, as in Beethoven's case. Modern medical opinion holds that cirrhosis of the liver is *not* necessarily caused by alcoholism, though its exact cause is as yet unknown. Improper diet over a long period of time may have something to do with it. Dropsy is treated today by a low salt diet, by dehydrating medicines, and by tapping—very much as in Beethoven's day, except that instead of inserting a tube, a thin hollow needle is inserted and the excess fluid is drained off slowly.

** It must have! There was no anesthesia.

He bore himself like a knight—he who had so often complained about his ailments. The wound became infected; the infection was with difficulty brought under control.

Karl had to be got ready for the army. A formal visit had to be made to Lieutenant Field Marshal Stutterheim, questionnaires filled out, uniforms bought, and so on. Stephan von Breuning was ill, but as soon as he recovered he helped Karl. The Conversation Book gives pathetic evidence of the fact that Beethoven thought of accompanying Karl on his journey to Moravia. Karl left on January 2, 1827. The very next day Beethoven wrote to Dr. Bach, stating that Karl was to be "my sole and universal heir."

About that time Beethoven's intestinal cavity again swelled up, the fluids accumulating once more, and Dr. Wawruch was pondering the necessity of a second operation. According to Gerhard, who seems to have been present every single day,* Beethoven now lost faith in his physician, and whenever Wawruch's name was pronounced, Beethoven turned his face to the wall and sighed, "Oh, that ass!" Gerhard tried to cheer him. Entries in the Conversation Book by Gerhard:

> How are you? ... • Has your belly become smaller? • You are supposed to perspire more.... • How was your enema? • You should take several. • Have you read Walter Scott already? • Would you perhaps like to read some Schiller? The world history by Schröckh? • Descriptions of summer travel? • I will bring them to you tomorrow.

The second operation took place on January 8. There were no complications. Beethoven was plagued by a continuous thirst.** Dr. Wawruch prescribed raspberry syrup and water flavored with wine. He was cautioned not to imbibe liquids freely.

From the Conversation Book:

> Brother Johann: The simpler one lives, the healthier. Breuning drinks hardly any wine all week, only water. Healthful. Newton, Voltaire, Rousseau lived very simply in their old age *** ... Newton ate only chicken with rice for many years.

---

* The boy was so eager that he flew into the room, panting. Entry in the Conversation Book: "I am not coughing, but I ran up the stairs."
** Facts about Beethoven's last sickness have been newly synthesized in an article by Dr. M. Piroth, "Beethoven's Last Sickness," which appeared in the *Beethoven Jahrbuch* 1959–60, published by the Beethoven House in 1962.
*** Johann mentioned these three men perhaps because he knew that Beethoven admired them.

Gerhard: I hear today that bedbugs are plaguing you and disturbing you, so that every moment you are awakened from your sleep. Sleep is good for you now; therefore I will bring you something to chase the bedbugs away.

Schindler: Somebody had the good idea of proposing that the water which was drawn from you be saved and be pumped in considerable quantities into other composers; they might get some inspiration from it.

When Beethoven began to doubt Wawruch's competency, his friends knew that he might trust only one physician, that famous man who years ago had been his friend and with whom he later quarreled, Dr. Johann Malfatti. Ten years had elapsed, and Schindler now tried to effect a reconciliation. According to an account published later (1842), he begged Malfatti to come to see Beethoven, who was sinking rapidly after the second operation. Malfatti answered:

> "Say to Beethoven that he, as a master of harmony, must know that I must also live in harmony with my colleagues." Beethoven wept bitter tears when I brought him this reply, which, hard as it was, I had to do, so that he might no longer look for help to that quarter. (TQ).

However, Malfatti relented. He came. Beethoven greeted him with open arms. Malfatti must at once have realized that the case was hopeless, that the man lying there was doomed. He concentrated his efforts on giving Beethoven relief and cheering him up. He threw out the medicines and prescribed frozen punch. The ice cooled and the alcohol acted as a kind of anesthetic.

Malfatti also thought that a sort of sweat bath would be stimulating. A bath of hot water in which hayseeds were steeped was prepared. The bath affected him badly: Beethoven's body, emptied of water by the third tapping which had just taken place, absorbed the moisture. He swelled visibly in the tub, and a fourth operation became necessary on February 27. It was the last.

After the fourth operation, Dr. Malfatti gave up whatever little hope he might still have harbored. He allowed Beethoven to have as much frozen punch as he wanted and to drink whatever wine he liked. The doctor even made him a present of wine. Beethoven was in a state of euphoria. He wrote Schindler a note; * he spoke of "truly a miracle," his previous very learned physicians

---

* Schindler happened to be away, probably because he was indisposed. He was most faithful in attending Beethoven during the last illness.

having both been beaten; "and it is only thanks to Malfatti's skill that my life is being saved."

The rumor of Beethoven's sickness spread through Vienna and abroad. Wegeler wrote one of those cheerful and untruthful letters one writes to a dying friend (February 1, 1827). He told Beethoven that he would send one of his patients to Karlsbad and go there with him as soon as Beethoven would find it convenient to journey to Karlsbad for his own convalescence. Then the two friends would meet again and could travel through Germany together and finally visit the home of their childhood. Eleonore sent a postscript saying that she looked forward to their reunion.

Zmeskall sent greetings. He himself was confined within his four walls. Beethoven answered—now the dilatory letter writer became punctual—and hoped that Zmeskall's pain would soon be alleviated.

After the fourth operation the fluid flowed across the floor to the middle of the room and the bedclothes were soaked. The filth was obviously bad enough to attract bedbugs. Yet people came to call, and the sickroom must have resembled the salon of a prince: Haslinger, Streicher, Bernard, Wolfmayer,* Schuppanzigh, Linke, Diabelli, Gleichenstein, and Moritz Lichnowsky are some of the names of which we have a record.

For some days Beethoven maintained his hope for recovery. He thought of his tenth symphony, to be composed for London. What troubled him most was finances, this time with good cause. Practically no money was coming in, not enough to meet his rent, as he wrote to Sir George Smart. Galitzin did not pay, and there were no further compositions to be sold. Probably the friends helped. He himself appealed to his friends in London, to Stumpff, Moscheles, Smart. A bitter irony lies in the fact that in the last year of Beethoven's life Vienna was passing through good times economically. There was peace in Austria, peace in most of Europe. A war was going on in Greece, where the Turks were to storm the Acropolis in another two months, and one in Persia, against which Russia had declared war the previous September. But these battles were far away. In Vienna the people were undisturbed. A book published anonymously in Leipzig in 1827, titled *Vienna as It Is: Portrait of its Character and Morals,* says that "Prosperity is extraordinarily great" and describes the smiling faces, the well-dressed women of the middle class, and even

---

* Entry in the Conversation Book by Gerhard: "Wolfmayer loves you very much. When he said good-bye, he said with tears in his eyes: 'The great man, oh! Oh!' "

the prosperous-looking factory workers, day laborers, and apprentices parading on a Sunday. There was no such prosperity surrounding Beethoven.

He asked the Schott brothers to send him some "very good old Rhine wine." The Schotts forwarded not only a case of twelve bottles of Rüdesheimer, but four bottles (two pure and two mixed with herbs to be used as medicine) by special post, so that Beethoven might receive them more quickly. Pasqualati sent over various refreshments: stewed fruit, a dish of cooked food, and champagne. Beethoven, with many thanks, also asked for stewed peaches, a cherry compote, and a light pudding.

Finally Beethoven realized that he was dying. Dr. Wawruch reported:

> No words of comfort could brace him up, and when I promised him alleviation of his sufferings with the coming of the vitalizing weather of spring he answered with a smile: "My day's work is finished. If there were a physician who could help me 'his name shall be called Wonderful!'" (TQ).

It is a reference to Handel's *Messiah,* where the phrase occurs.

Among his last visitors were Johann Nepomuk Hummel and Ferdinand Hiller. Hiller was barely sixteen years old and was a pupil of Hummel. He later became a famous conductor and friend of Chopin, Meyerbeer, Berlioz, and Liszt. He kept a diary, from which the following excerpts are taken: *

March 8th

> Through a spacious anteroom in which high cabinets were piled with thick, tied-up parcels of music we reached—how my heart beat!—Beethoven's living-room, and were not a little astonished to find the master sitting in apparent comfort at the window. He wore a long, gray sleeping robe, open at the time, and high boots reaching to his knees.** Emaciated by long and severe illness he seemed to me, when he arose, of tall stature; he was unshaved, his thick, half-gray hair fell in disorder over his temples. The expression of his features heightened when he caught sight of Hummel, and he seemed to be extraordinarily glad to meet him. The two men embraced each other most cordially. Hummel introduced me. Beethoven showed himself extremely kind and I was permitted to sit opposite him at the window. . . .

> Beethoven asked about Goethe's health with extraordinary solicitude and we were able to make the best of reports, since only a few days before the great poet had written in my

---

* They are published also in Thayer and in K. Benyouszky, *J. N. Hummel, Man and Artist,* 1934.
** Hüttenbrenner told Thayer that when Hummel came, Beethoven said, "I cannot receive him in bed," immediately got up, put on a lounging robe, and received him with due respect.

album. Concerning his own state, poor Beethoven complained much. "Here I have been lying for four months," he cried out, "one must at last lose patience...."

March 13th

We found his condition to be materially worse. He lay in bed, seemed to suffer great pains, and at intervals groaned deeply despite the fact that he spoke much and animatedly. Now he seemed to take it much to heart that he had not married. Already at our first visit he had joked about it with Hummel, whose wife he had known as a young and beautiful maiden. "You are a lucky man," he said to him now smilingly, "you have a wife who takes care of you, who is in love with you—but poor me!" and he sighed heavily. He also begged Hummel to bring his wife to see him, she not having been able to persuade herself to see in his present state the man whom she had known at the zenith of his powers. A short time before he had received a present of a picture of the house in which Haydn was born. He kept it close at hand and showed it to us. "It gave me a childish pleasure," he said, "the cradle of so great a man." Then he appealed to Hummel in behalf of Schindler, of whom so much was spoken afterwards. "He is a good man," he said, "who has taken a great deal of trouble on my account. He is to give a concert soon at which I promised my cooperation. But now nothing is likely to come of that. Now I should like to have you do me the favor of playing. We must always help poor artists." As a matter of course, Hummel consented. The concert took place—ten days after Beethoven's death—in the Josephstadt-Theater. Hummel improvised in an obviously exalted mood on the Allegretto of the A major Symphony; the public knew why he participated and the performance and its reception formed a truly inspiring incident.

March 20th

When we stood again at his bedside ... he was very weak and spoke only in faint and disconnected phrases. "I shall, no doubt, soon be going above," he whispered after our first greeting. Similar remarks occurred frequently. In the intervals, however, he spoke of projects and hopes which were destined not to be realized....

His eyes, which were still lively when we saw him last, dropped and closed today and it was difficult from time to time for him to raise himself. It was no longer possible to deceive one's self—the worst was to be feared.

March 23rd

He lay, weak and miserable, sighing deeply at intervals. Not a word fell from his lips; sweat stood upon his forehead. His handkerchief not being conveniently at hand, Hummel's wife took her fine cambric handkerchief and dried his face several times. Never shall I forget the grateful glance with which his broken eye looked upon her. (TQ).

One of the last recorded conversations (in a Conversation Book about three weeks before his death) shows that Beethoven still held fast to his life-long loves: the subject was Shakespeare.

Though Beethoven had made his testament, the question had been left open as to what was to happen to the inheritance should his nephew Karl die. A simple statement was prepared by Breuning and shown to Beethoven. In the statement it was stipulated that the estate was to go to Karl's "legitimate" heirs. Beethoven was not satisfied with this clause and substituted the words "natural or testamentary" for "legitimate." Breuning called his attention to the fact that this change might cause controversy, but Beethoven insisted on having the wording his way. Schindler wrote, "This was his last contradiction." The copying of the few words cost Beethoven a great effort. What he wrote in a shaking hand was this:

Mein Nefffe [1] Karl Soll allein Erbe sein, das Kapital meines Nachlalasses [2] soll jedoch Seinen natürlichen oder Testamentarischschen [3] Erben zufallen —

Wien am März 1827 —

luwig [4] van Beethoven

[1] Instead of "Neffe"
[2] Instead of "Nachlasses"
[3] Instead of "Testamentarischen"
[4] Instead of "Ludwig"

("My nephew Karl is to be sole heir. The principal of my estate is to pass to his natural or testamentary heirs.")

Schindler relates that on the day Beethoven signed the last document, he turned to him and Breuning and said, *"Plaudite, amici, comoedia finita est."* ("Applaud, friends, the play is finished.") It is a frequently used last line in ancient Roman comedy.

When his end was near, Beethoven's friends and Dr. Wawruch urged him to call a priest. Dr. Wawruch reported that he wrote the suggestion on a piece of paper, that Beethoven read the paper slowly and thoughtfully, and that there was peace in his countenance: "Cordially and solemnly he held out his hand to me and said, 'Have the priest called.'" Then he lay quietly, lost in a reverie.

About midday, on March 24, the special shipment of the four bottles of wine arrived from Mainz. Schindler showed them to Beethoven, who murmured, "Pity, pity, too late!" He spoke no more. A little of the wine was given to him in spoonfuls as long as he could still swallow it. Toward evening he lost consciousness.

The death struggle was a long one, the process of dissolution of the powerful body being a slow and fearful spectacle. He breathed stertorously, and according to Gerhard, "the rattle could be heard at a distance."

Anselm Hüttenbrenner, who lived in Graz and was a long-time admirer of Beethoven, hurried from Graz to Vienna with the hope of seeing him once more. He called about eight days before Beethoven's death, and again on March 26, at about three o'clock. According to his recollection, given in a letter to Thayer many years later (August 20, 1860), there were present Stephan von Breuning, Gerhard, Schindler (?), Therese Beethoven, and a Joseph Teltscher, a painter. Teltscher began to sketch the face of the dying man; this offended Breuning and he protested, whereupon the painter left the room. Then Breuning and Schindler went away to choose a plot for the grave. Hüttenbrenner says that Therese and he were the only ones present during the last moments of Beethoven's life. However, he was almost certainly mistaken: his acquaintance with Therese was of the slightest, and according to Gerhard and Stephan von Breuning, who had no recollection of ever having seen either of the sisters-in-law in Beethoven's rooms, the woman present was a housekeeper, Sali, whom Hüttenbrenner mistook for Therese.

The day was very cold; snow had fallen. Around five o'clock a sudden thunderstorm obscured the sky. It became very dark. Suddenly there was a great flash of lightning which illuminated the death chamber, accompanied by violent claps of thunder.* At the flash of lightning, Beethoven opened his eyes, raised his tightly clenched right hand, and fell back dead. It was about 5:15 P.M., March 26, 1827.

One thinks of the lines from *Julius Caesar:*

> When beggars die, there are no comets seen;
> The heavens themselves blaze forth the death of princes.

When Breuning and Schindler returned, having selected a spot in the cemetery of Währing, they were greeted with the words, "It is finished."

---

* This abnormality of Nature, a thunderstorm in March, has been verified by the Vienna Meteorological Bureau and other sources.

·∘[3]∘·

The friends now had to occupy themselves with the preparations for the funeral, the ordering of the death mask, the safeguarding of Beethoven's possessions, the notification of the nearest of kin, Johann * and Karl, the question of an autopsy, and so on.

Breuning, Schindler, Johann, and Holz met the day after Beethoven's death to bring some order into Beethoven's papers and to look for the seven bank shares which now belonged to Karl.** They searched everywhere but could not find them. Johann let fall a hint that he suspected somebody had done away with them. This infuriated Breuning and he left the house. But he returned in the afternoon and the search was continued. Holz then pulled out a protruding nail in a cabinet. A drawer fell out. In it were the shares, the letter to the Immortal Beloved, the portrait which Therese Brunsvik had given him, and possibly (the question has never been resolved with certainty) another portrait of an unidentified woman.

On the same day, March 27, an autopsy was performed by a Dr. Johann Wagner in the presence of Dr. Wawruch. Dr. Wagner was particularly interested in an examination of Beethoven's ears, and so the temporal bones were sawed out and carried away. A young painter, Joseph Dannhauser, received permission from Breuning to make a death mask. The cast has little value, because it was made after the autopsy, and Beethoven's face appears disfigured. (The original report of the postmortem was lost, but Seyfried made a copy of it, and all subsequent medical judgments have been based on this copy.)

Beethoven was dead—and some who had never grasped what he meant now realized with a shock the extent of their loss. Rosenbaum wrote in his diary:

> Monday the 26th. Freezing. Frequent snow flurries. North wind. It got dark after four o'clock—snowstorm and thunder and lightning. Nature in revolution. Three powerful claps followed. At the same hour funeral of Bab. Beck [not identified] ... Ludwig van Bethhowen's death, in the evening, toward six o'clock, of dropsy in his 56th year. He is no longer! His names lives in fame's illumination.

---

* Johann wrote a statement on his brother's last sickness and claimed that Beethoven died in his arms. This is almost certainly untrue, since it is at variance with the accounts of Hüttenbrenner, the two Breunings, and Schindler. (Discussed by Stephan Ley in *Truth, Doubt, and Error in the Knowledge of Beethoven's Life,* Wiesbaden, 1955.)

** There were eight originally. Beethoven had to sell one in 1823 to pay debts.

Wednesday, the 28th. Variable, not so cold. At Haslinger's [music] shop I spoke with Steiner about Bethhowen's testament. He left seven bank shares and 1000 fls from London as *Fidey-Commiss* for his ne'er-do-well nephew, the cadet. A violin quartet was his swan song. Haslinger gave me an invitation to the funeral.

Beethoven's body lay in state, and a continuous procession passed it. The room no longer resembled the familiar chamber. The papers had been locked up, the disorder had been cleaned up.

The funeral took place on March 29 in the afternoon. Cards of invitation had been printed and distributed to those who had known Beethoven and to people of importance. Numerous though the invitations were, the last ticket was gone by the day before. Uninvited citizens gathered around the Schwarzspanierhaus and in its spacious court until it could no longer hold the dense crowd. The gate had to be locked. The invited guests and pallbearers assembled around noon, pushing through the crowd. They wore rose bouquets with white silk scarves, placed on their left sleeves. Poems by Castelli and Seidl (another Viennese poet) had been printed and were given out as souvenirs. Before three o'clock the crowd increased and they threatened to storm the entrance. There were many children, since the schools of Vienna had been closed for the day. Breuning had procured military assistance from a nearby barracks in the Alserstrasse, but the soldiers were hardly able to control the crowd. The coffin was closed at three o'clock and carried down to the court. Nine priests blessed the dead man. A group of choristers from the Court Opera sang a chorale. The singers then lifted the coffin and began the procession toward the church, while a military band played the funeral march from Opus 26. This was the piano sonata (No. 12) which Beethoven had dedicated to Prince Lichnowsky. It was in Lichnowsky's Palace in the Alserstrasse that Beethoven had first found fame.

He was now being carried to the Alserstrasse, to the Trinity Church of the Minorites. Although the distance from the courtyard to the church was little more than one long city block, it took more than an hour and a half to traverse it. The number of people milling around the coffin was estimated by Schindler to be 20,000 (Thayer gives the same figure) and by the *Allgemeine Theater Zeitung* (April 12) to be 15,000.

The list of pallbearers, torchbearers, and the honorary escort, men who carried candles wrapped in crepe, reads like a roll call of memories, names familiar to us from Beethoven's life: Wranitzky, Hummel, Kreutzer, Seyfried, Gyrowetz, Weigl, Bernard, Böhm, Castelli, Czerny, Grillparzer, Haslinger,

Holz, Linke, Schubert, Streicher, Schuppanzigh, Steiner, Wolfmayer. Johann followed the coffin, as did Stephan and Gerhard Breuning.* Was Therese there? Was Johanna? We do not know. Karl returned from Moravia, but did not arrive in time for the funeral.

At the entrance of the church there was further confusion. The soldiers on duty did not want to admit anyone after the coffin had been carried inside, and the invited guests succeeded only with great difficulty in reaching their places. The crowd again became unruly; several people fainted and had to be taken to the nearby hospital.

The church was splendidly lighted. Wolfmayer at his own expense had ordered candles for all the altars, the wall brackets, and chandeliers. Nine priests chanted. People sobbed.

After the religious service, a ceremonial carriage transported the coffin to the Währing Cemetery. At the gate two priests were waiting, the coffin was carried into the cemetery church, and further musical selections were heard. Then the bearers again took up the bier, many hundreds still following the procession, with the neighborhood children being supervised by their teachers. At the cemetery gates the famous tragedian Heinrich Anschütz delivered a funeral oration written by Grillparzer.

The day, which had been mild, now came to an end. A gentle twilight began to fall. The body was lowered into the grave, and those standing nearest threw earth on the coffin. Then the torches were extinguished.

·◦[4]◦·

The memorial services were held shortly after, one on April 3 in the Church of St. Augustin, where Mozart's *Requiem* was given, and one on April 5 in the St. Charles Church, when Cherubini's *Requiem* was performed. The famous bass Lablache, a man as huge as he was generous, who had been a torchbearer at the funeral, sang in the Mozart *Requiem*. A long-standing ruling by Barbaja forbade any member of his opera troupe to sing outside the Court Opera, under penalty of a fine. Lablache sang—and not only paid the fine but paid the other singers as well. In the history of music he has the extraordinary distinction of having sung not only at Beethoven's memorial but, before that, at a service in Naples in 1809 commemorating Haydn's death, and later at Bellini's obsequies in 1835.

---

* Schindler's name does not appear. He was probably busy with the funeral arrangements.

Beethoven's household effects were sold in April to dealers in secondhand merchandise. His manuscripts, notes, notebooks, sketches, books, printed music —including the edition of Handel in forty volumes—were auctioned off in November of that year. There was lively bidding, entered into particularly by the publishers, such as Artaria, Haslinger, Steiner, and Diabelli. The prices which the items fetched were reported as "extraordinarily high"—for those days, of course! Much material was thus dispersed, some of it never to be found again. Griesinger wrote to Dresden:

VIENNA, April 7, 1827

The churches [for the memorial services] are stiflingly full. The funeral was a most solemn occasion. It is a great exaggeration to describe Beethoven as poor as a churchmouse. Seven or nine bank shares (five to six thousand thalers) were found in his legacy; he had a pension of 3000 thalers from Archduke Rudolph. And the publishers paid whatever he demanded for his compositions. He could have earned a lot more, but particularly in his younger days he was totally unconcerned with money, so much so that his brothers exercised a kind of guardianship over him....

VIENNA, April 25th

Beethoven always had a lot of admirers. Up to now our local papers have published [only] short accounts about him.* As yet I have not heard of anyone who plans to erect a detailed biographical monument to him. It is true that his history was simple and his real life lay in his works. About these a knowledgeable writer could say much, but perhaps that would interest only musicians. In the end one could sum him up in a few words: *His mighty genius drove him on!* To this natural gift he owed almost everything, not to his instruction by Haydn, of which he used to speak to me from time to time with a smile. Because he was completely deaf in the last years, I no longer met with him....

Beethoven's grave in the Währing Cemetery was surmounted by the simplest kind of pyramid bearing only one word, BEETHOVEN. The grave was neglected, and in 1863 the Society of the Friends of Music in Vienna had the body exhumed and reburied. In 1888 the remains of Beethoven and Schubert were buried side by side in the Central Cemetery in Vienna. As one drives in from the Vienna Airport, one passes the Central Cemetery. A taxi driver once said to me, "The *real* Vienna lies there."

---

* Wrong. The obituaries were long, including a finely written tribute by Rochlitz in the *Allgemeine Theater Zeitung* of April 14.

CHAPTER 24

"THE GENERAL
OF THE MUSICIANS"

A stranger arriving in Vienna on the day of Beethoven's funeral saw the city black with people swarming in the streets. "What is happening?" the stranger asked an old woman standing beside her stall in the market. "Don't you know?" the woman replied; "they are burying the General of the Musicians."

The story is probably apocryphal, as such stories usually are. If she did say it, the old woman gave Beethoven an appropriate memorial. In the Viennese dialect of the time *Herr General* carried no military connotation: it simply meant "headman," "chief," "leader."

To millions of men and women of every nationality Beethoven represents the headman of music. To many he is the very symbol and credo of music. Whether we consider music to be the food of love or ordained to "refresh the mind of man, after his studies or his usual pain," we turn to him when we reach for the highest. He is valued equally in Verona or Vienna, Boston or Burgos, Oslo or Osaka. (He is the most popular composer of modern Japan.) Our connection with him is as close—and occasionally as careless—as friend to good friend. Some of his work has become overfamiliar—the Fifth, the *Moonlight Sonata,* the *Eroica*—yet none of it has ceased to exercise its spell. That spell is compounded of our feeling that we will never understand his music to the full, will never plumb its depths—and yet that we do understand it very well.

It is the function of art to bring to us emotions, thoughts, states of mind and heart which are larger and more exalted and more intense than those we can produce ourselves, but which we can still recognize as possible within the compass of our imagination, still lying within our capacity for thinking and feeling. There is nothing unrecognizable in Beethoven's music, even at its most

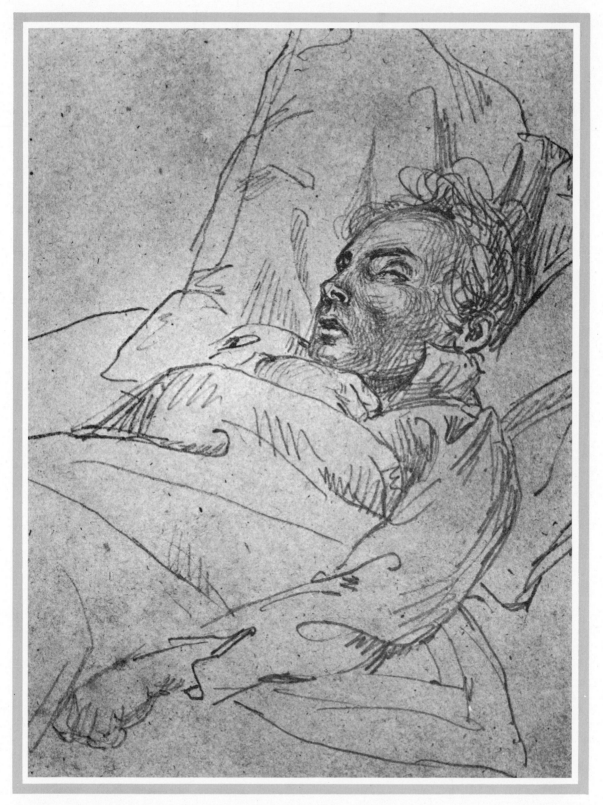

Beethoven in a coma, sketched by J. Teltscher. At one time this drawing was owned by Stefan Zweig.

difficult. Balzac wrote of the gift many people possess which he called "the genius of admiration, of comprehension, the sole faculty whereby an ordinary man becomes the brother of a great poet." * Beethoven makes it easy for any one of us to become the brother of a great poet.

The quality of greatness, but of a greatness which could be comprehended, signalized itself to the audiences in the Redoutensaal or the Theater-an-der-Wien. Yes, there were those who were puzzled by the rougher language of the music; they missed grace and lightness. There were many more, however, who found inspiration and illumination as they listened for the first or second time. Beethoven wanted it so: he wrote "for the public." If anybody had told him that he was to be understood only by a coterie, or that he was to be the Mohammed of a sect of believers, he would have laughed his loud, raucous laugh. He was far from despising success, and he assumed as a matter of course that the artist is to come to the public. He would have had no patience with the modern notion that the public must come to the artist. It would never have occurred to him not to strive for wide and intelligible communication.

We have noted that insofar as his music has any connection with concepts which can be described in words, much of it expresses struggle and suffering. As J. W. N. Sullivan wrote:

> ... to the vast majority of people suffering is still one of the fundamental characteristics of life, and it is their realization that an experience of suffering, pure and profound, enters as an integral part into Beethoven's greatest work, that helps to give that work its unique place in the minds and hearts of men.**

Yet Beethoven never succumbs. He is never defeated, his view never goes limp, the color of his work never turns wan or smudgy. Nor does it contain an iota of cynicism. He never denies life. He balances suffering with solace. The legacy he leaves us is an assertion of strength.

In this one characteristic the work parallels the man. Almost to the last he gave the impression of strength to those who knew him. They spoke of his "lion's voice," "broad shoulders," "jaws that can crack nuts," "square nose like a lion's," "strong frame," and "carriage proudly erect." He does not give this impression in his letters, where he so frequently complains, bemoaning his fate. It would be a mistake to judge him by these letters, many of which were written

---

* In *Le Cousin Pons*.
** In *Beethoven: His Spiritual Development*.

for the purpose of voicing a grievance or protesting an injury, real or fancied. In them and in his self-pitying journal notes he sometimes seems to ask, "What is the use of it all?" In his art he never asked that question. It is significant that this man, often maddeningly unjust, was so greatly beloved by his companions. Moritz Lichnowsky would submit himself to an insulting shock—"I despise what is false"—and come back. He and the others knew that the hail which pelted them would melt in a trice, to reveal the warm sun of Beethoven's soul and the strong, positive light of his mind.

The positive light of his artistic mind—a mind which had room for anger, pity, play, sweetness, exaltation, but not despair—helps to explain why his work is so firmly embedded in our artistic consciousness, why his value to us has remained constant. He is an immortal who is "true-fix'd."

Even immortality is subject to relativity. It can vary from a kind of museum respect to impassioned involvement. An artist long dead, his work long assayed, his fame secure, may yet be "alive" in the thought and feeling of one generation while to another his message is of but historic interest. The voice of the artist does not change; our willingness to listen changes. Immortal artists are statues. At certain times the statues, like the dancers in an old-fashioned ballet, come to life at the stroke of midnight. They walk into our room and the visitors are entertained by us with much joy. At other times and with other hosts, the reception is less friendly; then the guests return to their pedestals to await their turn.

The pertinence of artists is in a state of flux. There are periods of ebb and of flood. John Donne is relatively more important to us today than John Milton, Ibsen less than Shaw, Renoir more than Watteau, Proust more than Balzac. Tolstoy's *War and Peace* is an immortal novel, but during World War II we felt a special relationship to it. We particularly needed it then. Even Shakespeare's immortality has in the past been subject to relativity.

Is this merely a matter of fashion? Of course, fashion operates in art as it does in shoes. Fifteen years ago the French painters of the 18th century, David or Boucher or Ingres, were virtually dismissed from favor because of the public's exclusive occupation with the Impressionists. Now appreciation is slowly veering. Twenty-five years ago practically nobody except a Harvard professor of music cared much about Vivaldi or Telemann or most of the storehouse of Baroque music. Today musicians are running to the libraries to dig up the least-known works by these composers.

We have in the course of the last half-century changed our receptivity toward

Mozart and Bach. Mozart, who in sheer beauty brought music to its purest sheen, has become more mysterious. Bach, that magnificently intricate genius, has become less mysterious and more "human." In the early decades of our century, Wagner was taken seriously as a philosopher. Later we realized that many of his pronouncements rang with thumping hollowness and Teutonic arrogance, and this reaction affected our estimate of Wagner the musician. Today we are re-evaluating him as a composer.*

There are a few artists who seem impervious to relativity. They have never let go their hold on us, being as important to sons as to fathers. Rembrandt is such an artist, Sophocles another, Michelangelo another. Beethoven is such an artist. Berenson ** has pointed out that "Our reaction toward a creation of the past begins to be increasingly different from what it was in those who first enjoyed it. This feeling is continuously changing." Very true. *Not* true of Beethoven. Beethoven always impresses us as a contemporary.

It is remarkable how quickly he achieved appreciation in cities and countries other than Vienna and Austria. We have seen that London welcomed the Ninth in 1825. In the same year Ries performed it in the little town of Godesberg, though in a truncated version. It was enthusiastically received. Ries told Beethoven that had he written nothing else, it would have made him immortal. In Paris, Habeneck and the Conservatoire Orchestra thought it worth while to work at the symphony through three winters, in the 1830's, before they gave a performance of it. In Dresden, Richard Wagner conducted it in 1846 in a performance "such as had never before been heard in Dresden, or indeed in any other German town" (Carse). Mendelssohn conducted it in Leipzig about ten years previously.

In New York, however, the Ninth was a failure at its first performance, on March 21, 1846, given by the Philharmonic Society in Castle Garden. The failure was as much due to maladroit programming as to the obtuseness of the audience. The purpose of the concert was to raise funds for the erection of a concert hall suited to the purposes of the Philharmonic Society. It started with the Overture to *Der Freischütz,* followed by an aria sung by Miss Northall, followed by the Overture to *The Magic Flute,* followed by an aria sung by

---

* Robert W. Gutman writes in *Richard Wagner, the Man, His Mind and His Music:* "Though he has returned as a classic, entitled to a place among his peers, his art has yet to recover fully from the blight his theories have put upon it. Music alone cannot preach; it can reveal nothing about a composer's character; it is either good or bad. But Wagner's great music is often allied to texts and episodes typifying the despicable points of view elaborated in his essays."
** In *Aesthetics and History,* 1954.

Mme. Otto, followed by Mendelssohn's Piano Concerto—soloist, Mr. Timm—followed by Mme. Pico singing a Verdi aria which was encored. And after all that came Beethoven's Ninth. The correspondent for *The Evening Post* informed his readers that Beethoven had been "deaf as a post" when he composed the symphony and it was reasonable to suppose that he had never heard it. "If he had, being a man of a high order of musical taste and sensibility, it is probable he never would have been inclined to hear it the second time." Somebody on the staff of the newspaper became angry and put a footnote at the end of this report: "We do not agree in this criticism of our correspondent. The symphony was certainly too long for the late hour of the evening at which it was introduced, but it seemed to us one of the grandest musical compositions that we ever listened to. . . ."

The critic of the *Tribune* regretted that the audience, "though good-looking, well-behaved," was not numerous enough:

> We suppose the calculation was injudicious and that, in taking so large a hall, the tickets should have been put at a lower rate, for it is well known that the economies of our people lead them to prefer paying eight quarters of a dollar eight times for eight bad books, rather than two whole dollars, all at once, for one good book; and it follows they would prefer paying four half dollars for four ordinary entertainments, rather than two dollars for an excellent one. [As to the symphony]: . . . at this first time of hearing, it overshadowed like a tower the wandering mind; we could only feel it, and should need long acquaintance to disentangle our impression.

But it did not need "long acquaintance." Within a very few seasons Beethoven's symphonies, including the Ninth, had become the pillars of New York's Philharmonic Society.* They serve today a similar structural function for the recorded repertoire. Since its release in 1952 to the end of 1968, Toscanini's recording of the Ninth has sold 440,000 copies in the United States. It is estimated that complete editions of all nine symphonies are in 750,000 United States homes. World figures would show similar proportions.

---

* The society played Beethoven's Fifth at its inaugural concert on December 7, 1842. Ureli Corelli Hill was the conductor. This was not the first performance of the Fifth in the United States, but the date of the first performance is impossible to establish. Dr. Otto Kinkeldey in an article in *The Musical Quarterly,* April 1927, pointed out that it is difficult to fix musical "firsts" for the period of 1800 to 1850, a somewhat "dark age" in American musical history.

No one composing music after Beethoven could escape his influence. Who would want to? Only now is he being denied and only by those who believe that the musical elements to which we respond—melody, rhythm, harmony, counterpoint—must be thrown into the ashcan. "The symphonic form is dead, finished," said Leonard Bernstein on his fiftieth birthday. Perhaps the form is not dead—but men who can use it are not around. To composers who think that the confusion of the world must be expressed in musical structures unanchored in tonality and floating like jetsam on a muddy sea, or to those deglutinated halfwits who believe that art must dispense with form and structure, Beethoven's name may now be an unwelcome shibboleth. But to hundreds of composers who came after him, from Schubert to Richard Strauss and Mahler and Prokofiev and Stravinsky, he was a preceptor from whom one could depart —as he himself departed from the classicists of the Enlightenment—but to whom one owed a deep debt.

The works of his middle period acted seminally on the music of full-blown Romanticism. In creating these works, Beethoven himself was influenced by the early Romantic Movement, as it was expressed in poetry, the novel, painting, philosophy. Beethoven was the springtime; a rich summer followed, lasting till the end of the 19th century. Liszt, the arch-Romantic, wrote grandiloquently:

> To us musicians the work of Beethoven parallels the pillars of smoke and fire which led the Israelites through the desert, a pillar of smoke to lead us by day, and a pillar of fire to light the night, so that we may march ahead both day and night. His darkness and his light equally trace for us the road we must follow; both the one and the other are a perpetual commandment, an infallible revelation.*

The year Beethoven died, Schubert, who had only one more year to live, composed *Die Winterreise.* (The year before, he had sent a Petition to His Majesty Emperor Franz asking for the position of "Vice-Court Kapellmeister" and enumerating his qualifications. Franz ignored Schubert as he had ignored Beethoven.) When Beethoven died, Wagner and Verdi were fourteen years old, Mendelssohn was eighteen and had written the Overture to *A Midsummer Night's Dream,* Berlioz was twenty-four and was shortly to complete the *Sinfonie Fantastique,* Chopin and Schumann were seventeen. Brahms was born

---

* From a letter to Wilhelm von Lenz in 1852.

six years after Beethoven's death, Tchaikovsky thirteen. The music these men composed was no more an isolated expression of the artistic spirit than Beethoven's was in his time. Composers stimulated one another; artists in other fields stimulated them; and vice versa. It was one of the best of times for art; the interaction of Romanticism helped to make it so. In the last years of Beethoven's life the first part of Pushkin's *Eugen Onegin* appeared (1822), Manzoni's *I Promessi Sposi* (1825), and Heinrich Heine's *Buch der Lieder.* Shortly after came Balzac's *La Comédie Humaine,* Stendhal's *The Red and the Black,* Alfred Lord Tennyson's "The Lotus-Eaters," and Thomas Carlyle's *Sartor Resartus.* Constable, Turner, Delacroix—who in his Journal frequently mentions Beethoven—and Pierre Rousseau painted, and Daumier began his career. Tolstoy was born the year after Beethoven's death.

Beethoven's interests took in almost every form of music.* In the symphony, overture, piano concerto, piano sonata, quartet, and trio he achieved "the high Supremacie of Heav'n." There is only one opera—but it is *Fidelio.* There is only one violin concerto—but it is *the* Violin Concerto. We have hardly mentioned the violin sonatas: he wrote ten, of which eight are youthful works. He composed five sonatas for violoncello and piano. Only in song—he wrote some seventy songs **—is he less than master. E. T. A. Hoffman thought that "Beethoven, who is more of a Romantic than any composer who has existed" (he wrote this in 1813), is less successful with words because "words present sentiments already fixed and experienced."

The world he built for himself was wide, his life was narrow. He never went to London or saw Italy and he never once caught a glimpse of the ocean. But on the sea of thought he was an assured explorer. Criticism of his course did not swerve him. As he wrote ten months before he died: "I hold with Voltaire 'that a few midge-bites cannot hold up a lively horse in his canter.' " (A-1484, May 10, 1826). Yet he was far from stupidly conceited: "One should not want to be so like a god as not to have to correct something here and there in one's created works," he wrote to Breitkopf and Härtel in 1809. (A-199). Hope was in him even when he lay dying. He wrote to Wegeler: "I still hope to create a few great works and then like an old child to finish my earthly course somewhere among kind people." (A-1542).

---

* Quantitatively his output was small. Schubert, who died at thirty-one, composed more than 600 *Lieder,* 8 symphonies, 6 masses, 17 overtures, 15 string quartets, 22 piano sonatas, a number of operas, *Singspiele,* etc.

** Not counting the arrangements of folk songs he did for Thomson of Edinburgh.

Funeral orations are usually unctuous speeches; an interment is not an occasion for telling the truth. Yet Grillparzer, in the words he wrote to be read at Beethoven's grave, paid a truthful tribute to his friend:

> He fled the world because in the depths of his loving nature he found no means by which to deal with the world. If he withdrew from men it was because they did not want to climb up to him and he could not descend to them. He dwelt alone, because he found no second Self. Yet to the end his heart beat for all men. . . .
>
> Thus he was, thus he died, thus will he live till the end of time.*

---

* From the original text as furnished by Grillparzer to Stephan Breuning. When Grillparzer published the speech, he changed the wording slightly.

Appendixes

A Note on the Conversation Books

The Conversation Books are frequently quoted in this biography. A number of the quotations have not been published before, and the reader may like to know how this came about.

Beethoven's Conversation Books (*Konversationshefte*) are bound memorandum pads. After he became deaf, he kept a supply of them always handy, carrying one with him when he left the house. Offering a pencil to his conversational partner—sometimes more than one at the same time—he invited him or her to write his remarks or questions. Thus, these books were the chief means of communication used by Beethoven's relatives, friends, publishers, callers, etc. (Other means were writing on a slate, scribbling on loose sheets of paper, or merely gesturing.)

After Beethoven's death Stephan von Breuning inherited the Conversation Books. There were then 400 of them. When Anton Schindler began his project of writing the biography of the composer, Breuning gave him the books as a gift. After some years Schindler sold the collection to the Royal Prussian Library in Berlin. He told S. W. Dehn, then the custodian of the library, that Beethoven himself had expressed the wish "to have these original documents, as well as the major part of his mental legacy, deposited as a whole in a suitable public place, so that they could be available to everybody" (1846). But what arrived at the library was not 400 books: there were only 136 (or 137 if one counted two small, incomplete volumes separately). Where were the missing 264? Schindler told Dehn that he had destroyed some of them. He justified his action by stating that the missing books were of small importance and that they contained compromising political remarks. Two books particularly, said Schindler, contained uncouth and unbridled invectives against the Emperor, the Crown Prince, and other high members of the Imperial Family. He wrote to Dehn: "I am convinced that if Your Excellency had had knowledge of the contents of these writings, you yourself would at once have ordered them burned, so that the Royal Library could not be regarded as a repository of licentious assaults against persons in highest places." It is generally agreed that there is little truth in these statements and that Schindler willfully destroyed these books because they may have contained facts about or allusions to Beethoven's private life detrimental to the image of the "Master" he was trying to create; or, equally probably, that they contained unflattering remarks about Schindler himself.

The Conversation Books were examined by Thayer, who quotes from them in the *Life of Beethoven,* and by several other scholars. Walter Nohl, nephew of the Beethoven scholar Ludwig Nohl, began a critical edition in 1923, but got only as far as half a volume. His work was taken up by Georg Schünemann. Between 1941 and 1943 he published three volumes. His work too was left unfinished: he only got as far as the Conversation Book of July, 1823. A French scholar, Jacques-Gabriel Prod'homme, penetrated a little farther, publishing further excerpts at random (*Les Cahiers de Conversation de Beethoven,* Paris, 1946).

Amazing as it seems, no complete edition of these important documents— ranging from 1818, when Beethoven was forty-eight years old, to three weeks before his death in 1827—has ever been published.

In the division of Berlin, the Royal Prussian Library, now renamed the *Deutsche Staatsbibliothek,* was ceded to the Eastern Zone. Dr. Karl-Heinz Köhler, director of the Music Division of the library, with his staff of assistants, has now embarked on the task of editing and publishing all the Conversation Books. The work is progressing very slowly, since he is attempting to clear up every single name and reference mentioned. The first volume under his editorship, beginning where Schünemann left off, has been published in 1968. It will be many years before all the books will be ready for publication. Fortunately, Dr. Köhler is a young man and in good health.

The deciphering of the Conversation Books entails such problems as these: parts have almost completely faded and now need to be brought back to legibility; this is being accomplished through a special photographic process developed by the Institute for Criminology of the Humboldt University, Berlin. Some curious signs were discovered which, on being submitted to an expert, turned out to be stenographic marks. The system of shorthand used was one developed around 1823 and is now obsolete.

A NOTE ON THE CONVERSATION BOOKS

Through the courtesy of Dr. Köhler I have been able to gain access to all the Conversation Books in their unedited stage, and to quote from them at will. I journeyed to the library in East Berlin: there I sat and read extensively, using, at Dr. Köhler's suggestion, a handwritten transcript. When a point seemed doubtful, when for example I wasn't sure who was writing, I was able to consult the original books. Dr. Köhler unlocked a huge safe; I must say it was quite a thrill to hold in my hand these unretouched testimonies of life as it was lived in Beethoven's room. The force of his personality, which exercised so magic an effect on his friends, transpires through the lines.

Only rarely did Beethoven himself write in the books. He usually replied *viva voce*. He talked, and according to the testimony of his friends he talked vivaciously and forcefully until his final illness. Therefore what you read is dialogue in which the voice of the main actor is absent. Yet one can reconstruct some of Beethoven's remarks and imagine others. When he did write, it was usually when he was afraid of being overheard, or when he wanted to jot down a reminder, or, as happened once or twice, when he spoke to another deaf person.

The Conversation Books have had a curious recent history. In the early 1950's they were stolen by an expert thief, specializing in the purloining of valuable documents. This Arsene Lupin, who made away with papers instead of jewels, spirited the Conversation Books away from the Eastern Zone into West Germany and offered them for sale, posing as a German patriot who had "saved this important legacy from the Russians." He was eventually caught and tried. The court took a negative view of his supposedly patriotic gesture and restored the books to the library.

The subjects covered in the Conversation Books range from the lofty to the most trivial. Musical discussions occur rarely. Beethoven thought about music while he was alone and noted his thoughts in a shorthand of his own in his Sketchbooks. In the Conversation Books we have political, philosophic, and literary exchanges with his friends, many discussions of a business nature—prices to be asked for compositions, arrangements to be made for concerts, evaluations of one publisher against another—and no end of evidence of the minutiae of existence, proving that a great man was as subject to indigestion or as receptive to praise as all of us are. The Conversation Books show Beethoven at his most human. For example:

He is in a restaurant. Beethoven writes: "To charge 1 florin 20 for fried chicken is monstrous! He [the proprietor of the restaurant] makes a profit of at least 40 kr. . ." His companion: "I have had enough. I only empty the bottle so that the innkeeper won't make too great a profit. . ." B: "I do not think we will come here again very often."

Nephew Karl interviews a servant who says that in the past, when she was placed in more "fortunate circumstances," she spoke French like a native French girl and Italian like an Italian. Thereupon Karl spoke in French with her but discovered that "her French was no better than her German spelling." He finds her unsatisfactory.

Karl, probably chiming in with Beethoven's brother Johann: "Don't give your original manuscripts away. They can always be sold for a good sum. Some day they will be worth more. You can tell that by the autographs of famous men. For example, Schiller—his letters are worth a lot." (Beethoven did not heed this advice.)

A note by Beethoven: "Woolens and flannels are to be washed in water as hot as possible. As soon as they are clean, dip them quickly in cold water and then hang them up to dry. To remove snails and worms from vegetables and plants, soak them in salt water. That will kill them." One can only guess that Beethoven read these household hints somewhere and wanted to make a note of them; having at that moment no paper conveniently handy, he used a Conversation Book. Why should Beethoven have been interested in such domestic details? Was it to instruct a servant?

Karl: At the *Wilden Mann* [an inn] you are known among the waiters as Baron Beethoven. The other day a waiter said to his assistant, "Quick, a plate for Baron Beethoven."

A friend of Holz: All the churches of Vienna have their eye on you. You will simply *have* to become pious [*gottesfürchtig*].

Beethoven's deep interest in history and his reading tastes are documented here. I discuss the substance of his reading in Chapter IX, but the books reveal further literary notations. For example, a year before his death he talks with Holz about Aeschylus and calls him "the greatest" of the tragic poets, preferring his *Oresteia* to the plays of Sophocles and Euripides. Beethoven writes that he wants a six-volume work of *Explanatory Comments on Homer* and he makes a memorandum of the address of a dealer in rare books (*Antiquar*) who has Xenophon's *Speeches and Deeds of Socrates* in stock. The poet August Kanne borrows Beethoven's copy of Goethe's *Theory of Color.*

"Schiller and Goethe are two names worthy to stand side by side," * writes Dr. Bach, Beethoven's friend and lawyer, and urges him to turn Schiller's *Fiesco* into an opera. Beethoven inquires about an edition of Sir Walter Scott— in thirty volumes!

As to history—some of the works noted in the Conversation Books are: *History of the Hellenic Tribes and Cities* by Otfried Müller, *Universal History* by Johannes Müller (who was a follower of Rousseau) in twenty-four volumes, M. I. Wikosch's *Outline of Universal History,* which Karl mentions, and *History of the Germans* by J. H. Voss, the translator of Homer. Beethoven's interest in the cultures of the past extends to Egypt, and he makes a memorandum of a collection of Egyptian Antiquities in Vienna, with the times at which it can be seen and the price of admission. He plans to inspect a mummy from Thebes in the possession of a member of the Hungarian Legation. Kuffner, the poet, writes: ". . . the lightning rod, the invention of which is attributed to Franklin, was most certainly known to the Egyptians and the Etruscans." Beethoven's interest in painting is slight, but friend Peters does report that a Heinrich Seelig, innkeeper of the "City of Triest," owns "an exceptionally beautiful Leonardo da Vinci" (most probably a spurious one). Seelig himself calls on Beethoven, brings him a bottle of fine Hungarian wine, and asks "for the honor of a visit any morning."

Karl tells his uncle what he has learned in school. The housekeeper suggests menus. Beethoven scribbles financial calculations, trying to convert old currency into new or foreign currency into Austrian.

It is just this mixture of the transitory and the revelatory, of the requirements of a minute and the requirements of a mind, that makes these books moving and instructive to the biographer. Eventually their contents will become accessible to everybody. In the meantime, I am glad to have had the opportunity to turn their pages.

---

* The question of who was the greater was endlessly discussed by Beethoven's contemporaries. Goethe said to Eckermann: "Now the public is fighting as to who is greater, Schiller or I. They ought to be glad that there exist in the world a few fellows worth fighting about."

A
Beethoven
Calendar

The Calendar does not attempt to present a complete chronicle of musical, literary, scientific, or political events of the years 1770 to 1827. Its purpose is orientation: that is, to set Beethoven's biographical data within the frame of his world. I have given preference to such events and developments as may have impinged on Beethoven's life and thought. Dates of composition of his works are not always ascertainable. I have used the generally accepted dates wherever possible.

G.R.M.

DATE	BEETHOVEN'S LIFE AND PRINCIPAL WORKS	MUSICAL EVENTS	CULTURAL AND SCIENTIFIC EVENTS	PRINCIPAL POLITICAL EVENTS
1770	Beethoven born in Bonn; baptized December 17	Mozart: *Mitridate* Gluck: *Paris and Helena*	Gainsborough: *Blue Boy* Paul D'Holbach: *Système de la Nature* James Cook discovers Botany Bay	Dauphin of France marries Marie Antoinette, daughter of Maria Theresa of Austria
1771		Haydn: Quartets Op. 17	Klopstock: *Odes*	Russia conquers Crimea.
1772		Haydn: *Farewell Symphony*	James Bruce traces Blue Nile to White Nile. Daniel Rutherford discovers nitrogen. Lessing: *Emilia Galotti*	First partition of Poland Samuel Adams forms committee for concerted action against British
1773	Death of Beethoven's grandfather (61)	Charles Burney publishes *The Present State of Music in Germany, The Netherlands, and the United Provinces*	Herder: *Von Deutscher Art und Kunst* Klopstock: *Messiah* Goethe: *Götz von Berlichingen* Goldsmith: *She Stoops to Conquer*	Boston Tea Party
1774		Gluck: *Iphigenia in Aulis*	J. Priestley discovers oxygen Goethe: *Sorrows of Werther*	Accession of Louis XVI of France Philadelphia Congress of 13 American Colonies
1775	Beginning of music lessons, given by his father	Mozart: *La Finta Giardiniera, Il Re Pastore,* Six Clavier Sonatas and Four Violin Sonatas	James Watt perfects steam engine Critical edition of New Testament Sheridan: *The Rivals* Beaumarchais: *Barber of Seville* German translation of Shakespeare's plays begun (Eschenburg)	Beginning of War for American Independence
1776		Mozart: *Haffner Serenade*	Adam Smith: *An Inquiry into the Nature and Causes of the Wealth of Nations* Gibbon: *Decline and Fall of the Roman Empire* (Publication begun)	France: Financial reform under Turgot; he is dismissed by Louis XVI. American Declaration of Independence
1777	Beethoven enters school (probably)	Gluck: *Armide*		Burgoyne capitulates at Saratoga, New York
1778	Makes his first appearance at a small concert. Gets lessons from Van den Eeden	Feud between Gluck and Piccini in Paris	James Cook surveys Bering Strait. Death of Rousseau (66) and Voltaire (83)	France aids American Colonies. Washington defeats British

Date	Beethoven's Life and Principal Works	Musical Events	Cultural and Scientific Events	Principal Political Events
1779	Takes lessons from Pfeifer.	Mozart: Symphonies K. 318 and K. 319 Gluck: *Iphigenia in Tauris*	Lessing: *Nathan the Wise* Samuel Johnson: *Lives of the Poets* (Publication begun)	Spain declares war on Britain.
1780		Paisiello: *Barber of Seville* Erard constructs the first "modern" pianoforte.		Death of Maria Theresa of Austria Succession of Joseph II
1781	Becomes pupil of Neefe. Learns various instruments and assists as organist at the Minorite Church.	Mozart: Production of *Idomeneo*. Is dismissed from Salzburg post. Remains in Vienna. Haydn: *Russian* String Quartets Gewandhaus concerts founded in Leipzig.	Pestalozzi develops his educational theory. Herschel discovers the planet Uranus. Voss: German translation of Homer's *Odyssey* Kant: *Critique of Pure Reason* Rousseau: *Confessions* published.	Victory of Washington and Lafayette at Yorktown Joseph II abolishes serfdom in Austria.
1782	Assists Neefe as organist.	Mozart: *Haffner Symphony*, K. 385; *Abduction from the Seraglio*	Choderlos de Laclos: *Dangerous Acquaintances*	Joseph II: Patent of Tolerance U.S. War for Independence ends.
1783	First-published composition. Appointed cembalo player and accompanist on Neefe's recommendation.	Mozart: *Mass in C Minor*, K. 427	Herschel: *Motion of the Solar System in Space* Moses Mendelssohn: *Jerusalem* First paddle-wheel steamboat	Peace of Versailles: U.S.A.
1784	Death of Elector Maximilian Friedrich. Maximilian Franz is new Elector, reorganizes musical staff. Beethoven appointed organist with small salary.	Mozart: Piano Concertos, K. 449–51, 453, 459	Beaumarchais: *The Marriage of Figaro* Schiller: *Kabale und Liebe*	Pitt's India Act

A BEETHOVEN CALENDAR

Date	Beethoven's Life and Principal Works	Musical Events	Cultural and Scientific Events	Principal Political Events
1785	Works in Bonn as Court musician.	Haydn: *The Seven Last Words of Christ* Mozart: Several string quartets, piano concertos.		James Madison's Religious Freedom Act
1786		Mozart: *Marriage of Figaro* Haydn: Six *Paris* Symphonies	Robert Burns: *Poems*	Death of Frederick the Great (74), succeeded by Frederick William II.
1787	First visit to Vienna and meeting with Mozart. Death of his mother.	Mozart: *Don Giovanni, Prague Symphony, Eine Kleine Nachtmusik* Death of Gluck (73)	John Wesley: *Sermons* Schiller: *Don Carlos* Goethe: *Iphigenie auf Tauris*	Catherine the Great forms alliance with Joseph II in Crimea. U.S. Constitution signed.
1788	Friendship with Breunings and Waldstein.	Haydn: *Oxford Symphony* Mozart: Last 3 symphonies	Goethe: *Egmont*	Joseph II declares war on Turkey.
1789	Becomes head of family.	Mozart: *Così fan Tutte*	Saint-Pierre: *Paul et Virginie* Volta pioneers study of electricity.	George Washington President Fall of the Bastille French Revolution begins.
1790	Haydn visits Bonn, meets Beethoven. Cantata on death of Joseph II. Cantata on accession of Leopold II.	Haydn goes to London at invitation of Salomon.	Kant: *Critique of Judgment* Bruce: *Travels to discover the Source of the Nile, 1768–73*	Leopold II succeeds Joseph II as Holy Roman Emperor. French Revolution continues with Robespierre and Danton in power. Death of Benjamin Franklin (84)
1791	Plays in Mergentheim.	Mozart: *Magic Flute, Requiem* Death of Mozart (35) Haydn: *Surprise Symphony* Begins composition of *Salomon* Symphonies	Thomas Paine: *The Rights of Man, Part I* Boswell: *Life of Johnson* Birth of Grillparzer	

A BEETHOVEN CALENDAR

Date	Beethoven's Life and Principal Works	Musical Events	Cultural and Scientific Events	Principal Political Events
1792	Second journey to Vienna. Takes lessons from Haydn. Death of his father.	Rossini born. Cimarosa: *Il Matrimonio Segreto*		Franz II succeeds Leopold II. France declares war on Austria—First Coalition. French Royal Family imprisoned.
1793	Studies with various teachers. Acquaintance with Prince Lichnowsky and Baron van Swieten.	Haydn: Symphony No. 99	Eli Whitney invents the cotton gin. The Louvre becomes French National Art Gallery.	Louis XVI executed. Reign of Terror begins. Murder of Marat. Marie Antoinette executed. French war. Napoleon captures Toulon.
1794	In Vienna, becomes famous as piano virtuoso.	Haydn: Second visit to London, for which he composes Symphonies Nos. 102 to 104.		Execution of Danton and Desmoulins; later of Robespierre and Saint-Just. French troops reach Rhine, occupy Bonn; invade Spain, Holland.
1795	First public appearance in concert; plays B-flat Piano Concerto. Publishes 3 Piano Trios Op. 1 and 3, Piano Sonatas Op. 2. *Adelaide.*	Haydn: *Drum Roll Symphony*	Goethe: *Wilhelm Meister* Goya paints "Duchess of Alba."	Austrians beaten in Upper Italy. Armistice with France Bread riots in Paris French Directory Third Partition of Poland
1796	Tours to Prague, Berlin. Produces chamber music.		Jenner: Smallpox vaccination	Napoleon renews war with Austria. Freedom of press in France
1797		Schubert born. Donizetti born. Cherubini: *Médée*	Schelling: *Philosophy of Nature* Coleridge: *Kubla Khan* Hölderlin: *Hyperion*	Further Napoleonic victories against Austria. Cisalpine and Ligurian Republics established. Peace of Campo Formio
1798	Meets Bernadotte and through him Kreutzer. Piano Sonatas Op. 10.	Haydn: *The Creation*		French occupy Rome; Napoleon conquers Egypt. Switzerland invaded. Nelson's victory over French fleet
1799	Three Violin Sonatas Op. 12. *Pathétique* Sonata Op. 13. Two Piano Sonatas Op. 14. Signs of deafness.	First public performance of *The Creation*, Vienna	Herder attacks Kant's philosophy (*Metakritik*). Schiller: *Wallenstein*	Renewal of war, Austria vs. France William Pitt's Second Coalition Napoleon ends the Directory and becomes First Consul.

A BEETHOVEN CALENDAR

Date	Beethoven's Life and Principal Works	Musical Events	Cultural and Scientific Events	Principal Political Events
1800	First public performance of Septet at concert of his works at which First Symphony is played. Composes 6 Quartets, Piano Concerto No. 3, *Creatures of Prometheus.* Takes Czerny as pupil.	Cherubini: *Les Deux Journées*	Thomas Young: *Outlines and Experiments Respecting Sound and Light* Novalis: *To the Night* Jean Paul: *Titan* Wordsworth publishes manifesto of Romanticism. Schiller: *Maria Stuart*	Napoleon defeats Austrians. Battle of Marengo. Thomas Jefferson elected President.
1801	Signs of deafness and confession of it to two friends. Relationship with Countess Guicciardi. *Moonlight Sonata.* F. Ries becomes pupil. Stephan Breuning arrives in Vienna.	Haydn: *The Seasons* Bellini born.	Elgin Marbles brought to London. Schiller: *The Maid of Orléans*	Peace of Lunéville between Austria and France Assassination of Czar Paul I, succeeded by Alexander I.
1802	Heiligenstadt Testament. Second Symphony begun.			Napoleon becomes First Consul for life; annexes Piedmont, Parma, Piacenza.
1803	First performance of Second Symphony. *Kreutzer Sonata.* First performance of Piano Concerto No. 3. Oratorio: *Christus am Ölberge.* Begins composition of *Eroica Symphony.*	Berlioz born.	Robert Fulton: Steamboat	U.S. purchases Louisiana from France. Britain renews war with France.
1804	*Eroica* completed. Piano Sonatas Op. 53 and 54 composed.		*Code Napoléon.* Thomas Brown: *Inquiry into the Relation of Cause and Effect* Schiller: *William Tell*	Napoleon proclaimed Emperor.
1805	First public performance of *Eroica. Fidelio* premiere a failure.	Paganini begins to tour Europe.		Napoleon crowned King of Italy. Nelson defeats Franco-Spanish fleet at Trafalgar. Napoleon occupies Vienna, defeats combined Russo-Austrian forces at Austerlitz; forces Austria to sign Peace of Pressburg.
1806	*Fidelio* revived briefly. First performance of Violin Concerto by Clement. *Appassionata Sonata* composed. Fourth Symphony begun. Three *Rasoumovsky Quartets* composed.		Ernst Arndt: *Spirit of the Age;* promotes German nationalism.	Death of William Pitt. Holy Roman Empire ends. Franz II becomes Franz I, Emperor of Austria. Russian-French War. Napoleon victorious at Jena; occupies Berlin and Warsaw.

Date	Beethoven's Life and Principal Works	Musical Events	Cultural and Scientific Events	Principal Political Events
1807	End of relationship with Josephine Brunsvik. Concerts at Lobkowitz Palace. First performances of Fourth Symphony, *Coriolan Overture,* and Piano Concerto No. 4. Mass in C Major, for Esterházy.	Spontini: *La Vestale*	Alexander von Humboldt publishes report of his voyages in the New World. Charles Bell: *System of Comparative Surgery* Wordsworth: "Ode: Intimations of Immortality"	Treaty of Tilsit virtually isolates Britain from her allies.
1808	Composes Fifth and Sixth Symphonies. Is offered appointment to Court of Jerome Bonaparte, King of Westphalia. Friendship with Countess Erdödy	Haydn appears at festival performance of *The Creation.*	Fichte: *Addresses to the German Nation* Canova: "Pauline as Venus" (sculpture) Goethe: *Faust, Part I*	Napoleon abolishes the Inquisition in Spain and Italy. Reoccupies Rome and invades Spain. Austria creates military guard (*Landwehr*).
1809	Archduke Rudolph, Lobkowitz, and Kinsky sign contract of lifetime support of Beethoven. *Emperor Concerto.* Piano Sonata Op. 78, *Les Adieux Sonata* Op. 81a. String Quartet Op. 69.	Death of Haydn (77) Birth of Mendelssohn Spontini: *Cortez*	Goethe: *Elective Affinities*	New War, Napoleon against Austria. Second occupation of Vienna. Austrians victors at Aspern, defeated at Wagram. Metternich becomes Chief Minister. Napoleon is divorced from Josephine. Peace of Schönbrunn, Austria ceding large portions of territory.
1810	Friendship with Bettina Brentano. *Egmont·*music, Quartet Op. 95	Chopin born. Schumann born. Rossini's first opera performed: *La Cambiale di Matrimonio*	Goya: "Disasters of War" (engravings)	Napoleon marries Marie Louise of Austria.
1811	Publishes *Les Adieux Sonata.* Works on Seventh and Eighth Symphonies. Pension reduced because of Lobkowitz financial difficulties and money devaluation. Visits Teplitz.	Liszt born.	Fouqué: *Undine* Goethe: *Dichtung und Wahrheit*	Austrian "Finanz Patent" devalues currency. George III insane; Prince of Wales becomes Prince Regent.
1812	In Teplitz. Letter to Immortal Beloved (?). Meets Goethe. Trouble with brother Johann.		Byron: *Childe Harold's Pilgrimage* J. and W. Grimm: *Fairy Tales*	U.S. declares war on Britain. Napoleon's Russian campaign. Burning of Moscow. Retreat and destruction of *Grande Armée.* Wellington victorious in Spain.

DATE	BEETHOVEN'S LIFE AND PRINCIPAL WORKS	MUSICAL EVENTS	CULTURAL AND SCIENTIFIC EVENTS	PRINCIPAL POLITICAL EVENTS
1813	Friendship with Mälzel. *Wellington's Victory*. First performance of it and Seventh Symphony great success.	Verdi born. Wagner born. Schubert composes First Symphony. Rossini: *Tancredi*. Philharmonic Society of London founded.	Jane Austen: *Pride and Prejudice* Chamisso: *Peter Schlemihl*	Wellington routs French at Vitoria. Metternich-Napoleon interview. Austria declares war against France. "Battle of the Nations" at Leipzig.
1814	*Fidelio*, 3rd version, performed with great success. Concert for Vienna Congress. Zenith of his fame. Quarrel with Mälzel.		First steam locomotive runs. Goya: "May 2" and "May 3" (paintings)	Austria and Allies enter Paris. Napoleon abdicates to Elba. Louis XVIII King. End of war, Britain—U.S. Congress of Vienna opens.
1815	Annuity payments reinstated, including Lobkowitz's. Death of brother Carl. Becomes nephew Karl's guardian.	Schubert: *Der Erlkönig*		Napoleon enters Paris. "The Hundred Days." Congress of Vienna ends. Wellington and Blücher defeat Napoleon at Waterloo. Napoleon banished to St. Helena.
1816	Karl's mother makes court appeal against Beethoven's guardianship. Negotiations with London Philharmonic Society.	Schubert: Fifth Symphony Rossini: *Barber of Seville*	Froebel founds educational center in Thuringia. Coleridge: *Kubla Khan* (published)	
1817	Involved in troubles with nephew. His health suffers.	Rossini: *La Cenerentola* and *Gazza Ladra* Clementi: *Gradus ad Parnassum*	E. T. A. Hoffmann: *Night Pieces* Hegel: *Encyclopedia of Philosophy* Byron: *Manfred*	Monroe fifth U.S. President.
1818	Lawsuit. Karl at home with him. *Missa Solemnis* begun.		Keats: *Endymion* Mary Shelley: *Frankenstein*	Bernadotte becomes King of Norway and Sweden.
1819	Finishes *Hammerklavier* Sonata Op. 106. Works on *Missa* and Ninth Symphony. Lower court finds against him re Karl. He appeals. Deafness. "Conversation Books."	Schubert: *Trout Quintet*	First steamship (the *Savannah*) crosses Atlantic. Schopenhauer: *The World as Will and Idea* Goethe: *West-Östlicher Divan*	Kotzebue's assassination gives Metternich opportunity to formulate oppressive "Karlsbad Decrees."

Date	Beethoven's Life and Principal Works	Musical Events	Cultural and Scientific Events	Principal Political Events
1820	Court of Appeals decides in his favor. Composes *Piano Sonata Op. 109.*		Ampere formulates laws of electrodynamics. *Venus de Milo* discovered. Scott: *Ivanhoe* Pushkin: *Russlan and Ludmilla*	Death of George III. Succeeded by Prince Regent as George IV.
1821	Various attacks of illness. Composes last two piano sonatas, Op. 110 and 111.	Weber: *Der Freischütz*	Heine: *Poems* De Quincey: *Confessions of an English Opium Eater*	Greek war against Turks begun. Mexico, Peru, Guatemala, Panama, Colombia, etc., break away from Spain. Simon Bolivar defeats Spanish Army. Death of Napoleon
1822	Negotiates for *Missa Solemnis* with various publishers. Works on Ninth Symphony. *Fidelio* again performed after lapse of three years. Prince Galitzin orders three string quartets. Visit of Rossini.	Schubert: "Unfinished" Symphony César Franck born.	Pushkin: *Eugen Onegin*	Greek Independence
1823	*Missa Solemnis* finished. Solicits subscriptions for *Missa.* Further negotiations with England. Works with Grillparzer on opera projects. *Diabelli Variations* Op. 120. Ninth Symphony finished.	Schubert: *Rosamunde, Schöne Müllerin* song cycle Weber: *Euryanthe* Rossini: *Semiramide*		Monroe Doctrine
1824	First performance of *Missa Solemnis* in St. Petersburg. After long hesitation, first performance of Ninth Symphony with parts from the *Missa* in Vienna. Great ovation. Renewed invitation from London Philarmonic Society to come to London. Finishes String Quartet Op. 127.	Smetana born. Bruckner born.	Ranke: *History of the Roman and Teutonic People* Byron (36) dies at Missolonghi, aiding Greeks against Turkey.	
1825	Beethoven moves to his final lodgings, the Schwarzspanierhaus. Is severely ill. Composes String Quartets Op. 132 and 130. Relationship with nephew deteriorates. Visit of George Smart from England.	Johann Strauss, Jr. born. Cherubini: *Coronation Mass* Chopin publishes Op. 1, Rondo in C Minor.	Faraday isolates benzene. Manzoni: *I Promessi Sposi* Pushkin: *Boris Godunov*	Austrian Emperor reconvenes Hungarian Diet after 13 years because of widespread discontent in Hungary. Czar Alexander I succeeded by Nicholas I. Decembrist rising in Russian Army is crushed.

Date	Beethoven's Life and Principal Works	Musical Events	Cultural and Scientific Events	Principal Political Events
1826	String Quartet Op. 131 composed. Public performance of Quartet Op. 130. Karl attempts suicide. Beethoven takes Karl to brother Johann's estate at Gneixendorf. There he composes Quartet Op. 135 and a new finale for Op. 130 to replace the "Great Fugue." Returns to Vienna, develops pneumonia and dropsy. Is tapped for dropsy for the first time at the end of the year.	Weber: *Oberon* Weber (39) dies. Bellini: *Il Pirata* Schubert: *Death and the Maiden Quartet* Mendelssohn: *Overture to a Midsummer Night's Dream*		Russo-Persian Wars begin.
1827	Beethoven undergoes three further operations. London Philharmonic Society sends 100 pounds. Dies March 26.			

Who's Who
of People Important
in Beethoven's Life

Albrechtsberger, Johann Georg (1736–1809). Famous teacher of theory who taught Beethoven in Vienna.

Amenda, Karl (1771–1836). For a short time intimate friend of Beethoven, to whom we owe a vivid account. Returned to his native Courland in 1799; they never saw each other again.

Artaria, Family of. Prominent Viennese music publishers. Beethoven quarreled with Carlo(1747–1808), but his nephew Domenico (1775–1842) was returned to favor in the composer's last years.

Bach, Johann Baptist (1779–1847). Viennese lawyer. Beethoven consulted him about many difficulties, particularly in the matter of his nephew.

BEETHOVEN, Family of:

> Ludwig (1712–1773). Grandfather. Rose to important post of Kapellmeister in Bonn. Married Maria Josepha Poll.
>
> Johann (1740?–1792). Father. Married Maria Magdalena Keverich. Musician and voice teacher. Died while Beethoven was in Vienna.
>
> Maria Magdalena (1746–1787). Mother. Died when Beethoven was not yet seventeen.
>
> Caspar Anton Carl (1774–1815). Brother. Married Johanna Reiss. Bank employee.
>
> Nikolaus Johann (1776–1848). Brother. Apothecary. Became wealthy. Married Therese Obermayer.
>
> Karl (1806–1858). Son of Carl. Beethoven's nephew.

Bernadotte, Jean Baptiste (1764–1844). French Ambassador to Vienna, 1797. May have suggested idea of *Eroica* to Beethoven. Through him Beethoven met Kreutzer. Became Charles XIV of Norway and Sweden.

Bernard, Josef Karl (1775–1850). Journalist and editor. Intimate friend. Frequently mentioned in Conversation Books.

Bertolini, Dr. Andreas (Dates uncertain). Beethoven's physician between 1806 and 1816. Suppressed medical evidence about Beethoven.

Bigot, Marie (1786–1820). Superb pianist and piano teacher. Played *Appassionata Sonata* from manuscript, 1806.

Blöchinger, Joseph (1788–1855). Director of boarding school for boys. Karl attended his school for four years.

Böhm, Joseph (1795–1876). Hungarian violinist. Played last chamber works of Beethoven.

Browne-Camus, Count Johann Georg (1767–1827). Officer in the Russian army. One of Beethoven's early patrons.

Breitkopf and Härtel. Prominent Leipzig music publishers. Published complete edition of Beethoven's works.

Brentano, Elisabeth (Bettina) (1785–1859). Charming and unreliable friend of Goethe, Beethoven, etc. Married the poet Achim von Arnim, 1811.

Brentano, Franz (1765–1844). Half brother of Bettina. Merchant and senator in Frankfurt. Friend of Beethoven. Married Antonie von Birkenstock. Daughter Maximiliane born 1802.

BREUNING, Family of:

> Hélène (1750–1838). Widowed in 1777. In Bonn, earliest motherly friend of Beethoven and of paramount influence in his education.

> *Children:*

> Eleonore (1771–1841). Beethoven was probably seriously in love with her. Married Dr. Franz Gerhard Wegeler, settled in Koblenz, 1807.

> Christoph (1773–1841). Studied law, settled in Bonn.

> Stephan (1774–1827). Studied law. Was appointed to I. R. War Council in Vienna, 1801. One of Beethoven's closest friends, a friendship which lasted a lifetime.

> Lorenz (Lenz) (1777–1798). Studied medicine in Vienna. Died at the age of twenty-one.

> Gerhard (1813–1892). Son of Stephan. Devoted young admirer of Beethoven. Nicknamed "Trouser-button" by Beethoven. Published book of reminiscences in 1874.

Bridgetower, George Polgreen (1779–1860). Mulatto violinist. Played *Kreutzer Sonata* in Vienna.

PEOPLE IMPORTANT IN BEETHOVEN'S LIFE

BRUNSVIK, Family of:

Hungarian aristocratic family, whose lives were intertwined with that of Beethoven. Important are two of the sisters:

Therese (1775–1861). Often chosen as the Immortal Beloved. Never married. Kept diary and wrote reminiscences.

Josephine (1779–1821), with whom Beethoven was undoubtedly in love. Married 1799 to Count Joseph Deym, in 1810 to Baron Christoph von Stackelberg. Contender for Immortal Beloved until thirteen letters from Beethoven to her were discovered.

Franz (1777–1849). Only son. Intimate friend.

Castelli, Ignaz Franz (1781–1862). Viennese playwright, poet, and humorist. Friend of Beethoven who wrote several anecdotes about him.

Clement, Franz (1780–1842). Violinist. The first to play the Violin Concerto. He became director of the orchestra of the Theater-an-der-Wien.

Clementi, Muzio (1752–1832). Composer and pianist. Also successful music publisher.

Collin, Heinrich Joseph (1771–1811). Playwright. Wrote the tragedy *Coriolan*.

Cramer, Johann Baptist (1771–1858). Pianist, pupil of Clementi, and publisher. Instrumental in promoting Beethoven's cause in England.

Czerny, Carl (1791–1857). Great piano virtuoso and piano teacher in Vienna. First pupil, then devoted friend of Beethoven.

Deym, Count Joseph (1750 or 1752–1804), alias Müller. Known through his Gallery of Statues, which Beethoven visited. First husband of Josephine Brunsvik.

Diabelli, Anton (1781–1858). Composer and publisher in Vienna. Associated with Steiner. Known for the *Diabelli Variations*. Beethoven was one of the composers who contributed a set of variations on a theme by him.

Eeden, Heinrich van den (1710?–1782). Court organist in Bonn and probably Beethoven's first formal teacher.

Erdödy, Countess Anna Maria (1779–1837). Intimate friend, great admirer. Probably was instrumental in bringing about the agreement to pay Beethoven an annuity. Mystery and scandal beclouded her life.

Ertmann, Dorothea von (1781–1849). His "Dorothea Caecilia." Their relationship lasted over many years, even after she and her husband, General Stephan von Ertmann, moved to Milan. Immortal Beloved? One of the greatest interpreters of his music.

660

Esterházy, Prince Nikolaus II (1765–1833). Commissioned Beethoven to write a Mass for the name day of his wife, Marie Hermengild, née Liechtenstein. Later not on friendly terms with Beethoven.

Fischer, Gottfried and Cäcilia (brother and sister, dates uncertain). Bonn family. Gottfried wrote copious recollections of Beethoven.

Fischhoff, Joseph (1804–1857). Professor of music at Vienna University. Copied biographical material, the so-called Fischhoff Manuscript.

Franz I (1768–1835). Emperor of Austria, under whose reign Beethoven lived. Napoleon's adversary. Franz paid almost no attention to Beethoven.

Fries, Moritz, Count von (1777–1826). Important patron of Beethoven. Wealthy banker. Later lost his money.

Galitzin, Prince Nikolas Boris (1795–1866). Russian admirer who commissioned three of the last Quartets and was active in promoting the premiere of the *Missa Solemnis* in St. Petersburg.

Gallenberg, Wenzel Robert, Count von (1783–1839). Ballet composer and director. Husband of Giulietta Guicciardi.

Gelinek, Joseph Abbé (1758–1825). Piano virtuoso. Prolific composer for the piano, nicknamed "The Variation-smith." Was defeated by Beethoven in a piano-playing contest.

Gerhardi, Christine (dates unknown). Singer and admirer of Beethoven. Married Dr. Joseph von Frank, a Viennese physician; he, too, was a friend of Beethoven.

Gleichenstein, Ignaz, Baron von (1778–1828). One of Beethoven's best and kindest friends. Married Anna Malfatti, sister of Therese.

Goethe, Johann Wolfgang von (1749–1832). The great German poet. Met Beethoven in 1812.

Griesinger, Georg August von (1769–1845). Saxon chargé d'affaires in Vienna and friend of Haydn. His letters give valuable information about musical conditions in Vienna.

Grillparzer, Franz von (1791–1872). Austrian national poet. Friend of Beethoven. Planned an opera with him. Wrote the funeral oration.

Guicciardi, Giulietta, Countess (1784–1856). Related to the Brunsvik family. Beethoven was undoubtedly in love with her and dedicated the *Moonlight Sonata* to her. Married Count Gallenberg. Schindler's choice for the Immortal Beloved.

Gyrowetz, Adalbert (1763–1850). Prolific and popular composer. Not much love was lost between him and Beethoven.

Haslinger, Tobias (1787–1842). Music publisher, associated with Steiner.

Haydn, Franz Joseph (1732–1809). Austria's most celebrated composer when Beethoven was a youth. Made Beethoven's acquaintance in Bonn. Later gave Beethoven some lessons.

Hiller, Ferdinand (1811–1885). Composer. Pupil of Hummel. One of the last to visit Beethoven.

Hoffmann, Ernst Theodor Amadeus (1776–1822). German author and composer, one of the leading figures of the Romantic movement. Early appreciated Beethoven's music.

Holz, Karl (1798–1858). One of the last close friends of Beethoven. Schindler was jealous of him.

Hotschevar, Jakob (dates unknown). Relative of Johanna Beethoven; aided her in her fight for the guardianship of her son.

Hummel, Johann Nepomuk (1778–1837). Pupil of Mozart. Pianist and composer. One of the last to see Beethoven alive.

Hüttenbrenner, Anselm (1794–1868). Composer, pupil of Salieri and friend of Schubert. Was present when Beethoven died.

Kanka, Johann (1772–1865). Lawyer in Prague. Helpful in settling Beethoven's annuity with the Kinsky estate.

Kinsky, Prince Ferdinand Johann Nepomuk (1781–1812). One of the three donors of Beethoven's annuity. Beethoven called on him in Prague in 1812.

Koch (dates uncertain). A widow who ran an inn in Bonn, the Zehrgarten, which the town's intellectuals frequented. Her daughter Barbara (Babette) was a beauty and friend of Eleonore Breuning.

Kotzebue, August (1761–1819). Playwright whom Beethoven admired. Assassinated by a German student.

Kraft (Krafft), Anton (1752–1820). Cellist who played Beethoven's Triple Concerto.

Kreutzer, Rodolphe (1766–1831). Violinist, attached to Bernadotte, to whom Beethoven dedicated the Sonata Op. 47.

Krumpholz, Wenzel (1750–1817). Violinist. One of Beethoven's oldest friends. He introduced Czerny to Beethoven.

Kuffner, Christoph (1777–1846). Poet and critic; occasionally part of the Beethoven circle.

LICHNOWSKY, Family of:

> Karl, Prince (1756–1814). Beethoven's earliest patron in Vienna, whose house welcomed the composer. Intimate and generous friend, in spite of disagreements.

Maria Christiane (1765–1841). One of "The Three Graces" of Vienna. Wife of Karl. Her mother, Countess Wilhelmine Thun, was a patron of Mozart and became one of Beethoven's protective friends.

Moritz, Count (1771–1837). Younger brother of Karl. Highly talented musician and lifelong friend.

Linke, Joseph (1783–1837). Cellist. Attached to the household of Marie Erdödy.

Liszt, Franz (1811–1886). Unique piano virtuoso. Composer. Beethoven met him when Liszt was thirteen years old.

Lobkowitz, Prince Josef Franz Max (1772–1816). One of the leading personalities of the Austro-Hungarian Empire. Active in political and artistic life. His great palace—still standing—was a center of activity. Early patron and indefatigable admirer of Beethoven. One of the three guarantors of the subsidy. In financial difficulties in 1811. Beethoven dedicated many works to him, including the *Eroica*.

Malfatti, Dr. Johann (1776–1858). Famous physician. Founder of the Vienna Medical Society. Treated Beethoven until Beethoven quarreled with him. Returned to him in the last days.

Malfatti, Therese (1792–1851). Niece of the doctor. Beethoven was in love with her.

Mälzel, Johann Nepomuk (1772–1838). Inventor of the metronome and other mechanical devices. Suggested idea of *Battle Symphony*. Beethoven treated him badly.

Maximilian Franz (1756–1801). Habsburg Archduke. Youngest of the four sons of Empress Maria Theresa. Became Elector of Cologne in 1784. Employed and favored the young Beethoven.

Maximilian Friedrich, Count von Königsegg-Aulendorf (1708–1784). Elector of Cologne, under whose reign Beethoven was born.

Milder-Hauptmann, Anna Pauline (1785–1838). Famous singer. Admired by Haydn. Beethoven's first Leonore.

Moscheles, Ignaz (1794–1870). Pianist, composer, and conductor. Friend of Beethoven, for whom he did the piano reduction of *Fidelio*. Conducted first performance of *Missa Solemnis* in London. Helped Beethoven shortly before the composer's death.

Neate, Charles (1784–1877). British composer, pianist. One of the members of the London Philharmonic Society. A staunch friend in England.

Neefe, Christian Gottlob (1748–1798). Composer. Active in Bonn. Beethoven's first important teacher.

Oliva, Franz (?–1848). Bank employee. Friend of Beethoven and the Varnhagens.

PEOPLE IMPORTANT IN BEETHOVEN'S LIFE

Pachler-Koschak, Marie Leopoldine (1794–1855). Pianist. Enthusiastic admirer. Sometimes called Beethoven's autumnal love.

Paer, Ferdinando (1771–1839). Italian composer. For a time active in Vienna. Friend of Beethoven.

Palffy de Erdöd, Count Ferdinand (1774–1840). Hungarian nobleman. Director of the Court Theaters. Not particularly amicable toward Beethoven.

Pasqualati, Johann, Freiherr von Osterberg (1777–1830). Good friend. Owned house on the Mölkerbastei, where Beethoven lived.

Pfeifer (Pfeiffer), Tobias Friedrich (dates unknown). Musician and actor. Supposed to have taught the child Beethoven for a short time.

Potter, Philip Cipriani (1792–1871). British composer and pianist. We are indebted to him for interesting recollections of his visits to Beethoven.

Punto, Johann Wenzel (1748–1803). Horn player. Real name Stich. First to play Sonata Op. 17.

Rasoumovsky, Andrei Kirillovich, Count then Prince (1752–1836). Russian Ambassador in Vienna, patron and friend of Beethoven, for whom Beethoven composed the *Rasoumovsky Quartets*. One of the richest men in Europe, his palace one of Vienna's showplaces. Brilliant personality and active during Congress of Vienna.

Reicha, Anton (1770–1836). Composer and friend.

Reichardt, Johann Friedrich (1752–1814). Composer, writer, and music critic. Traveled extensively and wrote the famous "Confidential Letters Written on a Journey to Vienna" (1808), which contains much information about Beethoven.

Rellstab, Heinrich (1799–1860). German writer. Wrote memoirs with extensive recollections of his visits to Beethoven in 1825.

RIES, Family of:

> Franz Anton (1755–1846). Concertmaster and later music director of the Bonn Electoral Orchestra. Taught Beethoven the rudiments of violin playing.

> Ferdinand (1784–1838). Pianist and composer. First pupil, then friend of Beethoven. Played extremely important part in Beethoven's life, particularly in London. Co-author with Wegeler of source book, *Biographische Notizen über Ludwig van Beethoven.*

Rio (del Rio), Cajetan Giannatasio (dates unknown). Owner of the boarding school to which Beethoven sent his nephew. He and his two daughters, Fanny (born 1790) and Nanni (born 1792), became close friends of Beethoven. Fanny wrote recollections of the composer.

Rochlitz, Johann Friedrich (1769–1842). Leading music critic and editor of the *Allgemeine Musikalische Zeitung*. Recognized Beethoven's worth to a remarkable degree. Beethoven wanted him to write his biography but Rochlitz declined.

Röckel, Josef August (1783–1870). Singer. Florestan in the revival of *Fidelio*. Gave Thayer a full account of what happened in Prince Lichnowsky's house when changes in the opera were suggested.

Rudolph, Habsburg Archduke of Austria (1788–1832). Son of Leopold II. Gifted pupil of Beethoven, to whom the composer dedicated many works and for whom he wrote the *Missa Solemnis*. Became Archbishop of Olmütz.

Russell, John (1792–1863 or 1878). Wrote *A Tour in Germany* (published in Edinburgh, 1824). Reported a visit to Beethoven which probably took place in the autumn, 1821. May have been the famous Liberal leader, Lord Russell.

Salieri, Antonio (1750–1825). Operatic composer. Active in Vienna. Gave Beethoven some lessons in the early Vienna days.

Salomon, Johann Peter (1745–1815). Conductor, violinist, concert manager, great friend of Haydn. Born in Bonn, he died in London. Promoted Beethoven's popularity with London Philharmonic Society.

Schenk, Johann (1753–1836). Composer and teacher of theory. Gave Beethoven lessons in the early Vienna days.

Schikaneder, Emanuel Johann (1748–1812). Actor, poet, composer, theater manager, librettist (of Mozart's *The Magic Flute*), and one of Vienna's most eccentric personalities. Recognized Beethoven's importance and engaged him for the Theater-an-der-Wien.

Schindler, Anton Felix (1795–1864). Friend and devoted "slave" of Beethoven during the last twelve years of the composer's life. Wrote biography, published in 1840; third edition, thoroughly revised, 1860. Unreliable reporter.

Schlesinger. Family of publishers. Moritz Adolf (1798–1871) founded the French firm and knew Beethoven well. Adolf Martin (1769–1839), his father, ran the Berlin branch.

Schlösser, Louis (1800–1886). German musician and composer. Left several valuable recollections of Beethoven.

Schmidt, Dr. Johann Adam (1759–1808). One of Beethoven's eminent physicians.

Schott, Family of. Music-publishing company founded by Bernhard Schott in Mainz in 1773. Published a number of Beethoven's works, including the *Missa Solemnis*.

Schröder-Devrient, Wilhelmina (1804–1860). Great singer whom Wagner heard in the role of Leonore.

Schuppanzigh, Ignaz (1776–1830). Eminent violinist specializing in chamber music.

One of Beethoven's most intimate and devoted friends, a relationship which began in 1804 and lasted until Beethoven's death. Beethoven nicknamed him Falstaff, because he was fat.

Sebald, Amalie (1787–1846). Singer, with whom Beethoven may have been in love. One of the candidates for the Immortal Beloved.

Seyfried, Ignaz Xaver, Ritter von (1776–1841). Composer and Kapellmeister for Schikaneder and at the Theater-an-der-Wien. Wrote personal recollections of the composer.

Simrock, Nikolaus (1752–1833). Bonn musician. Horn player in the Electoral orchestra. Later became music publisher, publishing several of Beethoven's works. His son, Peter Joseph (1792–1868), carried on the business.

Smart, Sir George Thomas (1776–1867). British conductor. Active in promoting music in England. Gave many Beethoven performances and visited the composer in Vienna.

Smetana, Dr. Karl von (1774–1827). Surgeon. Operated on Nephew Karl. Beethoven summoned him when Karl attempted suicide.

Sonnleithner, Joseph (1766–1835). Austrian diplomat. Active in theatrical life. Largely responsible for the formation of Viennese Society of the Friends of Music. Librettist of the original version of *Fidelio*.

Sontag, Henrietta (1806–1854). Singer. Soloist in first performance of the Ninth Symphony.

Spohr, Ludwig (Louis) (1784–1859). Composer. Author of a well-known autobiography which contains recollections of Beethoven.

Staudenheim, Dr. Jakob, Ritter von (1764–1830). Personal physician to Emperor Franz. One of Beethoven's physicians.

Steiner, Sigmund Anton (1773–1838). Music publisher in Vienna. Nicknamed "Lieutenant-General" by Beethoven.

Streicher, Johann Andreas (1761–1833) and wife Nanette (1769–1833). Piano manufacturer. Friend of Schiller. Nanette, daughter of the piano manufacturer Johann Andreas Stein of Augsburg, whom Beethoven visited as a youth, was an accomplished pianist and was helpful to Beethoven in his domestic affairs. Numerous notes and letters attest to this.

Stumpff, Johann Andreas (1769–1846). Musician and harp manufacturer. Lived in London.

Stutterheim, Joseph, Freiherr von (1764–1831). High-ranking Austrian officer. Obtained military post for nephew Karl, and Beethoven dedicated Quartet Op. 131 to him in gratitude.

PEOPLE IMPORTANT IN BEETHOVEN'S LIFE

Swieten, Baron Gottfried van (1733–1803). Diplomat and panjandrum of music in Vienna. One of Beethoven's early patrons.

Thayer, Alexander Wheelock (1817–1897). American consul in Trieste. Beethoven's great biographer, a work he never finished, despite his lifelong dedication to it.

Thomson, George (1757–1851). Scottish publisher. Gave Beethoven several commissions, most of which the composer refused. There was much haggling about fees. Beethoven did arrange a collection of Scottish, Welsh, and Irish songs for him.

Tiedge, Christoph August (1752–1841). Poet. Lived for many years with Elisabeth von der Recke. Beethoven met him in Teplitz in 1811.

Tomaschek, Johann Wenzel (1774–1850). Composer. Wrote recollections of Beethoven in his autobiography.

Treitschke, Georg Friedrich (1776–1842). Playwright, actor, and stage director. Helpful to Beethoven. Recast libretto of *Fidelio* for revival in 1814.

Trémont, Baron Louis-Philippe-Joseph Girod de Vienney (1779–1852). One of Napoleon's diplomats. Musical enthusiast. Wrote important account of his visit to Beethoven.

Umlauf, Michael (1781–1842). Conductor. Conducted first performance of the Ninth Symphony in 1824.

Unger, Caroline (1803–1877). Singer. Sang in the premiere of the Ninth Symphony.

Varena, Joseph von (1769–1843). One of the founders of the Graz Music Society. Met Beethoven in Teplitz in 1811.

Varnhagen von Ense, Karl August (1785–1858). Diplomat and poet. Husband of Rahel Levin. Friend of Beethoven, whom he met in Teplitz in 1811.

Vering, Dr. Gerhard von (1755–1823). One of Beethoven's physicians.

Vigano, Salvatore (1769–1821). Dancer and choreographer for whom Beethoven composed *Prometheus*.

Waldstein, Ferdinand Ernst (1762–1823). Met the young Beethoven in Bonn. Became a helpful friend. Later Waldstein fell on evil fortune and died poverty-stricken. Immortal because of the *Waldstein Sonata*.

Wawruch, Dr. Andreas Johann (1782–1842). Last physician of Beethoven.

Weber, Carl Maria von (1786–1826). Famous composer. At first unsympathetic to Beethoven.

Wegeler, Dr. Franz Gerhard (1765–1848). Knew Beethoven in Bonn. Co-author with

Ferdinand Ries (*q.v.*) of *Notizen*. Went to Vienna for medical study. Married Eleonore von Breuning, lived with her in Koblenz. Became professor of medicine.

Weigl, Joseph (1766–1846). Successful Viennese composer and Kapellmeister to the Court.

Weissenbach, Dr. Alois (1766–1821). Physician and writer. Published popular book about his trip to Vienna.

Willmann, Magdalene (1775–1801). Singer. Beethoven met her in Bonn and again in Vienna and was supposed to have offered her his hand in marriage. She refused.

Wolfmayer, Johann Nepomuk (dates unknown). Textile manufacturer. Admirer of Beethoven, particularly in the last years. Saw Beethoven during his last days.

Wranitzky, Paul (1756–1808). Viennese composer. Beethoven wrote Variations on one of the melodies from his ballet *Das Waldmädchen*.

Zmeskall, Nikolaus von Domanowitz (Domanovetz) (1759–1833). Formed a friendship with Beethoven, soon after the composer's arrival in Vienna, which lasted until Beethoven's death. Probably through him Beethoven met the leading Hungarian families in Vienna, such as the Brunsviks. Zmeskall carefully preserved numerous letters and notes. Suffered badly with gout in his last years.

Bibliography

Books and publications from which specific points were taken are mentioned in the text. The following books also were frequently consulted:

Anderson, Emily, ed., *Letters of Mozart and His Family.* 3 vols. London, 1938.

————, *The Letters of Beethoven.* 3 vols. London, 1961.

Bachmann, L. G., *Beethoven contra Beethoven: The History of a Famous Lawsuit.* Munich, 1963.

Bagar, Robert, and Biancolli, Louis, *The Concert Companion.* New York, 1947.

Barea, Ilsa, *Vienna, Legend and Reality.* London, 1966.

Benz, Richard, *Goethe und Beethoven.* Stuttgart, 1948.

Berlioz, Hector, *A Critical Study of Beethoven's Nine Symphonies.* London.

Bory, Robert, ed., *Ludwig van Beethoven: His Life and Work in Pictures.* London, 1966.

Boucourechliev, André, *Beethoven.* Paris.

Breuning, Gerhard von, *Aus dem Schwarzspanierhause.* Revised edition of the Vienna 1874 edition. Berlin and Leipzig, 1907.

Brockway, Wallace, ed., *High Moment: Stories of Supreme Crises in the Lives of Great Men* (Ernest Newman on Beethoven; C. S. Forester on Napoleon). New York, 1955.

Brockway, Wallace, and Weinstock, Herbert, *Men of Music.* New York, 1939.

Bruck, A. Moeller van den, *Beethoven der Deutsche.* Minden.

Burk, John N., *The Life and Works of Beethoven.* New York, 1943.

Carse, Adam, *The Orchestra.* New York, 1949.

————, *The Orchestra from Beethoven to Berlioz.* Cambridge, 1948.

Chandler, David, *The Campaigns of Napoleon.* New York, 1966.

Deutsch, Otto Erich, ed., *Mozart: A Documentary Biography.* Stanford, California, 1965.

————, *The Schubert Reader.* New York, 1947.

Durant, Will and Ariel, *Rousseau and Revolution.* New York, 1967.

————, *The Age of Voltaire.* New York, 1965.

Einstein, Alfred, *Essays on Music.* New York, 1956.

Engel, Eduard, *Geschichte der deutschen Literatur.* 2 vols. Vienna and Leipzig, 1917.

————, *Goethe.* Berlin, 1910.

Ewen, David and Frederic, *Musical Vienna.* New York, 1939.

Ferguson, Donald N., *Masterworks of the Orchestral Repertoire.* Minneapolis, 1954.

Forster, Walther, *Beethovens Krankheiten und ihre Beurteilung.* Wiesbaden, 1955.

Friedenthal, Richard, *Goethe: His Life and Times.* Cleveland, 1963.

Frimmel, Theodor von, *Beethoven Handbuch.* 2 vols. Leipzig, 1926.

————, *Beethoven Studien.* 2 vols. Munich and Leipzig, 1904, 1906.

————, *Ludwig van Beethoven.* 6th revised edition. Berlin, 1922.

———, *Neue Beethoveniana*. Vienna, 1890.

Gal, Hans, *The Golden Age of Vienna*. New York, 1948.

Gay, Peter, *Age of Enlightenment*. New York, 1966.

———, *The Enlightenment: An Interpretation*. New York, 1966.

Giannatasio del Rio, Fanny, Ludwig Nohl, ed., *An Unrequited Love*. London, 1876.

Goethe, Johann Wolfgang von, *Works*. Edition of Bibliographisches Institut. 30 vols. Leipzig and Vienna.

Grillparzer, Franz, *Works*. Edition of Bibliographisches Institut. 5 vols. Leipzig and Vienna.

Groner, Richard, *Wien wie es war*. Vienna, 1965.

Grove, George, *Beethoven and His Nine Symphonies*. London, 1898.

Grove's Dictionary of Music and Musicians. 7 vols. Edition of Philadelphia, 1927.

Hamburger, Michael, ed., *Beethoven: Letters, Journals and Conversations*. London, 1951.

Hamerow, Theodore S., *Restoration, Revolution, Reaction*. Princeton, 1958.

Herriot, Édouard, *Beethoven*. German edition. Frankfurt, 1930.

———, *The Life and Times of Beethoven*. English edition. New York, 1935.

de Hevesy, A., *Petites Amies de Beethoven*. Paris, 1910.

Holborn, Hajo, *The History of Modern Germany, 1648–1840*. New York, 1964.

Hrussoczy, Marie Edle von, *Recollections of Countess Theresa Brunswick*. London, 1893.

Jacob, H. E., *Joseph Haydn*. New York, 1950.

Jahn, Otto, *W. A. Mozart*. Leipzig, 1905.

Kalischer, Alfred Christian, ed., *Beethovens Sämtliche Briefe*. 5 vols. Berlin and Leipzig, 1906.

———, *Die Unsterbliche Geliebte Beethovens*. Dresden, 1891.

Kaznelson, Siegmund, *Beethovens Ferne und Unsterbliche Geliebte*. Zurich, 1954.

Kerman, Joseph, *The Beethoven Quartets*. New York, 1967.

Kerst, Friedrich, and Krehbiel, Henry Edward, eds., *Beethoven the Man and the Artist, as Revealed in His Own Words*. New York, 1964.

Kobald, Karl, *Beethoven. Seine Beziehungen zu Wiens Kunst und Kultur, Gesellschaft und Landschaft*. Vienna, Munich, Zurich, 1964.

Köhler, Karl-Heinz, and Herre, Grita, eds., *Ludwig van Beethoven Konversationshefte*, Vol. IV. Leipzig, 1968.

Kohn, Hans, *The Mind of Germany*. New York, 1960.

Komroff, Manuel, *Beethoven and the World of Music*. New York, 1961.

Kralik, Heinrich, *The Vienna Opera*. Vienna, 1963.

Kruseman, Philip, ed., *Beethoven's Own Words*. London, 1947.

Landon, H. C. Robbins, *Das Kleine Haydnbuch*. Salzburg, 1967.

———, ed., *The Collected Correspondence and London Notebooks of Joseph Haydn*. London, 1959.

Lang, Paul Henry, *Music in Western Civilization*. New York, 1941.

Leitzmann, Albert, ed., *Beethovens persönliche Aufzeichnungen*. Leipzig.

Ley, Stephan, *Wahrheit, Zweifel und Irrtum in der Kunde von Beethovens Leben*. Wiesbaden, 1955.

Lipsius, Ida Maria, *Beethovens Unsterbliche Geliebte*. Leipzig, 1909.

Ludwig, Emil, *Beethoven: Life of a Conqueror*. New York, 1943.

Lux, Joseph August, *Ludwig van Beethoven*. Berlin, 1927.

Magnani, Luigi, *Beethovens Konversationshefte*. Munich, 1967.

————, *I Quaderni di Conversazione di Beethoven*. Milan, 1962.

Mann, Golo, *The History of Germany Since 1789*. London, 1968.

Marx, Adolf Bernhard, *Ludwig van Beethoven Leben und Schaffen*. Berlin, 1863.

Mason, Daniel Gregory, *The Quartets of Beethoven*. New York, 1947.

McGuigan, Dorothy Gies, *The Habsburgs*. New York, 1966.

McNeill, William H., *A World History*. New York, 1967.

Mies, Paul, and Schmidt-Görg, Joseph, eds., *Beethoven Jahrbuch*. 4 vols. Bonn, 1954, 1956, 1959, 1962.

Misch, Ludwig, *Beethoven Studies*. University of Oklahoma, 1953.

Moscheles, Ignaz, *Recent Music and Musicians*. London, 1879.

Naumann, Emil, *Musikgeschichte*. 2 vols. Berlin and Stuttgart.

Nettl, Paul, *Beethoven and the Medical Profession* (Ciba Symposium). Basel, 1966.

————, *Beethoven Handbook*. New York, 1956.

Newman, Ernest, *The Unconscious Beethoven*. New York, 1927.

Nicolson, Harold, *The Congress of Vienna*. London, 1946.

Nohl, Ludwig, *Beethovens Brevier*. Leipzig, 1901.

————, *Beethovens Leben*. 4 vols. 2nd edition. Berlin, 1909.

Nottebohm, Gustav, *Beethovens Studien*. Leipzig and Winterthur, 1873.

Orel, Alfred, ed., *Ein Wiener Beethoven Buch*. Vienna, 1921.

Palmer, Alan, *Napoleon in Russia*. New York, 1967.

Perfahl, Jost, ed., *Wien Chronik*. Salzburg, 1961.

Priestley, J. B., *Literature and Western Man*. New York, 1960.

Pryce-Jones, Alan, *Beethoven*. New York, 1933.

Radant, Else, ed., *Die Tagebücher von Joseph Carl Rosenbaum, 1770–1829* (Haydn *Jahrbuch* V). Vienna, 1968.

Reeser, Dr. Eduard, *The History of the Waltz*. Stockholm.

Reinitz, Dr. Max, *Beethoven im Kampfe mit dem Schicksal*. Vienna, 1924.

Rolland, Romain, *Beethoven the Creator*. London, 1929.

San Galli, Thomas Wolfgang Alexander, *Beethoven und die Unsterbliche Geliebte*. Munich, 1910.

Schauffler, Robert Haven, *Beethoven: The Man Who Freed Music*. 2 vols. Garden City, 1929.

Schenk, H. G., *The Mind of the European Romantics*. New York, 1966.

Schering, Arnold, *Beethoven in neuer Deutung*. Leipzig, 1934.

————, *Beethoven und die Dichtung*. Leipzig, 1936.

Schiedermair, Ludwig, *Der Junge Beethoven*. Leipzig, 1925.

Schiller, Friedrich von, *Selected Works*. Edition of Das Bergland-Buch. 2 vols. Salzburg.

Schindler, Anton Felix, Donald W. Mac-

Ardle, ed., *Beethoven As I Knew Him.* London, 1966.

Schmidt-Görg, Joseph, *Dreizehn Unbekannte Briefe an Josephine Gräfin Deym geb. v. Brunsvik* (Facsimile edition). Bonn, 1957.

Schünemann, Georg, ed., *Ludwig van Beethoven Konversationshefte.* 3 vols. Berlin, 1941–1943.

Scott, Marion M., *Beethoven.* London, 1934.

Sedgwick, Henry Dwight, *Vienna.* Indianapolis, 1939.

Slonimsky, Nicolas, ed., *Lexicon of Musical Invective.* New York, 1953.

Sonneck, O. G., ed., *Beethoven: Impressions of Contemporaries.* New York, 1926.

———, *The Riddle of the Immortal Beloved.* New York, 1927.

Spohr, Louis, Henry Pleasants, ed., *The Musical Journeys of Louis Spohr.* University of Oklahoma, 1961.

Steichen, Dana, *Beethoven's Beloved.* Garden City, 1959.

Sterba, Editha and Richard, M.D., *Beethoven and His Nephew.* New York, 1954.

Sullivan, J. W. N., *Beethoven: His Spiritual Development.* New York, 1927.

Talmon, J. L., *Romanticism and Revolt, Europe 1815–1848.* London, 1967.

Thayer, Alexander Wheelock, Elliot Forbes, ed., *The Life of Beethoven.* 2 vols. Princeton, 1964.

———, Henry Edward Krehbiel, ed., *The Life of Ludwig van Beethoven.* 3 vols. New York, 1921.

Thompson, Oscar, ed., *The International Cyclopedia of Music and Musicians.* New York, 1939.

Tovey, Donald Francis, *Beethoven.* London, 1945.

———, *Essays in Musical Analysis.* 7 vols. London, 1935–1944.

Unger, Max, *Auf Spuren von Beethovens "Unsterblicher Geliebten."* Langensalza (Germany), 1911.

Valentin, Erich, *Beethoven: A Pictorial Biography.* London, 1958.

Vallotton, Henry, *Metternich.* Heide (Germany), 1966.

Various Authors, *Beethoven, Das Genie und Seine Welt* (Symposium). Munich, 1963.

Various Authors, *Beethovens Symphonien* (Symposium). Berlin.

Vaughan Williams, R., *Some Thoughts on Beethoven's Choral Symphony.* London, 1953.

Wagner, Richard, *"Beethovens Heroische Symphonie." "Zum Vortrag der Neunten Symphonie Beethovens." "Eine Pilgerfahrt zu Beethoven."* From Complete Edition of Wagner's Writing. 10 vols. Leipzig, 1888.

Waldegg, Richard, *Sittengeschichte von Wien.* Stuttgart, 1957.

Warrack, John, *Carl Maria von Weber.* New York, 1968.

Wegeler, Dr. F. G., and Ries, Ferdinand, *Biographische Notizen über Ludwig van Beethoven.* Koblenz, 1838.

Weinstock, Herbert, *Handel.* New York, 1946.

———, *Rossini.* New York, 1968.

Wells, H. G., *The Outline of History.* New York, 1920.

Wetzler, H. H., *Wege zur Musik (Analogien bei Shakespeare und Beethoven).* Zurich, 1938.

Williams, Neville, *Chronology of the Modern World.* New York, 1966.

Index

INDEX

674

INDEX

INDEX

INDEX

INDEX

INDEX

INDEX

694

INDEX